MODERN
Real Estate
Practice IN
ILLINOIS

Fillmore W. Galaty

Wellington J. Allaway

Robert C. Kyle

Laurie MacDougal
Consulting Editor

Dearborn™
Real Estate Education

This publication is designed to provide accurate and authoritative information in regard to the subject matter covered. It is sold with the understanding that the publisher is not engaged in rendering legal, accounting, or other professional service. If legal advice or other expert assistance is required, the services of a competent professional should be sought.

President: Mehul Patel
Executive Director of Product Development: Kate DeVivo
Managing Editor: Anne Huston
Managing Editor: Tony Peregrin
Director of Production: Daniel Frey
Production Editor: Samantha Raue
Senior Production Artist: Virginia Byrne
Creative Director: Lucy Jenkins
Vice President of Product Management: Dave Dufresne
Director of Product Management: Melissa Kleeman

Published by Dearborn™ Real Estate Education
30 South Wacker Drive
Chicago, Illinois 60606-7481
(312) 836-4400
www.dearbornRE.com

Printed in the United States of America

09 10   10   9   8   7   6   5   4   3   2

The Library of Congress has cataloged the previous edition as follows:

Galaty, Fillmore W.
Modern real estate practice in Illinois / Fillmore W. Galaty, Wellington J. Allaway,
Robert C. Kyle. — 5th ed.
p.cm.
Includes bibliographical references and index.
ISBN 0-7931-8835-0
I. Allaway, Wellington J.II. Kyle, Robert C.III. Title
KFI1482.R4 G352004
346.77304'37—dc21   2004004996

Contents

Preface

Whether you are preparing for the Illinois real estate licensing examination, fulfilling a college or university requirement, looking for specific guidance about buying a home or investment property, or simply expanding your understanding of this fascinating field, you can rely on *Modern Real Estate Practice in Illinois*, 6th Edition, for accurate and comprehensive information in a format that is easy to use.

■ TEXT FEATURES

- *Key Terms,* useful for review and study, appear at the beginning of each chapter. They reinforce important vocabulary words and concepts covered in that chapter.
- *Illinois-specific laws and practice issues* are clearly highlighted for easy study and classroom emphasis.
- The *For Example* feature, also clearly set off, adds real-life examples and case studies to illustrate key concepts.
- *In Practice* sections reinforce course material by showing how the concepts are likely to be played out in actual practice.
- *Math Concepts,* marked with an icon, help students learn basic real estate math skills and their applications.
- *Margin Boxes* direct readers' attention to important concepts and contain tips for more effective studying.
- Inclusive *Chapter Summaries* help students easily refer to and retain key information from the chapter.
- *Chapter review questions and practice exams*, containing national and Illinois-specific questions, provide a good sampling of the types of questions on the real estate licensing examination.
- The *Math FAQs* section contains over 30 pages covering real estate problems involving fractions, decimals, and measurements. Twenty-five sample questions and an answer key with solutions are included.
- The latest **AMP Outline** for the national salesperson's exam is included, along with chapter references for each topic.

■ NEW TO THE SIXTH EDITION

- Illinois laws and regulations have been updated/added, including:
  — Homeowner's Exemption
  — Senior Citizen's Homestead Exemption
  — Senior Citizen's Freeze Homestead Exemption
  — Homestead Improvement Exemption
  — Equity in Eminent Domain Act
  — Illinois Radon Awareness Act

- New content topics have been added, such as:
  - Manufactured Housing
  - Electronic contracting
  - Fee for services
  - Do Not Call, CAN-SPAM, and Junk Fax legislation
  - Minimum service requirements for exclusive brokerage agreements
  - Special service areas
  - Brownfields Legislation
- All forms are updated to include the latest editions; new radon disclosure form has been added.
- Questions and answers are updated to reflect the new sixth edition and the current business climate.
- Web links are now are located in a separate Web Link Appendix, in chapter-by-chapter order.

One thing, however, has stayed the same. The two fundamental goals of *Modern Real Estate Practice in Illinois* are to help students understand the dynamics of the real estate industry in Illinois and pass their state licensing exam. In this edition, we've met that challenge, providing the critical information students need to pass the real estate examination, buy or sell property, or establish a real estate career.

■ A FINAL NOTE

We like to hear from our readers. Like the many instructors who have helped us develop each edition and the real estate professionals who have been willing to share their expertise, you are a partner in the *Modern Real Estate Practice* book series. The only way we can be sure we've succeeded—and know what we need to improve—is if you tell us.

Your comments help us evaluate the current edition and continue to improve future editions. Please take a few moments to let us know what you thought of this edition of *Modern Real Estate Practice in Illinois*. Did it help you? Has your understanding of the real estate industry increased? How did you do in your real estate course or on your license exam? What additional or different information would improve the book? Please indicate that you used the 6th edition of *Modern Real Estate Practice in Illinois* and send your comments to Dearborn™ Real Estate Education, Attention: Editorial Group, 30 South Wacker Drive, Chicago, Illinois 60606-7481.

Thank you for your help and for joining the ranks of successful users of *Modern Real Estate Practice in Illinois*.

Acknowledgments

The authors express their gratitude and appreciation to the instructors and other real estate professionals whose invaluable suggestions and advice help *Modern Real Estate Practice in Illinois* remain the state's leading real estate principles text.

■ CONSULTING EDITOR

The authors would like to express special appreciation to the Consulting Editor, Laurie MacDougal, for her invaluable assistance in revising and preparing this text's 6th Edition.

Laurie MacDougal has worked in the real estate industry since 1975. She presently is a real estate educator with the Chicago Association of REALTORS® and its affiliates. She has taught all levels of real estate licensing courses, and is best known for her ongoing involvement with real estate broker prelicensing, continuing education, and sales training courses. In addition, she founded and operates Laurmac Learning Center, which provides customized training for the real estate and mortgage brokerage industries.

Laurie served as consulting editor on *Modern Real Estate Practice in Illinois*, fifth edition and fifth edition update as well as on Dearborn's *Illinois Broker Management* course. Beyond the classroom, Laurie's real estate experience of three-plus decades includes industrial and commercial development, property management, economic development, and residential real estate sales. Currently, she provides consulting services to numerous real estate–related organizations regarding license law and compliance issues.

Laurie is a member of the Chicago Association of REALTORS® Education Foundation and the Triton College Education Foundation. She broadcasts a weekly radio show, *Radio Real Estate*, from Triton College.

Laurie has appeared as an industry expert on NBC *Nightly News* and CLTV segments, discussing real estate–related news.

■ REVIEWERS

This edition of *Modern Real Estate Practice in Illinois* would not have been possible without the input of real estate instructors and the feedback of real estate professionals. For their comments, suggestions, and contributions, the authors wish to especially thank Michael Fair, Director, Illinois Academy of Real Estate; Wayne Paprocki, Wayne Jay and Associates; Francis Patrick Murphy, JD, Chicago Association of REALTORS®; and Sam Martin, *SamTheTutor.com*.

Each new edition of *Modern Real Estate Practice in Illinois* builds on earlier editions. The authors would like to thank the following individuals for their assistance with prior editions of this book:

Jean Bartholomew
Elyse Berns
Maureen Cain
Patrick Cal
William Carmody
Sandra CeCe
Michael Fair
Kerry Kidwell
Maureen LeVanti
Deborah Lopes
Vincent Lopez
Laurie MacDougal
Lynda McKay
Clarke Marquis

Susan Miranda
Rose McDonald
Robert Mocella
Francis Patrick Murphy
Wayne Paprocki
Joyce Bea Sterling
Dawn Svenningsen
Alan Toban
Casey Voris
Barry Ward
Terry W. Watson
Mary Wezeman
Martha Williams

Fillmore W. Galaty

Wellington J. Allaway

Robert C. Kyle

CHAPTER 1

Introduction to the Real Estate Business

■ **LEARNING OBJECTIVES** *When you've finished reading this chapter, you should be able to*

- ■ **identify** the various careers available in real estate and the professional organizations that support them.

- ■ **describe** the five categories of real property.

- ■ **explain** the operation of supply and demand in the real estate market.

- ■ **distinguish** the economic, political, and social factors that influence supply and demand.

- ■ **define** the following *key terms*:

broker	market	supply and demand
Federal Reserve Board	salesperson	

■ A VERY BIG BUSINESS

Real estate transactions are taking place all around us, all the time. When a commercial leasing company rents space in a mall or the owner of a building rents an apartment to a retired couple, it's a real estate transaction. If an appraiser gives an expert opinion of the value of farmland or a bank lends money to a professional corporation to purchase an office building, it's a real estate transaction. Most common of all, when a family sells its old home to buy a new one or steps into the housing market for the first time, it's a real estate transaction. Consumers of real estate services include home buyers and sellers, tenants and landlords, investors and developers. Nearly everyone at some time is an active participant in the real estate industry.

All this adds up to big business—complex transactions that involve billions of dollars every year in the United States alone.

The services of millions of highly trained individuals are required: attorneys, bankers, trust company representatives, abstract and title insurance agents, architects, surveyors, accountants, tax experts, home inspectors, and many others, in addition to buyers and sellers. All these people depend on the skills, knowledge, and integrity of licensed real estate professionals.

■ REAL ESTATE: A BUSINESS OF MANY SPECIALIZATIONS

Despite the size and complexity of the real estate business, many people think of it as being made up of only brokers and salespersons. Actually, the real estate industry is much broader than that. Appraisal, property management, financing, subdivision and development, counseling, and education are all separate businesses within the real estate field. To succeed in this complex industry, every real estate professional must have a basic knowledge of these specialties.

Brokerage—*Brokerage* is the business of bringing people together in a real estate transaction. A **broker** (or the broker's designated representative—a salesperson or associate broker) acts as a point of contact between two or more people in negotiating the sale, purchase, or rental of property. A broker may be the agent for the buyer, for the seller, or for both. The property may be residential, commercial, or industrial. A **salesperson** is a licensee employed by the broker. The salesperson conducts brokerage activities on behalf of the broker. *Leasing agents* bring together tenants and prospective rental properties. The *sponsoring broker* is ultimately responsible for the actions of salespersons, other brokers, leasing agents, or licensed personal assistants working under the umbrella of that particular firm.

Appraisal—*Appraisal* is the process of estimating a property's market value based on established methods and the appraiser's professional judgment. Although real estate training will give brokers and salespersons some understanding of the valuation process, most lenders require that a professional appraisal by a licensed appraiser accompany a loan package. The appraisal substantiates the sales price of the home and assists the lender in determining maximum loan amount. Appraisals are also used for refinancing and insurance purposes. Detailed expertise in all the methods of valuation is required. Appraisers must be licensed or certified for any federally related loan transaction.

Property management—A *property manager* is a person or company hired to maintain and manage property on behalf of its owner. By hiring a property manager, the owner is relieved of many day-to-day management tasks, such as finding new tenants, collecting rents, altering or constructing new space for tenants, ordering repairs, and generally maintaining the property. The scope of the manager's work depends on the terms of the individual employment contract, known as a *property* *management agreement.* Whatever tasks are specified, the property manager must protect the owner's investment and maximize the owner's return on his or her investment.

Financing—*Financing* is the business of providing the funds that make real estate transactions possible. Most transactions are financed by means of mortgage loans or trust deed loans secured by the property. Individuals involved in financing real estate may work in commercial banks, savings associations, mortgage banking, or mortgage brokerage companies. A growing number of real estate brokerage firms affiliate with mortgage brokers to provide consumers with one-stop-shopping real estate services. Mortgage brokers and the loan officers working for them must be licensed and registered in Illinois.

Subdivision and development—*Subdivision* is the splitting of a single property into smaller parcels. *Development* involves the construction of improvements on the land. These improvements may be either on-site or off-site. Off-site improvements such as water lines and storm sewers are made on public lands to serve the new development. On-site improvements such as new buildings, private swimming pools, or private wells are made on individual parcels. While subdivision and development normally are related, they are independent processes that can occur separately.

Home inspection—*Home inspection* is a profession that allows practitioners to combine their interest in real estate with their professional skills and training in the construction trades or in engineering. Professional home inspectors conduct a thorough visual survey of a property's structure, systems, and site conditions and prepare an analytical report that is valuable to both purchasers and homeowners. Home inspectors require a license in Illinois.

Professional inspections occur on other types of property as well. Commercial properties may undergo an environmental assessment to determine the probability of hazardous substances being present on the property.

Counseling—*Counseling* involves providing clients with competent independent advice based on sound professional judgment. A real estate counselor helps clients choose among the various alternatives involved in purchasing, using, or investing in property. A counselor's role is to furnish clients with the information needed to make informed decisions. Professional real estate counselors must have a high degree of industry expertise.

Education—*Real estate education* is available to both practitioners and consumers. Colleges and universities, private schools, and trade organizations all conduct real estate courses and seminars, from the principles of a prelicensing program to the technical aspects of tax and exchange law. State licensing laws establish the minimum educational requirements for obtaining—and keeping—a real estate license. Continuing education (CE) helps ensure that licensees keep their skills and knowledge current.

Auctioning—Buying or selling real estate at auction is an intriguing process. The concept of using an open and competitive bidding process to transfer property has become an acceptable alternative to the negotiated sale method of property disposition. In Illinois, as in many states, auctioneers have licensing requirements.

Other areas—Many other real estate career options are available. Practitioners will find that real estate specialists are needed in a variety of business settings. *Lawyers* who specialize in real estate are always in demand. Large *corporations* with extensive land holdings often have their own *real estate* and *property tax departments*. Local governments must staff both *zoning boards* and *assessment offices*.

■ PROFESSIONAL ORGANIZATIONS

Many trade organizations serve the real estate business. The largest is the National Association of REALTORS® (NAR). NAR sponsors various affiliated organizations that offer professional designations to brokers, salespersons, and other professionals who complete required courses in areas of special interest. Members subscribe to a Code of Ethics and are entitled to be known as REALTORS® or REALTOR-ASSOCIATES®. You must be a member of NAR to use the term REALTOR® to describe yourself. These REALTOR® associations have ongoing political and educational activities as valuable member services. By way of a special three-way agreement, member REALTORS® who participate at the local level become members of all three.

Among the other professional associations is NAREB (the National Association of Real Estate Brokers), a group whose code of ethics pledges members to strive toward ending racial discrimination in housing and promoting diversity. Its members are called *Realtists*, and they are found throughout the country, most prominently in New England.

Professional appraisers' associations include the Appraisal Institute, the American Society of Appraisers (ASA), and the National Association of Independent Fee Appraisers (NAIFA). The Real Estate Educators Association (REEA) includes both individuals and institutions. The growth in buyer brokerage led to the formation of organizations such as the Real Estate Buyer's Agent Council (REBAC), now associated with NAR, and the National Association of Exclusive Buyer Agents (NAEBA). Additionally, the American Society of Home Inspectors® (ASHI), the Building Owners and Managers Association International (BOMA), the Institute of Real Estate Management (IREM), the Commercial Investment Real Estate Institute (CIREI), the CCIM Institute (commerical real estate), the Association of Real Estate License Law Officials (ARELLO), and the American Society of Real Estate Counselors (ASREC) are all among recognized professional societies or affiliations. Web addresses for these organizations are contained in the Web Link Appendix.

■ TYPES OF REAL PROPERTY

Five Categories of Real Property

1. Residential
2. Commercial
3. Industrial
4. Agricultural
5. Special Purpose

Just as there are areas of specialization within the real estate industry, there are different types of property in which to specialize. Real estate can be classified as

- *residential*—all property used for single-family or multifamily housing, whether in urban, suburban, or rural areas;
- *commercial*—business property, including office space, shopping centers, stores, theaters, hotels, and parking facilities;
- *industrial*—warehouses, factories, land in industrial districts, and power plants;
- *agricultural*—farms, timberland, ranches, and orchards; or
- *special purpose*—churches, schools, cemeteries, and government-held lands.

The market for each of these types of property can be subdivided into the *sales market*, which involves the transfer of title and ownership rights, and the *rental market*, in which space is used temporarily by lease.

IN PRACTICE

Although it is possible for a single real estate firm or an individual real estate professional to perform all the services and handle all the classes of property discussed in this chapter, this rarely is done. While a broad range of services at one firm may be available in small towns, most firms and professionals specialize to some degree, especially in urban areas. Some licensees perform only one service for one type of property or client, such as residential sales or commercial leasing. Under one brokerage firm's roof, however, there may be many specializations.

"One-stop shopping" (collecting many specialties under one roof) has become a major umbrella for today's specialization trend, allowing those specialized parts to form a cohesive whole. Having one firm offer brokerage, appraisal, financing, and title insurance services provides added value, convenience, and possible cost savings to the consumer while adding increased profitability to brokerage companies. On the other hand, there is the potential for a conflict of interest. Consult an attorney to ensure proper procedures are followed.

■ THE REAL ESTATE MARKET

A **market** is a place where goods can be bought and sold. A market may be a specific place, such as the village square, or it may be a vast, complex, worldwide economic system for moving goods and services. In either case, the function of a market is to provide a setting in which supply and demand can establish market value, making it advantageous for buyers and sellers to trade.

Supply and Demand

The forces of **supply and demand** in the market determine how prices for goods and services are set. Essentially, when supply increases and demand remains stable, prices go down; when demand increases and supply remains stable, prices go up. Greater supply means producers need to attract more buyers, so they lower prices. Greater demand means producers can raise their prices because buyers compete for the product.

Supply and demand in the real estate market.   Two characteristics of real estate govern the way the market reacts to the pressures of supply and demand: uniqueness and immobility. *Uniqueness* means that no matter how similar two parcels of real estate may appear, they are never *exactly* alike. Each occupies its own unique geographic location, and two properties are never exactly the same inside. *Immobility* refers to the fact that property cannot be relocated to satisfy demand where supply is low. Nor do buyers necessarily make relocation decisions based on greater housing supply in a certain locale. For these reasons, real estate markets are *local markets*. Each geographic area has different types of real estate and different conditions that drive prices. In these defined hubs of activity, real estate offices can keep track of types of property in demand and specific parcels available.

> When supply increases and demand remains stable, prices go down. When demand increases and supply remains stable, prices go up.

IN PRACTICE   Technological advances and market changes have widened the real estate professional's local market. Computers, the Internet, e-mail, cell phones, and a growing arsenal of other technologies all help real estate practitioners stay on top of their wide-ranging markets.

> *Uniqueness* and *immobility* are the two characteristics of land that have the most impact on market value.

Because of real estate's uniqueness and immobility, the market generally adjusts slowly to the forces of supply and demand. Although a home offered for sale can be withdrawn in response to low demand and high supply, it is much more likely that oversupply will result in lower price.

When *supply* is low, a high demand may not be met because development and construction are lengthy processes. As a result, development tends to occur in uneven spurts of activity.

> **Demand and Price**
> Price follows demand: High demand, high prices; low demand, low prices.

Even when supply and demand can be forecast with some accuracy, natural disasters such as tornados and flooding can disrupt market trends. Similarly, sudden changes in financial markets or local events such as plant relocations or industry shifts or environmental factors can dramatically disrupt a seemingly stable market.

Because some forces in these cycles are unpredictable, the best approach is to assume that "good markets don't always last." Skilled real estate professionals are aware of and recognize predictable indicators of the cycles so they can better assist clients in making intelligent sales and purchase decisions.

Factors Affecting Supply

Factors that tend to affect the *supply side* of the real estate market's supply and demand balance include the labor force, construction and material costs, government controls, and financial policies.

Labor force and construction costs.   A shortage of skilled labor or building materials or an increase in the cost of materials can decrease the amount of new construction. Construction permit fees and high property transfer costs can also discourage development. An attempt may be made to pass increased construction costs along to buyers and tenants in the form of higher prices and increased rents, which can further slow the market.

Government controls and financial policies.   The government's monetary policy can have a substantial impact on the real estate market. The **Federal Reserve Board** establishes a discount rate of interest for the money it lends to its member banks. That rate has a direct impact on the interest rates that banks charge to borrowers. These interest rates play a significant part in people's ability to buy homes. The Federal Reserve Board attempts to keep the rates at a level that will keep the market moving without leading to inflation.

Governmental agencies, such as the Federal Housing Administration (FHA) and the Department of Veterans Affairs (VA), also have impact by insuring or guaranteeing loans. They are intended to benefit the economy, the consumer, and housing purchases.

Virtually any government action has some effect on the real estate market. Even eminent domain used to "take" land for a highway project may shift the supply or value of land in a local market.

Policies on the taxation of real estate can have both significant and complex effects on the real estate market. Real estate taxation is a necessary source of revenue for local governments. High taxes may deter investors, but may be necessary to maintain an excellent school system, for instance. Tax incentives, however, can attract new business and industries. And, of course, along with these enterprises come increased employment and expanded residential real estate markets.

Local governments also can influence supply. Land-use controls, building codes, and zoning ordinances help shape the character of a community and control the use of land. Careful planning helps stabilize and even increase real estate values.

Factors Affecting Demand

Factors that tend to affect the *demand side* of the real estate market include population, demographics, and employment and wage levels.

Population.   Shelter is a basic human need, so the demand for housing grows with the population. Although the total population of the country continues to rise, the demand for real estate increases at a faster rate in some areas than in others. In some locations, growth has ceased altogether as the population has declined. This may be due to economic changes (such as plant closings), social concerns (such as the quality of schools or a desire for more open space), or population changes (such as population shifts from colder to warmer climates). The result can be a drop in demand for real estate in one area at the same time that demand increases elsewhere.

Demographics.   *Demographics* is the study and description of population. The population of a community is a major factor in determining the quantity and type of housing in that community. Family size, the ratio of adults to children, the ages of children, the number of retirees, family income, lifestyle, and the growing number of single-parent and empty-nester households are all demographic factors that contribute to the amount and type of housing needed.

Niche marketing is the phrase used to refer to the targeted marketing of specific demographic populations. For example, as baby boomers age and look for retirement housing, their need or demand is considered a niche market.

Employment and wage levels.   Decisions about whether to buy or rent and how much to spend on housing are closely related to income. When job

---

Sidebar (left column):

Factors that affect the supply of real estate are
- labor force,
- construction costs,
- government controls, and
- government financial policies.

Factors that affect the demand for real estate are
- population,
- demographics, and
- employment and wage levels.

IN PRACTICE

opportunities are scarce or wage levels low, demand for real estate usually drops. A local market often is drastically affected by a single major employer moving in or shutting down. For this reason, licensees must be aware of business plans of local employers.

■ SUMMARY

As we've seen, the real estate market depends on a variety of economic forces, such as interest rates and employment levels. To be successful, licensees must follow economic trends and anticipate where they will lead. How people use their income depends on consumer confidence. Consumer confidence is based not only on perceived job security but also on the availability of credit, the impact of inflation, and actions of the Federal Reserve Board. General trends in the economy, such as the availability of mortgage money and the interest rate that must be paid to have it, will strongly influence an individual's decision to invest in real estate.

Although brokerage is the most widely recognized real estate activity, the industry provides many other services. These include appraisal, property management, property development, counseling, property financing, and education. Most real estate firms specialize in only one or two of these areas; however, the highly complex and competitive nature of our society requires that a real estate agent be knowledgeable in a number of fields.

Real property can be classified by its general use as residential, commercial, industrial, agricultural, or special purpose. Although many brokers deal with more than one type of real property, they usually specialize to some degree. The trend toward one-stop shopping has added value to the consumers while increasing profitability for brokerage companies.

A market is a place where goods and services can be bought and sold and where price levels can be established based on supply and demand. Because of its unique characteristics, real estate is usually relatively slow to adjust to the forces of supply and demand.

Real estate supply and demand is affected by many factors, including changes in population and demographics, wage and employment levels, influx or loss of industry, construction costs, availability of labor, and governmental monetary policy and controls. Supply itself can have an impact on perceived demand (e.g., a low supply of colonial homes can create perceived demand for them; too many houses for sale on one block can decrease perceived demand). Demand always influences supply. High demand depletes properties for sale and drives up prices.

Governmental agencies influence the market by insuring or guaranteeing loans.

QUESTIONS

1. A professional estimate of a property's market value, based on established methods and using trained, professional judgment, is performed by a
   a. real estate broker.
   b. real estate appraiser.
   c. real estate counselor.
   d. home inspector.

2. In general, when the supply of a certain commodity increases,
   a. prices tend to rise.
   b. prices tend to drop.
   c. demand tends to rise.
   d. demand is unchanged.

3. Which factor tends to affect supply in the real estate market?
   a. Population
   b. Demographics
   c. Government controls
   d. Employment

4. Which factor would most likely influence the demand for real estate?
   a. Labor force
   b. Construction costs
   c. Wage levels and employment opportunities
   d. Government financial policies

5. Property management, leasing, appraisal, financing, and development are all examples of
   a. factors affecting demand.
   b. specializations within the real estate industry.
   c. non-real estate professions.
   d. government regulation of the real estate industry.

6. A REALTOR® is
   a. a specially licensed real estate salesperson.
   b. any real estate broker or salesperson who assists buyers, sellers, landlords, or tenants in any real estate transaction.
   c. a member of the National Association of Real Estate Brokers who specializes in residential properties.
   d. a real estate licensee who is a member of the National Association of REALTORS®.

7. A major manufacturer of automobiles announces that it will relocate one of its factories, along with 2,000 employees, to Smallville. What effect will this announcement likely have on Smallville's housing market?
   a. Houses likely will become less expensive as a result of the announcement.
   b. Houses likely will become more expensive as a result of the announcement.
   c. The announcement involves an issue of demographics, not a supply and demand issue; housing prices will stay about the same.
   d. The announcement involves an industrial property; residential housing will not be affected.

8. Mario holds a real estate license and has several years of experience in the industry. However, Mario has "retired" from actively marketing properties. Now Mario helps clients choose among the various alternatives involved in purchasing, using, or investing in property. What is Mario's profession?
   a. Real estate counselor
   b. Real estate appraiser
   c. Real estate educator
   d. REALTOR®

CHAPTER 2

Real Property and the Law

■ **LEARNING OBJECTIVES** *When you've finished reading this chapter, you should be able to*

■ **identify** the rights that convey with ownership of real property and the characteristics of real estate.

■ **describe** the difference between real and personal property, and the various types of personalty.

■ **explain** the types of laws that affect real estate.

■ **distinguish** among the concepts of land, real estate, and real property.

■ **define** the following *key terms:*

accession	emblements	Real Estate License Act of 2000
air rights	fixture	
appurtenance	improvement	real property
attachment	land	severance
bill of sale	location	situs
bundle of legal rights	manufactured housing	subsurface rights
chattels	personal property	surface rights
deed	real estate	trade fixture

■ LAND, REAL ESTATE, AND REAL PROPERTY

The words *land*, *real estate*, and *real property* often are used interchangeably. To most people, they mean the same thing. Strictly speaking, however, these terms

FIGURE 2.1

Land, Real Estate, and Real Property

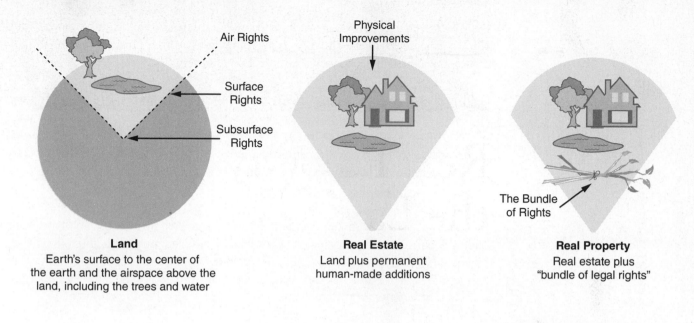

Air Rights

Surface Rights

Subsurface Rights

Land
Earth's surface to the center of the earth and the airspace above the land, including the trees and water

Physical Improvements

Real Estate
Land plus permanent human-made additions

The Bundle of Rights

Real Property
Real estate plus "bundle of legal rights"

refer to different aspects of the same idea. To fully understand the nature of real estate and the laws that affect it, licensees must be aware of these subtle yet important differences.

Land

Land is defined as *the earth's surface extending downward to the center of the earth and upward to infinity.* The term includes permanent natural objects such as trees and water. (See Figure 2.1.)

Land, then, means not only the surface of the earth but also the underlying soil. *Land* also refers to objects that are naturally attached to the earth's surface, such as boulders and plants. Land includes the minerals and substances that lie far below the earth's surface (*subsurface*). It even includes the air above the earth, all the way up into space (*airspace*).

Real Estate

Real estate is defined as *land at, above, and below the earth's surface, plus all things permanently attached to it.* These attachments may be natural or artificial, such as buildings. (See Figure 2.1.)

The term *real estate* is similar to the term land, but it means much more. *Real estate* includes the natural land along with all human-made improvements. An **improvement** is any artificial addition to land, such as a building or a fence.

The term *improvement,* as used in the real estate industry, refers to any addition to the land. The word is neutral. It doesn't matter whether the artificial attachment makes the property better-looking or more useful, more valuable or less valuable; the land still is said to be *improved.* Land also may be improved by streets, utilities, sewers, and other additions that make it suitable for building.

> **Memory Tip**
> **Land**—No improvements
> **Real Estate**—Land with improvements
> **Real Property**—Land with improvements plus rights

Real Property

The term *real property* is the broadest of all. It includes both land and real estate. **Real property** is defined as *the interests, benefits, and rights that are automatically included in the ownership of land and real estate*. (See Figure 2.1.)

Real property includes the surface, subsurface, airspace, any improvements, and the *bundle of legal rights*—the legal rights of ownership that attach to ownership of a parcel of real estate (discussed later in this chapter).

Real property often is coupled with the word **appurtenance**. An appurtenance is anything associated with the property, although not necessarily a direct part of it. Typical appurtenances include parking spaces in multiunit buildings, easements, water rights, and other improvements. An appurtenance is connected to the property, and ownership of the appurtenance normally transfers to the new owner when the property is sold.

IN PRACTICE   When consumers talk about buying or selling homes, office buildings, and land, they often will call all these properties *real estate*. For practical purposes, the term is synonymous with *real property* as defined here. In everyday usage, then, remember that *real estate* has come to include the legal rights of ownership specified in the formal definition of *real property*. Sometimes people also use the term *realty* instead.

Surface, subsurface, and air rights.   The right to use the surface of the earth is referred to as a **surface right**. However, real property ownership also can include **subsurface rights**, which are the rights to the natural resources lying below the earth's surface. Although it may be difficult to imagine, the two rights are distinct. An owner may transfer his or her surface rights without transferring the subsurface rights.

■ **FOR EXAMPLE** Annie sells the rights to any oil and gas found beneath her farm to an oil company. Later, she sells the remaining interests (the surface, air, and limited subsurface rights) to Bradley, reserving the rights to any coal that may be found in the land. Bradley sells the remaining land to Charles, but Bradley retains the farmhouse, stable, and pasture. Based on these sales, four parties now have ownership interests in the same real estate: (1) The oil company owns all the oil and gas; (2) Annie owns all the coal; (3) Bradley owns the farmhouse, stable, and pasture; and (4) Charles owns the rights to the remaining real estate. (See Figure 2.2.)

The rights to use the air above the land, provided the rights have not been preempted by law, may be sold or leased independently. **Air rights** can be an important part of real estate, particularly in large cities where air rights over railroads must be purchased to construct office buildings. Examples of construction based on air rights include the MetLife Building in New York City and the Prudential Building in Chicago. To construct such a building, the developer must purchase not only the air rights but also numerous small portions of the land's surface for the building's foundation supports.

Before air travel was common, a property's air rights were considered to be unlimited, extending upward into the farthest reaches of outer space. Today, however, the courts permit reasonable interference with air rights, such as might be needed by aircraft (and presumably spacecraft), so long as the owner's right

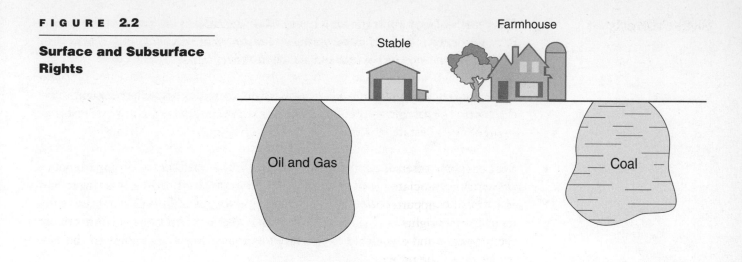

FIGURE 2.2

Surface and Subsurface Rights

to use and occupy the land is not unduly lessened. Governments and airport authorities often purchase adjacent air rights to provide approach patterns for air traffic.

With the continuing development of solar power, air rights, solar rights, and even "view" rights are being closely examined by the courts. A proposed tall building that blocks sunlight from a smaller, existing building may be held to be interfering with the smaller building's right to sunlight, especially if the smaller building is solar-powered. Air and solar rights are established by laws and ordinances that very widely from state to state.

■ REAL PROPERTY AND PERSONAL PROPERTY

Personal property, sometimes called *personalty*, is *all property that does not fit the definition of real property.*

An important distinction between the two is that personal property is movable. Items of personal property, also referred to as **chattels**, include such tangibles as chairs, tables, clothing, money, bonds, and bank accounts. Trade fixtures are included in this category. They, too, are frequently referred to as *chattels*.

Manufactured Housing

Manufactured housing is defined as *dwellings that are not constructed at the site but are built off-site and trucked to a building lot where they are installed or assembled.* Manufactured housing includes modular, panelized, precut, and mobile homes. Generally, however, the term *mobile home* is used to refer to factory-built housing constructed before 1976. Use of the term *mobile home* was phased out with the passage of the National Manufactured Housing Construction and Safety Standards Act of 1976 when manufactured homes became federally regulated. Nevertheless, the term *mobile home* is still commonly used among licensees. Most states have agencies that administer and enforce the federal regulations for manufactured housing.

The distinction between real and personal property is not always obvious. Manufactured housing, for example, is generally considered personal property even though its mobility may be limited to a single trip to a park or development to be hooked up to utilities. Manufactured housing may, however, be considered real property if it becomes permanently affixed to the land. The distinction is generally one of state law. Whether manufactured housing is characterized as real or personal property may have an effect on how it is taxed. Real estate licensees should be familiar with local laws before attempting to sell manufactured housing. Some states permit only specially licensed dealers to sell such housing; other states require no special licensing.

Plants

Trees and crops generally fall into one of two classes. Trees, perennial shrubbery, and grasses that do not require annual cultivation are considered real estate. They obviously attach to the land. Annual plantings or crops of wheat, corn, vegetables, and fruit, known as **emblements**, generally are considered personal property. As long as an annual crop is growing, it will stay with the real property unless other provisions are made in the sales contract.

> **In Illinois**

When Illinois farmland is sold, it is customary for possession to be transferred to the buyer on March 1. March 1 is chosen because it falls after the last year's crops have been harvested and before the new crops are planted. Because of this "standard" date, no special provisions are required regarding the annual crops. However, when possession is transferred to the buyer on March 1, it also is customary for the buyer to assume full payment of the current year's tax bill *without proration*; this is because he or she will receive the full benefit of the new crop for that tax year.

> The term used in the law for plants that do not require annual cultivation (such as trees and shrubbery) is *fructus naturales* (fruits of nature); emblements are known in the law as *fructus industriales* (fruits of industry).

If the sale is closed at another time during the year and before the crops are harvested, the sales contract should indicate whether the growing crops are included in the sales price. Sometimes, when the crop is included in the sale, the buyer reimburses the seller for crop-related costs already incurred, such as seed, planting, fertilizing, and spraying. As for farm leases, if an owner wishes to break a lease with a tenant, notification must be given by November 1. This produces the least interference with the cycle of spring planting and fall harvesting. ■

An item of real property can become personal property by **severance**. For example, a growing tree is *real estate* until the owner cuts it down, *severing* it from the property. Similarly, an apple becomes personal property once it is picked from a tree, and a wheat crop becomes personal property once harvested.

It also is possible to change personal property into real property; for example, a landowner buys cement, stones, and sand; mixes them into concrete; and constructs a sidewalk across his or her land. This landowner has effectively converted personal property (cement, stones, and sand) into real property (a sidewalk). This process is called **attachment** (annexation).

Licensees need to know whether property is real or personal for many reasons. An important distinction arises, for instance, when the property is transferred from one owner to another. *Real property* is conveyed by **deed**, while *personal property* is conveyed by a **bill of sale**.

Classifications of Fixtures

In considering the differences between real and personal property, it is necessary to distinguish between a *fixture* and *personal property*.

FIGURE 2.3

Legal Tests of a Fixture

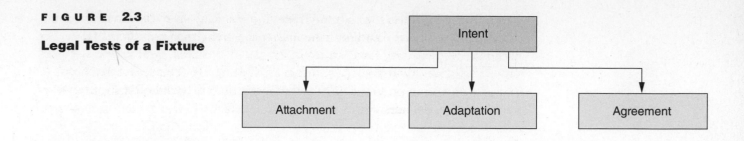

FIGURE 2.3

Legal Tests of a Fixture

Legal Tests of a Fixture

1. Method of attachment
2. Adaptation to real estate
3. Agreement

Fixtures.   A fixture is *personal property that has been so attached to land or a building that, by law, it becomes part of the real estate.* Examples of fixtures are heating systems, elevator equipment in highrise buildings, radiators, kitchen cabinets, attached bookcases, light fixtures, and plumbing fixtures. Almost any item that has been added as a permanent part of a building is considered a fixture. During the course of time, the same materials may be both real and personal property, depending on their use and location.

Legal tests of a fixture.   The overall test that is used in determining whether an item is a fixture or personal property is a question of intent. (See Figure 2.3.)

Did the person who installed the item intend for it to remain permanently on the property or for it to be removable in the future? In determining intent, courts use three basic tests:

1. *Method of attachment*—How permanent is the method of attachment? Can the item be removed without causing damage to the surrounding property?
2. *Adaptation to real estate*—Is the item being used as real property or personal property?
3. *Agreement*—Have the parties agreed in writing on whether the item is real or personal property? What does the contract say?

Although these tests may seem simple, court decisions have occasionally been inconsistent. Property that appears to be permanently affixed sometimes has been ruled to be personal property, while property that seems removable has been ruled a fixture. It is important that an owner clarify what is to be sold with the real estate at the very beginning of the sales process.

IN PRACTICE

At the time a property is listed, the seller and real estate agent should discuss which items will be included in the sale. Any item that the seller does not want included in the sale should be replaced prior to public viewing. The written sales contract between the buyer and the seller should *list articles included in the sale if any doubt exists as to whether they are personal property or fixtures.*

Trade fixtures.   A special category of fixture includes property used in the course of business. An article owned by a tenant and attached to a rented space or building or used in conducting a business is a trade fixture, also called a *chattel fixture.* Some examples of trade fixtures are bowling alleys, store shelves, bars, and restaurant equipment. Agricultural fixtures, such as chicken coops and toolsheds, also are included in this category. Trade fixtures must be removed on or before the last day the property is rented. The tenant is responsible for any damage caused by the removal of a trade fixture. Trade fixtures that are not removed become the real property of the landlord. Acquiring the property in this way is known as accession.

Personal property that "turns into" real property does so by **attachment**. However, in commercial real estate if trade fixtures (personal property) are left unremoved, they become real property belonging to the lessor by **accession**.

■ **FOR EXAMPLE** Paul's Pizza leases space in a small shopping center. Paul bolted a large iron oven to the floor of the unit. When Paul's Pizza goes out of business or relocates, Paul will be able to take his pizza oven with him on or before the last day of his occupancy. (Paul needs to repair the bolt holes left in the floor.)

Trade fixtures differ from other fixtures in these ways:

■ Fixtures belong to the owner of the real estate, but trade fixtures are usually owned and installed by a tenant for the tenant's use.
■ Fixtures are considered a permanent part of a building, but trade fixtures are removable. Trade fixtures may be attached to a building so they appear to be fixtures, then later carefully removed.

Legally, fixtures are real property, so they are included in any sale or mortgage. Trade fixtures, however, are considered personal property and are not included in the sale or mortgage of real estate, except by written agreement.

■ OWNERSHIP OF REAL PROPERTY

Traditionally, ownership of real property is described as a **bundle of legal rights.** In other words, a purchaser of real estate actually buys the rights of ownership held by the seller. These rights include the

■ right of possession;
■ right to control the property within the framework of the law;
■ right of enjoyment (that is, to use the property in any legal manner);
■ right of exclusion (to keep others from entering or using the property); and
■ right of disposition (to sell, will, transfer, or otherwise dispose of or encumber the property).

The concept of a bundle of rights comes from old English law. In the Middle Ages, a seller transferred property by giving the purchaser a handful of earth or a bundle of bound sticks from a tree on the property, symbolizing the whole property. The purchaser, who accepted the bundle in a ceremony, became owner of the tree producing the sticks *and* the land to which the tree was attached. Because the rights of ownership (like the sticks) can be separated and individually transferred, the sticks became symbolic of those rights. (See Figure 2.4.)

■ CHARACTERISTICS OF REAL ESTATE

Real estate possesses seven basic characteristics that define its nature and affect its use. These characteristics fall into two broad categories—*economic* characteristics and *physical* characteristics.

FIGURE   2.4

The Bundle of Legal Rights

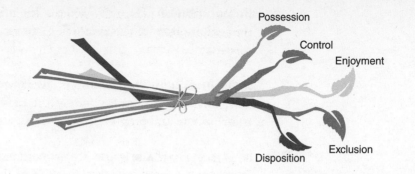

Possession
Control
Enjoyment
Exclusion
Disposition

Economic Characteristics

The economic characteristics of land affect its investment value. These four characteristics are *scarcity, improvements, permanence of investment,* and *location (situs).*

Scarcity.   We usually do not consider land a rare commodity, but only a quarter of the earth's surface is dry land; the rest is water. The total available supply of land is not limitless. While a considerable amount of land remains unused or uninhabited, the supply in a given location or of a particular quality is generally considered to be limited.

Improvements.   Building an improvement on one parcel of land can affect the land's value and use as well as that of neighboring tracts and whole communities. For example, constructing a new shopping center or selecting a nuclear power site or toxic waste dump can dramatically shift land values in a large area.

Permanence of investment.   The capital and labor used to build an improvement represent a large fixed investment. Although even a well-built structure can be razed to make way for a newer building, improvements such as drainage, electricity, water, and sewage systems often remain. The return on such investments tends to be long term and relatively stable.

Location.   This economic characteristic, sometimes called area preference or **situs,** does not directly refer to a geographic location but rather to people's preferences for given areas. It is the unique quality of these preferences that results in different values for similar units. *Location is the most important economic characteristic of land.*

■ **FOR EXAMPLE** A river runs through Bedford Falls, dividing the town more or less in half. On the north side of the river, known as North Town, houses sell for an average of $170,000. On the south side of the river, known as Southbank, identical houses sell for more than $200,000. The only difference is that homebuyers think that Southbank is a better neighborhood, even though no obvious difference exists between the two equally pleasant sides of town.

> **Four Economic Characteristics of Real Estate**
> 1. Scarcity
> 2. Improvements
> 3. Permanence of investment
> 4. Location

Physical Characteristics

Land has three main physical characteristics: *immobility, indestructibility,* and *uniqueness.*

Immobility. It is true that some of the substances of land are removable and that topography may shift. Nevertheless, *the geographic location of any given parcel of land can never be changed*. It is fixed or *immobile*.

Indestructibility. Land also is *indestructible*. This permanence of land, coupled with the long-term nature of most improvements, tends to stabilize investments in real estate.

The fact that land is indestructible does not change the fact that man-made *improvements* on land depreciate and can become obsolete, which *may* dramatically reduce the land's value. This gradual depreciation should not be confused with the knowledge that the economic desirability of a given location can change.

Uniqueness. No two parcels of land are ever exactly the same. Although they may be substantially similar, all parcels differ geographically because each parcel has its own location. The characteristics of each property, no matter how small, differ from those of every other. An individual parcel has no substitute because each is unique. The uniqueness of land also is referred to as its *heterogeneity* or *nonhomogeneity*.

■ **FOR EXAMPLE** Because of the uniqueness of property, a person who contracts to buy a new condominium apartment, say, Unit 305, cannot have Unit 307 substituted at the closing, even though the two units appear to be identical. The buyer could sue for *specific performance* (asking the seller to "perform" on the promise of Unit 305) based on the *uniqueness* of real estate.

> **Physical Characteristics of Real Estate**
> 1. Immobility
> 2. Indestructibility
> 3. Uniqueness

■ LAWS AFFECTING REAL ESTATE

The unique nature of real estate has given rise to an equally unique set of laws and rights. Even the simplest real estate transaction involves a body of complex laws. Licensees must have a clear and accurate understanding of the laws that affect real estate.

The specific areas important to the real estate practitioner include law of contracts, general property law, law of agency, and the state's real estate license law. All of these will be discussed at length later in this book. Federal regulations (such as environmental laws) as well as federal, state, and local tax laws also play an important role in real estate transactions. Finally, state and local land-use and zoning laws, as well as environmental regulations, have a significant impact on the practice of real estate, too.

Laws come from seven different sources. They are the *United States Constitution*, *laws passed by Congress*, *rules of the regulatory agencies*, *state constitutions*, *state statutes*, *local ordinances*, and *common law* (common usage and court decisions).

> **Seven Sources of Law**
> 1. United States Constitution
> 2. Laws passed by Congress
> 3. Rules of the regulatory agencies
> 4. State constitutions
> 5. State statutes
> 6. Local ordinances
> 7. Common law

A real estate practitioner can't be an expert in all areas of real estate law. However, licensees should know and understand some basic principles. Perhaps most important is the ability to recognize which problems should be referred to a real estate attorney. Only attorneys are trained and licensed to prepare documents defining or transferring rights in property and to give advice on matters of law.

Under no circumstances may a broker or salesperson act as an attorney unless he or she is also a licensed attorney representing a client in only that capacity. This includes filling in the blanks in deeds or mortgages.

In Illinois

The practice of real estate in Illinois is governed by the **Real Estate License Act of 2000**, as amended from time to time by the legislature, and by the rules established by the Illinois Department of Financial and Professional Regulation. This license law, which replaced the Real Estate Licensing Act of 1983, is *Public Act 91-0245, Chapter 225 of the Illinois Compiled Statutes, Act 454.* Other laws affecting real estate in Illinois may be found throughout the Illinois compiled statutes, but many of those addressing real property are in *Chapter 765, ILCS.* ■

Key Law for Illinois

The Illinois Real Estate License Act of 2000
■ Click on *www.ilga.gov*
■ Click on *Illinois Compiled Statutes*
■ Click on *Chapter 225 Professions and Occupations*
■ Scroll to *225 ILCS 454*

Because brokers and salespersons are involved with other people's real estate and money, the need for regulation of their activities has long been recognized. The purpose of real estate license law is to protect the public from fraud, dishonesty, and incompetence in real estate transactions. All 50 states, the District of Columbia, and all Canadian provinces have passed laws that require real estate brokers and salespersons to be licensed. Although state license laws are similar in many broad respects, they may differ on key points, from the amount of education required for a license to appropriate approaches for handling agency relationships. In practice, those differences sometimes are quite significant.

Note: The License Act of 2000 and the Rules are discussed in Chapter 14.

■ SUMMARY

Although most people think of land as the surface of the earth, land actually includes the earth's surface, the mineral deposits under the earth, and the air above the earth. The term real estate further expands this definition to include all natural and man-made improvements attached to the land. The term real property describes real estate plus the bundle of legal rights associated with its ownership.

The various rights to the same parcel of real estate may be owned and controlled by different parties. For instance, one person may own the surface rights, one the air rights, and one the subsurface rights.

All property that does not fit the definition of real estate is classified as personal property (or chattels). When articles of personal property are attached to real estate, they may become fixtures and as such are considered part of the real estate. However, personal property attached to real property by a tenant for business purposes is called a trade fixture, and it remains personal property, transportable by the tenant at the end of the lease. The special nature of land as an investment is apparent in both its economic and physical characteristics. The economic characteristics are scarcity, improvements, permanence of investment, and location (situs). The physical characteristics of land are that it is immobile, indestructible, and unique.

Even the simplest real estate transaction reflects a complex body of laws. They are the United States Constitution, laws passed by Congress, rules of the regulatory agencies, state constitutions, state statutes, local ordinances, and common law (shaped by common usage and court decisions). A buyer of real estate purchases from the seller the legal rights to use the land in certain ways, going back to the old English transfer of bundle rights—the symbolic few branches from a tree on the land.

All 50 states, the District of Columbia, and Canadian provinces have some type of licensing requirement for real estate brokers and salespersons. Real estate professionals have an obligation to be familiar with the real estate laws and licensing requirements not only for their own states but for any areas into which their practice may extend.

QUESTIONS

1. One defining difference between real estate (real property) and personal property is
   a. real estate includes land and all things permanently attached, while personal property includes property that is movable.
   b. real estate includes land and the rights and interests inherent in the ownership of land, while personal property includes only air and mineral rights.
   c. real estate includes the trees and air rights, while personal property includes the house and its contents.
   d. real estate includes annual crops, while personal property includes mineral rights.

2. Helen owns a building in a commercial area of town. Trudy rents space in the building and operates a bookstore. In Trudy's bookstore, there are large tables fastened to the walls where customers are encouraged to sit and read. Shelves create aisles from the front of the store to the back. The shelves are bolted to both the ceiling and the floor. Which of the following best characterizes the contents of Trudy's bookstore?
   a. The shelves and tables are trade fixtures and will be sold when Helen sells the building.
   b. The shelves and tables are trade fixtures and must be removed before Trudy's lease expires.
   c. Because Trudy is a tenant, the shelves and tables are fixtures and may not be removed except with Helen's permission.
   d. Because the shelves and tables are attached to the building, they are treated the same way as other fixtures.

3. The term *nonhomogeneity* refers to
   a. scarcity.
   b. immobility.
   c. uniqueness.
   d. indestructibility.

4. Another term for personal property is
   a. realty.
   b. fixtures.
   c. chattels.
   d. fructus naturales.

5. When an owner of real estate sells the property to someone else, which of the "sticks" in the bundle of legal rights is he or she using?
   a. Exclusion
   b. Legal enjoyment
   c. Control
   d. Disposition

6. Omar inherited Rolling Hills Farm from his uncle. The first thing Omar did with the vacant property was to remove all the topsoil, which he sold to a landscaping company. Omar then removed a thick layer of limestone and sold it to a construction company. Finally, Omar dug 40 feet into the bedrock and sold it for gravel. When Omar died, he left Rolling Hills to his daughter, Patty. Which of the following statements is *TRUE?*
   a. Patty inherits nothing because Rolling Hills no longer exists.
   b. Patty inherits a large hole in the ground, but it is still Rolling Hills, down to the center of the earth.
   c. Patty owns the gravel, limestone, and topsoil, no matter where it is.
   d. Omar's estate must restore Rolling Hills to its original condition.

7. The buyer and the seller of a home are debating whether a certain item is real or personal property. The buyer says it is real property and should convey with the house; the seller says it is personal property and would not convey without a separate bill of sale. In determining whether an item is real or personal property, a court would *NOT* consider which of the following?
   a. The cost of the item when it was purchased
   b. Whether its removal would cause severe damage to the real estate
   c. Whether the item is clearly adapted to the real estate
   d. Any relevant agreement of the parties in their contract of sale

8. Which of the following would *BEST* describe the *economic characteristics* of real estate?

   a. Location, uniqueness, and indestructibility
   b. Scarcity, immobility, and improvements
   c. Heterogeneity, location, and improvements
   d. Scarcity, improvements, and area preference

9. An owner decides to sell her house and takes the antique front door with her when she moves. In the absence of any provision in the contract, is the owner allowed to remove the door?

   a. Yes, the owner can remove the door, and the act would be known as *accession*.
   b. No, this act of *severance* is not allowed at time of selling because the door is a fixture.
   c. No, this would be *conversion*.
   d. Yes, the owner can remove the door, and the act would be known as *separation*.

10. When the buyer moved into a newly purchased home, the buyer discovered that the seller had taken the electric lighting units that were installed over the vanity in the bathroom. The seller had not indicated that these would be removed. Which of the following is *TRUE*?

    a. Installed lighting units normally are considered to be real estate fixtures.
    b. The lighting fixtures belong to the seller because he installed them as personal property.
    c. These lighting fixtures are considered trade fixtures, and could be removed.
    d. Original lighting fixtures are real property, but replacement lighting would be personal property and can be taken by the seller.

11. Jamal is building a new enclosed front porch on his home. A truckload of lumber has been left on Jamal's driveway for use in building the porch. At this point, the lumber is considered what kind of property?

    a. A fixture, because it will be permanently affixed to existing real property
    b. Personal property
    c. A chattel that is real property
    d. A trade fixture or chattel fixture

12. Intent of the parties, method of attachment, adaptation to real estate, and agreement between the parties are the legal tests for determining whether an item is

    a. a trade fixture or personal property.
    b. real property or real estate.
    c. a fixture or personal property.
    d. an improvement.

13. Parking spaces in multiunit buildings, water rights, and other improvements are classified as

    a. trade fixtures.
    b. emblements.
    c. subsurface rights.
    d. appurtenances.

14. Yolanda purchases Greenacre, a parcel of natural forest. She immediately cuts down all the trees and constructs a large shed out of old sheets of rusted tin, where she stores turpentine, varnish, and industrial waste products. Which of the following statements is *TRUE* about this rusty shed?

    a. Yolanda's action constitutes improvement of the property.
    b. Yolanda's shed is personal property.
    c. If Yolanda is in the business of storing toxic substances, her shed is a trade fixture.
    d. Altering the property in order to construct a shed is not included in the bundle of rights.

CHAPTER 3

Concepts of Home Ownership

■ **LEARNING OBJECTIVES** *When you've finished reading this chapter, you should be able to*

- ■ **identify** the various types of housing choices available to home buyers.

- ■ **describe** the issues involved in making a home ownership decision.

- ■ **explain** the tax benefits of home ownership and the provisions of changes to the Tax Code.

- ■ **distinguish** the various types of homeowner's insurance policy coverage.

- ■ **define** the following *key terms:*

actual cost value policies	coinsurance clause	homeowner's insurance policy
Comprehensive Loss Underwriting Exchange (CLUE)	equity guaranteed replacement cost policies	liability coverage replacement cost

■ HOME OWNERSHIP

People buy homes for both psychological and financial reasons. To many, home ownership is a sign of financial stability. It is an investment that can appreciate in value and provide federal income tax deductions. Home ownership also imparts benefits that are less tangible but no less valuable: pride, security, and a sense of belonging to the community.

Types of Housing

As our society evolves, the needs of its homebuyers become more specialized. Various forms of housing respond to the demands of a diverse marketplace.

Apartment complexes are groups of apartment buildings with any number of units in each building. The buildings may be lowrise or highrise, and the amenities may include parking, security, clubhouses, swimming pools, tennis courts, and even golf courses.

The *condominium* is a popular form of residential ownership, particularly for people who want the security of owning property without the care and maintenance a house demands. Condominium owners share ownership of common facilities such as halls, elevators, swimming pools, clubhouses, tennis courts, and surrounding grounds. Management and maintenance of building exteriors and common facilities are provided by the governing association or by outside contractors, with expenses paid out of monthly assessments charged to owners.

A *cooperative* is similar to a condominium in that it also may offer units with shared common facilities. The owners, however, do not actually own the units. Instead, they buy *shares of stock* in the corporation that holds title to the building. Owners receive proprietary leases that entitle them to occupy particular units. Like condominium unit owners, cooperative unit owners pay their share of the building's expenses.

Planned unit developments (PUDs), sometimes called *master-planned communities*, merge such diverse land uses as housing, recreation facilities, and commercial concerns in one self-contained development. PUDs are planned under special zoning ordinances. These ordinances permit maximum use of open space by reducing lot sizes and street areas. A community association is formed to maintain these areas, with fees collected from the owners.

Retirement communities, many of them in temperate climates, often are structured as PUDs. They may provide shopping, recreational opportunities, and healthcare facilities in addition to residential units.

Highrise developments, sometimes called *mixed-use developments* (MUDs), combine such elements as office space, stores, theaters, and apartment units into a single vertical community. MUDs are self-contained, offering convenient options (such as a spa or exercise facility) to those living there.

Converted-use properties are factories, warehouses, office buildings, hotels, schools, churches, and other structures that have been converted to residential use. Developers often find renovation of such properties more aesthetically and economically appealing than demolishing a perfectly sound structure to build something new. An abandoned warehouse may be transformed into luxury loft condominium units, a closed hotel may reopen as an apartment building, or an old factory may be recycled into a profitable shopping mall.

Manufactured housing, including mobile homes, was once considered useful only as temporary residences. Now, however, such homes are more often permanent principal residences or stationary vacation homes. Increased living space now available in the newer models combined with low cost has made such homes an attractive option for many. Housing parks make residential environments possible with community facilities; semipermanent home foundations; and hookups for gas, water, and electricity.

Modular homes offer another lower-cost ownership option. Each room is preassembled at a factory, driven to the building site on a truck, then lowered onto its foundation by a crane. Later, workers finish the structure and connect plumbing and wiring. Entire developments can be built at a fraction of the time and cost of conventional construction.

Through *time-shares*, multiple purchasers share ownership of a single property, usually a vacation home. Each owner is entitled to use the property for a certain period of time each year, usually a specific week. In addition to the purchase price, each owner pays an annual maintenance fee.

■ HOUSING AFFORDABILITY

Housing costs have become a major issue in many areas. Location is a huge variable. Because more homeowners mean more business opportunities, however, real estate and related industry groups have a vital interest in ensuring continued affordable housing for all segments of the population.

Certainly, not everyone wants to own a home. Home ownership involves substantial commitment and responsibility. People whose work requires frequent moves or whose financial position is uncertain particularly benefit from renting. Renting also provides more leisure time by freeing tenants from management and maintenance.

Those who choose home ownership must evaluate many factors before they decide to purchase property. The purchasing decision must be weighed carefully in light of each individual's financial circumstances. Renters can probably make a higher mortgage payment than their current rent payment, without requiring a pay increase, because of the tax savings realized by home ownership.

The decision of buying or renting property involves considering

- how long a person wants to live in a particular area,
- a person's financial situation,
- housing affordability,
- current mortgage interest rates,
- tax consequences of owning versus renting property, and
- what may happen to home prices and tax laws in the future.

Mortgage Terms

Liberalized mortgage terms and payment plans today open up real estate ownership to many who would otherwise not qualify. Low down payment mortgage loans are available under special programs sponsored by the Federal Housing Administration (FHA) and the Department of Veterans Affairs (VA) along with an increasing number of creative mortgage loan programs. Specific programs may offer lower closing costs to purchasers in targeted neighborhoods or to first-time buyers anywhere. Increasing numbers of innovative loans are tailored to suit younger buyers or persons whose income is expected to increase in coming years, as well as retirees looking to supplement their income by utilizing the equity in their home.

Ownership Expenses and Ability to Pay

Home ownership involves many expenses, including utilities (such as electricity, natural gas, and water), trash removal, sewer charges, and maintenance and repairs. Owners also must pay real estate taxes and buy property insurance, and they must repay the mortgage loan with interest.

A home purchased at a price of $350,000 ($70,000 down) on a 30-year loan, 6 percent interest, will ultimately cost the consumer more than $590,000.

To determine whether a prospective buyer can afford a certain purchase, lenders traditionally have used this basic formula: the monthly cost of buying and maintaining a home (mortgage payments—both principal and interest—plus monthly taxes and insurance payments) should not exceed 28 percent of gross monthly income. *The payments on all long-term debts combined with the house payment should not exceed 36 percent of gross monthly income.* These formulas may vary, however, depending on the type of loan program and the borrower's earnings, credit history, number of dependents, and other factors.

■ **FOR EXAMPLE** A consumer wants to know how much house he or she can afford. That consumer has a gross monthly income of $5,000, with $800 in monthly debt. Allowable housing expense using the 28 percent and 36 percent ratios may be calculated as follows:

Ratio 1: $5,000 gross monthly income x 28% = $1,400 total housing expense allowed.

Ratio 2: $5,000 gross monthly income x 36% = $1,800 total housing expense and other long-term debt allowed.

BOTH ratios need to be met independently in most loan scenarios.

In this case, $1,400 (Ratio 1) plus existent debt ($800 indicated) = $2,200. $2,200 exceeds the dollar amount for Ratio 2 (a maximum of $1,800), so *Ratio 2 is not met.*

If actual debts exceed the amount allowed and the borrower is unable to reduce them, the monthly payment would have to be lowered proportionately using some other loan package or by purchasing a less expensive property. *Debts and housing payment combined should not exceed 36 percent of gross monthly income.*

Memory Tip

The basic costs of owning a home—mortgage *Principal, Interest, Taxes,* and *Insurance*—can be remembered by the acronym **PITI**.

Investment Considerations

Current market value – Property debt = Equity

Purchasing a home offers several financial advantages to a buyer. First, if the property's value increases, a sale could bring in more money than the owner paid, creating a long-term gain. Second, as the total mortgage debt is reduced through monthly payments, the owner's actual ownership interest in the property increases. This increasing ownership interest is called **equity** and represents the paid-off share of the property held free of any mortgage. A tenant accumulates a good credit rating by paying the rent on time, but a homeowner's *mortgage payments build equity and so increase net worth.* Equity also builds when the property's value rises through area appreciation. The third financial advantage of home ownership is in tax deductions available to homeowners but not to renters.

Tax Benefits

To encourage home ownership, the federal government allows homeowners certain income tax advantages. Homeowners may deduct from their income some or all of the mortgage interest paid as well as real estate taxes and certain other expenses identified on page 28. Tax considerations may be an important part of any decision to purchase a home.

The federal government excludes $500,000 from capital gains tax on sale profits from a principal residence as long as the taxpayers are married, filing jointly. Taxpayers who file singly are entitled to a $250,000 exclusion. The exemption may be used repeatedly, as long as the homeowners have occupied the property as their principal residence for *two out of the last five years*.

Yet another reform benefits the real estate market by making it easier for people to obtain down payments. First-time homebuyers may make penalty-free withdrawals from their tax-deferred individual retirement funds (IRAs) to make a down payment on a home; however, these withdrawals are still subject to income tax. The limit on such withdrawals is $10,000 and must be spent entirely within 120 days on a down payment to avoid the 10 percent penalty.

In short, the changes in tax laws have generally benefited home ownership, which is good news for homeowners and real estate professionals.

The *Jobs & Growth Tax Relief Reconciliation Act of 2003* provides tax breaks in several areas. As it relates to homeownership, the tax rate for capital gains was reduced. The maximum tax rate on individual's capital gains was reduced to 15 percent in 2003 through 2008. For taxpayers in the 10 percent and 15 percent ordinary income tax rate brackets, the rate on capital gains was reduced to 5 percent in 2003 through 2007, and to zero percent for 2008 through 2010. These rates apply to capital gains realized on or after May 6, 2003.

Another tax benefit is the 1031 exchange. An *exchange* is a transaction in which all or part of the consideration for the purchase of real property is the transfer of property of "like kind." The tax-free exchange involves the exchange of property held for investment, or the production of income for property of a like kind (which includes improved and unimproved property). In such an exchange, payment of capital gains tax is not avoided but rather is deferred until the property is later disposed of in a taxable transaction. The underlying philosophy behind an exchange is that income tax should not apply as long as an investment remains intact in the form of real estate. The exchange of a personal residence does not qualify for this tax-deferred treatment. One disadvantage to an investor in a tax-free exchange is that the basis in the new property is lower than it would have been had the new property been purchased and the old property been sold in separate transactions. Such a reduced basis thus results in smaller depreciation deductions. It is important that the contract indicate the taxpayer's intention to exchange rather than sell the property.

It is rare to find two properties of equal value and equity; therefore, to balance the equities, one party usually also pays some money or assumes a larger amount of underlying debt. If received by the party seeking the tax-free exchange, this money or additional debt from which a person is relieved would be treated as "boot," and gain will be taxable to the extent of that boot.

In many cases, the exchangor needs time to locate the replacement property. Under special delayed exchange rules, the exchange need not be simultaneous, although there are strict time periods in which to locate and close the replacement property measured from the time of sale of the relinquished property. The replacement property must be located within the United States if the exchanged property is U.S. property. It is permissible to exchange foreign property for foreign property. If the exchangors are married, the spouse should release any marital rights.

Tax deductions.   Homeowners may deduct from their gross income any of the following:

- Real estate taxes
- Mortgage interest payments on most first and second homes (The combined amount of acquisition indebtedness cannot exceed $1,000,000 and the combined amount of home equity indebtedness cannot exceed $100,000.)
- Loan origination fees in the year of purchase (Rules differ for refinance and equity loans.)
- Loan discount points in the year of purchase (Rules differ for refinance and equity loans.)
- Loan prepayment penalties

When a homeowner adds to a property's value in preparation for its sale, the homeowner may deduct certain expenses such as paint, carpeting, and wallpaper and the cost of other repairs from any gain in determining the adjusted sales price for capital gains purposes. In addition, all expenses incurred to complete the sales transaction may be used to reduce the sales price such as commission, attorney fees, closing fees, etc. Be sure to contact a CPA or tax attorney for further discussion.

IN PRACTICE   Note that appraisal fees, notary fees, preparation costs, mortgage insurance premiums, and VA funding fees are not interest but are part of the cost of acquiring a home. When it is sold at a later date, these charges can be figured into the cost *basis*. Points are deductible in the year of a house purchase if certain criteria are met. Points are deducted over the life of the loan for a refinance. Note that real estate licensees should not provide tax advice and homeowners should consult with accountants or attorneys about home ownership or investment tax deductions. The rules are complicated and constantly changing.

■ HOMEOWNER'S INSURANCE

A home is often the largest investment people will ever make. Most homeowners see the wisdom in protecting such an important investment by insuring it. Lenders usually require that a homeowner obtain insurance when a debt is secured by the property. While owners can purchase individual policies that insure against destruction of property by fire or windstorm, injury to others, and theft of personal property, most buy packaged **homeowner's insurance policies** to cover all these risks.

Coverage and Claims   The most common homeowner's policy is called a *basic form*. It provides property coverage against

- fire and lightning,
- glass breakage,

- windstorm and hail,
- explosion,
- riot and civil commotion,
- damage by aircraft,
- damage from vehicles,
- damage from smoke,
- vandalism and malicious mischief,
- theft, and
- loss of property removed from the premises when it is endangered by fire or other perils.

A broad-form policy also is available. It covers

- falling objects;
- damage due to the weight of ice, snow, or sleet;
- collapse of all or part of the building;
- bursting, cracking, burning, or bulging of a steam or hot water heating system or of appliances used to heat water;
- accidental discharge, leakage, or overflow of water or steam from within a plumbing, a heating, or an air-conditioning system;
- freezing of plumbing, heating, and air-conditioning systems and domestic appliances; and
- injury to electrical appliances, devices, fixtures, and wiring from short circuits or other accidentally generated currents.

Further insurance is available from policies that cover almost all possible perils. For instance, apartment and condominium policies generally provide fire and windstorm, theft, and public liability coverage for injuries or losses sustained within the unit. However, they do not usually cover losses or damages to the structure. The basic structure, in such cases, is insured by either the landlord or the condominium owner's association.

A third party, such as an insurance company, often settles any covered insurance claim. When this happens, the third party generally acquires the right to any legal damages available to the insured. This right is called *subrogation*. (In other words, if a house burns down due to a utility company's negligence, and the insured accepts compensation from the insurance company, then the insurance company gains the rights related to possible further payment for damages from the utility company.)

When determining what will be paid to the insured, **actual cash value policies** usually subtract depreciation from the value of the property and may result in lower-than-market-value compensation for a structure. Many homeowner's insurance policies, however, contain a **coinsurance clause**. **Guaranteed replacement cost policies** (with coinsurance) usually require that the owner maintain insurance equal to at least 80 percent of the replacement cost of the dwelling. *An owner who has this type of policy may make a claim for the full cost of the repair/replacement of the damaged structure without first depreciating it.* If the homeowner carries less than 80 percent of the full replacement cost, however, the claim will be handled in one of two ways. Either the loss will be settled for the *actual cash value* (replacement cost minus depreciation) or it may be prorated by dividing actual insurance percentage by the recommended percentage of coinsurance (usually 80 percent). The resulting percentage times estimated loss equals payout.

■ **FOR EXAMPLE** Tom's insurance policy is for 80 percent of the replacement cost of his home, or $80,000. His home is valued at $100,000, and the land is valued at $40,000. Tom sustains $30,000 in fire damage to his house. Tom can make a claim for the full cost of the repair or replacement of the damaged property, without deduction for depreciation. However, if Tom had insurance of only $70,000, his claim would be handled in one of two ways. He would receive either actual cash value (replacement cost of $30,000 less depreciation cost of say $3,000, or $27,000), or his claim would be prorated by dividing the percentage of replacement cost actually covered (.70) by the policy minimum coverage requirement (.80). So, .70 divided by .80 equals .875, and $30,000 multiplied by .875 equals $26,250.

Comprehensive Loss Underwriting Exchange

Comprehensive Loss Undewriting Exchange (CLUE) is a database of consumer claim history that enables insurance companies to access prior claim information in the underwriting and rating process. The database contains up to five years of personal property claim history. The reports include policy information such as name, date of birth, policy number, and claim information date (date and type of loss, amounts paid, and description of property covered).

IN PRACTICE   Water-related problems have emerged in some properties over time. In particular, significant problems can occur with synthetic stucco exterior finishes and mold. The *exterior insulating finishing system* (EIFS) is a highly effective moisture barrier that also tends to *seal in* moisture—trapping water in the home's walls and resulting in massive wood rot. Frequently, the effects of the rotting cannot be seen until the damage is extensive and sometimes irreparable. If a homeowner suspects that EIFS was used on their home and is causing damage, the homeowner should have the property inspected. Some insurance companies refuse to cover homes with EIFS exteriors, and class action lawsuits have been brought against builders by distressed homeowners.

■ FEDERAL FLOOD INSURANCE PROGRAM

The National Flood Insurance Act of 1968 was enacted by Congress to assist owners of property in flood-prone areas by subsidizing flood insurance and by taking land-use and land-control measures to improve future management for floodplain areas. The Federal Emergency Management Agency (FEMA) administers the flood insurance program, and the Army Corps of Engineers has prepared detailed maps that identify specific flood-prone areas throughout the country. To finance property with federal or federally related mortgage loans, owners in flood-prone areas must obtain flood insurance. If they do not obtain the insurance, they will not receive the loan.

In designated areas, flood insurance is required on all types of buildings—residential, commercial, industrial, and agricultural—for either the value of the property or the amount of the mortgage loan, subject to the maximum limits available. Policies are written annually and can be purchased from any licensed property insurance broker, the National Flood Insurance Program (NFIP), or the designated servicing companies in each state. However, if a borrower can produce a survey showing that the lowest part of the building is located above the 100-year flood mark, the borrower may be exempted from the flood insurance requirement, even if the property is in a flood-prone area.

■ SUMMARY

Current trends in home ownership include cooperatives, apartment complexes, condominiums, planned unit developments (PUDs), retirement communities, highrise developments, converted-use properties, modular homes, mobile homes, time-shares/time-uses, and of course, residential housing. Prospective buyers should be aware of the many pluses and minuses in home ownership. While a homeowner gains financial security and pride of ownership, both the initial price and the continuing expenses must be considered.

One of the many income tax benefits available to homeowners is the ability to deduct mortgage interest payments (with certain limitations) and property taxes from federal income taxes. Up to $250,000 (filing singly) or $500,000 (married, filing jointly) in house sale profits can now be excluded from capital gains tax. The exemption may be used repeatedly, but the homeowners must have occupied the property for at least two years out of the last five.

To protect their investment in real estate, most homeowners purchase insurance. A standard homeowner's insurance policy covers fire, theft, and liability, and it can be extended to cover other risks. Many homeowner's policies contain a coinsurance clause that stipulates that the policyholder must maintain insurance in an amount equal to 80 percent of the replacement cost of the home. If this percentage is not met, the policyholder receives only partial compensation for repair costs if a loss occurs. Guaranteed replacement cost policies, with coinsurance met, offer the most security. Actual cash value policies usually subtract depreciation before determining compensation and result in lower compensation.

The federal government requires flood insurance for federally regulated or federally insured mortgage loans for properties in flood-prone areas. Many such areas are covered by federally subsidized insurance programs. Lenders may notify buyers of the need for flood insurance during the loan acquisition process, but many buyers will want to know prior to purchase. Sellers who know of a floodplain on their property must disclose it. Floodplain maps, which change from time to time, may be acquired through local government offices or insurance companies.

The Comprehensive Loss Underwriting Exchange (CLUE) is a database of consumer claim history that enables insurance companies to access prior claim information in the underwriting and rating process.

QUESTIONS

1. Which is *NOT* a cost or expense of owning a home?
   a. Interest paid on borrowed capital
   b. Homeowners' insurance
   c. Maintenance and repairs
   d. Taxes on personal property

2. Mr. and Mrs. Homeowner paid $56,000 for their property 20 years ago. Today the market value is $119,000, and they owe $5,000 on their mortgage. With regard to this situation, which of the following is *TRUE*?
   a. The $63,000 difference between the original investment and the market value is their tax basis.
   b. The $114,000 difference between the market value and the mortgage is their equity.
   c. The $63,000 difference between the original investment and the market value will be used to compute the capital gains.
   d. The $114,000 difference between the market value and the mortgage is their replacement cost.

3. A building that is remodeled into residential units and is no longer used for the purpose for which it was originally built is an example of a(n)
   a. converted-use property.
   b. urban homesteading.
   c. planned unit development.
   d. modular home.

4. A highrise development that includes office space, stores, theaters, and apartment units is an example of which of the following?
   a. Planned unit development (PUD)
   b. Mixed-use development (MUD)
   c. Converted-use property
   d. Special cluster zoning

5. Danuta, a single person, bought her home 18 months ago and has found a new job in another city. Ursula and Vincent are a married couple who file jointly but have owned their nine-bedroom home for only three years. Now, Ursula and Vincent want to move to a small condominium unit. Walter, a single person, has owned his home for 17 years and will use the proceeds from his sale to purchase a larger house. Based on these facts, which of these people is entitled to the $500,000 exclusion?
   a. Danuta only
   b. Ursula and Vincent only
   c. Ursula, Vincent, and Walter only
   d. Walter and Danuta only

6. If a married, filing jointly homeowner realizes a profit from the sale of his or her home that exceeds $500,000, what is the result?
   a. The homeowner will not pay capital gains tax if he or she is over 55.
   b. Up to $125,000 of the excess profit will be taxed as a capital gain.
   c. The excess gain will be taxed at the homeowner's income tax rate.
   d. The excess gain will be taxed at the current applicable capital gains rate.

7. Theft, smoke damage, and damage from fire are covered under which type of homeowners' insurance policy?
   a. Basic form
   b. Broad form
   c. Coinsurance
   d. National Flood Insurance Program policies

8. One result of the capital gains tax law is that most homeowners
   a. will pay capital gains tax at an 8 percent lower rate on their home sales.
   b. may use a one-time $500,000 exclusion if they file their taxes jointly.
   c. may use a $250,000 exclusion if they lived in the property for two out of the last five years.
   d. will be permitted to use the $125,000 over-55 exclusion more than once.

9. In 2008 Lorenzo purchased his home and paid two discount points at the closing. Which of the following is *NOT* deductible from his gross income?

a. Mortgage interest payments on a principal residence
b. Real estate taxes (except for interest on overdue taxes)
c. The gain realized from the sale or exchange of a principal residence
d. Loan discount points

10. A lot is valued at $25,000 and the house is valued at $75,000. If the house is totally destroyed by fire, under a *standard insurance policy with a coinsurance clause*, which of the following would *MOST LIKELY* occur?

a. The insurance company would pay $100,000 to the owner.
b. The insurance company would pay $75,000 to the owner.
c. The insurance company would pay $60,000 to the owner.
d. The insurance company would pay $80,000 to the owner.

11. Janis has a basis of $80,000 in her primary residence, which she has lived in for three years. She sells the condo for $135,000. The broker's commission was 5.5 percent, and other selling expenses amounted to $1,200. What is Janis's taxable gain on this transaction?

a. $61,425
b. $47,575
c. $0
d. $46,375

12. Marco incurs the following expenses: (1) $9,500 in interest on a mortgage loan on his residence; (2) $800 in real estate taxes plus a $450 late payment penalty; and (3) a $1,000 loan origination fee paid in the course of purchasing his home. How much may be deducted from Marco's gross income?

a. $9,800
b. $10,500
c. $11,300
d. $11,750

CHAPTER 4

Real Estate Agency

■ **LEARNING OBJECTIVES** *When you've finished reading this chapter, you should be able to*

■ **identify** the various types of agency relationships common in the real estate profession and the characteristics of each.

■ **describe** the fiduciary duties involved in an agency relationship.

■ **explain** the process by which agency is created and terminated and the role of disclosure in agency relationships.

■ **distinguish** the duties owed by an agent to his or her client from those owed to customers.

■ **define** the following *key terms:*

agency
agency coupled with an
    interest
agent
Article 15 of the Real
    Estate License Act of
    2000
brokerage agreement
buyer agency
buyer agency agreement
client
commingling
confidentiality
co-op commission
consumer

customer
designated agent
dual agency
express agency
express agreement
fiduciary relationship
fraud
general agency
general agent
gratuitous agency
implied agency
implied agreement
latent defect
law of agency
listing agreement

material fact
Megan's Law
ministerial acts
negligent
    misrepresentation
principal
puffing
ready, willing, and able
    buyer
seller disclosure form
single agency brokerage
special agent
subagent
universal agent

■ INTRODUCTION TO REAL ESTATE AGENCY

The relationship between a real estate licensee and the parties involved in a real estate transaction is not a simple one. In addition to the parties' assumptions and expectations, the licensee is subject to a wide range of legal and ethical requirements designed to protect the seller, the buyer, and the transaction itself. **Agency** is the word used to describe that special relationship between a real estate licensee and the person he or she represents. Agency is governed by two kinds of law: *common law* (the rules of a society established by tradition and court decisions) and *statutory law* (the laws, rules, and regulations enacted by legislatures and other governing bodies).

> In Illinois

Agency relationships in Illinois are now governed by statutes that replace common law. The body of law on which Illinois agency is based is *Article 15 of the Real Estate License Act of 2000*. ■

The History of Agency

The basic historical framework of the law that governs the legal responsibilities of the broker to the people he or she represents is known as **common-law law of agency**. The fundamentals of agency law have remained largely unchanged for hundreds of years. However, the application of the law has changed dramatically, particularly in residential transactions. As states enact legislation that defines and governs the broker-client relationship, brokers are reevaluating their services. They must determine whether they will represent the seller, the buyer, or both (or the lessor, lessee, or both) in a transaction. They also must decide how they will cooperate with other brokers. In short, the brokerage business is undergoing many changes as brokers focus on ways to enhance their services to buyers and sellers.

> "Do my actions and words represent my client's best interests?" The answer should always be "Yes."

Even as the laws change, however, the underlying assumptions that govern the agency relationship remain intact. The principal-agent relationship evolved from the master-servant relationship under English common law. In that relationship, the servant owed absolute loyalty to the master. This loyalty superseded the servant's personal interests as well as any loyalty the servant might owe to others.

In a modern-day agency relationship, the agent still owes the principal loyalty and duty—above any personal interests of the agent. The real estate professional is regarded as an expert on whom the principal can rely for specialized professional advice.

■ LAW OF AGENCY

> In Illinois

The **law of agency** defines the rights and duties of the principal and the agent. It applies to a variety of business transactions. Both contract law and real estate licensing laws—in addition to the law of agency—interpret the relationship between real estate licensees and their clients. The law of agency is a common-law concept. In Illinois the *Real Estate License Act of 2000* is given precedence in defining legal real estate agency concepts. Insofar as real estate is considered, Illinois is a designated agency state that has replaced common-law duties with statutory duties. ■

Definitions

Real estate brokers and salespersons are commonly called *real estate agents*. In real estate, agency is a relationship that a broker, associate broker, or salesperson (representing the broker) may have with buyers, sellers, or prospective tenants who are *clients*. Consumers and customers may become clients and acquire their own "agents" through a contractual relationship (or in some cases by oral agreement, actions, or even implication). It is at this point that the real estate professional actually becomes a legal, loyal agent obligated to work for the client's best interests at all times, so long as those interests are within the law.

The Term *Agency*

In a broader sense than the agent-client relationship, the relationship of the salesperson or associate broker with the firm's broker is also properly called an *agency*: a **general agency**. In this case, the salesperson or associate broker is called a *general agent* because he or she represents the broker in all daily actions. Contracts most effectively establish the client/agent relationship.

Definitions—Statutory (Real Estate License Act of 2000)

In Illinois

Key terms of the law of agency under *Article 15 of the Real Estate License Act of 2000* are defined as follows:

- **Agency**—a relationship in which a real estate broker or licensee, whether directly or through an affiliated licensee, represents a consumer by the consumer's consent, whether express or implied, in a real property transaction.
- **Brokerage agreement**—a written or oral agreement for brokerage services to be provided to a consumer in return for compensation or the right to receive compensation from another.
- **Client**—a person who is being represented by a licensee.
- **Consumer**—a person or entity seeking or receiving licensed activities.
- **Customer**—a consumer who is not being represented by a licensee, but for whom the licensee is performing ministerial acts.
- **Ministerial acts**—those acts that a licensee may perform for a consumer that are informative or clerical in nature and do not rise to the level of active representation on behalf of a consumer. ■

An agent works for the client and with the customer.

There is a distinction between the level of services a licensee (as agent) provides to a **client** and the level of services a licensee may provide to a **customer**. The client is the **principal** to whom his or her agent gives advice and counsel. The agent is entrusted with certain confidential information and has fiduciary responsibilities (sometimes called *statutory responsibilities*) to the principal.

In contrast, the customer is entitled to factual information and honest dealings as a consumer but never receives advice and counsel or confidential information about the principal. The real estate professional may provide small acts of assistance to the customer but, as an agent, *works for* the client. Essentially, the agent is an advocate for the principal, but cannot be one for the customer.

The relationship between the principal and agent must be consensual; that is, the principal delegates authority and the agent consents to act as the agent of the principal. Alternatively, the broker may designate a salesperson to act as agent. The parties must agree to form the relationship. An agent may be authorized by the principal to use the assistance of others. Just as the agent owes certain duties to the principal, the principal has responsibilities toward the agent. The principal's primary duties are to comply with the brokerage agreement and cooperate with the agent; that is, the principal must not hinder the agent and must deal with the agent in good faith. The principal also must compensate the agent according to the terms of the brokerage agreement.

Fiduciary/Statutory Responsibilities

The agency agreement usually authorizes the broker to act for the principal. The agent's **fiduciary relationship** of trust and confidence with the principal means that the broker owed the principal certain specific duties. These duties were not simply moral or ethical; they formed the common law of agency and now are the basis for statutory laws governing real estate transactions. *Under the common law of agency, an agent owes the principal the duties of care, obedience, loyalty, disclosure, accounting, and confidentiality.*

Care.   The agent must exercise a reasonable degree of care while transacting the business entrusted to him or her by the principal. The principal expects the agent's skill and expertise in real estate matters to be superior to that of the average person. The agent should know all facts pertinent to the principal's affairs, such as the physical characteristics of the property being transferred and the type of financing being used. If the agent represents the seller, care and skill include helping the seller arrive at an appropriate listing price, discovering and disclosing facts that affect the seller, and properly presenting the contracts that the seller signs. It also means properly marketing the property and helping the seller evaluate the terms and conditions of offers to purchase.

> **Memory Tip**
> **Remember COLD AC**
>
> The six common-law fiduciary duties may be remembered by the acronym **COLD AC:** **C**are, **O**bedience, **L**oyalty, **D**isclosure, **A**ccounting, and **C**onfidentiality.

An agent who represents the buyer is expected to help the buyer locate suitable property and evaluate property values, neighborhoods and property conditions, financing alternatives, and offers and counteroffers with the buyer's interest in mind.

An agent who does not make a reasonable effort to properly represent the interests of the principal could be found by a court to have been negligent. The agent is liable to the principal for any loss resulting from the agent's negligence or carelessness. The standard of care will vary from market to market and depends on the expected behavior for a particular type of transaction in a particular area.

IN PRACTICE   Because real estate licensees have, under the law, enormous exposure to liability, nearly all brokers purchase errors and omissions (E&O) insurance policies for their firms. Similar to malpractice insurance in the medical and legal fields, E&O policies cover liability for errors and negligence in the usual listing and selling activities of a real estate office. Errors and omissions insurance is required by virtually all brokers in Illinois. However, n*o insurance policy will protect a licensee from litigation arising from deliberate criminal acts.* Insurance companies normally exclude coverage for violations of fair housing laws and antitrust laws as well.

Obedience.   The fiduciary relationship obligates the agent to act in good faith at all times, obeying the principal's instructions in accordance with the contract. However, *the agent must not obey instructions that are unlawful or unethical.* Because illegal acts do not serve the principal's best interests, obeying such instructions also violates the broker's duty of care.

■ **FOR EXAMPLE**   A seller tells the listing agent, "I don't want you to show this house to any minorities." Because refusing to show a property to someone on the basis of race is illegal, the agent must not follow the seller's instructions and should withdraw from the agency. Violating fair housing laws is illegal, and the duty of obedience never extends to illegal actions.

An agent who exceeds the authority assigned in the contract will be liable for any losses that the principal suffers as a result. While the agent represents the principal, it is the principal who must ultimately make *all* of the decisions. The agent then *obeys* those decisions within the law.

Loyalty. The duty of loyalty requires that the agent place the principal's interests above all others, including the agent's own self-interest. Because the agent may not act out of self-interest, *any negotiations must be conducted without regard to how much the agent will earn in commission.* All states forbid agents to *buy* property listed with them for their own accounts or for accounts in which they have a personal interest without first disclosing that interest and receiving the principal's consent. Also, neither brokers nor salespersons may *sell* property in which they have a personal interest without informing the purchaser of that interest.

In Illinois

Illinois license law prohibits an agent from acting as a dual agent in any transaction to which the agent is a party. ■

The agent must be particularly sensitive to any possible conflicts of interest.

Disclosure. *Disclosure* is the agent's duty to keep the principal informed of all facts or information that could affect a transaction. The duty of disclosure includes disclosure of relevant information or material facts that the agent knows or that the courts might later say he or she "should have known."

The agent is obligated to discover facts that a reasonable person would feel are important in choosing a course of action, regardless of whether those facts are favorable or unfavorable to the principal's position. The agent may be held liable later for a mistake on these issues.

In Illinois

Much of this is covered by the **seller disclosure form**, which is required in Illinois. This form is called the Illinois Residential Real Property Disclosure form and it shifts the responsibility for full disclosure from the real estate agent to the seller. It requires that sellers of one-unit to four-unit residential properties fill out property disclosure forms revealing any material defects they are aware of in the real estate for sale. The completed forms shall be given to buyers before an offer is made. If the disclosure form is delivered after the offer has been accepted and if it has any negative disclosures, the buyer has three days to cancel the contract. Furthermore, *if the seller learns of a new problem after a contract is signed and up until closing, disclosure must be made in writing to the buyer.* In the latter case, the buyer does *not* have the power to simply cancel the contract. Compensation may be negotiated or the problem remedied by the seller. ■

Typically, the disclosure form is completed by the seller prior to or at the time the seller signs the listing agreement. The use of the disclosure form does not alleviate a broker's responsibility to disclose all known material defects and it does not alleviate responsibility in the event a real estate agent is aware of misrepresentation or a seller's failure to fully disclose. *An agent for a buyer must disclose deficiencies of a property as well.* (See Figure 4.1.)

Accounting.   Most states' license laws require that agents periodically report the status of all funds or property received from or on behalf of the principal. Similarly, most state license laws require that brokers give accurate copies of all documents to all affected parties and keep copies on file for a period of time.

In Illinois	*Illinois brokers are required to deliver true copies of all executed sales contracts to the people who signed them within 24 hours.* In Illinois, all funds entrusted to a broker must be deposited in a special escrow account by the next business day following the signing of a sales contract or lease. **Commingling** such monies with the broker's personal or general business funds is illegal. **Conversion** is the practice of using those escrow funds as the broker's own money, which is illegal as well. Brokers should be aware that records of escrow account transactions and reconciliations must be kept on file for at least *five years.* ■

Confidentiality.   **Confidentiality** about the principal's personal affairs is a key element of loyalty. An agent may not, for example, disclose the principal's financial condition. When the principal is the seller, the agent may not reveal such things as the principal's willingness to accept less than the listing price or his or her anxiousness to sell, *unless* the principal has authorized the disclosure. If the principal is the buyer, the agent may not disclose that the buyer will pay more than the offered price if necessary, that the buyer is under a tight schedule for moving, or any other fact that might harm the principal's bargaining position.

An agent may not disclose personal, confidential information about his or her principal. However, known material facts about the property's physical condition or its environs must always be disclosed. A **material fact** is any fact that, if known, might reasonably be expected to affect the course of events.

Opinion versus Fact

Brokers, salespersons, and other staff members always must be careful about the statements they make. They must be sure that the customer understands whether the statement is an opinion or a fact. Statements of *opinion* are permissible only as long as they are offered as opinions and without any intention to deceive.

Statements of *fact* must be accurate. Exaggeration of a property's benefits is called **puffing.** While puffing is legal, licensees must ensure that none of their statements can be interpreted as fraudulent. **Fraud** is the intentional misrepresentation of a material fact in such a way as to harm or take advantage of another person. That includes not only making false statements about a property but also intentionally concealing or failing to disclose important facts.

The misrepresentation or omission does not have to be intentional to result in broker liability. *A **negligent misrepresentation** occurs when the broker should have known that a statement about a material fact was false.* If the buyer relies on the broker's statement, the broker is liable for any damages that result. Similarly, if a broker accidentally fails to perform some act the broker may be liable for damages that result from such a negligent omission.

Residential Real Property Disclosure Form

Illinois Association of REALTORS®
RESIDENTIAL REAL PROPERTY DISCLOSURE REPORT

NOTICE: THE PURPOSE OF THIS REPORT IS TO PROVIDE PROSPECTIVE BUYERS WITH INFORMATION ABOUT MATERIAL DEFECTS IN THE RESIDENTIAL REAL PROPERTY. THIS REPORT DOES NOT LIMIT THE PARTIES RIGHT TO CONTRACT FOR THE SALE OF RESIDENTIAL REAL PROPERTY IN "AS IS" CONDITION. UNDER COMMON LAW SELLERS WHO DISCLOSE MATERIAL DEFECTS MAY BE UNDER A CONTINUING OBLIGATION TO ADVISE THE PROSPECTIVE BUYERS ABOUT THE CONDITION OF THE RESIDENTIAL REAL PROPERTY EVEN AFTER THE REPORT IS DELIVERED TO THE PROSPECTIVE BUYER. COMPLETION OF THIS REPORT BY SELLER CREATES LEGAL OBLIGATIONS ON SELLER THEREFORE SELLER MAY WISH TO CONSULT AN ATTORNEY PRIOR TO COMPLETION OF THIS REPORT.

Property Address: _____

City, State & Zip Code: _____

Seller's Name: _____

This report is a disclosure of certain conditions of the residential real property listed above in compliance with the Residential Real Property Disclosure Act. This information is provided as of _____, 20____, and does not reflect any changes made or occurring after that date or information that becomes known to the seller after that date. The disclosures herein shall not be deemed warranties of any kind by the seller or any person representing any party in this transaction.

In this form, "am aware" means to have actual notice or actual knowledge without any specific investigation or inquiry. In this form a "material defect" means a condition that would have a substantial adverse effect on the value of the residential real property or that would significantly impair the health or safety of future occupants of the residential real property unless the seller reasonably believes that the condition has been corrected.

The seller discloses the following information with the knowledge that even though the statements herein are not deemed to be warranties, prospective buyers may choose to rely on this information in deciding whether or not and on what terms to purchase the residential real property.

The seller represents that to the best of his or her actual knowledge, the following statements have been accurately noted as "yes", (correct), "no" (incorrect) or "not applicable" to the property being sold. If the seller indicates that the response to any statement, except number 1, is yes or not applicable, the seller shall provide an explanation, in the additional information area of this form.

YES	NO	N/A	
1. ____	____	____	Seller has occupied the property within the last 12 months. (No explanation is needed.)
2. ____	____	____	I am aware of flooding or recurring leakage problems in the crawlspace or basement.
3. ____	____	____	I am aware that the property is located in a flood plain or that I currently have flood hazard insurance on the property.
4. ____	____	____	I am aware of material defects in the basement or foundation (including cracks and bulges).
5. ____	____	____	I am aware of leaks or material defects in the roof, ceilings or chimney.
6. ____	____	____	I am aware of material defects in the walls or floors.
7. ____	____	____	I am aware of material defects in the electrical system.
8. ____	____	____	I am aware of material defects in the the plumbing system (includes such things as water heater, sump pump, water treatment system, sprinkler system, and swimming pool).
9. ____	____	____	I am aware of material defects in the well or well equipment.
10. ____	____	____	I am aware of unsafe conditions in the drinking water.
11. ____	____	____	I am aware of material defects in the heating, air conditioning, or ventilating systems.
12. ____	____	____	I am aware of material defects in the fireplace or woodburning stove.
13. ____	____	____	I am aware of material defects in the septic, sanitary sewer, or other disposal system.
14. ____	____	____	I am aware of unsafe concentrations of radon on the premises.
15. ____	____	____	I am aware of unsafe concentrations of or unsafe conditions relating to asbestos on the premises.
16. ____	____	____	I am aware of unsafe concentrations of or unsafe conditions relating to lead paint, lead water pipes, lead plumbing pipes or lead in the soil on the premises.
17. ____	____	____	I am aware of mine subsidence, underground pits, settlement, sliding, upheaval, or other earth stability defects on the premises.
18. ____	____	____	I am aware of current infestations of termites or other wood boring insects.
19. ____	____	____	I am aware of a structural defect caused by previous infestations of termites or other wood boring insects.
20. ____	____	____	I am aware of underground fuel storage tanks on the property.
21. ____	____	____	I am aware of boundary or lot line disputes.
22. ____	____	____	I have received notice of violation of local, state or federal laws or regulations relating to this property, which violation has not been corrected.

108 Revised 1/00

Source: Published with permission, Illinois Association of REALTORS®.

F I G U R E   4.1 (CONTINUED)

Residential Real Property Disclosure Form

Note: These disclosures are not intended to cover the common elements of a condominium, but only the actual residential real property including limited common elements allocated to the exclusive use thereof that form an integral part of the condominium unit.

   Note: These disclosures are intended to reflect the current condition of the premises and do not include previous problems, if any, that the seller reasonably believes have been corrected.

If any of the above are marked "not applicable" or "yes", please explain here or use additional pages, if necessary:
_____
_____
_____

Check here if additional pages used: _____

Seller certifies that seller has prepared this statement and certifies that the information provided is based on the actual notice or actual knowledge of the seller without any specific investigation or inquiry on the part of the seller. The seller hereby authorizes any person representing any principal in this transaction to provide a copy of this report, and to disclose any information in the report, to any person in connection with any actual or anticipated sale of the property.

Seller: _____ Date: _____
Seller: _____ Date: _____

PROSPECTIVE BUYER IS AWARE THAT THE PARTIES MAY CHOOSE TO NEGOTIATE AN AGREEMENT FOR THE SALE OF THE PROPERTY SUBJECT TO ANY OR ALL MATERIAL DEFECTS DISCLOSED IN THIS REPORT ("AS IS"). THIS DISCLOSURE IS NOT A SUBSTITUTE FOR ANY INSPECTIONS OR WARRANTIES THAT THE PROSPECTIVE BUYER OR SELLER MAY WISH TO OBTAIN OR NEGOTIATE. THE FACT THAT THE SELLER IS NOT AWARE OF A PARTICULAR CONDITION OR PROBLEM IS NO GUARANTEE THAT IT DOES NOT EXIST. PROSPECTIVE BUYER IS AWARE THAT HE MAY REQUEST AN INSPECTION OF THE PREMISES PERFORMED BY A QUALIFIED PROFESSIONAL.

Prospective Buyer: _____ Date: _____ Time: _____
Prospective Buyer: _____ Date: _____ Time: _____

108 Revised 1/00   COPYRIGHT © BY ILLINOIS ASSOCIATION OF REALTORS®

Residential Real Property Disclosure Form

RESIDENTIAL REAL PROPERTY DISCLOSURE ACT
SENATE BILL 828 (PUBLIC ACT 88-111) EFFECTIVE OCTOBER 1, 1994

AN ACT relating to disclosure by the seller of residential real property.

Section 1. Short title. This Act may be cited as the Residential Real Property Disclosure Act.

Section 5. As used in this Act, unless the context otherwise requires the following terms have the meaning given in this section:

"Residential real property" means real property improved with not less than one nor more than four residential dwelling units; units in residential cooperatives; or, condominium units including the limited common elements allocated to the exclusive use thereof that form an integral part of the condominium unit.

"Seller" means every person or entity who is an owner, beneficiary of a trust, contract purchaser or lessee of a ground lease, who has an interest (legal or equitable) in residential real property. However, "seller" shall not include any person who has both (i) never occupied the residential real property and (ii) never had the management responsibility for the residential real property nor delegated such responsibility for the residential real property to another person or entity.

"Prospective buyer" means any person or entity negotiating or offering to become an owner or lessee of residential real property by means of a transfer for value to which this Act applies.

Section 10. Except as provided in Section 15, this Act applies to any transfer by sale, exchange, installment land sale-contract, assignment of beneficial interest, lease with an option to purchase, ground lease or assignment of ground lease of residential real property.

Section 15. The provisions of this Act do not apply to the following:

(1) Transfers pursuant to court order, including, but not limited to, transfers ordered by a probate court in administration of an estate, transfers between spouses resulting from a judgment of dissolution of marriage or legal separation, transfers pursuant to an order of possession, transfers by a trustee in bankruptcy, transfers by eminent domain and transfers resulting from a decree for specific performance.

(2) Transfers from a mortgagor to a mortgagee by deed in lieu of foreclosure or consent judgement, transfer by judicial deed issued pursuant to a foreclosure sale to the successful bidder or the assignee of a certificate of sale, transfer by a collateral assignment of a beneficial interest of a land trust, or a transfer by a mortgagee or a successor in interest to the mortgagee's secured position or a beneficiary under a deed in trust who has acquired the real property by deed in lieu of foreclosure, consent judgement or judicial deed issued pursuant to a foreclosure sale.

(3) Transfers by a fiduciary in the course of the administration of a decedent's estate, guardianship, conservatorship, or trust.

(4) Transfers from one co-owner to one or more other co-owners.

(5) Transfers pursuant to testate or intestate succession.

(6) Transfers made to a spouse, or to a person or persons in the lineal line of consanguinity of one or more of the sellers.

(7) Transfers from an entity that has taken title to residential real property from a seller for the purpose of assisting in the relocation of the seller, so long as the entity makes available to all prospective buyers a copy of the disclosure form furnished to the entity by the seller.

(8) Transfers to or from any governmental entity.

(9) Transfers of newly constructed residential real property that has not been occupied.

Section 20. A seller of residential real property shall complete all applicable items in the disclosure document described in Section 35 of this Act. The seller shall deliver to the prospective buyer the written disclosure statement required by this Act before the signing of a written agreement by the seller and prospective buyer that would, subject to the satisfaction of any negotiated contingencies, require the prospective buyer to accept a transfer of the residential real property.

Section 25. Liability of seller. (a) The seller is not liable for any error, inaccuracy, or omission of any information delivered pursuant to this Act if (i) the seller had no knowledge of the error, inaccuracy, or omission, (ii) the error, inaccuracy, or omission was based on a reasonable belief that a material defect or other matter not disclosed had been corrected, or (iii) the error, inaccuracy, or omission was based on information provided by a public agency or by a licensed engineer, land surveyor, structural pest control operator, or by a contractor about matters within the scope of the contractor's occupation and the seller had no knowledge of the error, inaccuracy or omission.

(b) The seller shall disclose material defects of which the seller has actual knowledge.

(c) The seller is not obligated by this Act to make any specific investigation or inquiry in an effort to complete the disclosure statement.

Section 30. Disclosure supplement. If prior to closing, any seller has actual knowledge of an error, inaccuracy, or omission in any prior disclosure document after delivery of that disclosure document to a prospective buyer, that seller shall supplement the prior disclosure document with a written supplemental disclosure.

Section 35. Disclosure report form. The disclosures required of a seller by this Act, shall be made in the following form: [form on reverse side]

Section 40. Material defect. If a material defect is disclosed in the Residential Real Property Disclosure Report, after acceptance by the prospective buyer of an offer or counter-offer made by a seller or after the execution of an offer made by a prospective buyer that is accepted by the seller for the conveyance of the residential real property, then the Prospective Buyer may, within three business days after receipt of that Report by the prospective buyer, terminate the contract or other agreement without any liability or recourse except for the return to prospective buyer of all earnest money deposits or down payments paid by prospective buyer in the transaction. If a material defect is disclosed in a supplement to this disclosure document, the prospective buyer shall not have a right to terminate unless the material defect results from an error, inaccuracy, or omission of which the seller had actual knowledge at the time the prior disclosure document was completed and signed by the seller. The right to terminate the contract, however, shall no longer exist after the conveyance of the residential real property. For purposes of this Act the termination shall be deemed to be made when written notice of termination is personally delivered to at least one of the sellers identified in the contract or other agreement or when deposited, certified or registered mail, with the United States Postal Service, addressed to one of the sellers at the address indicated in the contract or agreement, or, if there is not an address contained therein, then at the address indicated for the residential real property on the Report.

Residential Real Property Disclosure Form

Section 45. This Act is not intended to limit or modify any obligation to disclose created by any other statute or that may exist in common law in order to avoid fraud, misrepresentation, or deceit in the transaction.

Section 50. Delivery of the Residential Real Property Disclosure Report provided by this Act shall be by:

1) personal or facsimile delivery to the prospective buyer;

2) depositing the report with the United States Postal Service, postage prepaid, first class mail, addressed to the prospective buyer at the address provided by the prospective buyer or indicated on the contract or other agreement, or

3) depositing the report with an alternative delivery service such as Federal Express, UPS, or Airborne, delivery charges prepaid, addressed to the Prospective buyer at the address provided by the prospective buyer or indicated on the contract or other agreement.

For purposes of this Act, delivery to one prospective buyer is deemed delivery to all prospective buyers. Delivery to authorized individual acting on behalf of a prospective buyer constitutes delivery to all prospective buyers. Delivery of the Report is effective upon receipt by the prospective buyer. Receipt may be acknowledged on the Report, in an agreement for the conveyance of the residential real property, or shown in any other verifiable manner.

Section 55. Violations and damages. If the seller fails or refuses to provide the disclosure document prior to the conveyance of the residential real property, the buyer shall have the right to terminate the contract. A person who knowingly violates or fails to perform any duty prescribed by any provision of this Act or who discloses any information on the Residential Real Property Disclosure Report that he knows to be false shall be liable in the amount of actual damages and court costs, and the court may award reasonable attorney fees incurred by the prevailing party.

Section 60. No action for violation of this Act may be commenced later than one year from the earlier of the date of possession, date of occupancy or date of recording of an instrument of conveyance of the residential real property.

Section 65. A copy of this Act excluding Section 35, must be printed on or as a part of the Residential Real Property Disclosure Report form.

Section 99. This Act takes effect on October 1, 1994.

PUBLIC ACT (88-111), REPRINTED IN ITS ENTIRETY

As amended, effective date 1-1-98

■ **FOR EXAMPLE** 1. While showing a potential buyer a very average-looking house, Broker Quinn described even its plainest features as "charming" and "beautiful." Because the statements were obviously Quinn's personal opinions, designed to encourage a positive feeling about the property (obvious puffing), their truth or falsity is not an issue.

2. Broker Georgia neglected to inform the buyer that the lot next to the house the buyer was considering had been sold to a waste disposal company for use as a toxic dump. This is an example of fraudulent misrepresentation.

If a contract to purchase real estate is obtained as a result of fraudulent misstatements, the contract may be disaffirmed or renounced by the purchaser. In such a case, the broker not only loses a commission but can be liable for damages if either party suffers loss because of the misrepresentation. If the licensee's misstatements were based on the owner's own inaccurate statements and the licensee had no independent duty to investigate their accuracy, the broker may be entitled to a commission, even if the buyer rescinds the sales contract.

In Illinois

An Illinois licensee may be held liable to the buyer under the *Illinois Consumer Fraud and Deceptive Practices Act*. Licensees found in violation of this act may be required to pay the plaintiffs' attorneys' fees and court costs in addition to damages. The act prohibits the use, within a trade or profession, of any deception, fraud, false promise, misrepresentation or concealment, suppression or omission of any material fact with the intent that others rely on it. A real estate brokerage business clearly fits within the meaning of the Act, and the courts of Illinois have ruled accordingly. ■

Latent Defects

The seller has a duty to disclose any known latent defects that threaten structural soundness or personal safety. A **latent defect** is a hidden structural defect that would not be discovered by ordinary inspection. Buyers have been able to either rescind the sales contract or receive damages when a seller fails to reveal known latent defects. The courts also have decided in favor of the buyer when the seller neglected to reveal violations of zoning or building codes.

In addition to the seller's duty to disclose latent defects, the agent has an independent duty to conduct a reasonably competent and diligent inspection of the property. It is the licensee's duty to discover any material facts that may affect the property's value or desirability, whether or not they are known to or disclosed by the seller. Any such material facts discovered by the licensee must be disclosed to prospective buyers. If the licensee should have known about a substantial defect that is detected later by the buyer, the agent may be liable to the buyer for any damages resulting from that defect. The statute of limitations is one year for buyer action.

■ **FOR EXAMPLE** Broker Kelley knew that a house had been built on a landfill. A few days after the house was listed, one of Kelley's salespersons noticed that the living room floor was uneven and sagging in places. Both Kelley and the salesperson have a duty to conduct further investigations into the structural soundness of the property. They cannot simply ignore the problem or place throw rugs over particularly bad spots and hope buyers won't look underneath.

| In Illinois | The Illinois Appellate Court, in *Munjal v. Baird & Warner, Inc. et al.*, 2nd Dist. (1985), held that a broker or salesperson has no duty to discover "latent material defects" in a property if a seller has not disclosed these defects to him or her prior to sale. This decision underscored the need to find ways by which a broker could obtain relevant information about a listed property from the seller to avoid future litigation from unhappy buyers. ■

Stigmatized Properties

In recent years, questions have been raised about stigmatized properties—properties that society has branded undesirable because of events that occurred there. *Stigma* is the continuing negative association with or feeling about the property. Typically, the stigma is a criminal event such as homicide, illegal drug manufacturing, or gang-related activity or a tragedy such as suicide. However, properties even have been stigmatized by rumors that they are haunted. Because of the potential liability to a licensee for inadequately researching and disclosing material facts concerning a property's condition, licensees should seek competent counsel when dealing with a stigmatized property.

| In Illinois | *Article 15 of the Real Estate License Act of 2000* states that in dealing with specific situations related to disclosure, *"no cause of action shall arise against a licensee for the failure to disclose that an occupant of that property was afflicted with HIV or any other medical condition or that the property was the site of an act or occurrence which had no effect on the physical condition of the property or its environment or the structures located thereon."*

Article 15, Section 15–20, continues:

- ■ ". . . no cause of action shall arise against a licensee for the failure to disclose a fact situation on property that is not the subject of the transaction."
- ■ ". . . no cause of action shall arise against a licensee for the failure to disclose physical conditions located on property that is not the subject of the transaction that do not have a substantial adverse effect on the value of the real estate that is the subject of the transaction."

For any action brought under Article 15, "the court may in its discretion, award only actual damages and court costs or grant injunctive relief, when appropriate."

Any action brought under Article 15 must commence within two years after the person bringing the action knew or should have known of such act or omission. In no event can the action be brought more than five years after the date on which the act or omission occurred. If the person entitled to bring the action is under the age of 18 or under legal disability, the period of limitation shall not begin to run until the disability is removed. ■

The *buyer's agent* is the one to suggest the *highest range of prices* the buyer should consider, based on comparable values and current market. The agent's aim is to help the buyer get the *lowest price possible, given all other buyer concerns and needs.* The buyer's agent discloses information about how long a property has been listed or why the owner is selling, if known. Of course, a *seller's* agent who discloses such information violates the agent's fiduciary/statutory duties of loyalty to the seller.

The seller's disclosure form is a good guide to follow for what *must* be disclosed to all parties by the listing side of a transaction. In all other respects, unless it is illegal or a material fact about the property itself, the seller's agent should follow the seller's lawful instructions. A buyer's agent should be on watch and do what research is possible. When in doubt, consult the sponsoring broker.

Megan's Law

At the state level, Megan's Law is a general name for laws requiring law enforcement authorities to make information available to the public regarding registered sex offenders. Individual states decide what information will be made available and how it is to be disseminated. Commonly included information includes the offender's name, picture, address, incarceration date, and nature of crime. The information is often displayed on public sites, but can also be published in newspapers and pamphlets or disseminated through various other means.

At the federal level, Megan's Law is known as the Sexual Offender Act of 1994 and requires persons convicted of sex crimes against children to notify local law enforcement of any change of address or employment after release from custody (such as prison or a psychiatric facility). The notification requirement may be imposed for a fixed period of time—usually at least ten years—or permanently.

Some states may legislate registration for all sex crimes, even if no minors were involved. It is a felony in most jurisdictions to fail to register or fail to update information.

In Illinois

As noted, Article 15, Section 15–20, of the act states, "No cause of action shall arise against a licensee for the failure to disclose . . . fact situations on property that is not the subject of the transaction . . ."

Listing agents have no legal duty to disclose that a known sex offender resides in a property near a listed home, but skilled buyer's agents should be watchful for any signals of hard to identify issues. Sex offender location lists are public information and a buyer's agent should refer a buyer client to such lists if asked. When in doubt, consult an attorney. ■

In Illinois

These statutory duties, based on (but replacing) common law duties, are set forth in *Article 15 of the Real Estate License Act of 2000*. According to this statute, the agent must

1. perform the terms of the brokerage agreement.
2. promote the best interests of the client by

   ■ seeking a transaction at the price and terms stated in the brokerage agreement or at a price and terms otherwise acceptable to the client;

   ■ timely presenting all offers to and from the client, unless the client has waived this duty;

   ■ disclosing to the client material facts concerning the transaction of which the licensee has actual knowledge, unless that information is confidential information;

   ■ timely accounting for all money and property received in which the client has, may have, or should have an interest;

   ■ obeying specific directions of the client that are not otherwise contrary to applicable statutes, ordinances, or rules; and

■ acting in a manner consistent with promoting the client's best interests as opposed to a licensee's or any other person's self-interest.

3. exercise reasonable skill and care in the performance of brokerage services.

4. keep confidential all confidential information received from the client. Confidentiality is not limited to the term of the agreement; client confidentiality is forever.

5. comply with all the requirements of the law, including fair housing and civil rights. ■

Creation of Agency

An agency relationship may be based on a formal agreement between the parties, an **express agency,** or it may result from the parties' behavior, an **implied agency**.

Express agency.   The principal and agent may enter into a contract, or an **express agreement,** in which the parties formally express their intention to establish an agency and state its terms and conditions. The agreement may be either oral or written. An agency relationship between a seller and a broker generally is created by a written employment contract, commonly referred to as a **listing agreement,** that authorizes the broker to find a buyer or tenant for the owner's property. An express agency relationship between a buyer and a broker is created by a **buyer agency agreement.** Similar to a listing agreement, it stipulates the activities and responsibilities the buyer expects from the broker in finding the appropriate property for purchase or rent.

| In Illinois |

Illinois law requires that all exclusive brokerage agreements must be in writing. ■

Implied agency.   An agency also may be created by **implied agreement.** This occurs when the actions of the parties indicate that they have mutually consented to an agency. A person acts on behalf of another as agent; the other person, as principal, delegates the authority to act. Agency relationships sometimes occur without having been consciously intended.

■ **FOR EXAMPLE** Nancy tells Phillip, a real estate broker, that she is thinking about selling her home. Phillip immediately contacts several prospective buyers. One of them makes an attractive offer. Phillip goes to Nancy's house and presents the offer, which Nancy accepts. Although no formal agency agreement was entered into either orally or in writing, Phillip's actions to seller Nancy implied to prospective purchasers that Phillip was acting as Nancy's agent. If Phillip made any misrepresentations to the buyer, Phillip may be held liable.

Compensation.   *The source of compensation does not determine agency.* An agent does not necessarily represent the person who pays his or her commission. In fact, agency can exist even if no fee is involved; it is called a **gratuitous agency.** The written brokerage agreement should state how the agent is being compensated and explain all the alternatives available.

| In Illinois |

In Illinois, both buyer's and seller's agents are often paid by the seller in a "co-op" arrangement. The seller first pays the listing broker, and the listing broker cuts a check to the "cooperating" broker. Sometimes the seller pays only the listing broker and the buyer pays the buyer's broker. In any case, all parties to the transaction have a right to know compensation sources. *This information must be disclosed in writing.* ■

Termination of Agency   An agency may be terminated for any of the following reasons:

- Death or incapacity of either the client or the broker
- Destruction or condemnation of the property
- Expiration of the terms of the agency
- Mutual agreement by all parties to the contract
- Breach by one of the parties, in which case the breaching party might be liable for damages
- By operation of law, as in bankruptcy of the principal (bankruptcy terminates the agency contract, and title to the property transfers to a court-appointed receiver)
- Completion, performance, or fulfillment of the purpose for which the agency was created

In Illinois   *A definite termination date must be included in an agency agreement under Illinois law. Automatic extension clauses are illegal in Illinois.* ■

An **agency coupled with an interest** is an agency relationship in which the agent has an interest in the subject of the agency, such as the property being sold. An agency coupled with an interest cannot be revoked by the principal or be terminated on the principal's death.

■ **FOR EXAMPLE** A broker agrees to provide the financing for a condominium building being constructed by a developer in exchange for the exclusive right to sell the units once the building is completed. The developer may not revoke the listing agreement once the broker has provided the financing because this is an agency coupled with an interest.

■ TYPES OF AGENCY RELATIONSHIPS

What an agent may do as the principal's representative depends solely on what the principal authorizes the agent to do.

Limitations on an Agent's Authority   A **universal agent** is a person empowered to do anything the principal could do personally. The universal agent's authority to act on behalf of the principal is *virtually unlimited*.

In Illinois   In Illinois, a written power of attorney is required to create a universal agency. ■

A general agent represents the principal *generally*; a special agent represents the principal only for a *specific act*, such as the sale of a house.

A **general agent** may represent the principal in a broad range of matters related to a particular business or activity. The general agent may, for example, bind the principal to any contract within the scope of the agent's authority. The salespersons and associate brokers are *general agents on the broker's behalf*. A property manager also is often a general agent.

A **special agent** is authorized to represent the principal in one specific act or business transaction only, under detailed instructions. *A real estate broker usually is a "special" agent to a client.* If hired by a seller, the broker is limited to finding a ready, willing, and able buyer for the property. A special agent for a buyer (buyer's agent) has the limited responsibility of finding a property that fits the buyer's criteria.

As a special agent, the broker may not bind the principal to a contract. The principal makes all contractually related decisions and will sign on his or her own. A *special power of attorney* is another legal means of authorizing an agent to carry out only a specified act or acts.

Finally, a **designated agent** is a person authorized by the broker to act as the agent of a specific principal. A designated agent is the *only* salesperson or associate broker in the company who has a fiduciary responsibility toward that principal. When one salesperson in the company is a designated agent, the others are free to act as agents for the other party in a transaction. In this way, two salespersons from the same real estate company may represent opposite sides in a property sale without it being considered a dual agency. This is acceptable because each side is fully represented by its own designated agent.

In Illinois

Designated agency is standard in Illinois. A sponsoring broker by his or her signature "designates" a salesperson or associate broker within the firm as the exclusive agent of a client. The firm's sponsoring broker will not be considered a dual agent as long as there is a single "designated agent" for each party in a single transaction.

Most Illinois licensees are
- "designated agents" to clients (designated by their sponsoring broker).
- "general agents" of the sponsoring broker.

Article 15, Section 15-35, discusses agency relationship disclosure. It requires that a consumer be advised that a designated agency relationship exists, unless there is a written agreement between the sponsoring broker and the consumer providing for a different brokerage relationship. This must occur no later than the time of entering into a brokerage agreement with the sponsoring broker. The name or names of his or her designated agent or agents must be in writing and the sponsoring broker's compensation and policy with regard to cooperating with brokers who represent other parties in a transaction must be disclosed.

A licensee must also disclose in writing to a customer that the licensee is not acting as the agent of the customer. This must be done at a time intended to prevent disclosure of confidential information from a customer to a licensee, and in no event later than the preparation of a sales contract or lease with an option to purchase. (See Figure 4.2.) ∎

F I G U R E   4.2

Designated Agency Disclosure Language

The copy below appears as part of many standard Illinois contracts. This language allows the sponsoring broker to "designate" one of his or her salespeople as the designated agent for the client.

   **CHICAGO ASSOCIATION OF REALTORS®**
EXCLUSIVE BUYER - BROKER AGREEMENT
Rev. 01/2008

23   **6.   DESIGNATED AGENT.** Broker and Seller hereby agree that (a) _____, a sponsored licensee
24   of Broker, is Seller's exclusive designated agent ("***Designated Agent***") under this Agreement with Broker, and (b) neither Broker nor other
25   sponsored licensees of Broker will be acting as agent for Seller. Seller understands and agrees that Broker and any of Broker's other
26   sponsored licensees may enter into agreements with prospective buyers of the Property as agents of those buyers.

Source: Published with permission, Chicago Association of REALTORS®.

FIGURE 4.3

Dual Agency

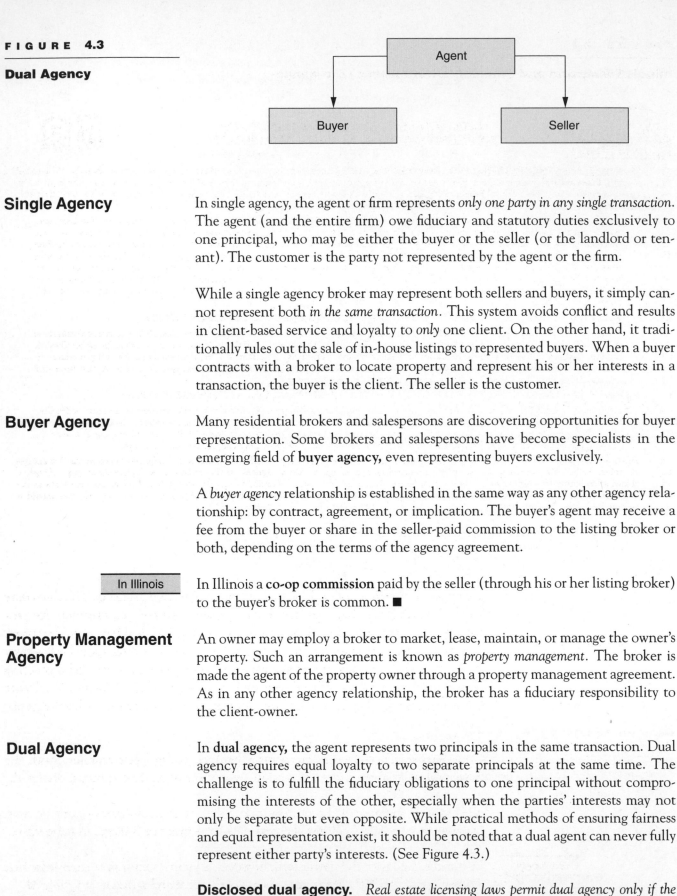

Single Agency

In single agency, the agent or firm represents *only one party in any single transaction.* The agent (and the entire firm) owe fiduciary and statutory duties exclusively to one principal, who may be either the buyer or the seller (or the landlord or tenant). The customer is the party not represented by the agent or the firm.

While a single agency broker may represent both sellers and buyers, it simply cannot represent both *in the same transaction.* This system avoids conflict and results in client-based service and loyalty to *only* one client. On the other hand, it traditionally rules out the sale of in-house listings to represented buyers. When a buyer contracts with a broker to locate property and represent his or her interests in a transaction, the buyer is the client. The seller is the customer.

Buyer Agency

Many residential brokers and salespersons are discovering opportunities for buyer representation. Some brokers and salespersons have become specialists in the emerging field of **buyer agency,** even representing buyers exclusively.

A *buyer agency* relationship is established in the same way as any other agency relationship: by contract, agreement, or implication. The buyer's agent may receive a fee from the buyer or share in the seller-paid commission to the listing broker or both, depending on the terms of the agency agreement.

| In Illinois |

In Illinois a **co-op commission** paid by the seller (through his or her listing broker) to the buyer's broker is common. ■

Property Management Agency

An owner may employ a broker to market, lease, maintain, or manage the owner's property. Such an arrangement is known as *property management.* The broker is made the agent of the property owner through a property management agreement. As in any other agency relationship, the broker has a fiduciary responsibility to the client-owner.

Dual Agency

In **dual agency,** the agent represents two principals in the same transaction. Dual agency requires equal loyalty to two separate principals at the same time. The challenge is to fulfill the fiduciary obligations to one principal without compromising the interests of the other, especially when the parties' interests may not only be separate but even opposite. While practical methods of ensuring fairness and equal representation exist, it should be noted that a dual agent can never fully represent either party's interests. (See Figure 4.3.)

Disclosed dual agency.   *Real estate licensing laws permit dual agency only if the buyer and seller are informed and consent to the broker's representation of both in the same transaction.* Although the possibility of conflict of interest still exists, disclosure is intended to minimize the risk for the broker by ensuring that both principals

FIGURE 4.4

Illinois Disclosure and Consent to Dual Agency Language

CHICAGO ASSOCIATION OF REALTORS®
EXCLUSIVE BUYER - BROKER AGREEMENT
Rev. 01/2008

56   **10. DUAL REPRESENTATION.** By checking "yes" and writing its initials below, Seller acknowledges and agrees that the Designated
57   Agent ("**Licensee**") may undertake a dual representation (represent both seller and buyer or landlord and tenant, as the case may be) in
58   connection with any Transfer of Property. Seller acknowledges and agrees that Seller has read the following prior to executing this
59   Agreement:

60   Representing more than one party to a transaction presents a conflict of interest since both parties may rely upon the Licensee's
61   advice and the parties' respective interests may be adverse to each other. The Licensee will undertake the representation of more
62   than one party to a transaction only with the written consent of **ALL** parties to the transaction. Any parties who consent to dual
63   representation expressly agree that any agreement between the parties as to any terms of the contract, including the final contract
64   price, results from each party negotiating on its own behalf and in its own best interest. Seller acknowledges and agrees that (a)
65   Broker has explained the implications of dual representation, including the risks involved, and (b) Seller has been advised to seek
66   independent counsel from its advisors and/or attorneys prior to executing this Agreement or any documents in connection with this
67   Agreement.

68   **WHAT A LICENSEE <u>CAN</u> DO FOR CLIENTS WHEN UNDERTAKING DUAL REPRESENTATION:**

69   1. Treat all clients honestly. 2. Provide information about the property to the buyer or tenant. 3. Disclose all latent material defects in
70   the property that are known to the Licensee. 4. Disclose the financial qualification of the buyer or tenant to the seller or landlord. 5.
71   Explain real estate terms. 6. Help the buyer or tenant arrange for property inspections. 7. Explain closing costs and procedures. 8.
72   Help the buyer compare financing alternatives. 9. Provide information to seller or buyer about comparable properties that have sold
73   so both clients may make educated decisions on what price to accept or offer.

74   **WHAT A LICENSEE <u>CANNOT</u> DO FOR CLIENTS WHEN UNDERTAKING DUAL REPRESENTATION:**

75   1. Disclose confidential information that the Licensee may know about either client without that client's express consent. 2. Disclose
76   the price the seller or landlord will take other than the listing price without the express consent of the seller or landlord. 3. Disclose
77   the price the buyer or tenant is willing to pay without the express consent of the buyer or tenant. 4. Recommend or suggest a price the
78   buyer or tenant should offer. 5. Recommend or suggest a price the seller or landlord should counter with or accept.

79   Seller acknowledges having read these provisions regarding the issue of dual representation. Seller is not required to accept this Paragraph
80   10 unless Seller wants to allow the Licensee to proceed as a dual agent ("**Dual Agent**") in this transaction. By checking "yes", initialing
81   below, and signing this Agreement, Seller acknowledges that it has read and understands this Paragraph 9 and voluntarily consents to the
82   Licensee acting as a Dual Agent (that is, to represent **BOTH** the seller and buyer or landlord and tenant, as the case may be) should it
83   become necessary. (***check one***) ____ Yes _____ No _____ (*Seller initials*) _____ (*Seller initials*).

Source: Published with permission, Chicago Association of REALTORS®.

are aware of the effect of dual agency on their respective interests. The disclosure alerts the principals that they may have to assume greater responsibility for protecting their interests than they would if each had independent representation. The broker must reconcile how, as agent, he or she will discharge the fiduciary duties on behalf of both principals, particularly providing loyalty and protecting confidential information. (See Figure 4.4 for the required Dual Agency Disclosure Language and see Figure 4.5 for the Confirmation of Consent to Dual Agency Language.)

Considerable debate focuses on whether brokers can properly represent both the buyer and seller in the same transaction, even though the dual agency is disclosed.

Nevertheless, because of the obvious risks inherent in dual agency—ranging from conflicts of interest to outright abuse of trust—the practice is illegal in some states.

> **In Illinois**

In Illinois, dual agency is permitted; however, all parties must give their informed written consent. *Dual agency must always be disclosed and agreed to in writing.* ■

F I G U R E   4.5

Confirmation of Consent to Dual Agency Language

MULTI-BOARD RESIDENTIAL REAL ESTATE CONTRACT 4.0

452 ____ ___ ___ ___   **41. CONFIRMATION OF DUAL AGENCY**: The Parties confirm that they have previously consented to
453 _____ (Licensee) acting as a Dual Agent in providing brokerage services
454 on their behalf and specifically consent to Licensee acting as a Dual Agent with regard to the transaction referred to in this Contract.

Source: Published with permission, Illinois Real Estate Lawyers Association, all rights reserved.

■ **F O R   E X A M P L E** Martin, a real estate broker, is the agent for the owner of Roomy Manor, a large mansion. Josef, a prospective buyer, comes into Martin's office and asks Martin to represent him in his search for a modest home. After several weeks of activity, including two offers unsuccessfully negotiated by Martin, Josef spots the For Sale sign in front of Roomy Manor. She tells Martin she wants to make an offer and asks for Martin's advice on a likely price range. Martin is now in the difficult position of being a dual agent: Martin represents the seller (who naturally is interested in receiving the highest possible price) and also represents the buyer (who is interested in making a successful low offer).

Undisclosed dual agency.   A broker may not intend to create a dual agency. However, a salesperson's words and actions may create a dual agency unintentionally. Sometimes the cause is carelessness. Other times the salesperson does not fully understand his or her fiduciary responsibilities. Some salespeople lose sight of legal obligations when they focus intensely on bringing buyers and sellers together. For example, a salesperson representing the seller might tell a buyer that the seller will accept less than the listing price to entice the buyer into making an offer. Or the listing salesperson might try to persuade the seller to accept an offer that is really in the buyer's interest.

A listing agent giving a buyer any specific advice on how much to offer can lead the buyer to believe that the salesperson is an advocate for him or her. These actions create an implied agency with the buyer and violate the duties of loyalty and confidentiality to the principal-seller. Because neither party has been informed of that situation and been given the opportunity to seek separate representation, the interests of both are jeopardized. This type of undisclosed dual agency is a violation of licensing laws. It can result in rescission of the sales contract, forfeiture of commission, or filing of a suit for damages.

Disclosure of Agency

Mandatory agency disclosure laws now exist in every state. These laws stipulate when, how, and to whom disclosures must be made. Frequently, printed brochures outlining agency alternatives are available to a firm's clients and customers.

In Illinois

Licensees are presumed to be representing the consumer with whom they are working as the consumer's designated agent, unless there is a written agreement between them specifying another relationship or if the licensee is performing only ministerial acts on the consumer's behalf.

Ministerial acts are defined as acts that are informative in nature—that is, acts that do not rise to the level of active representation. Examples of ministerial acts include

- responding to phone inquiries by consumers as to the availability and pricing of brokerage services;
- responding to phone inquiries from a consumer concerning the price or location of property;
- attending an open house and responding to questions about the property from a consumer;
- setting an appointment to view property;
- responding to questions of consumers walking into a licensee's office concerning brokerage services offered or a particular property;
- accompanying an appraiser, inspector, contractor, or similar third party on a visit to a property;
- completing business or factual information for a consumer on an offer or contract to purchase on behalf of a client;
- showing a client through a property being sold by an owner on his or her own behalf; or
- referring to another broker or service provider.

On the other hand, if a licensee searches for suitable properties for the consumer to view, shows the properties to the consumer, helps negotiate a sales price for the consumer, and walks the consumer through the closing process, the licensee would be going well beyond the concept of ministerial acts. Instead, he or she would be considered an *implied agent* for that consumer.

If the other party is represented by another agent, no disclosures are necessary. A licensee who is acting as the designated agent of a party must disclose in writing to any customer that the agency relationship exists. Understanding the scope of the service a party can expect from the broker allows customers to make an informed decision about whether to seek their own representation.

According to *Article 15 of the Real Estate License Act of 2000*, a consumer must receive the following disclosures no later than the time *when a brokerage agreement is created*:

- A clear indication that a designated agency relationship will exist unless there is a written agreement providing otherwise
- A summary of any other agency relationships available through the broker
- The names of any designated agents who will be involved with the client
- The amount and manner of the broker's compensation
- An indication of whether the broker will share the compensation with brokers who represent other parties in a transaction

A licensee must disclose to an unrepresented customer in writing that the licensee is not acting as the customer's agent. The disclosure must be made at a time intended to prevent disclosure of confidential information by the customer to the licensee. The licensee may perform ministerial acts for a customer without violating any brokerage agreement with a client. *Merely performing ministerial acts does not create a brokerage agreement.* However, under the *Real Estate License Act of 2000*, agency is presumed if nothing else is stated or disclosed. ■

■ CUSTOMER-LEVEL SERVICES

Even though an agent's primary responsibility is to the principal, the agent also has duties to third parties. Any time a licensee works with a third party or a customer, the licensee is responsible for adhering to state and federal consumer protection laws as well as to the ethical requirements imposed by professional associations and state regulators.

In Illinois

An agent's primary responsibility is to the principal, and Illinois courts have long held that the contractual principal-agent relationship as defined in a listing agreement or buyer agency agreement gives the seller or buyer a cause of action against the licensee who breaches his or her fiduciary duties to the client. The courts have not demanded fiduciary duty to third parties. However, Illinois license law does set forth the duties that licensees owe to third-party customers (buyers or sellers). Licensees are to treat all customers honestly. They cannot negligently or knowingly give customers false information. Finally, licensees must disclose all material adverse facts about the physical condition of the property to the customer that are actually known by the licensee and that could not be discovered by a reasonably diligent inspection of the property by the customer.

An agent owes a customer the duties of *reasonable care* and *skill, honest and fair dealing,* and *disclosure of known facts.*

In Illinois, *a licensee may be held liable to a seller or buyer if the licensee misrepresents material facts about a property and if the seller or buyer suffers monetary loss through reliance on these statements.* The licensee's loyalty to the principal is no defense, even though the principal may have ordered the agent to misrepresent. *Licensees have a duty to prospective sellers and buyers to disclose all material information within their knowledge.* If the licensee knowingly makes untrue statements, Illinois courts will have no difficulty in finding the licensee liable to the appropriate party.

Furthermore, liability may be imposed when the licensee is aware of facts that tend to indicate he or she is making a false statement. For instance, if the seller tells his or her agent/licensee that "the roof was replaced last year," and the agent has good reason to believe that statement is untrue, the licensee should attempt to ascertain the truth and pass the correct information on to the buyer. However, if false information was provided by the client and the licensee did not have knowledge that the information was false, the licensee will not be held liable to the customer.

Brokers who attempt to avoid liability to buyers through the use of a waiver or an exculpatory clause in the sales contract will probably be unsuccessful. In the Illinois Appellate Court case of *Zimmerman v. Northfield Real Estate, Inc.,* 1st Dist. (1986), the broker included the following language in the sales contract:

> *Purchaser acknowledges . . . that neither the seller, broker or any of their agents have made any representations with respect to any material fact relating to the real estate unless such representations are in writing and further that the purchaser has made such investigations as purchaser deems necessary or appropriate to satisfy that there has been no deception, fraud, false pretenses, misrepresentations, concealments, suppressions or omission of any material fact by the seller, the broker, or any of their agents relating to the real estate, its improvements and included personal property.*

The court refused to enforce the clause because it clearly *violated public policy*, particularly that expressed within the Illinois Real Estate License Act and the Rules. ■

■ SUMMARY

The common law of agency has historically governed the principal-agent relationship. Agency relationships may be expressed either by the words of the parties or by written agreement, or they may be implied by the parties' actions. In single agency relationships, the broker or agent represents one party, either the buyer or the seller, in the transaction. In some states, if the agent elicits the assistance of other brokers who cooperate in the transaction, the other brokers may become subagents of the principal. Any offering of subagency by a multiple listing service (MLS) in Illinois is illegal.

Many states, including Illinois, are dominated by non-single agency firms. These firms work with both buyers and sellers, including buyers and sellers in the same transaction. They will consider dual agency in the event it develops or will assign designated agents to each of the two parties (usually a seller and a buyer) should a conflict develop. Many states, including Illinois, have adopted statutes that replace the common law of agency and amplify it.

Representing two opposing parties in the same transaction constitutes dual agency. Licensees must be careful not to create dual agency when none was intended. This unintentional or inadvertent dual agency can result in the sales contract being rescinded and the commission being forfeited or in a lawsuit. Disclosed dual agency requires that both principals be informed of and consent to the broker's multiple representation. In any case, the prospective parties in any transaction should be informed about agency alternatives and the ways in which client-level versus customer-level services differ. Many states, including Illinois, have mandatory agency disclosure laws. The source of compensation for the client services does not determine which party is represented.

Licensees have certain duties and obligations to their customers as well. Consumers are entitled to fair and honest dealings and to the information necessary for them to make informed decisions. This includes accurate information about the property. Some states, including Illinois, have mandatory property disclosure laws.

Real estate license laws and regulations govern the professional conduct of brokers and salespersons. The license laws are enacted to protect the public by ensuring a standard of competence and professionalism in the real estate industry.

Stigmatized housing remains a controversial issue in many states. In many states, buyers' agents bear more burden for disclosure of known stigmas than do sellers' (listing) agents.

| In Illinois |

Article 15 of the Real Estate License Act of 2000 has fully superseded any previous agency law. Illinois agency law currently presumes that a salesperson or broker who is working with a seller represents the seller (client relationship). A licensee working with a buyer is presumed to represent the buyer. Disclosure is required for any other arrangement.

The Illinois *Real Estate License Act of 2000* along with the rules governing permitted dual agency, always must be disclosed, and in writing, to be legal. Merely designating one salesperson to represent sellers and another to represent buyers does not by itself constitute dual agency. Licensees operate as designated agents most of the time. Agency relationship disclosures require written notice to the consumer of the name or names of the designated agent; that a designated agency relationship exists, unless there is a written agreement providing otherwise; and the sponsoring broker's compensation and policy with regard to compensation cooperation with other brokers. Dual agency, however, occurs if the same agent represents both parties in a transaction. Then additional designated agents sometimes need to be made so that two licensees are involved (each representing only one party) unless a disclosed dual agency is agreed to in writing. Even disclosed dual agency is frowned upon by many and is likely to continue to be controversial.

Stigmas to a property are disclosed only when they constitute a material fact and affect the physical condition of the property. Normally ghosts or past crimes on a property would not be disclosed. Federal law prohibits disclosure of HIV or other medically related conditions except by permission or direction of the seller/ owner. ■

QUESTIONS

1. Which of the following best describes an agent?
   a. A person who gives someone else the legal power to act on his or her behalf
   b. A person who is in a customer-agent relationship
   c. A person who is placed in a position of trust and confidence
   d. Two agents who work for the same brokerage firm

2. Sam just listed his property with SXS Realty. The agency relationship between Sam and the broker would be what type of agency?
   a. Special
   b. General
   c. Implied
   d. Universal

3. Which of the following statements is *TRUE* of a real estate broker acting as the agent of the seller?
   a. The broker is obligated to render faithful service to the seller.
   b. The broker can disclose personal information to a buyer if it increases the likelihood of a sale.
   c. The broker can agree to a change in price without the seller's approval.
   d. The broker can accept a commission from the buyer without the seller's approval.

4. Louise is a real estate broker. Kristen lists a home with Louise for $289,500. Later that same day, Jerry comes into Louise's office and asks for general information about homes for sale in the $250,000 to $300,000 price range. Based on these facts, which of the following statements is *TRUE*?
   a. Both Kristen and Jerry are Louise's customers.
   b. Kristen is Louise's client; Jerry is a customer.
   c. Louise owes fiduciary duties to both Kristen and Jerry.
   d. If Jerry asks Louise to be Jerry's buyer representative, Louise must decline because of the preexisting agreement with Kristen.

5. A licensee who has contracted with a condo owner to manage a highrise apartment is probably a
   a. transactional broker.
   b. buyer's agent.
   c. general agent.
   d. special agent.

6. Which of the following events will terminate an agency in a broker-seller relationship?
   a. The broker discovers that the market value of the property is such that he or she will not make an adequate commission.
   b. The owner declares personal bankruptcy.
   c. The owner abandons the property.
   d. The broker appoints other brokers to help sell the property.

7. In Illinois, a real estate broker hired by an owner to sell a parcel of real estate must comply with
   a. the federal common law of agency, although a state agency statute may exist that abrogates common law.
   b. undisclosed dual agency requirements.
   c. the concept of caveat emptor as codified in Illinois law.
   d. the Illinois statute governing agency relationships.

8. Broker Andre is hired by a first-time buyer to help the buyer purchase a home. The buyer confides to Andre that being approved for a mortgage loan may be complicated by the fact that the buyer filed for bankruptcy two years ago. When the buyer offers to buy Mr. and Mrs. Thompson's home, what is Andre's responsibility?

    a. Andre should discuss with the buyer Andre's duty to disclose the buyer's financial situation to the local multiple listing service.

    b. Andre has a duty of honest dealing toward Mr. and Mrs. Thompson; he should not lie about the buyer's financial circumstances but may present them in the best possible terms.

    c. Andre should have the buyer qualified by a lender, and then politely refuse to answer any questions that would violate the duty of confidentiality.

    d. Andre has no responsibility whatsoever toward Mr. and Mrs. Thompson because Andre is the buyer's agent.

9. Broker Miguel lists Kim's residence. For various reasons, Kim must sell the house quickly. To expedite the sale, Miguel tells a prospective purchaser that Kim will accept at least $5,000 less than the asking price for the property. Based on these facts, which of the following statements is TRUE?

    a. Miguel has not violated his agency responsibilities to Kim.

    b. Miguel should have disclosed this information, regardless of its accuracy.

    c. The disclosure was improper, regardless of Miguel's motive.

    d. The relationship between Miguel and Kim is referred to as a general agency relationship.

10. A buyer who is a client of the broker wants to purchase a house that the broker has listed for sale. Which of the following statements is TRUE?

    a. Illinois law no longer regulates this situation.

    b. The broker should refer the buyer to another broker to negotiate the sale.

    c. The seller and buyer must be informed of the situation and agree to the broker's representing both of them.

    d. The buyer should not have been shown a house listed by the broker.

11. Bob is a real estate broker. Saul is a for sale by owner who has a home advertised for $198,000. Vera comes into Bob's office and asks Bob to represent her while she searches for a home in the $190,000 to $200,000 price range. Bob calls Saul and asks if he can show Saul's home to Vera. Based on these facts, which of the following statements is TRUE?

    a. Both Saul and Vera are Bob's customers.

    b. Saul is Bob's customer; Vera is a client.

    c. Vera is Bob's customer; Saul is Bob's client.

    d. Bob is now a dual agent.

12. A real estate licensee was representing a buyer. At their first meeting, the buyer explained that he planned to operate a dog-grooming business out of any house he bought. The licensee did not check the local zoning ordinances to determine in which parts of town such a business could be conducted. Which agency duty did the licensee violate?

    a. Care

    b. Obedience

    c. Loyalty

    d. Accountability

13. Broker Elliot tells a prospective buyer, "This property has the most beautiful view." In fact, the view includes the back of a shopping center. In a separate transaction, broker Phyllis fails to mention to some enthusiastic potential buyers that a six-lane highway is planned for construction within ten feet of a house the buyers think is perfect. Based on these facts, which of the following statements is TRUE?

    a. Broker Elliot has committed fraud.

    b. Broker Phyllis has committed puffing.

    c. Both broker Elliot and broker Phyllis are guilty of intentional misrepresentation.

    d. Broker Elliot merely is puffing; broker Phyllis has misrepresented the property.

14. Under Illinois agency law, which of the following is *TRUE*?

    a. The law codifies the common-law concept of caveat emptor by eliminating any assumption of a buyer's right to representation or disclosure.
    b. Brokers may designate which agent represents which party.
    c. Sellers are not legally obligated to make any disclosures regarding the known physical condition of the property.
    d. Dual agency is outlawed.

15. A broker listed and sold Martin's home. Martin told the broker that the home was structurally sound. This information was passed on to a prospective buyer by the broker's salesperson. If the broker has no way of knowing that this information is false, who will likely be held liable if a latent defect is later discovered?

    a. Only the salesperson
    b. The seller
    c. The seller and the salesperson
    d. The buyer will lose because a buyer must carefully inspect or bear the loss

CHAPTER 5

Real Estate Brokerage

■ **LEARNING OBJECTIVES** *When you've finished reading this chapter, you should be able to*

- ■ **identify** the role of technologies, personnel, and license laws in the operation of a real estate business.

- ■ **describe** the various types of antitrust violations common in the real estate industry and the penalties involved with each.

- ■ **explain** how a broker's compensation is usually determined.

- ■ **distinguish** employees from independent contractors and explain why the distinction is important.

- ■ **define** the following *key terms*:

allocation of customers or markets	employees	price-fixing
antitrust laws	group boycotting	procuring cause
brokerage	independent contractor	ready, willing, and able
CAN-SPAM Act of 2003	Junk Fax Prevention Act of 2005	buyer
commission	National Do Not Call	salesperson
cooperative commission	Registry	tie-in agreement
electronic contracting	personal assistant	transactional broker

■ REAL ESTATE BROKERAGE

Brokerage is simply the business of bringing parties together. A real estate broker is defined as an individual, partnership, limited liability company, corporation, or registered limited liability partnership other than a real estate salesperson or leasing agent who for another and for compensation, or with the intention or expectation of receiving compensation, either directly or indirectly, sells, exchanges, purchases, rents, or leases real estate.

A **brokerage** business may take many forms. It may be a sole proprietorship (a single-owner company), a corporation, or a partnership with another broker. The office may be independent or part of a regional or national franchise. The business may consist of a single office or multiple branches. The broker's office may be located in a downtown highrise, a suburban shopping center, or the broker's home, provided it meets municipal requirements.

A typical real estate brokerage may specialize in one type of transaction or service or may offer an array of services.

No matter what its form, a real estate brokerage firm incurs the same demands, expenses, and rewards as any other small business. The real estate industry, after all, is made up of thousands of individual businesses operating in defined local markets. Real estate brokers face many of the same challenges as do any other entrepreneurs, but they also must master the complexities of real estate transactions and real estate law. They must set effective policies for every aspect of the brokerage operation: maintaining space and equipment; keeping technology updated; attracting skillful agents; determining compensation; directing staff and marketing efforts; and staying abreast of all current legal and professional standards issues.

Broker-Salesperson Relationship

Although brokerage firms vary widely in size and style, few brokers today perform their duties without the assistance of salespersons and other brokers associated with the firm (sometimes called *associate brokers*). Much of the business's success hinges on the broker-salesperson relationship.

A real estate **salesperson** is any person licensed to perform real estate activities on behalf of a licensed real estate broker. The broker is fully responsible for the actions performed in the course of the real estate business by all persons licensed under him or her. In turn, all of an associate broker's or salesperson's activities must be performed in the name of this sponsoring broker. The salespersons and associate brokers, as general agents of the sponsoring broker, act on the broker's behalf in all real estate-related matters. These licensees may list a house or procure buyer clients without direct supervision, but it is all done under the sponsoring broker's flag and as his or her designated agent. That is why brokerage agreements (listing and buyer agency agreements) require the broker's signature before they are valid. Also, as an agent acting on behalf of the broker, the salesperson cannot receive compensation from any other party. The broker also carries responsibility for the acts of any sponsored licensees representing the firm.

Independent contractor versus employee.   Every broker who hires licensees or has an independent contractor relationship with a licensee must have a *written employment agreement* with each licensee. The agreement defines the employment or independent contractor relationship, including supervision, duties, compensation, and termination. State license laws generally affect licensees who are employees or independent contractors without differentiating between the two. However, choosing employee or independent contractor status has a big impact on an individual's taxes, job responsibilities, and the broker's responsibility to pay and withhold taxes from an individual's earnings.

Independent Contractors:

- Do not work employer-determined hours
- Do not receive scheduled salaries
- Must be self-starters
- Decide how to do their work and when
- Are paid irregularly based on project completion (e.g., a completed sale)
- Cannot be required to attend office meetings

A broker can exercise somewhat greater control over salespersons who are **employees**. The broker may require that an employee follow rules governing such matters as working hours, office routine, attendance at sales meetings, assignment of sales quotas, and adherence to dress codes. When dealing with employees, a broker is required by the federal government to withhold Social Security tax and income tax from wages paid to those employees. The broker also is required to pay unemployment compensation tax on wages paid to one or more employees, as defined by state and federal laws. In addition, employees might receive benefits such as health insurance, profit-sharing plans, or workers' compensation.

A broker's relationship with a salesperson who is an **independent contractor** is very different. As the name implies, an independent contractor operates more independently than does an employee, and a broker may not exercise the same degree of control over this person's daily activities. While the broker may determine *what* the independent contractor does (especially because the independent contractor is still representing the broker as his or her agent) the broker *cannot dictate how to do it*. Independent contractors are responsible for paying their own income and Social Security taxes and may receive nothing from brokers that might be construed as an employee benefit. An independent contractor's income is usually commission-based.

The Internal Revenue Service often investigates the independent contractor/employee situation in real estate offices. Under the qualified real estate agent category in the Internal Revenue Code, meeting three requirements can establish an independent contractor status:

1. The individual must have a current real estate license.
2. He or she must have a written contract with the broker that specifies that the salesperson will not be treated as an employee for federal tax purposes.
3. At least 90 percent of the individual's income as a licensee must be based on sales production and not on the number of hours worked.

IN PRACTICE

A broker must have a written employment agreement for all licensees sponsored by the employing broker both for independent contractors and for employees including licensed personal assistants. Specific legal and tax questions regarding independent contractors should be referred to a competent attorney or an accountant.

Broker Compensation

There are clearly defined approaches for how a brokerage firm's compensation practices must be handled. Compensation to the brokerage firm is specified in the contract with the principal (the seller or the buyer, and in some cases the lessor or the lessee). License laws usually stipulate that a *written agreement must establish compensation for it to be paid*. Compensation can be in the form of a brokerage fee commission (computed as a percentage of the total sales price), a flat fee, or an hourly rate. The amount of a broker's **commission** is fully negotiable in every case. However, it is important for the broker and the client to agree on a negotiated rate before the agency relationship is established.

In Illinois

Only a licensed broker may collect a commission in Illinois; the broker then may share it with any salespersons or associate brokers who are directly involved in or responsible for a given transaction. To collect a commission on a real estate transaction, the agent must have been "hired" by way of an agreement in which the principal (seller or buyer) agreed to pay a specified commission for services. The percentage of sales price or dollar amount of commission must have been expressed clearly in the agreement. If another real estate office "brought in" the buyer, the concept of **cooperative commission** allows the *listing broker* to pay the *selling broker* the amount of *cooperative (co-op) commission* advertised in advance on the multiple listing service (MLS) listing. This check is issued by the listing broker's office to the selling broker's office, and checks then are cut by each of these sponsoring brokers to any respective salespersons (or other brokers working within the firm) who were directly involved in the transaction.

"Co-op" Commission

Commission paid by the listing broker to the "cooperating broker" who has the buyer.

A commission is usually considered to be earned when the work for which the broker was hired has been accomplished. In Illinois, this means that the listing broker generally is entitled to a commission after procuring a *full-price offer with no contingencies from a buyer who is ready, willing, and able to buy on the seller's terms* as set forth in the listing. ∎

If the offer does not agree with the terms of the original listing, and the offer is acceptable, *the broker is entitled to a commission if terms have been clearly indicated by a contract of sale signed by both buyer and seller.* This is certainly true when the property closes, and sometimes even if it does not close. If a buyer cannot meet a stated contract contingency (such as acquiring financing) and bows out by the stated contingency date, then no commission is earned. Once contingency dates have passed and the buyer has failed to opt out of the deal, litigation for performance and/or for commission becomes more likely.

In reality, brokers only occasionally will risk alienating their clients and the public with suits for commission. For one thing, even if the buyer is at fault, the only suit *usually* possible for commission is against the seller if the seller was responsible for commission (as is still often the case in Illinois). Such a suit must be initiated by the seller's listing broker as a "suit for earned commission." *Courts may prevent a broker from receiving a commission on even a full-price offer if it can be shown the broker knew in advance that the buyer was unable to perform.*

To be a *procuring cause*, the broker must have started a chain of events that resulted in a sale.

Procuring cause is defined as *the uninterrupted chain of events, without abandonment or estrangement, which leads to the sale of property on the seller's terms.* To be considered the procuring cause of sale, the broker must have taken action to start or to cause a chain of events that resulted in the sale. Procuring cause issues have become less troublesome with buyer agency, because buyer agency agreements leave little doubt as to whose client is whose.

IN PRACTICE

Procuring cause disputes between brokers are usually settled through an arbitration hearing conducted by the local board or association. Disputes between a broker and a client may go to court.

A *ready, willing, and able buyer* is one prepared to buy on the seller's terms and ready to complete the transactions.

Finally, sales commissions are usually *payable* when the sale is consummated by delivery of the seller's deed. This provision is specifically stipulated in the listing agreement and/or in the real estate sales contract. The commission generally is earned when a completed sales contract has been executed by a **ready, willing, and able buyer**; when it has been accepted and executed (signed) by the seller; and when signed copies of the contract are in the possession of all parties. However, it usually is not paid until closing and deed transfer.

In Illinois

In Illinois, the closing of the sale is the usual proof in a court of law that the broker has produced a buyer and earned a commission. ■

Even if a transaction is not consummated, the brokers *may still be entitled to a commission* if the seller

- has a change of mind and refuses to sell,
- has a spouse who refuses to sign the deed prior to or at closing,
- has a title with uncorrected defects,
- commits fraud with respect to the transaction,
- is unable to deliver possession within a reasonable time,
- insists on terms not in the listing (for example, the right to restrict the use of the property), or
- has a mutual agreement with the buyer to cancel the transaction.

A listing broker generally is said to be "due a commission" if a sale is not consummated because of the seller's default.

Sales Force Compensation

The amount of compensation a salesperson receives from a sale is shaped by mutual agreement between the salesperson and his sponsoring broker. This compensation agreement is included in the employment agreement. A sponsoring broker may agree to pay a fixed salary or a predetermined percentage based on transactions originated by a specific licensee. Some brokers require that sales staff pay all or part of the expenses of advertising listed properties; this may be subtracted from commissions by agreement or be billed separately to the licensee.

In Illinois

In many states, including Illinois, it is illegal for a sponsoring broker to pay a commission to anyone *other than*

- a salesperson (or associate broker) licensed under that same sponsoring broker; or
- another firm's sponsoring broker (co-op commission) who then pays his or her own salesperson involved.

Fees, commissions, or other compensation *cannot* be paid to unlicensed persons for services that legally require a real estate license. "Other compensation" includes certain items of personal property, such as a new television, or other premiums, such as vacations, given to nonlicensed persons to perhaps acquire names of "leads." This is not to be confused with referral fees paid between brokers for "leads," which are legal as long as the individuals are licensed.

Illinois brokers may pay the salesperson or associate broker his or her commissions directly, or, under the *Real Estate License Act of 2000*, a licensee may form a *solely owned corporation* for the purpose of receiving compensation. That solely owned corporation cannot be licensed as a broker by the IDFPR. ■

IN PRACTICE

Sponsoring brokers *always* handle money that goes in and out of real estate offices. This includes but is not limited to incentive prizes for selling agents, earnest money deposits, escrows, commissions, referral fees, wages for licensed personal assistants, bonuses, thank-you surprises from buyers or sellers, and other monies or awards.

In Illinois

Commissions and disclosures.   The sponsoring broker's compensation and policy with cooperating brokers who represent other parties in a transaction must always be disclosed. If there is compensation from two parties to a transaction—from both the buyer and the seller—that needs to be disclosed in writing also. If an agent refers the client to another source for services related to the transaction and the agent has an interest greater than 1 percent in that source, it must be disclosed. ■

Commission Structures

Commission "splits" earned by salespersons and associate brokers vary. Some firms have adopted a 100 percent commission plan. Salespersons in these offices pay a monthly service charge or desk fee to their brokers to cover the costs of office space, telephones, and supervision in return for keeping 100 percent of the commissions from the sales they negotiate. The 100 percent commission salesperson pays all of his or her own expenses.

Other companies offer graduated commission splits based on a salesperson's achieving specified production goals. For instance, a broker might agree to split commissions 50/50 with a certain salesperson until the broker has earnings of $25,000 for the year from that salesperson; 60/40 until the broker's tally reaches $50,000; and then past that point the salesperson's portion of the split might go to 70 percent, 80 percent, or even 100 percent. Commission splits 80/20 or 90/10 are not unheard of for high producers. No matter how the licensee's compensation package is structured *only the sponsoring broker can pay it*.

In cooperating transactions (usually stated as "co-op: X%" on the MLS sheet), the commission is paid by the sponsoring broker of the "list side" to the sponsoring broker of the "sell side," and then paid to the salesperson who worked for or with the buyer. The listing agent is similarly paid by the listing broker.

In Illinois

If the commission is from a listing that has sold, the sponsoring broker of the listing firm is first paid by the seller. Then the sponsoring broker pays the salesperson (or broker associate) involved at the listing office and also pays the cooperating broker at any other firm involved in the transaction. The cooperating sponsoring broker in turn issues the appropriate amount to the salesperson involved at his or her office, based on their agreed on split. Sometimes a commission or fee does not involve a seller. It might come from a buyer who has agreed to a buyer agent fee. The same procedure applies: Incoming funds always go to the sponsoring broker first; from there they are dispersed to others involved.

If a salesperson had earned a commission but his or her employment had been terminated prior to the payment of the commission, the former employing broker may pay the commission directly to the former associate, even if that former associate has a new sponsoring broker. ■

MATH CONCEPTS

SHARING COMMISSIONS

A commission might be shared by many people: The listing broker, the listing salesperson, the selling broker, and the selling salesperson. Drawing a diagram can help you determine which person is entitled to receive what amount of the total commission.

For example, salesperson Ed, while working for broker Harry, took a listing on a $73,000 house at a 6 percent commission rate. Salesperson Tom, while working for broker Matt, found the buyer for the property. If the property sold for the listed price, the listing broker and the selling broker shared the commission equally and the selling broker kept 45 percent of what he received, how much did salesperson Tom receive? (If the broker retained 45 percent of the total commission he received, his salesperson would receive the balance: 100% – 45% = 55%.)

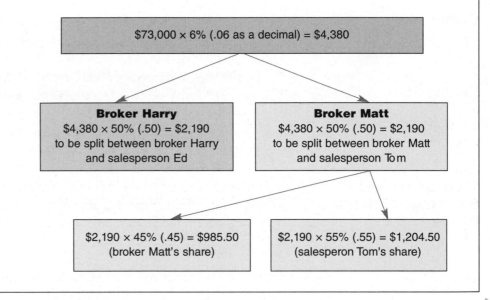

$73,000 × 6% (.06 as a decimal) = $4,380

Broker Harry
$4,380 × 50% (.50) = $2,190
to be split between broker Harry
and salesperson Ed

Broker Matt
$4,380 × 50% (.50) = $2,190
to be split between broker Matt
and salesperson Tom

$2,190 × 45% (.45) = $985.50
(broker Matt's share)

$2,190 × 55% (.55) = $1,204.50
(salesperon Tom's share)

Transactional Brokerage

A **transactional broker** (also called a *nonagent, facilitator, coordinator,* or *contract broker*) is not an agent of either party. A transactional broker's job is simply to help both the buyer and the seller with the necessary paperwork and formalities involved in transferring ownership of real property. The buyer and the seller negotiate the sale without representation or advocacy, much like a closer would at a title company.

The transactional broker is expected to treat all parties honestly and competently, to locate qualified buyers or suitable properties, to provide needed forms, and to assist in the closing of the transaction. Transactional brokers are equally responsible to both parties and must disclose known defects in a property. However, they may not negotiate on anyone's behalf or disclose confidential information to either party. No agency representation is provided. Transactional brokerage is legal only in a few states.

> In Illinois

Transactional brokerage is not legal in Illinois. ■

Legal Rights and Obligations

As each contract is prepared for signature during a real estate transaction, the broker should advise the parties of the desirability of securing legal counsel to protect their interests. *Only a lawyer can offer legal advice.* Licensees are prohibited from practicing law.

Personal Assistants

A licensed **personal assistant**, also known as a *real estate assistant* or *professional assistant*, is often a combination office manager, marketer, organizer, and facilitator with a fundamental understanding of the real estate industry. While an assistant does not need to have a real estate license, he or she is allowed to perform many more duties if licensed. (*In Illinois, the license would usually be a salesperson's license. There is no specific assistant's license.*)

The extent to which the assistant can help the broker or salesperson with transactions is usually determined by state license laws. An unlicensed assistant may perform duties ranging from clerical and secretarial functions to answering phones. A licensed assistant can set up and host open houses, deal more extensively with clients, actively show houses, and assist in all aspects of a real estate transaction.

| In Illinois |

Section 1450.165 of the administrative rules specifies the permitted activities in which an unlicensed real estate assistant may engage. (See Figure 5.1.)

The Real Estate License Act of 2000 clearly indicates that *licensed personal assistants must have an employment agreement with the sponsoring broker* of the firm in which they are working, even though they are in practice working for a salesperson or broker associate in the firm. Wages earned by these personal assistants must be paid to them by the sponsoring broker. ■

Technology and Brokerage of the Future

In addition to assistants, a wide range of technologies continues to be available to brokerage firms and licensees. Computers are a necessary staple in any modern real estate brokerage, and REALTORS® often utilize notebooks, tablets, and iPhones to make their "desks" portable.

MLSs and tax information are accessible to licensees in their own homes on the Internet. In many areas, MLS listings can be designed specifically for real estate professionals, and generic word-processing and spreadsheet software is available. There are programs to help real estate brokers and salespersons with such office management tasks as billing, accounting, and timekeeping. Other software helps with marketing and advertising properties and services, complete with postcards, prewritten letter templates, or suggested ad copy for newspapers.

Continuing education requirements may be met through the use of continuing education software or online courses. Real estate Web sites, home pages, and computer networks help licensees keep in touch, and some cable and satellite television channels are dedicated solely to real estate programming for both consumers and licensees.

As for selling properties, voicemail systems can track caller response to advertisements and give callers preprogrammed information about specific properties (using a coded ID system for the various properties) when the broker or salesperson is unavailable. Yard signs are available that broadcast details about a property on an AM radio band, so drivers passing by can tune in for information.

Blogs are used by licensees to exchange information. NAR maintains a blog in order to inform licensees of the latest technological trends in the industry and to provide a forum for asking questions.

FIGURE 5.1

Licensed and Unlicensed Real Estate Assistants

An Unlicensed Real Estate Assistant May . . .

- answer the telephone, take messages, and forward calls to a licensee
- submit listings and changes to an MLS
- follow up on a transaction after a contract has been signed
- assemble documents for a closing
- secure public information documents from a courthouse, sewer district, water district, or other repository of public information
- have keys made for a company listing
- draft advertising and promotional materials for approval by a licensee
- place advertising in media
- record and deposit earnest money, security deposits, and rents
- complete contract forms with business and factual information at the direction of and with approval by a licensee
- monitor licenses and personnel files
- compute commission checks and perform bookkeeping activities
- place signs on property
- order items of routine repair as directed by a licensee
- prepare and distribute flyers and promotional information under the direction of and with approval by a licensee
- act as a courier to deliver documents, pick up keys, etc.
- place routine telephone calls on late rent payments
- schedule appointments for the licensee (does not include making phone calls, telemarketing, or performing other activities to solicit business on behalf of the licensee)
- respond to questions by quoting from published information
- sit at a property for a broker tour that is not open to the public
- gather feedback on showings
- perform maintenance, engineering, operations, or other building trades work and answer questions about such work
- provide security
- provide concierge services and other similar amenities to existing tenants
- manage or supervise maintenance, engineering, operations, building trades, and security
- perform other administrative, clerical, and personal activities for which a license under the act is not required

An Unlicensed Real Estate Assistant May NOT. . .

- host open houses, kiosks, home show booths, or fairs
- show property
- interpret information on listings, titles, financing, contracts, closings, or other information related to a real estate transaction
- explain or interpret a contract, listing, lease agreement, or other real estate document with anyone outside the employing licensee's firm
- negotiate or agree to any commission, commission split, management fee, or referral fee on behalf of a licensee
- perform any other activity for which a real estate license under the act is required

SOURCE: Sec. 1450.165, Rules for the Administration of the Real Estate License Act of 2000.

Vlogs are also being used by licensees. Vlogs are video blogs and are useful for targeting out-of-area consumers looking for homes. Visitors to vlogs download videos and can see virtual tours of properties. Creating a vlog can be costly because it requires a webcam, camcorder, or digital camera with video capabilities, as well as video editing software.

Real estate brokers and salespersons must make careful decisions about which technologies best suit their needs and invest in them to have a cutting edge on today's market.

IN PRACTICE

Home listings are becoming available to the general public on the Internet through such Web sites as *www.realtor.com* and *cyberhomes.com* or through major newspapers' property-finding services. It is true that by accessing such services, potential buyers can preview photographs of properties and narrow their searches by price range, number of bedrooms, school district, or other parameters. However, consumers will always need licensees for key transaction elements—seeing the home, gaining advice on purchases, acquiring an intelligent comparative market analysis (CMA), and negotiating advice.

Security

As technology becomes more available and convenient, it brings security problems for both licensees and clients. Systems can be subject to attack by viruses, worms, adware, and spyware, placing personal information and databases at risk. Phishing e-mails may ask for personal information that should not be shared. It is important for a licensee to take security seriously to avoid placing one's firm and the information provided by clients at risk. Following are a few security measures to keep in mind:

- Place firewalls on servers and computers
- Keep virus and spyware protective software up to date
- Use passwords, changed with some frequency, and encryption, especially when using public hotspots to convey information
- Be reluctant to open e-mail and especially e-mail attachments from unknown sources
- Be aware that wireless environments, including those used by computers, phones, and PDAs may be subject to content viewing and listening in by others
- Stay attentive to phishing scams
- Keep current on software security patches
- Practice good back-up procedures and have off-site storage for back-up records
- Research carefully those companies a real estate firm outsources for its information technology (IT) and Web services
- Talk with your IT personnel about suspicious situations regarding the computer system or wireless environment

Electronic Contracting

Electronic contracting is a growing field in real estate practice because it quickly and efficiently integrates information in a real estate transaction between clients, lenders, title and closing agents. The transactions are conducted through e-mail or fax.

Two federal Acts govern electronic contracting: the **Uniform Electronic Transactions Act (UETA),** and the **Electronic Signatures in Global and National Commerce Act (E-Sign).**

The UETA sets forth rules for entering an enforceable contract using electronic means and has been enacted in most states. The primary purpose of the UETA is to remove barriers in electronic commerce that would otherwise prevent enforceability of contracts. The UETA validates and effectuates electronic records and signatures in a procedural manner. It is intended to complement any state's digital signature statute. The UETA does not in any way require parties to use electronic means. Following are UETA's four key provisions:

1. A contract cannot be denied its legal effect just because an electronic record was used.
2. A record or signature cannot be denied its legal effect just because it is in an electronic format.
3. If a state's law requires a signature on a contract, an electronic signature is sufficient.
4. If a state's law requires a written record, an electronic record is sufficient.

E-Sign functions as the electronic transactions law in states that have not enacted the UETA, and some sections of E-Sign apply to states that have enacted the UETA. The purpose of the E-Sign is to make contracts (including signatures) and records legally enforceable regardless of the medium in which they are created. For example, contracts formed using e-mail have the same legal significance as those formed on paper.

Fee-for-Services

One of the more notable impacts of the Internet is that it has allowed buyers and sellers to have tremendous access to information about real estate, housing, financing, and law. As a result, the average consumer is now much more knowledgeable about real estate matters. With knowledge and information, a consumer is more innovative and independent. The advent of the Internet has also meant that the consumer is privy to information immediately. Consumers now want instant access to real estate information.

The successful licensee will understand and encourage consumers' innovation. In the process, it is critical for the licensee to identify what services he or she can provide and underscore the value of those services. While emphasizing the services that a licensee provides, it may be important for the licensee to think of himself or herself as a *consultant*. While consumers are more independent, real estate expertise is almost always needed.

It may be important for licensees to be more flexible and open to seeing their occupation as a *bundle of services* that can be unbundled. Note that unbundling fee-for-services is different from discounted real estate services. *Fee-for-services* is the arrangement where the consumer decides which services he or she needs and then works with and pays the licensee solely for those services. *Discounted real estate services* is the arrangement where a consumer receives all of the real estate services, but at a discounted price.

Unbundling services means offering services in a piecemeal fashion. For example, a consultant may want to offer a seller the following services:

- Helping the seller prepare the property for sale
- Performing a competitive market analysis (CMA) and pricing the property
- Assisting with marketing the property using the MLS and any Web sites
- Locating and screening a buyer
- Drafting a purchase sales agreement and helping with negotiations
- Assisting with the closing transaction

Other services include those for a buyer. For example, a consultant may offer a buyer the following services:

- Consulting on renting versus owning
- Helping a buyer with a mortgage preapproval
- Consulting on a buyer's desired location
- Visiting properties with a buyer and checking property information
- Completing a real estate sale contract and helping with negotiations
- Assisting with closing the transaction

While licensees want to encourage consumers to use all of their services (*full-service*) for a commission rate, when it becomes apparent that a consumer wants help with one or several services only, then it would be helpful for the licensee to have in mind the best compensation model. Many licensees use either an hourly rate or a flat fee for particular services. In determining a flat fee, licensees consider the amount of hours it would take to do a particular task and multiply that by an hourly rate. In order to avoid a price-fixing claim, it is important that brokers independently establish their fees and do not develop their fees based on a "norm" in the industry.

Licensees may also want to develop their own lists of services for sellers and buyers, as well as a list of specific services to help those consumers selling their home on their own (FSBOs).

Communicating with consumers and identifying their real estate needs are key. Knowledgeable and independent consumers can seem threatening to a licensee; however, the licensee has the opportunity to emphasize the value and variety of real estate services offered, for varying fees. Remember that it is ultimately the broker who decides whether an unbundling of services is good for the company.

■ **FOR EXAMPLE** Chris wants to buy a house without contracting with a licensee but needs help writing an offer. Chris asks Sally, a broker friend of hers, to write an offer to purchase. Sally consults with Chris, writes the offer to purchase, and charges Chris a set fee for her service.

■ ANTITRUST LAWS

The real estate industry is subject to federal and state **antitrust laws.** These laws prohibit monopolies and any contracts, combinations, and conspiracies that unreasonably restrain trade—that is, acts that interfere with the free flow of goods and services in a competitive marketplace. The most common antitrust violations are price-fixing, group boycotting, allocation of customers or markets, and tie-in agreements.

Price-Fixing

Price-fixing is the practice of setting prices for products or services rather than letting competition in the open market establish those prices. In real estate, price-fixing occurs when competing brokers agree to set standard sales commissions, fees, or management rates or if they attempt illegal tying arrangements. Price-fixing is illegal. Brokers must independently determine any minimum commission rates or minimum fees. These decisions must be based on a broker's business judgment and revenue requirements without input from other brokers.

Antitrust violations include

- price-fixing;
- group boycotting;
- allocation of customers;
- allocation of markets; and
- tie-in agreements.

MLSs, Boards of REALTORS®, and other professional organizations may not set fees or commission splits. Nor can they deny membership to brokers based on the fees the brokers charge. Either practice could lead the public to believe that the industry not only sanctions the unethical practice of withholding cooperation from certain brokers but also encourages the illegal practice of restricting open-market competition.

The broker's challenge is to avoid even the impression of price-fixing. Hinting to prospective clients that there is a "going rate" of commission or a "normal" fee also implies that rates are, in fact, standardized, which must be avoided. The broker must make it clear to clients that any stated minimum is *only the firm's minimum*. The specific commission is negotiable in a fair market.

Group Boycotting

Group boycotting occurs when two or more businesses conspire against another business or agree to withhold their patronage to reduce competition. Group boycotting is illegal under the antitrust laws.

■ **FOR EXAMPLE** Lilly and Nick, the only real estate brokers in Potterville, agree that there are too many apartment finder services in town. They decide to refer all prospective tenants to the service operated by Lilly's niece rather than handing out a list of all providers, as they have done in the past. As a result, Lilly's niece runs the only apartment finder service in Potterville by the end of the year.

Allocation of Customers or Markets

Allocation of customers or markets involves an agreement among brokers to divide their markets and refrain from competing for each other's business. Allocations may be made on a geographic basis, with brokers agreeing to specific territories within which they will operate exclusively. The division also may occur by markets, such as by price range or category of housing. These agreements result in reduced competition.

Tie-in Agreements

Tie-in agreements, also known as *tying agreements*, are agreements to sell one product only if the buyer purchases another product as well. The sale of the first (desired) product is "tied" to the purchase of a second, less desirable, product.

■ **FOR EXAMPLE** Dion, a real estate broker, owns a vacant lot in a popular area of town. Brent, a builder, wants to buy the lot and build three new homes on it. Dion refuses to sell the lot to the builder unless Brent also agrees to purchase three other less desirable lots further east. This sort of tie-in arrangement violates antitrust laws.

Penalties

The penalties for violating antitrust laws are severe. For instance, under the *Sherman Antitrust Act*, people who fix prices or allocate markets may be subject to fines and imprisonment.

■ OTHER CONSUMER PROTECTION MEASURES

National Do Not Call Registry

In 2003, the Federal Communications Commission (FCC) established the **National Do Not Call Registry**. The registry is a list of phone numbers of consumers who do not want to be contacted by commercial telemarketers. It is managed by the FTC and is enforced by the FTC, the FCC, and state officials.

The do-not-call rules cover the sale of goods or services by telephone. Political organizations, charities, telephone surveyors, or companies with which a consumer has an existing business relationship are exempt from the do-not-call rules. A company may call a consumer, even if that consumer is on the registry, for 18 months after that consumer's last purchase, delivery, or payment; or a company may call a consumer for three months after a consumer makes an inquiry or submits an application to the company. If the consumer asks the company not to call again, the company must honor the request, even if the consumer is not on the do-not-call registry.

For example, it is permissible for a real estate agent to call expired listings for the purpose of listing the property because the established business relationship exception permits the listing agent, as well as other agents from the same company, to contact the seller for up to 18 month after the listing expiration date. Keep in mind that companies must also maintain a company-specific do-not-call list that applies as well.

Accessing the National Do Not Call Registry

Sellers, telemarketers, and other service providers must register to access the registry. The do-not-call registry may not be used for any purpose other than preventing telemarketing calls to the telephone numbers on the registry.

Regulators say that brokerage companies must have a do-not-call policy even if they do not engage in cold calling. A company that is a seller or telemarketer could be in violation of the law for placing any telemarketing calls (even to numbers *not* on the do-not-call registry) if the company does not have a policy for access to the registry. Violators may be subject to fines of up to $11,000 for each call placed.

To successfully avoid penalties ("safe harbor"), the seller or telemarketer must demonstrate the following:

- It has written procedures to comply with the do-not-call requirements.
- It trains its personnel in those procedures.
- It monitors and enforces compliance with these procedures.
- It maintains a company-specific list of telephone numbers it may not call.
- It accesses the national registry every 30 days before calling any consumer and maintains records documenting this process.
- It must show that any call made in violation of the do-not-call rules was the result of an error.

The best source of information about complying with the do-not-call rules is the FTC's Web sites: *www.donotcall.gov* and *www.ftc.gov*. They include business information about the registry.

The CAN-SPAM Act

The **CAN-SPAM Act of 2003** (Controlling the Assault of Non-Solicited Pornography and Marketing Act) establishes requirements for sending commercial e-mail; spells out penalties for those that don't comply, not just "spammers"; and gives consumers the right to have e-mailers stop e-mailing them. The law covers e-mail whose primary purpose is advertising or promoting a commercial product or service, including Web site content. A "transactional or relationship message" (e-mail that facilitates an agreement upon transaction or updates a customer in an existing business relationship) may not contain false or misleading routing information but otherwise is exempt from most provisions of the CAN-SPAM Act.

The FTC is authorized to enforce the CAN-SPAM Act and gives the Department of Justice the authority to enforce its criminal sanctions. Other federal and state agencies have the authority to enforce the law against organizations under their jurisdiction. Companies that provide interstate access may regulate violators as well.

Briefly, the CAN-SPAM Act requires the following:

- *False or misleading header information is banned.* An e-mail's "From," "To," and routing information—including the original domain name and e-mail address—must be accurate and identify the person who initiated the e-mail.
- *Deceptive subject lines are prohibited.* The subject line cannot mislead the recipient about the contents or subject matter of the message.
- *E-mail recipients must have an opt-out method.* You must provide a return e-mail address or another Internet-based response mechanism that allows a recipient to ask you not to send future e-mail messages to that e-mail address and requests must be honored.
- *Commercial e-mail must be identified as an advertisement and include the sender's valid physical postal address.*

Each violation is subject to fines of up to $11,000. Deceptive commercial e-mails are also subject to laws banning false or misleading advertising. Additional fines are provided for commercial e-mailers who violate the rules and do any of the following:

- "Harvest" e-mail addresses from Web sites or Web services that have published a notice prohibiting the transfer of e-mail addresses for the purpose of sending e-mail
- Generate e-mail addresses using a "dictionary attack"—combining names, letters, or numbers into multiple permutations
- Use scripts or other automated ways to register for multiple e-mail or user accounts to send commercial e-mail
- Relay e-mails through a computer or network without permission— for example, taking advantage of open relays or open proxies without notification.

The Junk Fax Prevention Act

The **Junk Fax Prevention Act of 2005** does not legalize unsolicited fax advertisements or solicitations but does allow for an established business relationship exception. As a general rule, a real estate licensee could not legally send an unsolicited commercial fax message without express written consent or without an established business relationship with the recipient.

Following are the provisions of the fax law:

- Reaffirms the long-standing established business relationship (EBR) exception to the ban on unsolicited commercial faxes by establishing explicit statutory authority for the EBR
- Places no time limit on an EBR
- Requires all commercial faxes to include an opt-out provision on the first page of the fax and provide a cost-free, 24/7 means for the recipient to request removal from a fax distribution list
- Requires that, after the date of enactment, fax numbers to which advertising is sent be obtained either directly from the recipient by oral or written

consent or, if sent within the context of a newly established business relationship, from a public source to which the recipient gave the number willingly for publication (i.e., a Web site or advertisement)

■ Allows senders, in the case of an earlier EBR, to use fax numbers in their possession prior to the effective date

■ Requires, in the case of an EBR that existed prior to enactment but for which the sender did not possess a fax number at the time of enactment of this legislation, that a fax number be obtained either directly from the recipient by oral or written consent or from a public source to which the recipient gave the number willingly for publication

■ Authorizes the FCC, after not less than three months from enactment, to review this matter and, if the FCC determines that there are significant abuses of faxes sent under the EBR exception, may reconsider imposing limitations on the EBR

It is also important to know that despite adoption of this federal law, state laws on the sending of unsolicited faxes are not preempted.

■ STATE LICENSE LAWS

All 50 states, the District of Columbia, and all Canadian provinces license and regulate the activities of real estate brokers and salespersons. While the laws share a common purpose, the details vary from state to state. Uniform policies and standards for administering and enforcing state license laws are promoted by an organization of state license law officials known as *ARELLO*—the Association of Real Estate License Law Officials.

Real estate license laws have been enacted to *protect the public* by ensuring a standard of competence and professionalism in the real estate industry. The laws achieve this goal by

■ establishing basic requirements for obtaining a real estate license and, in many cases, requiring continuing education to keep a license;

■ defining which activities require licensing;

■ describing the acceptable standards of conduct and practice for licensees; and

■ enforcing those standards through a disciplinary system.

The purpose of these laws is not merely to regulate the real estate industry. Their main objective is to make sure that the rights of purchasers, sellers, tenants, and owners are protected from unscrupulous or sloppy practices.

The laws are not intended to prevent licensees from conducting their businesses successfully nor are they meant to interfere in legitimate transactions. Laws cannot create an ethical or a moral marketplace. However, by establishing minimum levels of competency and limits of permitted behavior, laws can make the marketplace safer and more honest.

Each state has a licensing authority—a commission, a department, a division, a board, or an agency—that serves the needs of real estate brokers and salespersons while protecting the public. This authority has the power to issue licenses, to make real estate information available to licensees and the public, and to enforce the statutory real estate law.

<table>
<tr><td>In Illinois</td><td>Illinois has had a *Real Estate License Act* since January 1, 1921. The current law—The *Real Estate License Act of 2000*—is administered by the Bureau of Real Estate Professions (BRE). The act governs the licensing and activities of brokers and salespeople. The act's intent is to evaluate the competency of persons engaged in the real estate business and to regulate this business for the protection of the public. Illinois license law consists of the "act" itself as well as the "rules" which interpret and implement it. ∎</td></tr>
</table>

■ SUMMARY

Real estate brokerage is the act of bringing people together, for a fee or commission, for the purpose of buying, selling, exchanging, or leasing real estate. New technologies are changing the way that brokerage offices are managed and operated. Many new Web sites are available both to the public and real estate licensees, as well as new technology including notebooks, tablets, iPhones, blogs, and vlogs.

The use of licensed assistants is another way a real estate agent may advance in a busy, demanding business. Licensed assistants must have an agreement with the sponsoring broker and must be paid by him or her. An unlicensed assistant may only engage in administrative or clerical functions on behalf of the licensee.

The broker's compensation in a real estate sale may take the form of a percentage commission, a flat fee, or an hourly rate. The broker is considered to have earned a commission when he or she procures a ready, willing, and able buyer for a seller. Salespersons or brokers who work under a sponsoring broker do so either as an employee or as an independent contractor. Either way, there must be a written employment agreement signed by both parties.

Two federal acts govern electronic contracting: the Uniform Electronic Transactions Act (UETA) and the Electronic Signatures in Global and National Commerce Act (E-sign).

The Internet has allowed buyers and sellers tremendous access to real estate information. As consumers become more innovative, it may be important for licensees to view their occupation as a bundle of services that can be unbundled and offered separately.

Federal and state antitrust laws prohibit brokers from conspiring to fix prices, engage in boycotts, allocate customers or markets, or establish tie-in agreements.

The National Do Not Call Registry is a list of consumer telephone numbers that do not want to be contacted by businesses who sell goods or services. Violators are subject to fines of up to $11,000 for each illegal call placed.

The CAN-SPAM Act establishes requirements for commercial e-mail, spells out penalties for e-mail senders, and gives consumers the right to have e-mailers stop sending e-mails to them. It is enforced by the FTC and the Department of Justice with fines of up to $11,000 per transgression.

The Junk Fax Prevention Act prohibits faxing unsolicited fax advertisements or solicitations but does allow for an established business relationship exception.

Real estate license laws and regulations govern the professional conduct of brokers and salespersons. The license laws are enacted to protect the public by ensuring a standard of competence and professionalism in the real estate industry.

In Illinois

In Illinois, the *Real Estate License Act of 2000* provides the primary guidelines for compliance in handling real estate activities. ■

QUESTIONS

1. Which of the following statements best explains the meaning of this sentence: "To recover a commission for brokerage services, a broker must be employed as the agent of the seller"?
   a. The broker must work in a real estate office.
   b. The seller must have made an express or implied agreement to pay a commission to the broker for selling the property.
   c. The broker must have asked the seller the price of the property and then found a ready, willing, and able buyer.
   d. The broker must have a salesperson employed in the office.

2. An Illinois real estate salesperson who is engaged as an independent contractor
   a. is considered an employee by the IRS for tax purposes.
   b. must have a written contract with the broker.
   c. must be covered by workers' compensation.
   d. may work as an independent contractor for two or more brokers.

3. In Illinois, the usual "proof" that the listing broker has earned his or her commission is the
   a. submission to the seller of a signed offer from a ready, willing, and able buyer.
   b. closing of the sale.
   c. signing of an exclusive listing contract.
   d. deposit of the buyer's earnest money into escrow.

4. Broker Sierra listed Brock's home for $300,000. Before the listing contract expired, Sierra brought Brock a full-price offer on Brock's terms, containing no contingencies. Brock then decided not to sell. Which of the following statements is *TRUE*?
   a. Sierra has no reason to collect a commission in this case.
   b. Brock probably is liable for the commission.
   c. Sierra must immediately file suit against Brock.
   d. Brock's only liability is to the buyer.

5. Gerald is an unlicensed real estate assistant. Under Illinois law, which of the following may Gerald do?
   a. Negotiate compensation
   b. Engage in prospecting
   c. Host an open house for the public
   d. Host a broker open house

6. According to the Illinois license law, a real estate salesperson may not
   a. represent both buyer and seller.
   b. buy or sell real estate for himself or herself.
   c. accept a commission from another broker unless previously earned.
   d. engage in dual agency.

7. A sponsoring broker must have a written employment agreement with which of these individuals?
   a. Independent contractors
   b. Licensed personal assistants
   c. Licensed salespersons
   d. All of the above

8. Broker Mark and Broker Ivan agreed to boycott the services of the MNM Title Company so that the new TSK Title Company can take over MNM's market share. What is the act that Mark and David are violating?
   a. Antiboycotting Act
   b. Illinois Lincoln Antitrust Act
   c. Sherman Antitrust Act
   d. Land of Lincoln Fair Trade Act

9. Juan's first commission as a broker was $8,200. If his commission rate was 6 percent, what was the selling price of the property?
   a. $136,666.67
   b. $154,232.50
   c. $132,666.67
   d. $175,452.48

10. Jack received $2,520 as his firm's 50 percent share of a commission. If the property sold for $72,000, what was the commission rate?
    a. 7 percent
    b. .07 percent
    c. 8 percent
    d. 6.5 percent

11. One general rule of the Federal Do Not Call regulations is
    a. states must maintain separate do-not-call lists.
    b. the national registry must be updated once a year.
    c. it is illegal to make an unsolicited phone call to a number listed on the national registry.
    d. real estate offices are exempt from the laws because they are not considered telemarketers.

12. Federal regulations on unsolicited e-mail
    a. require prior permission of recipients in order to send e-mail to them.
    b. require that e-mail lists be scrubbed every 31 days.
    c. exempt phone calls to individuals with whom the real estate office has a prior business relationship.
    d. require commercial e-mails to include a physical address, among other things, for the sender.

13. Which statement is *TRUE* regarding the Junk Fax Prevention Act of 2005?
    a. Real estate licensees are not required to search the national registry before making telemarketing calls to solicit listings or to solicit potential buyers.
    b. Real estate licensees are exempt from telemarketing laws.
    c. Real estate licensees may phone or fax any visitors to an open house who provide their phone numbers on a sign-in sheet, but only where the visitor is given either an option to opt out or notice that they will be called.
    d. Real estate licensees may not advertise their listings by faxing promotional flyers to a list of potential homebuyers with whom they do not have an existing business relationship.

CHAPTER 6

Brokerage Agreements

■ **LEARNING OBJECTIVES** *When you've finished reading this chapter, you should be able to*

■ **identify** the different types of listing and buyer representation agreements and their terms.

■ **describe** the ways in which a listing may be terminated.

■ **explain** the listing process and the parts of the listing agreement.

■ **distinguish** among the characteristics of the various types of listing and buyer representation agreements.

■ **define** the following *key terms:*

buyer agency agreement
comparative market
  analysis
exclusive-agency listing
exclusive-right-to-sell
  listing

market value
minimum services
multiple listing service
net listing
open listing

option listing
statute of frauds

■ BROKERAGE AGREEMENTS

Listing and buyer representation agreements are *employment contracts* rather than real estate sales contracts. They are contracts for the personal professional services of the broker, not for the transfer of real estate. In most states, either by **statutes of frauds** or by specific rules from real estate licensing authorities, listings are required to be in writing to be enforceable in court. Oral listings are sometimes permitted but rarely recommended.

Illinois requires that *any exclusive brokerage agreement, whether with a buyer or seller, must be in writing* (Section 1450.195 of the Rules). ■

Employment contracts with buyers and sellers create special agency relationships between the principal (the person who is being represented by the broker) and the broker (the agent). As agent, the broker is authorized to represent the principal to third parties.

Under both the law of agency and most state license laws, only a broker can act as the legal agent to list, sell, rent, or purchase another person's real estate and provide other services to a principal. A salesperson (or a broker who works under the auspices of a sponsoring broker) who performs these acts does so in the name of and under the supervision of the sponsoring broker. Throughout this chapter, unless otherwise stated, the terms *broker, agent,* and *firm* are intended to include both the broker and a salesperson working for the broker. A broker employment contract is ultimately between the principal (buyer or seller) and the sponsoring broker of the firm.

■ LISTING AGREEMENTS WITH SELLERS

Types of Listing Agreements

Several types of listing agreements exist. The type of contract determines the specific rights and obligations of the parties.

Exclusive-right-to-sell listing:

One authorized broker receives a commission regardless of who sells the property.

Exclusive-right-to-sell listing.   In an **exclusive-right-to-sell listing** one broker is appointed as the seller's sole agent. The broker is given the exclusive right, or *authorization*, to market the seller's property. If the property is sold while the listing is in effect, the seller must pay the broker a commission *regardless of who sells the property*. In other words, if the seller finds a buyer without the broker's assistance, the seller still must pay the broker a commission. Sellers benefit from this form of agreement because the broker feels more free to spend time and money actively marketing the property, making a timely and profitable sale more likely. From the broker's perspective, an exclusive-right-to-sell listing offers the greatest opportunity to receive a commission.

IN PRACTICE   The majority of residential listing agreements in Illinois are exclusive-right-to-sell listing agreements.

Exclusive-agency listing:

■ There is one authorized broker.
■ Broker receives a commission only if he or she is the procuring cause.
■ Seller retains the right to sell without obligation.

Exclusive-agency listing.   In an **exclusive-agency listing** one broker is authorized to act as the exclusive agent of the principal. However, the seller retains the right to sell the property without obligation to the broker. The seller is obligated to pay a commission to the broker only if the broker has been the procuring cause of a sale.

Open listing.   In an **open listing** (known in some areas as a *nonexclusive listing* or a *general listing*), the seller retains the right to employ any number of brokers as agents. The brokers can act simultaneously, and the seller is obligated to pay a commission to only that broker who successfully produces a ready, willing, and able buyer. If the seller personally sells the property without the aid of any of the brokers, the seller is not obligated to pay a commission.

Negotiated terms of an open listing should be in writing to protect the broker's ability to collect an agreed-on fee from the seller. Written terms may be in the form of a listing agreement (if the broker represents the seller) or a fee agreement (if the broker represents the buyer or the seller does not wish to be represented).

Net listing. A **net listing** provision specifies that the seller will receive a net amount of money from any sale, with the excess going to the listing broker as commission. The broker is free to offer the property at any price greater than the net amount the seller wants; the difference is the broker's fee. Because a net listing can create a clear conflict of interest between the broker's fiduciary responsibility to the seller and the broker's profit motive, net listings are illegal in many states and are discouraged in others.

In Illinois, they are legal but not recommended due to the potential for fraud. ■

In a net listing: Actual Sale Price – Seller-Required Sale Price = Broker Profit.

■ **FOR EXAMPLE** A broker lists a property. The agreement states that the minimum amount acceptable to the seller is $190,000. The list price is set much higher, but the only profit the broker will gain is the amount the property sells for *over* the $190,000 amount.

A number of situations could occur that make net listings ill-advised on the above property. For instance:

1. The broker advertises the property for $250,000. Given the above agreement, the broker pockets $40,000 when an offer and sale for $230,000 is made. *(Actual sale price [$230,000] minus seller-required sale price [$190,000] equals broker profit [$40,000]).* This is likely to provoke charges that the broker deliberately estimated fair market value on the low side so as to reap larger rewards. The seller loses money, and the broker may have his or her integrity questioned.

2. The property is marketed at $200,000. It sells for $190,000, with the seller accepting. The broker earns nothing, given the stated agreement, and must pay for his or her advertising campaign. If such a possibility is foreseen by a broker, owing to the very small gap between seller's desired list price and seller's required price, the agent may not feel motivated to spend money advertising or promoting the listing because it is anticipated that little or no commission may result. Both seller and broker may lose.

Option listing. An **option listing** provision gives the broker the right to purchase the listed property at some point in the future. The specific length of the time period is by agreement, and usually matches the length of the listing. Use of an option listing may open the broker to charges of fraud unless the broker is scrupulous in fulfilling all obligations to the property owner. In some states, a broker who chooses to exercise such an option must first inform the property owner of the broker's profit in the transaction and secure in writing the owner's agreement to it.

Note: an *option listing* differs from an *option contract,* the latter involving a consumer's option to purchase a given property.

Sometimes, brokers and sellers enter into *guaranteed sale agreements*, in which the broker agrees to buy the listed property if it fails to sell before the end of the listing period. Typically, these guarantees are made to the seller as an inducement to list the property with the broker.

In Illinois

In Illinois, any such agreement must be in writing and is subject to other legal requirements, noted in detail in the Illinois *Real Estate License Act of 2000*. ■

Special Listing Provisions

Multiple listing.   A *multiple listing clause* frequently is included in an exclusive listing. It is a marketing tool used by brokers who are members of a **multiple listing service** (MLS). An MLS is a marketing organization whose broker members make their listings available for showing and sale through all the other member brokers.

An MLS offers advantages to both brokers and sellers. Brokers develop a sizable inventory of properties to be sold and are assured a portion of the commission if they list property or participate in the sale of another broker's listing. Sellers gain because the property is exposed to a much larger market.

The contractual obligations among the member brokers of an MLS vary widely. Most MLSs require that a broker turn over new listings to the service within a specific, fairly short period of time after the broker obtains the listing. The length of time during which the listing broker can offer a property to the public on his or her own without involving the MLS varies. Of course, sellers must be informed and give their written consent for any delay in notifying the MLS. This gives the listing company a strong chance to sell its own listing.

Under the provisions of most MLSs, a participating broker makes a unilateral offer of cooperation and compensation to other member brokers when the listing enters the MLS. The broker must have the written consent of the seller to include the property in an MLS.

In Illinois

Under Illinois law, a broker working with a buyer is *not* considered to be a sub-agent of the seller. *No offer of subagency can be made through an MLS in Illinois today.* Illinois law states that a buyer is represented as a client by the licensee with whom he or she is working unless that consumer *chooses* not to be. This approach makes it clear to all parties who is represented by whom.

Today it is illegal to offer subagency through an MLS in Illinois.

While a few buyers choose to remain as customers without representation, even that lack of agency is now subject to disclosure—*the licensee must be certain the consumer understands what is at stake in refusing agency. If nothing is said about agency, the consumer may now legally presume he or she has an agent: the salesperson or broker working for him or her as described in Article 15 of the act.*

In spite of these relatively clear lines with regard to whose agent is whose, sellers often still pay the fees for both agents in a transaction. These fees are called *cooperative commissions*. In an Illinois MLS listing data sheet, this is typically stated as "co-op: X% or as a flat fee." *Paying someone a commission does not create agency in Illinois.* ■

IN PRACTICE   Technology has enhanced the benefits of MLS membership. In addition to providing instant access to information about the status of listed properties, MLSs often offer a broad range of other useful information about mortgage loans, real estate taxes and assessments, municipalities, and school districts. They are extremely helpful to licensees who need to make a comparative market analysis (CMA) to determine the value of a particular property before suggesting an appropriate range of prices.

■ EXPIRATION OF LISTING PERIOD

| In Illinois | All listings in Illinois must specify a definite period of time during which the broker is to be employed. ■

Automatic Extension

Courts in most states have discouraged the use of automatic extension clauses in exclusive listings. Automatic extension clauses are illegal in some states, and many listing contract forms specifically provide that there can be no automatic extensions of the agreement.

| In Illinois | The failure to specify a definite termination date in a listing agreement is grounds for suspension or revocation of a real estate license in this state. *Illinois law forbids automatic extension clauses.* ■

Broker Protection

Some listing contracts, in Illinois and elsewhere, contain a *broker protection clause*, also called a *safety clause*. This clause provides that the property owner will pay the listing broker a commission if, within a specified time period after the listing expires, the owner transfers property title to someone who saw the property while it was listed with the broker. Normally such a fee will cover commissions for both the listing broker and whatever brokerage firm brought in the buyer. The protection clause protects a broker from losing a commission on a sale involving buyers who saw the property while it was listed. It also is designed to discourage others from trying to reach private arrangements with sellers.

The length of time for a protection clause is set by agreement. Any new buyers the seller might procure on his or her own after expiration of the listing are not affected. To protect the owner and prevent liability of the owner for two separate commissions, this clause cannot be enforced if the property is relisted under a new contract with another brokerage firm.

The broker protection clause can be enforced on commercial property even if the property is relisted with another brokerage firm.

■ THE LISTING PROCESS

Before signing a contract, the broker and seller must discuss a variety of issues. The seller's most critical concerns typically are the selling price of the property and the net amount he or she can expect to receive from the sale. The broker has several professional tools available to provide information about a property's value and to calculate the proceeds from a sale.

Pricing the Property

While it is the responsibility of the broker or salesperson to advise and assist, it is the seller who must determine the listing price for the property. Because the average seller does not have the skills needed to determine a market-based listing price, real estate agents must be prepared to offer their knowledge and expertise.

The CMA

A *comparative market analysis* or **CMA** is an analysis of market activity among comparable properties; it is not the same as a formal appraisal.

A salesperson can help the seller determine a listing price for the property by using a **comparative market analysis** (CMA). This is a comparison of the prices of similar properties recently sold, similar properties currently on the market, and properties that did not sell. The comparisons must be made with properties similar in location, size, age, style, and amenities. Although a CMA is not viewed as a formal appraisal, the salesperson uses many of the appraiser's methods and techniques in arriving at a reasonable value range. If no adequate comparisons can be made, or if the property is unique in some way, the real estate agent may wish to suggest that the seller pay to have a professional appraiser conduct a detailed, formal estimate of the property's value. In most situations, the real estate professional's sense of the local market and detailed knowledge of properties in a neighborhood contribute to a quality CMA.

Market Value

Market value is the most probable price a property would bring in an arm's-length transaction under normal conditions on the open market.

The figure sought in both CMAs and appraisals is the property's market value. **Market value** is *the most probable price a property would bring in an arm's-length transaction under normal conditions on the open market*. A CMA estimates market value as likely to fall within a range of values (e.g., $335,000 to $340,000). A formal appraisal indicates a specific value rather than a range. In both cases, the seller/principal must make the final decision on his or her asking price.

While it is the property owner's privilege to set whatever listing price he or she chooses, a broker should consider rejecting any listing in which the price is substantially exaggerated or severely out of line with the indications of the CMA or appraisal. These tools provide the best indications of what a buyer will likely pay for the property. An unrealistic listing price will make it difficult for the broker to properly market the seller's property within the agreed upon listing period. Furthermore, a seller who is unreasonable about the property's value may prove uncooperative on other issues later on.

IN PRACTICE

When helping a seller determine an appropriate listing price, the broker must give an estimate of value that is reasonable and as accurate as possible. Overpriced listings cost the broker time and money in wasted marketing and advertising and give sellers false hopes of riches to come. Additionally, some research suggests that listings priced too high in the beginning sell for less in the end than if they had been more moderately priced at the outset.

Seller's Return

The broker easily can calculate roughly how much the seller will net from a given sales price or what sales price will produce a desired net amount. (The Math Concepts accompanying this section illustrate how the various formulas are applied.)

Information Needed for Listing Agreements

Once the real estate licensee and the owner agree on a listing price, the licensee must obtain specific, detailed information about the property. Obtaining as many facts as possible ensures that most contingencies can be anticipated. This is particularly important when the listing will be shared with other brokers through an MLS and the other licensees must rely on the information taken by the listing agent.

MATH CONCEPTS

CALCULATING SALES PRICES, COMMISSIONS, AND NETS TO SELLER

When a property sells, the sales price equals 100 percent of the money being transferred. Therefore, if a broker is to receive a 6 percent commission, 94 percent will remain for the seller's other expenses and equity. To calculate a commission using a sales price of $80,000 and a commission rate of 6 percent, multiply the sales price by the commission rate:

$$\$80,000 \times 6\% = \$80,000 \times .06 = \$4,800 \text{ commission}$$

To calculate a sales price using a commission of $4,550 and a commission rate of 7 percent, divide the commission by the commission rate:

$$\$4,550 \div 7\% = \$4,550 \div .07 = \$65,000 \text{ sales price}$$

To calculate a commission rate using a commission of $3,200 and a sales price of $64,000, divide the commission by the sales price:

$$\$3,200 \div \$64,000 = .05, \text{ or } 5\% \text{ commission rate}$$

To calculate the net to the seller using a sales price of $85,000 and a commission rate of 8 percent, multiply the sales price by 100 percent minus the commission rate:

$$\$85,000 \times (100\% - 8\%) = \$85,000 \times (1 - .08) = \$85,000 \times .92 = \$78,200$$

The same result could be achieved by calculating the commission ($85,000 × .08 = $6,800) and deducting it from the sales price ($85,000 − $6,800 = $78,200); however, this involves unnecessary extra calculations.

You may use this circle formula to help you with these calculations. In the circle, C is the commission amount, R is the rate, and P is the price of the property. If you know two of the figures, you can determine the third.

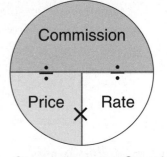

In summary: Sales price × Commission rate = Commission
Commission ÷ Commission rate = Sales price
Commission ÷ Sales price = Commission rate
Sales price × (100% − Commission rate) = Net to seller

The information needed for a listing agreement typically includes

- the names and relationship, if any, of the owners;
- the street address and legal description of the property;
- the size, type, age, and construction of improvements;
- the number of rooms and their sizes;
- the dimensions of the lot;

- existing loans, including such information as the name and address of each lender, the type of loan, the loan number, the loan balance, the interest rate, the monthly payment and what it includes (principal, interest, real estate tax impounds, hazard insurance impounds, mortgage insurance premiums), whether the loan may be assumed by the buyer and under what circumstances, and whether the loan may be prepaid without penalty;
- the possibility of seller financing;
- the amount of any outstanding special assessments and whether they will be paid by the seller or assumed by the buyer;
- the zoning classification of the property;
- the current (or most recent year's) property taxes;
- neighborhood amenities (for instance, schools, parks and recreational areas, churches, and public transportation);
- any real property to be removed from the premises by the seller and any personal property to be included in the sale for the buyer (both the listing contract and the subsequent purchase contract should be explicit on these points);
- any additional information that would make the property more appealing and marketable; and
- any required disclosures concerning agency representation and property conditions.

Disclosures

Disclosure of agency relationships and property conditions has become the focus of consumer safeguards in recent years. Property condition disclosures normally cover a wide range of structural, mechanical, and other conditions that a prospective purchaser should know about to make an informed decision. Agents should caution sellers to make truthful, careful disclosures to avoid litigation arising from fraudulent or careless misrepresentations. It is the agent's responsibility to see that the seller is aware of these mandatory disclosures.

| In Illinois |

Like most other states, *Illinois requires that agents disclose whose interests they legally represent if the other party has no agent.* It is important that the seller be informed of the brokerage company's policies about cooperating with other brokers. Seller disclosure of property conditions is also required by Illinois law. ■

■ THE LISTING AGREEEMENT

A wide variety of listing agreement forms are available. Some brokers have attorneys draft contracts, some use forms prepared by their local REALTOR® association, and some use forms produced by state real estate licensing authorities. Some brokers use a separate information sheet (also known as a *profile* or *data sheet*) for recording property features. That sheet is wed to a second form containing the contractual obligations between the seller and the broker: listing price, duration of the agreement, signatures of the parties, and so forth. Other brokers use a single form. A sample listing agreement appears in Figure 6.1.

| In Illinois |

The listing contracts most commonly in use are prepared by local REALTOR® associations and their attorneys. These forms may vary slightly from area to area. ■

F I G U R E   6.1

Sample Listing Agreement

CHICAGO ASSOCIATION OF REALTORS®
EXCLUSIVE LISTING AGREEMENT
Rev. 01/2008

1. **BROKER.** This Exclusive Listing Agreement (**"Agreement"**) is entered into this by and between _____ (**"Broker"**) and _____ (**"Seller"**). In consideration of the following agreements and Broker's efforts to procure an acquiring party for the property and improvements described below (including the undivided interest in the common elements and accumulated reserves, if any) (collectively, **"Property"**), .Seller hereby grants Broker the exclusive right (**"Exclusive Right"**) to sell the Property (or, at Seller's direction, lease, exchange, joint venture or grant an option to purchase) the Property (**"Transfer of Property"**) pursuant to the terms and conditions set forth below.

2. **TERM.** Broker's Exclusive Right shall extend from the Effective Date, as set forth on page 3 (**"Commencement Date"**) until 11:59 P.M. on _____, 20___, at which time this Agreement shall automatically terminate (**"Termination Date"**). From the date of Seller's acceptance of any offer and execution of a contract for the Transfer of Property (**"Accepted Offer"**), unless the Accepted Offer is expressly subject to the continual marketing of the Property, Broker shall have no further obligation to market, advertise for sale or show the Property. Once all of the contingencies for the Accepted Offer have been satisfied or waived, Broker shall have no further obligation to Seller except to present Seller with any offers or counteroffers pertaining to the Property.

3. **PRICE.** In the event that the Transfer of Property is a sale, Seller authorizes Broker to market the Property at a price of $_____ (**"Purchase Price"**). If the Transfer of Property is a lease, Seller authorizes Broker to market the Property at a price of $_____ per month (**"Rental Price"**). The Purchase Price and Rental Price may be changed from time to time at Seller's direction.

4 **PROPERTY.**
Address:_____ Unit Number(s): _____
City:_____ State:_____ Zip Code:_____
Parking Space Number(s):_____ (**check all that apply**) ☐ Deeded; ☐ Limited Common Element; ☐ Assigned; ☐ Indoor; ☐ Outdoor

5. **POSSESSION.** Seller shall surrender possession of the Property and remove all debris and Seller's personal property not conveyed to Buyer no later than the closing date set forth in the purchase and sale agreement.

6. **DESIGNATED AGENT.** Broker and Seller hereby agree that (a) _____, a sponsored licensee of Broker, is Seller's exclusive designated agent (**"Designated Agent"**) under this Agreement with Broker, and (b) neither Broker nor other sponsored licensees of Broker will be acting as agent for Seller. Seller understands and agrees that Broker and any of Broker's other sponsored licensees may enter into agreements with prospective buyers of the Property as agents of those buyers.

7. **MINIMUM SERVICES.** Pursuant to the Illinois Real Estate License Act of 2000 (265 ILCS 454/1 et seq.), as amended, Broker, through the Designated Agent, must provide to Seller, at a minimum, the following services: (a) accept delivery of and present to Seller offers and counteroffers to buy, sell, lease or otherwise transfer any interest in the Property or any portion thereof; (b) assist Seller in developing, communicating, negotiating and presenting offers, counteroffers and notices that relate to the offers and counteroffers until a lease or purchase agreement is fully executed and all contingencies are satisfied or waived; and (c) answer Seller's questions relating to the offers, counteroffers, notices and contingencies.

8. **SELLER OBLIGATIONS.** From and after the Commencement Date of this Agreement, Seller agrees to:
(i) cooperate fully with Broker and the Designated Agent; (ii) refer all inquiries to Broker and the Designated Agent; (iii) allow inspection of the Property and entry at convenient times by Broker, the Designated Agent and/or cooperating brokers (whether alone or accompanied by Broker or the Designated Agent) for the purpose of showing the Property to prospective buyers; (iv) conduct all negotiations through Broker or the Designated Agent; (v) pay to Broker on demand for Broker's out-of-pocket advertising and marketing costs in the amount of $_____; and (vi) pay Broker a commission or compensation pursuant to the terms of Paragraph 9 below.

9. **COMMISSION.** In the event Broker produces a buyer ready, willing and able to close on the Transfer of Property on the terms provided in this Agreement, then Seller shall pay Broker a commission in the amount of _____ % [percent] of the Purchase Price (**"Sale Commission"**) plus $_____ (**"Additional Fee"**). In the event Seller enters into a leasing agreement with a tenant during the term of this Agreement, Seller agrees to pay Broker a rental commission of _____ (**"Rental Commission"**) plus $_____ (**"Additional Rental Fee"**). In the event the Property is later purchased by the tenant, or an option to purchase is later granted to and exercised by tenant, then in addition to the Rental Commission and Additional Rental Fee, Seller must pay Broker the Sale Commission and Additional Fee. The Sale Commission, Additional Fee, Rental Commission and Additional Rental Fee are referred to collectively as **"Commission"**. Broker shall be entitled to the Commission pursuant to this Agreement (a) upon the closing of any Transfer of Property prior to the Termination Date, regardless of whether the Transfer of Property resulted from the service and/or effort of the Broker, Designated Agent, Seller or any other persons or entities; or (b) upon the closing of any Transfer of Property within 180 days after the Termination Date to any person to whom the Property was submitted prior to the Termination Date. Notwithstanding the foregoing, if (i) the Property is residential property of four units or less, (ii) the Termination Date has passed, and (iii) Seller has entered into a valid, bona fide, written listing agreement with another licensed real estate broker during the 180 day period, then Broker shall not be entitled to any Commission pursuant to this Agreement on any Transfer of Property. For Property which is not residential property of four units or less, if the Property is listed with another licensed real estate broker during the 180 day period following the Termination Date, Seller shall be liable for the entire Commission, which shall be shared by the Broker and the other licensed real estate broker. The actual allocation of the Commission will be determined pursuant to a separate agreement between Broker and the other licensed real estate broker.

10. **DUAL REPRESENTATION.** By checking "yes" and writing its initials below, Seller acknowledges and agrees that the Designated Agent (**"Licensee"**) may undertake a dual representation (represent both seller and buyer or landlord and tenant, as the case may be) in connection with any Transfer of Property. Seller acknowledges and agrees that Seller has read the following prior to executing this Agreement:

Representing more than one party to a transaction presents a conflict of interest since both parties may rely upon the Licensee's advice and the parties' respective interests may be adverse to each other. The Licensee will undertake the representation of more than one party to a transaction only with the written consent of **ALL** parties to the transaction. Any parties who consent to dual representation expressly agree that any agreement between the parties as to any terms of the contract, including the final contract

Seller Initials:_____ Seller Initials:_____

1 of 4

Broker Initials:_____ Broker Initials:_____

F I G U R E   6.1 (CONTINUED)

Sample Listing Agreement

64 price, results from each party negotiating on its own behalf and in its own best interest. Seller acknowledges and agrees that (a)
65 Broker has explained the implications of dual representation, including the risks involved, and (b) Seller has been advised to seek
66 independent counsel from its advisors and/or attorneys prior to executing this Agreement or any documents in connection with this
67 Agreement.

68 **WHAT A LICENSEE <u>CAN</u> DO FOR CLIENTS WHEN UNDERTAKING DUAL REPRESENTATION:**

69 1. Treat all clients honestly. 2. Provide information about the property to the buyer or tenant. 3. Disclose all latent material defects in
70 the property that are known to the Licensee. 4. Disclose the financial qualification of the buyer or tenant to the seller or landlord. 5.
71 Explain real estate terms. 6. Help the buyer or tenant arrange for property inspections. 7. Explain closing costs and procedures. 8.
72 Help the buyer compare financing alternatives. 9. Provide information to seller or buyer about comparable properties that have sold
73 so both clients may make educated decisions on what price to accept or offer.

74 **WHAT A LICENSEE <u>CANNOT</u> DO FOR CLIENTS WHEN UNDERTAKING DUAL REPRESENTATION:**

75 1. Disclose confidential information that the Licensee may know about either client without that client's express consent. 2. Disclose
76 the price the seller or landlord will take other than the listing price without the express consent of the seller or landlord. 3. Disclose
77 the price the buyer or tenant is willing to pay without the express consent of the buyer or tenant. 4. Recommend or suggest a price the
78 buyer or tenant should offer. 5. Recommend or suggest a price the seller or landlord should counter with or accept.

79 Seller acknowledges having read these provisions regarding the issue of dual representation. Seller is not required to accept this Paragraph
80 10 unless Seller wants to allow the Licensee to proceed as a dual agent ("***Dual Agent***") in this transaction. By checking "yes", initialing
81 below, and signing this Agreement, Seller acknowledges that it has read and understands this Paragraph 9 and voluntarily consents to the
82 Licensee acting as a Dual Agent (that is, to represent **BOTH** the seller and buyer or landlord and tenant, as the case may be) should it
83 become necessary. (***check one***) _____ Yes _____ No _____ *(Seller initials)* _____ *(Seller initials)*.
84

85 **11. ADDITIONAL TERMS AND PROPERTY INFORMATION.** Seller represents that the following information is true and correct as of
86 the date of this Agreement:

87 (a) Property P.I.N. #_____.   Homeowner's Exemption: _____ Yes /_____No
88   Real estate taxes for the year 20___ equal $_____.   Senior Citizen's Exemption: _____ Yes /_____No
89   Senior Freeze Exemption: _____Yes/_____No

90 (b) Current monthly assessment equals $_____ and includes _____.

91 (c) Percentage of interest in common elements is _____%.   Waiver of Right of First Refusal necessary _____Yes / ___No

92 (d) Seller (***check one***) ____ is _____ is not aware of a proposed special assessment. Seller shall keep listing Broker informed of all Board of
93   Directors/Managers actions. Seller shall keep Broker informed of all changes to the above.

94 (e) If applicable, the amount of special assessment is $_____ with a remaining balance due of $_____ payable through
95   _____. Special assessments are payable (*check all that apply*) ☐ Annually; ☐ Semi-Annually; ☐ Quarterly; ☐ Monthly; ☐ Other.

96 (f) The lot size is approximately _____. Approximate square feet of Property:_____.

97 (g) Heating cost is approximately: $_____/Month $_____/Year.

98 (h) Additional Information: If this property is new construction, the following information is required:

99   R Factor   Thickness   Type
100   Exterior Walls   _____   _____   _____
101   Interior Walls   _____   _____   _____
102   Ceiling   _____   _____   _____

103 (i) If the Property is income or commercial property, Seller shall provide Broker with accurate copies of all leases, income and expense
104 statements, a rent roll, existing environmental reports and relevant information necessary to market the property within 14 days after the
105 date of this Agreement.

106 (j) For residential properties located within the City of Chicago, local ordinances require that all properties must have smoke and carbon
107 monoxide detectors present and in working condition. Seller shall comply with these ordinances. In addition, Seller shall provide Broker
108 with the following, if applicable, at least 72 hours immediately prior to the closing date set forth in the Accepted Offer: (a) Residential Real
109 Property Disclosure Report; (b) Heat Disclosure; (c) Lead Paint Disclosure; (d) Radon Disclosure; and (e) Zoning Certificate.
110

111 **12. FIXTURES AND PERSONAL PROPERTY.** In conjunction with any Accepted Offer, Seller agrees to transfer by a bill of sale, all
112 heating, electrical, and plumbing systems that serve the Property together with the following to the buyer (*check or enumerate applicable*
113 *items*):

114 ☐ Refrigerator___   ☐ Sump Pump___   ☐ Central air conditioner__   ☐ Fireplace screen   ☐ Built-in or attached
115 ☐ Oven/Range___   ☐ Smoke and carbon monoxide   ☐ Window air conditioner__   and equipment___   shelves or cabinets__
116 ☐ Microwave___   detectors__   ☐ Electronic air filter___   ☐ Fireplace gas log_ ☐ Ceiling fan___
117 ☐ Dishwasher___   ☐ Intercom system___   ☐ Central humidifier___   ☐ Firewood___   ☐ Radiator covers___
118 ☐ Garbage disposal_ ☐ Security system___ *(rented or owned)* *(strike one)*   ☐ Attached gas grill_ ☐ All planted vegetation_
119 ☐ Trash compactor___ ☐ Satellite Dish___   ☐ Lighting fixtures___   ☐ Existing storms   ☐ Outdoor play set/swings
120 ☐ Washer___   ☐ T.V. antenna___   ☐ Electronic garage door(s)   and screens___   ☐ Outdoor shed
121 ☐ Dryer___   ☐ LCD/plasma/multimedia equipment_ with ___ remote unit(s)__ ☐ Window treatments___
122 ☐ Water Softener_   ☐ Stereo speakers/surround sound__ ☐ Wall-to-wall carpeting__ ☐ Home warranty *(as attached)*___

123 Seller also transfers the following:_____.

124 The following items are excluded:_____.

Seller Initials:_____   Seller Initials:_____   Broker Initials:_____ Broker Initials:_____
2 of 4

F I G U R E   6.1 (CONTINUED)

Sample Listing Agreement

125   THIS AGREEMENT INCLUDES THE GENERAL PROVISIONS ON THE FOLLOWING PAGE.

126

127   **SELLER'S INFORMATION:**

128   Seller's Signature:_____

129   Seller's Signature:_____

130   Date:_____

131

132   Seller's Name (print):_____

133   Address:_____

134   City:_____ State:_____ Zip:_____

135   Office Phone:_____

136   Home Phone:_____

137   Cell Phone:_____

138   Fax:_____

139   Email Address:_____

140

141   Seller's Name (print):_____

142   Address:_____

143   City:_____ State:_____ Zip:_____

144   Office Phone:_____

145   Home Phone:_____

146   Cell Phone:_____

147   Fax:_____

148   Email Address:_____

149
150
151
152
153
154
155
156
157
158
159
160
161
162
163
164
165
166
167
168
169

170

171   **BROKER'S INFORMATION:**

172   Managing Broker's Signature:_____

173   Date:_____ (*"Effective Date"*)

174

175

176

177   Broker Company Name (print):_____

178   Office Address:_____

179   City:_____ State:_____ Zip:_____

180   Office Phone:_____

181   Home Phone:_____

182   Cell Phone:_____

183   Fax:_____

184   Email Address:_____

185

186   Designated Agent Name (print):_____

187   Designated Agent Identification Number:_____

188   Office Address:_____

189   City:_____ State:_____ Zip:_____

190   Office Phone:_____

191   Home Phone:_____

192   Cell Phone:_____

193   Fax:_____

194   Email Address:_____

Seller Initials:_____   Seller Initials:_____   Broker Initials:_____   Broker Initials:_____

F I G U R E 6.1 (CONTINUED)

Sample Listing Agreement

195 GENERAL PROVISIONS:

196 A. **Fair Housing Act.** IT IS ILLEGAL FOR EITHER THE SELLER OR THE BROKER TO REFUSE TO DISPLAY, LIST, LEASE OR SELL, OR REFUSE
197 TO NEGOTIATE FOR THE LEASE OR SALE OF, OR OTHERWISE MAKE UNAVAILABLE OR DENY. REAL ESTATE TO ANY PERSON BECAUSE OF
198 ONE'S MEMBERSHIP IN A PROTECTED CLASS, E.G.: RACE, COLOR, RELIGION, NATIONAL ORIGIN, SEX, ANCESTRY, AGE, MARITAL STATUS,
199 PHYSICAL OR MENTAL HANDICAP, FAMILIAL STATUS, OR ANY OTHER CLASS PROTECTED BY ARTICLE 3 OF THE ILLINOIS HUMAN RIGHTS
200 ACT. SELLER AND BROKER ACKNOWLEDGE THAT THEY SHALL ALSO BE BOUND BY THE PROVISIONS OF STATE AND LOCAL (CITY AND/OR
201 COUNTY) HUMAN RIGHTS OR FAIR HOUSING ORDINANCES IF ANY AND AGREE TO COMPLY WITH SAME.

202 B. **Obligations of Seller.** Seller shall comply with the Real Estate Settlement Procedures Act of 1974, as amended, if applicable, and furnish all information
203 required for compliance with the Act, and, if applicable, Seller agrees to comply with the Residential Real Property Disclosure Act, as amended.

204 C. **Illinois Condominium Property Act.** If the property is a condominium, then no later than 15 days from the date of this Agreement, Seller shall furnish to
205 Broker a complete set of condominium documents, including the declaration, bylaws, and if available, a survey. If the Property is a cooperative, then, no later than 15
206 days from the date hereof Seller shall furnish to broker a complete set of cooperative documents, including the proprietary lease or trust agreement, bylaws, and if
207 available, a survey. If the Property is a townhouse or condominium and dependent upon the condominium association's governing documents, either upon execution of
208 this Agreement or upon Seller's acceptance of an offer by buyer, Seller shall promptly notify the appropriate representative of the condominium association or any
209 affiliated organization of the contemplated transaction. Seller shall furnish to the buyer a statement from an authorized officer or agent of the condominium association
210 certifying payment of assessments for condominium common expenses, and if applicable, proof of waiver or termination of any right of refusal or general option
211 contained in the declaration of condominium together with any other documents required by the declaration of condominium or its bylaws as a precondition to the
212 transfer of ownership. At closing, Seller shall deliver to the buyer all appropriate documents properly endorsed and a survey or plat of the condominium unit showing the
213 location of all improvements of the unit and further showing any parking spaces or garages that will be conveyed. Seller shall comply with all of the conditions and
214 stipulations of the Illinois Condominium Property Act (765 ILCS 605/1 et seq.), as amended, as may be applicable.

215 D. **Title.** **At least 5 days prior to closing,** Seller shall furnish an owner's title insurance policy in the amount of the purchase price showing good and merchantable
216 title, and execute and deliver, or cause to be executed and delivered to the buyer a proper instrument of conveyance.

217 E. **Survey.** If the Property is not a condominium or a cooperative, then prior to closing, Seller shall furnish to the buyer at least 5 days prior to closing a survey by a
218 licensed land surveyor dated not more than 6 months prior to date of closing (as defined in the Seller's Real Estate Sale Contract) showing the present location of all
219 improvements on the Property. If the buyer or buyer's mortgagee desires a more recent or extensive survey, then the survey shall be obtained at buyer's expense.

220 F. **Lock Box.** Seller hereby authorizes Broker and its agent to place an electronic or combination lock box on the Property in accordance with the terms and
221 conditions of this Agreement for the purpose of keeping a key to the Property for access by cooperating real estate agents. Seller shall hold Broker, its agents, and any
222 Multiple Listing Service of which Broker is a participant harmless from any and all liability, claims, judgments, obligations, or demands against Broker and/or agent as
223 a result of Seller's authorization to use a "Lock Box," including, but not limited to, any and all liabilities and costs, including reasonable attorneys' fees incurred by
224 Broker and/or agents as a result of this authorization, except for any criminal or gross negligence on the part of the Broker and/or agents.

225 G. **Seller's Personal Property.** Seller has been advised by Broker of the importance of safeguarding or removing valuables now located within the Property and the
226 need to obtain personal property insurance through Seller's insurance company. If the Property is leased, Seller acknowledges that Seller has in fact notified and
227 advised the tenant/occupant of the foregoing and that the tenant/occupant agrees to the terms and provisions of these Paragraphs F and G of the General Provisions.

228 H. **Indemnity.** Seller hereby indemnifies and holds Broker and Broker's agents harmless, from any and all claims, disputes, litigation, judgments, costs and legal
229 fees from the defense of Broker and Broker's agents, including reasonable attorneys' fees and costs, arising from any misrepresentation by the Seller or other incorrect
230 information supplied by the Seller to Broker or any third party.

231 I. **Authority.** Seller warrants that Seller has the authority to execute this Agreement and to deal with and on behalf of the Property as provided in this Agreement.

232 J. **Broker's Duty.** Broker's sole duty is to use Broker's best efforts to effect a Transfer of Property, and Broker is not charged with the custody of the Property, its
233 management, maintenance, upkeep or repair.

234 K. **Disbursement of Earnest Money.** If a dispute arises between Seller and the buyer as to whether a default had occurred, Broker shall hold the earnest money
235 and pay it out as agreed in writing by Seller and the buyer or as directed by a court of competent jurisdiction. In the event of a dispute Seller agrees that Broker may
236 deposit the funds with the Clerk of the Circuit Court by the filing of an action in the nature of an Interpleader. Seller agrees that Broker may be reimbursed from the
237 earnest money for all costs, including reasonable attorneys' fees and court costs related to the filing of the Interpleader and hereby agrees to indemnify and hold Broker
238 harmless from any and all claims and demands, including the payment of reasonable attorneys' fees, costs and expenses arising out of the default, claims and demands.
239 If Seller defaults, earnest money, at the option of the buyer, and upon written direction by Seller and the buyer or as directed by a Court of competent jurisdiction, shall
240 be refunded to the buyer and Seller shall not be released from any of its obligations under this Agreement. Notwithstanding anything in this Agreement to the contrary,
241 disbursement of earnest money shall be in accordance with the Real Estate License Act, as amended.

242 L. **Commission.** No amendment or alteration with respect to the amount of commission or time of payment of commission shall be valid or binding unless made in
243 writing and signed by the parties hereto. Broker's commission is to be paid at time of execution and delivery of deed, option, lease, joint venture agreement, or
244 installment agreement for deed, whichever occurs first, and Broker is authorized to deduct the commission and expenses from the earnest money deposit at time.
245 BROKER IS AUTHORIZED TO ACCEPT AN EARNEST MONEY DEPOSIT FROM THE BUYER. IF THE BUYER DEFAULTS AND SELLER DECLARES A
246 FORFEITURE OF THE EARNEST MONEY, THE EARNEST MONEY SHALL BE APPLIED FIRST TO PAYMENT OF BROKER'S COMMISSION AND ANY
247 EXPENSES INCURRED, AND THE BALANCE SHALL BE PAID TO SELLER, EXCEPT AS OTHERWISE STATED BELOW IN PARAGRAPH "O" OF THE
248 GENERAL PROVISIONS OF THIS AGREEMENT.

249 M. **Representation of Multiple Sellers.** Seller understands and agrees that Broker may from time to time represent or assist other sellers who may be interested
250 in selling property to the buyers with whom Broker has a buyer agency contract or with whom Broker is working as a customer. The Seller consents to Broker's
251 representation of other sellers before, during and after the expiration of this Agreement and expressly waives any claims, including, but not limited to, breach of
252 fiduciary duty or breach of contract, based solely upon Broker's representation or assistance of other sellers who may be interested in selling property to the buyers with
253 whom Broker has a buyer agency contract or with whom Broker is working as a customer.

254 N. **Promoting and Advertising Property.** Broker is hereby authorized to promote and advertise the Property as Broker deems appropriate, including but not
255 limited to (i) displaying signs on the Property, (ii) placing the Property in any multiple listing service in which Broker participates, (iii) promoting the Property on any
256 internet homepage and/or any other advertising medium to which Broker may subscribe, and (iv) releasing information as to the amount of the selling price, type of
257 financing, and number of days to sell this Property to any multiple listing service in which Broker participates at the time a contract is executed. Broker is authorized to
258 share Broker's compensation or commission with all cooperating brokers regardless of any cooperating broker's agency relationship to Seller, Broker or the buyer.

259 O. **Cancellation of Agreement.** In the event this Agreement is cancelled by Seller pursuant to the terms of this Agreement, unless mutually agreed to in writing by
260 Broker and Seller, Seller shall pay to Broker, upon written demand by Broker within 4 business days of the written demand, reimbursement of Broker's out-of-pocket
261 expenses, including but not limited to: marketing, advertising, office expenses, Multiple Listing Service (MLS) fees, printing, attorneys' fees and court costs. The amount
262 of Broker's out-of-pocket expenses shall be determined solely by Broker. In cases of the Seller's breach of this Agreement, Seller shall pay to Broker the commission or
263 compensation previously described within this Agreement payable on the Transfer of Property to compensate Broker for Broker's time, expenses and services involved in
264 marketing the Property.

265 P. **Dispute Resolution.** The parties agree that any dispute, controversy or claim arising out of or relating to this Agreement, or any breach of this Agreement by
266 either party, shall be resolved by arbitration in accordance with the Code of Ethics and Arbitration Manual of the National Association of REALTORS, as amended from
267 time to time, through the facility of the Chicago Association of REALTORS. The parties agree to be bound by any award rendered by any professional standards
268 arbitration hearing panel of the Chicago Association of REALTORS and further agree that judgment upon any award rendered by a professional standards arbitration
269 hearing panel of the Chicago Association of REALTORS may be entered in any court having jurisdiction. The parties agree to execute any arbitration agreements,
270 consents and documents as may be required by the Chicago Association of REALTORS to facilitate any arbitration.

271 Q. **Miscellaneous.**

272 (1) Where applicable, the singular form shall include the plural, and the masculine form shall include the feminine and neuter, and vice versa.

273 (2) This Agreement shall be binding upon and inure to the benefit of the heirs, executors, administrators, successors, and assigns of the parties to this Agreement.

274 (3) Any reference in this Agreement to "day" or "days" shall mean business days, not calendar days, including Monday, Tuesday, Wednesday, Thursday, and Friday,
275 and excluding all official federal and state holidays.

Seller Initials:_____   Seller Initials:_____   Broker Initials:_____   Broker Initials:_____

In Illinois	Illinois law requires that the following disclosures be included with listing contracts.

Disclosure of material facts.   A licensee must not withhold material facts concerning a property of which he or she has knowledge from any purchaser, prospective purchaser, seller, lessee, lessor, or other party to the transaction. *Material facts* are any facts on which a reasonable person would base a contractual decision.

Disclosure of interest.   A licensee must disclose in writing to the parties to the transaction his or her status as a licensee and any direct or indirect interest he or she has or may have in the subject property. For example, if the buyer or seller is a licensed salesperson or broker, this must be clearly stated in the contract.

Disclosure of special compensation.   A licensee is prohibited from accepting "any finder fees, commissions, discounts, kickbacks, or other compensation from any financial institution, title insurance company, or any other person other than another licensee, without full disclosure in writing of such receipt to all parties to the transaction." Sales agents receive any such compensation only through their respective brokers.

Earnest money and purchaser default.   When any written listing includes a provision that the seller will not receive the earnest money deposit if the purchaser defaults, this fact must appear emphasized in letters larger than those otherwise used in the listing agreement.

Disclosure of property condition.   Seller disclosure of property conditions is required by law in Illinois. These disclosures normally cover a wide range of structural, mechanical, and other conditions that a prospective purchaser should know about to make an informed decision. Agents should caution sellers to make truthful disclosures to avoid litigation arising from fraudulent or careless misrepresentations. A Property Disclosure Report must be given to the buyer before an offer is made and accepted, or the buyer will have three days in which to rescind the contract, based on any negative disclosures. In Illinois, many listing agents choose with their sellers to leave the disclosure statement on display and available in the home itself for all showings.

Once a listing agreement has been finalized and signed by the broker and seller, Illinois law prohibits the licensee from making any addition to, deletion from, or alteration of the written listing without the written consent of the principal. The licensee must return a true copy of the listing agreement, signed by the seller and by the sponsoring broker, to the principal within 24 hours of execution. ■

Listing Agreement Issues

Regardless of which standard form of listing agreement is used, the same considerations arise in most real estate transactions. This means that all listing contracts tend to require similar information. However, licensees should review the specific forms used in their areas and refer to their states' laws for any specific requirements. Some of the considerations covered in a typical contract are discussed in the following paragraphs.

In Illinois There is no required state form for any real estate contract in Illinois. However, all written exclusive listing agreements must include

- the list price of the property,
- the agreed-upon amount of commission and the time of payment,
- the time duration of the agreement,
- the names of the broker and seller,
- the address or legal description of the property,
- minimum services,
- a statement of nondiscrimination, and
- a statement regarding antitrust.

Licensees may not obtain written listings that contain blank spaces to be filled in later. ■

Type of listing agreement.   The contract may be an exclusive-right-to-sell listing (the most common type), an exclusive-agency listing, an open listing, or a net listing (the last not recommended). The type of listing agreement determines the extent of a broker's authority to act on the principal's behalf. Most MLSs do not permit open listings to be posted in their systems.

Broker's authority and responsibilities.   The contract should specify whether the broker may place a sign on the property and advertise and market the property. Another major consideration is whether the broker is permitted to authorize buyers' brokers through an MLS and the Internet. Will the contract allow the broker to show the property at reasonable times and on reasonable notice to the seller? May the broker accept earnest money deposits on behalf of the seller, and what are the broker's responsibilities in holding the funds? Without the written consent of the seller, the broker cannot undertake any of these or other important activities.

Names of all parties to the contract.   Anyone who has an ownership interest in the property must be identified and must sign the listing to validate it.

In Illinois If a married couple is living in the listed property, both spouses must sign the listing, even if only one owns the property, in order to release homestead rights. If the property is in the possession of a tenant, that should be disclosed and instructions given on how the property is to be shown to a prospective buyer. ■

Brokerage firm.   The brokerage company name, the employing broker, and the *designated agent* of the sponsoring broker are all identified.

Listing price.   This is the proposed gross sales price. The seller's proceeds will be reduced by unpaid real estate taxes, special assessments, mortgage or trust deed debts, and any other outstanding obligations.

Real property and personal property.   Any personal property that will be left with the real estate when it is sold must be explicitly identified. Similarly, any items of real property that the seller expects to remove at the time of the sale must be specified as well. Some of these items may later become points of negotiation when a ready, willing, and able buyer is found for the property. Typical items to consider include major appliances, swimming pool and spa equipment, fireplace accessories, storage sheds, window treatments, stacked firewood, and stored heating oil.

Leased equipment. Will any leased equipment—security systems, cable television boxes, water softeners, special antennas—be left with the property? If so, the seller is responsible for notifying the equipment's lessor of the change of property ownership.

Description of the premises. In addition to the street address, the legal description, lot size, and tax parcel number (property index number or PIN) may be required for future insertion into a purchase offer.

In Illinois

The street address of the property is sufficient for listing agreements to be valid and enforceable under Illinois law. However, it is advisable to include the parcel number (or property index number, or PIN), and most listing agreements include a blank for it. This number can be acquired from the tax database. ∎

Proposed dates for the closing and the buyer's possession. These dates should be based on an anticipated sale date. The listing agreement should allow adequate time for the paperwork involved once a contract comes in (including the buyer's qualification for any financing) and the physical moves to be arranged by the seller and the buyer. Frequently, TBA (*to be arranged* or *to be agreed*) is indicated because so many unpredictable variables are not known at the time of listing.

Closing issues. Details of the closing—such as a closing attorney, title company, or escrow company—may be considered even at this early stage. Who will complete the settlement statements and disburse the funds? Who will file the proper forms, such as documents to be recorded, documents to be sent to the Internal Revenue Service, and documents to be submitted for registering foreign owners? By pointing out a few of these issues at listing presentation, the seller will become aware of the need for a competent real estate attorney for guidance on closing matters.

In some states brokers are more actively involved in this area. In Illinois, the attorney, title company, and lender dominate closing issues.

Evidence of ownership. The most commonly used proofs of title are either a title insurance policy or an abstract of title and lawyer's opinion.

Encumbrances. Which liens will be paid in full at the closing by the seller and which liens will be assumed by the buyer? It is unrealistic to expect most buyers to absorb any liens on the property unless it is a multiple offer situation. Advice on issues such as encumbrances falls under the attorney's responsibilities. You might wish to ask a seller if there are any major outstanding liens apart from the mortgage, and in such a case advise the seller to seek legal counsel.

As for physical encroachments on the property (such as a fence) and their legal implications, these, too, are questions best referred to an attorney, although they should be noted for the listing file and for use in properly preparing listing display sheets.

Home warranty program.   In some situations, it may be advisable to offer a "home warranty" with the property. If so, the listing contract should answer these questions: What items does the warranty cover? Is the seller willing to pay for it? If not, will it be available to the buyer at the buyer's expense? What are the deductibles?

Sellers are not often aware of various home warranty packages available. Skillful agents are able to explain these warranties, as they often can benefit both the seller and the buyer. Most real estate offices have information about the different home warranty programs available to homeowners for use in licensees' presentations. (*Agents must disclose in writing any monies sent to them by a home warranty company.*)

Commission.   The circumstances under which a commission will be paid must be stated specifically: Is payment earned only on the sale of the property or on *any* transfer of interest created by the broker? Will it be a percentage or a flat fee? When will it be paid? Negotiation of commission is a key element of discussions leading up to a listing contract, and the commission amount is fully negotiable between parties.

Antitrust wording.   Remember that any assertion that a "set" or "standard" commission exists violates antitrust laws. Any sponsoring broker is free to set a *minimum* commission that will be accepted within a given office, but there is *no such thing as a standard commission.* The contract should indicate that all commissions have been negotiated between the seller and the broker. It is illegal for commissions to be set by any regulatory agency, trade association, or other industry organization.

| In Illinois |

By law, written listing agreements in Illinois must state that no change in the amount of the commission or time of payment will be valid or binding unless the change is made in writing and signed by the parties. ■

Termination of the contract.   A contract should provide some way for the parties to end it. Under what circumstances will the contract terminate? Can the seller arbitrarily refuse to sell or cooperate with the listing broker?

Broker protection ("carryover") clause.   As previously discussed, brokers may be well advised to protect their interests against possible fraud or a reluctant buyer's change of heart. Under what circumstances will the broker be entitled to a commission after the agreement terminates? How long will the clause remain in effect? These issues are set at listing time.

Warranties by the owner.   The owner is responsible for certain assurances and disclosures that are vital to the agent's ability to market the property successfully. Is the property suitable for its intended purpose? Does it comply with the appropriate zoning and building codes? Will it be transferred to the buyer in essentially the same condition as it was originally presented, considering repairs or alterations to be made as provided for in a purchase contract? Are there any known defects?

Indemnification ("hold harmless") wording.   The seller and the broker may agree to hold each other harmless for any incorrect information supplied by one to the other. Indemnification may be offered regardless of whether the inaccuracies are intentional or unintentional.

| In Illinois | A client shall not be vicariously liable for the acts or omissions of a salesperson or broker in providing brokerage services for or on behalf of the client. ■ |

Nondiscrimination (equal opportunity) wording.   The seller must understand that the property will be shown and offered without regard to the race, color, creed, or religious preference, national origin, family status, sex, age, or disability of the prospective buyer. Federal, state, and local fair housing laws protect a variety of different groups and individuals. For instance, on the state and local level, sexual orientation and source of finances are also often protected.

| In Illinois | All Illinois written listing agreements must clearly state that it is illegal for either the owner or the broker to refuse to sell or show property to any person because of race, color, religion, national origin, sex, familial status, ancestry, citizenship status, age 40 and over, marital status, physical or mental handicap, military service, unfavorable military discharge, or sexual orientation and/or preference. |

The Illinois Human Rights Act and information pertaining to it are available on the Internet. ■

Minimum Services

| In Illinois | The sponsoring broker, through its sponsored licensees, must provide the following three required **minimum services**: |

1. Accept delivery of and present to the client all offers and counteroffers to buy, sell, or lease the client's property or the property the client seeks to purchase or lease
2. Assist the client in developing, communicating, negotiating, and presenting offers, counteroffers, and notices that relate to the offers and counteroffers until a lease or purchase agreement is signed and all contingencies are satisfied or waived
3. Answer the client's questions relating to the offers, counteroffers, notices, and contingencies ■

The signatures of the parties.   All parties identified in the listing contract must sign it, including all individuals who have a legal interest in the property.

The date the contract is signed.   This date may differ from the date the contract actually becomes effective, particularly if an agent takes the listing and then must have his or her broker sign the contract to accept employment under its terms.

IN PRACTICE

Anyone who takes a listing should use only the appropriate documents provided by the broker. Most brokers are conscientious enough to use only documents that have been carefully drafted or reviewed by an attorney so that their construction and legal language comply with the appropriate federal, state, and local laws. Such contracts also should give consideration to local customs, such as closing dates and the proration of income and expenses, with which most brokers and local real estate attorneys are very familiar.

■ BUYER AGENCY AGREEMENTS

Like a listing agreement, a **buyer agency agreement** is an employment contract. In this case, however, the broker is employed as the buyer's agent. The buyer, rather than the seller, is the principal. The purpose of the agreement is to find a suitable property. A buyer agency agreement gives the buyer a degree of representation possible only in a fiduciary relationship. A buyer's broker must protect the buyer's interests at all points in the transaction.

Types of Buyer Agency Agreements

Three basic types of buyer agency agreements exist:

1. **Exclusive buyer agency agreement**—Also known as an *exclusive right to represent*, this is a true exclusive agency agreement. The buyer is legally bound to compensate the agent whenever the buyer purchases a property of the type described in the contract. The broker is entitled to payment regardless of whether he or she locates the property. Even if the buyer finds the property independently, the broker is entitled to payment. A sample exclusive buyer agency contract appears in Figure 6.2.
2. **Exclusive-agency buyer agency agreement**—Like an exclusive buyer agency agreement, this is an exclusive contract between the buyer and the broker. However, this agreement limits the broker's right to payment. The broker is entitled to payment only if he or she locates the property the buyer ultimately purchases. The buyer is free to find a suitable property without obligation to pay the broker.
3. **Open buyer agency agreement**—This agreement is a nonexclusive contract between a broker and a buyer. It permits the buyer to enter into similar agreements with an unlimited number of brokers. The buyer is obligated to compensate only the broker who locates the property the buyer ultimately purchases.

Buyer Representation Issues

A number of issues must be discussed by a broker and a buyer before they sign a buyer agency agreement. For instance, the licensee should make the same disclosures to the buyer that the licensee would make in a listing agreement. The licensee should explain the forms of agency available and the parties' rights and responsibilities under each type. The specific services provided to a buyer-client should be clearly explained. Compensation issues need to be addressed as well. Buyers' agents may be compensated in the form of a flat fee for services, an hourly rate, or a percentage of the purchase price. The agent may require a retainer fee at the time the agreement is signed to cover initial expenses. The retainer can usually be applied as a credit toward any fees due at the closing.

As in any agency agreement, the source of compensation is not the factor that determines the relationship. A buyer's broker may be compensated by either the buyer or the seller. Issues of compensation are always negotiable.

Because the agency contract employs the agent to represent the buyer and locate a suitable property, the licensee must obtain detailed specifications from the buyer as to what he or she can afford. Often this is in concert with a loan officer's prequalifying the buyer. In addition, the buyer's agent needs information about the buyer's specific parameters for a suitable property.

F I G U R E   6.2

Exclusive Buyer Representation Agreement

CHICAGO ASSOCIATION OF REALTORS®
EXCLUSIVE BUYER - BROKER AGREEMENT
Rev. 01/2008

1   **1.   BROKER.** This Exclusive Buyer-Broker Agreement ("***Agreement***") is entered into by and between _____
2   _____ ("***Broker***") and _____ ("***Buyer***").
3   Broker agrees to appoint a sales associate affiliated with Broker to act as the Buyer's designated agent ("***Buyer's Designated Agent***") for the
4   purpose of assisting Buyer in identifying and negotiating the acquisition of residential real estate ("***Property***") and Buyer agrees to grant
5   Buyer's Designated Agent the exclusive right ("***Exclusive Right***") to represent Buyer in such acquisition per the terms and conditions set forth
6   in this Agreement. The terms "acquire" or "acquisition" shall mean the purchase (title transfer or Articles of Agreement for deed), lease,
7   exchange, or contract for the option to purchase Property by Buyer or anyone acting on Buyer's behalf.

8   **2.   TERM.** Broker's Exclusive Right shall extend from the Effective Date, as set forth on page 3 ("***Commencement Date***"), until 11:59
9   P.M. on _____, 20___, at which time this Agreement shall automatically terminate ("***Termination Date***").

10 **3.   COMPENSATION.** Broker shall seek to be paid a commission from the listing broker under a cooperative brokerage arrangement
11 or from the seller if there is no listing broker. In the event that the seller or listing broker does not pay Broker a commission, then Buyer
12 shall pay Broker at the time of closing compensation equal to _____% [percent] of the purchase price of the Property which Buyer acquires
13 during the Term of this Agreement ("***Acquisition Commission***"), whether or not the Property has been identified by Broker to Buyer. If
14 Buyer leases Property or enters into a lease/purchase contract during this Agreement, and the landlord does not agree to pay Broker a leasing
15 commission, then Buyer shall pay to Broker for the duration of the lease, including all renewals and extensions, a commission of 5% of each
16 rental payment paid by Buyer to landlord ("***Rental Commission***"). The Rental Commission and the Acquisition Commission are together
17 referred to as "***Compensation***". Furthermore, if Buyer acquires (or enters into an agreement to acquire) Property that was identified to
18 Buyer by Broker during the Term of this Agreement within _____ **days / months** *(strike one)* following the Termination Date
19 ("***Compensation Deadline***"), then Buyer shall pay Broker at closing or upon the commencement of any lease, as the case may be, the
20 Compensation set forth above. If Buyer enters into an agreement to acquire Property and the closing does not occur because of any fault on the
21 part of Buyer, then Broker shall still be entitled to the Compensation set forth above. In no event shall Broker be obligated to advance funds to
22 Buyer to facilitate the closing of any acquisition. *(strike the following sentence if NOT applicable)* Buyer shall pay Broker's Designated
23 Agent a non-refundable retainer fee of $_____ which shall be due and payable to, and shall be considered earned by, Broker upon
24 signing this Agreement. Buyer's obligations under this Paragraph 3 shall survive the termination of this Agreement.

25 **4.   MINIMUM SERVICES.** Pursuant to the Real Estate License Act of 2000, as amended, Broker must provide, at a minimum, the
26 following services: (a) accept delivery of and present to the Buyer offers and counteroffers to sell or lease any Property that Buyer seeks to
27 acquire; (b) assist the Buyer in developing, communicating, negotiating and presenting offers, counteroffers and notices that relate to the
28 offers and counteroffers until a lease or agreement for the acquisition of the Property is signed and all contingencies have been satisfied or
29 waived; and (c) answer the Buyer's questions relating to the offers, counteroffers, notices and contingencies.

30 **5.   BUYER'S DESIGNATED AGENT.** Broker and Buyer agree that (a) _____, a
31 sponsored licensee of Broker, is Broker's Designated Agent under this Agreement with Broker, and (b) neither Broker nor other sponsored
32 licensees of Broker will be acting as agent for Buyer. Buyer understands and agrees that Broker and any of Broker's other sponsored
33 licensees may enter into agreements with other prospective purchasers and sellers of Property as agents of those purchasers and sellers.

34 **6.   BUYER'S DESIGNATED AGENT'S DUTIES.** Buyer's Designated Agent shall: (a) use best efforts to identify Properties
35 available for acquisition that meet the Buyer's specifications relating to location, purchase price, features and amenities; (b) arrange, to the
36 extent available, inspections of Properties identified by Buyer as potentially appropriate for acquisition; (c) negotiate a contract acceptable to
37 Buyer for the acquisition of Property; (d) safeguard and protect any confidential or proprietary information that Buyer discloses to Buyer's
38 Designated Agent; (e) disclose to Buyer any information known to Buyer's Designated Agent that would materially affect Buyer's decision to
39 acquire the Property; and (f) assist Buyer, once a contract for acquisition is signed, in securing financing or other commitments or services as
40 may be necessary to close the transaction.

41 **7.   LIMITATIONS ON BUYER'S DESIGNATED AGENT'S DUTIES.** Buyer acknowledges and agrees that Broker's Designated
42 Agent: (a) may enter into exclusive brokerage relationships with other buyers of Property and may show the same or similar Properties in
43 which Buyer is interested to other prospective buyers that Buyer's Designated Agent represents; (b) is not an expert with regard to matters
44 which could have been revealed through a survey, title search or inspection of the Property; the condition of Property or items within the
45 Property; building products and construction techniques; the necessity or cost of any repairs to the Property; hazardous or toxic materials;
46 termites and other wood destroying organisms; the tax and legal consequences of any acquisition; the availability and cost of utilities and
47 community amenities; appraised or future value of the Property (or matters relating to financing for which Buyer is hereby advised to seek
48 independent expert advice); and conditions off the Property which may affect the Property; (c) is not responsible for the accuracy of room
49 dimensions, lot size, square feet, variances, zoning or use restrictions which may or may not be reflected in the Multiple Listing Service
50 ("***MLS***") or other sources; (d) shall owe no duties to Buyer nor have any authority on behalf of buyer other than what is set forth in the
51 Agreement; (e) may make disclosures as required by law; (f) may show Buyer Property which is listed in the MLS by Broker or Broker's
52 Designated Agent; and (g) IS NOT OBLIGATED TO SHOW PROPERTIES THAT ARE FOR SALE BUT NOT IN THE MLS IN WHICH
53 BROKER OR BUYER'S DESIGNATED AGENT PARTICIPATE, UNLESS REQUESTED TO DO SO BY BUYER IN WRITING, AND THE
54 PROPERTY IS AVAILABLE FOR SHOWING BY BUYER'S DESIGNATED AGENT.

55 **8.   BUYER'S DUTIES.** Buyer must (a) work EXCLUSIVELY with Buyer's Designated Agent to identify and acquire Property during
56 the Term of this Agreement; (b) comply with reasonable requests of Buyer's Designated Agent to supply relevant financial information that
57 may be necessary to permit Buyer's Designated Agent to fulfill its obligations under this Agreement; (c) be available upon reasonable notice
58 and at reasonable hours to inspect Properties that are potentially appropriate for acquisition by Buyer; (d) identify to Buyer's Designated

Buyer Initials:_____ Buyer Initials:_____   Broker Initials: _____ Broker Initials:_____

1 of 3

F I G U R E   6.2 (CONTINUED)

Exclusive Buyer Representation Agreement

59 Agent those specific Properties not in the MLS that Buyer would want to inspect; (e) otherwise cooperate with Buyer's Designated Agent in
60 its efforts to fulfill its obligations under this Agreement; and (f) pay Broker, or cause seller's listing broker or seller to pay Broker, the
61 Compensation set forth in Paragraph 3 of this Agreement.

62 **9.   DISCLAIMER.** Buyer acknowledges and agrees that Broker and Buyer's Designated Agent are being retained solely as real estate
63 professionals and NOT as attorney, tax advisor, surveyor, structural engineer, home inspector, environmental consultant, architect,
64 contractor, or other professional service advisor. Buyer understands and agrees that such other professional service providers are available to
65 render advice or services to Buyer, if desired, at Buyer's expense.

66 **10.   INDEMNIFICATION OF BROKER.** Buyer hereby indemnifies and holds Broker and Buyer's Designated Agent harmless from
67 and against any and all claims, disputes, litigation, judgments, costs, and legal fees arising from (i) misrepresentations by Buyer or other
68 incorrect or incomplete information supplied by Buyer; (ii) earnest money handled by anyone other than Broker; and (iii) injuries to persons
69 on the Property and/or loss or damage to the Property or any portions of the Property.

70 **11.   ARBITRATION.** Any controversy or claim arising out of or relating to this Agreement, or the breach of this Agreement, shall be
71 settled by arbitration in accordance with the rules of the Chicago Association of REALTORS, and judgment upon the award rendered by the
72 arbitrator may be entered in any court having jurisdiction.

73 **12.   LIMITATION ON BROKER'S LIABILITY.** Neither Broker nor Buyer's Designated Agent shall, under any circumstances, have
74 any liability pursuant to this Agreement which is greater than the amount of the Compensation paid to Broker by Buyer or seller's listing
75 broker or seller, as the case may be (and excluding any commission amount retained by the listing broker, if any).

76 **13.   REAL ESTATE SETTLEMENT PROCEDURES ACT COMPLIANCE.** Buyer shall comply with the Real Estate Settlement
77 Procedures Act of 1974, as amended ("**Act**"), if applicable, and furnish all information required for compliance with the Act.

78 **14.   DUAL REPRESENTATION.** By checking "yes" and writing its initials below, Buyer acknowledges and agrees that Buyer's
79 Designated Agent ("**Licensee**") may undertake a dual representation (represent both seller and buyer or landlord and tenant, as the case may
80 be) in connection with any acquisition of Property. Buyer acknowledges and agrees that Buyer has read the following prior to executing this
81 Agreement:

82   Representing more than one party to a transaction presents a conflict of interest since both parties may rely upon the Licensee's
83   advice and the parties' respective interests may be adverse to each other. The Licensee will undertake the representation of more
84   than one party to a transaction only with the written consent of **ALL** parties to the transaction. Any parties who consent to dual
85   representation expressly agree that any agreement between the parties as to any terms of the contract, including the final contract
86   price, results from each party negotiating on its own behalf and in its own best interest. Buyer acknowledges and agrees that (a)
87   Broker has explained the implications of dual representation, including the risks involved, and (b) Buyer has been advised to seek
88   independent counsel from its advisors and/or attorneys prior to executing this Agreement or any documents in connection with this
89   Agreement.

90 **WHAT A LICENSEE _CAN_ DO FOR CLIENTS WHEN UNDERTAKING DUAL REPRESENTATION:**

91   1. Treat all clients honestly. 2. Provide information about the property to the purchaser or tenant. 3. Disclose all latent material
92   defects in the property that are known to the Licensee. 4. Disclose the financial qualification of Buyer to the seller or landlord. 5.
93   Explain real estate terms. 6. Help the Buyer arrange for property inspections. 7. Explain closing costs and procedures. 8. Help the
94   Buyer compare financing alternatives. 9. Provide information to seller or Buyer about comparable properties that have sold so both
95   clients may make educated decisions on what price to accept or offer.

96 **WHAT A LICENSEE _CANNOT_ DO FOR CLIENTS WHEN UNDERTAKING DUAL REPRESENTATION:**

97   1. Disclose confidential information that the Licensee may know about either client without that client's express consent. 2.
98   Disclose the price the seller or landlord will take other than the listing price without the express consent of the seller or landlord.
99   3. Disclose the price the purchaser or tenant is willing to pay without the express consent of the purchaser or tenant. 4.
100   Recommend or suggest a price the Buyer should offer. 5. Recommend or suggest a price the seller or landlord should counter with
101   or accept.

102 Buyer acknowledges having read these provisions regarding the issue of dual representation. Buyer is not required to accept this Paragraph
103 14 unless Buyer wants to allow the Licensee to proceed as a dual agent ("**Dual Agent**") in this transaction. By checking "yes", initialing
104 below, and signing this Agreement, Buyer acknowledges that it has read and understands this Paragraph 14 and voluntarily consents to the
105 Licensee acting as a Dual Agent (that is, to represent **BOTH** the seller and purchaser or landlord and tenant, as the case may be) should it
106 become necessary. (**check one**) ____ Yes ____ No _____ (Buyer initials) _____ (Buyer initials).

107 **15.   NONDISCRIMINATION. BROKER, ITS AGENTS AND EMPLOYEES AND BUYER'S DESIGNATED AGENT SHALL
108 NOT ACT IN ANY WAY TO INDUCE OR DISCOURAGE BUYER FROM ACQUIRING A PARTICULAR PROPERTY BASED ON
109 THE RACE, COLOR, RELIGION, NATIONAL ORIGIN, SEX, ANCESTRY, AGE, MARITAL STATUS, PHYSICAL OR MENTAL
110 HANDICAP OR FAMILIAL STATUS (OR ANY OTHER CLASS PROTECTED BY ARTICLE 3 OF THE ILLINOIS HUMAN
111 RIGHTS ACT) OF THE SELLER AND/OR BUYER. THE PARTIES TO THIS AGREEMENT AGREE TO COMPLY WITH ALL
112 APPLICABLE FEDERAL, STATE AND LOCAL FAIR HOUSING LAWS.**

Buyer Initials:_____   Buyer Initials:_____   Broker Initials:_____   Broker Initials:_____

F I G U R E   6.2 (CONTINUED)

Exclusive Buyer Representation Agreement

113 **16.** <u>**MISCELLANEOUS PROVISIONS.**</u>

114   A.   <u>Amendments</u>. No amendment or alteration of this Agreement shall be valid or binding unless made in writing and signed by
115   the Broker, Buyer's Designated Agent and Buyer.

116   B.   <u>Gender Neutral</u>. Where applicable in this Agreement, the singular form of any word shall include the plural and the
117   masculine form shall include the feminine and neuter, and vice versa.

118   C.   <u>Successors and Assigns</u>. This Agreement shall be binding upon and inure to the benefit of the heirs, executors, administrators,
119   successors and assigns of the parties.

120   D.   <u>Days</u>. Any reference in this Agreement to "day" or "days" shall mean business days, not calendar days, including Monday,
121   Tuesday, Wednesday, Thursday, and Friday, and excluding all official federal and state holidays.

122 **BUYER INFORMATION:**   **BROKER INFORMATION:**

Buyer's Signature:_____   Managing Broker's Signature:_____

Buyer's Signature:_____   Date:_____ (**"Effective Date"**)

Date:_____

Buyer's Name (print):_____   Broker Company Name (print):_____

Address:_____   Office Address:_____

City:_____ State:_____ Zip:_____   City:_____ State:_____ Zip:_____

Office Phone:_____   Office Phone:_____

Home Phone:_____   Cell Phone:_____

Cell Phone:_____   Fax:_____

Fax:_____   Email Address:_____

Email Address:_____

Buyer's Name (print):_____   Designated Agent Name (print):_____

Address:_____   Designated Agent Number:_____

City:_____ State:_____ Zip:_____   Office Address:_____

Office Phone:_____   City:_____ State:_____ Zip:_____

Home Phone:_____   Office Phone:_____

Cell Phone:_____   Cell Phone:_____

Fax:_____   Fax:_____

Email Address:_____   Email Address:_____

Buyer Initials:_____ Buyer Initials:_____   Broker Initials:_____ Broker Initials:_____

IN PRACTICE   In Illinois, it is common that the buyer's broker may be paid by the seller under a "cooperative" arrangement, as previously noted. However, this is a clear case where commission does not equate to agency or representation. Discussions regarding a commission or fee provided by the buyer may still take place. An agent is free to negotiate for compensation from any buyer to whom he or she provides service in an agency capacity, but if the broker receives compensation from more than one source in a transaction, it always needs to be disclosed in writing to the involved parties.

■ TERMINATION OF BROKER EMPLOYMENT AGREEMENTS

A broker employment agreement is a personal service contract between a broker and a property owner or buyer. Its success depends on the broker's personal, professional efforts. Because the broker's services are unique, he or she cannot turn over the contract to another broker without the principal's written consent. The client cannot force the broker to perform, but the broker's failure to work diligently toward fulfilling the contract's terms constitutes abandonment of the contract. In the event the contract is abandoned or revoked by the broker, the principal is entitled to sue the broker for damages.

Of course, the principal also might fail to fulfill the terms of the agreement. For instance, a property owner who refuses to cooperate with the broker's reasonable requests, such as allowing the broker to show the property to prospective buyers, or who refuses to proceed with a completed sales contract, could be liable for damages to the broker. If either party cancels the contract, he or she may be liable for damages to the other.

An employment agreement may be canceled for the following reasons:

■ When the agreement's purpose is fulfilled.
■ When the agreement's term expires without a successful transfer.
■ If the property is destroyed or its use is changed by some force outside the client's control, such as a zoning change or condemnation by eminent domain.
■ If title to the property is transferred by operation of law, as in the case of the client's bankruptcy.
■ If the broker and client mutually agree to end the agreement or if one party ends it unilaterally (in which case he or she may be liable to the other party for damages).
■ If either the broker or the client dies or becomes incapacitated.
■ If either the broker or client breaches the contract, the agreement is terminated and the breaching or canceling party may be liable to the other for damages.

■ SUMMARY

To acquire an inventory of property to sell, brokers must obtain listings. Types of listings include exclusive-right-to-sell, exclusive-agency, and open listings. With an exclusive-right-to-sell listing, the seller employs only one broker and must pay that broker a commission regardless of whether it is the broker or the seller who finds a buyer, provided the buyer is found within the listing period.

Under exclusive agency, the broker is given the exclusive right to represent the seller, but the seller can avoid paying the broker a commission by selling the property to someone not procured by the broker.

With an open listing, to obtain a commission, the broker must find a ready, willing, and able buyer on the seller's terms before the property is sold by the seller or by another broker.

A multiple listing service (MLS) provision may appear in an exclusive-right-to-sell or an exclusive-agency listing. It gives the broker the additional authority and obligation to distribute the listing to other members of the broker's multiple listing organization, which enhances the odds of the property selling.

A net listing, which is illegal in some states and considered somewhat unethical in most areas, is based on the net price the seller will receive if the property is sold. The broker is free to offer the property for sale at the highest available price and will receive as commission any amount exceeding the seller's stipulated net. Net listings are legal in Illinois.

An option listing, which also must be handled with caution, gives the broker the option to purchase the listed property, sometimes if it does not sell in a specified amount of time.

When listing a property for sale, the seller is concerned about the selling price and the net amount he or she will receive from the sale. A comparative market analysis (CMA) compares the prices of recently sold properties that are similar to the seller's property. The CMA or a formal appraisal report can be used to help the seller determine a reasonable listing price. The approximate amount the seller will net from the sale is calculated by subtracting the broker's commission, any other seller expenses (attorney, title search), and any existing liens (such as the mortgage) from the approximate sales price.

Listing contract forms typically are preprinted forms that include such information as the type of listing agreement, the broker's authority and responsibility under the listing, the listing price, the duration of the listing, information about the property, terms for the payment of commission, details regarding buyer's possession, and nondiscrimination and antitrust laws. Detailed information about the property may be included in the listing contract or on a separate property data sheet.

Disclosure of the broker's agency relationships and agency policies are required. The seller will be expected to comply honestly with legally required disclosures of property conditions.

A buyer agency agreement ensures that a buyer's interest will be represented. Different forms of buyer agency agreements exist—an exclusive buyer agency; an exclusive-agency buyer agency, and open buyer agency. In an exclusive buyer agency, the broker is compensated regardless of whether the broker locates the property. In an exclusive-agency buyer agency, the broker is compensated only if the broker locates the property the buyer purchases. In open buyer agency, the buyer is obligated to compensate only the broker who locates the property the buyer purchases.

A buyer's broker is obligated to find a suitable property for the client, who is owed fiduciary or statutory duties of agency. Buyer agency is regulated by Illinois agency laws.

Listings and buyer agency agreements may be terminated for the same reasons as any other agency relationship.

In Illinois   In Illinois, a written exclusive or exclusive-right-to-sell listing agreement must include the list price, the basis for and time of payment of the commission, the term of the listing, the names and signatures of the listing broker and seller, and the address or legal description of the property.

All exclusive brokerage agreements must be in writing according to the Rules accompanying the *Real Estate License Act of 2000*. In addition, under the act, all exclusive brokerage agreements must provide for minimum services.

Detailed information about a property should be included for the record in the listing contract or on a separate property data sheet. Full disclosure of the broker's agency relationship, any interest the broker has in the subject property, material facts pertaining to the property, any guaranteed sales agreement, or any special bonus or fee provided to an agent is required by Illinois law. ■

QUESTIONS

1. A listing taken by a real estate salesperson is an agreement between the seller and the
   a. sponsoring broker.
   b. local multiple listing service.
   c. salesperson (or a broker associated with the firm).
   d. local REALTOR® association.

2. Which of the following is a similarity between an exclusive-agency listing and an exclusive-right-to-sell listing?
   a. Under both, the seller retains the right to sell the real estate without the broker's help and without paying the broker a commission.
   b. Under both, the seller authorizes only one particular salesperson to show the property.
   c. Both types of listings give the responsibility of representing the seller to one broker only.
   d. Both types of listings are open listings.

3. The listing agreement between broker Betty and seller Theo states that it expires on May 2. Which event would *NOT* terminate the listing?
   a. The agreement is not renewed after May 2.
   b. Betty dies on April 29.
   c. On April 15, Theo tells Betty that he is dissatisfied with Betty's marketing efforts.
   d. Theo's house is destroyed by fire on April 25.

4. The seller has listed his property under an exclusive-agency listing with the broker. If the seller sells the property himself during the term of the listing to someone introduced to the property by the seller, he will owe the broker
   a. no commission.
   b. the full commission.
   c. a partial commission.
   d. only reimbursement for the broker's costs.

5. A broker sold a residence for $235,000 and received $12,925 as her commission in accordance with the terms of the listing. What was the broker's commission rate?
   a. 5.5 percent
   b. 5.7 percent
   c. 6.25 percent
   d. 6.5 percent

6. Under a listing agreement, the broker is entitled to sell the property for any price, as long as the seller receives $85,000. The broker may keep any amount over $85,000 as a commission. This type of listing is called a(n)
   a. exclusive-right-to-sell listing.
   b. exclusive-agency listing.
   c. open listing.
   d. net listing.

7. Which of the following is a similarity between an open listing and an exclusive-agency listing?
   a. Under both, the seller avoids paying the broker a commission if the seller sells the property to someone the broker did not procure.
   b. Both grant a commission to any broker who procures a buyer for the seller's property.
   c. Under both the broker earns a commission regardless of who sells the property as long as it is sold within the listing period.
   d. Both grant an exclusive right to sell to whatever broker procures a buyer for the seller's property.

8. The listed price for a property should be determined by the
   a. agent based on information from the local MLS.
   b. agent and the appraiser.
   c. agent and seller equally.
   d. seller based on the agent's CMAs.

9. Which of the following statements is *TRUE* of a listing contract?
   a. It is an employment contract for the personal and professional services of the broker.
   b. It obligates the seller to convey the property if the broker procures a ready, willing, and able buyer.
   c. It obligates the broker to work diligently for both the seller and the buyer.
   d. It automatically binds the owner, broker, and MLS to the agreed provisions.

10. A real estate broker sold a property and received a 6.5 percent commission. The broker gave the listing salesperson 40 percent of the commission, or $9,750. What was the selling price of the property?

    a. $55,000
    b. $150,000
    c. $250,000
    d. $375,000

11. A seller hired broker Nathan under the terms of an open listing. While that listing was still in effect, the seller, without informing broker Nathan, hired broker Frank under an exclusive-right-to-sell listing for the same property. If broker Nathan produces a buyer for the property whose offer the seller accepts, then the seller must pay a

    a. full commission only to broker Nathan.
    b. full commission to broker Frank and broker Nathan.
    c. at least a one-third commission to broker Nathan.
    d. half commission to both broker Nathan and broker Frank.

12. Seller Grace listed her residence with broker Diane. Broker Diane brought an offer at full price and terms of the listing from buyers who were ready, willing, and able to pay cash for the property. However, seller Grace changed her mind and rejected the buyers' offer. In this situation, seller Grace

    a. must sell her property.
    b. owes a commission to broker Diane.
    c. is liable to the buyers for specific performance.
    d. is liable to the buyers for compensatory damages.

13. Which statement regarding open buyer agency is *TRUE?*

    a. The buyer may enter into agreements with multiple brokers and is obligated to pay only the broker who locates the property that the buyer ultimately purchases.
    b. While the buyer may enter into agreements with multiple brokers, he or she is under no obligation to pay the broker; the seller bears all brokerage expenses.
    c. Because multiple brokers may be involved, an open buyer agency agreement involves reduced fiduciary duties.
    d. The buyer may not look for or make offers on properties on his or her own.

14. Broker Jane and buyer Nadia enter into an exclusive-agency buyer agency agreement. This means

    a. Nadia is obligated to compensate Jane regardless of who locates the property ultimately purchased.
    b. Jane is entitled to payment only if she, or any broker acting under her authority, locates the property Nadia ultimately purchases.
    c. Nadia may enter into similar agreements with any number of other brokers.
    d. if Nadia finds the property without any help from Jane, Nadia must pay Jane a reduced compensation.

15. A comparative market analysis

    a. is the same as an appraisal.
    b. can help the seller price the property.
    c. by law must be completed for each listing taken.
    d. should not be retained in the property's listing file.

16. A property was listed with a broker who belonged to a multiple listing service and was sold by another member broker for $153,500. The total commission was 6 percent of the sales price. The selling broker received 60 percent of the commission, and the listing broker kept the balance. What was the listing broker's commission?

    a. $3,684
    b. $4,464
    c. $5,526
    d. $36,840

17. Shane signs a listing agreement with broker Keith to sell Shane's home. The agreement states that Keith will receive a 5.5 percent commission. The home sells for $387,000. What is the net amount that Shane will receive from the sale?

    a. $4,785
    b. $21,285
    c. $365,715
    d. $369,585

18. A real estate broker and a seller enter into a listing agreement that contains the following language: "Seller will receive $100,000 from the sale of the subject property. Any amount greater than $100,000 will constitute Broker's sole and complete compensation." Which of the following statements is *TRUE* regarding this agreement?

    a. This agreement is an example of an option listing.
    b. If the seller's home sells for exactly $100,000, the broker still will be entitled to receive the standard commission in the area.
    c. The broker may offer the property for any price over $100,000, but the agreement may be unethical.
    d. This type of listing is known as an *open listing,* because the selling price is left open.

19. Most states require that listing agreements contain a

    a. multiple listing service (MLS) clause.
    b. definite contract termination date.
    c. automatic extension clause.
    d. broker protection clause.

20. Broker George enters into an agreement with a client. The agreement states, "In return for the compensation agreed upon, Broker will assist Client in locating and purchasing a suitable property. Broker will receive the agreed compensation regardless of whether Broker, Client, or some other party locates the property ultimately purchased by Client." What kind of agreement is this?

    a. Exclusive-agency listing
    b. Exclusive-agency buyer agency agreement
    c. Exclusive buyer agency agreement
    d. Open buyer agency agreement

In Illinois

21. Illinois salespeople may

    a. submit a listing to the local MLS.
    b. refuse to show a property to racial minorities if their sellers so instruct them.
    c. advertise in their own name as long as they hold independent contractor status.
    d. never take open listings.

Interests in Real Estate

■ **LEARNING OBJECTIVES** *When you've finished reading this chapter, you should be able to*

■ **identify** the kinds of limitations on ownership rights that are imposed by government action and the form of conveyance of property.

■ **describe** the various estates in land and the rights and limitations they convey.

■ **explain** concepts related to encumbrances and water rights.

■ **distinguish** the various types of police powers and how they are exercised.

■ **define** the following *key terms:*

accretion	encroachment	license
appurtenant easement	encumbrance	lien
avulsion	Equity in Eminent Domain	life estate
condemnation	Act	life tenant
deed restrictions	erosion	littoral rights
doctrine of prior	escheat	party wall
appropriation	estates in land	police power
dominant tenement	fee simple absolute	quick-take
easement	fee simple defeasible	remainder interest
easement by	fee simple determinable	reversionary interest
condemnation	fee simple estates	riparian rights
easement by necessity	freehold estate	servient tenement
easement by prescription	future interests	taxation
easement in gross	homestead	Uniform Probate Code
eminent domain	leasehold estates	

■ LIMITATIONS ON THE RIGHTS OF OWNERSHIP

Ownership of real estate is not absolute, that is, a landowner's power to control his or her property is subject to other interests. Keep in mind that a landowner's power to control his or her property relates to the landowner having title of the property and the bundle of legal rights that accompanies the title. Even the most complete ownership the law allows is limited by public and private restrictions. These restrictions are intended to ensure that one owner's use or enjoyment of his or her property does not interfere with others' use or enjoyment of their property or with the welfare of the general public. Licensees should have a working knowledge of the restrictions that might limit current or future owners. A zoning ordinance that will not allow a doctor's office to coexist with a residence, a condo association bylaw prohibiting resale without board approval, or an easement allowing the neighbors to use the private beach may not only burden today's purchaser but also deter a future buyer.

This chapter puts the various interests in real estate in perspective—what rights they confer and how use of the ownership may be limited.

■ GOVERNMENT POWERS

Individual ownership rights are subject to certain powers, or rights, held by federal, state, and local governments. These limitations on the ownership of real estate are imposed for the general welfare of the community and, therefore, supersede the rights or interests of the individual. Government powers include the following: Police power, Eminent domain, Taxation, and Escheat.

| In Illinois | The state and local government powers discussed in this section are all held by the state of Illinois and various county and municipal governing bodies. ■

Police Power

Every state has the power to enact legislation to preserve order, protect the public health and safety, and promote the general welfare of its citizens. That authority is known as a state's **police power**. The state's authority is passed on to municipalities and counties through legislation called *enabling acts*.

> **Memory Tip**
>
> Remember the four government powers as **PETE**:
> *Police power,*
> *Eminent domain,*
> *Taxation, and*
> *Escheat.*

What is identified as being "in the public interest" varies widely from state to state and region to region. A state's police power generally is used to enact environmental protection laws, zoning ordinances, and building codes. Regulations that govern the use, occupancy, size, location, and construction of real estate also fall within the police powers. Police powers may be used to achieve a community's needs or goals. If a city deems growth to be desirable, it may exercise its police powers to enact laws encouraging the purchase and improvement of land. Or, an area that wishes to retain its current character may enact laws that discourage development and population growth.

As with rights of ownership, the state's power to regulate land use is not absolute. The laws must be uniform and nondiscriminatory. They may not operate to the advantage or disadvantage of any one particular owner or group of owners.

Eminent Domain

Eminent domain is the right of the government to acquire privately owned real estate for public use. *Condemnation* is the process by which the government exercises this right, by either judicial or administrative proceedings. In the taking of property, just compensation must be paid to the owner, and the rights of the property owner must be protected by due process of law. Appraisals are used to determine a fair price.

In Illinois

Local units of government and quasi-governmental bodies are given the power of eminent domain by the Illinois Constitution and by the Illinois Code of Civil Procedure. In certain situations, Illinois law permits a summary proceeding in which a plaintiff/condemnor may obtain immediate fee simple title to real property, including the rights of possession and use. Such a proceeding in Illinois is termed a **quick-take**.

> *Eminent domain* is the government's right to seize property.
> *Condemnation* is the way the right is exercised.

In quick-take, the plaintiff must deposit a sum with the county treasurer that is preliminarily considered by the court to be *just compensation*; this can be litigated later. A quick-take might be appropriate, for instance, in the following circumstances:

- The state of Illinois or the Illinois Toll Highway Authority takes property to construct, maintain, and operate highways.
- A sanitary district takes property to remove obstructions in a river, such as the Des Plaines River or Illinois River.
- An airport authority takes property to provide additional land for airport purposes. ■

Generally, the states delegate their power of eminent domain to quasi-public bodies and publicly held companies responsible for various facets of public service. For instance, a public housing authority might take privately owned land to build low-income housing, or the state's land-clearance commission or redevelopment authority could use the power of eminent domain to make way for urban renewal. If there were no other way to accomplish its aims, a railway, utility company, or highway department might acquire farmland or residential properties for key endeavors. Such projects might include a railroad track, delivery of electricity to a remote new development, or a new highway.

In the past, the proposed use for taking property was to be for the public good. However, in June 2005, the U.S. Supreme Court in *Kelo v. City of New London*, significantly changed the definition of public use. The court held that local governments can condemn homes and businesses for private or economic development purposes.

In *Kelo v. City of New London*, a development agent, on behalf of the city, initiated condemnation proceedings on land owned by nine property owners who refused to have their property taken. The development plan involved land for commercial, residential, and recreational purposes. The court noted that the development plan was not going to benefit a particular class of identifiable individuals. Further, although the owners' properties were not blighted, the city determined that a program of economic rejuvenation was justified and entitled to deference. *Economic development* fit within the broad definition of *public purpose*. The court found that the city's proposed disposition of petitioners' properties qualified as a *public use* within the meaning of the Takings Clause of the 5th Amendment of the U.S. Constitution.

In this case, the city had invoked a state statute that authorized the use of eminent domain to promote economic development. The court decision leaves it to the states to establish rules that cities must follow when exercising eminent domain powers. In response to this court decision, many state legislators are drafting legislation to impose a narrow definition of *public use* in eminent domain proceedings to stop condemnations justified on purely economic grounds.

| In Illinois | The **Equity in Eminent Domain Act** became effective in Illinois on January 1, 2007, following the *Kelo v. New London* eminent domain Supreme Court case. The law places the obligation on government to prove that an area is blighted before forcing property owners to sell their property for private development projects. In addition, the act helps property owners receive fair market value for their property, requires relocation costs for displaced residents and businesses, and pays attorneys' fees when property owners successfully sue to keep their property. ∎

Taxation

Taxation is a charge on real estate to raise funds to meet the public needs of a government. When real estate taxes are left unpaid for too long, the government has the right to sell property at a tax sale.

Escheat

Although **escheat** is not a limitation on ownership, it is an avenue by which the state may acquire privately owned real or personal property. State laws provide for ownership to transfer, or escheat, to the state when an owner dies without a will or any identifiable heirs. Escheat is intended to prevent property from being ownerless or abandoned.

| In Illinois | In Illinois, real property will *escheat to the county* in which it is located rather than to the state. ∎

■ ESTATES IN LAND

Historically, **estates in land** have been classified as *freehold estates* and *leasehold estates*. The two types of estates are distinguished by their duration and depth. As a practical matter, freehold estates involve property ownership; leaseholds involve property rental.

Freehold estates last for an indeterminable length of time, such as for a lifetime or forever. They include *fee simple* (also sometimes called an *indefeasible fee*), *defeasible fee,* and *life estates*. The first two of these estates continue for an indefinite period and may be passed along to the owner's heirs. A life estate is based on the lifetime of a person and ends when that individual dies. Freehold estates are illustrated in Figure 7.1.

Leasehold estates last for a fixed period of time. They include estates for years and estates from period to period. Estates at will and estates at sufferance also are leaseholds, though by their operation they are not generally viewed as being for fixed terms.

FIGURE   7.1

Freehold Estates

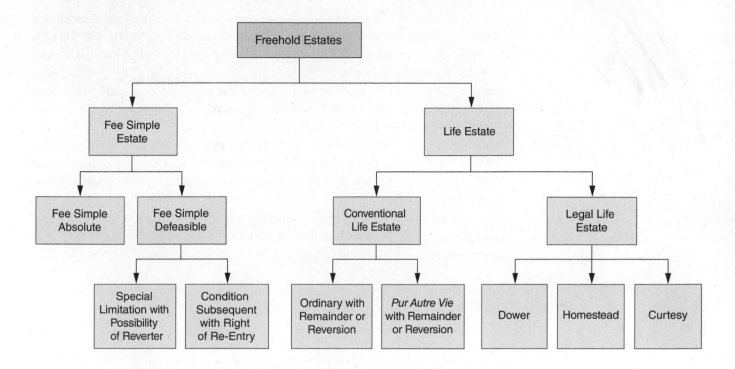

In Illinois The traditional freehold and leasehold estates found in most states are also recognized under Illinois law. ■

Fee Simple Estate

Because **fee simple estates** are of unlimited duration, they are said to run "forever." On the death of the owner a fee simple passes to the owner's heirs or as provided by will. A *fee simple estate* is also referred to as an *estate of inheritance* (because that is how it passes unless the owner chooses to sell the property) or simply as *fee ownership*. There are two major divisions of fee ownership: fee simple absolute and fee simple defeasible.

Fee simple with condition subsequent: "on the condition that"
Fee simple determinable: "so long as" "while" "during"

Fee simple absolute. A **fee simple absolute** estate is the highest interest in real estate recognized by law. Fee simple ownership is absolute ownership: the holder is entitled to all rights to the property. It is limited only by certain public and private restrictions, such as zoning laws and restrictive covenants.

Fee simple defeasible. A **fee simple defeasible** (or *defeasible fee*) estate is a qualified estate—that is, it is subject to the occurrence or nonoccurrence of some specified event. Two types of defeasible estates exist: those *subject to a condition subsequent* and those *qualified by a special limitation (determinable fees)*.

A fee simple estate may be qualified by a *condition subsequent*. This means that the new owner must not perform some action or activity. The former owner retains a *right of re-entry* so that *if the condition is broken, the former owner can retake possession of the property through legal action*. Conditions in a deed under "condition subsequent" are different from restrictions or covenants because of the grantor's right to reclaim ownership. Possible reclamation of ownership does not exist under private restrictions made by builders or homeowner associations.

■ **FOR EXAMPLE** A grant of land "on the condition that" there be no consumption of alcohol on the premises is a *fee simple subject to a condition subsequent*. If alcohol is consumed on the property, the former owner has the right to reacquire full ownership. It will be necessary for the grantor (or the grantor's heirs or successors) to go to court to assert that right, however.

A fee simple estate also may be qualified by a *special limitation*. The estate ends automatically on the current owner's failure to comply with the limitation. The former owner retains a *possibility of reverter*. The reversion is automatic if the restriction on the deed is broken. If the limitation is violated, the former owner (or his or her heirs or successors) reacquires full ownership, *with no need to reenter the land or go to court*. A fee simple with a special limitation is also called a **fee simple determinable**—it may end automatically in a way that has already been determined. Words used to distinguish a special limitation—*as long as* or *while* or *during*—are key to legally creating this estate.

> **Memory Tip**
> ■ *Determinable Fee = predetermined events (reversion)*
> ■ *Special Limitation = specifically limited in advance*
> ■ *Defeasible with Condition Subsequent = court subsequently must sanction re-entry*

The right of reentry and possibility of reverter may never take effect. If they do, it will be only at some time in the future. Therefore, each of these rights is considered a **future interest.**

church

■ **FOR EXAMPLE** A grant of land from an owner to her church "so long as the land is used only for religious purposes" is set up as a *fee simple determinable* with a *special limitation*. If the church ever decides to use the land for a nonreligious purpose, title will revert *automatically* to the previous owner (or her heirs or successors).

> **In Illinois**

Because the right of re-entry and possibility of reverter can happen only in the future, they are considered *future interests*. While the condition passes from owner to owner forever, Illinois allows the original grantor's right of reverter to continue for only 40 years. After that time, the condition still may be enforced but no longer by the threat of losing the property. ■

Life Estate

A **life estate** is a freehold estate limited in duration to the life of the owner or the life of some other designated person or persons. Unlike other freehold estates, a life estate is not inheritable. It passes to future owners according to the prearranged provisions of the life estate.

Golddigger

A life tenant is entitled to the rights of ownership, that is, the life tenant can enjoy both possession and the ordinary use and profits arising from ownership, just as if the individual were a fee owner. The ownership may be sold, mortgaged, or leased, but it is always subject to the limitation of the life estate.

A life tenant's ownership rights, however, are not absolute. The life tenant may not injure the property, such as by destroying a building or allowing it to deteriorate. In legal terms, such injury is known as *waste*. Those who eventually will own the property could seek an injunction against the life tenant or sue for damages if waste occurs.

Because the ownership will terminate on the death of the person against whose life the estate is measured, a purchaser, lessee, or lender can be affected if the life tenant has sold his or her rights. Because the interest is less desirable than a fee simple estate, the life tenant's limited rights must be disclosed if the property is sold. The new purchaser will lose the property at whatever point in time the original life tenant would have lost it.

Conventional life estate.   A *conventional life estate* is created intentionally by the owner. It may be established either by deed at the time the ownership is transferred during the owner's life or by a provision of the owner's will after his or her death. The estate is conveyed to an individual who is called the life tenant. The **life tenant** has full enjoyment of the ownership for the duration of his or her life. When the life tenant dies, the estate ends and its ownership passes, often as a fee simple to another designated individual, or returns to the previous owner.

■ **F O R   E X A M P L E** Anna, who has a fee simple estate in Blackacre, conveys a life estate to Phil for Phil's lifetime. Phil is the life tenant. On Phil's death, the life estate terminates, and Anna once again owns Blackacre. If Phil's life estate had been created by Anna's will, however, subsequent ownership of Blackacre would be determined by the provisions of the will.

Life estate pur autre vie.   A life estate also may be based on the lifetime of a person other than the life tenant. This is known as a life estate *pur autre vie* ("for the life of another"). Although a life estate is not considered an estate of inheritance, a life estate pur autre vie provides for the life tenant's "ownership" only until the death of the person against whose life the estate is measured.

■ **F O R   E X A M P L E** Rita has a good friend, Harry, who has always struggled with his finances, and Harry often has trouble paying for his small rental apartment. Rita sets up a life estate pur autre vie for Harry, making him the life tenant for a Wisconsin cottage Rita no longer uses. Based on Rita's instructions, the estate is based on the life of Harry's father, Richard. Rita knows that Harry's father is willing Harry a beautiful home by the lake, so after the father dies Harry will no longer need the cottage. Rita plans it so Harry's life estate from Rita will then end (*pur autre vie*—for the life of another), and the cottage will either revert to Rita, Rita's heirs, or pass to a designated *remainderman*, perhaps a relative of Rita's.

Remainder and reversion.   The fee simple owner who creates a conventional life estate must plan for future ownership. When the life estate ends, it is replaced by a fee simple estate. The future owner of the fee simple estate may be designated in one of two ways:

1. **Remainder interest:** The creator of the life estate may name a *remainderman* as the person to whom the property will pass when the life estate ends. ("Remainderman" is the legal term; neither the term *remainderperson* nor the term *remainderwoman* is used legally.) (See Figure 7.2.)
2. **Reversionary interest:** The creator of the life estate may choose *not* to name a remainderman. In that case, the creator will recapture ownership when the life estate ends. The ownership is said to "revert to the original owner." (See Figure 7.3.)

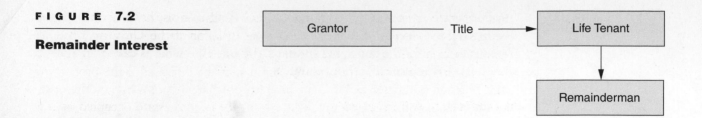

FIGURE 7.2

Remainder Interest

■ **FOR EXAMPLE** Craig conveys Blackacre to Jean for Jean's lifetime and designates James to be the remainderman. While Jean is still alive, James owns a remainder interest, which is a *nonpossessory estate;* that is, James does not possess the property, but has an interest in it nonetheless. This is a future interest in the fee simple estate. If Jean should die, James automatically becomes the fee simple owner. On the other hand, Craig may convey a life estate in Blackacre to Jean during and based on Jean's life. On Jean's death, ownership of Blackacre reverts to Craig. Craig has retained a *reversionary interest* (also called a *nonpossessory estate*). Craig has a future interest in the ownership and may reclaim the fee simple estate when Jean dies. If Craig dies before Jean, Craig's heirs (or other individuals specified in Craig's will) will assume ownership of Blackacre whenever Jean dies.

IN PRACTICE

Assisting a client with life estates, determinable fees, or fees with "conditions subsequent" should be the job of a skilled real estate attorney. Noting such situations in a sales transaction is, however, a responsibility of careful listing agents. In day-to-day practice, however, basic fee simple absolute—the simplest to understand form of ownership—will dominate.

Legal life estate.   A *legal life estate* is not created voluntarily by an owner. Rather, it is a form of life estate established by state law. It becomes effective automatically when certain events occur. *Dower, curtesy,* and *homestead* are the legal life estates currently used in many states.

Dower and curtesy provide the nonowning spouse with a means of support after the death of the owning spouse. *Dower* is the life estate that a wife has in the real estate of her deceased husband. *Curtesy* is an identical interest that a husband has in the real estate of his deceased wife. In some states, dower and curtesy are referred to collectively as either dower or curtesy.

Dower and curtesy provide that the nonowning spouse has a right to a *one-half or one-third interest* in the real estate for the rest of her or his life, even if the owning spouse wills the estate to others. Because a nonowning spouse might claim an interest in the future, both spouses may have to sign the proper documents when real estate is conveyed. The signature of the nonowning spouse would be needed to release any potential common-law interests in the property being transferred.

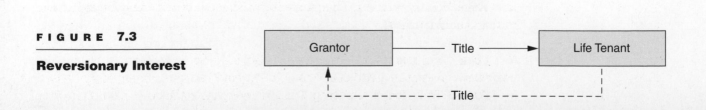

FIGURE 7.3

Reversionary Interest

| In Illinois | Most separate or *marital property* states, including Illinois, have abolished the common-law concepts of dower and curtesy in favor of the **Uniform Probate Code**, which gives the surviving spouse a right to take what is called an *elective share* on the death of the other spouse. ■ |

Homestead.   A **homestead** is a legal life estate in real estate occupied as the family home. In effect, the home (or at least some part of it) is protected from unsecured creditors during the occupant's lifetime. In states that have homestead exemption laws, a portion of the area or value of the property occupied as the family home is exempt from certain judgments for debts such as charge accounts and personal loans. The homestead is not protected from real estate taxes levied against the property or from a mortgage for the purchase or cost of improvements. In other words, if the debt is secured by the property, the property cannot be exempt from a judgment on that debt.

How does the homestead exemption actually work? The homestead merely reserves a certain amount of money for the family in the event of a court sale. On such a sale, any debts secured by the home, such as a mortgage, unpaid taxes, or mechanics' liens are paid from the proceeds first. Then the family receives the amount reserved by the homestead exemption. Whatever remains from sale proceeds is applied to the family's unsecured debts.

| In Illinois | Every homeowner in Illinois is entitled to a homestead estate up to a value of $15,000 in the land and buildings he or she occupies as a principal residence. Homestead estates of a husband and wife can be combined for a total of $30,000. The estate extends to all types of residential property including condominiums, cooperatives, and beneficial interests in land trusts. Single persons, as well as householders with spouses and families, qualify. |

No notice has to be recorded or filed to establish a homestead in Illinois. Therefore, prospective purchasers, lienholders, and other concerned parties are charged with inspecting a property to see if it serves as the residence of the potential debtor and if homestead estate rights can be claimed.

A family can have only one homestead at any one time. The Illinois homestead exemption is not applicable between co-owners but is applicable to any co-tenant's unsecured creditors. The exemption continues after the death of an individual for the benefit of the surviving spouse as long as she or he continues to occupy the homestead residence. It also extends for the benefit of all children living there until the youngest reaches 18 years of age.

A release, waiver, or conveyance of homestead is not valid unless it is expressed in writing and signed by the individual and his or her spouse, if applicable. The signatures of both spouses are always required on residential sales contracts, listing agreements, notes, mortgages, deeds, and other conveyances to release possible homestead rights, even if the property in question is owned solely by either the husband or the wife. ■

■ **FOR EXAMPLE** Greenacre is Tony's Illinois homestead. In Illinois, the homestead exemption is $15,000. At a court-ordered sale, the property is purchased for $60,000. First, Tony's remaining $15,000 mortgage balance is paid; then Tony receives $15,000. The remaining $30,000 is applied to Tony's unsecured debts. Of course, no sale would be ordered if the court could determine that nothing would remain from the proceeds for the unsecured creditors.

■ ENCUMBRANCES

Physical Encumbrances

- Restrictions
- Easements
- Licenses
- Encroachments

An **encumbrance** is a claim, charge, or liability that attaches to real estate. An encumbrance does not have a possessory interest in real property; it is not an estate.

Encumbrances may be divided into two general classifications:

1. Encumbrances that affect title (*liens*—usually monetary charges) and
2. Encumbrances that affect the use or physical condition of the property (restrictions, easements, licenses, and encroachments).

Liens

A **lien** is a charge against property that provides security for a debt or an obligation of the property owner. If the obligation is not repaid, the lienholder is entitled to have the debt satisfied from the proceeds of a court-ordered or forced sale of the debtor's property. Real estate taxes, mortgages and trust deeds, judgments, and mechanics' liens all represent possible liens against an owner's real estate.

Restrictions

Deed restrictions, also referred to as *covenants, conditions, and restrictions,* or *CC&Rs,* limit uses of property and can create affirmative obligations of the land owner. They may be imposed by an owner of real estate and included in the seller's deed to the buyer. Typically, however, restrictive covenants are imposed by a developer or subdivider to maintain specific standards in a subdivision. Such restrictive covenants are listed in the original development plans for the subdivision filed in the public record, usually held by the county.

Easements

An **easement** is the right to use the land of another for a particular purpose. An easement may exist in any portion of the real estate, including the airspace above or a right-of-way across the land. Easements are by agreement at any time or created by a seller when a property is conveyed.

Memory Tip

Servient Tenement = the land that *serves* the other party

Dominant Tenement = the *dominating* party benefitted by the easement

An **appurtenant easement** is annexed to the ownership of one parcel and allows the owner the use of a neighbor's land. For an appurtenant easement to exist, *two adjacent parcels of land must be owned by two different parties*. The parcel over which the easement runs is known as the **servient tenement;** the neighboring parcel that benefits is known as the **dominant tenement.** (See Figure 7.4 and Figure 7.5.)

An appurtenant easement is part of the dominant tenement. If the dominant tenement is conveyed to another party, the beneficial easement transfers with the title, or *"runs with the land."* It will transfer with the deed of the dominant tenement forever unless the holder of the dominant tenement releases that right. Easements are considered encumbrances for disclosure, especially so for the servient tenement whose land is being used. While the easement must also be mentioned for a dominant tenement, the fact that it exists is often a marketing plus (such as an easement accessing a beach).

FIGURE 7.4

Easement Appurtenant

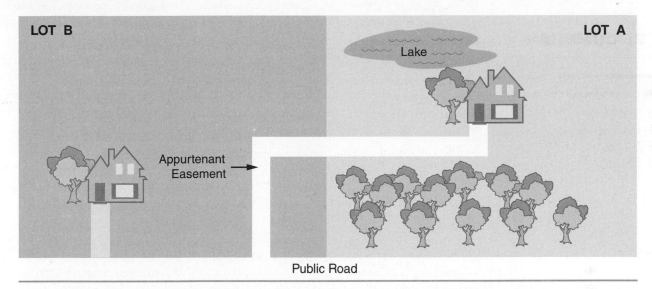

The owner of Lot A has an appurtenant easement across Lot B to gain access to his property from the paved road. Lot A is dominant, and Lot B is servient.

FIGURE 7.5

Easement Appurtenant and Easement in Gross

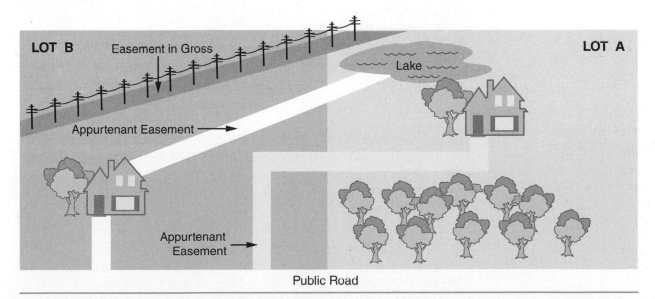

The owner of Lot B has an appurtenant easement across Lot A to gain access to the lake. Lot B is dominant and Lot A is servient. The utility company has an easement in gross across both parcels of land for its power lines. Note that Lot A also has an appurtenant easement across Lot B for its driveway. Lot A is dominant and Lot B is servient.

■ **FOR EXAMPLE** Carol and Jess own adjoining parcels of land near a lake. Carol's property borders the lake, and Jess's does not. Carol grants Jess an easement, established by a deed properly delivered and accepted. The easement gives Jess the right to cross Carol's property to reach the lake. This is an easement appurtenant. When Carol sells the lakefront property to Ruth Peters, the easement is automatically included, even if Carol inappropriately fails to mention it. Jess's easement has become a limitation on the ownership rights of Carol's land.

Creating an easement.   An easement is commonly created by a written agreement between parties that establishes the easement right. It also may be created by the grantor in a deed of conveyance, where the grantor either reserves an easement over the sold land or grants the new owner an easement over the grantor's remaining land. An easement may be created by longtime usage, as in an easement by prescription, by necessity, or by implication (the parties' actions or the land use implies intent to create an easement).

The creation of an easement always involves two separate parties, one of whom is the owner of the land over which the easement runs. It is impossible by definition for the owner of a parcel of property to have an easement over his or her own land.

Party wall easement.   A **party wall** can be an exterior wall of a building that straddles the boundary line between two lots, or it can be a commonly shared partition wall between two connected properties. Each owner holds in severalty that cross-portion of the wall on his or her tract subject to an easement, called a cross-easement, by the other owner for use of the wall as a perimeter wall of each owner's respective building and for its support. A party wall may be created by agreement, deed, or implied grant. Because a party wall involves an easement, the agreement should be in writing, as required by the statute of frauds. The right to a party wall can also arise by prescription, as where a surveyor's error causes a wall to encroach on adjoining land and such encroachment continues for the prescriptive period. The duty to repair a party wall falls equally on both owners, and one owner may not use his or her rights to the wall in such a way as to damage a neighbor. A *party driveway* shared by and partly on the land of adjoining owners must also be created by written agreement, specifying responsibility for expenses.

Easement by necessity.   An appurtenant easement that arises when an owner sells part of his or her land that has no access to a street or public way (except over the seller's remaining land) is an **easement by necessity.** An *easement by necessity is created by court order.* Such an easement arises because all owners have the right to enter and exit their land (the right of ingress and egress)—they cannot be landlocked. Remember: This form of easement is called an easement by *necessity;* it is not merely for convenience and is not imposed simply to validate a shortcut.

Easement by prescription.   When the claimant has made use of another's land for a certain period of time as defined by state law, an **easement by prescription,** or a *prescriptive easement,* may be acquired. The prescriptive period may vary from 10 years to 21 years in states. The claimant's use must have been continuous, exclusive, and without the owner's approval ("adverse"). The use must be visible, open, and notorious; that is, the owner must have been able to learn of it. A visible fence, continuous gardening on the back lot, or driving over property so often that ruts are visible are all examples.

| In Illinois | To establish an easement by prescription in Illinois, the use must be adverse, exclusive, under claim of right, and continuous and uninterrupted for a period of *20 years*. Illinois law permits owners of pedestrian walkways in shopping centers and large commercial or industrial buildings to prevent the establishment of prescriptive easements by the public. To block the establishment of a prescriptive easement, the owner of any property must display signs *or* send a certified letter stating that access to or use of the property is by permission (and thus not adverse). |

The concept of *tacking* provides that successive periods of continuous occupation by different parties may be combined (tacked) to reach the required total number of years necessary to establish a claim for a prescriptive easement. To tack on one person's possession to that of another, the parties must have been "successors in interest," such as an ancestor and his or her heir, a landlord and tenant, or a seller and buyer. ■

■ **FOR EXAMPLE** Jana's property is located in a state with a prescriptive period of 20 years. For the past 22 years, Frank has driven his car across Jana's front yard every day to reach his garage with ease. Frank has an easement by prescription.

■ For 25 years, Linda has driven across Jana's front yard two or three times a year to reach her property when she's in a hurry. She does *not* have an easement by prescription because her use has not been continuous.

■ For 15 years, Elliot parked his car on Jana's property, next to Jana's garage. Six years ago, Elliot sold his house to Ned, who continued to park his car next to Jana's garage. Last year, Ned acquired an easement by prescription through *tacking*.

Easement in gross.   An **easement in gross** is an individual interest in or right to use someone else's land. For instance, a railroad's right-of-way is an easement in gross. So is the right-of-way for a pipeline or high-tension power line (utility easements). Commercial easements in gross may be assigned, conveyed, and inherited. However, personal easements in gross usually are not assignable. A personal easement in gross typically terminates on the death of the easement owner. An easement in gross is often confused with the similar but less formal *personal right of license*, discussed later in this chapter.

Easement by condemnation.   An **easement by condemnation** is acquired for a public purpose, through the right of *eminent domain*. The owner of the servient tenement must be compensated for any loss in property value.

Terminating an easement.   An easement may be ended

■ when the purpose for which the easement was created no longer exists;

■ when the owner of either the dominant or the servient tenement becomes the owner of both properties (also known as *termination by merger*);

■ by release of the right of easement to the owner of the servient tenement;

■ by abandonment of the easement (the intention of the parties is legally important);

- by nonuse of a prescriptive easement;
- by adverse possession by the owner of the servient tenement;
- by destruction of the servient tenement (e.g., the demolition of a party wall);
- by lawsuit (*"action to quiet title"*) against someone claiming an easement; or
- by property conversion (e.g., a residential use is converted to a commercial purpose).

Note: an easement may *not* automatically terminate for those reasons. Certain legal steps may be required.

License

A **license** is a personal *privilege* (not a right) to enter the land of another for a specific purpose. A license differs from an easement in that it can be terminated or canceled by the *licensor* (the person who granted the license) at any time. If the use of another's property is given orally or informally, it generally is considered to be a license rather than a personal easement in gross. A license ends on the death of either party or the sale of the land by the licensor.

■ **FOR EXAMPLE** Bud asks Ruth for permission to park a boat in Ruth's driveway. Ruth says, "Sure, Bud, go ahead!" Bud has a license, but Ruth may tell Bud to move the boat at any time. Similarly, a ticket to a theater or sporting event is a license: the holder is permitted to enter the facility and is entitled to a seat. But if the ticketholder becomes rowdy or abusive, he or she may be asked to leave.

Encroachments

Survey Sketch—Sketches only lot outline
Spot Survey—Sketches lot *and* buildings

An **encroachment** occurs when all or part of a structure (such as a building, fence, or driveway) illegally extends beyond the land of its owner or beyond the legal building lines. An encroachment usually is disclosed by either a physical inspection of the property or a spot survey. A *spot survey* shows the location of all improvements located on a property and whether they extend over the lot or building lines. A spot survey is more informational and useful than a simple *survey sketch* with only the lot dimensions. If a spot survey and physical inspection show that a building encroaches on adjoining land, the neighbor may be able to either recover damages or secure removal of the portion of the building that encroaches. Unchallenged encroachments that last beyond a state's prescriptive period, however, may give rise to easements by prescription.

IN PRACTICE   Because an undisclosed encroachment could create a serious situation if discovered late in a transaction, any known encroachments should be noted in a listing agreement and in the sales contract. Spot surveys provide evidence of encroachments. However, the new survey may only become available fairly late in the transaction process. For this reason, listing agents often encourage sellers to attach an existent survey to listing materials if one is available.

■ NATURE AND WATER: RIGHTS AND RESTRICTIONS

Whether for agricultural, recreational, or other purposes, waterfront real estate has always been desirable. Each state has strict laws that govern the ownership and use of water as well as the adjacent land. The laws vary among the states, but all are closely linked to climatic and topographic conditions. Where water is plentiful, for instance, many states rely on the simple parameters set by the

FIGURE   7.6

Riparian Rights

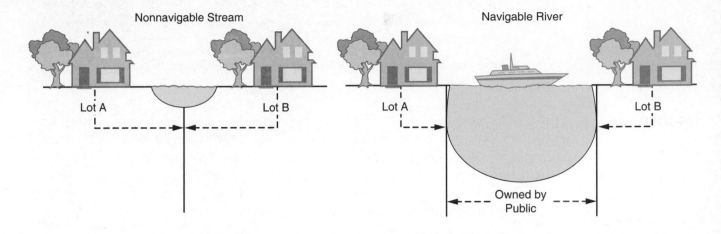

common-law doctrines of riparian and littoral rights. Where water is scarce, a state may control all but limited domestic use of water according to the doctrine of prior appropriation.

Riparian Rights

Riparian rights are common-law rights granted to owners of land along the course of a river, stream, or similar body of flowing water. Although riparian rights are governed by laws that vary from state to state, they generally include the unrestricted right to use the water. As a rule, the only limitation on the owner's use is that it cannot interrupt or alter the flow of the water or contaminate it in any way. In addition, an owner of land that borders a nonnavigable waterway (that is, a body of water unsuitable for commercial boat traffic) owns the land under the water to the exact center of the waterway.

> **Memory Tip**
>
> *Ri*parian refers to *ri*vers, streams, and similar waterways; *L*ittoral refers to *l*akes, oceans, and similar bodies of water.

Land adjoining commercially navigable rivers, on the other hand, usually is owned to the water's edge, with the state holding title to the submerged land. (See Figure 7.6.) Navigable waters are considered public waterways on which the public has an easement or right to travel.

Littoral Rights

Closely related to riparian rights are the **littoral rights** of owners whose land borders commercially navigable lakes, seas, and oceans. Owners with littoral rights enjoy unrestricted use of available waters, but own the land adjacent to the water only up to the mean high-water mark. (See Figure 7.7.) All land below this point is owned by the public.

Riparian and littoral rights are appurtenant (attached) to the land. The right to use the water belongs to whoever owns the bordering land and cannot be retained by a former owner after the land is sold.

Accretion, Erosion, and Avulsion

The amount of land an individual owns may be affected by the natural action of water. An owner is entitled to all land created through **accretion**—increases in the land resulting from the deposit of soil by the water's action. (Such deposits are called *alluvion* or *alluvium*.) If water recedes, new land is acquired by *reliction*.

FIGURE 7.7

Littoral Rights

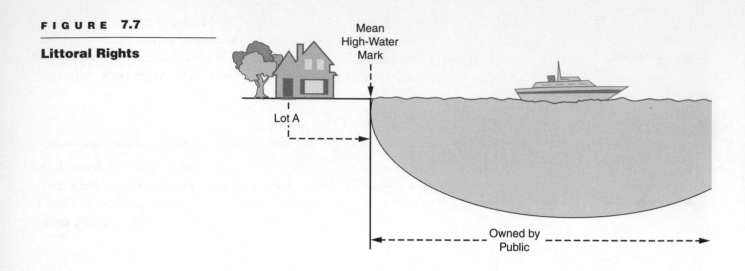

■ **FOR EXAMPLE** One famous example of soil deposits is visible in Galena, Illinois. The river running through town was large enough 150 years ago to help Galena become a major river port—the "largest in the West." Today, high and dry banks and old silt deposits can be seen that mark only faint memories of flowing water. In this case, accretion had a negative result. Because of silt deposits, the river became impassable by large ships within a few decades, changing the town's direction forever. Today, Galena is no longer a large trade port, but it has become a popular tourist destination with a rich history. It is also a prime example of major land, economic, and real estate development changes imposed by nature.

On the other hand, an owner may *lose land* through **erosion**. Erosion is the gradual and imperceptible wearing away of the land by natural forces such as wind, rain, and flowing water. Fortunately, erosion usually takes hundreds of years to have any noticeable effect on a person's property. Flash floods or heavy winds can increase the speed of erosion.

Avulsion is the sudden removal of soil by an act of nature. A major earthquake or a mudslide, for instance, can cause an individual's land holdings to become much smaller very quickly.

In Illinois

Those who sell Illinois real estate should be aware of the New Madrid fault, located mainly in Missouri but with potential impact on southern Illinois. Many geologists predict a serious New Madrid quake could occur at any time. ■

Doctrine of Prior Appropriation

In states where water is scarce, ownership and use of water are often determined by the **doctrine of prior appropriation**. Under this doctrine, the right to use any water, with the exception of limited domestic use, is *controlled by the state* rather than by the landowner adjacent to the water.

To secure water rights in prior appropriation states, a landowner must demonstrate to a state agency that she or he plans a *beneficial use* for the water, such as crop irrigation. If the state's requirements are met, the landowner receives a permit to use a specified amount of water for the limited purpose of the beneficial use. Although statutes governing prior appropriation vary from state to state, the priority of water rights is usually determined by the oldest recorded permit date.

Once granted, water rights attach to the land of the permit holder. The permit holder may sell a water right to another party. Issuance of a water permit does not automatically grant access to the water source. All rights of access over the land of another (easements) must be obtained by agreement from the property owner.

■ SUMMARY

Ownership of real estate is not absolute, since a landowner's power to control his or her property is subject to public controls and private restrictions. Individual ownership rights are subject to certain powers held by federal, state, and local governments. Government powers include police power, eminent domain, taxation, and escheat.

An estate is the degree, quantity, nature, and extent of interest a person holds in land. Freehold estates are estates of indeterminate length and last until they are sold or the owner dies, and then they pass freely by will to stated parties. Less-than-freehold estates are called *leasehold estates*, and they involve landlords and rent rather than sales contracts and owners.

A freehold estate may be a fee simple estate or a life estate. A fee simple estate can be absolute (sometimes just called a *fee*) or defeasible (rights affected by the happening of some event). A fee simple absolute is the highest form of real estate ownership, and comes with the most rights attached.

One type of defeasible fee, the fee simple determinable, is especially restrictive: The property automatically reverts to the original owner if a given promise or restriction is broken. Defeasible fees with condition subsequent must go to court for the original owner to gain right of re-entry over similar issues. Illinois limits right of reverter or re-entry by the original owner to a maximum length of 40 years. After that, the restrictions may still be enforced but the original owner may not take back the property.

A conventional life estate is created by the owner of a fee estate and involves measuring limited ownership rights by the life of the owner, the life tenant, or a third party. On the death of this individual, ownership shifts based on the original owner's instructions in the life estate.

Legal life estates are created by law and are quite different from other life estates: these life estates involve long-lived (for the life of the property) monetary rights granted to homeowners and spouses of homeowners. Common legal life estates in the United States include dower and curtesy and homestead rights.

In Illinois | In Illinois, dower and curtesy has been replaced by spousal "elective shares," based on the Uniform Probate Code. Illinois offers homestead rights of $15,000 per individual. This amount is protected from unsecured creditors. ■

Encumbrances against real estate can be legal or physical: liens, deed restrictions, easements such as driveways, licenses to use a property for a stated purpose, and physical encroachments such as fences or sheds built over a property line are all examples.

An easement is a right to use another's real estate. Easements are classified as interests in real estate but are not large enough in concept to be estates in land. There are two types of easements. Appurtenant easements involve two separately owned tracts. The tract benefited is known as the *dominant tenement;* the tract over which the easement is found is called the *servient tenement.* An easement in gross is a personal right, such as that granted to utility companies to maintain poles, wires, and pipelines. Personal easements in gross are possible and resemble a formalized license.

Easements may be created by agreement, express grant or reservation in a deed, by necessity, by prescription, or condemnation. An easement can be terminated when the purpose of the easement no longer exists, by merger of both interests, or by release or abandonment of the easement.

A license is permission to enter another's property for a specific purpose. A license usually is created orally and is temporary; it can easily be ended by the property owner. A personal easement in gross is more formal than a license, in writing, and cannot be terminated without cause.

Ownership of land encompasses not only the land itself but also the right to use the water on or adjacent to it. Many states subscribe to the common-law doctrine of riparian rights, which allows ownership of nonnavigable streams to their midpoint. Littoral rights are held by owners of land next to lakes and oceans; land rights here go to the mean high-water mark. In states where water is scarce, water use from natural flowing water is by doctrine of prior appropriation, and permits for water use are required, such as for watering crops.

| In Illinois | Local units of government and quasi-governmental bodies are granted the power of *eminent domain* by the Illinois Constitution. A *quick-take* in Illinois is a fast proceeding to obtain title, such as for highway construction. |

The Equity in Eminent Domain Act places the obligation on government to prove that an area is blighted before forcing property owners to sell their property for private development projects.

Real property escheats to the county in which it is located if no will was left and no heirs are found.

The period for an easement by prescription in Illinois is 20 years. ■

QUESTIONS

1. A city decides to build a new library. Which of the following terms would *BEST* describe the action taken by the city to acquire the land for the new library?

   a. Zoning would allow the city to take the land by granting a variance for the library.

   b. County laws permit the city to take the land by escheat so long as the property owners are paid just compensation.

   c. The city has the right to take the land by eminent domain as long as just compensation is paid the property owners.

   d. The sheriff would sell the property at a public sale and pay the owners just compensation, then the city could build the library.

2. A purchaser of real estate learned that his ownership rights could continue forever and that no other person could claim to be the owner or exert any ownership control over the property. This person owns a

   a. fee simple absolute interest.

   b. life estate.

   c. determinable fee estate.

   d. fee simple on condition.

3. Julia owned the fee simple title to a vacant lot adjacent to a hospital and was persuaded to make a gift of the lot. She wanted to have some control over its use, so her attorney prepared her deed to convey ownership of the lot to the hospital "so long as it is used for hospital purposes." After completion of the gift, the hospital will own a

   a. fee simple absolute estate.

   b. license.

   c. fee simple determinable.

   d. leasehold estate.

4. After Dennis had purchased his house and moved in, he discovered that his neighbor regularly used Dennis's driveway to reach a garage located on the neighbor's property. Dennis's attorney explained that ownership of the neighbor's real estate includes an easement over the driveway. Dennis's property is properly called

   a. the dominant tenement.

   b. a freehold.

   c. a leasehold.

   d. the servient tenement.

5. Bonnie is the owner of Blueacre. During her lifetime, Bonnie conveys a life estate in Blueacre to Carla. Under the terms of the grant, Carla's life estate will terminate when Bonnie's uncle dies. However, Carla herself dies shortly after moving to Blueacre, while Bonnie's uncle remains alive. Carla's will states, "I leave everything to Donald." Which of the following *BEST* describes the interests that the parties now hold?

   a. Carla possessed a life estate pur autre vie, measured by the life of Bonnie's uncle. Donald now has the same interest as Carla had. Donald's interest in Blueacre will end when Bonnie's uncle dies.

   b. Carla possessed a life estate pur autre vie, measured by the life of Bonnie's uncle. Donald is the remainderman and holds a nonpossessory estate until Bonnie's uncle dies. When Bonnie's uncle dies, Blueacre will escheat to the state.

   c. Carla possessed a determinable life estate in Blueacre. Bonnie's uncle is the measuring life. When Carla died, her interest passed directly to Donald. When Bonnie's uncle dies, Bonnie may regain ownership of Blueacre only by suing Donald.

   d. Bonnie has a remainder interest in the conventional life estate granted to Carla. Because the grant was to Carla alone, the estate may not pass to Donald. When Carla died before Bonnie's uncle, the estate automatically ended and Bonnie now owns Blueacre in fee simple.

6. Wendell owns a home in a state that recognizes homestead exemption. Which of the following statements is *TRUE* if Wendell is sued by his creditors?

   a. The creditors can have the court sell Wendell's home and apply the full proceeds of sale to the debts.

   b. The creditors have no right to have Wendell's home sold.

   c. The creditors can force Wendell to sell the home to pay them.

   d. The creditors can request a court sale and apply the sale proceeds, in excess of the statutory exemption and secured debts, to Wendell's unsecured debts.

7. If the owner of real estate does not take action against a persistent trespasser before the statutory period has passed, the trespasser may acquire

   a. an easement by necessity.
   b. a license.
   c. title by eminent domain.
   d. an easement by prescription.

8. Mark wants to use water from a river that runs through his property to irrigate a potato field. To do so, Mark is required by his state's law to submit an application to the Department of Water Resources describing in detail the beneficial use he plans for the water. If the department approves Mark's application, he will receive a permit to divert a limited amount of river water into his field. Based on these facts, it can be assumed that Mark's state relies on which of the following rules of law?

   a. Common-law riparian rights
   b. Common-law littoral rights
   c. Doctrine of prior appropriation
   d. Doctrine of highest and best use

9. Which is *NOT* a governmental power?

   a. Easement in gross
   b. Police power
   c. Eminent domain
   d. Taxation

10. Property deeded to a town "so long as" it is used "for recreational purposes" conveys a

    a. fee simple absolute.
    b. fee simple on condition precedent.
    c. leasehold interest.
    d. fee simple determinable.

11. Tonya has the legal right to pass over the land owned by her neighbor. This is a(n)

    a. estate in land.
    b. easement.
    c. police power.
    d. encroachment.

12. Which is *NOT* considered a legal life estate?

    a. Leasehold
    b. Husband's curtesy
    c. Homestead
    d. Wife's dower

13. A father conveys ownership of his residence to his daughter but reserves for himself a life estate in the residence. The interest the daughter owns during her father's lifetime is

    a. pur autre vie.   c. a reversion.
    b. a remainder.   d. a leasehold.

14. Kendra has just fenced her property. The fence extends one foot onto the property of a neighbor, Sophie. The fence is an example of a(n)

    a. license.
    b. encroachment.
    c. easement by necessity.
    d. easement by prescription.

15. Encumbrances on real estate

    a. include easements and encroachments.
    b. make it impossible to sell the encumbered property.
    c. must all be removed before the title can be transferred.
    d. established by condition subsequent.

16. Ken has permission from Aaron to hike on Aaron's property during the autumn months when the leaves are most colorful. Ken has a(n)

    a. easement by necessity.
    b. easement by prescription.
    c. determinable freehold interest.
    d. license.

17. In Illinois, the homestead exemption

    a. must be recorded with the county recorder to be in effect.

    b. is limited to $15,000 per person.

    c. can never be released.

    d. is limited to $15,000 per residence.

18. A conveyance of residential real estate by a married person also should be executed by that person's spouse

    a. to ensure the release of any potential homestead rights.

    b. only if the property is owned by both parties.

    c. to release dower rights.

    d. to comply with Illinois's community property laws.

19. In Illinois, a prescriptive easement may be

    a. established by 15 years of continuous, uninterrupted use without the owner's approval or permission.

    b. prevented by posting a "No Trespassing" sign in a prominent place on or near the boundary of the property.

    c. established by 20 years of continuous, uninterrupted, exclusive use under claim of right and without the owner's permission.

    d. defeated by showing that the adverse possession was not exercised by a single individual for the requisite period, but by successive parties in interest.

20. In Illinois, which of the following is *TRUE* when there is escheat of a decedent's real property?

    a. The decedent's heirs must receive just compensation for the property's fair market value, measured at the time of the decedent's death.

    b. The state laws of eminent domain apply.

    c. Ownership of the property goes to the county in which it is located.

    d. Ownership of the property goes to the state.

21. George died, leaving a lakefront cottage to his girlfriend for her use as long as she lives, with the provision that title shall pass equally to her children upon her death. The estate that George's girlfriend holds is a(n)

    a. fee simple estate.

    b. estate at will.

    c. determinable fee estate.

    d. life estate.

22. Illinois does *NOT* recognize

    a. curtesy.

    b. homestead.

    c. leasehold.

    d. fee simple determinable.

23. David made a gift of a house to Rhonda for Rhonda's lifetime, with a provision that the real estate will pass to Simone after Rhonda dies. Which of the following statements accurately describes these facts?

    a. Rhonda holds a life estate; Simone holds a reversionary interest; David has retained a reversionary interest.

    b. Rhonda holds a life estate; Simone holds a remainder interest.

    c. Rhonda holds an estate for years; Simone holds a life estate pur autre vie, measured by the life of Rhonda.

    d. Rhonda holds a life estate pur autre vie; Simone holds no interest in the house until after Rhonda dies; David has retained fee simple ownership under these facts.

24. In 2008, Evan conveyed Longacre to Ben in fee simple, on the condition that Longacre is never used as a theme park. Under Illinois law, when may Ben open a theme park on Longacre without fear of automatically losing ownership of the property?

    a. In the year 2028, 20 years after the date of the original conveyance, Ben will own Longacre free of any condition or limitation.

    b. In the year 2048, 40 years after the date of the original conveyance, Evan's condition may still be enforced, but Evan's right of reverter will expire.

    c. In the year 2058, 50 years after the date of the original conveyance, Evan's limitation will no longer be enforceable, and Evan's right of reverter will expire.

    d. There is no expiration period on conveyances of real property in Illinois.

CHAPTER 8

Forms of Real Estate Ownership

■ **LEARNING OBJECTIVES** *When you've finished reading this chapter, you should be able to*

■ **identify** the four basic forms of co-ownership.

■ **describe** the ways in which various business organizations may own property.

■ **explain** how a tenancy in common, joint tenancy, and tenancy by the entirety are created and how they may be terminated.

■ **distinguish** cooperative ownership from condominium ownership.

■ **define** the following *key terms:*

common elements	limited liability company	syndicate
community property	limited partnership	tenancy by the entirety
condominium	marital property	tenancy in common
cooperative	partition	time-share estate
co-ownership	partnership	time-share ownership
corporation	proprietary lease	time-share use
general partnership	right of survivorship	trust
joint tenancy	separate property	
joint venture	severalty	

■ **FORMS OF OWNERSHIP**

As we've seen in Chapter 7, many different interests in land exist—fee simple, life estates, and easements, for instance. Licensees also need to understand how these interests in real property may be held. Although questions about forms of ownership always should be referred to an attorney, brokers and salespersons must understand the fundamental types of ownership so they will know who must sign various documents. They also must know what form of ownership a purchaser wants and what options are possible when more than one individual will take title.

Although the forms of ownership available are controlled by state laws, a fee simple estate may be held in three basic ways:

- In *severalty*, where title is held by one individual
- In *co-ownership*, where title is held by two or more individuals
- In *trust*, where a third individual holds title for the benefit of another

■ OWNERSHIP IN SEVERALTY

When title to real estate is owned by *one individual*, that individual is said to have ownership in **severalty.** The term comes from the fact that this sole owner is "severed" or "cut off" from other owners. The severalty owner has sole rights to the ownership and sole discretion over the transfer of the ownership. When either a husband or wife owns property in severalty, state law may affect how ownership is held.

| In Illinois | Sole ownership of property is quite common in Illinois, and title held in severalty presents no unique legal problems. However, when either a husband or wife owns property in severalty, lenders, grantees, and title insurers in Illinois usually do require that the spouse sign in order to release any potential homestead rights. This is true for both listing and sales contracts. *A nonowning spouse who is a minor also will have to sign.* ■ |

■ CO-OWNERSHIP

When title to one parcel of real estate is held by two or more individuals, those parties are called *co-owners* or *concurrent owners*. Most states commonly recognize various forms of **co-ownership.** Individuals may co-own property as tenants in common, joint tenants, or tenants by the entirety, or they may co-own *community property* in states recognizing community property.

| In Illinois | Illinois recognizes co-ownership and most traditional forms of co-ownership as discussed in this chapter *except* for community property (Illinois is a *marital property* state). Illinois also recognizes ownership in trust, in partnership, and by commercial entities such as corporations and limited liability companies. ■ |

Tenancy in Common   A parcel of real estate may be owned by two or more people as tenants in common. In a **tenancy in common,** each tenant holds what is called an *undivided fractional interest* in the property. A tenant in common may hold, for example, a one-half or one-third interest in a property. *The physical property, however, is not divided into a specific half or third.* That is why it is called an undivided fractional interest. The co-owners have *unity of possession;* that is, they are entitled to *possession* of the whole property. It is the ownership interest, not the property, that is divided.

FIGURE 8.1

Tenancy in Common

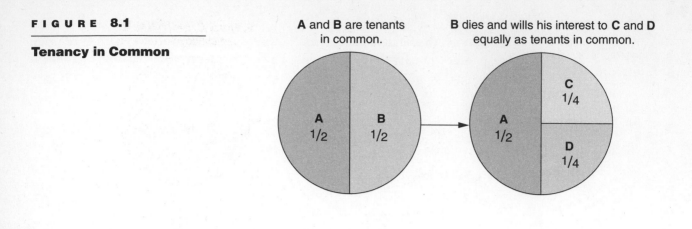

The deed creating a tenancy in common may or may not state the fractional interest held by each co-owner. If no fractions are stated, the tenants are presumed to hold equal shares. For example, if five people hold title, each would own an undivided one-fifth interest if nothing else is stated.

In Illinois

In Illinois, a single deed may show the proportional interests of each tenant in common, *or* a separate deed issued to each tenant may show his or her individual proportional interest. When a single deed is used, lack of a description of each tenant's share means all tenants hold equal, undivided shares.

Tenants in common also hold their ownership interests in *severalty*. In other words, because the co-owners own separate interests, each can sell, convey, mortgage, or transfer his or her interest. *The consent of the other co-owners is not needed.* When one co-owner dies, the tenant's undivided interest passes according to his or her will. (See Figure 8.1.)

In Illinois, the law presumes that two or more owners hold title as tenants in common if the deed does not state specifically how title is to be held. ∎

Joint Tenancy

Most states recognize some form of **joint tenancy** in property owned by two or more people. The feature that distinguishes a joint tenancy from a tenancy in common is *unity of ownership*. Title is held as though all owners collectively constitute one unit. The death of one joint tenant does not destroy the ownership unit; it only reduces by one the number of people who make up the unit. This occurs because of the **right of survivorship.** The joint tenancy continues until only one owner remains. This owner then holds title in severalty. The right of survivorship applies only to the co-owners of the joint tenancy; it cannot pass to their heirs.

As each successive joint tenant dies, the surviving joint tenants acquire the deceased tenant's interest. The last survivor takes title in severalty and has all the rights of sole ownership, including the right to pass the property to his or her heirs. (See Figure 8.2.)

Four Forms of Co-Ownership

1. Tenancy in common
2. Joint tenancy
3. Tenancy by the entirety
4. Community property

Creating joint tenancies. A joint tenancy can be created only by the intentional act of conveying a deed or giving the property by will. It cannot be implied or created by operation of law. The deed must specifically state the parties' intention to create a joint tenancy, and the parties must be explicitly identified as joint tenants. Some states have abolished the right of survivorship as the distinguishing

FIGURE   8.2

Joint Tenancy With Right of Survivorship

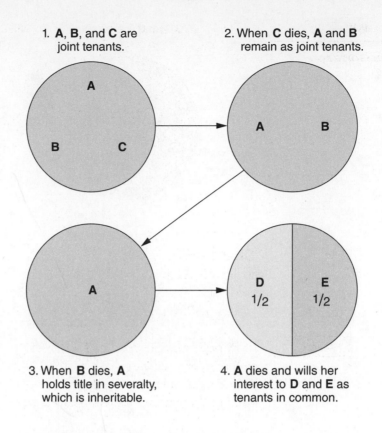

1. **A**, **B**, and **C** are joint tenants.

2. When **C** dies, **A** and **B** remain as joint tenants.

3. When **B** dies, **A** holds title in severalty, which is inheritable.

4. **A** dies and wills her interest to **D** and **E** as tenants in common.

characteristic of joint tenancy. In these states, the deed must explicitly indicate the intention to create the right of survivorship for that right to exist.

Four "unities" are required to create a joint tenancy:

1. Unity of *possession*—all joint tenants holding an undivided right to possession
2. Unity of *interest*—all joint tenants holding equal ownership interests
3. Unity of *time*—all joint tenants acquiring their interests at the same time
4. Unity of *title*—all joint tenants acquiring their interests by the same document

The four unities are present when the following requirements are met:

1. Title is acquired by one deed.
2. The deed is executed and delivered at one time.
3. The deed conveys equal interests to all of the parties.
4. The parties hold undivided possession of the property as joint tenants.

Because the unities must be satisfied, many states require the use of an intermediary when a sole owner wishes to create a joint tenancy between himself or herself and others. The owner conveys the property to a *nominee*, or *straw man*. Then the nominee conveys it back, naming all the parties as joint tenants in the deed. As a result, all the joint tenants acquire title at the same time by one deed.

Typical wording in a deed creating a joint tenancy would be: "*To A and B as joint tenants and not as tenants in common.*"

Memory Tip

The four unities necessary to create a joint tenancy may be remembered by the acronym **PITT:** *Possession, Interest, Time,* and *Title*.

In Illinois

Illinois has eliminated this "legal fiction," and it allows a sole owner to execute a deed to himself or herself and others "as joint tenants and not as tenants in common" in order to create a valid joint tenancy. In the 1983 Illinois Supreme Court case *Minonk State Bank v. Gassman*, the court held that a joint tenant may

FIGURE 8.3

Combination of Tenancies

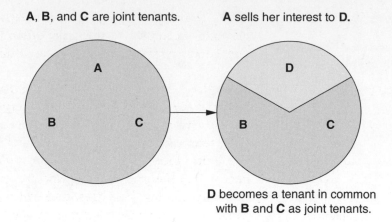

A, B, and C are joint tenants.

A sells her interest to D.

D becomes a tenant in common
with B and C as joint tenants.

unilaterally sever the tenancy by *conveying to himself or herself as a tenant in common even without the consent of co-owners.* This means that any owner holding property in a joint tenancy may elect at any time to become a tenant in common, at which time that particular owner may will his or her interest to heirs or sell it. Any joint tenancy may be severed by mutual agreement of all co-tenants, by conveying to third parties, or through a partition suit in the courts. ■

Terminating joint tenancies.   A joint tenancy is destroyed when any one of the four unities of joint tenancy is terminated. If a tenant conveys his or her interest in the jointly held property, doing so destroys the unity of interest. The new owner cannot become a joint tenant and will hold interest as a tenant in common. Rights of other joint tenants, however, are unaffected.

■   **FOR EXAMPLE**   A, B, and C hold title to Blackacre as joint tenants. A conveys her interest to D. D now owns a fractional interest in Blackacre as a tenant in common with B and C, who continue to own their undivided interest as joint tenants. (See Figure 8.3.) D is presumed to have a one-third interest, which may be reconveyed or left to D's heirs.

Termination of Co-Ownership by Partition Suit

Cotenants who wish to terminate their co-ownership may file an action in court to partition the property. **Partition** is a legal way to dissolve the relationship when the parties do not voluntarily agree to its termination. (A partition suit is also sometimes referred to as a *suit to partition.*)

In Illinois

An Illinois partition suit may be filed by one or more of the owners in the circuit court of the county in which the subject parcel is located. The court appoints one or three commissioners who must, if possible, divide the property by legal description among the owners in title. If such division cannot be made without harming the rights of the co-owners, the commissioners must report a valuation of the property. The property is then offered for public sale at a price not less than two-thirds of the value as set by the commissioners.

All defendants to the suit (the co-owners who object to the partition) are required to pay their proportionate share of court costs and the lawyer fees of the plaintiff (the co-owner who is seeking partition). However, this requirement may be waived if the defendants have a sound and substantial defense. On completion of the sale, confirmation of the sale by the court, and delivery of a proper conveyance to the purchaser at the sale, the proceeds of the sale are delivered to the former cotenants according to the court order. Generally, the proceeds of the sale are divided among the former owners according to their fractional interests. ∎

Tenancy by the Entirety

Some states, including Illinois, allow husbands and wives to use a special form of co-ownership called **tenancy by the entirety** for their personal residence. In this form of ownership, each spouse has an equal, undivided interest in the property. (The term *entirety* refers to the fact that the owners are considered one indivisible unit: Under early common law, a married couple was viewed as one "legal person.") A husband and wife who are tenants by the entirety have rights of survivorship. During their lives, they can convey title only by a deed *signed by both parties*. One party may not convey a one-half interest, and generally they have no right to partition or divide.

> Tenancy by the Entirety for Married Couples (a special joint tenancy):
> - Right of survivorship
> - No probate delays
> - If lawsuits against spouse—no liens
> - No half-interests
> - To convey, *both* must sign
> - Only for personal residence

The main reason married couples own property by the entirety is that a lawsuit against one of the spouses will not put a lien on the house. A married couple owning property by the entirety would be eligible for homestead protection in the event of a judgment against either the husband or the wife. In addition, on the death of one spouse, the survivor automatically becomes the sole owner. Married couples often take title to property as tenants by the entirety so the surviving spouse can enjoy the benefits of ownership without the delay of probate proceedings.

In Illinois

Tenancy by the entirety is recognized in Illinois. To create a tenancy by the entirety, the deed must

- indicate that the property is to be owned "*not as joint tenants or tenants in common, but as tenants by the entirety*."

A tenancy by the entirety may be terminated in several ways:

Memory Tip

The methods of terminating a tenancy by the entirety may be remembered by the acronym *JSDAD: Judgment Sale, Death Agreement,* or *Divorce*

- By a court-ordered sale of the property to satisfy a judgment against the husband and wife as joint debtors (the tenancy is dissolved so that the property can be sold to pay the judgment)
- By the death of either spouse (the surviving spouse becomes sole owner in severalty)
- By agreement between both parties (through the execution of a new deed)
- By divorce (which leaves the parties as tenants in common) ∎

Community Property

Community property laws are based on the idea that a husband and wife, rather than merging into one entity, are equal partners in the marriage. Any property acquired during a marriage is considered to be obtained by mutual effort. Various states' community property laws vary widely. Essentially, however, all community property states recognize two kinds of property: separate property and community property.

Separate property is real or personal property that was owned solely by either spouse before the marriage. It also includes property acquired by gift or inheritance during the marriage, as well as any property purchased with separate funds during the marriage. Any income earned from a person's separate property belongs to that individual. Separate property can be mortgaged or conveyed by the owning spouse without the signature of the nonowning spouse.

Community property consists of all other property, both real and personal, acquired by either spouse during the marriage. Any conveyance or encumbrance of community property requires the signatures of both spouses. When one spouse dies, the survivor automatically owns one-half of the community property. The other half is distributed according to the deceased spouse's will.

If a community property spouse dies without a will, the other half is inherited by the surviving spouse or by the decedent's other heirs, depending on state law. *Community property does not provide an automatic right of survivorship as do joint tenancy and tenancy by the entirety.*

In Illinois

Illinois is *not* a community property state. However, as a **marital property** state, Illinois bears certain similarities to community property states, but with important differences. It, too, breaks property down into two major categories based on marital status: marital property and nonmarital property. Illinois law recognizes that a husband and wife acquire joint rights in all property acquired after the date of marriage for the duration of the marriage. Illinois labels such property *marital property*, all of which will be divided between the two parties in the event of a divorce.

Nonmarital property is property that was acquired prior to the marriage *or by gift or inheritance at any time*, even during the marriage. If nonmarital property is exchanged for other property, if it increases in value, or if it returns income, the exchange, increase, or income also would be considered *nonmarital property* (property belonging to the individual). If nonmarital property is commingled with marital property, however, a presumption of *transmutation* is created: the resulting "mixed" property is presumed to be marital property. The spouses may execute an express contract agreeing to exclude certain property from being classified as marital property.

The *Illinois Marriage and Dissolution of Marriage Act* gives the courts flexibility in determining the precise division of marital property. This is a difference from community property states, which often impose a strict 50-50 division unless a prenuptial agreement is in place. ■

See Table 8.1 for a brief description of the forms of co-ownership.

■ TRUSTS

A **trust** is a device by which one person transfers ownership of property to someone else to hold or manage for the benefit of a third party. Perhaps a grandfather who wishes to ensure the college education of his granddaughter transfers his oil field to the grandchild's mother. He instructs the mother to use income from the trust to pay for the grandchild's college tuition. In this case, the grandfather is the *trustor*—the person who creates the trust. The granddaughter is the *beneficiary*—the person who benefits from the trust. The mother is the *trustee*—the party who holds legal title to the property and is entrusted with carrying out the trustor's instructions regarding the purpose of the trust. The trustee is a *fiduciary*, who acts

TABLE 8.1		Property Held	Property Conveyed
Forms of Co-Ownership	Tenancy in Common	Each tenant holds a fractional undivided interest.	Each tenant can convey or devise his or her interest, but not entire interest.
	Joint Tenancy	Unity of ownership. Created by intentional act; unities of possession, interest, time, title.	Right of survivorship; cannot be conveyed to heirs.
	Tenancy by the Entirety	Husband and wife have equal undivided interest in their personal residence.	Right of survivorship; convey by deed signed by both parties. One party can't convey one-half interest.
	Community Property	Husband and wife are equal partners in marriage. Real or personal property acquired during marriage is community property.	Conveyance requires signature of both spouses. No right of survivorship; when spouse dies, survivor owns one-half of community property. Other one-half is distributed according to will or, if no will, according to state law.

in confidence or trust and has a special legal relationship with the beneficiary. The trustee's power and authority are limited by the terms of the trust agreement, will, or deed in trust.

IN PRACTICE

The legal and tax implications of setting up a trust are complex and vary widely from state to state. Attorneys and tax experts should always be consulted on the subject of trusts.

Most states allow real estate to be held in trust. Depending on the type of trust and its purpose, the trustor, trustee, and beneficiary can all be either people or legal entities such as corporations. Trust companies are corporations set up for this specific purpose.

In Illinois

Illinois permits real estate to be held in trust as part of a living or testamentary trust or as the sole asset in a land trust. ∎

Real estate can be owned under living or testamentary trusts and land trusts. It also can be held by a group of investors in a *real estate investment trust (REIT)*.

Living and Testamentary Trusts

A property owner *may provide for his or her own financial care or for that of the owner's family by establishing a trust.* This trust may be created by agreement during the property owner's lifetime (*living trust*, also called *inter vivos trust*) or established by will after the owner's death (*testamentary trust*).

The person who creates the trust conveys real or personal property to a trustee (usually a corporate trustee), with the understanding that the trustee will assume certain duties. These duties may include the care and investment of the trust assets to produce an income. After paying the trust's operating expenses and trustee's fees, the income is paid to or used for the benefit of the beneficiary. The trust may continue for the beneficiary's lifetime, or the assets may be distributed when the beneficiary reaches a certain age or when other conditions are met.

Land Trusts

A few states, including Illinois, permit the creation of *land trusts, in which real estate is the only asset.* As in all trusts, the title to the property is conveyed to a trustee, and the beneficial interest belongs to the beneficiary. In the case of land trusts, however, the beneficiary usually is also the trustor. While the beneficial interest is personal property, the beneficiary retains management and control of the real property and has the right of possession and the right to any income or proceeds from its sale.

> **Land Trusts**
> - Trustor often is beneficiary
> - Trustee often is bank
> - Beneficiary Interest = Personal Property
> - Fully private ownership
> - Useful in probate proceedings

One of the distinguishing characteristics of a land trust is that the public records usually do not name the beneficiary. A land trust may be used for secrecy when assembling separate parcels. There are other benefits as well. A beneficial interest in a land trust is personal property and can be transferred by assignment, making the formalities of a deed unnecessary. The beneficial interest in property can be pledged as security for a loan without having a mortgage recorded. Because the beneficiary's interest is personal, it passes at the beneficiary's death under the laws of the state in which the beneficiary lived. If the deceased owned property in several states, additional probate costs and inheritance taxes can be avoided.

In Illinois Land trusts are used in Illinois. However, Illinois law requires that the trustee disclose the beneficiary's name to certain parties under specific circumstances.

The beneficiary's name must be revealed

- to the concerned housing authority within ten days after receiving a complaint of a violation of a building ordinance or law.
- when applying to any state of Illinois agency for a license or permit affecting the entrusted real estate.
- if selling the entrusted property by land contract (seller financing).
- if the trustee is named as a defendant in a private lawsuit or criminal complaint regarding the subject real estate. The beneficiary's identity can then be "discovered" by the plaintiff.
- if a fire inspector or another officer is investigating arson. ■

A land trust ordinarily continues for a definite term, such as 20 years. If the beneficiary (who may also be the trustor, or original owner) does not extend the trust term when it expires, the trustee usually is obligated to sell the real estate and return the net proceeds to the beneficiary.

IN PRACTICE

Licensees should be cautious in using the term *trust deed.* It can mean both a *deed in trust* (which relates to the creation of a living, testamentary, or land trust) and a *deed of trust* (a financing document similar to a mortgage). Because these documents are not interchangeable, using an inaccurate term can cause serious misunderstandings.

Real Estate Investment Trust

A real estate investment trust (REIT) is a method of pooling investment money using the trust form of ownership. In the 1960s Congress provided favored tax treatments for certain business trusts by exempting from corporate tax certain qualified REITs that invest at least 75 percent of their assets in real estate and that distribute 95 percent or more of their annual real estate ordinary income to their investors. As an alternative to the partnership or corporate methods of investing in real estate, the REIT offers some of the flow-through tax advantages of a partnership or syndication while retaining many of the attributes and advantages of a corporate operation. Investors purchase certificates of ownership in the trust, which in turn invests the money in real property and then distributes any profits to the investors free of corporate tax. As a part owner of real property, the shareholder pays normal income tax on the ordinary income from the trust and receives capital gains treatment for any capital gains distribution.

Some advantages of the REIT are avoidance of corporate tax, centralized management, continuity of operation, transferability of interests, diversification of investment and the benefit of skilled real estate advice. Some of the disadvantages are that investments are passive in nature and usually restricted to very large real estate transactions; losses cannot be passed through to the investor to offset his or her income and usually the trust must be registered with the Securities and Exchange Commission.

The rules for REITs have been liberalized, making them a more attractive investment vehicle. The new law eases shareholder income, and asset requirements for the first year that an entity qualifies as a REIT. Income and asset requirements are eased for the first year after a REIT receives new equity capital or certain new debt capital. In addition to these breaks, REITs will be permitted to hold assets in wholly owned subsidiaries.

Other rules have been eased for when a sale constitutes a prohibited transaction, the amount of capital gain dividends a REIT may pay, penalties on distributions of deficiency dividends, definitions of rents and interest, treatment of shared appreciation mortgage income and distribution requirements relating to income not accompanied by the receipt of cash.

■ OWNERSHIP OF REAL ESTATE BY BUSINESS ORGANIZATIONS

A business organization is a legal entity that exists independently of its members. Ownership by a business organization makes it possible for many people to hold an interest in the same parcel of real estate. Investors may be organized to finance a real estate project in various ways. Some provide for the real estate to be owned by the entity; others provide for direct ownership by the investors.

Partnerships

A **partnership** is an association of two or more persons who carry on a business for profit as co-owners. In a **general partnership,** all the partners participate in the operation and management of the business and share full liability for business losses and obligations. A **limited partnership,** on the other hand, consists of one or more general partners as well as limited partners. The business is run by the general partner or partners. The limited partners are not legally permitted to participate, and each can be held liable for business losses only to the extent of his or her investment. The limited partnership is a popular method of organizing investors because it permits investors with small amounts of capital to participate in large real estate projects with a minimum of personal risk.

In Illinois

Illinois has adopted the federal *Uniform Partnership Act* (UPA), which permits real estate to be held in the partnership name. The *Uniform Limited Partnership Act* (ULPA) also has been widely adopted. It establishes the legality of the limited partnership entity and provides that realty may be held in the limited partnership's name. Profits and losses are passed through the partnership to each partner, whose individual tax situation determines the tax consequences. ∎

General partnerships are dissolved and must be reorganized if one partner dies, withdraws, or goes bankrupt. In a limited partnership, however, the partnership agreement may provide for the continuation of the organization following the death or withdrawal of one of the partners.

Corporations

A **corporation** is a legal entity (an artificial person) created under the authority of the laws of the state from which it receives its charter. A corporation is managed and operated by its *board of directors*. The *charter* sets forth the powers of the corporation, including its right to buy and sell real estate (based on a resolution by the board of directors). Because the corporation is a legal entity, it can own real estate in severalty or as a tenant in common. Some corporations are permitted by their charters to purchase real estate for any purpose; others are limited to purchasing only the land necessary to fulfill the entities' corporate purposes.

In Illinois   The creation and regulation of corporations in Illinois are governed by the *Illinois Business Corporation Act*. The federal *Uniform Partnership Act* also applies. ∎

As a legal entity, a corporation continues to exist until it is formally dissolved. The death of one of the officers or directors does not affect title to property owned by the corporation.

Individuals participate, or invest, in a corporation by purchasing stock. Because stock is personal property, shareholders do not have direct ownership interest in real estate owned by a corporation. Each shareholder's liability for the corporation's losses is usually limited to the amount of his or her investment.

One of the main disadvantages of corporate ownership of income property is that the profits are subject to double taxation. As a legal entity, a corporation must file an income tax return and pay tax on its profits. The portion of the remaining profits distributed to shareholders as dividends is taxed again as part of the shareholders' individual incomes.

An alternative form of business ownership that provides the benefit of a corporation as a legal entity but avoids double taxation is known as an *S corporation*. Only the shares of the profits that are passed to the shareholders are taxed. The profits of the S corporation are not taxed. Though there is no limitation on the amount of corporate income for an S corporation, the shareholders are limited to 100. S corporations are subject to strict requirements regulating their structure, membership, and operation. If the IRS determines that an S corporation has failed to comply with these detailed rules, the entity will be redefined as some other form of business organization, and its favorable tax treatment will be lost.

Syndicates and Joint Ventures

Generally speaking, a **syndicate** is two or more people or firms joined together to make and operate a real estate investment. A syndicate is not in itself a legal entity; however, it may be organized into a number of ownership forms, including co-ownership (tenancy in common, joint tenancy), partnership, trust, or corporation. A **joint venture** is a form of partnership in which two or more people or firms carry out a single business project. The joint venture is characterized by a time limitation resulting from the fact that the joint venturers do not intend to establish a permanent relationship.

Limited Liability Companies

The **limited liability company** (LLC) is a relatively recent form of business organization. An LLC combines the most attractive features of limited partnerships and corporations. The members of an LLC enjoy the limited liability offered by a corporate form of ownership and the tax advantages of a partnership. In addition, the LLC offers flexible management structures without the complicated requirements of S corporations or the restrictions of limited partnerships. The structure and methods of establishing a new LLC or of converting an existing entity to the LLC form vary from state to state.

> In Illinois

With passage of the *Illinois Limited Liability Company Act* in 1994, Illinois joined the majority of states that recognize limited liability companies as legitimate business organizations. ■

■ CONDOMINIUMS, COOPERATIVES, AND TIME-SHARES

Home ownership does not refer only to ownership of a brick bungalow on a grassy lawn surrounded by a white picket fence. A growing urban population, diverse lifestyles, changing family structures, and heightened mobility have created a demand for new types of real estate and ownership. Condominiums, cooperatives, and time-share arrangements creatively addressed our society's changing real estate needs.

Condominium Ownership

Condominium properties have become increasingly popular throughout the United States. Condominium laws, often called *horizontal property acts*, have been enacted in every state. Under these laws, the owner of each unit holds a fee simple title to the unit. The individual unit owners also own a specified share of the undivided interest in the remainder of the building and land, known as the **common elements.** Common elements typically include such items as land, courtyards, lobbies, the exterior structure, hallways, elevators, stairways, and the roof, as well as recreational facilities such as swimming pools, tennis courts, and golf courses. (See Figure 8.4.) The individual unit owners own these common elements as *tenants in common*. As such, each has a fractional, undividable interest in the common locations, meaning the interest can be sold (along with the condo), but not any actual part of the common elements. State law usually provides, however, that unit owners do not have the same right to partition that other tenants in common have.

Condominium ownership is not restricted to highrise buildings. Lowrises, town houses (also known as row houses), and detached structures can all be owned using the condominium model for common elements and governing boards for group decisions.

Creation of a condominium.   Many states have adopted the *Uniform Condominium Act* (UCA). Under its provisions, a condominium is created and established when the owner of an existing building (or the developer of unimproved property) executes and records a detailed report and description of the property called a *declaration of condominium*.

FIGURE 8.4

Condominium Ownership

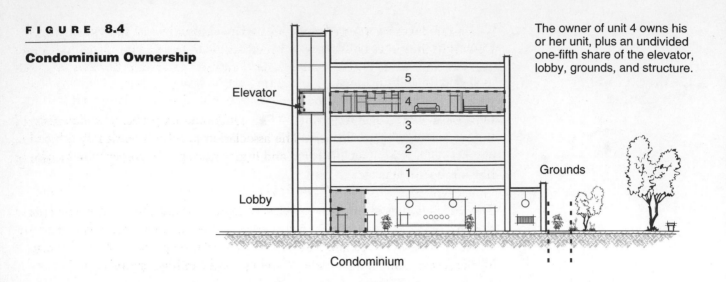

The owner of unit 4 owns his or her unit, plus an undivided one-fifth share of the elevator, lobby, grounds, and structure.

Elevator

Lobby

Grounds

Condominium

In Illinois

Illinois has not adopted the *Uniform Condominium Act*. In Illinois, creation of condominiums is governed by the *Illinois Condominium Property Act (765 ILCS 605/)*. Under this law, an owner/developer may elect to submit a parcel of real estate as a condominium situation by recording a declaration to which is attached a three-dimensional plat of survey of the parcel showing the location and size of all units in the building. (*A building built on leased land may not be submitted for condominium designation in Illinois.*) Every unit purchaser acquires the fee simple title to his or her unit, together with the percentage of ownership of the common elements that is set forth in the declaration and that belongs to that unit. This percentage is computed on the basis of the initial list prices of each unit.

The survey required with each declaration of condominium ownership must indicate the dimensions of each unit. This survey will show the outlines of the lot, the size and shape of each apartment, and the elevation or height above base datum for the upper surface of the floor level and the lower surface of the ceiling level. The difference between these two levels represents the airspace owned in fee simple by the unit owner.

Illinois Condominium Property Act

www.legis.state.il.us
- Click on Illinois Compiled Statutes
- Click on Chapter 765
- Click on 765 ILCS 605/

Many Illinois municipalities have adopted *conversion ordinances* to protect tenants in rental buildings whose owners wish to convert to condominiums. The ordinances also protect prospective purchasers. These laws typically allow tenants an opportunity to extend their leases and often guarantee first purchase rights. Additional protections often include disclosure of all material information, structural soundness of the building, adequacy of parking, and a variety of other concerns. These ordinances generally have been upheld by the courts as a valid exercise of police power. ■

Ownership. Once the property is established as a condominium, each unit becomes a separate parcel of real estate that is owned in fee simple and may be held by one or more persons in any type of ownership or tenancy recognized by state law. A condominium unit may be mortgaged like any other parcel of real estate. The unit usually can be sold or transferred to whomever the owner chooses, unless the condominium association provides for a right of first refusal. In this case, the owner is required to offer the unit at the same price to the other owners in the condominium or the association before accepting an outside purchase offer.

Real estate taxes are assessed and collected on each unit as an individual property. Default in the payment of taxes or a mortgage loan by one unit owner may result in a foreclosure sale of that owner's unit. One owner's default, however, does not affect the other unit owners.

Operation and administration.   The condominium property is administered by an *association of unit owners*. The association may be governed by a board of directors or another official entity, and it may manage the property on its own or hire a property manager.

The association must enforce any rules it adopts regarding the operation and use of the property. The association is responsible for the maintenance, repair, cleaning, and sanitation of the common elements and structural portions of the property. It also must maintain fire, extended-coverage, and liability insurance.

The expenses of maintaining and operating the building are paid by the unit owners in the form of fees and assessments. Both fees and assessments are imposed and collected by the owners' association. Recurring fees (referred to as *assessments* or *condo fees*) are paid by each unit owner. The fees often are due monthly, but the schedule may be quarterly, semiannually, or annually, depending on the provisions of the bylaws. The size of an individual owner's fee is generally determined by the size of his or her unit. For instance, the owner of a three-bedroom unit pays a larger share of the total expense than the owner of a one-bedroom unit. If the fees are not paid, the association may seek a court-ordered judgment to have the delinquent owner's unit sold to cover the outstanding amount.

Special assessments are special payments required of unit owners to address some specific expense, such as a new roof. Assessments are structured in the same way as condo fees: owners of larger units pay proportionately higher assessments.

In Illinois

While the above condominium guidelines generally apply under the *Condominium Property Act* in Illinois, the property may be removed from condominium status at any time by the unanimous consent of all owners and all lienholders, as evidenced by a recorded written instrument. All owners would then be tenants in common. ■

Cooperative Ownership

In a **cooperative**, a corporation holds title to the land and building. The corporation offers shares of stock to prospective tenants.

The price the corporation sets for each apartment becomes the price of the stock. The purchaser becomes a shareholder in the corporation by virtue of this stock ownership and receives a **proprietary lease** to the apartment for the life of the corporation. *Because stock is personal property, the cooperative tenant-owners do not own real estate.* Instead, they own an interest in a corporation that has only one asset: the building.

Operation and management.   The operation and management of a cooperative are determined by the corporation's bylaws. *Through their control of the corporation, the shareholders of a cooperative control the property and its operation.* They elect officers and directors who are responsible for operating the corporation and its real estate assets. Individual shareholders are obligated to abide by the corporation's bylaws.

An important issue in most cooperatives is the method by which shares in the corporation may be transferred to new owners. The bylaws may require that the board of directors approve any prospective shareholders. In some cooperatives, a tenant-owner must sell the stock back to the corporation at the original purchase price so that the corporation realizes any profits when the shares are resold. In others, if the stock is sold for the latest "going price" on the unit, stock profits may go to the departing tenant or at least be shared.

■ **FOR EXAMPLE** In a highly publicized incident, former President Richard Nixon's attempt to move into an exclusive Manhattan cooperative apartment building was blocked by the cooperative's board. In refusing to allow the ex-president to purchase shares, the board cited the unwanted publicity and media attention other tenants would suffer.

The corporation incurs costs in the operation and maintenance of the entire parcel, including both the common property and the individual apartments. These costs include real estate taxes and any mortgage payments the corporation may have. The corporation also budgets funds for such expenses as insurance, utilities, repairs and maintenance, janitorial and other services, replacement of equipment, and reserves for capital expenditures. Funds for the budget are assessed to individual shareholders, generally in the form of monthly fees similar to those charged by a homeowners' association in a condominium.

Unlike in a condominium association, which has the authority to impose a lien on the title held by a unit owner who defaults on maintenance payments, the burden of any defaulted payment in a cooperative falls on the remaining shareholders. Each shareholder is affected by the financial ability of the others. For this reason, approval of prospective tenants by the board of directors frequently involves financial evaluation. If the corporation is unable to make mortgage and tax payments because of shareholder defaults, the property might be sold by court order in a foreclosure suit. This could destroy the interests of all shareholders, including those who have paid their assessments.

Advantages. Cooperative ownership, despite its risks, has become desirable in recent years for several reasons. Lending institutions view the shares of stock as acceptable collateral for financing. The availability of financing extends the possible transfer of shares to modest purchasers in many co-ops. As a tenant-owner, rather than a tenant who pays rent to a landlord, the shareholder has some control over the property. Tenants in cooperatives also enjoy certain income tax advantages in regard to deductability of property taxes and mortgage loan interest. Finally, owners enjoy freedom from maintenance.

In Illinois

Illinois real estate brokers and salespersons are permitted to list and sell cooperative units and interests without obtaining a securities license. ■

Time-Share Ownership

Time-share ownership permits multiple purchasers to buy interests in real estate, usually a resort property. Each purchaser receives the right to use the facilities for a certain period of time. A *time-share estate* includes a real property interest in condominium ownership; a *time-share use* is a contract right in which a third party retains ownership of the real estate.

In Illinois

The promotion or sale of all time-share units is strictly regulated by the Illinois *Real Estate Time-Share Act of 1999 (765 ILCS 101)*. The *Time-Share Act* applies to both in-state and out-of-state time-share sales. In addition, a person who engages in the sale of time-shares must have a real estate license pursuant to the *Real Estate License Act of 2000*. Certain exemptions to the licensing requirement apply:

■ An exchange company registered under the *Real Estate Time-Share Act of 1999* and their regular employees

■ An existing time-share owner who, for compensation, refers prospective purchasers, but only if the existing time-share owner refers no more than 20 prospective purchasers in any calendar year; receives no more than $1,000 or its equivalent, for referrals in any calendar year; and limits his or her activities to referring prospective purchasers of time-share interests to the developer or the developer's employees or agents, and does not show, discuss terms or conditions of purchase, or otherwise participate in negotiations with regard to time-share interests ■

A **time-share estate** is a fee simple interest. The owner's occupancy and use of the property are limited to the contractual period purchased. The owner is assessed for maintenance and common area expenses based on the ratio of the ownership period to the total number of ownership periods in the property. Time-share estates theoretically never end because they are real property interests. However, the physical life of the improvements is limited and must be looked at carefully when considering such a purchase.

The principal difference between a time-share estate and a time-share use lies in the interest transferred to an owner by the developer of the project. A **time-share use** consists of the right to occupy and use the facilities for a certain number of years. At the end of that time, the owner's rights in the property terminate. In effect, the developer has sold only a right of occupancy and use to the owner, not a fee simple interest.

In Illinois

The Illinois *Real Estate Time-Share Act of 1999* requires that all developers and their agents must register with the IDFPR. Each purchaser must be given a detailed *public offering statement* before signing the contract, disclosing extensive information about the property, time periods, percentage of common expenses for each unit, use and occupancy restrictions, and total number of units. The statement also must include information about the developer and property management.

Any purchase contract entered into by a purchaser of a time-share interest shall be voidable by the purchaser, without penalty, within five calendar days after the receipt of the public offering statement or the execution of the purchase contract, whichever is later. The purchase contract shall provide notice of the five-day cancellation period, together with the name and mailing address to which any notice of cancellation shall be delivered.

Upon such cancellation, the developer or resale agent shall refund to the purchaser all payments made by the purchaser, less the amount of any benefits actually received pursuant to the purchase contract. The refund shall be made within 20 calendar days after the receipt of the notice of cancellation, or receipt of funds from the purchaser's cleared check, whichever occurs later.

The *Real Estate Time-Share Act of 1999* places developers and their agents under strict requirements regarding potential misrepresentation, such as predicting specific or immediate market value increases or disclosure of details of any prizes offered. Violations can result in the suspension or revocation of a certificate or permit issued under the act. ■

Membership camping is similar to time-share use. The owner purchases the right to use the developer's facilities, which usually consist of an open area with minimal improvements (such as camper and trailer hookups and restrooms). Normally, the owner is not limited to a specific time for using the property; use is limited only by weather and access.

IN PRACTICE

The laws governing the development and sale of time-share units are complex. In addition, the sale of time-share properties may be subject to federal securities laws. In many states, time-share properties are now subject to subdivision requirements. Real estate professionals providing assistance on time-shares need to be well-versed in the laws, benefits, and risks of such ownership.

■ SUMMARY

Sole ownership, or ownership in severalty, means that title is held by one natural person or legal entity. Under co-ownership, title can be held concurrently by more than one person or legal entity in several ways.

Tenancy in common provides that each party holds separate title but shares possession of the whole property with the other owners, each of which has separate interests. Upon the death of a tenant in common, his or her interest passes to any legal heirs. When two or more parties hold title to real estate in Illinois, they do so as tenants in common by default unless they express another intention.

Joint tenancy indicates two or more owners with the right of survivorship. The intention of the parties to establish a joint tenancy must be stated clearly. The four unities of possession, interest, time, and title (PITT) must be present.

Tenancy by the entirety, in those states where it is recognized (including Illinois), is a type of joint tenancy between husband and wife. It gives the couple the right of survivorship in all lands they acquired during marriage. During their lives, both must sign the deed for any title to pass to a purchaser. Liens may not be placed on a property held in this way if such liens are the result of one spouse's legal problems. Community property exists only in certain states, such as California. Usually, the property acquired by combined efforts during the marriage is community property, and each spouse owns one-half, but with no right of survivorship. (Properties acquired by a spouse before the marriage and through inheritance or gifts during the marriage are considered separate property.)

In Illinois

Illinois is a marital property state. Any property acquired during the marriage is likely to be viewed as marital, shared property unless it is by gift or inheritance to only one spouse. This is true even for real estate set up as ownership in severalty during the marriage. If nonmarital inherited property or gift monies are commingled, transmutation can legally transform them into marital property. Divorce laws in Illinois give courts flexibility in distributing marital property. ■

Real estate ownership may be held in trust. All trusts involve three conceptual parts: trustor, trustee, and beneficiary. In a land trust (common in Illinois), the trustor and the beneficiary are typically the same party. To create any trust, the trustor conveys title and visible control to a third-party trustee, for the benefit of the beneficiary. Names of the owners of a land trust are not usually available, except in court suits or building violations involving the subject property, arson investigations, or other legally noted exceptions.

Various types of business organizations may own real estate. A corporation is a legal entity and can hold title to real estate in severalty. While a partnership is technically not a legal entity, the Uniform Partnership Act and the Uniform Limited Partnership Act, adopted by most states, recognize a partnership as an entity that can own property in the partnership's name. A limited liability company (LLC) combines the limited liability offered by a corporate form with the tax advantages of a partnership without the complicated requirements of S corporations or the restrictions of limited partnerships. A syndicate is simply an association of two or more people or firms that invest in real estate. Many syndicates are joint ventures assembled for only a single project.

Cooperatives are a form of ownership in which actual title is held by one entity (a corporation or trust) which pays taxes, mortgage interest, and principal, as well as all operating expenses. Shareholders occupy the units, buy initial stock, and/ or also pay monthly assessments in order to do so. They sometimes share in stock profits when they depart the building and their "shares" are sold.

In a condominium setting, each owner-occupant holds fee simple title to a unit plus a share of the common elements. Each unit owner receives an individual tax bill and may mortgage the unit. His or her bankruptcy or default does not affect other building occupants. Expenses for operating the building are collected by an owners' association through monthly assessments.

Time-sharing enables multiple purchasers to own estates or "use interests" in real estate, with the right to use the property for a part of each year.

QUESTIONS

1. The four unities of possession, interest, time, and title are associated with which of the following?
   a. Community property
   b. Severalty ownership
   c. Tenants in common
   d. Joint tenancy

2. What is the difference between tenancy in common and joint tenancy?
   a. Tenancy in common is characterized by right of survivorship; joint tenancy is characterized by unity of possession.
   b. Tenancy in common ownership must contain specific wording; joint tenancy is presumed by the law when two or more people own property unless the deed states otherwise.
   c. Under tenancy in common ownership each owner has the right to sell, mortgage, or lease his or her interest without the consent of the other owners; this is not true in joint tenancy.
   d. Tenancy in common is an inheritable estate; joint tenancy is characterized by the right of survivorship.

3. Martin, Bianca, and Francine are joint tenants with rights of survivorship in a tract of land. Francine conveys her interest to Victor. Which of the following statements is *TRUE*?
   a. Martin and Bianca are still joint tenants.
   b. Martin, Bianca, and Victor are joint tenants.
   c. Martin, Bianca, and Victor are tenants in common.
   d. Victor now has severalty ownership.

4. Hanna owns one of 20 townhouses in the Luxor Lakes development. Hanna owns the townhouse in fee simple and a 5 percent ownership share of the parking facilities, recreation center, and grounds. What does Hanna own?
   a. Cooperative
   b. Condominium
   c. Time-share
   d. Land trust

5. John conveys a vineyard in trust to Raul, with the instruction that any income derived from the vineyard is to be used for Tina's medical care. Which of the following statements most accurately describes the relationship of these parties?
   a. John is the trustee, Raul is the trustor, and Tina is the beneficiary.
   b. John is the trustor, Raul is the trustee, and Tina is the beneficiary.
   c. John is the beneficiary, Raul is the trustor, and Tina is the trustee.
   d. John is the trustor, Raul is the beneficiary, and Tina is the trustee.

6. Dan and Sara are married. Under the laws of their state, any real property that either owns at the time of their marriage remains separate property. Further, any real property acquired by either party during the marriage (except by gift or inheritance) belongs to both of them equally. This form of ownership is called
   a. a partnership.
   b. joint tenancy.
   c. tenancy by the entirety.
   d. community property.

7. Emma, Jack, and Igor were co-owners of a parcel of real estate. Jack died, and his interest passed according to his will to become part of his estate. Jack was a
   a. joint tenant.
   b. tenant in common.
   c. tenant by the entirety.
   d. severalty owner.

8. A legal arrangement under which the title to real property is held to protect the interests of a beneficiary is a
   a. trust.
   b. corporation.
   c. limited partnership.
   d. general partnership.

9. Which statement is *TRUE* regarding a cooperative?
   a. Title to the land and building are held by different owners.
   b. Unit owners hold real property interests.
   c. Maintaining and operating a cooperative is paid for by the corporation from charges assessed to unit owners, generally in the form of monthly fees.
   d. Because their proprietary leases are real property, unit owners are exempt from the fees or assessments condominium owners are often required to pay for building maintenance and operation.

10. Ollie purchases an interest in a house in Beachfront. Ollie is entitled to the right of possession only between July 10 and August 4 of each year. Which of the following is *MOST LIKELY* the type of ownership Ollie purchased?
    a. Cooperative
    b. Condominium
    c. Time-share estate
    d. Life estate

11. Because a corporation is a legal entity (an artificial person), real estate owned by it is owned in
    a. trust.
    b. partnership.
    c. severalty.
    d. survivorship tenancy.

12. Which is a form of co-ownership?
    a. Severalty
    b. Sole owner
    c. Tenancy at will
    d. Joint tenancy

13. Terri and Ron are married and co-own Blueacre, with a right of survivorship. Theirs is most likely
    a. severalty ownership.
    b. community property.
    c. a tenancy in common.
    d. an estate by the entirety.

14. Which involves a fee simple interest?
    a. Tenancy for years
    b. Ownership in severalty
    c. Tenancy at will
    d. Tenancy at sufferance

15. Goldacre is owned by Frank, George, and Hank as tenants in common. When George dies, to whom will his interest pass?
    a. Frank and Hank equally
    b. George's heirs
    c. The state, by the law of escheat
    d. Frank and Hank in joint tenancy

16. Which of the following best proves one's right to live in a cooperative?
    a. Tax bill for the individual unit
    b. Existence of a reverter clause
    c. Shareholder's stock certificate
    d. Right of first refusal

17. Shellie lives in the elegant Howell Tower. Her possessory interest is evidenced by a proprietary lease. What does Shellie own?
    a. Condominium unit
    b. Cooperative unit
    c. Time-share
    d. Leasehold

18. Which of the following statements applies to both joint tenancy and tenancy by the entirety?
    a. There is no right to file a partition suit.
    b. The survivor becomes a severalty owner.
    c. A deed signed by one owner will convey a fractional interest.
    d. A deed will not convey any interest unless signed by both spouses.

19. Theo owns a fee simple interest in a lakefront cottage, along with 5 percent of the parking lot, laundry room, and boat house. Theo owns a
    a. membership camping interest.
    b. time-share estate.
    c. cooperative unit.
    d. condominium unit.

20. If property is held by two or more owners as tenants with survivorship rights, the interest of a deceased cotenant will be passed to the
    a. surviving owner or owners.
    b. heirs of the deceased.
    c. state under the law of escheat.
    d. trust under which the property was owned.

21. Which of the following statements is *TRUE* according to the Illinois Real Estate Time-Share Act?

    a. Developers, but not their agents, are required to register with the IDFPR.

    b. Purchasers must be given a disclosure statement about the property immediately after signing the purchase contract.

    c. Purchasers have 24 hours in which to request a disclosure statement from a developer.

    d. The statute guarantees purchasers a five-day right to rescind a time-share purchase contract.

22. The names of the beneficiaries of a land trust must be revealed by the trustee to

    a. any member of the public who is interested in the beneficiary's identity.

    b. any Illinois agency when applying for a license or permit affecting the entrusted real estate.

    c. any unsecured creditor of the beneficiary.

    d. a licensed real estate broker, if the broker is assisting in the sale or rental of the entrusted property.

23. Every co-owner of real estate in Illinois has the right to file a suit for partition when the property is held in which of the following ways?

    a. Joint tenancy or tenancy in common

    b. Land trust

    c. Condominium or cooperative

    d. Time-share use or estate

24. Title to land in Illinois may be held and conveyed in which of the following ways?

    a. In the name of a partnership

    b. As joint tenants only if the property is owned by a husband and wife as their principal residence

    c. As tenants in common with rights of survivorship

    d. All of the above

25. If the deed of conveyance to Illinois land transfers title to two or more co-owners without defining the character of the co-ownership, which of the following statements is *TRUE*?

    a. The property is construed as being held in joint tenancy.

    b. The co-owners are tenants in common.

    c. While proper in some states, such a deed would be an invalid conveyance under Illinois law.

    d. By statute, such co-owners would have the right of survivorship.

26. Ben and Cheri held title to an apartment building as joint tenants with rights of survivorship. Ben and Cheri had an argument, and Ben didn't like the possibility that Cheri would acquire total ownership of the building if Ben died. Therefore, Ben executed a deed to himself as a tenant in common and later willed his interest to Jenna. If these facts occurred in Illinois, which of the following statements accurately describes Ben's action?

    a. Ben's action is illegal under Illinois law.

    b. While not necessarily illegal, Ben's action has no effect on the joint tenancy.

    c. Ben's goal of severing the joint tenancy can be accomplished only by a partition suit.

    d. Ben's action legally severs the joint tenancy.

27. Which of the following is necessary to convert an apartment building to condominium ownership in Illinois?

    a. The owner records a condominium declaration with a three-dimensional plat.

    b. The owner must record a certificate stating that the current tenants have been duly surveyed and that a majority of all tenants are in favor of the conversion.

    c. The existing tenants elect a board of directors having the power to act as legal administrator for the property, and the board petitions the state under the Condominium Property Act for certification as a condominium.

    d. The owner must execute and record a declaration of condominium under the Uniform Condominium Act as adopted in Illinois.

Legal Descriptions

■ **LEARNING OBJECTIVES** *When you've finished reading this chapter, you should be able to*

■ **identify** the three methods used to describe real estate.

■ **describe** how a survey is prepared.

■ **explain** how to read a rectangular survey description.

■ **distinguish** the various units of land measurement.

■ **define** the following *key terms:*

air lots	government survey system	point of beginning
base lines	legal description	principal meridians
bench marks	lot-and-block (or recorded plat) system	ranges
correction line	metes-and-bounds method	rectangular survey system
datum	monuments	sections
fractional sections	plat map	townships
government check		township lines
government lots		township squares
		township tiers

■ DESCRIBING LAND

People often refer to real estate by its street address, such as "1234 Main Street." While that usually is enough for the average person to find a particular building, it is not precise enough to be used on documents affecting the ownership of land. For instance, sales contracts, deeds, mortgages, and trust deeds require a much more specific, *legally sufficient*, description of property to be binding.

Courts have stated that a description is "legally sufficient" if it allows a competent surveyor to locate the parcel. In this context, however, "locate" means *the surveyor must be able to define the exact boundaries of the property*. The street address "1234 Main Street" would not tell a surveyor how large the property is or where it begins and ends. Several alternative systems of identification have been developed that express a **legal description** of real estate.

■ METHODS OF DESCRIBING REAL ESTATE

Three basic methods can be used to describe real estate:

1. Metes and bounds
2. Rectangular (or government) survey
3. Lot and block (recorded plat)

Although each method can be used independently, the methods may be combined in some situations. Some states use only one method; others use all three.

Metes-and-Bounds Method

The **metes-and-bounds method** is the oldest type of legal description. *Metes* means distance, and *bounds* means compass directions or angles. The method relies on a property's physical features to determine the boundaries and measurements of the parcel. A metes-and-bounds description always starts at a designated place on the parcel, called the **point of beginning** (POB). From there, the surveyor proceeds around the property's boundaries. The boundaries are recorded by referring to linear measurements, natural and artificial landmarks (called *monuments*), and directions. A metes-and-bounds description always ends back at the POB so that the tract being described is completely enclosed.

Monuments are fixed objects used to identify the POB, the ends of boundary segments, or the location of intersecting boundaries. A monument may be a natural object, such as a stone, large tree, lake, or stream. It may also be a man-made object, such as a street, highway, fence, canal, or markers (iron pins or concrete posts) placed by surveyors. Measurements often include the words "more or less" because the location of the monuments is more important than the distances given in the wording. In other words, the actual distance between monuments takes precedence over any linear measurements in the description.

An example of a metes-and-bounds description of a parcel of land (pictured in Figure 9.1) follows:

> *A tract of land located in Red Skull, Boone County, Virginia, is described as follows: Beginning at the intersection of the east line of Jones Road and the south line of Skull Drive; then east along the south line of Skull Drive 200 feet; then south 15° east 216.5 feet, more or less, to the center thread of Red Skull Creek; then northwesterly along the center line of said creek to its intersection with the east line of Jones Road; then north 105 feet, more or less, along the east line of Jones Road to the point of beginning.*

FIGURE 9.1

Metes-and-Bounds Tract

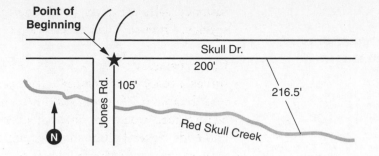

When used to describe property within a town or city, a metes-and-bounds description may begin as follows:

> *Beginning at a point on the southerly side of Kent Street, 100 feet easterly from the corner formed by the intersection of the southerly side of Kent Street and the easterly side of Broadway; then. . . .*

In this description, the POB is given by reference to the corner intersection. *Again, the description must eventually close by returning to the POB.*

IN PRACTICE

Metes-and-bounds descriptions can be complex and should be handled with extreme care. When they include detailed compass directions or concave and convex lines, these descriptions can be hard to understand. Natural deterioration or destruction of the monuments in a description can make boundaries difficult to identify. For instance, "Raney's Oak" may have died long ago, and "Hunter's Rock" may no longer exist. Computer programs are available that convert the data of the compass directions and dimensions to a drawing that verifies that the description represents a closed figure. *Professional surveyors should be consulted for definitive interpretations of any legal description.*

In Illinois

Metes-and-bounds descriptions are used in Illinois when describing irregular tracts, portions of a recorded lot, or fractions of a section. Such descriptions always incorporate the rectangular survey method and refer to the section, township, range, and principal meridian of the land. These elements are described in the following section. ■

Rectangular (Government) Survey System

The **rectangular survey system**, sometimes called the **government survey system**, was established by Congress in 1785 to standardize the description of land acquired by the newly formed federal government. This system is based on two sets of intersecting lines: principal meridians and base lines. The **principal meridians** run north and south, and the **base lines** run east and west. Both are located by reference to degrees of longitude and latitude. Each principal meridian has a name or number and is crossed by a base line. Each principal meridian and its corresponding base line are used to survey a definite area of land, indicated on the map by boundary lines.

Each principal meridian describes only specific areas of land by boundaries. No parcel of land is described by reference to more than one principal meridian. The meridian used is not necessarily the nearest one.

FIGURE 9.2

**Rectangular Survey
System Map**

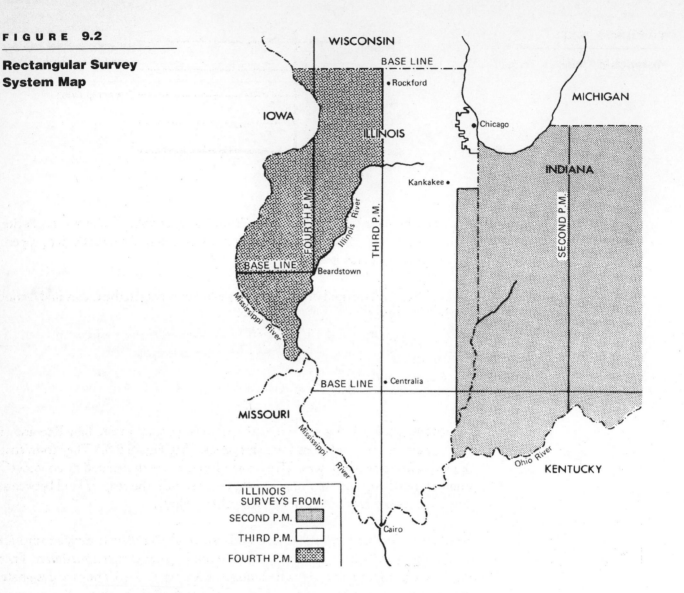

In Illinois Locations in Illinois are described by their relation to one of the three meridians shown on the map in Figure 9.2. Note that only two of these three meridians actually run through Illinois, but nevertheless all are sometimes referenced in legal descriptions for Illinois properties.

The *Second Principal Meridian* is located in Indiana and controls that portion of Illinois lying south and east of Kankakee. The *Third Principal Meridian* begins at Cairo, at the junction of the Ohio and Mississippi rivers, and extends northward toward Wisconsin and near Rockford to the Illinois-Wisconsin border. The *Fourth Principal Meridian* begins near Beardstown and extends northward to the Canadian border. Surveys of land located in the western portion of Illinois use a base line for the Fourth Principal Meridian at Beardstown. Surveys of land in Wisconsin and eastern Minnesota are made from the Fourth Principal Meridian using a base line that is on the Illinois-Wisconsin border.

Not all property is described by reference to the nearest principal meridian. Looking at the Illinois map in Figure 9.2, you will see that a property on the western border of the Third Principal Meridian and just west of Rockford will nevertheless be

FIGURE 9.3

Township Lines

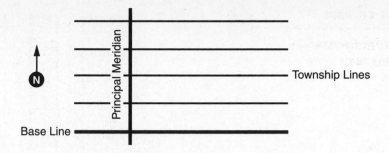

described by reference to the Fourth Principal Meridian. There are no options with regard to the meridians and base lines used to describe a particular property; *once made, a legal description will not change.* ■

Further divisions are used in the same way as monuments in the metes-and-bounds method. They are

- townships,
- ranges,
- sections, and
- quarter-section lines.

Township tiers.   Lines running east and west, parallel to the base line and six miles apart, are referred to as **township lines.** (See Figure 9.3.) They form strips of land called **township tiers.** These township tiers are designated by consecutive numbers north or south of the base line. For instance, the strip of land between 6 and 12 miles north of a base line is Township 2 North.

Ranges.   The land on either side of a principal meridian is divided into six-mile-wide strips by lines running north and south, parallel to the meridian. These north-south strips of land are called **ranges.** (See Figure 9.4.) They are designated by consecutive numbers east or west of the principal meridian. For example, Range 3 East would be a strip of land between 12 and 18 miles east of its principal meridian.

Township squares.   When the horizontal township lines and the vertical range lines intersect, they form squares. These **township squares** are the basic units of the rectangular survey system. (See Figure 9.5.) **Townships** are 6 miles square and contain 36 square miles (23,040 acres).

FIGURE 9.4

Range Lines

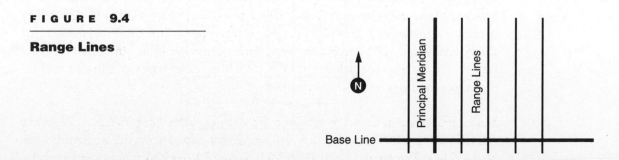

FIGURE 9.5

Townships in the Rectangular Survey System

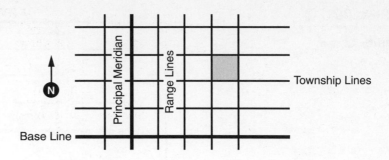

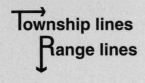
Note that although a township *square* is part of a township *tier*, the two terms do not refer to the same thing. Township tiers are the very long strips of six-mile-wide land running east and west. In this discussion, the word *township* used by itself refers only to the *township squares* formed by the vertical range lines intersecting the tiers.

Each township is given a legal description. The township's description includes the following:

■ Designation of the township tier in which the township is located
■ Designation of the range strip
■ Name or number of the principal meridian for that area

■ **FOR EXAMPLE** In Figure 9.5, the township indicated by a gray box is described as Township 3 North, Range 4 East of the Principal Meridian (an Illinois legal description would name the 2nd, 3rd, or 4th principal meridian, naming the meridian specifically). This township is the third strip, or tier, north of the base line, and it designates the township number and direction. The township is also located in the fourth range strip (those running north and south) east of the principal meridian. Finally, reference is made to the principal meridian because the land being described is within the boundary of land surveyed from that meridian. An actual description, then, might be abbreviated as T3N, R4E 4th Principal Meridian.

Sections. Each township contains *36 sections. Each section is one square mile, or 640 acres. Sections* are numbered 1 through 36, as shown in Figure 9.6. Section 1 is always in the northeast, or upper right-hand, corner. The numbering proceeds right to left (backward), beginning in the upper right-hand corner. From there,

FIGURE 9.6

Sections in a Township

			N		
6	5	4	3	2	1
7	8	9	10	11	12
18	17	16	15	14	13
19	20	21	22	23	24
30	29	28	27	26	25
31	32	33	34	35	36

W (left) E (right) S (bottom)

FIGURE 9.7

A Section

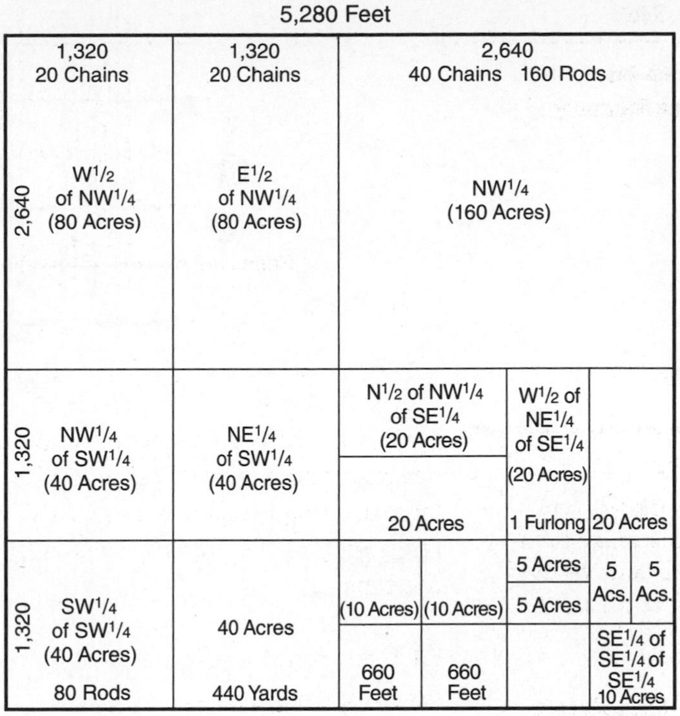

5,280 Feet

1,320 20 Chains	1,320 20 Chains	2,640 40 Chains 160 Rods			
2,640 — W½ of NW¼ (80 Acres)	E½ of NW¼ (80 Acres)	NW¼ (160 Acres)			
1,320 — NW¼ of SW¼ (40 Acres)	NE¼ of SW¼ (40 Acres)	N½ of NW¼ of SE¼ (20 Acres) —— 20 Acres	W½ of NE¼ of SE¼ (20 Acres) 1 Furlong	20 Acres	
1,320 — SW¼ of SW¼ (40 Acres) 80 Rods	40 Acres 440 Yards	(10 Acres) 660 Feet	(10 Acres) 660 Feet	5 Acres 5 Acres	5 Acs.	5 Acs. SE¼ of SE¼ of SE¼ 10 Acres

the numbers drop down to the next tier and continue from left to right, then back from right again to left. By law, each section number 16 is set aside for school purposes. The sale or rental proceeds from section 16 were originally available for township school use. The schoolhouse was often located in this section so it would be centrally located for all of the students in the township. As a result, *Section 16 is always referred to as the school section.*

Sections (see Figure 9.7) are divided into halves (320 acres) and quarters (160 acres). In turn, each of those parts may be further divided into halves and quarters. The southeast quarter of a section, which is a 160-acre tract, is abbreviated SE¼. The SE¼ of the SE¼ of the SE¼ of Section 1 would be a ten-acre square in the lower right-hand corner of Section 1.

The rectangular survey system sometimes uses a shorthand method in its descriptions. For instance, a comma may be used in place of the word *of*: SE¼, SE¼, SE¼, Section 1. It is possible to combine portions of a section, such as NE¼ of SW¼ and N½ of NW¼ of SE¼ of Section 1, which could also be written NE¼, SW¼; N½, NW¼, SE¼ of Section 1. A semicolon means "and." Because of the word *and* in this description, tallying first the total amount of land on each side of "and" (or the semicolon), then adding those two numbers together for area, gives 60 acres.

Correction lines.   Range lines are parallel only in theory. Due to the curvature of the earth, *range lines gradually approach each other.* If they are extended northward, they eventually meet at the North Pole. The fact that the earth is not flat, combined with the crude instruments used in early days, means that few townships are exactly six-mile squares or contain exactly 36 square miles. *The system compensates for this "round earth problem" with correction lines.* (See Figure 9.8.) Every fourth township line, both north and south of the base line, is designated

Memory Tip

Townships are numbered in a backward **S-curve**, beginning at the upper right; right to left, then curving left to right, then right to left.

FIGURE 9.8

Correction Lines and Guide Meridians

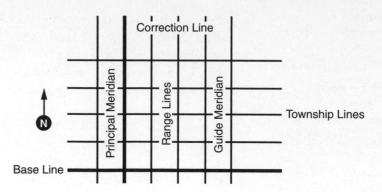

a **correction line**. On each correction line, the range lines are measured to the full distance of six miles apart. Guide meridians run north and south at 24-mile intervals from the principal meridian. A **government check** is the irregular area created by these corrections; such an area is about 24 miles square.

Because most townships do not contain exactly 36 square miles, surveyors follow well-established rules of adjustment. These rules provide that any irregularity in a township must be adjusted in those sections adjacent to its north and west boundaries (Sections 1, 2, 3, 4, 5, 6, 7, 18, 19, 30, and 31). These are called *fractional sections* (discussed below). All other sections are exactly one square mile and are known as *standard sections*. These provisions for making corrections explain some of the variations in township and section acreage under the rectangular survey system of legal description.

Fractional sections and government lots. Undersized or oversized sections are classified as **fractional sections**. Fractional sections may occur for a number of reasons. In some areas, for instance, the rectangular survey may have been made by separate crews, and gaps less than a section wide remained when the surveys met. Other errors may have resulted from the physical difficulties encountered in the actual survey. For example, part of a section may be submerged in water.

Areas smaller than full quarter-sections were numbered and designated as **government lots** by surveyors. These lots can be created by the curvature of the earth, by land bordering or surrounding large bodies of water, or by artificial state borders. An *overage* or a *shortage* was corrected whenever possible by placing the government lots in the north or west portions of the fractional sections. For example, a government lot might be described as *Government Lot 2 in the northwest quarter of fractional Section 18, Township 2 North, Range 4 East of the Salt Lake Meridian*.

Reading a rectangular survey description. To determine the location and size of a property described in the rectangular (or government) survey style, start at the end and work backward to the beginning. In other words, *analyze the legal description right to left*. For example, consider the following description:

The S½ of the NW¼ of the SE¼ of Section 11, Township 8 North, Range 6 West of the Fourth Principal Meridian.

To locate this tract of land from the citation alone, first search for the Fourth Principal Meridian on a map of the United States. Then, on a regional map, find the township in which the property is located by counting six range strips west of the Fourth Principal Meridian and eight townships north of its corresponding base line. After locating Section 11, divide the section into quarters. Then divide the SE¼ into quarters, and then the NW¼ of that into halves. The S½ of that NW¼ contains the property in question.

In computing the size of this tract of land, first determine that the SE¼ of the section contains 160 acres (640 acres divided by 4). The NW¼ of that quarter-section contains 40 acres (160 acres divided by 4), and the S½of that quarter-section—the property in question—contains 20 acres (40 acres divided by 2).

In general, if a rectangular survey description does not use the conjunction *and* or a semicolon (indicating two or more parcels are combined), the *longer* the description, the *smaller* the tract of land it describes.

Legal descriptions should always include the name of the county and state in which the land is located because meridians often relate to more than one state and occasionally relate to two base lines.

For example, the description "the southwest quarter of Section 10, Township 4 North, Range 1 West of the Fourth Principal Meridian" could refer to land in either Illinois or Wisconsin.

Metes-and-bounds descriptions within the rectangular survey system.   Land in states that use the rectangular survey system also may require a metes-and-bounds description. This usually occurs in one of three situations: when describing an irregular tract; when a tract is too small to be described by quarter-sections; or when a tract does not follow the lot or block lines of a recorded subdivision or section, quarter-section lines, or other fractional section lines. The following is an example of a combined metes-and-bounds and rectangular survey system description (see Figure 9.9):

> *That part of the northwest quarter of Section 12, Township 10 North, Range 7 West of the Third Principal Meridian, bounded by a line described as follows: Commencing at the southeast corner of the northwest quarter of said Section 12 then north 500 feet; then west parallel with the south line of said section 1,000 feet; then south parallel with the east line of said section 500 feet to the south line of said northwest quarter; then east along said south line to the point of beginning.*

Must-Know Measurements

Sections are smaller than townships.

Township = 6 miles × 6 miles = 36 sections per township.

Section = 1 mile × 1 mile = 1 square mile

43,560 = square feet per acre

5,280 feet in a mile (one side of a section)

FIGURE 9.9

Metes and Bounds with Rectangular Survey

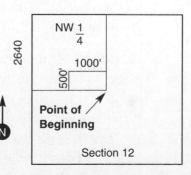

"Section 12, T10N, R7W, Third Principal Meridian"

| In Illinois |

Metes-and-bounds descriptions may be included in the rectangular survey system used in Illinois when describing irregular or small tracts. ■

Lot-and-Block System

The third method of legal description is the **lot-and-block** (or **recorded plat**) system. This system uses *lot-and-block numbers* referred to in a **plat map** filed in the public records of the county where the land is located. The lot-and-block system is often used to describe property in subdivisions.

A lot-and-block survey is performed in two steps. First, a large parcel of land is described either by metes and bounds or by rectangular survey. Once this large parcel is surveyed, it is broken into smaller parcels. As a result, a lot-and-block legal description is always a smaller part of a metes-and-bounds or rectangular survey description. For each parcel described under the lot-and-block system, the *lot* refers to the numerical designation of any particular parcel. The *block* refers to the name of the subdivision under which the map is recorded. The block reference is drawn from the early 1900s, when a city block was the most common type of subdivided property.

The lot-and-block system starts with the preparation of a *subdivision plat* by a licensed surveyor or an engineer. (See Figure 9.10.) On this plat, the land is divided into numbered or lettered lots and blocks, and streets or access roads for public use are indicated. Lot sizes and street details must be described completely

F I G U R E   9.10

Subdivision Plat Map

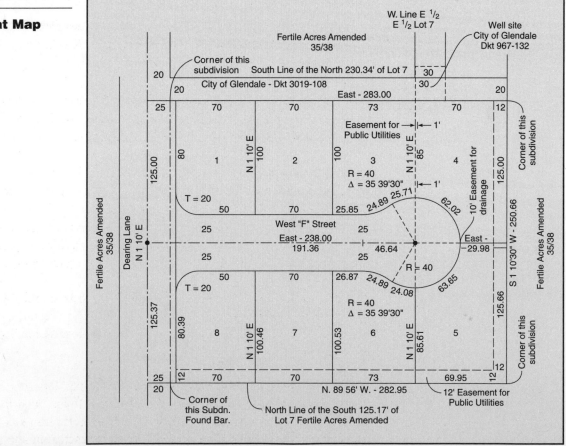

and must comply with all local ordinances and requirements. When properly signed and approved, the subdivision plat is recorded in the county in which the land is located.

The plat becomes part of the legal description. In describing a lot from a recorded subdivision plat, three identifiers are used:

1. Lot-and-block number
2. Name or number of the subdivision plat
3. Name of the county and state

The following is an example of a lot-and-block description:

> *Lot 71, Happy Valley Estates 2, located in a portion of the southeast quarter of Section 23, Township 7 North, Range 4 East of the Seward Principal Meridian in _____ County, State of _____.*

Anyone who wants to locate this parcel would start with the map of the Seward Principal Meridian to identify the township and range reference. Then he or she would consult the township map of Township 7 North, Range 4 East, and the section map of Section 23. From there, he or she would look at the quarter-section map of the southeast quarter. The quarter-section map would refer to the plat map for the subdivision known as the second unit (second parcel subdivided) under the name of Happy Valley Estates.

Some subdivided lands are further divided by a later resubdivision. In the following example, one developer (Western View) purchased a large parcel from a second developer (Homewood). Western View then resubdivided the property into different-sized parcels:

> *Lot 4, Western View Resubdivision of the Homewood Subdivision, located in a portion of the west half of Section 19, Township 10 North, Range 13 East of the Black Hills Principal Meridian, _____ County, State of _____.*

In Illinois

The lot-and-block system is used in Illinois. Subdivision descriptions are the predominant method of describing developed land in this state. The plat of Prairie Acres Estates that appears in Figure 9.11 illustrates a subdivision map.

Under the *Illinois Plat Act,* when an owner divides a parcel of land into two or more parts, any of which is less than five acres, the parts must be surveyed and a plat of subdivision recorded. An exception to this would be the division of lots or blocks of less than one acre in any recorded subdivision that does not involve the creation of any new streets or easements of access. When a conveyance is made, the county recorder may require an affidavit that an exception exists.

The provisions of the *Illinois Plat Act* are complicated and subject to interpretation by each county recorder. Anyone attempting to record a document conveying land should consult a lawyer and the county recorder about the requirements involved. ■

IN PRACTICE

Real estate offices routinely have plat books available. These books have all the lots drawn and numbered for a given township area. If you have the legal description or the *property index number* (PIN) for a property, you can locate its basic dimensions and location using these books. The legal description and the PIN are the two

FIGURE 9.11

Plat Map of Prairie Acres Estates

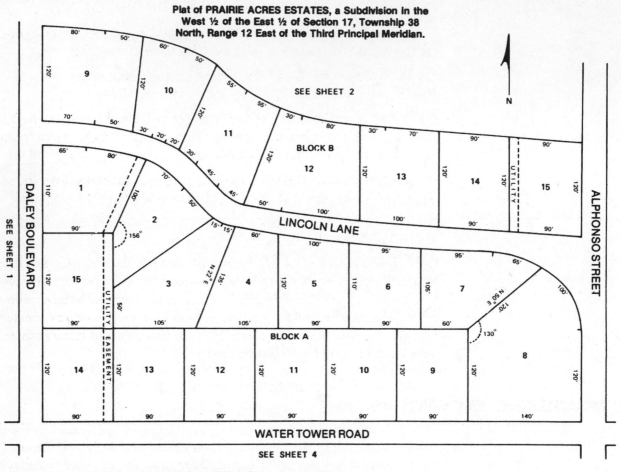

Plat of PRAIRIE ACRES ESTATES, a Subdivision in the West ½ of the East ½ of Section 17, Township 38 North, Range 12 East of the Third Principal Meridian.

Recorded January 14, 1969, in Book 275, Page 1346, in Prairie County, Illinois.

non–street address forms of property identification commonly used. PINs are basically a condensed version of a legal description; they can be found for a given property by examining a survey, checking the tax database, or by calling the county.

■ PREPARING A SURVEY

Legal descriptions should not be altered or combined without adequate information from a surveyor or title attorney. A licensed surveyor is trained and authorized to locate and determine the legal description of any parcel of land. The surveyor does this by preparing two documents: a survey and a survey sketch. The *survey* states the property's legal description. The *survey sketch* shows the location and dimensions of the parcel. When a survey also shows the location, size, and shape of buildings on the lot, it is referred to as a *spot survey*.

IN PRACTICE Because legal descriptions, once recorded, affect title to real estate, they should be prepared only by a professional surveyor.

MATH CONCEPTS · LAND ACQUISITION COSTS

To calculate the cost of purchasing land, use the same unit in which the cost is given. Costs quoted per square foot must be multiplied by the proper number of square feet; costs quoted per acre must be multiplied by the proper number of acres; and so on.

To calculate the cost of a parcel of land of three acres at $1.10 per square foot, convert the acreage to square feet before multiplying:

43,560 square feet per acre × 3 acres = 130,680 square feet
130,680 square feet × $1.10 per square foot = $143,748

To calculate the cost of a parcel of land of 17,500 square feet at $60,000 per acre, convert the cost per acre into the cost per square foot before multiplying by the number of square feet in the parcel:

$60,000 per acre ÷ 43,560 square feet per acre = $1.38 (rounded) per square foot
17,500 square feet × $1.38 per square foot = $24,150

Legal descriptions should be copied with extreme care. An incorrectly worded legal description in a sales contract may result in a conveyance of more or less land than the parties intended. Title problems can arise for the buyer who seeks to convey the property at a future date. Even if the contract can be corrected before the sale is closed, a licensee might create a difficult set of circumstances just by improperly copying a legal description.

■ MEASURING ELEVATIONS

Just as surface rights must be identified, surveyed, and described, so must rights to the property above the earth's surface. Elevations are measured to determine the legal descriptions of air rights and condominium apartments. As discussed earlier, land includes the space above the ground. In the same way land may be measured and divided into parcels, the air itself may be divided. An owner may subdivide the air above his or her land into air lots. **Air lots** are composed of the airspace within specific boundaries located over a parcel of land.

Datum

A **datum** is a point, line, or surface from which elevations are measured or indicated. For the purpose of the *U.S. Geological Survey (USGS)*, *datum* is defined as the mean sea level at New York Harbor. A surveyor would use a datum in determining the height of a structure or establishing the grade of a street.

The condominium laws passed in all states require that a registered land surveyor prepare a plat map that shows the elevations of floor and ceiling surfaces and the vertical boundaries of each unit with reference to an official datum (discussed below). A unit's floor, for instance, might be 60 feet above the datum, and its ceiling, 69 feet. Typically, a separate plat is prepared for each floor in the condominium building.

Subsurface rights can be legally described in the same manner as air rights. They are measured *below* the datum rather than above it. Subsurface rights are used

TABLE 9.1

Units of Land Measurement

Unit	Measurement
mile	5,280 feet; 1,760 yards; 320 rods
rod	16.5 feet; 5.50 yards
sq. mile	640 acres (5,280 × 5,280 = 27,878,400 ÷ 43,560)
acre	43,560 sq. feet; 160 sq. rods
cu. yard	27 cu. feet
sq. yard	9 sq. feet
sq. foot	144 sq. inches
chain	66 feet; 4 rods; 100 links
township	36 square miles; 6 miles × 6 miles
section	1 square mile; 640 acres; 1 mile × 1 mile

not only for coal mining, petroleum drilling, and utility line location but also for multistory condominiums—both residential and commercial—that have several floors below ground level.

In Illinois

The general datum plane used by Illinois surveyors is the USGS datum. ■

Bench marks. As discussed earlier in this chapter, monuments traditionally are used to mark surface measurements between points. A monument could be a marker set in concrete, a piece of steel-reinforcing bar (rebar), a metal pipe driven into the soil, or simply a wooden stake stuck in the dirt. Because such items are subject to the whims of nature and vandals, their accuracy is sometimes suspect. As a result, surveyors instead rely heavily on bench marks to mark their work accurately and permanently.

Bench marks are permanent reference points that have been established throughout the United States. They are usually embossed brass markers set into solid concrete or asphalt bases. While used to some degree for surface measurements, their principal reference use is for marking datums.

IN PRACTICE

All large cities have established a local official datum used in place of the USGS datum. For instance, the official datum for Chicago is known as the *Chicago City Datum*. It is a horizontal plane that corresponds to the low-water level of Lake Michigan in 1847 (the year in which the datum was established) and is considered to be at zero elevation. Although a surveyor's measurement of elevation based on the USGS datum will differ from one computed according to a local datum, it can be translated to an elevation based on the USGS.

Location:
22 West 300 Birchwood Drive, Glen Ellyn, IL
Bench mark:
22 miles west of Chicago's State Street Benchmark

Cities with local datums also have designated official local bench marks, which are assigned permanent identifying numbers. Local bench marks simplify surveyors' work because the basic bench marks may be miles away. A major one in Chicago is located at State and Madison Streets. It references noncity addresses extending far west of Cook County. County addresses beginning with 33 West or 25 West refer to number of miles west of State Street *(as the crow flies!).* Numbers 1 North or 4 South refer to miles north or south of Madison Street.

■ LAND UNITS AND MEASUREMENTS

It is important to understand land units and measurements because they are integral parts of legal descriptions. Some commonly used measurements are listed in Table 9.1.

■ SUMMARY

A legal description is a precise method of identifying a parcel of land. Three methods of legal description can be used: metes-and-bounds method, rectangular (or government) survey system, and lot-and-block (plat map) system. A property's description should always be noted by the same method as the one used in previous documents.

The metes and bounds method uses direction and distance measurement to establish precise boundaries for a parcel. Monuments are fixed objects that establish these boundaries. Their physical location takes precedence over the written linear measurement in a document. When property is described by metes and bounds, the description begins and ends at the point of beginning (POB).

The rectangular (or government) survey system is used in most states. Illinois legal descriptions refer to three principal meridians, one of which is in Indiana (the second). Meridians in and near Illinois number from left to right on the map. A given property is not necessarily referenced by the closest meridian. Once a legal description has been made, it is permanent. With rectangular survey, each principal meridian and its corresponding base line are the primary reference points. Any parcel of land is surveyed from only one principal meridian and one base line.

East and west lines parallel with the base line form six-mile-wide strips called township tiers. North and south lines parallel with the principal meridian form six-mile-wide range strips. The resulting squares are 36 square miles in area and are called townships.

A sample legal description might partially read: Township 3 North, Range 4 East of the 2nd Principal Meridian. Legal descriptions are read left to right but are best analyzed right to left. Townships are divided into 36 sections, one square mile each. Each section has 640 acres, and each acre has 43,560 square feet. Section 16 is traditionally the school section; all other sections are numbered off in the township backwards in S-curves, starting with Section 1 in the upper right-hand corner.

Irregularities in using a square system to match a round planet are adjusted in the rectangular system by correction lines, which in turn form pockets of land called government checks.

When a tract of land is irregular a surveyor can prepare a combination of methods: for instance, rectangular survey and metes-and-bounds description. Lot-and-block combined with rectangular survey is even more frequently utilized in describing suburban America.

Land in every state can be subdivided into lots and blocks by means of a plat map. An approved plat of survey is filed for record in the recorder's office of the county in which the land is located. A plat of subdivision gives the legal description of a building site in a town or city by lot, block, and subdivision in a section, township, and range of a principal meridian in a county and state. Lot and block, section, and township also comprise the essentials given in a property identification number (PIN), which also appears on tax information, surveys, and contracts.

Air lots, condominium descriptions, and other measurements of vertical elevations may be computed from the U.S. Geological Survey datum, which is the mean sea level in New York Harbor. Most large cities have established local survey datums for surveying within the areas—the Chicago City Datum is based on the low-level water mark of Lake Michigan in 1847. The elevations from these datums are further supplemented by reference points, called bench marks, placed at fixed intervals from the datums. Bench marks are used for vertical reference points but often supplement surface measurements.

QUESTIONS

1. What is the proper description of this shaded area of a section?

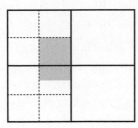

   a. SW¼ of the NE¼ and the N½ of the SE¼ of the SW¼
   b. N½ of the NE¼ of the SW¼ and the SE¼ of the NW¼
   c. SW¼ of the SE¼ of the NW¼ and the N½ of the NE¼ of the SW¼
   d. S½ of the SW¼ of the NE¼ and the NE¼ of the NW¼ of the SE¼

2. When surveying land, a surveyor refers to the principal meridian that is
   a. nearest the land being surveyed.
   b. in the same state as the land being surveyed.
   c. not more than 40 townships or 15 ranges distant from the land being surveyed.
   d. within the rectangular survey system area in which the land being surveyed is located.

3. The N½ of the SW¼ of a section contains how many acres?
   a. 20
   b. 40
   c. 60
   d. 80

4. In describing real estate, the system that uses feet, degrees, and natural and artificial markers as monuments is
   a. rectangular survey.
   b. metes and bounds.
   c. government survey.
   d. lot and block.

Questions 5 through 8 refer to the following illustration of a whole township and parts of the adjacent townships.

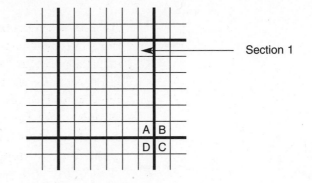

5. The section marked A is which of the following?
   a. School section
   b. Section 31
   c. Section 36
   d. Government lot

6. Which of the following is Section 6?
   a. A
   b. B
   c. C
   d. D

7. The section directly below C is
   a. Section 7.
   b. Section 12.
   c. Section 25.
   d. Section 30.

8. Which of the following is Section D?
   a. Section 1
   b. Section 6
   c. Section 31
   d. Section 36

9. Which of these shaded areas of a section depicts the NE¼ of the SE¼ of the SW¼?

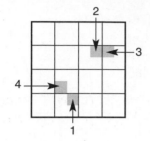

a. Area 1
b. Area 2
c. Area 3
d. Area 4

10. Janice purchases a one-acre parcel from Sheila for $2.15 per square foot. What is the selling price of the parcel?

a. $344
b. $774
c. $1,376
d. $93,654

11. The proper description of the shaded township area in this illustration is

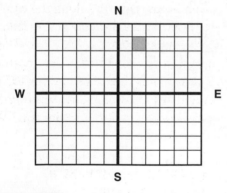

a. T7N R7W.
b. T4W R7N.
c. T4N R2E.
d. T4N R7E.

12. If a farm described as "the NW¼ of the SE¼ of Section 10, Township 2 North, Range 3 West of the 6th P.M." sold for $1,500 an acre, what would the sales price be?

a. $30,000
b. $15,000
c. $45,000
d. $60,000

13. The legal description "the northwest ¼ of the southwest ¼ of Section 6, Township 4 North, Range 7 West" is defective because there is no reference to

a. lot numbers.
b. boundary lines.
c. a principal meridian.
d. a record of survey.

14. To keep the principal meridian and range lines as near to six miles apart as possible, a correction known as a *government check* is made. How large is a government check?

a. 1 square mile
b. 20 square miles
c. 6 miles square
d. 24 miles square

15. Fractional sections in the rectangular survey system along the northern or western borders of a check that are less than a quarter-section in area are known as

a. fractional parcels.
b. government lots.
c. portional sections.
d. fractional townships.

16. Tara purchased 4.5 acres of land for $78,400. An adjoining owner wants to purchase a strip of Tara's land measuring 150 feet by 100 feet. What should this strip cost the adjoining owner if Tara sells it for the same price per square foot originally paid for the property?

a. $3,000
b. $6,000
c. $7,800
d. $9,400

17. A property contained ten acres. How many 50-foot by 100-foot lots could be subdivided from the property if 26,000 square feet were dedicated for roads?

a. 80
b. 81
c. 82
d. 83

18. A parcel of land is 400 feet by 640 feet. The parcel is cut in half diagonally by a stream. How many acres are there in each half of the parcel?

    a. 2.75
    b. 2.94
    c. 5.51
    d. 5.88

19. What is the shortest distance between Section 4 and Section 32 in the same township?

    a. 3 miles
    b. 4 miles
    c. 5 miles
    d. 6 miles

20. The section due west of Section 18, Township 5 North, Range 8 West, is

    a. Section 19, T5N, R8W.
    b. Section 17, T5N, R8W.
    c. Section 13, T5N, R9W.
    d. Section 12, T5N, R7W.

21. In any township, which section is traditionally designated as the school section?

    a. 1
    b. 16
    c. 25
    d. 36

In Illinois

22. Legal descriptions of land in Illinois usually are based on the

    a. rectangular survey system.
    b. Third, Fourth, and Fifth Principal Meridians.
    c. three base lines running through the central part of the state.
    d. nearest principal meridian.

23. Rebecca has a 10-acre tract of land. If she wants to divide the tract into four 2½-acre lots and sell the lots for residences, Rebecca must

    a. establish a datum for the area.
    b. have a spot survey made of the proposed lots.
    c. record a copy of the plat before offering lots for sale.
    d. sell each of the lots before applying for a plot license.

24. Land in the northwest corner of Illinois is described with reference to which Principal Meridian?

    a. Second
    b. Third
    c. Fourth
    d. Fifth

Answer questions 25, 26, and 27 using the information given on the plat of Prairie Acres Estates in Figure 9.11.

25. How many lots have easements?

    a. 3
    b. 4
    c. 6
    d. 7

26. Which of the following lots has the most frontage on Lincoln Lane?

    a. Lot 10, block B
    b. Lot 11, block B
    c. Lot 7, block A
    d. Lot 8, block A

27. "Beginning at the intersection of the east line of Daley Boulevard and the south line of Lincoln Lane and running south along the east line of Daley Boulevard a distance of 230 feet; then easterly parallel to the north line of Water Tower Road a distance of 195 feet; then northeasterly on a course of N22°E a distance of 135 feet; and then northwesterly along the south line of Lincoln Lane to the point of beginning." Which lots are described here?

    a. Lots 13, 14, and 15, block A
    b. Lots 9, 10, and 11, block B
    c. Lots 1, 2, 3, and 15, block A
    d. Lots 7, 8, and 9, block A

Real Estate Taxes and Other Liens

■ **LEARNING OBJECTIVES** *When you've finished reading this chapter, you should be able to*

■ **identify** the various classifications of liens.

■ **describe** how real estate taxes are applied through assessments, tax liens, and the use of equalization ratios.

■ **explain** how nontax liens, such as mechanics' liens, mortgage liens, and judgment liens are applied and enforced.

■ **distinguish** the characteristics of voluntary, involuntary, statutory, and equitable liens.

■ **define** the following *key terms*:

ad valorem tax	inheritance taxes	special service areas
appropriation	involuntary lien	special assessment
attachment	judgment	redemption
encumbrance	lien	specific lien
equalization factor	lien waivers	statutory lien
equitable lien	lis pendens	subordination agreement
estate taxes	mechanic's lien	tax deed
general lien	mill	tax liens
general real estate tax	mortgage lien	tax sale

■ LIENS

A **lien** is a charge or claim against property that is made to enforce the payment of money. Whenever someone borrows money, the lender generally requires some form of security. *Security* (also referred to as *collateral*) is something of value that the borrower promises to give the lender if the borrower fails to repay the debt. When the lender's security is in the form of real estate, the security is called a lien.

All liens are encumbrances, but not all encumbrances are liens.

Liens are not limited to security for borrowed money (such as *mortgage liens*). Liens can be enforced against property by a government agency to recover taxes owed by the owner (*tax liens*). A lien can be used to compel the payment of an assessment or other special charge as well. A *mechanic's lien* represents an effort to recover payment for work performed.

A lien represents only an interest in property; it does not constitute actual ownership of the property. It is an *encumbrance* on the owner's title. An **encumbrance** is any charge or claim that attaches to real property and lessens its value or impairs its use. An encumbrance does not necessarily prevent the transfer or conveyance of the property, but because it is "attached" to the property, it transfers along with it. Liens differ from other encumbrances, however, because they are financial or monetary in nature and attach to the property because of a debt.

Types of Liens

There are many different types of liens. One way liens are classified is by how they are created. A **voluntary lien** is created intentionally by the property owner's action, such as when someone takes out a mortgage loan. An **involuntary lien**, on the other hand, is not a matter of choice: it is created by law. It may be either statutory or equitable. A **statutory lien** is created by statute. A real estate tax lien, then, is an involuntary, statutory lien. It is created by statute without the property owner taking it on voluntarily. An **equitable lien** is created by a court to ensure the payment of a judgment as well as by agreement.

Memory Tip

The four ways of creating a lien may be remembered by the acronym *VISE*: *Voluntary, Involuntary, Statutory,* and *Equitable*.

Liens also may be classified according to the type of property involved. **General liens** affect all the property, both real and personal, of a debtor. This includes judgments, estate and inheritance taxes, decedent's debts, corporate franchise taxes, and Internal Revenue Service taxes. A lien on real estate differs from a lien on personal property. A lien *attaches* to real property *at the moment it is filed*. In contrast, a lien does not attach to personal property until the personal property actually is levied on or seized by the sheriff. **Specific liens** are secured by specific property and affect only that particular property. Specific liens on real estate include mechanics' liens, mortgage liens, real estate tax liens, and liens for special assessments and utilities. Specific liens can also secure personal property, as when a lien is placed on a car to secure payment of a car loan.

Effects of Liens on Title

The existence of a lien does not necessarily prevent a property owner from conveying title to someone else. The lien might reduce the value of the real estate, however, because few buyers will take on the risk of a property that has a lien on it.

Because the lien attaches to the property, not the property owner, a new owner could lose the property if the creditors take court action to enforce payment. Once properly established, a lien runs with the land and will bind all successive owners until the lien is paid in full.

IN PRACTICE

A buyer should insist on a title search before closing a real estate transaction so that any recorded liens are revealed. If liens are present, the buyer may decide to purchase at a lower price or at better terms, require the liens be paid, or refuse to purchase.

Priority of liens. Priority of liens refers to the order in which claims against the property will be satisfied. In general, the rule for priority of liens is "first to record, first in right." Liens take priority from the date they are recorded in the public records of the county in which the property is located.

There are some notable exceptions to this rule. For instance, real estate taxes and special assessments generally take priority over all other liens, regardless of the order in which the liens are recorded. This means that outstanding real estate taxes and special assessments are paid from the proceeds of a court-ordered sale first. The remainder of the proceeds is used to pay other outstanding liens in the order of their priority. *Mechanics' liens take priority as provided by state law but never over tax and special assessment liens.*

■ **FOR EXAMPLE** Mottley Mansion is ordered sold by the court to satisfy Barry's debts. The property is subject to a $50,000 judgment lien, incurred as a result of a mechanic's lien suit. $295,000 in interest and principal remains to be paid on Mottley Mansion's mortgage. This year's unpaid real estate taxes amount to $5,000. The judgment lien was entered in the public record on February 7, 1998, and the mortgage lien was recorded January 22, 1996. If Mottley Mansion is sold at the tax sale for $375,000, the proceeds of the sale will be distributed in the following order:

1. $5,000 to the taxing bodies for this year's real estate taxes

2. $295,000 to the mortgage lender (the entire amount of the mortgage loan outstanding as of the date of sale)

3. $50,000 to the creditor named in the judgment lien

4. $25,000 to Barry (the proceeds remaining after paying the first three items)

However, if Mottley Mansion sold for $325,000, the proceeds would be distributed as follows:

1. $5,000 to the taxing bodies for this year's real estate taxes

2. $295,000 to the mortgage lender (the entire amount of the mortgage loan outstanding as of the date of sale)

3. $25,000 to the creditor named in the judgment lien

4. $0 to Barry

Although the creditor is not repaid in full, this outcome is considered fair for two reasons:

1. The creditor's interest arose later than the others, so the others' interests took priority.

2. The creditor knew (or should have known) about priority creditors when credit was extended to Barry, so the risk involved was clear (or should have been clear).

Subordination agreements are written agreements between lienholders to change the priority of mortgage, judgment, and other liens. Under a subordination agreement, the holder of a superior or prior lien agrees to permit a junior lienholder's interest to move ahead of his or her lien.

■ REAL ESTATE TAX LIENS

The ownership of real estate is always subject to certain government powers. One of these is the right of state and local governments to impose (levy) taxes to pay for their functions. Because the location of real estate is permanently fixed, the government can levy taxes with a high degree of certainty that the taxes will be collected. The annual taxes levied on real estate usually have priority over previously recorded liens, so they may be enforced by a court-ordered sale.

There are two types of real estate taxes: *general real estate taxes* (also called *ad valorem taxes*) and *special assessments* (or *improvement taxes*). Both are levied against specific parcels of property and automatically become **tax liens** on those properties.

General Tax (Ad Valorem Tax)

The **general real estate tax,** or **ad valorem tax,** is made up of the taxes levied on real estate by various governmental agencies and municipalities. These taxing bodies include

- states;
- counties;
- cities, towns, and villages;
- school districts (local elementary and high schools, publicly funded junior colleges and community colleges);
- drainage districts;
- water districts;
- sanitary districts; and
- parks, forest preserves, recreation, and other public-use districts.

Ad valorem is Latin for "according to value." *Ad valorem* taxes are *based on the value of the property being taxed.* They are specific, involuntary, statutory liens. General real estate taxes are levied to fund the operation of the government agency that imposes the taxes.

Exemptions from general taxes.   Most state laws exempt certain real estate from taxation. Such property must be used for tax-exempt purposes, as defined in the statutes. The most common exempt properties are owned by

- various municipal organizations (such as schools, parks, and playgrounds),
- cities and counties,
- state and federal governments,
- religious and charitable organizations,
- hospitals, and
- educational institutions.

Many state laws also allow special exemptions to reduce real estate tax bills for certain property owners or land uses. For instance, senior citizens frequently are granted reductions in the assessed values of their homes. Some state and local governments offer real estate tax reductions to attract industries and sports franchises. Many states also offer tax reductions for agricultural land.

In Illinois

Properties in Illinois that are totally exempt from paying general real estate taxes include schools, religious institutions, cemeteries, and charitable institutions, as well as those owned by federal, state, county, and local governments. Taxing districts may elect to exempt certain other properties (within limits), such as commercial and industrial properties.

Illinois property taxes are adjusted to reflect certain concessions given on owner-occupied residences. These properties are designated as *homesteads*. The *homestead exemption* (not to be confused with the *homestead estate*) reduces the assessed value of a property subject to taxes. Here are the basic exemptions:

1. The ***Homeowner's Exemption*** applies to owners of single-family homes, condominiums, cooperatives, and one-unit to six-unit apartment buildings. In some counties, owners must apply to the assessor for the exemption each year; in others, the exemption is automatically applied. The amount of exemption is the increase in the current year's equalized assessed value up to a maximum of $5,500 and increased again to $6,000 for the 2009 tax year.
2. The ***Senior Citizen's Homestead Exemption*** is available to homeowners over the age of 65. Seniors must prove age and ownership to the County Assessor by December 31 for this exemption to become valid for the following year. Thereafter the exemption becomes automatic. These exemption amounts are subtracted from the property's equalized assessed value before the tax rate is applied. This exemption reduces the equalized assessed value of a senior's home by $4,000.
3. The ***Senior Citizen's Assessment Freeze Homestead Exemption*** program allows Illinois seniors to freeze their assessed valuation for the remainder of their lifetime once they have turned 65, if household income does not exceed $55,000. Annual application and proof of income must be filed by March 1 with the county assessor.
4. The ***Homestead Improvement Exemption*** allows any Illinois homeowner who has recently improved his or her home (by adding a new family room, for instance) to forestall an increase in the home's overall assessed value for up to *four years*. This exemption is available up to an improvement value of $75,000. If the value of the addition or work exceeds $75,000, the homeowner will be assessed for any amount above that without the delay period.

Property owners may qualify for other tax concessions based on their status as disabled veterans or by virtue of improvements to the property, certain maintenance and repair expenses, solar heating, airport land, farmland, rehabilitation of historic buildings, and location within enterprise zones or tax concession districts. ■

IN PRACTICE

If there is a new addition or remodeling, *buyers' agents* should be aware of

■ mechanics' liens, and
■ four-year homestead improvement exemptions.

Assessment. Real estate is valued for tax purposes by county or township assessors or appraisers. This official valuation process is called *assessment*. A property's *assessed value* generally is based on the sales prices of comparable properties, although practices may vary. Land values may be assessed separately from buildings or other improvements, and different valuation methods may be used for different types of property. State laws may provide for property to be reassessed periodically.

In Illinois

Counties with populations over one million may divide their county into three geographic areas. Each area is then assessed once every three years, as in Cook County. All assessments are published in full in a newspaper of general circulation serving the area of the property, and a written notice is sent to the taxpayer of record. Assessment officials may adjust assessed values as often as annually for parcels whose use has changed during the intervening time.

In all counties except Cook, real property is assessed at 33⅓ percent of fair market value. (Depending on how the property is classified, real property in Cook County is assessed based on a sliding scale of percentages of fair market value, from 16 to 38 percent.) *Real property* is defined by the Illinois Revenue Act as including land, buildings, structures, improvements, and any other permanent fixtures *attached to land.*

Taxpayers who believe that errors were made in their property's assessment may file a complaint directly with the assessment official (variously called the *county assessor* or the *supervisor of assessments*). If the taxpayer's complaint is denied, the decision may be appealed to an administrative board of review (in Cook County, the Board of Appeals). Alternatively, the taxpayer can bypass the county official and go directly to the board of review. If the taxpayer is dissatisfied with the board's decision, he or she may file an administrative appeal or request a review of the decision by the circuit court of the county in which the property is located. ■

To Determine Taxes

1. Locate assessed value (usually ⅓ market value)
2. Always "equalize" assessed value *first!*
3. Subtract any exemptions
4. Multiply adjusted assessed value by tax rate = real estate taxes

Equalization. In some jurisdictions, when it is necessary to correct inequalities in statewide tax assessments, an **equalization factor** is used to achieve uniformity. An equalization factor may be applied to raise or lower assessments in a particular district or county. The basic assessed value of each property in the area is multiplied by the equalization factor to acquire an "equalized assessment," then any exemptions are subtracted, and last, the tax rate is applied.

■ **FOR EXAMPLE** The assessments in Laslo County are 20 percent lower than the average assessments throughout the rest of the state. This underassessment can be corrected by requiring the application of an equalization factor of 125 percent (1.25) to each assessment in Laslo County. Therefore, a parcel of land assessed for tax purposes at $98,000 would be taxed on an equalized value of $122,500 ($98,000 × 1.25 = $122,500). At this point, the $5,500 homestead exemption would be subtracted. Then, if there were a $4,000 senior exemption it would be subtracted, too ($122,500 − $5,500 − $4,000 = $113,000 adjusted assessed value). Using this final equalized, adjusted assessed value, taxes would then be computed by multiplying by the proper tax rate.

| In Illinois |

The assessed valuation of real estate is adjusted yearly in each county by applying an equalization factor determined by the Property Tax Administration Bureau of the Department of Revenue. Assessed values are compared with selling prices to arrive at the equalization factor, and each county is assigned a multiplier to be used for equalization purposes. The equalizer is always applied first (equalizer times the basic value) before applicable homeowner's exemptions (if any) are subtracted from value. From the final equalized, adjusted assessed value, taxes are computed. *Any given parcel receives a full reassessment on a quadrennial (four-year) basis*, as mandated by the state. ■

Budgets and tax rates. The process of arriving at a real estate tax rate begins with the adoption of a *budget* by each taxing district. Each budget covers the financial requirements of the taxing body for the coming fiscal year. The fiscal year may be the January through December calendar year or some other 12-month period designated by statute. The budget must include an estimate of all expenditures needed for the year. In addition, the budget must indicate the amount of income expected from all fees, revenue sharing, and other sources. The net amount remaining to be raised from real estate taxes is then determined by the difference between these figures.

The next step is to spread out the needed monies among all the homeowners proportionately (based on values). The total monies needed for the coming fiscal year are divided by the total valuations of all real estate located within the taxing body's jurisdiction.

Proposed expense ÷ Total assessed property values = Tax rate

■ **FOR EXAMPLE** A taxing district's budget indicates that $800,000 must be acquired from real estate taxes to pay for needed expenditures. The assessment roll (assessor's record) of all taxable real estate within the district equals $10 million. The tax rate is computed as follows:

$800,000 ÷ $10,000,000 = .080 or 8%

What's in a Mill?

1 mill = 1/1,000 of a dollar, or .001, or $1 per $1,000 of assessed value.

The tax rate may be stated in a number of ways. In many areas, it is expressed in mills. A **mill** is 1/1,000 of a dollar, or $.001. The tax rate may be expressed as a mill per dollar ratio, as in dollars per hundred, or in dollars per thousand. A tax rate of .08, or 8 percent, could be expressed as 80 mills, as $8 per $100 of assessed value, or as $80 per $1,000 of assessed value.

■ **FOR EXAMPLE** A property is valued at $350,000. If it is taxed at 2 mills, what amount of tax needs to be paid?

Approach 1: *If the problem is expressed in mills:* 2 mills = .002 or 2 thousandths per dollar of valuation. You may multiply the valuation number directly by thousandths. $350,000 × .002 = $700.

Approach 2: *If the problem is expressed in dollars per thousand*: 2 mills is the same as $2 per $1,000 of valuation. You could divide property value into sets of 1,000 to start. In this case, $350,000 ÷ 1,000 = 350 sets of $1,000. Now multiply 350 × $2 = $700 in taxes.

Approach 3: *If the problem is expressed in dollars per hundred:* 2 mills is the same as $.2 (2 tenths) dollar (20 cents) per $100 of valuation. Use Approach 2 here as well, except divide property value into sets of 100. In this case, $350,000 divided by 100 = 3,500 sets of $100. Now multiply. 3,500 × $.2 = $700 in taxes.

Appropriation.   Formal **appropriation** is the way a taxing body actually authorizes the expenditure of funds and provides for the sources of the funding. Appropriation generally involves the adoption of an ordinance or the passage of a law that states the specific terms of the proposed taxation. The amount to be raised from the general real estate tax is then imposed on property owners through a tax levy. A *tax levy* is the formal action taken to impose the tax, usually by way of a vote of the taxing district's governing body.

Creating the tax bills.   After appropriation, a property owner's tax bill is computed by applying the tax rate to the assessed valuation of the property.

Generally, one tax bill that incorporates all real estate taxes levied by the various taxing districts is prepared for each property. Some tax purposes or tax targets (like the park district) are split out and easily identifiable on most bills. In some areas, however, separate bills are prepared by each taxing body.

In Illinois   The county collector prepares and issues only one combined tax bill to each parcel of property. ■

■ **FOR EXAMPLE** If a property is assessed for tax purposes at $160,000, and the tax rate is 3 percent or 30 mills, the tax will be $4,800 ($160,000 × .03). (This assumes no equalization factor.)

Let's say the equalization factor is 120 percent. Thus, the equalized, assessed value is $192,000 ($160,000 × 1.20). From there, apply the tax rate of 3 percent (.03) to arrive at taxes of $5,760 ($192,000 × .03).

In Illinois   General real estate taxes are levied annually for the calendar year and become a *prior first lien*, superior to all other liens, on January 1 of that tax year. However, they are not due and payable until the following year.

General real estate taxes are payable in two equal installments in the year *after* they are levied: one-half by *June 1* and the second half by *September 1* (except in Cook County, as noted below). Taxes in Illinois, then, are said to be *paid in arrears*. The payment due dates are also called *penalty dates*, after which a 1.5 percent-per-month penalty is added to any unpaid amount. Because bills must be issued 30 days prior to a penalty date, the penalty date for an installment may be delayed if the county collector is late in preparing the bills.

Penalty dates of March 1 and August 1 have been authorized for Cook County taxes under an accelerated billing procedure. With this accelerated procedure, the billing for the installment due on March 1 is sent before the actual tax has been determined. The amount of this first accelerated installment is one-half the amount of the tax bill for the previous year. The second installment then is billed after the tax has been determined. It is for the actual tax less the amount billed as the first installment.

Additional information on the Illinois Tax Code and specific tax situations can be found in Chapter 35 of the Illinois Compiled Statutes ■

Enforcement of tax liens.   Real estate taxes must be valid to be enforceable. That means they must be levied properly, must be used for a legal purpose, and must be applied equitably to all property. Real estate taxes that have remained delinquent for the statutory period can be collected through a **tax sale.**

In Illinois

The statutory requirements for enforcement of tax liens are complex. When a property owner fails to pay taxes on real estate in this state, the property ultimately may be sold in one of three ways:

1. At an *annual tax sale*
2. At a *forfeiture sale*
3. At a *scavenger sale*

Annual sale.   If the taxes on a property have not been paid by the due date of the second installment, the county collector can enforce the tax lien and request that the circuit court order a tax sale. The county has notification requirements that are prescribed by statute. These requirements include publication in a newspaper of general circulation within the community and a certified or registered mailing to the last known address of the taxpayer. The court will render judgment in favor of the county if the taxes are shown to be delinquent and proper notice has been given. *The court order allows only the sale of the tax lien, not the property itself.*

Prior to the time of sale, the owner and any other party with a legal interest (except undisclosed beneficiaries of a land trust) may redeem the property and stop the sale by paying the delinquent taxes, applicable interest, and publication costs. Successful purchasers at the sale are those who offer to pay all outstanding taxes, interest, publication costs, processing charges, and the county treasurer's indemnity fund fee.

If competitive bidding results, the bid is for the lowest rate of interest that will be accepted by the bidder in case of redemption during the first six months of the redemption period. The only persons not allowed to bid at the sale are owners, persons with legal interest, and/or their agents. The successful bidder must pay with cash, cashier's check, or certified check. Upon payment, the purchaser receives a *certificate of purchase*. The certificate will ripen into a **tax deed** if no redemption is made within the statutorily prescribed period.

The statutory time period allowed for redemption on most property is two years after the sale. Properties with six or fewer units where the owner resides must be redeemed within 2½ years after the sale. If the property is not redeemed by the owner within the period allowed, the tax sale purchaser is required to give notice to the delinquent owner and other parties who hold any interest in the property before applying for a tax deed. A tax deed must be recorded within one year after the expiration of the redemption period or it becomes null and void.

Forfeiture sale.   If there are no bids on a property at the annual tax sale, the property is forfeited to the state, although title does not really change. The owner still may redeem the property after forfeiture by paying delinquencies, publication costs, and interest. On the other hand, *anyone who wants to purchase the property for the outstanding taxes may make application to the county.* If this happens and the owner does not claim the property within 30 days of notification, the applicant will be issued a *certificate of purchase* once he or she pays the outstanding taxes, interest, and other fees. If redemption is later made by the original owner, the certificate holder must be compensated based on 12 percent interest for each six months the certificate was held.

Scavenger sale.   If the taxes have not been paid on a property for two years or more, the property may be sold at a *scavenger sale.* The county must go through the same court process as it would for tax sales and receive an order of sale. The successful bidder at these sales is the one who is willing to pay the highest cash price for the property. The buyer is not required to pay the tax lien but must pay current taxes. In this case, former owners may not bid on their delinquent properties, either in person or through an agent. Nor may a person who already owns property that is two or more years delinquent bid on the property.

As noted earlier, redemption rights apply. However, the redemption period for vacant nonfarm real estate, commercial or industrial property, or property improved with seven or more residential units is only six months. *For redemption to occur, all past-due taxes plus interest and penalties must be paid by the redeemer. In addition, the owner of the certificate of purchase must be paid back his or her bid price plus interest.*

Note: Geography affects which approach is emphasized. Cook County generally holds scavenger sales. Other counties, such as Kane and Du Page, redeem the properties and then sell them to return them to the tax rolls. ■

Special Assessments (Improvement Taxes)

Special assessments are taxes levied on real estate to fund public improvements to the property. Property owners living nearest to the improvements are required to pay for them because their properties benefit directly from the improvements. For example, the installation of paved streets, curbs, gutters, sidewalks, storm sewers, or street lighting increases the values of the affected properties. The owners, in effect, reimburse the levying authority. However, dollar-for-dollar increases in value are rarely the result.

Special assessments are always specific and statutory, but they can be either involuntary or voluntary liens. Improvements initiated by a public agency create involuntary liens. However, when property owners petition the local government to install a public improvement for which the owners agree to pay (such as a sidewalk or paved alley), the assessment lien is voluntary.

Whether the lien is voluntary or involuntary, each property in the improvement district is charged a prorated share of the total amount of the assessment. The share is determined either on a fractional basis (four houses may equally share the cost of one streetlight) or on a cost-per-front-foot basis (wider lots incur a greater cost than narrower lots for street paving and curb and sidewalk installation).

| In Illinois |

Special assessments usually are due in equal annual installments, plus interest, over a period of five years to ten years, with the first installment usually due during the year following the public authority's approval of the assessment. The first bill includes one year's interest on the property owner's share of the entire assessment; subsequent bills include one year's interest on the unpaid balance. Property owners have the right to prepay any or all installments to avoid future interest charges. The annual due date for assessment payments in Illinois is generally January 2. ■

Special Service Areas

| In Illinois |

Special Service Areas (SSAs) are special taxing districts in municipalities that are established by ordinance, often at the request of developers of new housing subdivisions, in order to pass on the costs of the streets, landscaping, water lines, and sewer systems to homeowners who reside within the SSA. The SSA assessments pay off the municipal bonds that are issued to pay for the infrastructure. Assessments are billed annually on property tax bills, generally for a period of 20 to 30 years.

Even though these assessments appear on property tax bills, they are only tax-deductible if they are for the repairs or maintenance of existing infrastructure. The assessments are not tax-deductible if they are for new infrastructure. The interest portion of the assessment is tax-deductible only if the taxpayer has an itemized statement that clearly delineates or allocates the dollar amount of the interest from the principal, which is not done in most counties. ■

■ OTHER LIENS ON REAL PROPERTY

In addition to real estate tax and special assessment liens, a variety of other liens may be charged against real property.

Mortgage Liens (Deed of Trust Liens)

A **mortgage lien**, or a deed of trust lien, is a voluntary lien on real estate given to a lender by a borrower as security for a real estate loan. It becomes a lien on real property when the lender records the documents in the county where the property is located. Lenders generally require a preferred lien, referred to as a *first mortgage lien*. This means that no other liens against the property (aside from real estate taxes) would take priority over the mortgage lien. Subsequent liens are referred to as *junior liens*.

Mechanics' Liens

A **mechanic's lien** is a specific, involuntary lien that gives security to persons or companies that perform labor or furnish material to improve real property. A mechanic's lien is available to contractors, subcontractors, architects, equipment lessors, surveyors, laborers, and other providers. This type of lien is filed when the owner has not fully paid for the work or when the general contractor has been compensated but has not paid the subcontractors or material suppliers.

| In Illinois |

To be entitled to a mechanic's lien, the person who did the work must have had a contract (express or implied) with the owner or the owner's authorized representative. Releases of lien or lien waivers should be sought by the seller once work is paid, with signatures from the general and the subs. Also, a "no-lien contract" filed on the project precludes any liens. If improvements that were not ordered by the property owner have commenced, the property owner may execute a document called a *notice of nonresponsibility* to attempt to relieve himself or herself from possible mechanics' liens. By posting this notice in some conspicuous place on the property and recording a verified copy of it in the public record, the owner gives notice that he or she is not responsible for the work done.

In Illinois, contractors whose bills have not been paid and who wish to enforce their lien rights against an owner must file their lien notices within four months after the work is completed. Subcontractors have the right in Illinois to file for their unpaid claims as well, even when the general contractor has been paid in full.

Priority.   In Illinois, mechanics' liens can take priority over a previously recorded lien if the work done has enhanced the value of the property. *The lien attaches as of the date when the work was ordered or the contract was signed by the owner.* The date of attachment establishes the lien's priority over other liens. From the point of view of the public or a prospective purchaser, an unpaid contractor has a "secret lien" until the notice is recorded. ■

Waiver and disclaimer.   The names of all subcontractors must be listed by the general contractor in a sworn statement. This list is presented to the landowner who ordered the work. **Lien waivers** (or *waivers of lien*) should be collected by the landowner from each contractor and subcontractor to create a continuing record that all lien claimants have released their lien rights. Materials suppliers and property managers should also be approached for releases.

In Illinois

Expiration of lien right and commencement of suit.   In Illinois, the contractor's lien right will expire two years after completion of that contractor's work, unless he or she files suit within that time to foreclose the lien. Suits to enforce mechanic's liens must be filed within two years after the last labor and/or materials were supplied. Under Section 34 of the Illinois Mechanic's Lien Act, a property owner can demand that the suit be commenced in 30 days. This suit can force the sale of the real estate through a court order to provide funds to pay the claimant's lien. ■

Judgments

A **judgment** is an order issued by a court that settles and defines the rights and obligations of the parties to a lawsuit. When the judgment establishes the amount a debtor owes and provides for money to be awarded, it is referred to as a *money judgment.*

A judgment is a *general, involuntary, equitable lien* on both real and personal property owned by the debtor. A judgment is not the same as a mortgage because no specific parcel of real estate was given as security at the time the debt was created. A lien usually covers only property located within the county in which the judgment is issued. As a result, a notice of the lien must be filed in any county to which a creditor wishes to extend the lien coverage.

In Illinois	A judgment becomes a general lien on all of the defendant's real and personal property in a county at the time the judgment is recorded in the county recorder's office. For the lien to be effective in another county, a memorandum of judgment must be recorded in that county.

Judgment liens are effective in Illinois for seven years and may be renewed for another seven-year term.

In Cook County, an experimental *arbitration* approach to dealing with mechanics' claims has been undertaken for cases under $50,000 or any case in which both parties are open to arbitration. Decisions are nonbinding and either party can accept or reject. If the dispute remains unsolved, the court is free to consider the arbitration's findings as part of its later final decision on the matter.

To enforce an actual judgment, the creditor must obtain a *writ of execution* from the court. A writ of execution directs the sheriff to seize and sell as much of the debtor's property as is necessary to pay both the debt and the expenses of the sale. A judgment does not become a lien against *personal property* (as opposed to real property) of a debtor until the creditor orders the sheriff to levy the property and the levy actually is made. When property is sold, the debtor should demand a *satisfaction of judgment* (or *satisfaction piece*) to clear the record. ∎

Lis pendens. There is often a considerable delay between the time a lawsuit is filed and the time final judgment is rendered. When any suit is filed that affects title to real estate, a special notice, known as a **lis pendens** (Latin for "litigation pending") is recorded. A *lis pendens* is not itself a lien, but rather notice of a possible future lien. Recording a *lis pendens* notifies prospective purchasers and lenders that there is a potential claim against the property. It also establishes a priority for the later lien: the lien is backdated to the recording date of the *lis pendens*.

Attachments. Special rules apply to realty that is not mortgaged or similarly encumbered. To prevent a debtor from conveying title to such previously unsecured real estate while a court suit is being decided, a creditor may seek a **writ of attachment**. By this writ, the court retains custody of the property until the suit concludes. First, the creditor must post a surety bond or deposit with the court. The bond must be sufficient to cover any possible loss or damage the debtor may suffer while the court has custody of the property. In the event the judgment is not awarded to the creditor, the debtor will be reimbursed from the bond.

Estate and Inheritance Tax Liens

Federal **estate taxes** and **state inheritance** taxes (as well as the debts of decedents) are *general, statutory, involuntary liens* that encumber a deceased person's real and personal property. These are normally paid or cleared in probate court proceedings.

Liens for Municipal Utilities

Municipalities often have the right to impose a *specific, equitable, involuntary lien* on the property of an owner who refuses to pay bills for municipal utility services.

Bail Bond Lien

A real estate owner who is charged with a crime for which he or she must face trial *may post bail in the form of real estate* rather than cash. The execution and recording of such a bail bond creates a *specific, statutory, voluntary lien* against the owner's

TABLE 10.1

Real Estate–Related Liens

	General	Specific	Voluntary	Involuntary
General Real Estate Tax (Ad Valorem Tax) Lien		•		•
Special Assessment (Improvement Tax) Lien		•	• or	•
Mortgage Lien		•	•	
Deed of Trust Lien		•	•	
Mechanic's Lien		•		•
Judgment Lien	•			•
Estate Tax Lien	•			•
Inheritance Tax Lien	•			•
Debts of a Decedent	•			•
Municipal Utilities Lien		•		•
Bail Bond Lien		•	•	
Corporation Franchise Tax Lien	•			•
Federal Income Tax Lien	•			•

real estate. If the accused fails to appear in court, the lien may be enforced by the sheriff or another court officer.

Corporation Franchise Tax Lien

State governments generally levy a *corporation franchise tax* on corporations as a condition of allowing them to do business in the state. Such a tax is a *general, statutory, involuntary lien* on all real and personal property owned by the corporation.

IRS Tax Lien

A *federal tax lien*, or Internal Revenue Service (IRS) tax lien, results from a person's failure to pay any portion of federal taxes, such as income and withholding taxes. A federal tax lien is a *general, statutory, involuntary lien* on all real and personal property held by the delinquent taxpayer. Its priority, however, is based on the date of filing or recording; it does not supersede previously recorded liens.

| In Illinois |

The *Commercial Real Estate Broker Lien Act* permits commercial brokers to place a lien on property in the amount of the commission they are entitled to receive for leasing as well as for a sale under a written brokerage agreement in the event they are not paid for their services. The lien applies to commercial property only, and it must be recorded before closing to be enforceable. ■

A summary of the real estate–related liens discussed in this chapter appears in Table 10.1.

■ **SUMMARY**

Liens are claims of creditors or taxing authorities against the real and personal property of a debtor. A lien is a type of encumbrance. Liens are either general, covering all real and personal property of a debtor-owner, or specific, covering only identified property. They also are either voluntary, arising from an action of the debtor, or involuntary, created by statute (statutory) or based on the concept of fairness (equitable).

With the exception of tax liens and special assessment liens, which are always paid first, the priority of liens generally is determined by the order in which they are placed into the public record. This of course is in the county in which the property is located.

Real estate taxes are levied annually by local taxing authorities and are generally given priority over other liens when they are not paid.

Taxes are determined by first determining total cost of public needs, then dividing the cost for these needs into the sum value of taxable property (equalized and adjusted) to determine a tax rate.

Payments for property taxes are required in each county before stated dates, after which penalties accrue. An owner may lose title to property for nonpayment of taxes because such tax-delinquent property can be sold at a tax sale. Some states allow a time period during which a defaulted owner can utilize right of redemption to save his or her real estate from tax sale.

Special assessments are levied to allocate the cost of public improvements to the specific parcels of real estate that benefit from them. Assessments usually are payable annually over a five-year or ten-year period, together with interest due on the balance of the assessment.

Special service areas are special taxing districts in municipalities that are established by ordinance in order to pass on the costs of the streets, landscaping, water lines, and sewer systems to homeowners who reside within the SSA. They are billed annually, generally for a period of 20 to 30 years.

Mortgage liens (or deed of trust liens) are voluntary, specific liens given to lenders to secure payment for real estate loans.

Mechanics' liens protect general contractors, subcontractors, property managers, and material suppliers whose work enhances the value of real estate. Lien waivers protect property owners when these debts have been paid.

A judgment is a court decree obtained by a creditor, usually for a monetary award from a debtor. A judgment lien can be enforced by court issuance of a writ of execution and sale by the sheriff to pay the judgment amount and costs.

Attachment is a means of preventing a defendant from conveying property before completion of a suit in which a judgment is sought.

Lis pendens is a recorded notice of a lawsuit that is pending in court and that may result in a judgment affecting title to a parcel of real estate.

Federal estate taxes and state inheritance taxes are general liens against a deceased owner's property.

Liens for water charges or other municipal utilities and bail bond liens are specific liens, while corporation franchise tax liens are general liens.

IRS tax liens are general liens against the property of a person who is delinquent in paying IRS taxes.

| In Illinois | The Homeowner's Exemption is an annual concession that reduces the assessed value of a property. The basic homeowner's exemption in many counties must be applied for every year. The Senior Homestead Exemption is available to a homeowner over age 65 and renews automatically. The Seniors' Freeze Exemption, an even stronger alternative, freezes assessed valuation for the rest of a senior citizen's life if he or she applies and is over age 65. The Homestead Improvement Exemption gives any homeowner improving his or her home a four-year delay before the increased home value affects taxes. |

General real estate taxes are payable in two equal installments in the year after they are levied—June 1 and September 1. Full reassessments for tax purposes take place every four years in Illinois.

When a property owner fails to pay taxes on his or her real estate, the property may be sold at an annual tax sale, a forfeiture sale, or a scavenger sale.

Mechanics' liens must be filed by contractors, electricians, plumbers, or other hired home improvement personnel within four months after work was completed. However, such liens are retroactive (making mechanics' liens the so-called secret liens). These liens attach (become legal and enforceable based on date) as of the time the work was ordered or when the contract was first signed by the owner.

A judgment becomes a general lien on all the defendant's real and personal property located in the county at the time the judgment was recorded. A judgment lien stays in effect in Illinois for seven years and is renewable for another seven. During such time, if the property is sold, the lien amount is usually paid from the proceeds. ■

QUESTIONS

1. Warren was sued and found guilty in a court of law. A judgment was placed against all real and personal property that he owned. This is an example of which of the following types of liens?
   a. Specific
   b. Voluntary
   c. Statutory
   d. General

2. Priority of liens refers to which of the following?
   a. Order in which a debtor assumes responsibility for payment of obligations
   b. Order in which liens will be paid if property is sold to satisfy a debt
   c. Dates liens are filed for record
   d. Fact that specific liens have greater priority than general liens

3. Consuelo purchased a house that was 50 years old. When it rained, the old sewer system could not handle the flow of water, and it caused water to back up in the homes on the street. The city decided to put new lines down the street. The property owners will have to pay a(n)
   a. mechanic's lien.
   b. special assessment.
   c. *ad valorem.*
   d. utility lien.

4. Which of the following would be classified as a general lien?
   a. Mechanic's lien
   b. Bail bond lien
   c. Judgment
   d. Real estate taxes

5. Which of the following liens would usually be given highest priority?
   a. Mortgage dated last year
   b. Real estate taxes due
   c. Mechanic's lien for work started before the mortgage was made
   d. Judgment rendered yesterday

6. A specific parcel of real estate has a market value of $80,000 and is assessed for tax purposes at 35 percent of market value. The tax rate for the county in which the property is located is 30 mills. The tax bill will be
   a. $50.
   b. $60.
   c. $720.
   d. $840.

7. Taxes generally are used to distribute the cost of public services among all taxpayers. Which of the following taxes would target homeowners in particular?
   a. Personal property tax
   b. Sales tax
   c. Real property tax
   d. Luxury tax

8. A homeowner decided to add a family room onto his house. An electrician was hired to wire the room and has not been paid. The electrician would have the right to
   a. tear out his or her work.
   b. record a notice of the lien.
   c. record a notice of the lien and file a court suit within the time required by state law.
   d. have personal property of the owner sold to satisfy the lien.

9. What is the annual real estate tax on a property valued at $135,000 and assessed for tax purposes at $47,250, with an equalization factor of 125 percent, when the tax rate is 25 mills?
   a. $945
   b. $1,181
   c. $1,418
   d. $1,477

10. Which of the following is a voluntary, specific lien?
   a. IRS tax lien
   b. Mechanic's lien
   c. Mortgage lien
   d. Special assessment

11. In two weeks, a general contractor will file a suit against a homeowner for nonpayment. The contractor just learned that the homeowner has listed the property for sale with a real estate broker. In this situation, which of the following will the contractor's attorney use to protect the contractor's interest?

    a. Seller's lien
    b. Buyer's lien
    c. Assessment
    d. *Lis pendens*

12. Which of the following statements *BEST* describes special assessment liens?

    a. They are general liens.
    b. They are paid on a monthly basis.
    c. They take priority over mechanics' liens.
    d. They cannot be prepaid in full without penalty.

13. Which of the following is a lien on real estate?

    a. Easement running with the land
    b. Unpaid mortgage loan
    c. License
    d. Encroachment

14. Which of the following statements is *TRUE* of both a mortgage lien and a judgment lien?

    a. They must be entered by the court.
    b. They involve a debtor-creditor relationship.
    c. They are general liens.
    d. They are involuntary liens.

15. A mechanic's lien would be available to which of the following?

    a. Listing broker
    b. Buyer's broker
    c. Taxing authority
    d. Contractor

16. Which of the following is a specific, involuntary, statutory lien?

    a. Real estate tax lien
    b. Income tax lien
    c. Estate tax lien
    d. Judgment lien

17. General real estate taxes levied for the operation of the government are called

    a. assessment taxes.
    b. *ad valorem* taxes.
    c. special taxes.
    d. improvement taxes.

18. In Illinois, a broker's lien would be available to which of the following?

    a. A commercial or residential real estate broker
    b. Any licensed broker or salesperson dealing with residential property valued at more than $50,000
    c. A real estate broker seeking to recover a commission under a written or oral listing agreement
    d. A commercial real estate broker dealing with commercial property

19. The equalization factor used in Illinois taxation is designed to

    a. increase the tax revenues of the state.
    b. correct discrepancies between the assessed values of similar parcels of land in various counties.
    c. correct inequities in taxes for senior citizens and disabled persons.
    d. decrease taxes for the poor and unemployed.

20. Homeowner Nancy contracted with the Belding Construction Company to add a bedroom to her house on June 17. The job was completed on August 28, but Nancy still had not paid for the work by November 28. The Belding Company records a mechanic's lien against the property. When does this lien take effect?

    a. As of June 17
    b. As of August 28
    c. As of November 28
    d. Four months after the contract date

21. Brett owns a condominium town house in Cook County and a weekend retreat in Sangamon County, Illinois. Brett also owns investment property in Montana. If one of his creditors sues him in a Cook County court and a judgment is issued against him and is recorded in Cook County, which of the following is *TRUE*?

a. The judgment becomes a lien on the town house, Brett's two cars, and other items of personal property in Cook County.

b. The judgment becomes a lien on the weekend retreat, Brett's speedboat, and all other items of real and personal property in Sangamon and Cook counties.

c. The judgment becomes a lien on all of Brett's real and personal property, wherever located.

d. The judgment becomes a lien on the Cook County town house only.

22. Which of the following statements is *TRUE* of the successful bidder on property offered at an annual tax sale?

a. He or she owns the property after paying the outstanding taxes.

b. He or she bids the highest percentage of interest he or she will accept if the property is redeemed.

c. He or she may obtain a tax deed if the property is not redeemed within the redemption period.

d. He or she receives a tax deed at the time of the sale.

23. With an accelerated billing procedure, such as that used in Cook County, the first installment of the tax bill

a. is one half of the previous year's bill.

b. is due on April 1.

c. includes special assessments for the current year.

d. is billed after the actual amount of the current year's tax is determined.

24. The Valmonts own a home valued at $80,000 that is assessed for tax purposes at 33⅓ percent of market value. The equalization factor for the county in which the residence is located is 0.9500, and the tax rate is $6 per $100. The first half of the Valmonts' real estate tax would be approximately how many dollars?

a. $760

b. $841

c. $1,518

d. $1,682

25. Branham owns a primary residence and two apartment buildings. He pays property taxes on two of the three properties. The delinquent taxes will result in a lien on

a. all three properties.

b. all real and personal property that he owns.

c. his primary residence only.

d. the property on which he has not paid the taxes.

CHAPTER

11

Real Estate Contracts

■ **LEARNING OBJECTIVES** *When you've finished reading this chapter, you should be able to*

- **identify** the requirements for a valid contract.

- **describe** the various types of contracts used in the real estate business.

- **explain** how contracts may be discharged.

- **distinguish** among bilateral and unilateral, executed and executory, and valid, void, and voidable contracts.

- **define** the following key terms:

assignment	executed contract	suit for specific
bilateral contract	executory contract	performance
breach of contract	express contract	time is of the essence
commingling	implied contract	unenforceable contract
consideration	installment contract	Uniform Vendor and
contingencies	land contract	Purchaser Risk Act
contract	liquidated damages	unilateral contract
conversion	novation	valid
counteroffer	offer and acceptance	void
earnest money	option	voidable
equitable title	statute of frauds	

■ CONTRACT LAW

> A contract is a voluntary, legally enforceable promise between two competent parties to perform some legal act in exchange for consideration.

A **contract** is a voluntary agreement or promise between legally competent parties, supported by legal consideration, to perform (or refrain from performing) some legal act. That definition may be easier to understand if its various parts are examined separately. A contract must be

- ■ *voluntary*—no one may be forced into a contract;
- ■ *an agreement or a promise*—a contract is essentially a legally enforceable promise;
- ■ made by *legally competent parties*—the parties must be viewed by the law as capable of making a legally binding promise;
- ■ supported by *legal consideration*—a contract must be supported by something of value that induces a party to enter into the contract, and that something must be legally sufficient to support a contract; and
- ■ having to do with a *legal act*—no one may legally contract to do something illegal.

Brokers and salespersons use many types of contracts and agreements to carry out their responsibilities to sellers, buyers, and the general public. The general body of law that governs such agreements is known as *contract law*.

IN PRACTICE   Real estate professionals are advised to use preprinted and preapproved forms provided by their employing brokers or associations, if they are members of a REALTOR® association. Also, remember that practitioners should be careful to not practice law without a license. Both the buyer and the seller have the option of seeking legal counsel for form preparation.

Express and Implied Contracts

A contract may be *express* or *implied*, depending on how it is created. An **express contract** exists when the parties state the terms and show their intentions in *words*. An express contract may be oral or written. Under the **statute of frauds**, *certain types of contracts (including those for the sale of real property) must be in writing to be enforceable in a court of law*. (*Enforceable* means that the parties may be forced to comply with the contract's terms and conditions.) In an **implied contract**, the agreement of the parties is demonstrated by their *acts and conduct*.

■ **FOR EXAMPLE** Sam signs a contract to purchase Sally's house for $350,000. Sally signs the contract in agreement. This is an *express* contract. Ken goes into a restaurant and orders a meal. Ken has entered into an *implied* contract with the restaurant to pay for the meal, even though payment was not mentioned before the meal was ordered.

In Illinois   The Illinois *Statute of Frauds* requires that any contracts for the sale of land, or for leases that will not be fulfilled within one year from the *date they are entered into, must be in writing to be enforceable in court*. The Illinois Real Estate License Act of 2000 also indicates that certain contracts must be in writing such as employment agreements between broker and salesperson. ■

Bilateral and Unilateral Contracts

Contracts may be classified as either *bilateral* or *unilateral*. In a **bilateral contract**, both parties promise to do something; one promise is given in exchange for another. A real estate sales contract is a bilateral contract because the seller promises to sell a parcel of real estate and convey property title to the buyer, who in turn promises to pay a certain sum of money for the property. An exclusive right to sell listing agreement is a bilateral contract.

A **unilateral contract**, on the other hand, is a one-sided agreement. One party makes a promise to induce a second party to do something. *The second party is not legally obligated to act.* However, if the second party does comply, the first party is then obligated to keep the promise. An option contract to retain one's option to possibly make a purchase later is another example of a unilateral contract.

Bi- means "two"—a *bilateral contract* must have two promises. *Uni-* means "one"—a *unilateral contract* has only one promise

■ **FOR EXAMPLE** Beatrice puts up a sign that says, "If you paint my house today, I will pay you $1,550." If Henry paints Beatrice's house, Beatrice will be legally obligated to pay Henry. Beatrice and Henry have a unilateral contract.

Executed and Executory Contracts

A contract may be classified as either *executed* or *executory*, depending on whether the agreement is performed. An **executed contract** is one in which all parties have fulfilled their promises: the contract has been performed. This sometimes can be confused with the word *execute*, which refers to the act of signing a contract. An **executory contract** exists when one or both parties still have an act to perform. A sales contract is an executory contract from the time it is signed until closing: ownership has not yet changed hands, and the seller has not received the sales price. At closing, the sales contract is executed.

Table 11.1 highlights the formation of a contract, which will be discussed in detail in this chapter.

Essential Elements of a Valid Contract

A contract must meet certain minimum requirements to be considered legally valid. The following are the basic essential elements of a contract.

Elements of a Contract:

■ Offer and acceptance
■ Consideration
■ Legally competent parties
■ Consent
■ Legal purpose

Offer and acceptance ("mutual assent"). There must be an offer by one party that is accepted by the other. The person who makes the offer is the *offeror*. The person who accepts the offer is the *offeree*. This requirement also is called *mutual assent*. It means that there must be a *meeting of the minds*, or complete agreement about the purpose and terms of the contract. Courts look to the objective intent of the parties to determine whether there was intent to enter into a binding agreement. In cases where the statute of frauds applies, the **offer and acceptance** must be in writing. The wording of the contract must express all the agreed-on terms and must be clearly understood by the parties.

An *offer* is a promise made by one party, requesting something in exchange for that promise. The offer is made with the intention that the offeror will be bound

TABLE 11.1

Contract Formation

Preformation	Formation	Postformation
Essential Elements	Classification	Discharge
Offer, Acceptance, Consideration, Legal Purpose, Legal Capacity	Valid, Void, Voidable, Enforceable, Unenforceable, Express, Implied, Unilateral, Bilateral, Executory, Executed	Performance, Breach, Remedies (Damages, Specific Performance, Recision)

to the terms if the offer is accepted. The terms of the offer must be definite and specific and must be communicated to the offeree.

An *acceptance* is a promise by the offeree to be bound by the exact terms proposed by the offeror. The acceptance must be communicated to the offeror.

Proposing any deviation from the terms of the offer constitutes a rejection of the original offer and *becomes a new offer*. This is known as a **counteroffer**, and it must be communicated to the original offering party. The counteroffer must be accepted by the original offering party for a contract to exist.

A *counteroffer* is a *new offer*; it voids the original offer.

IN PRACTICE

The process of negotiating usually follows the same basic pattern and protocol. First, the buyer makes an offer. The seller then has three options: to accept the offer, reject it, or make a counteroffer. If the seller accepts or rejects the offer, the process is over; either there is a contract or there is not. If the seller makes a counteroffer, he or she essentially is starting the process over again; the buyer now has the same three options. Through this back-and-forth process, the parties hope to come to a meeting of the minds. It's important for the broker to help the parties stay aware of where they are in the negotiating process so as to avoid confusion about what offers are (or are not) still active, because each counteroffer negates the offer that preceded it.

Besides being terminated by a counteroffer, an offer may be terminated by the offeree's outright rejection of it. Alternatively, an offeree may fail to accept the offer before it expires if a time frame was attached to the offer. The offeror may *revoke* the offer at any time before receiving the acceptance. This revocation must be communicated to the offeree by the offeror, either directly or through the parties' agents. The offer also is considered revoked if the offeree learns of the revocation and observes the offeror acting in a manner that indicates that the offer no longer exists. (See Figure 11.1.)

IN PRACTICE

The licensee must transmit all offers, acceptances, or other responses *as soon as possible* to avoid charges of deliberate delay and possible communication problems. Also, such speed is sometimes critical to the client's interests. If an agent is representing the buyer, what if another better offer comes in on the house? The house may be

FIGURE 11.1

The Negotiation Process: Offer, Counteroffer, and Acceptance Flowchart

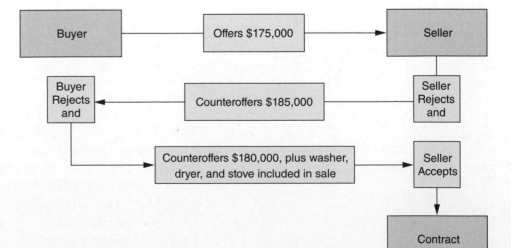

lost, or the price needed to acquire the property may escalate in a "multiple offer." If an agent represents the seller, what if a similar house down the block, with a nicer kitchen and a bigger backyard, comes on the market for a lower price? If a sales contract hasn't been signed, a seller's prospective buyer may move to make an offer on the other property. Both of these scenarios have happened!

Consideration.   The contract must be based on consideration. **Consideration** is something of legal value offered by one party and accepted by another as an inducement to perform or to refrain from performing some act. There must be a definite statement of consideration in a contract to show that something of value was given (or promised) in exchange for the other party's promise.

Consideration must be "good and valuable" between the parties. The courts do not inquire into the adequacy of consideration. Adequate consideration ranges from as little as a promise of "love and affection" to a substantial sum of money. Anything that has been bargained for and exchanged is legally sufficient to satisfy the requirement for consideration. The only requirements are that the parties agree to the consideration and that no undue influence or fraud occurred.

Reality of consent.   Under the doctrine of *reality of consent*, a contract must be entered into as the free and voluntary act of each party. Each party must be able to make a prudent and knowledgeable decision without undue influence. A mistake, misrepresentation, fraud, undue influence, or duress deprives a person of that ability. If any of these circumstances is present, the contract is voidable by the injured party. If the other party were to sue for breach, the injured party could use lack of voluntary assent as a defense.

Legally competent parties.   All parties to the contract must have legal capacity. That is, they must be of legal age and have enough mental capacity to understand the nature or consequences of their actions in the contract.

Validity of Contracts

A contract can be described as *valid, void, voidable,* or *unenforceable,* depending on the circumstances.

A contract is **valid** when it meets all the essential elements that make it legally sufficient or enforceable.

A contract is **void** when it has no legal force or effect because it lacks some or all of the essential elements of a contract.

A contract that is **voidable** appears on the surface to be valid but may be rescinded or disaffirmed by one or both parties based on some legal principle. If it is not disaffirmed, *a voidable contract may nevertheless end up being executed. A voidable contract is considered by the courts to be valid if the party who has the option to disaffirm the agreement does not do so within a period of time prescribed by state law.* A contract entered into under duress or intoxication or as a result of fraud, mistake, or misrepresentation is always voidable by the compelled or defrauded party. A contract with a minor is also voidable; minors are permitted to disaffirm real estate contracts at any time while underage and for a certain period of time after reaching majority age. Finally, a contract entered into by a mentally ill person usually is voidable *during* the mental illness and for a reasonable period after recovery.

A contract may be
- **Valid**—has all legal elements; fully enforceable;
- **Void**—lacks one or all legal elements;
- **Voidable**—has all legal elements; may be rescinded or disaffirmed; or
- **Unenforceable**—has all legal elements; enforceable only between the parties.

On the other hand, a contract made by a person who has been adjudicated insane (that is, found to be insane by a court) is void at the outset based on insanity judgments being a matter of public record.

In Illinois

Illinois law provides that all persons come of "legal age" on their 18th birthday. *Contracts entered into by a minor in Illinois are voidable until the minor reaches majority and for a reasonable time afterward.* There is no statutory period within which a person may void a contract after reaching majority in Illinois. What is considered "reasonable" depends on the circumstances of each case, although the courts tend to allow a maximum of six months.

Contracts made by a minor for what the law terms *necessaries* are generally enforceable. "Necessaries" include items such as food, clothing, shelter, and medical expenses. While a real estate sales contract with a minor probably would not be enforceable in Illinois, *leases or rental agreements signed by minors generally are enforceable* because short-term housing is usually considered a necessity. ■

IN PRACTICE

Mental capacity to enter into a contract is not the same as medical sanity. The test is whether the individual in question is capable of understanding what he or she is doing. A party may suffer from a mental illness but have a clear understanding of the significance of his or her actions. This is a thorny legal and psychological question that requires consultation with experts.

An **unenforceable contract** may seem on the surface to be valid; however, neither party can sue the other to force performance. A contract may be unenforceable because it is not in writing, as may be required under the statute of frauds.

■ **FOR EXAMPLE** An oral agreement for the sale of a parcel of real estate would be "unenforceable." An unenforceable contract is said to be "valid as between the parties." There is, however, a distinction between a suit to force performance and a suit for damages; *suits for damages are permissible in an oral agreement.* This means that once the agreement is fully executed and both parties are satisfied, neither has reason to initiate a lawsuit to force performance.

IN PRACTICE

If a contract contains any ambiguity, the courts generally interpret the agreement against the party who prepared it.

■ DISCHARGE OF CONTRACTS

A contract is discharged when the agreement is terminated. Obviously, the most desirable case is when a contract terminates because it has been completely performed, with all its terms carried out. However, a contract may be terminated for other reasons, such as a party's breach or a default.

Performance of a Contract

Each party has certain rights and duties to fulfill. The question of when a contract must be performed is an important factor. Many contracts call for a specific time by which the agreed on acts must be completely performed. In addition, many contracts provide that **time is of the essence**. This means that the contract must be performed within the time limit specified. A party who fails to perform on time is liable for breach of contract.

When a contract does not specify a date for performance, the acts it requires should be performed within a reasonable time. The interpretation of what constitutes a reasonable time depends on the situation. Generally, *unless the parties agree otherwise, if the act can be done immediately, it should be performed immediately.* Courts sometimes have declared contracts to be invalid because they did not contain a time or date for performance.

In Illinois

In Illinois, a deed or contract executed on a Sunday or legal holiday is valid and enforceable. However, when the last day on which a deed or contract must be executed is a holiday or a Sunday, the deed or contract may be executed on the next regular business day. ■

Assignment

Assignment is a transfer of rights or duties under a contract. Rights may be assigned to a third party (called the *assignee*) unless the contract forbids it. Obligations also may be assigned (or *delegated*), but the original party remains primarily liable unless specifically released. An assignment may be made without the consent of the other party unless the contract includes a clause that permits or forbids assignment.

■ **FOR EXAMPLE** Bill, widowed and in his 80s, is looking to move closer to his children. Bill has had his house up for sale for some time, and when a buyer makes an offer to purchase, Bill is sick in the hospital. Bill assigns his contract rights to his son, Andrew, so that his property may be sold in a real estate closing transaction without Bill being present or signing documents.

Novation

Assignment = *substitution of parties*
Novation = *substitution of contracts*

A contract may be performed by **novation**—that is, the substitution of a new contract in place of the original. The new agreement may be between the same parties, or a new party may be substituted for either (this is *novation of the parties*). The parties' intent must be to discharge the old obligation. For instance, when a real estate purchaser assumes the seller's existing mortgage loan, the lender may choose to release the seller and substitute the buyer as the party primarily liable for the mortgage debt. When a contract is performed by novation, both parties must consent to novation.

Breach of Contract

A contract may be terminated if it is *breached* by one of the parties. A **breach of contract** is a violation of any of the terms or conditions of a contract without legal excuse. For instance, a seller who fails to deliver title to the buyer breaches a sales contract. The breaching or defaulting party assumes certain burdens, and the nondefaulting party has certain remedies.

Buyer Remedies
■ Suit for specific performance
■ Suit for damages
■ Rescind contract

When a contract is signed by both the buyer and the seller, the buyer acquires equitable title. If the seller breaches a real estate sales contract, the buyer *can have the seller deliver legal title with a suit for* **specific performance** unless the contract specifically states otherwise. In a s**uit for specific performance**, the buyer asks the court to force the seller to go through with the sale and convey the property as previously agreed. The buyer may choose to sue for damages, in which case he or she asks that the seller pay for any costs and hardships suffered by the buyer as a result of the seller's breach. Alternatively, the buyer may *rescind* (cancel) the contract, and the seller must return any earnest money deposit.

Seller Remedies
- Suit for specific performance
- Suit for damages
- Declare contract forfeited

If the buyer defaults, the seller can sue for damages or sue for the purchase price. A suit for the purchase price is essentially a suit for specific performance: The seller tenders the deed and asks that the buyer be compelled to pay the agreed price. Or the seller may declare the contract forfeited, in which case the contract usually permits the seller to retain the buyer's earnest money as *liquidated damages*. In addition, the seller may sue for *compensatory damages* if the buyer's breach resulted in further financial losses for the seller.

The contract may limit the remedies available to the parties. A *liquidated damages clause* permits the seller to keep the earnest money deposit and any other payments received from the buyer as the seller's sole remedy. The clause may limit the buyer's remedy to a return of the earnest money and other payments should the seller default.

Statute of limitations. Every state has laws that limit the time within which parties to a contract may bring legal suit to enforce their rights. *The statute of limitations varies for different legal actions.*

In Illinois

In Illinois, the statute of limitations for oral contracts is five years; for written contracts, ten years. Any rights not enforced within the applicable time period are lost. ■

Other Reasons for Termination

Contracts may also be discharged or terminated when any of the following occurs:

- *Partial performance* of the terms, along with a written acceptance by the other party.
- *Substantial performance*, in which one party has substantially performed on the contract but does not complete all the details exactly as the contract requires. (Such performance may be enough to force payment, with certain adjustments for any damages suffered by the other party.) For instance, if a newly constructed addition to a home were finished except for polishing the brass doorknobs, the contractor would be entitled to the final payment.
- *Impossibility of performance*, in which an act required by the contract cannot be legally accomplished.
- *Mutual agreement* of the parties to cancel.
- *Operation of law*—such as in the voiding of a contract by a minor—as a result of fraud, due to the expiration of the statute of limitations, or because a contract was altered without the *written consent of all parties involved*.
- *Rescission*—one party may cancel or terminate the contract as if it had never been made. Cancellation terminates a contract without a return to the original position. Rescission, however, returns the parties to their original positions before the contract, so any monies that have been exchanged must be returned. Rescission is normally a contractual remedy for a breach, but a contract may also be rescinded by the mutual agreement of the parties.

■ CONTRACTS USED IN THE REAL ESTATE BUSINESS

The written agreements most commonly used by brokers and salespersons are

■ listing agreements and buyer agency agreements,
■ real estate sales contracts,
■ options,
■ land contracts or contracts for deed, and
■ leases and escrow agreements.

Contract forms.   Because so many real estate transactions are similar in nature, preprinted forms are available for most kinds of contracts. The use of preprinted forms raises three problems: (1) what to write in the blanks, (2) what words and phrases should be ruled out by drawing lines through them because they don't apply, and (3) what additional clauses or agreements (called *riders* or *addenda*) should be added. All changes and additions are usually initialed in the margin or on the rider by both parties when a contract is signed.

IN PRACTICE

It is essential that both parties to a contract understand exactly what they are agreeing to. Poorly drafted documents, especially those containing extensive legal language, may be subject to various interpretations and lead to litigation. The parties to a real estate transaction should be advised to have sales contracts and other legal documents examined by their lawyers before they sign to ensure that the agreements accurately reflect their intentions. When preprinted forms do not sufficiently address the unique provisions of a transaction, the parties should have an attorney draft an appropriate contract.

In Illinois

The 1966 Illinois Supreme Court decision in the case of *Chicago Bar Association, et al. v. Quinlan and Tyson, Inc.*, placed certain limitations on brokers and salespersons in drafting a contract of sale. The court ruled that *brokers and salespersons are authorized only to fill in blanks on printed form contracts* that are customarily used in the real estate community. Real estate sales contracts that fit the "customarily used" requirement typically have been drafted by local bar associations and approved by the local REALTOR® associations.

All insertions and deletions must be at the direction of the *principals*, based on the negotiations. Advising a buyer or seller of the legal significance of any part of the contract or writing any change to the form language constitutes the unauthorized practice of law.

A licensee may not request or encourage a party to sign a contract or document that contains blank spaces to be "filled in later," after signing, or make changes to a signed contract without the written consent of the parties. If changes are made by the agreement of all the principals, the buyers and sellers must initial any changes *they* agree to add. All licensees are required to give each person signing or initialing the contract an original "true copy" *within 24 hours* of the time of signing.

A licensee also must not prepare or complete any document subsequent to the sales contract or related to its implementation, such as a deed, bill of sale, affidavit of title, note, mortgage, or other legal instrument. ■

Listing and Buyer Agency Agreements

Listing and buyer agency agreements are employment contracts. A *listing agreement* establishes the rights and obligations of the broker as agent and the seller as principal. A buyer agency agreement establishes the relationship between a buyer as principal and his or her agent. (Refer to Chapter 6 for a complete discussion.)

Customary Terms of Real Estate Sales Contracts

A real estate sales contract contains the complete agreement between the buyer of a parcel of real estate and the seller. Depending on the area, this agreement may be known as an *offer to purchase*, a *contract of purchase and sale*, a *purchase agreement*, an *earnest money agreement*, a *deposit receipt*, or a *sales contract*.

In Illinois

In Illinois, a licensee should not use any form titled "Offer to Purchase" if the form is intended to become a binding real estate contract. Illinois law requires that sales contracts indicate at the top "**Real Estate Sales Contract**" in bold type. ■

Whatever the contract is called, it is an *offer to purchase* real estate as soon as it has been prepared and signed by the purchaser. If the document is accepted and signed by the seller, it becomes a contract of sale. This transformation is referred to as *ripening* the contract.

The *contract of sale* is the most important document in the sale of real estate. It establishes the legal rights and obligations of the buyer and seller. In effect, it dictates the contents of the deed.

Parts of a sales contract.   All real estate sales contracts can be divided into a number of separate parts. Although each form of contract contains these divisions, their location within a particular contract may vary. Most sales contracts include the following information:

- The purchaser's name and a statement of the purchaser's obligation to purchase the property, including how the purchaser intends to take title.
- An adequate description of the property, such as the street address. (Note that while a street address may be adequate for a sales contract, it is not legally sufficient as a description of the real property being conveyed, as discussed in Chapter 12.)
- The seller's name and a statement of the type of deed a seller agrees to give, including any covenants, conditions, and restrictions that apply to the deed.
- The purchase price and how the purchaser intends to pay for the property, including earnest money deposits, additional cash from the purchaser, and the conditions of any mortgage financing the purchaser intends to obtain or assume.
- The amount and form of the down payment or earnest money deposit and whether it will be in the form of a check or promissory note.
- A provision for the closing of the transaction and the transfer of possession of the property to the purchaser by a specific date.
- A provision for title evidence (abstract and legal opinion, certificate of title, or title insurance policy).
- The method by which real estate taxes, rents, fuel costs, and other expenses are to be prorated.
- A provision for the completion of the contract should the property be damaged or destroyed between the time of signing and the closing date.

- A liquidated damages clause, a right-to-sue provision, or another statement of remedies available in the event of default.
- Contingency clauses (such as the buyer's obtaining financing or selling a currently owned property or the seller's acquisition of another desired property or clearing of the title; attorney approval and home inspection are other commonly included contingencies).
- The dated signatures of all parties (the signature of a witness is not essential to a valid contract). In some states, the seller's nonowning spouse may be required to release potential marital or homestead rights. An agent may sign for a principal if the agent has been expressly authorized to do so. When sellers are co-owners, all must sign if the entire ownership is being transferred.
- In most states, an agency disclosure statement.

Additional provisions.   Many sales contracts provide for the following:

- Any personal property to be left with the premises for the purchaser (such as major appliances or lawn and garden equipment)
- Any real property to be removed by the seller before the closing (such as a storage shed)
- The transfer of any applicable warranties on items such as heating and cooling systems or built-in appliances
- The identification of any leased equipment that must be transferred to the purchaser or returned to the lessor (such as security systems, cable television boxes, and water softeners)
- The appointment of a closing or settlement agent
- Closing or settlement instructions
- The transfer of any impound or escrow account funds
- The transfer or payment of any outstanding special assessments
- The purchaser's right to inspect the property shortly before the closing or settlement (often called the walk-through)
- The agreement as to what documents will be provided by each party and when and where they will be delivered

In Illinois   It is not unusual to include in the sale of a residence personal property, such as drapes, as well as items that are fixtures, such as screens and storm windows, or a built-in range. In Illinois, any fixtures that might be questioned as fixtures are listed in the sales contract. This can help to eliminate possible arguments at the time of the final walk-through. Even attached bookcases and sometimes shrubbery have managed to disappear if they are not listed. Title to personal property usually is transferred by a *bill of sale, prepared by the attorney.* (A typical Illinois residential sales contract is reproduced in Figure 11.2.) ∎

Earnest money deposits.   It is customary (although not legally required) for a purchaser to provide a deposit when making an offer to purchase real estate. This deposit, usually in the form of a check, is referred to as **earnest money**. The earnest money deposit is evidence of the buyer's intention to carry out the terms of the contract in good faith. Usually the check is given to the listing broker, who holds it for the parties in a special account. If the offer is not accepted, the earnest money deposit is returned immediately to the would-be buyer.

F I G U R E   11.2

Typical Residential Real Estate Sales Contract

MULTI-BOARD RESIDENTIAL REAL ESTATE CONTRACT 4.0

1   **1. THE PARTIES:** Buyer and Seller are hereinafter referred to as the "Parties".
2
3   Buyer(s) *(Please Print)* _____
4
5   Seller(s) *(Please Print)* _____
6
7   **If Dual Agency applies, complete Optional Paragraph 41.**
8
9   **2. THE REAL ESTATE:** Real Estate shall be defined to include the Real Estate and all improvements thereon. Seller
10 agrees to convey to Buyer or to Buyer's designated grantee, the Real Estate with the approximate lot size or acreage
11 of _____ commonly known as: _____
12   Address   City   State   Zip
13 _____
14 County   Unit # (if applicable)   Permanent Index Number(s) of Real Estate
15
16 **If Condo/Coop/Townhome Parking is Included:** # of space(s) ____; identified as Space(s) # _____;
17 *(check type)* ☐ deeded space; ☐ limited common element; ☐ assigned space
18
19 **3. FIXTURES AND PERSONAL PROPERTY.** All of the fixtures and personal property stated herein are owned by
20 Seller and to Seller's knowledge are in operating condition on the Date of Acceptance, unless otherwise stated herein.
21 Seller agrees to transfer to Buyer all fixtures, all heating, electrical, plumbing and well systems together with the
22 following items of personal property by Bill of Sale at Closing: *[Check or enumerate applicable items]*

23 x Refrigerator	x All Tacked Down Carpeting	__ Fireplace Screen(s)/Door(s)/Grate(s)	x Central Air Conditioning
24 x Oven/Range/Stove	xx All Window Treatments & Hardware	__ Fireplace Gas Logs	__ Electronic or Media Air Filter
25 x Microwave	x Built-in or Attached Shelving	x Existing Storms & Screens	x Central Humidifier
26 x Dishwasher	x Smoke Detector(s)	__ Security System(s) (owned)	x Sump Pump(s)
27 x Garbage Disposal	x Ceiling Fan(s)	__ Intercom System	__ Water Softener (owned)
28 __ Trash Compactor	__ TV Antenna System	__ Central Vac & Equipment	x Outdoor Shed
29 x Washer	__ Window Air Conditioner(s)	__ Electronic Garage Door Opener(s)	__ Attached Gas Grill
30 x Dryer	xx Planted Vegetation	with all Transmitters)	x Light Fixtures, as they exist
31 __ Satellite Dish	__ Outdoor Playsets	__ Invisible Fence System, Collar(s) and Box	__ Home Warranty $_____

32 **Other items included:** _____
33 **Items NOT included:** _____
34 Seller warrants to Buyer that all fixtures, systems and personal property included in this Contract shall be in operating
35 condition at possession, except: _____.
36 A system or item shall be deemed to be in operating condition if it performs the function for which it is intended,
37 regardless of age, and does not constitute a threat to health or safety.
38
39 **4. PURCHASE PRICE:** Purchase Price of $_____ shall be paid as follows: Initial
40 earnest money of $ _____ by ☐ check, ☐ cash **OR** ☐ note due on _____, 20___,
41 to be increased to a total of $_____ by _____, 20_____. The earnest money and the
42 original of this Contract shall be held by the Listing Company, as "Escrowee", in trust for the mutual benefit of the
43 Parties. The balance of the Purchase Price, as adjusted by prorations, shall be paid at Closing by wire transfer of funds,
44 or by certified, cashier's, mortgage lender's or title company's check (provided that the title company's check is
45 guaranteed by a licensed title insurance company).
46
47 **5. CLOSING:** Closing or escrow payout shall be on _____, 20___, or at such time as
48 mutually agreed upon by the Parties in writing. Closing shall take place at the title company escrow office situated
49 geographically nearest the Real Estate or as shall be agreed mutually by the Parties.
50
51 **6. POSSESSION:** Unless otherwise provided in Paragraph 39, Seller shall deliver possession to Buyer at the time of
52 Closing. Possession shall be deemed to have been delivered when Seller has vacated the Real Estate and delivered keys
53 to the Real Estate to Buyer or to Listing Office.

Buyer Initial _____ *Buyer Initial* _____ *Seller Initial* _____ *Seller Initial* _____
Address _____

Page 1

F I G U R E   11.2 (CONTINUED)

Typical Residential Real Estate Sales Contract

54 **7. RESIDENTIAL REAL ESTATE AND LEAD-BASED PAINT DISCLOSURES:** If applicable, prior to signing
55 this Contract, Buyer *[check one]* ☑ has ☐ has not received a completed Illinois Residential Real Property Disclosure
56 Report; *[check one]* ☑ has ☐ has not received the EPA Pamphlet, "Protect Your Family From Lead in Your Home";
57 *[check one]* ☑ has ☐ has not received a Lead-Based Paint Disclosure.
58
59 **8. PRORATIONS:** Proratable items shall include, without limitation, rents and deposits (if any) from tenants, Special
60 Service Area tax for the year of closing only, utilities, water and sewer, and homeowner or condominium association
61 fees (and Master/Umbrella Association fees, if applicable). Accumulated reserves of a Homeowner/Condominium
62 Association(s) are not a proratable item. Seller represents that as of the Date of Acceptance Homeowner/Condominium
63 Association(s) fees are $_____ per _____ (and, if applicable, fees for a Master/Umbrella Association are
64 $ _____ per _____). Seller agrees to pay prior to or at Closing any special assessments (governmental or
65 association) confirmed prior to Date of Acceptance. Installments due after the year of Closing for a Special Service Area
66 shall not be a proratable item. The general Real Estate taxes shall be prorated as of the date of Closing based on
67 ___100___% of the most recent ascertainable full year tax bill. All prorations shall be final as of Closing, except as
68 provided in Paragraph 20. If the amount of the most recent ascertainable tax bill reflects a homeowner, senior citizen or
69 other exemption, Seller has submitted or will submit in a timely manner all necessary documentation to the Assessor's
70 Office, before or after Closing, to preserve said exemption(s).
71
72 **9. ATTORNEY REVIEW:** The respective attorneys for the Parties may approve, disapprove, or make modifications to
73 this Contract, other than stated Purchase Price, within five (5) Business Days after the Date of Acceptance. Disapproval
74 or modification of this Contract shall not be based solely upon stated Purchase Price. Any notice of disapproval or
75 proposed modification(s) by any Party shall be in writing. **If written notice is not served within the time specified, this**
76 **provision shall be deemed waived by the Parties and this Contract shall remain in full force and effect. If prior to**
77 **the expiration of ten (10) Business Days after Date of Acceptance, written agreement is not reached by the Parties**
78 **with respect to resolution of proposed modifications, then this Contract shall be null and void.**
79
80 **10. PROFESSIONAL INSPECTIONS**: Buyer may secure at Buyer's expense (unless otherwise provided by
81 governmental regulations) a home, radon, environmental, lead-based paint and/or lead-based paint hazards (unless
82 separately waived), and/or wood destroying insect infestation inspection(s) of said Real Estate by one or more licensed
83 or certified inspection service(s). Buyer shall serve written notice upon Seller or Seller's attorney of any defects
84 disclosed by the inspection(s) which are unacceptable to Buyer, together with a copy of the pertinent page(s) of the
85 report(s) within five (5) Business Days (ten (10) calendar days for a lead-based paint and/or lead-based paint hazard
86 inspection) after Date of Acceptance. **If written notice is not served within the time specified, this provision shall be**
87 **deemed waived by the Parties and this Contract shall remain in full force and effect. If prior to the expiration of**
88 **ten (10) Business Days after Date of Acceptance, written agreement is not reached by the Parties with respect to**
89 **resolution of inspection issues, then this Contract shall be null and void.** The home inspection shall cover **only**
90 major components of the Real Estate, including but not limited to, central heating system(s), central cooling system(s),
91 plumbing and well system, electrical system, roof, walls, windows, ceilings, floors, appliances and foundation. A major
92 component shall be deemed to be in operating condition if it performs the function for which it is intended, regardless of
93 age, and does not constitute a threat to health or safety. The fact that a functioning component may be at the end of its
94 useful life shall not render such component defective for the purpose of this paragraph. Buyer shall indemnify Seller
95 and hold Seller harmless from and against any loss or damage caused by the acts or negligence of Buyer or any person
96 performing any inspection(s). **Buyer agrees minor repairs and routine maintenance items are not a part of this**
97 **contingency.** If radon mitigation is performed, Seller shall pay for a retest.
98
99 **11. MORTGAGE CONTINGENCY:** Seller *[check one]* ☐ has ☐ has not received a completed Loan Status
100 Disclosure (see page 11). This Contract is contingent upon Buyer obtaining a firm written mortgage commitment
101 (except for matters of title and survey or matters totally within Buyer's control) on or before _____, 20___
102 for a *[choose one]* ☐ fixed ☐ adjustable; *[choose one]* ☐ conventional ☐ FHA/VA ☐ other_____

| Buyer Initial _____ Buyer Initial _____ Seller Initial _____ Seller Initial_____ |
| Address _____ |

Typical Residential Real Estate Sales Contract

103 loan of $_____ or such lesser amount as Buyer elects to take, plus private mortgage insurance (PMI), if
104 required. The interest rate (initial rate, if applicable) shall not exceed _____% per annum, amortized over not less than
105 _____ years. Buyer shall pay loan origination fee and/or discount points not to exceed _____% of the loan amount.
106 Buyer shall pay the cost of application, usual and customary processing fees and closing costs charged by lender. (If
107 FHA/VA, complete Paragraph 35.) (If closing cost credit, complete Paragraph 33.) Buyer shall make written loan
108 application within five (5) Business Days after the Date of Acceptance. **Failure to do so shall constitute an act of**
109 **Default under this Contract. If Buyer, having applied for the loan specified above, is unable to obtain such loan**
110 **commitment and serves written notice to Seller within the time specified, this Contract shall be null and void. If**
111 **written notice of inability to obtain such loan commitment is not served within the time specified, Buyer shall be**
112 **deemed to have waived this contingency and this Contract shall remain in full force and effect. Unless otherwise**
113 **provided in Paragraph 31, this Contract shall not be contingent upon the sale and/or closing of Buyer's existing**
114 **real estate.** Buyer shall be deemed to have satisfied the financing conditions of this paragraph if Buyer obtains a loan
115 commitment in accordance with the terms of this paragraph even though the loan is conditioned on the sale and/or
116 closing of Buyer's existing real estate. If Seller at Seller's option and expense, within thirty (30) days after Buyer's
117 notice, procures for Buyer such commitment or notifies Buyer that Seller will accept a purchase money mortgage upon
118 the same terms, this Contract shall remain in full force and effect. In such event, Seller shall notify Buyer within five (5)
119 Business Days after Buyer's notice of Seller's election to provide or obtain such financing, and Buyer shall furnish to
120 Seller or lender all requested information and shall sign all papers necessary to obtain the mortgage commitment and to
121 close the loan.
122
123 **12. HOMEOWNER INSURANCE:** This Contract is contingent upon Buyer's securing evidence of insurability for an
124 Insurance Service Organization Homeowner 3 (ISOHO3) or applicable equivalent policy at Preferred Premium rates
125 within ten (10) Business Days after Date of Acceptance. **If Buyer is unable to obtain evidence of insurability and**
126 **serves written notice with proof of same to Seller within the time specified, this Contract shall be null and void. If**
127 **written notice is not served within the time specified, Buyer shall be deemed to have waived this contingency and**
128 **this Contract shall remain in full force and effect.**
129
130 **13. FLOOD INSURANCE**: Unless previously disclosed in the Illinois Residential Real Property Disclosure Report,
131 Buyer shall have the option to declare this Contract null and void if the Real Estate is located in a special flood hazard
132 area which requires Buyer to carry flood insurance. **If written notice of the option to declare this Contract null and**
133 **void is not given to Seller within ten (10) Business Days after Date of Acceptance or within the term specified in**
134 **Paragraph 11 (whichever is later), Buyer shall be deemed to have waived such option and this Contract shall**
135 **remain in full force and effect.** Nothing herein shall be deemed to affect any rights afforded by the Residential Real
136 Property Disclosure Act.
137
138 **14. CONDOMINIUM/COMMON INTEREST ASSOCIATIONS**: (If applicable) The Parties agree that the terms
139 contained in this paragraph, which may be contrary to other terms of this Contract, shall supersede any conflicting terms.
140   (a) Title when conveyed shall be good and merchantable, subject to terms, provisions, covenants and conditions of
141   the Declaration of Condominium/Covenants, Conditions and Restrictions and all amendments; public and utility
142   easements including any easements established by or implied from the Declaration of Condominium/Covenants,
143   Conditions and Restrictions or amendments thereto; party wall rights and agreements; limitations and conditions
144   imposed by the Condominium Property Act; installments due after the date of Closing of general assessments
145   established pursuant to the Declaration of Condominium/Covenants, Conditions and Restrictions.
146   (b) Seller shall be responsible for all regular assessments due and levied prior to Closing and for all special
147   assessments confirmed prior to the Date of Acceptance.
148   (c) Buyer has, within five (5) Business Days from the Date of Acceptance, the right to demand from Seller items as
149   stipulated by the Illinois Condominium Property Act, if applicable, and Seller shall diligently apply for same.
150   This Contract is subject to the condition that Seller be able to procure and provide to Buyer, a release or waiver
151   of any option of first refusal or other pre-emptive rights of purchase created by the Declaration of
152   Condominium/Covenants, Conditions and Restrictions within the time established by the Declaration of
153   Condominium/Covenants, Conditions and Restrictions. In the event the Condominium Association requires

Buyer Initial _____ *Buyer Initial* _____ *Seller Initial* _____ *Seller Initial*_____
Address _____

F I G U R E   11.2 (CONTINUED)

Typical Residential Real Estate Sales Contract

154   personal appearance of Buyer and/or additional documentation, Buyer agrees to comply with same.
155   (d) In the event the documents and information provided by Seller to Buyer disclose that the existing improvements
156   are in violation of existing rules, regulations or other restrictions or that the terms and conditions contained
157   within the documents would unreasonably restrict Buyer's use of the premises or would result in increased
158   financial obligations unacceptable to Buyer in connection with owning the Real Estate, **then Buyer may**
159   **declare this Contract null and void by giving Seller written notice within five (5) Business Days after the**
160   **receipt of the documents and information required by Paragraph 14 (c), listing those deficiencies which**
161   **are unacceptable to Buyer. If written notice is not served within the time specified, Buyer shall be deemed**
162   **to have waived this contingency, and this Contract shall remain in full force and effect.**
163   (e) Seller shall not be obligated to provide a condominium survey.
164   (f) Seller shall provide a certificate of insurance showing Buyer (and Buyer's mortgagee, if any) as an insured.
165
166   **15. THE DEED**: Seller shall convey or cause to be conveyed to Buyer or Buyer's designated grantee good and
167   merchantable title to the Real Estate by recordable general Warranty Deed, with release of homestead rights, (or the
168   appropriate deed if title is in trust or in an estate), and with real estate transfer stamps to be paid by Seller (unless
169   otherwise designated by local ordinance). Title when conveyed will be good and merchantable, subject only to: general
170   real estate taxes not due and payable at the time of Closing, covenants, conditions, and restrictions of record, building
171   lines and easements, if any, so long as they do not interfere with the current use and enjoyment of the Real Estate.
172
173   **16. TITLE:** At Seller's expense, Seller will deliver or cause to be delivered to Buyer or Buyer's attorney within
174   customary time limitations and sufficiently in advance of Closing, as evidence of title in Seller or Grantor, a title
175   commitment for an ALTA title insurance policy in the amount of the Purchase Price with extended coverage by a title
176   company licensed to operate in the State of Illinois, issued on or subsequent to the Date of Acceptance, subject only to
177   items listed in Paragraph 15. The requirement of providing extended coverage shall not apply if the Real Estate is vacant
178   land. The commitment for title insurance furnished by Seller will be conclusive evidence of good and merchantable title
179   as therein shown, subject only to the exceptions therein stated. If the title commitment discloses unpermitted exceptions,
180   or if the Plat of Survey shows any encroachments which are not acceptable to Buyer, then Seller shall have said
181   exceptions or encroachments removed, or have the title insurer commit to insure against loss or damage that may be
182   caused by such exceptions or encroachments. If Seller fails to have unpermitted exceptions waived or title insured over
183   prior to Closing, Buyer may elect to take the title as it then is, with the right to deduct from the Purchase Price prior
184   encumbrances of a definite or ascertainable amount. Seller shall furnish Buyer at Closing an Affidavit of Title covering
185   the date of Closing, and shall sign any other customary forms required for issuance of an ALTA Insurance Policy.
186
187   **17. PLAT OF SURVEY**: Not less than one (1) Business Day prior to Closing, except where the Real Estate is a
188   condominium (see Paragraph 14) Seller shall, at Seller's expense, furnish to Buyer or Buyer's attorney a Plat of Survey
189   dated not more than six (6) months prior to the date of Closing, prepared by an Illinois Professional Land Surveyor,
190   showing any encroachments, measurements of all lot lines, all easements of record, building set back lines of record,
191   fences, all buildings and other improvements on the Real Estate and distances therefrom to the nearest two lot lines. In
192   addition, the survey to be provided shall be a boundary survey conforming to the current requirements of the appropriate
193   state regulatory authority. The survey shall show all corners staked, flagged, or otherwise monumented. The survey shall
194   have the following statement prominently appearing near the professional land surveyor seal and signature: "This
195   professional service conforms to the current Illinois minimum standards for a boundary survey". A Mortgage Inspection,
196   as defined, is not a boundary survey, and is not acceptable.
197
198   **18. ESCROW CLOSING**: At the election of either Party, not less than five (5) Business Days prior to the Closing, this
199   sale shall be closed through an escrow with the lending institution or the title company in accordance with the provisions
200   of the usual form of Deed and Money Escrow Agreement, as agreed upon between the Parties, with provisions inserted
201   in the Escrow Agreement as may be required to conform with this Contract. The cost of the escrow shall be paid by the
202   Party requesting the escrow. If this transaction is a cash purchase (no mortgage is secured by Buyer), the Parties shall
203   share the title company escrow closing fee equally.
204

Buyer Initial _____ *Buyer Initial* _____ *Seller Initial* _____ *Seller Initial* _____
Address _____

FIGURE   11.2 (CONTINUED)

Typical Residential Real Estate Sales Contract

205 **19. DAMAGE TO REAL ESTATE PRIOR TO CLOSING**: If, prior to delivery of the deed, the Real Estate shall be
206 destroyed or materially damaged by fire or other casualty, or the Real Estate is taken by condemnation, then Buyer shall
207 have the option of either terminating this Contract (and receiving a refund of earnest money) or accepting the Real
208 Estate as damaged or destroyed, together with the proceeds of the condemnation award or any insurance payable as a
209 result of the destruction or damage, which gross proceeds Seller agrees to assign to Buyer and deliver to Buyer at
210 closing. Seller shall not be obligated to repair or replace damaged improvements. The provisions of the Uniform Vendor
211 and Purchaser Risk Act of the State of Illinois shall be applicable to this Contract, except as modified in this paragraph.
212

213 **20. REAL ESTATE TAX ESCROW**: In the event the Real Estate is improved, but has not been previously taxed for
214 the entire year as currently improved, the sum of three percent (3%) of the Purchase Price shall be deposited in escrow
215 with the title company with the cost of the escrow to be divided equally by Buyer and Seller and paid at Closing. When
216 the exact amount of the taxes prorated under this Contract can be ascertained, the taxes shall be prorated by Seller's
217 attorney at the request of either Party, and Seller's share of such tax liability after reproration shall be paid to Buyer from
218 the escrow funds and the balance, if any, shall be paid to Seller. If Seller's obligation after such reproration exceeds the
219 amount of the escrow funds, Seller agrees to pay such excess promptly upon demand.
220

221 **21. SELLER REPRESENTATIONS**: Seller represents that Seller has not received written notice from any
222 Governmental body or Homeowner Association regarding (a) zoning, building, fire or health code violations that have
223 not been corrected; (b) any pending rezoning; (c) any pending condemnation or eminent domain proceeding; or (d) a
224 proposed or confirmed special assessment and/or Special Service Area affecting the Real Estate. Seller represents,
225 however, that, in the case of a special assessment and/or Special Service Area, the following applies:
226   1. There *[check one]* is ☐ is not ☑ a proposed or pending unconfirmed special assessment affecting the Real
227   Estate not payable by Seller after date of Closing.
228   2. The Real Estate *[check one]* is ☐ is not ☑ located within a Special Service Area, payments for which will
229   not be the obligation of Seller after date of Closing.
230 **If any of the representations contained herein regarding non-Homeowner Association special assessment or**
231 **Special Service Area are unacceptable to Buyer, Buyer shall have the option to declare this Contract null and**
232 **void. If written notice of the option to declare this Contract null and void is not given to Seller within ten (10)**
233 **Business Days after Date of Acceptance or within the term specified in Paragraph 11 (whichever is later), Buyer**
234 **shall be deemed to have waived such option and this Contract shall remain in full force and effect.** Seller further
235 represents that Seller has no knowledge of boundary line disputes, easements or claims of easement not shown by the
236 public records, any hazardous waste on the Real Estate or any improvements for which the required permits were not
237 obtained. Seller represents that there have been no improvements to the Real Estate which are not either included in full
238 in the determination of the most recent real estate tax assessment or which are eligible for home improvement tax
239 exemption.
240

241 **22. CONDITION OF REAL ESTATE AND INSPECTION:** Seller agrees to leave the Real Estate in broom clean
242 condition. All refuse and personal property that is not to be conveyed to Buyer shall be removed from the Real Estate at
243 Seller's expense before possession. Buyer shall have the right to inspect the Real Estate, fixtures and personal property
244 prior to possession to verify that the Real Estate, improvements and included personal property are in substantially the
245 same condition as of the Date of Acceptance, normal wear and tear excepted.
246

247 **23. GOVERNMENTAL COMPLIANCE**: Parties agree to comply with the reporting requirements of the applicable
248 sections of the Internal Revenue Code and the Real Estate Settlement Procedures Act of 1974, as amended.
249

250 **24. BUSINESS DAYS/HOURS**: Business Days are defined as Monday through Friday, excluding Federal holidays.
251 Business Hours are defined as 8:00 A.M. to 6:00 P.M. Chicago time.
252

253 **25. FACSIMILE**: Facsimile signatures shall be sufficient for purposes of executing, negotiating, and finalizing this
254 Contract.

Buyer Initial _____ *Buyer Initial* _____ *Seller Initial* _____ *Seller Initial*_____
Address _____

F I G U R E   11.2 (CONTINUED)

Typical Residential Real Estate Sales Contract

255 **26. DIRECTION TO ESCROWEE:** In every instance where this Contract shall be deemed null and void or if this
256 Contract may be terminated by either Party, the following shall be deemed incorporated: "and earnest money refunded to
257 Buyer upon written direction of the Parties to Escrowee or upon entry of an order by a court of competent jurisdiction".
258

259 **27. NOTICE**: All Notices, except as provided otherwise in Paragraph 31(C) (2), shall be in writing and shall be served
260 by one Party or attorney to the other Party or attorney. Notice to any one of a multiple person Party shall be sufficient
261 Notice to all. Notice shall be given in the following manner:
262   (a) By personal delivery of such Notice; or
263   (b) By mailing of such Notice to the addresses recited herein by regular mail and by certified mail, return receipt
264   requested. Except as otherwise provided herein, Notice served by certified mail shall be effective on the date of
265   mailing; or
266   (c) By sending facsimile transmission. Notice shall be effective as of date and time of facsimile transmission,
267   provided that the Notice transmitted shall be sent on Business Days during Business Hours. In the event fax
268   Notice is transmitted during non-business hours, the effective date and time of Notice is the first hour of the next
269   Business Day after transmission; or
270   (d) By sending e-mail transmission. Notice shall be effective as of date and time of e-mail transmission, provided
271   that the Notice transmitted shall be sent during Business Hours, and provided further that the recipient provides
272   written acknowledgment to the sender of receipt of the transmission (by e-mail, facsimile, regular mail or
273   commercial overnight delivery). In the event e-mail Notice is transmitted during non-business hours, the
274   effective date and time of Notice is the first hour of the next Business Day after transmission; or
275   (e) By commercial overnight delivery (e.g., FedEx). Such Notice shall be effective on the next Business Day
276   following deposit with the overnight delivery company.
277

278 **28. PERFORMANCE: Time is of the essence of this Contract**. In any action with respect to this Contract, the Parties
279 are free to pursue any legal remedies at law or in equity and the prevailing Party in litigation shall be entitled to collect
280 reasonable attorney fees and costs from the non-Prevailing Party as ordered by a court of competent jurisdiction. There
281 shall be no disbursement of earnest money unless Escrowee has been provided written agreement from Seller and Buyer.
282 Absent an agreement relative to the disbursement of earnest money within a reasonable period of time, Escrowee may
283 deposit funds with the Clerk of the Circuit Court by the filing of an action in the nature of interpleader. Escrowee shall
284 be reimbursed from the earnest money for all costs, including reasonable attorney fees, related to the filing of the
285 interpleader action. Seller and Buyer shall indemnify and hold Escrowee harmless from any and all conflicting claims
286 and demands arising under this paragraph.
287

288 **29. CHOICE OF LAW/GOOD FAITH**: All terms and provisions of this Contract including, but not limited to, the
289 Attorney Review and Professional Inspection paragraphs, shall be governed by the laws of the State of Illinois and are
290 subject to the covenant of good faith and fair dealing implied in all Illinois contracts.
291

292 **30. OTHER PROVISIONS:** This Contract is also subject to those OPTIONAL PROVISIONS selected for use and
293 initialed by the Parties which are contained in the following paragraphs and attachments, if any: _____
294 _____
295

296 **THE FOLLOWING OPTIONAL PROVISIONS APPLY ONLY IF INITIALED BY ALL PARTIES**
297

298 ____ ____ ____ ____   **31. SALE OF BUYER'S REAL ESTATE**:
299   Initials

300 **(A) REPRESENTATIONS ABOUT BUYER'S REAL ESTATE:** Buyer represents to Seller as follows:
301   (1) Buyer owns real estate commonly known as (address):
302   _____
303   (2) Buyer *[check one]* ☐ has ☐ has not entered into a contract to sell said real estate. If Buyer has entered into a contract to
304   sell said real estate, that contract:
305   (a) *[check one]* ☐ is ☐ is not subject to a mortgage contingency.

Buyer Initial _____   *Buyer Initial* _____   *Seller Initial* _____   *Seller Initial*_____
Address _____

Page 6

Typical Residential Real Estate Sales Contract

306   (b) *[check one]* ☐ is ☐ is not subject to a real estate sale contingency.

307   (c) *[check one]* ☐ is ☐ is not subject to a real estate closing contingency.

308   (3) Buyer *[check one]* ☐ has ☐ has not listed said real estate for sale with a licensed real estate broker and in a local
309   multiple listing service.

310   (4) If Buyer's real estate is not listed for sale with a licensed real estate broker and in a local multiple listing service,
311   Buyer *[check one]*

312   (a) ☐ Shall list said real estate for sale with a licensed real estate broker who will place it in a local multiple listing
313   service within five (5) Business Days after the Date of Acceptance.
314   For information only: Broker: _____
315   Broker's Address: _____ Phone: _____

316   (b) ☐ Does not intend to list said real estate for sale.

317 **(B) CONTINGENCIES BASED UPON SALE AND/OR CLOSE OF BUYER'S REAL ESTATE:**

318   (1) This Contract is contingent upon Buyer having entered into a contract for the sale of Buyer's real estate that is in full force
319   and effect as of _____, 20_____. Such contract shall provide for a closing date not later than the Closing
320   Date set forth in this Contract. **If written notice is served on or before the date set forth in this subparagraph that**
321   **Buyer has not procured a contract for the sale of Buyer's real estate, this Contract shall be null and void. If written**
322   **notice that Buyer has not procured a contract for the sale of Buyer's real estate is not served on or before the close**
323   **of business on the date set forth in this subparagraph, Buyer shall be deemed to have waived all contingencies**
324   **contained in this Paragraph 31, and this Contract shall remain in full force and effect.** (If this paragraph is used, then
325   the following paragraph must be completed.)

326   (2) In the event Buyer has entered into a contract for the sale of Buyer's real estate as set forth in Paragraph 31 (B) (1) and that
327   contract is in full force and effect, or has entered into a contract for sale of Buyer's real estate prior to the execution of this
328   Contract, this Contract is contingent upon Buyer closing the sale of Buyer's real estate on or before
329   _____, 20____. **If written notice that Buyer has not closed the sale of Buyer's real estate is**
330   **served before the close of business on the next Business Day after the date set forth in the preceding sentence, this**
331   **Contract shall be null and void. If written notice is not served as described in the preceding sentence, Buyer shall be**
332   **deemed to have waived all contingencies contained in this Paragraph 31, and this Contract shall remain in full force**
333   **and effect.**

334   (3) If the contract for the sale of Buyer's real estate is terminated for any reason after the date set forth in Paragraph 31 (B) (1)
335   (or after the date of this Contract if no date is set forth in Paragraph 31 (B) (1)), Buyer shall, within three (3) Business Days
336   of such termination, notify Seller of said termination. **Unless Buyer, as part of said notice, waives all contingencies in**
337   **Paragraph 31 and complies with Paragraph 31 (D), this Contract shall be null and void as of the date of notice. If**
338   **written notice as required by this subparagraph is not served within the time specified, Buyer shall be in default**
339   **under the terms of this Contract.**

340 **(C) SELLER'S RIGHT TO CONTINUE TO OFFER REAL ESTATE FOR SALE:** During the time of this contingency, Seller
341 has the right to continue to show the Real Estate and offer it for sale subject to the following:

342   (1) If Seller accepts another bona fide offer to purchase the Real Estate while the contingencies expressed in subparagraph (B)
343   are in effect, Seller shall notify Buyer in writing of same. Buyer shall then have _____ hours after Seller gives such
344   notice to waive the contingencies set forth in Paragraph 31 (B), subject to Paragraph 31 (D).

345   (2) **Seller's notice to Buyer (commonly referred to as a "kick-out" notice) shall be served on Buyer, not Buyer's**
346   **attorney or Buyer's real estate agent.** Courtesy copies of such "kick-out" notice should be sent to Buyer's attorney and
347   real estate agent, if known. Failure to provide such courtesy copies shall not render notice invalid. Notice to any one of a
348   multiple-person Buyer shall be sufficient notice to all Buyers. Notice for the purpose of this subparagraph only shall be
349   served upon Buyer in the following manner:

350   (a) By personal delivery of such notice effective at the time and date of personal delivery; or

351   (b) By mailing of such notice to the addresses recited herein for Buyer by regular mail and by certified mail. Notice
352   served by regular mail and certified mail shall be effective at 10:00 A.M. on the morning of the second day following
353   deposit of notice in U.S. Mail; or

354   (c) By commercial overnight delivery (e.g., FedEx). Such notice shall be effective upon delivery or at 4:00 P.M. Chicago
355   time on the next delivery day following deposit with the overnight delivery company, whichever first occurs.

356   (3) If Buyer complies with the provisions of Paragraph 31 (D) then this Contract shall remain in full force and effect.

357   (4) If the contingencies set forth in Paragraph 31 (B) are NOT waived in writing within said time period by Buyer, this
358   Contract shall be null and void.

359   (5) Except as provided in subsections to subparagraph (C) (2) above, all notices shall be made in the manner provided by

Buyer Initial _____ *Buyer Initial* _____ *Seller Initial* _____ *Seller Initial* _____
Address _____

F I G U R E   11.2 (CONTINUED)

Typical Residential Real Estate Sales Contract

360   Paragraph 27 of this Contract.
361   (6) Buyer waives any ethical objection to the delivery of notice under this paragraph by Seller's attorney or representative.
362   **(D) WAIVER OF PARAGRAPH 31 CONTINGENCIES**: Buyer shall be deemed to have waived the contingencies in Paragraph
363   31 (B) when Buyer has delivered written waiver and deposited with the Escrowee the additional sum of $_____
364   earnest money within the time specified. **If Buyer fails to deposit the additional earnest money within the time specified, the**
365   **waiver shall be deemed ineffective and this Contract shall be null and void.**
366   **(E) BUYER COOPERATION REQUIRED:** Buyer authorizes Seller or Seller's agent to verify representations contained in
367   Paragraph 31 at any time, and Buyer agrees to cooperate in providing relevant information.
368
369   ____ ____ ____ ____ **32. CANCELLATION OF PRIOR REAL ESTATE CONTRACT:** In the event either Party has entered
370   into a prior real estate contract, this Contract shall be subject to written cancellation of the prior contract on or before
371   _____, 20____. **In the event the prior contract is not cancelled within the time specified, this Contract shall be**
372   **null and void. Notice to the purchaser under the prior contract should not be served until after Attorney Review and**
373   **Professional Inspections provisions of this Contract have expired, been satisfied or waived.**
374
375   ____ ____ ____ ____ **33. CLOSING COST CREDIT:** Provided Buyer's lender permits such credit to show on the HUD-1
376   Settlement Statement, **and if not, such lesser amount as the lender permits,** Seller agrees to credit to Buyer
377    $_____ at closing.
378
379   ____ ____ ____ ____ **34. INTEREST BEARING ACCOUNT**: Earnest money (with a completed W-9 and other required forms),
380   shall be held in a federally insured interest bearing account at a financial institution designated by Escrowee. All interest earned on
381   the earnest money shall accrue to the benefit of and be paid to Buyer. **Buyer shall be responsible for any administrative fee (not**
382   **to exceed $100) charged for setting up the account.** In anticipation of Closing, the Parties direct Escrowee to close the account no
383   sooner than ten (10) Business Days prior to the anticipated Closing date.
384
385   ____ ____ ____ ____ **35. VA OR FHA FINANCING**: If Buyer is seeking VA or FHA financing, this provision shall be applicable:
386   Buyer may terminate this Contract if the Purchase Price set forth herein exceeds the appraised value of the Real Estate, as
387   determined by the Veterans Administration (VA) or the Federal Housing Administration (FHA). However, Buyer shall have the
388   option of proceeding with this Contract without regard to the amount of the appraised valuation. If VA, the Funding Fee, or if FHA,
389   the Mortgage Insurance Premium (MIP) shall be paid by Buyer and *[check one]* ☐ shall ☐ shall not be added to the mortgage
390   loan amount. Seller agrees to pay additional miscellaneous expenses required by lender not to exceed $200.00. **Required FHA or**
391   **VA amendments shall be attached to this Contract.** It is expressly agreed that notwithstanding any other provisions of this
392   Contract, Buyer shall not be obligated to complete the purchase of the property described herein or to incur any penalty by forfeiture
393   of earnest money deposits or otherwise unless Buyer has been given, in accordance with HUD/FHA requirements, a written
394   statement by the Federal Housing Commissioner setting forth the appraised value of the property (excluding Closing costs) of not
395   less than $_____. Buyer shall have the privilege and option of proceeding with the consummation of the
396   Contract without regard to the amount of the appraised valuation. The appraised valuation is arrived at to determine the maximum
397   mortgage the Department of Housing and Urban Development will insure/guarantee. HUD and the mortgagee do not warrant the
398   value nor the condition of the property. Buyer should satisfy himself/herself that the price and condition of the property are
399   acceptable.
400
401   ____ ____ ____ ____ **36. INTERIM FINANCING**: This Contract is contingent upon Buyer obtaining a written commitment for
402   interim financing on or before _____, 20____ in the amount of $_____. **If Buyer is unable**
403   **to secure the interim financing commitment and gives written notice to Seller within the time specified, this Contract shall be**
404   **null and void. If written notice is not served within the time specified, this provision shall be deemed waived by the Parties**
405   **and this Contract shall remain in full force and effect.**
406
407   ____ ____ ____ ____ **37. WELL AND/OR SEPTIC/SANITARY INSPECTIONS**: Seller shall obtain at Seller's expense a well
408   water test stating that the well delivers not less than five (5) gallons of water per minute and including a bacteria and nitrate test (and
409   lead test for FHA loans) and/or a septic report from the applicable County Health Department, a Licensed Environmental Health
410   Practitioner, or a licensed well and septic inspector, each dated not more than ninety (90) days prior to Closing, stating that the well
411   and water supply and the private sanitary system are in proper operating condition with no defects noted. Seller shall remedy any
412   defect or deficiency disclosed by said report(s) prior to Closing; provided that if the cost of remedying a defect or deficiency and the
413   cost of landscaping together exceed $3,000.00, and if the Parties cannot reach agreement regarding payment of such additional cost,
414   then this Contract may be terminated by either Party. Additional testing recommended by the report shall be obtained at Seller's

Buyer Initial _____ *Buyer Initial* _____ *Seller Initial* _____ *Seller Initial*_____
Address _____

Typical Residential Real Estate Sales Contract

415 expense. If the report recommends additional testing after Closing, the Parties shall have the option of establishing an escrow with a
416 mutual cost allocation for necessary repairs or replacements, or either Party may terminate this Contract prior to Closing. Seller shall
417 deliver a copy of such evaluation(s) to Buyer not less than one (1) Business Day prior to Closing.
418
419 ____ ____ ____ ____ **38. WOOD DESTROYING INFESTATION:** Notwithstanding the provisions of Paragraph 10, within ten
420 (10) Business Days after the Date of Acceptance, Seller at Seller's expense shall deliver to Buyer a written report, dated not more
421 than six (6) months prior to the date of Closing, by a licensed inspector certified by the appropriate state regulatory authority in the
422 subcategory of termites, stating that there is no visible evidence of active infestation by termites or other wood destroying insects.
423 Unless otherwise agreed between the Parties, if the report discloses evidence of active infestation or structural damage, Buyer has
424 the option within five (5) Business Days of receipt of the report to proceed with the purchase or declare this Contract null and void.
425 This paragraph shall not apply to condominiums or to newly constructed property having been occupied for less than one year
426 following completion of construction.
427
428 ____ ____ ____ ____ **39. POST-CLOSING POSSESSION:** Possession shall be delivered no later than 11:59 P.M. on the date that
429 is _____ days after the date of Closing ("the Possession Date"). Seller shall be responsible for all utilities, contents and liability
430 insurance, and home maintenance expenses until delivery of possession. Seller shall deposit in escrow at Closing
431 with_____*[choose one]* ☐ one percent (1%) of the Purchase Price or ☐ the sum of $ _____
432 _____to be paid by Escrowee as follows: a) The sum of $ _____ per day for use and occupancy from and including the
433 day after Closing to and including the day of delivery of possession, if on or before the Possession Date; b) The amount per day
434 equal to five (5) times the daily amount set forth herein shall be paid for each day after the Possession Date specified in this
435 paragraph that Seller remains in possession of the real estate; and c) The balance, if any, to Seller after delivery of possession and
436 provided that the terms of Paragraph 22 have been satisfied. Seller's liability under this paragraph shall not be limited to the amount
437 of the possession escrow deposit referred to above. Nothing herein shall be deemed to create a Landlord/Tenant relationship
438 between the Parties.
439
440 ____ ____ ____ ____ **40. "AS IS" CONDITION:** This Contract is for the sale and purchase of the Real Estate and personal
441 property in its "As Is" condition as of the Date of Offer. Buyer acknowledges that no representations, warranties or guarantees with
442 respect to the condition of the Real Estate and personal property have been made by Seller or Seller's Agent other than those known
443 defects, if any, disclosed by Seller. Buyer may conduct an inspection at Buyer's expense. In that event, Seller shall make the
444 property available to Buyer's inspector at reasonable times. Buyer shall indemnify Seller and hold Seller harmless from and against
445 any loss or damage caused by the acts or negligence of Buyer or any person performing any inspection(s). **In the event the**
446 **inspection reveals that the condition of the improvements, fixtures or personal property to be conveyed or transferred is**
447 **unacceptable to Buyer and Buyer so notifies Seller within five (5) Business Days after the Date of Acceptance, this Contract**
448 **shall be null and void. Failure of Buyer to notify Seller or to conduct said inspection operates as a waiver of Buyer's right to**
449 **terminate this Contract under this paragraph and this Contract shall remain in full force and effect.** Buyer acknowledges the
450 provisions of Paragraph 10 and the warranty provisions of Paragraph 3 do not apply to this Contract.
451
452 ____ ____ ____ ____ **41. CONFIRMATION OF DUAL AGENCY**: The Parties confirm that they have previously consented to
453 _____ (Licensee) acting as a Dual Agent in providing brokerage services
454 on their behalf and specifically consent to Licensee acting as a Dual Agent with regard to the transaction referred to in this Contract.
455
456 ____ ____ ____ ____ **42. SPECIFIED PARTY APPROVAL:** This Contract is contingent upon the approval of the Real Estate by
457 _____, Buyer's specified party,
458 within five (5) Business Days after the Date of Acceptance. **In the event Buyer's specified party does not approve of the Real**
459 **Estate and written notice is given to Seller within the time specified, this Contract shall be null and void. If written notice is**
460 **not served within the time specified, this provision shall be deemed waived by the Parties and this Contract shall remain in**
461 **full force and effect.**
462
463 ____ ____/ ____ ____ **43. MISCELLANEOUS PROVISIONS:** Buyer's and Seller's obligations are contingent upon the Parties
464 entering into a separate written agreement consistent with the terms and conditions set forth herein, and with such additional terms
465 as either Party may deem necessary, providing for one or more of the following: *(check applicable box(es))*

466 ☐ Assumption of Seller's Mortgage   ☐ New Construction
467 ☐ Commercial/Investment/Starker Exchange   ☐ Vacant Land
468 ☐ Cooperative Apartment   ☐ Articles of Agreement for Deed or Purchase Money Mortgage

Buyer Initial _____ *Buyer Initial* _____ *Seller Initial* _____ *Seller Initial*_____
Address _____

F I G U R E   **11.2 (CONTINUED)**

Typical Residential Real Estate Sales Contract

469 **THIS DOCUMENT WILL BECOME A LEGALLY BINDING CONTRACT WHEN SIGNED BY ALL**
470 **PARTIES AND DELIVERED TO THE PARTIES OR THEIR AGENTS.**
471
472 The Parties represent that text of this form has not been altered and is identical to the official Multi-Board Residential
473 Real Estate Contract 4.0.
474 _____ 20____   _____ 20____
475 Date of Offer   **DATE OF ACCEPTANCE**
476
477 _____   _____
478 Buyer Signature   Seller Signature
479 _____   _____
480 Buyer Signature   Seller Signature
481 Print Buyer(s) Name(s) *[Required]*   Print Seller(s) Name(s) *[Required]*
482
483 Address   Address
484
485 City   State   Zip   City   State   Zip
486
487 Phone   E-mail   Phone   E-mail
488   *FOR INFORMATION ONLY*
489
490 Selling Office   MLS #   Listing Office   MLS #
491
492 Buyer's Designated Agent   MLS #   Seller's Designated Agent   MLS #
493
494 Phone   Fax   Phone   Fax
495
496 E-mail   E-mail
497
498 Buyer's Attorney   E-mail   Seller's Attorney   E-mail
499
500 Phone   Fax   Phone   Fax
501
502 Mortgage Company   Phone   Homeowner's/Condo Association (if any)   Phone
503
504 Loan Officer   Fax   Management Co./Other Contact   Phone
505

508
509   *Approved by the following organizations February 2006.*
510 Illinois Real Estate Lawyers Association, Aurora Tri-County Association of REALTORS®, Chicago Association of REALTORS®,
511 DuPage County Bar Association, Kane County Bar Association, Lake County Bar Association, McHenry County Association of
512 REALTORS®, North Shore - Barrington Association of REALTORS®, Northwest Suburban Bar Association, Oak Park Board of
513 REALTORS®, REALTOR® Association of the Fox Valley, REALTOR® Association of the Northwest Chicagoland, REALTOR®
514 Association of West/South Suburban Chicagoland, Three Rivers Association of REALTORS®, West Towns Board of REALTORS®
515
516
517
518
519
520 **Seller Rejection:** This offer was presented to Seller on _____ 20_____ at _____:_____ AM PM
521 and rejected on _____ 20_____ at ____:____ AM PM _____   _____
522   (Seller initials)   (Seller initials)
523 PDF Version 4.0.2 - 5/2/06

Buyer Initial _____ *Buyer Initial* _____ *Seller Initial* _____ *Seller Initial*_____
Address _____

Typical Residential Real Estate Sales Contract

Loan Status Disclosure

524
525 Borrowers/Buyers Name(s): _____
526 Current Address: _____
527   Street address
528   _____
529   City or Town   State   Zip code
530 Purchase Price dollar amount prequalified, pre-approved, or approved for:
531 $_____, Loan Amount $_____ with a total monthly payment not to
532 exceed $_____.
533
534 The current status of prequalification or application status of the borrowers/buyers is:
535
536 [ ] **Prequalification, WITHOUT credit review*:**
537 The borrowers/buyers listed on this form have **INQUIRED** with our firm about financing to purchase a home and the
538 documentation they provided regarding income and down payment has been reviewed by the loan originator listed
539 below. It is the opinion of said loan originator that the borrowers/buyers should/would qualify for the terms listed in the
540 attached letter.
541
542 [ ] **Prequalification, WITH credit review*:**
543 The borrowers/buyers listed on this form have **INQUIRED** with our firm about financing to purchase a home and the
544 documentation of income, down payment **and credit report** have been reviewed by the loan originator listed below. After
545 careful review, it is the opinion of said loan originator that the borrowers/buyers should/would qualify for the terms listed
546 in the attached letter.
547 This Prequalification is [ ] **WITH** or [ ] **WITHOUT** Automated Underwriting approval.
548
549 [ ] **Pre-Approval*:**
550 The borrowers/buyers have **APPLIED** with our firm for a mortgage loan to purchase a home and the loan application
551 has been approved by an Automated Underwriting System issued or accepted by FNMA, FHLMC, HUD or Nationally
552 recognized purchaser/pooler of mortgage loans, and a conditional commitment has been issued. See attached
553 commitment.
554
555 [ ] **Approval*:**
556 The borrowers/buyers have **APPLIED** with our firm for a mortgage loan to purchase a home and the loan application
557 has been reviewed by the actual lender's underwriter and conditional commitment has been issued. See attached
558 commitment.
559
560 *Please note that nothing contained herein constitutes a loan commitment or guarantee of financing and is used for
561 disclosure purposes only. See actual commitment letter for specific conditions/requirements of the lender. All approvals
562 are subject to satisfactory appraisal, title, and no material change to borrower(s) financial status.
563
564 <u>Information on mortgage company issuing the prequalification, pre-approval or approval:</u>
565
566 Originating Company's Name: _____
567
568 Company Address: _____
569   Street address   City or Town   State   Zip Code
570 Company Phone:(____)_____ Fax:(____)_____
571
572 Loan Originator's name:_____ LO Reg. # _____Date:_____
573
574 Loan Originator's signature:_____
575
576 **Use Recommended by: IAMB; IAR; and IRELA** Rev 1/24/04

Buyer Initial _____	*Buyer Initial* _____	*Seller Initial* _____	*Seller Initial* _____
Address _____			

The amount of the deposit is a matter to be agreed on by the parties. Under the terms of most listing agreements, a real estate broker is required to accept a "reasonable amount" as earnest money. The deposit should be an amount sufficient to

■ discourage the buyer from defaulting,
■ help the seller feel comfortable in taking the property off the market, and
■ cover any expenses the seller might incur if the buyer defaults.

In Illinois   Many contracts provide that the deposit becomes the seller's property as liquidated damages if the buyer defaults. To release earnest money in Illinois, for any reason, signatures of both parties are required.

Under the Administrative Rules established by the IDFPR through the Bureau of Real Estate Professions (BRE) for administering the Illinois *Real Estate License Act of 2000*, brokers who are holding earnest money deposits in sales and security deposits in leasing must establish special trust (or escrow) accounts for the deposit of funds entrusted to them in connection with real estate transactions. A broker need not open a special escrow account for *each* earnest money deposit received, however, but may deposit all earnest money funds in one account. The rules require that the escrow account be noninterest bearing, unless both parties agree in writing to interest-bearing. If interest is paid on the deposit, the disposition of any accrued interest must be designated by the parties in writing.

Each broker must maintain a complete journal and ledger of all earnest money transactions and notify the IDFPR of the name of the federally insured institution where the money is deposited. All funds must be deposited to that account no later than the end of the next business day following the acceptance of the real estate contract or lease agreement. Both the account itself and broker records are subject to inspection at any time. Broker records need to be produced within 24 hours upon official request. *Escrow reconciliations must be completed within ten days after receipt of the monthly bank statement and must be kept for a minimum of five years.*

Only the broker or an authorized agent may withdraw funds from the account. Fees and/or commissions earned by the broker that are to be paid from the funds in this account are to be disbursed by the broker from the account no earlier than the day the transaction is consummated or terminated and no later than the next business day after consummation or termination of the transaction.

Brokers are strictly prohibited from **commingling**, that is, mixing, their own funds with funds in special escrow accounts except for the purpose of maintaining a minimum running balance required by the depository. If a broker uses his or her own funds to avoid incurring service charges, scrupulous records must be kept. Brokers may never use escrow funds for personal use; this illegal act is known as **conversion.** ■

Equitable title.   When a buyer signs a contract to purchase real estate, he or she does not receive legal title to the land. Legal title transfers only on delivery and acceptance of a deed. However, after both buyer and seller have executed a sales contract, the buyer acquires an interest in the land. This interest is known as **equitable title**. Equitable title may give the buyer an insurable interest in the property.

Under the common law of contracts, the buyer always bore the risk of loss in the event the property was damaged or destroyed prior to closing. A few states still adhere to this common-law principle. The laws and court decisions of most states, however, have increasingly placed the risk of loss on the seller. Many of these states have adopted the **Uniform Vendor and Purchaser Risk Act**, which specifically states that the *seller bears any loss that occurs before the title passes or the buyer takes possession*. As a practical matter, the seller should be certain the property is fully insured for sale price value up until the closing is completed and possession has been given.

In Illinois

Illinois law subscribes to the *Uniform Vendor and Purchaser Risk Act*. If the entire premises or a material part of it is destroyed, the seller cannot enforce the contract against the buyer. Any earnest money must be returned. On the other hand, *if title or possession has been transferred to the buyer*, he or she must pay the full contract price, even in the event of partially or totally destroyed premises (e.g., the house burns while parties are at the closing). ■

Liquidated damages. To avoid a lawsuit if one party breaches the contract, the parties may agree on a certain amount of money that will compensate the nonbreaching party. That money is called **liquidated damages**. If a sales contract specifies that the earnest money deposit is to serve as liquidated damages in case the buyer defaults, the seller will be entitled to keep the deposit if the buyer refuses to perform without good reason. The seller who keeps the deposit as liquidated damages may not sue for any further damages if the contract provides that the deposit is the seller's sole remedy.

Contingencies. Additional conditions that must be satisfied before a sales contract is fully enforceable are called **contingencies**. A contingency includes the following three elements:

1. The specific actions necessary to satisfy the contingency
2. The time frame within which the actions must occur
3. Who is responsible for paying any costs involved

The most common contingencies include:

- **Mortgage contingency**—A mortgage contingency (sometimes called a financing contingency) protects the buyer's earnest money until a lender commits the mortgage loan funds.
- **Inspection contingency**—A sales contract may be contingent on the buyer's obtaining certain inspections of the property, within a set time frame. Inspections may include a basic home inspection or special inspections for radon, wood-boring insects, lead-based paint, structural and mechanical systems, sewage facilities, or various toxic materials.
- **Property sale contingency**—A purchaser may make the sales contract contingent on the sale of his or her current home by a certain date. This protects the buyer from owning two homes at the same time and also helps ensure the availability of cash for the purchase. A seller may insist on an

escape clause, a "continued to show" clause, or a "kick-out." This *kick-out clause*, also called *first right of refusal* in some locales, permits the seller to continue to market the property until all the buyer's contingencies have been satisfied or removed. The original buyer retains the right to drop his or her contingencies if the seller receives an offer that does not contain a property sale contingency.

Amendments and addendums.   An *amendment* is a change to an existing contract. For instance, the parties may agree to change a closing date or alter a list of personal property items included in the sale. Any time words or provisions are added to or deleted from the body of the contract, the contract has been amended. Amendments *must be signed or initialed by all parties*.

On the other hand, an *addendum* is any provision added to an existing contract *without* altering the content of the *original*.

Amendment = Change
Addendum = Addition

An addendum is essentially a new contract between the parties that includes the original contract's provisions "by reference"; that is, the addendum mentions the original contract. An addendum must be signed by the parties. For example, an addendum might be an agreement to split the cost of repairing certain flaws discovered in a home inspection. Such an addendum would be handled by the attorneys as a part of attorney modification.

In Illinois

Illinois requires several mandatory disclosures by sellers and agents, such as disclosure of property conditions and agency relationships. These disclosures are included in the sales contract by physical attachment or by reference. ∎

Options

An **option** is a contract by which an optionor (generally an owner) gives an optionee (a prospective purchaser or lessee) the right to buy or lease the owner's property at a fixed price within a certain period of time. The optionee pays a fee (agreed-on consideration) for this option right. The optionee has no other obligation until he or she decides to either exercise the option right or allow the option to expire. An option is *enforceable by only one party—the optionee*.

An option contract is *not* a sales contract. *At the time the option is signed by the parties, the owner does not sell and the optionee does not buy.* The parties merely agree that the optionee has the right to buy and the owner is obligated to sell if the optionee decides to exercise his or her right of option. Options must contain all the terms and provisions required for a valid contract.

The option agreement (which is a *unilateral contract*) requires that the optionor act only after the optionee gives notice that he or she elects to execute the option. If the option is not exercised within the time specified in the contract, both the optionor's obligation and the optionee's right expire. An option contract may provide for renewal, which often requires additional consideration. The optionee cannot recover the consideration paid for the option right. The contract may state whether the money paid for the option is to be applied to the purchase price of the real estate if the option is exercised.

A common application of an option is a lease that includes an option for the tenant to purchase the property. Options on commercial real estate frequently depend on some specific conditions being fulfilled, such as obtaining a zoning change or a building permit. The optionee may be obligated to exercise the option if the conditions are met. Similar terms could also be included in a sales contract.

Land Contracts

A real estate sale can be made by a **land contract**. A land contract may be called a *contract for deed*, an **installment contract**, or *articles of agreement for warranty deed*. Under a typical land contract, the seller (also known as the *vendor*) retains legal title. The buyer (called the *vendee*) takes possession and gains **equitable title** to the property. The buyer agrees to give the seller a down payment and pay regular monthly installments of principal and interest over a number of years. The buyer also agrees to pay real estate taxes, insurance premiums, repairs, and upkeep on the property.

Athough the buyer obtains possession under the initial land contract, the seller is *not* obligated to execute and deliver a deed to the buyer until the terms of the contract have been satisfied. Also, a land contract usually is assumable by subsequent purchasers, but this must be approved and agreed to by the seller.

IN PRACTICE

Legislatures and courts have not looked favorably on the harsh provisions of some real estate installment contracts. A seller and buyer contemplating such a sale should first consult an attorney to make sure that the agreement meets all legal requirements.

In Illinois

Installment contracts (or *articles of agreement or land contracts*) commonly are used in Illinois when creative seller financing is needed to consummate a sale. Real estate professionals keep them in mind to assist buyers who are having trouble getting a standard loan or for sellers who have a hard-to-sell property or who wish to retain ties to their property for some reason. While a real estate agent may assist in negotiating basic terms, in Illinois the actual *articles of agreement* must be drawn up by an attorney owing to the legal complexities involved.

Any provision in any installment contract or land contract is void if the document

- forbids the contract buyer to record the contract,
- provides that recording shall not constitute notice, or
- provides any penalty for recording.

Any installment contract for the sale of a dwelling that consists of 12 or fewer units is voidable at the option of the buyer unless either a certificate of compliance *or* an express warranty that no notice of a building code violation has been received within the past ten years is attached to or incorporated into the contract. If any notice has been received within the past ten years *and not complied with*, each notice must be listed with a detailed explanation. Neither buyer nor seller may waive this requirement.

A buyer who, under an installment contract, purchases residential property containing six or fewer units (which includes one unit) from a land trust must be told the names of all beneficiaries of the trust at the time the contract is executed. *The buyer has the option of voiding the contract if the names are not revealed.* ■

■ SUMMARY

A contract is a legally enforceable promise or set of promises that must be performed; if a breach occurs, the law provides a remedy.

Contracts may be classified according to whether the parties' intentions are express (i.e., expressed, stated) or merely implied by their actions. They may also be classified as bilateral (when both parties have obligated themselves to act) or unilateral (when one party is obligated to perform only if the other party acts). In addition, contracts may be classified according to their legal enforceability as valid, void, voidable, or unenforceable.

Many contracts specify a time for performance. In any case, all contracts must be performed within a reasonable time. An executed contract is one that has been fully performed. An executory contract is one in which some act remains to be performed.

The essentials of a valid contract are legally competent parties, offer and acceptance, consent, consideration, and legal purpose. A valid real estate contract must include a description of the property. It must be in writing and signed by all parties to be enforceable in court.

In many types of contracts, either of the parties may transfer his or her rights and obligations under the agreement by assignment or novation (substitution of a new contract).

Contracts usually provide that the seller has the right to declare a sale canceled if the buyer defaults. If either party suffers a loss because of the other's default, he or she may sue for damages to cover the loss. If one party insists on completing the transaction, he or she may sue the defaulter for specific performance of the terms of the contract; a court can order the other party to comply with the agreement if it was in writing.

Contracts frequently used in the real estate business include listing agreements, sales contracts, options, land contracts (often called installment contracts or articles of agreement), and leases.

A real estate sales contract binds a buyer and a seller to a definite transaction as described in detail within the contract. The buyer is bound to purchase the property for the amount stated in the agreement, and to perform by the various dates stipulated (financing, closing). The seller is bound to deliver title, free from liens and encumbrances (except those identified and agreed to in the contract).

Under an option agreement, the optionee purchases from the optionor, for a limited time period, the exclusive right to purchase or lease the optionor's property. A land contract or installment contract (articles of agreement for deed) is a seller financing agreement under which a buyer purchases a seller's real estate over time. The buyer takes possession of and responsibility for the property, but does not receive the deed immediately until all payments have been made in full. Instead, he or she receives equitable title.

In Illinois

The Illinois *Statute of Frauds* requires that all contracts for the sale of land and rental agreements that will not be fulfilled within one year must be in writing to be enforceable in court. Additionally, under the *Real Estate License Act of 2000*, any exclusive brokerage agreement must be in writing.

Real estate contracts undertaken prior to the legal age of 18 are usually voidable; however, leases by minors in Illinois are often enforceable as they may be classed as "necessaries" (food, water, shelter). Contracts made under duress or undertaken while intoxicated are also voidable. Those with mistakes, misrepresentations, or fraud are voidable by the damaged party. Contracts by legally adjudicated insane persons are void.

Brokers and salespersons may only fill in blanks on preprinted contract forms that are customarily used in the real estate industry. They may not write addendums or qualifying clauses. (*Chicago Bar Association, et al. v. Quinlan and Tyson, Inc.* is the famous Illinois real estate case dealing with this issue.)

Land contracts and options are used with some frequency in Illinois to facilitate transactions that might not otherwise occur. Licensees may negotiate basic terms in a land contract, but attorneys must prepare the articles of agreement.

Earnest money must be deposited in a special escrow or trust account, which bears interest if parties agree in writing. It is assumed this money will go to the seller as liquidated damages in the event of a buyer default unless some other arrangement is indicated in a typeface larger than the rest of the contract. ∎

QUESTIONS

1. A legally enforceable agreement under which two parties agree to do something for each other is known as a(n)
   a. escrow agreement.
   b. legal promise.
   c. valid contract.
   d. option agreement.

2. Doug approaches Betty and says, "I'd like to buy your house." Betty says, "Sure," and they agree on a price. What kind of contract is this?
   a. Implied
   b. Unenforceable
   c. Void
   d. There is no contract.

3. A contract is said to be bilateral if
   a. one of the parties is a minor.
   b. the contract has yet to be fully performed.
   c. only one party to the agreement is bound to act.
   d. all parties to the contract are bound to act.

4. During the period of time after a real estate sales contract is signed but before title actually passes, the status of the contract is
   a. voidable.
   b. executory.
   c. unilateral.
   d. implied.

5. A contract for the sale of real estate that does not state the consideration to be paid for the property and is not signed by the parties is considered to be
   a. voidable.
   b. executory.
   c. void.
   d. enforceable.

6. Nick and Keri sign a contract under which Nick will convey Blackacre to Keri. Nick changes his mind, and Keri sues for specific performance. What is Keri seeking in this lawsuit?
   a. Money damages
   b. New contract
   c. Deficiency judgment
   d. Conveyance of the property

7. In a standard sales contract, several words were crossed out; others were inserted. To eliminate future controversy as to whether the changes were made before or after the contract was signed, the usual procedure is to
   a. write a letter to each party listing the changes.
   b. have each party write a letter to the other approving the changes.
   c. redraw the entire contract.
   d. have both parties initial or sign in the margin, along with date, near each change.

8. Margaret makes an offer on Diane's house, and Diane accepts. Both parties sign the sales contract. At this point, Margaret has what type of title to the property?
   a. Equitable
   b. Voidable
   c. Escrow
   d. Contract

9. The sales contract says John will purchase only if his wife approves the sale by the following Saturday. His wife's approval is a
   a. contingency.
   b. reservation.
   c. warranty.
   d. consideration.

10. Charles verbally offers to buy Sharon's house for $150,000. No written real estate sales contract is drawn up, but Sharon agrees to the offer. What kind of contract is this?
    a. Unilateral
    b. Option
    c. Implied
    d. Unenforceable

11. Carl's property was listed for $100,000, and he agreed to enter into an option agreement with Keith. They agreed on a sale price of $95,000 and a term of three months. Two weeks later, Carl receives an offer of $100,000 from his neighbor to buy the property. An agent is not involved in the offer. Can he accept the second offer?

    a. Yes, because it is for the full list price.
    b. Yes, because Keith has not yet exercised his option.
    c. No, because an agent was not involved.
    d. No, a seller is bound to an option agreement for the term of the option.

12. Xander and Holly enter into a real estate sales contract. Under the contract's terms, Xander will pay Holly $500 a month for ten years. Holly will continue to hold legal title to Blueacre. Xander will live on Blueacre and pay all real estate taxes, insurance premiums, and regular upkeep costs. What kind of contract do Xander and Holly have?

    a. Option contract
    b. Contract for mortgage
    c. Unilateral contract
    d. Land, or installment contract

13. The purchaser of real estate under an installment contract

    a. generally pays no interest charge.
    b. receives title immediately.
    c. is not required to pay property taxes for the duration of the contract.
    d. is called a *vendee*.

14. Under the statute of frauds, all contracts for the sale of real estate must be

    a. originated by a real estate broker.
    b. on preprinted forms.
    c. in writing to be enforceable.
    d. accompanied by earnest money deposits.

15. The Froneks offer in writing to purchase a house for $120,000, including its draperies, with the offer to expire on Saturday at noon. The Whitmores reply in writing on Thursday, accepting the $120,000 offer but excluding the draperies. On Friday, while the Froneks consider this counteroffer, the Whitmores decide to accept the original offer, draperies included, and state that in writing. At this point, which of the following statements is *TRUE*?

    a. The Froneks are legally bound to buy the house although they have the right to insist that the draperies be included.
    b. The Froneks are not bound to buy.
    c. The Froneks must buy the house and are not entitled to the draperies.
    d. The Froneks must buy the house, but may deduct the value of the draperies from the $120,000.

16. Between June 5 and September 23, Martin suffered from a mental illness that caused delusions, hallucinations, and loss of memory. On July 1, Martin signed a contract to purchase Blueacre, with the closing set for October 31. On September 24, Martin began psychiatric treatment. He was declared completely cured by October 15. Which of the following statements is *TRUE* regarding Martin's contract to purchase Blueacre?

    a. The contract is voidable.
    b. The contract is void.
    c. The contract lacks reality of consent.
    d. The contract is fully valid and enforceable.

17. A broker has found a buyer for a seller's home. The buyer has indicated in writing his willingness to buy the property for $1,000 less than the asking price and has deposited $5,000 in earnest money with the broker. The seller is out of town for the weekend, and the broker has been unable to inform him of the signed document. At this point, the buyer has signed a(n)

    a. voidable contract.
    b. offer.
    c. executory agreement.
    d. implied contract.

18. A buyer and seller agree to the purchase of a house for $200,000. The contract contains a clause stating that "time is of the essence." Which of the following statements is TRUE?

   a. The closing may take place within a reasonable period after the stated date.

   b. A "time is of the essence" clause is not binding on either party.

   c. The closing date must be stated as a particular calendar date, and not simply as a formula, such as "two weeks after loan approval."

   d. If the closing date passes and no closing takes place, the contract may have been breached.

19. Cathy signs a contract under which she may purchase Yellowacre for $30,000 any time in the next three months. Cathy pays Yellowacre's current owner $500 at the time the contract is signed. Which of the following best describes this contract?

   a. Contingency
   b. Option
   c. Installment
   d. Sales

In Illinois
---

20. In preparing a sales contract, an Illinois broker may

   a. fill in factual and business details in the blank spaces of a customary preprinted form.

   b. draft riders to alter a preprinted contract to fit the transaction.

   c. fill out and sign an offer to purchase for the customer.

   d. advise a buyer or seller of the legal significance of certain parts of the contract.

21. On Tuesday, broker Loren received a $750 earnest money deposit from Gus. The seller accepted the offer on Thursday. Where and when must Loren deposit Gus's money?

   a. In Loren's personal checking account by Wednesday

   b. In a special trust account no later than midnight on Thursday

   c. In a special noninterest-bearing trust account by Friday

   d. In a special noninterest-bearing trust account by Wednesday

22. An Illinois broker does not need written consent of both parties to a transaction to do which of the following?

   a. Disburse interest accrued on an earnest money account

   b. Fill in the blanks on a sales offer as directed by principals

   c. Make changes in the terms of a signed sales contract

   d. Change the commission payment terms designated in the listing agreement

23. The unauthorized practice of law was dealt with in which Illinois Supreme Court case?

   a. *Illinois State Bar Association v. Illinois Board of* REALTORS®

   b. *Chicago Bar Association, et al. v. Quinlan and Tyson, Inc.*

   c. *Attorney Registration and Disciplinary Commission v. Illinois State Department of Professional Regulation*

   d. *Quinlan Associates, Inc. v. Illinois Real Estate Commission*

24. Which provision could legally be placed in an Illinois installment contract?

   a. "Buyer may not record this contract."
   b. "Seller will retain legal title."
   c. "Recording shall not constitute notice."
   d. "Buyer will forfeit $1,000 for recording."

25. Sam made an offer on Pam's property. For this contract to be valid, it must contain

   a. a contingency clause that allows Sam to secure financing.

   b. the date when the listing expires.

   c. a rescission clause.

   d. the consideration Sam is willing to pay.

26. A buyer made an offer of $350,000 on a property with no contingencies. The buyer intends to build a shopping center on the property, but no mention was made of this. The seller accepted the offer but before the closing, the buyer discovered he could not build a shopping center on the property. What is the status of the contract?

   a. Valid
   b. Void
   c. Voidable
   d. Unenforceable

CHAPTER 12

Transfer of Title

■ **LEARNING OBJECTIVES** *When you've finished reading this chapter, you should be able to*

- **identify** the basic requirements for a valid deed.

- **describe** the seven fundamental types of deeds.

- **explain** how property may be transferred through involuntary alienation.

- **distinguish** transfers of title by will from transfers by intestacy.

- **define** the following *key terms:*

acknowledgment	granting clause	testate
adverse possession	grantor	testator
bargain and sale deed	habendum clause	title
deed	heir	transfer tax
deed in trust	intestate	trustee's deed
devise	involuntary alienation	voluntary alienation
devisee	probate	will
general warranty deed	quitclaim deed	
grantee	special warranty deed	

■ TITLE

The term *title* has two meanings. **Title** to real estate means the right to ownership or actual ownership of the land; it represents the owner's bundle of rights. Title also serves as evidence of that ownership. A person who holds the title would, if challenged in court, be able to recover or retain ownership or possession of a parcel of real estate. Title is a way of referring to ownership; it is not an actual printed document. The document by which the owner transfers his or her title to another is the **deed**. The deed must be recorded to give public notice of new ownership.

Real estate may be transferred *voluntarily* by sale or gift. Alternatively, it may be transferred *involuntarily* by operation of law. Real estate may be transferred at any time while the owner lives or by will or descent after the owner dies. Title transfers or *passes* as a symbol of ownership.

■ VOLUNTARY ALIENATION

> A **grantor** conveys property to a grantee.
>
> A **grantee** receives property from a grantor.
>
> A **deed** is the instrument that conveys property from a grantor to a grantee.

Voluntary alienation is the legal term for the voluntary transfer of title. The owner may voluntarily transfer title by either making a gift or selling the property. To transfer during one's lifetime, the owner must use some form of deed of conveyance.

A deed is the written instrument by which an owner of real estate intentionally conveys the right, title, or interest in a parcel of real estate to someone else. *The statute of frauds requires that all deeds be in writing.* The owner who transfers the title is referred to as the **grantor.** The person who acquires the title is called the **grantee.** A deed is executed *only* by the grantor, or seller.

Requirements for a Valid Deed

The formal requirements for a deed are established by state law and thus vary from state to state.

> In Illinois

The following are the minimum requirements for a valid deed in Illinois:

- *Grantor*, who has the legal capacity to execute (sign) the deed
- *Grantee* named with reasonable certainty to be identified
- Recital of *consideration*
- *Granting clause* (words of conveyance, together with any words of limitation)
- Accurate *legal description* of the property conveyed
- Any relevant *exceptions* or *reservations*
- *Signature of the grantor*, sometimes with a seal, witness, or acknowledgment
- *Delivery* of the deed and *acceptance* by the grantee to pass title ■

Some states require a **habendum clause** to define ownership taken by the grantee. The habendum clause begins with the words to have and to hold. Its provisions must agree with those stated in the granting clause. If there is a discrepancy, the granting clause prevails.

Grantor.   A grantor must be of lawful age, at least 18 years old. A deed executed by a minor is usually *voidable*.

A grantor also must be of sound mind. Generally, any grantor who can understand the action is viewed as mentally capable of executing a valid deed. A deed executed by someone who was mentally impaired at the time is *voidable* but not *void* automatically. If, however, the grantor has been *judged* legally incompetent, the deed will be *void*. Real estate owned by someone who is legally incompetent can be conveyed only with a court's approval.

The grantor's name must be spelled correctly and consistently throughout the deed. If the grantor's name has been changed since the title was acquired, as when a person changes his or her name by marriage, both names should be shown—for example, "Mary Smith, formerly Mary Jones."

Grantee.   To be valid, a deed must name a grantee. The grantee must be specifically named so that the person to whom the property is being conveyed can be readily identified from the deed itself. However, *the grantee (new owner) is not required to sign the deed.*

■ **FOR EXAMPLE**   Phil wanted to convey Napa Ranch to his nephew, James Christian. In the deed, Phil wrote the following words of conveyance: "I, Phil, hereby convey to James all my interest in Napa Ranch." The only problem was that Phil also had a son named James, a cousin James, and a neighbor James. The grantee's identity could not be discerned from the deed itself. Phil should have conveyed Napa Ranch "to my nephew, James Christian."

If more than one grantee is involved, the granting clause should specify their rights in the property. The clause might state, for instance, that the grantees will take title as "joint tenants," "tenants in common," or "tenants by the entirety." This is especially important when specific wording is necessary to create a joint tenancy or tenancy by the entirety.

In Illinois

The purchaser's or grantee's *present address* is required in Illinois as an element of a valid deed. Also, if no specific form of ownership is selected, tenancy in common is assumed in Illinois. One can determine, then, how ownership is held by consulting the deed language. ■

Consideration.   A valid deed must contain a clause acknowledging that the grantor has received *consideration*. Generally, the amount of consideration is stated in dollars. When a deed conveys real estate as a gift to a relative, "love and affection" may be sufficient consideration. In most states, however, it is customary to recite at least a *nominal consideration*, such as "$10 and other good and valuable consideration."

Granting clause (words of conveyance).   A deed must contain a **granting clause** that states the grantor's intention to convey the property. Depending on the type of deed and the obligations agreed to by the grantor (discussed later in this chapter), the wording would be similar to one of the following:

■ "I, Kent Long, *convey and warrant . . .*" (creates a warranty deed)
■ "I, Kent Long, *remise, release, alienate, and convey. . .*" (creates a special warranty deed)
■ "I, Kent Long, *grant, bargain, and sell . . .*" (creates a bargain and sale deed)
■ "I, Kent Long, *remise, release, and quitclaim . . .*" (creates a quitclaim deed)

A deed that conveys the grantor's entire fee simple absolute interest usually contains wording such as "to Mary Goode *and to her heirs and assigns forever.*" If the grantor conveys less than his or her complete interest, such as a life estate, the wording must indicate this limitation—for example, "to Mary Goode for the duration of her natural life."

Legal description of real estate.   To be valid, a deed must contain an accurate *legal description* of the real estate conveyed. Land is considered adequately described if a competent surveyor can locate the property using the description.

Exceptions and reservations.   A valid deed must specifically note any encumbrances, reservations, or limitations that affect the title being conveyed. This might include such things as restrictions and easements that run with the land. In addition to citing existing encumbrances, a grantor may reserve some right to the land, such as an easement, for his or her own use. A grantor may also place certain restrictions on a grantee's use of the property. Developers often restrict the number of houses that may be built on each lot in a subdivision. Such private restrictions must be stated in the deed or contained in a previously recorded document, such as the subdivider's master deed, that is expressly referred to in the deed. Many of these deed restrictions have time limits and often include renewal clauses.

Signature of grantor.   To be valid, a deed must be signed by all grantors named in the deed. Some states also require witnesses to the grantor's signature.

Most states permit an attorney-in-fact to sign for a grantor. The attorney-in-fact must act under a *power of attorney*—the specific written authority to execute and sign one or more legal instruments for another person. Usually, the power of attorney is recorded in the county where the property is located. The power of attorney terminates when the person on whose behalf it is exercised dies. As a result, adequate evidence must be submitted that the grantor was alive at the time the attorney-in-fact signed the deed.

In some states a grantor's spouse is expected to sign any deed of conveyance to waive any marital or homestead rights. This requirement varies according to state law and depends on the manner in which title to real estate is held and whether the property is used as a homestead (residence).

Many states still require a seal (or simply the word *seal*) to be written or printed after an individual grantor's signature. The corporate seal may be required of a corporate grantor.

In Illinois | Seals are not required in Illinois for individual grantor's signatures. Also, corporations need not affix their official corporate seals to validate a deed when they are grantors. ■

Acknowledgment/notarization.   An **acknowledgment** (also called *notarization*) is a formal declaration that the person who signs a written document does so voluntarily and that his or her signature is genuine. The declaration is made before a notary public or an authorized public officer, such as a judge, a justice of the peace, or some other person as prescribed by state law. An acknowledgment usually states that the person signing the deed or other document is known to the officer or has produced sufficient identification to prevent a forgery. The form of acknowledgment required by the state where the property is located should be used even if the signing individual is a resident of another ("foreign") state.

In Illinois | In Illinois, acknowledgment is not essential to the validity of the deed. However, unless the deed is acknowledged, it may not be introduced as evidence in a court of law without some further proof of its execution. As a result, it is customary that virtually all documents conveying title are acknowledged/notarized. Recording offices as a rule also expect deeds to be notarized before they will record them. Most title insurance companies require acknowledgment/notarization for deeds covered by their policies. ■

Delivery and acceptance.   A title is not considered transferred until the deed is actually delivered to and accepted by the grantee. The grantor may deliver the deed to the grantee either personally or through a third party. The third party, commonly known as a *settlement agent* or *escrow agent*, will deliver the deed to the grantee as soon as certain requirements have been satisfied. In an arm's-length transaction, the title must be delivered during the grantor's lifetime and accepted during the grantee's lifetime. The effective date of the transfer of title from the grantor to the grantee is the date of delivery of the deed itself. When a deed is delivered in escrow, as often occurs in western states, the date of delivery generally relates back to the date of deposit with the escrow agent.

> Transfer of title requires both delivery and acceptance of deed.

Execution of Corporate Deeds

The laws governing a corporation's right to convey real estate vary from state to state. However, two basic rules must be followed. First, a corporation can convey real estate only by authority granted in its bylaws or upon resolution passed by its *board of directors*. If all or a substantial portion of a corporation's real estate is being conveyed, a resolution authorizing the sale must usually be secured from the *shareholders*. Second, deeds to corporate real estate can be signed only by an *authorized officer*.

Rules pertaining to religious corporations and not-for-profit corporations are complex and vary even more widely. Because the legal requirements must be followed exactly, an attorney should be consulted for all corporate conveyances.

Types of Deeds

A deed can take several forms, depending on the extent of the grantor's pledges to the grantee. Regardless of any guarantees the deed offers, however, the grantee will want additional assurance that the grantor has the right to offer what the deed conveys. To obtain this protection, grantees commonly seek evidence of title.

The most common deed forms are the

■ general warranty deed,
■ special warranty deed,
■ bargain and sale deed,
■ quitclaim deed,
■ deed in trust,
■ trustee's deed, and
■ deed executed pursuant to a court order.

General warranty deed.   A **general warranty deed** provides the greatest protection of any deed. It is called a *general warranty deed* because the grantor is legally bound by certain covenants or warranties (promises). In most states, the warranties are implied by the use of certain words specified by statute. The basic warranties are as follows:

General Warranty Deed

Five covenants:
1. Covenant of seisin
2. Covenant against encumbrances
3. Covenant of quiet enjoyment
4. Covenant of further assurance
5. Covenant of warranty forever

■ **Covenant of seisin**—The grantor warrants that he or she owns the property and has the right to convey title to it. (*Seisin* simply means "possession.") The grantee may recover damages up to the full purchase price if this covenant is broken.

■ **Covenant against encumbrances**—The grantor warrants that the property is free from liens or encumbrances, except for any specifically stated in the deed. Encumbrances generally include mortgages, mechanics' liens, and easements. If this covenant is breached, the grantee may sue for the cost of removing the encumbrances.

■ **Covenant of quiet enjoyment**—The grantor guarantees that the grantee's title will be good against third parties who might bring court actions to establish superior title to the property. If the grantee's title is found to be inferior, the grantor is liable for damages.

■ **Covenant of further assurance**—The grantor promises to obtain and deliver any instrument needed to make the title good. For example, if the grantor's spouse has failed to sign away dower rights, the grantor must deliver a quitclaim deed (discussed later) to clear the title.

■ **Covenant of warranty forever**—The grantor promises to compensate the grantee for the loss sustained if the title fails at any time in the future.

In Illinois

Illinois law provides that a deed using the *words "convey and warrant" implies and includes all covenants of general warranty*, which are as binding on the grantor, his or her heirs, and personal representatives as if written at length in the deed. These covenants in a general warranty deed are not limited to matters that occurred during the time the grantor owned the property; they extend back to its origins. The grantor defends the title against himself or herself and against all others as predecessors in title.

In addition, it is sufficient for a general warranty deed to recite only nominal consideration. ■

Special Warranty Deed

Two warranties:
1. Warranty that grantor received title
2. Warranty that property was unencumbered by grantor

Special warranty deed. A **special warranty deed** contains two basic warranties:

1. Warranty that the grantor received title
2. Warranty that the property was not encumbered *during the time the grantor held title*, except as otherwise noted in the deed

In effect, the grantor defends the title against himself or herself but not against previous encumbrances. The granting clause generally contains the words "Grantor remises, releases, alienates, and conveys." The grantor may include additional warranties, but they must be specifically stated in the deed. In areas where a special warranty deed is more commonly used, the purchase of title insurance is viewed as providing adequate protection to the grantee.

A special warranty deed may be used by fiduciaries such as trustees, executors, and corporations. A special warranty deed is appropriate for a fiduciary because he or she lacks the authority to warrant against acts of predecessors in title. A fiduciary may hold title for a limited time without having a personal interest in the proceeds. Sometimes a special warranty deed may be used by a grantor who has acquired title at a tax sale.

Deed in Trust

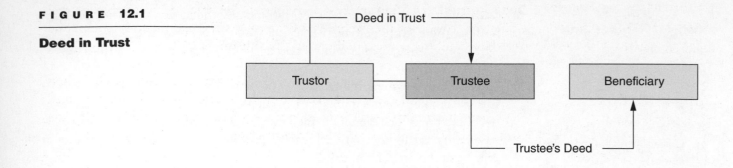

Bargain and sale deed. In some states, a **bargain and sale deed** contains no express warranties against encumbrances. It does, however, *imply* that the grantor holds title and possession of the property.

In Illinois

The words in the granting clause are "grant, bargain, and sell." A grant, bargain, and sale deed conveys a simple title with the following covenants: (1) the grantor holds a fee simple estate, (2) the title is free from encumbrances made by the grantor except those listed in the deed, and (3) the grantor warrants quiet enjoyment. An Illinois bargain and sale deed is similar to a warranty deed but less complete in its warranties. The buyer should purchase title insurance for protection. ■

Bargain and Sale Deed

No express warranties:
- Implication that grantor holds title and possession

Quitclaim Deed

No express or implied covenants or warranties:
- Used primarily to convey less than fee simple or to cure a title defect

Quitclaim deed. A **quitclaim deed** provides the grantee with the *least protection of any deed.* It carries no covenants or warranties and generally conveys only whatever interest the grantor may have when the deed is delivered. If the grantor has no interest, the grantee will acquire nothing. Nor will the grantee acquire any right of warranty claim against the grantor. A quitclaim deed can convey title as effectively as a warranty deed if the grantor has good title when he or she delivers the deed, but it provides none of the guarantees that a warranty deed does. Through a quitclaim deed, the grantor only "remises, releases, and quitclaims" his or her interest in the property, if any.

A quitclaim deed is the only type of deed that may be used to convey less than a fee simple estate. This is because a quitclaim deed conveys only the grantor's right, title, or interest without giving any kind of guarantee as to the quality or nature of title being conveyed.

A quitclaim deed frequently is used to cure a defect, called a *cloud on the title.* For example, if the name of the grantee is misspelled on a warranty deed filed in the public record, *a quitclaim deed with the correct spelling may be executed to the grantee to perfect the title.*

A quitclaim deed also is used when a grantor allegedly inherits property but is not certain that the decedent's title was valid. A warranty deed in such an instance could carry with it obligations of warranty, while a quitclaim deed would convey only the grantor's interest.

In Illinois

A quitclaim deed uses the words "convey and quit claim," and conveys in fee all the grantor's existing legal and equitable rights held at the time of delivery. ■

Deed in Trust

Conveyance from trustor to trustee.

Deed in trust.   A **deed in trust** is the means by which a trustor conveys real estate to a trustee for the benefit of a beneficiary. The real estate is held by the trustee to fulfill the purpose of the trust. (See Figure 12.1.)

Trustee's deed.   A deed executed by a trustee is a **trustee's deed.** It is used when a trustee conveys real estate held in the trust to the beneficiary. The trustee's deed must state that the trustee is executing the instrument in accordance with the powers and authority granted by the trust instrument.

Trustee's Deed

Conveyance from trustee to third party.

Deed executed pursuant to court order.   Executors' and administrators' deeds, masters' deeds, sheriffs' deeds, and many other types are all deeds executed pursuant to a court order. These deeds are established by state statute and are used to convey title to property that is transferred by court order or by will. The form of such a deed must conform to the laws of the state in which the property is located.

One common characteristic of *deeds executed pursuant to court order* is that the full consideration is usually stated in the deed. Instead of "$10 and other valuable consideration," for example, the deed lists the actual sales price.

Transfer Tax Stamps

Many states have enacted laws providing for a state transfer tax on conveyances of real estate. In some locations, there are local transfer stamps as well.

In Illinois

The Illinois Real Estate Transfer Act imposes a tax on conveying title to real estate in the amount of $0.50 per $500, and in all Illinois counties there is an additional transfer tax of $0.25 per $500. Total transfer tax to state and county combined is $0.75 per $500 or fraction thereof. Fifty percent of the tax collected is deposited into the Illinois Affordable Housing Trust Fund (under the Illinois *Affordable Housing Act of 1989*); 35 percent is deposited into the Open Space Land Acquisition and Development Fund; the remaining 15 percent goes to the Natural Areas Acquisition Fund. The seller generally pays the state and county transfer tax.

The **transfer tax** must be paid before the recording of the deed (or before transferring the beneficial interest in a land trust). This is done by purchasing *tax stamps* from the county recorder or the city offices if there are local stamps required. These stamps are literally affixed to the deed. ■

Local transfer tax.   Many local municipalities have their own tax as well. *Charts indicating these local transfer tax amounts are available from counties and individual municipalities. Local transfer tax can be paid by either buyer or seller so it is important to check each municipality.*

IN PRACTICE

Real estate professionals have an important role to play in letting buyers or sellers know about transfer taxes early. *For the sellers*, this comes at listing presentation time, when an *approximate* estimate of *total selling costs* for sellers is usually given—commission cost, mortgage payoff, attorney fee, survey, title insurance, and *transfer tax* (if payable by seller). *For buyers' agents*, it may mean mentioning transfer taxes any time the agent notes the buyer has an interest in homes located where buyer-paid taxes apply.

In Illinois	

Tax formula. The formula used in Illinois to determine the exact taxable consideration is as follows:

Full actual consideration (sales price)	$_____
Less value of personal property included in purchase	–_____
Less amount of mortgage to which property remains subject	–_____
Equals net TOTAL taxable consideration to be covered by stamps	=_____
Amount of Illinois state tax stamps ($.50 per $500 or taxable amount)	$_____
Amount of county tax ($.25 per $500)	+ $_____
Total transfer tax	= $_____

■ **FOR EXAMPLE** A parcel of real estate sold for $350,000. The purchaser agreed to assume the seller's existing mortgage of $128,000 and to pay $222,000 in cash upon receipt of the seller's deed. The purchase price includes $25,000 of personal property. What amount of county and state stamps must the seller affix to the deed?

The total transfer tax would be computed as follows:

Sales Price	$350,000
Less Personal Property	– $ 25,000
Less Assumable Mortgage	– $128,000
Equals Net Total Taxable Consideration	$197,000

To be covered by Stamps

$197,000 divided by $500 = 394 stamps x $.50 (State) =	$197.00
$197,000 divided by $500 = 394 stamps x $.25 (County) =	$ 98.50

$197.00 + $98.50 = $295.50 Total Transfer Tax ■

In Illinois	

Real Estate Transfer Declaration. The amount of consideration used for determining transfer taxes must be shown on the form entitled "Real Estate Transfer Declaration." The form must be signed by the buyer and seller or their agents, and it provides for the inclusion of the property description, manner of conveyance, and type of financing used. The financing data helps the Department of Revenue accurately determine equalization factors between different counties and eliminate inconsistencies caused by the use of nonconventional or creative financing.

A completed declaration must accompany every deed presented to the recorder for recording. (The Cook County Recorder's office has its own separate transfer form, which also must be presented with every deed.) A willful falsification or omission of any of the required data constitutes a Class B misdemeanor punishable by up to six months in jail. The information contained on the form is *not* confidential and is available for inspection by the public.

Exempted from the transfer tax are deeds such as those conveying real estate from or between any governmental bodies; those held by charitable, religious, or educational institutions; those securing debts or releasing property as security for a debt; partitions; tax deeds; deeds pursuant to mergers of corporations; deeds from subsidiary to parent corporations for cancellation of stock; and deeds subject to

FIGURE 12.2

Involuntary Alienation

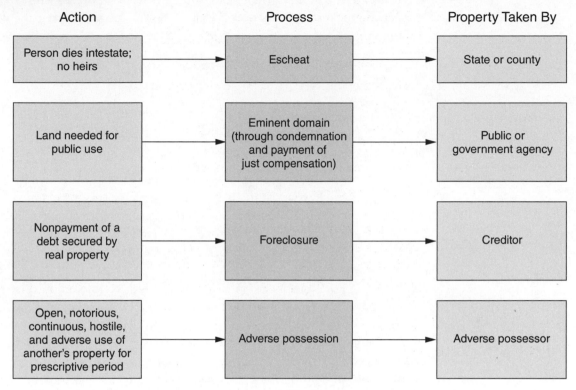

federal documentary stamp tax. *When the actual consideration for conveyance is less than $100, the transfer is considered a gift and is exempt from tax.* An Exemption Statement is usually typed on an exempted deed and signed before the deed is recorded.

Tax stamps and land trusts. Under the *Land Trust Recordation and Transfer Tax Act,* a land trustee has the obligation to record a facsimile of the assignment of beneficial interest. The names of the beneficiaries need not be disclosed, and privacy is maintained. The tax rate and the exemptions are the same for the assignment as for the transfer of real property. ■

■ INVOLUNTARY ALIENATION

Title to property may be transferred without the owner's consent by **involuntary alienation.** (See Figure 12.2.) Involuntary transfers are usually carried out by operation of law—such as by condemnation or a sale to satisfy delinquent tax or mortgage liens. When a person dies intestate and leaves no heirs, the title to the real estate passes to the county (in Illinois) by the state's power of escheat. Additional land may be acquired through the process of accretion or lost through erosion, and other acts of nature, such as earthquakes, hurricanes, sinkholes, and mudslides, may add to or eliminate a landowner's holdings.

Transfer by Adverse Possession

Adverse possession, sometimes referred to as *squatter's rights*, is another means of involuntary transfer. An individual who makes a claim to certain property, takes possession of it and *uses* it may take title away from an owner who fails to use or inspect the property for a period of years. The law recognizes that the use of land is an important function of its ownership. Usually, the possession by the claimant must be

- open,
- notorious,
- continuous and uninterrupted,
- hostile, and
- adverse to the true owner's possession.

In Illinois

The period of uninterrupted possession required to claim title by adverse possession is *20 years*. However, if the party whose property is being claimed has *color of title* (that is, if his or her apparently good title actually is invalidated by some flaw) and if the real estate taxes on the property are paid while satisfying the other statutory requirements, the possessory period may be shortened to seven years. ■

Through the principle of *tacking*, successive periods of different adverse possession by different adverse possessors can be combined, enabling a person who is not in possession for the entire required time to establish a claim. For instance, if Etha held a property in adverse possession for five years, then her daughter Diane held the same property for ten years, then Etha's other daughter Julie held the property for five more years, Julie would be able to claim the property by adverse possession even though she had not *personally* possessed the property for the full statutory 20 years.

IN PRACTICE

The right of adverse possession is a statutory right. State requirements must be followed carefully to ensure the successful transfer of title. The parties to a transaction that might involve adverse possession should seek legal counsel.

■ TRANSFER OF A DECEASED PERSON'S PROPERTY

A person who dies **testate** has prepared a will indicating how his or her property should be handled. In contrast, when a person dies **intestate** (without a will), real estate and personal property pass to the decedent's heirs according to the state's statute of *descent and distribution*. In effect, the state provides a will for an intestate decedent.

Legally, when a person dies, ownership of real estate *immediately* passes either to the heirs by descent or to the persons named in the will. Before these individuals can take full title and possession of the property, however, the estate must go through the judicial process of *probate*, and claims against the estate must be satisfied.

In Illinois

When the owner of real estate dies, *how title to the property was held* (rather than the laws of descent and distribution or the presence of a will) *may dictate who the new owners will be.*

- If the property was owned by a husband and wife in *tenancy by the entirety* or was held in *joint tenancy*, the surviving spouse (or other owner) will automatically be the new owner. If the property was held as a *life estate*, it automatically reverts to the former owner, or passes to a remainderman. In any case, no probate is required.

- If the property was not held in joint tenancy, tenancy by the entirety, or as a life estate, and the owner left a valid will (died testate), the devisees named in the will own the real estate.

- If the owner died without a will (intestate), relatives will inherit the property according to the Illinois Law of Descent. (In effect, the state makes a will for such decedents.)

- If the owner died without a will (intestate) and left no heirs, the real property will *escheat* to the Illinois county it lies in. ■

Transfer of Title by Will

A **will** is an instrument made by an owner to convey title to real or personal property after the owner's death. A will is a testamentary instrument; that is, it takes effect only after death. This differs from a deed, which must be delivered during the lifetime of the grantor and which conveys a present interest in property. While the **testator** (the person who makes a will) is alive, any property included in the will can still be conveyed by the owner. The parties named in a will have no rights or interests as long as the party who made the will lives; they acquire interest or title only after the owner's death.

Only property owned by the testator at the time of his or her death may be transferred by will. The gift of real property by will is known as a **devise**, and a person who receives property by will is known as a **devisee.** *The gift of personal property by will is known as a legacy or a bequest, and a person who receives the personal property by will is known as a legatee or beneficiary.*

For title to pass to the devisees, state laws require that on the death of a testator, the will must be filed with the court and probated. Probate is a legal procedure for verifying the validity of a will and accounting for the decedent's assets. The process can take several months to complete.

In Illinois

Legal requirements for making a will. Any person 18 or older, who is of sound mind and memory, may make a will. A will must be in writing and signed and declared by the maker (the *testator*) in the presence of two or more witnesses to be his or her last will and testament. Witnesses cannot be beneficiaries under the will, because their gifts will likely be voided by the probate court.

A modification of, an amendment of, or an addition to a previously executed will may be set forth in a separate document called a *codicil*.

A *holographic will* is written in the testator's own handwriting. A *nuncupative will*, such as a deathbed bequest, is given orally by a testator and is for personal property. Illinois courts recognize neither holographic wills nor noncupative wills unless also witnessed by two people in each case.

On the death of a testator, his or her will must be filed and a petition for probate initiated in the circuit court of the county in which the decedent resided. For six months after the executor has been appointed and the decedent's property has

FIGURE 12.3

Statutory Distributions Under the Illinois Law of Descent and Distribution

Descendent Status	Family Status	Property Passes . . .
Married, with surviving spouse	No children No other relatives	100% to surviving spouse
	Children	50% to surviving spouse; 50% shared by children or descendants of deceased child
Married, no surviving spouse	Children	Children share equally, with descendants of a deceased child taking their parent's share
Unmarried, no children	Other relatives	100% to parents, brothers, or sisters equally; however, if there is one surviving parent, that parent takes two shares and all others share equal portions; if no parents or brothers or sisters survive, the estate passes to other relatives as determined by the probate court.
	No other relatives	100% to the county in which the real estate is located, by escheat

been inventoried, claims may be presented to the executor for debts owed by the deceased. On completion of probate the executor's final account is filed with the court and the executor is discharged. The real estate is considered free from debts, claims, or taxes of the decedent.

While an individual may freely disinherit children or other previously named heirs in Illinois, *a surviving spouse may not be disinherited by the decedent spouse.* A surviving spouse who is disinherited by the decedent has a statutory right to renounce the will and claim a share of the estate as follows:

- If the deceased left no child or descendant(s) of a child, *one-half of the personal estate* and *one-half of each parcel of real estate* goes to the spouse if claimed.
- If the deceased left spouse and descendants, *one-third of the personal estate* and *one-third of each parcel of real estate* goes to the spouse if claimed.
- The will remains operative with respect to the balance of the estate. ■

Transfer of Title by Descent

When a person dies *intestate* (without leaving a valid will) his or her state's *law of descent* governs how and to whom his or her property will be distributed.

In Illinois

The Illinois *Law of Descent and Distribution* (in the Illinois *Probate Act*) provides that real estate located in Illinois owned by a deceased resident or nonresident *who did not leave a valid will* is distributed as indicated in Figure 12.3.

The estate of an intestate decedent must be probated to determine which statutory heirs will inherit, as well as to inventory the assets of and claims against the estate. Any **heir** or other interested person may petition the circuit court of the county in which the decedent last resided to probate the estate. Proof of heirship must be presented to the court. Probate generally proceeds as if the decedent had left a valid will. ■

Probate Proceedings

Probate is a formal judicial process that

- proves or confirms the validity of a will,
- determines the precise assets of the deceased person, and
- identifies the persons to whom the assets are to pass.

The purpose of probate is to see that the assets are distributed correctly. All assets must be accounted for and the decedent's debts must be satisfied before any property is distributed to the heirs. In addition, estate taxes must be paid before any distribution. The laws of each state govern the probate proceedings in that state and the functions of the individuals appointed to administer the decedent's affairs.

Assets that are distributed through probate are those that do not otherwise distribute themselves. For instance, *property held in joint tenancy or tenancy by the entirety passes immediately. Any probate proceedings will take place in the county in which the decedent resided.* If the decedent owned real estate in another county, probate would occur in that county as well.

The person who has possession of the will—normally the person designated in the will as *executor*—presents it for filing with the court. The court is responsible for determining that the will meets the statutory requirements for its form and execution. If a codicil or more than one will exists, the court will decide how these documents should be probated.

The court must rule on a challenge if a will is contested. Once the will is upheld, the assets can be distributed according to its provisions. Probate courts distribute assets according to statute only when no other reasonable alternative exists.

When a person dies intestate, the court determines who inherits the assets by reviewing proof from relatives of the decedent and their entitlement under the statute of descent and distribution. Once the heirs have been determined, the court appoints an *administrator* or a personal representative to administer the affairs of the estate—the role usually taken by an executor.

Whether or not a will is involved, the administrator or executor is responsible for having the estate's assets appraised and for ensuring that all the decedent's debts are satisfied. He or she is also responsible for paying federal estate taxes and state inheritance taxes out of the assets. Once all obligations have been satisfied, the representative distributes the remaining property according to the terms of the will or the state's law of descent.

IN PRACTICE

A broker entering into a listing agreement with the executor or administrator of an estate *in probate* should be aware that commission amount is fixed by the court and that a commission is payable only from the proceeds of the sale. *The broker will not be able to collect a commission unless the court approves the sale.*

■ SUMMARY

Title to real estate is the right to and evidence of ownership of the land. It may be transferred by voluntary alienation, involuntary alienation, will, and descent.

The voluntary transfer of an owner's title is made by a deed, executed (signed) by the owner, who is the grantor, to the purchaser (or donee) as grantee.

Among the most common requirements for a valid deed are a grantor with legal capacity to contract, a readily identifiable grantee, a granting clause, a legal description of the property, a recital of consideration, exceptions and reservations on the title, and the signature of the grantor. In addition, the deed should be properly witnessed and acknowledged/notarized before a notary public to provide evidence of a genuine signature and to facilitate recording. Title to the property passes when the grantor delivers a deed to the grantee and it is accepted. The level of guarantee a grantor offers is determined by the form of the deed.

A general warranty deed provides the greatest protection of any deed by binding the grantor to certain covenants or warranties. A special warranty deed warrants only that the real estate is not encumbered except as stated in the deed. A bargain and sale deed carries with it no warranties but implies that the grantor holds title to the property. A quitclaim deed carries with it no warranties whatsoever and conveys only the interest, if any, the grantor possesses in the property. The language of each deed is a key as to its type.

An owner's title may be transferred by his or her permission or without his or her permission by a court action or by death. The real estate of an owner who makes a valid will (who dies testate) passes to the devisees through the probating of the will. The title of an owner who dies without a will (intestate or intestatory) passes according to the provisions of the laws of descent and distribution of the state in which the real estate is located.

In Illinois

In Illinois, the requirements for a valid deed are a grantor with legal capacity to contract, a readily identifiable grantee, a granting clause, a legal description of the property, a recital of consideration, and the signature of the grantor. Title to the property passes when the grantor delivers a deed to the grantee and it is accepted. The obligation of a grantor is determined by the form of the deed. The specific words of conveyance in the granting clause are critical in determining the form of deed.

Acknowledgment and notarization are standard in county recorders' offices due to the protocol that has developed over time. Recording is absolutely required for tax deeds and if a deed is to be used as evidence in a court of law.

In Illinois, a bargain and sale deed includes covenants that make it similar to a special warranty deed. A quitclaim deed carries with it no warranties whatsoever and conveys only the interest, if any, the grantor possesses in the property.

Generally, state and county transfer tax stamps are paid for by the seller. This money goes to the state and county for affordable housing and land preservation.

Many municipalities have their own transfer tax as well, which can be paid by either the seller or the buyer.

The title of an owner who dies without a will (intestate) passes to the decedent's statutory heirs, according to the provisions of the Illinois Law of Descent and Distribution. Property conveyed by devise is property conveyed by will. Where a decedent leaves no statutory heirs, the real property escheats to the county in which it is located. ■

QUESTIONS

1. The basic requirements for a valid conveyance are governed by
   a. state law.
   b. local custom.
   c. national law.
   d. the law of descent.

2. Every deed must be signed by the
   a. grantor.
   b. grantee.
   c. grantor and grantee.
   d. devisee.

3. Hataraj, age 15, recently inherited many parcels of real estate from his late father and has decided to sell one of them. If Hataraj enters into a deed conveying his interest in the property to a purchaser, such a conveyance will be
   a. valid.
   b. void.
   c. invalid.
   d. voidable.

4. A husband who works for an international corporation has already moved to Germany. To authorize his wife to act on his behalf, he signed a(n)
   a. power of attorney.
   b. release deed.
   c. quitclaim deed.
   d. acknowledgment.

5. What is the major difference between a general warranty deed and a quitclaim deed?
   a. A general warranty deed provides the least protection for the buyer; a quitclaim deed provides the most protection for the buyer.
   b. A general warranty deed can be used only in foreclosure sales; a quitclaim deed is used only in residential sales.
   c. A general warranty deed provides the most protection for the buyer; a quitclaim deed provides the least protection for the buyer.
   d. A general warranty deed creates an indefeasible title; a quitclaim deed creates a defeasible title.

6. Lou receives a deed from Gary. The granting clause of the deed states, "I, Gary, hereby remise, release, alienate, and convey to Lou the property known as Yellowacre." What type of deed has Lou received?
   a. Special warranty
   b. Quitclaim
   c. General warranty
   d. Bargain and sale

7. Which of the following best describes the covenant of quiet enjoyment?
   a. The grantor promises to obtain and deliver any instrument needed to make the title good.
   b. The grantor guarantees that if the title fails in the future, he or she will compensate the grantee.
   c. The grantor warrants that he or she is the owner and has the right to convey title to the property.
   d. The grantor guarantees that the title will be good against the title claims of third parties.

8. A deed includes the following statement: "The full consideration for this conveyance is $125,480." Which type of deed is this most likely to be?
   a. Gift deed
   b. Trustee's deed
   c. Deed in trust
   d. Deed executed pursuant to court order

9. Which of the following types of deeds merely implies, but does not specifically warrant, that the grantor holds good title to the property?
   a. Special warranty
   b. Bargain and sale
   c. Quitclaim
   d. Trustee's

10. Step 1: Herbert decided to convey Blueacre to James. Step 2: Herbert signed a deed transferring title to James. Step 3: Herbert gave the signed deed to James, who accepted it. Step 4: James took the deed to the county recorder's office and had it recorded. At which step did title to Blueacre actually transfer or pass to James?

    a. Step 1
    b. Step 2
    c. Step 3
    d. Step 4

11. Andrea conveys property to Kurt by deed. The deed contains the following: (1) Kurt's name, spelled out in full; (2) a statement that Andrea has received $10 and Kurt's love and affection; and (3) a statement that the property is conveyed to Kurt "to have and to hold." Which of the following correctly identifies, in order, these three elements of the deed?

    a. Grantee; consideration; granting clause
    b. Grantee; consideration; habendum clause
    c. Grantor; habendum clause; legal description
    d. Grantee; acknowledgment; habendum clause

12. Teresa signed a deed transferring ownership of Whiteacre to Lynn. To provide evidence that Teresa's signature was genuine, Teresa executed a declaration before a notary. This declaration is known as an

    a. affidavit.
    b. acknowledgment.
    c. affirmation.
    d. estoppel.

13. Roland executes a deed to Philip as grantee, has it acknowledged, and receives payment from the buyer. Roland holds the deed, however, and arranges to meet Philip the next morning at the courthouse to give the deed to him. In this situation at this time

    a. Philip owns the property because he has paid for it.
    b. Legal title to the property will not officially pass until Philip has been given the deed the next morning.
    c. Legal title to the property will not pass until Philip has received the deed and records it the next morning.
    d. Philip will own the property when he signs the deed the next morning.

14. Title to real estate may be transferred during a person's lifetime by

    a. devise.
    b. descent.
    c. involuntary alienation.
    d. escheat.

15. Fran bought acreage in a distant county, never went to see the acreage, and did not use the ground. Harry moved his mobile home onto the land, had a water well drilled, and lived there for 22 years. Harry may become the owner of the land if he has complied with the state law regarding

    a. requirements for a valid conveyance.
    b. adverse possession.
    c. avulsion.
    d. voluntary alienation.

16. What do the terms *condemnation* and *escheat* have in common?

    a. They are examples of voluntary alienation.
    b. They are processes used in adverse possession claims.
    c. They are methods of transferring title by descent.
    d. They are examples of involuntary alienation.

17. A seller lists her property for $99,000. A buyer offers $99,000 for the property contingent on the seller's providing a general warranty deed. The seller accepts. Three months after the closing, a relative of the seller claims to have an interest in the property and sues. Does the seller have to protect the buyer?

    a. No, a general warranty deed does not provide protection to the buyer.
    b. No, because when the property was listed the seller only offered to give a quitclaim deed.
    c. Yes, the covenant of seisin promises the seller will protect the buyer from third parties.
    d. Yes, the covenant of quiet enjoyment guarantees that the seller will protect the buyer from third parties.

18. A deed contains a guarantee that the grantor will compensate the grantee for any loss resulting from the title's failure in the future. This is an example of which type of covenant?

    a. Warranty forever
    b. Further assurance
    c. Quiet enjoyment
    d. Seisin

19. A person who has died leaving a valid will is called a(n)

    a. devisee.
    b. testator.
    c. legatee.
    d. intestate.

20. Title to real estate can be transferred at death by which of the following documents?

    a. Warranty deed
    b. Special warranty deed
    c. Trustee's deed
    d. Will

21. Jameson, a bachelor, died owning real estate that he devised by his will to his niece, Karen. At what point does full title pass to his niece?

    a. Immediately on Jameson's death
    b. After his will has been probated
    c. After Karen has paid all inheritance taxes
    d. When Karen executes a new deed to the property

22. For Illinois courts to recognize a holographic will, the will must

    a. be handwritten.
    b. have no amendments.
    c. have two witnesses.
    d. be modified by codicil.

23. In Illinois, how many years are required to acquire title by adverse possession?

    a. 5
    b. 7
    c. 20
    d. 30

24. Which of the following statements is TRUE regarding the execution of a valid will in Illinois?

    a. The testator must be at least 21 years old and of sound mind.
    b. The will must be in writing, signed, and witnessed by two people.
    c. The will must be witnessed by three persons.
    d. The will must be notarized.

25. Which of the following statements is TRUE regarding a bargain and sale deed in Illinois?

    a. It warrants that the grantor has fee simple title.
    b. It warrants that the grantor will defend all suits against title.
    c. It conveys to the grantee any future title the grantor may acquire.
    d. It warrants that the premises are free from all encumbrances.

26. In Illinois, the transfer tax is

    a. customarily paid by the buyer.
    b. computed on the sales price less the amount of any existing mortgage to which the property remains subject.
    c. not required if the actual total consideration is less than $500.
    d. assessed at the rate of $1 per $1,000 of sales price.

27. Which deed requires the Illinois transfer tax?
    a. A deed conveying a property owned by a charitable institution
    b. A deed conveying a property owned by a government body
    c. Deeds for property valued at less than $100
    d. Deeds between relatives

28. Samuel, a longtime Illinois resident who owned considerable real and personal property, died testate, leaving only $1 to his wife, Marianne, who was his sole survivor. The balance of his estate was left to his trusted real estate broker. Marianne renounced the will. Which of the following is *TRUE*?
    a. The entire will is invalid.
    b. Marianne is entitled to a one-quarter share of all property.
    c. Marianne is entitled to one-half of the personal estate and one-half of each parcel of real estate.
    d. Because Samuel left no descendants, Marianne is entitled to the entire estate by the law of descent.

29. Robert, an Illinois resident, died intestate. Robert was survived by a mother and brother. Under these facts, which of the following correctly states how Robert's estate will be distributed?
    a. Robert's estate will be left entirely to his mother.
    b. The estate will be divided equally between the mother and brother.
    c. The estate will be divided so that Robert's mother receives two-thirds and Robert's brother receives one-third.
    d. Robert's mother receives one-third and Robert's brother receives two-thirds.

30. Jim owned Illinois real estate as a sole owner and died intestate, survived by a spouse and their one child. After Jim's debts and taxes are paid, the child will own
    a. two-thirds in fee simple.
    b. one-third in fee simple.
    c. one-half in fee simple.
    d. the entire estate in fee simple.

31. A parcel of Illinois real estate encumbered with a mortgage is being sold for $100,000. The purchaser agrees to assume this mortgage with a present balance of $48,000 and to pay $52,000 in cash upon receipt of the seller's deed. What amount of county and state stamps must the seller affix to the deed?
    a. $52
    b. $78
    c. $100
    d. $150

32. Millie sells her Springfield condominium to Jane for $80,000. Based on this transaction, which of the following statements is *TRUE*?
    a. If Millie takes back a purchase-money mortgage of $60,000, her total transfer tax due to the county and state will be $30.
    b. If Millie lets Jane take title subject to Millie's $50,000 mortgage, Millie will pay a total tax of $45 to the county and state.
    c. If the purchase price includes $10,000 of personal property, Millie's total tax due to the county and state will be $115.
    d. This transaction is exempt from real property taxation in Illinois.

33. A seller agreed to sell her home for $127,000. There is an existing mortgage on the property with an unpaid balance of $95,000. This mortgage has a prepayment option, and the seller will pay the $95,000 balance with the proceeds she receives from the sale. The purchaser, who has arranged for a mortgage loan of $100,000, will pay the remaining $27,000 in cash. Because of the two loan transactions, it is necessary to close the sale through an escrow. What amount of Illinois state and county transfer tax stamps is the seller required to affix to her deed conveying this property?

    a. $40.50
    b. $48.00
    c. $140.50
    d. $190.50

34. Karl has a deed prepared conveying a farm near Champaign to his son as a gift. The deed contains a statement that the farm was given in "consideration of $10 and love and affection." The farm has a market value of $73,000. Karl is required to attach what amount of transfer stamps to his executed deed?

    a. $0.00
    b. $73.00
    c. $109.00
    d. $109.50

CHAPTER 13

Title Records

■ **LEARNING OBJECTIVES** *When you've finished reading this chapter, you should be able to*

- ■ **identify** the various proofs of ownership.

- ■ **describe** recording, notice, and chain of title issues.

- ■ **explain** the process and purpose of a title search.

- ■ **distinguish** constructive and actual notice.

- ■ **define** the following *key terms:*

abstract and attorney's opinion of title	chain of title	subrogation
	constructive notice	suit to quiet title
abstract of title	marketable title	title insurance
actual notice	priority	title search
certificate of title	recording	

■ PUBLIC RECORDS

Public records contain detailed information about each parcel of real estate in a city or county. These records are crucial in establishing ownership, giving notice of encumbrances, and establishing priority of liens. They protect the interests of real estate owners, taxing bodies, creditors, and the general public. The real estate recording system includes written documents that affect title, such as deeds and mortgages. Public records regarding taxes, judgments, probate, and marriage also may offer important information about the title to a particular property. In most states, written documents must be recorded in the county where the land is located.

Public records are maintained by

- recorders of deeds,
- county clerks,
- county treasurers,
- city clerks,
- collectors, and
- clerks of court.

In Illinois

The recorder of deeds, county clerk, county treasurer, city clerk and collector, and clerks of various courts maintain these records. In Illinois, a recorder of deeds must be elected in each county with a population of 60,000 or more. In counties with a population of fewer than 60,000, the county clerk serves as the recorder of deeds.

Public records are just that: open to the public. This means that anyone interested in a particular property can review the records to learn about the documents, claims, and other issues that affect its ownership. A prospective purchaser, for example, needs to be sure that the seller can convey title to the property. If the property is subject to any liens or other encumbrances, a prospective buyer or lender will want to know. ■

IN PRACTICE

Although we speak of prospective purchasers conducting title searches, purchasers themselves rarely search the public records for evidence of title or encumbrances. Instead, title companies conduct searches before providing title insurance. An attorney also may search the title.

Recording

Recording is the act of placing documents in the public record. The specific rules for recording documents are a matter of state law. However, although the details may vary, recording essentially provides that any written document that affects any estate, right, title, or interest in land must be recorded in the county where the land is located to serve as public notice. That way, anyone interested in the title to a parcel of property will know where to look to discover the various interests of all other parties. Recording acts also generally give legal priority to those interests recorded first (the "first in time, first in right" or "first come, first served" principle).

To be eligible for recording, a document must be drawn and executed as stipulated in the recording acts of the state in which the real estate is located.

In Illinois

In most states, written documents that affect land *must be recorded in the county where the land is located.*

Illinois law does not require that most documents be filed or recorded within a specified period of time. However, when creditors and subsequent purchasers do not actually know the content of the documents affecting certain real estate interests, the courts will hold these creditors and purchasers responsible for "discovering" (knowing) that information only as of the date on which the documents are recorded. Tax deeds, by law, must be recorded within one year after the redemption period expires. A tax deed that is not recorded or filed within one year becomes null and void. *No instrument affecting title to real property may include any provision prohibiting recording.* Any such prohibiting provision is void as a matter of law.

The original document must be filed with the county recorder of deeds, and must meet specific requirements (in addition to the eight requirements of a valid deed):

- Grantor's name typed or printed below his or her signature
- Full address of the grantee
- Name and address of the person who prepared the deed
- Permanent tax index number (required only in some counties)
- Common address of the property (required only in some counties)
- 3½" × 5" blank space for use by the recorder
- Completed real estate transfer declaration
- Proof of payment of the state and county transfer taxes or indication of an applicable exemption
- Proof of payment of the municipal transfer tax (if applicable)

When the parcel of land being transferred is (1) a division of a larger parcel and (2) smaller than five acres, the recording provisions of the *Illinois Plat Act* apply. If the conveyance is exempt, an affidavit stating the reason for the exemption may be required by the recorder.

In some municipalities, the water department must declare, by way of an endorsement stamp on the municipal transfer declaration, that all outstanding water bills have been paid.

A deed in any language other than English, although valid between the parties, does not give constructive notice unless an official English translation of the document is attached at the time of recording. The translation must be prepared by a credible source, such as the local consulate of a country in which the language is used. ■

Notice

Anyone who has an interest in a parcel of real estate can take certain steps, called *giving notice*, to ensure that others know about the individual's interest. There are two basic types of notice: *constructive notice* and *actual notice*.

Constructive notice is the legal presumption that information may be obtained by an individual through diligent inquiry. Properly recording documents in the public record serves as constructive notice to the world of an individual's rights or interest. So does the physical possession of a property. Because the information or evidence is readily available to the world, a prospective purchaser or lender is responsible for discovering the interest.

> **Constructive Notice—** Could or should know with reasonable inquiry
> **Actual Notice—**Knows for certain by *direct* access to information

In contrast, **actual notice** means not only that the information is available, but that someone has been given the information and actually knows it. An individual who has searched the public records and inspected the property has actual notice. Actual notice is also known as *direct knowledge*. If an individual can be proven to have had actual notice of information, he or she cannot use a lack of constructive notice (such as an unrecorded deed) to justify a claim.

Priority.   **Priority** refers to the order of rights in time. Many complicated situations can affect the priority of rights in a parcel of real estate—who recorded first; which party was in possession first; who had actual or constructive notice. How the courts rule in any situation depends, of course, on the specific facts of the case. These are strictly legal questions that should be referred to the parties' attorneys.

■ **FOR EXAMPLE** In May, Ray purchased Grayacre from Arthur and received a deed. Ray never recorded the deed but began farming operations on the property in June. In November, Arthur (who was either forgetful or crafty) again sold Grayacre, this time to Carl. Carl accepted the deed and promptly recorded it. However, because Carl never inspected Grayacre to see whether someone was in possession, Ray has the superior right to the property even though Ray never recorded the deed. By taking possession, a purchaser gives constructive notice of his or her interest in the land. With no constructive notice given, had Ray not taken possession the result might have been different.

Unrecorded Documents

Certain types of liens are not recorded. Real estate taxes and special assessments are liens on specific parcels of real estate and usually are not recorded until some time after the taxes or assessments are past due. Inheritance taxes and franchise taxes are statutory liens. They are placed against all real estate owned by a decedent at the time of death or by a corporation at the time the franchise taxes became a lien. Like real estate taxes, they are not recorded.

Notice of these liens must be gained from sources other than the recorder's office. Evidence of the payment of real estate taxes, special assessments, municipal utilities, and other taxes can be gathered from paid tax receipts and letters from municipalities. Creative measures are often required to get information about these "off the record" liens.

In Illinois

A *mechanic's lien* that has not been recorded may nonetheless still have priority over other liens that have been recorded. ■

Chain of Title

A **chain of title** is the record of a property's ownership. Beginning with the earliest owner, title may pass to many individuals. Each owner is linked to the next so that a chain is formed. An unbroken chain of title can be traced through linking conveyances from the present owner back to the earliest recorded owner.

If ownership cannot be traced through an unbroken chain, it is said that there is a *gap* in the chain. In these cases, if a satisfaction of lien or a quitclaim deed cannot be provided, the cloud on the title makes it necessary to establish ownership by a court action called a **suit to quiet title**. A suit might be required, for instance, when a grantor acquired title under one name and conveyed it under another. Or there may be a forged deed in the chain, after which no subsequent grantee acquired legal title. All possible claimants are allowed to present evidence during a court proceeding; then the court's judgment is filed. Often, the simple procedure of obtaining any relevant quitclaim deeds is used to clear title and establish ownership.

Title Search and Abstract of Title

A **title search** is an examination of all of the public records to determine whether any defects exist in the chain of title. The records of the conveyances of ownership are examined, beginning with the present owner. Then the title is traced backward to its origin. The time back to which the title must be searched is limited in states that have adopted the *Marketable Title Act*. This law extinguishes certain interests and cures certain defects arising before the *root of the title*—the conveyance that establishes the source of the chain of title. Normally, the root is considered to be 40 years. Under most circumstances, then, it is necessary to search only from the current owner to the root.

In Illinois

For normal title searches in Illinois, the search goes back 40 years under the Illinois *Marketable Title Act.* When the possibility of litigation exists, the search must go back 75 years. Interestingly, in Cook and Du Page counties title searches cannot go back beyond 1871. In that year most records were destroyed in the Great Chicago Fire.

Other public records are examined to identify wills, judicial proceedings, and other encumbrances that may affect title. These include a variety of taxes, special assessments, and other recorded liens.

A title search usually is not ordered until after the major contingencies in a sales contract have been cleared—for instance, after a loan commitment has been secured. Before providing money for a loan, a lender or the attorney orders a title search to ensure that no lien is superior to its mortgage lien. In most cases, *the cost of the title search in Illinois is paid by the seller.* ∎

An **abstract of title** is a summary report of what the title search found in the public record. The person who prepares this report is called an *abstractor.* The abstractor searches all the public records, then summarizes the various events and proceedings that affected the title throughout its history. The report begins with the original grant (or root), then provides a chronological list of recorded instruments. All recorded liens and encumbrances are included, along with their current statuses. A list of all of the public records examined is also provided as evidence of the scope of the search.

IN PRACTICE

An abstract of title is a condensed history of those items that can be found in public records. It does not reveal such items as encroachments, forgeries, or any interests or conveyances that have not been recorded.

Marketable Title

Under the terms of the typical real estate sales contract, the seller is required to deliver **marketable title** to the buyer at the closing. To be marketable, a title must

- disclose no serious defects and not depend on doubtful questions of law or fact to prove its validity;
- not expose a purchaser to the hazard of litigation or threaten the *quiet enjoyment* of the property;
- convince a reasonably well-informed and prudent purchaser, acting on business principles and with knowledge of the facts and their legal significance, that he or she could sell or mortgage the property at a later time.

Although a title that does not meet these requirements still could be transferred, it contains certain defects that may limit or restrict its ownership. A buyer cannot be forced to accept a conveyance that is materially different from the one bargained for in the sales contract. However, questions of marketable title must be raised by a buyer before acceptance of the deed. Once a buyer has accepted a deed with an unmarketable title, the only available legal recourse is to sue the seller under any covenants of warranty contained in the deed.

■ PROOF OF OWNERSHIP

Proof of ownership is evidence that title is marketable. A *deed by itself is not considered sufficient evidence of ownership in Illinois.* Even though a warranty deed conveys the grantor's interest, it contains no proof of the condition of the grantor's title at the time of the conveyance. The grantee needs some assurance that he or she actually is acquiring ownership and that the title is marketable. A *certificate of title* or *title insurance* commonly are used to prove ownership.

Certificate of Title

A **certificate of title** is a statement of opinion regarding title status on the date the certificate is issued. A certificate of title is not a full guarantee of ownership. Rather, it certifies the condition of the title's history based on an actual examination of the public records—a title search. The certificate may be prepared by a title company, a licensed abstractor, or an attorney. An owner, a mortgage lender, or a buyer may request the certificate.

Although a certificate of title is used as evidence of ownership, it is not perfect. Unrecorded liens or rights of parties in possession cannot be discovered by a search of the public records. Hidden defects, such as transfers involving forged documents, incorrect marital information, incompetent parties, minors, or fraud, cannot be detected. A certificate offers no defense against these defects because they are unknown. The person who prepares the certificate is liable only for negligence in preparing the certificate.

Abstract and Attorney's Opinion of Title

An **abstract and attorney's opinion of title** are used in some areas, including Illinois, as evidence of title. This is an opinion of title status based on a review of the abstract by an attorney. Similar to a certificate of title, the opinion of title does not protect against defects that cannot be discovered from the public records. Many buyers purchase title insurance to defend the title from these defects.

Title Insurance

Title insurance is a contract under which the policyholder is protected from losses arising from defects in the title. A title insurance company determines whether the title is insurable based on a review of the public records. If so, a policy is issued. Unlike other insurance policies that insure against future losses, title insurance protects the insured from an event that occurred *before* the policy was issued. Title insurance is considered the best defense of title: The title insurance company will defend any lawsuit based on an insurable defect and pay claims if the title proves to be defective.

After examining the public records, the title company usually issues what may be called a *preliminary report of title* or a *commitment to issue a title policy.* This describes the type of policy that will be issued and includes

- the name of the insured party;
- the legal description of the real estate;
- the estate or interest covered;
- conditions and stipulations under which the policy is issued; and
- a schedule of all exceptions, including encumbrances and defects found in the public records and any known unrecorded defects.

The *premium* for the policy is paid once, at closing. The maximum loss for which the company may be liable cannot exceed the face amount of the policy (unless

	Standard Coverage	Extended Coverage	Not Covered by Either Policy
TABLE 13.1 **Owner's Title Insurance Policy**	1. Defects found in public records 2. Forged documents 3. Incompetent grantors 4. Incorrect marital statements 5. Improperly delivered deeds	Standard coverage plus defects discoverable through the following: 1. Property inspection, including unrecorded rights of persons in possession 2. Examination of survey 3. Unrecorded liens not known of by policyholder	1. Defects and liens listed in policy 2. Defects known to buyer 3. Changes in land use brought about by zoning ordinances

the amount of coverage has been extended by use of an *inflation rider*). When a title company makes a payment to settle a claim covered by a policy, the company generally acquires the right to any remedy or damages available to the insured. This right is called **subrogation**.

In Illinois *A title insurance policy is the most commonly used evidence* that an owner of Illinois real property tenders to a prospective purchaser or lender as proof of good title. Careful listing agents often request a copy of the first page of a title insurance policy for their files, so as to be certain those selling a property have the right to do so.

The Illinois *Title Insurance Act of 1990* requires that all producers of title insurance who own a part interest in a title company disclose this fact to clients. Producers of title insurance include lawyers and real estate brokers. Every time a sale is made, a new title insurance policy must be produced. These *producers* or *title agents* are permitted to recommend their own title companies, but they must be registered as title agents and must fill out mandatory disclosure forms for the buyer and seller. Failure to comply with the disclosure rules can result in loss of the privilege of doing business in the state. ■

Coverage.   Exactly which defects the title company will defend depends on the type of policy. (See Table 13.1.) A *standard coverage policy* normally insures the title as it is known from the public records. In addition, the standard policy insures against such hidden defects as forged documents, conveyances by incompetent grantors, incorrect marital statements, and improperly delivered deeds.

Extended coverage, as provided by an *American Land Title Association* (ALTA) policy, includes the protections of a standard policy plus additional protections. An extended or ALTA policy protects a homeowner against defects that may be discovered by inspection of the property: rights of parties in possession, examination of a survey, and certain unrecorded liens, to name a few. Most lenders require extended coverage title policies.

In Illinois An extended title insurance policy would offer the buyer protection against "secret liens," such as unrecorded mechanics' liens, and also is required by most lenders. ■

Title insurance does not offer guaranteed protection against all defects. A title company will not insure a bad title or offer protection against defects that clearly appear in a title search. The policy generally names certain uninsurable losses, called *exclusions*. These include zoning ordinances, restrictive covenants, easements, certain water rights, and current taxes and special assessments.

Types of policies.   The different types of policies depend on who is named as the insured. An owner's policy is issued for the benefit of the owner and his or her heirs or devisees. This policy is almost always paid for by the seller at the closing. A lender's policy is issued for the benefit of the mortgage company. This policy is usually paid for by the buyer at the closing. The amount of the coverage depends on the amount of the mortgage loan. As the loan balance is reduced, the coverage decreases.

A lessee's interest can be insured with a leasehold policy. Certificate of sale policies are available to insure the title to property purchased in a court sale.

■ SUMMARY

The purpose of the recording acts is to give legal, public, and constructive notice to the world of parties' interests in real estate. The recording provisions have been adopted to create an orderly system for real estate transfer. Without them, it would be virtually impossible to transfer real estate from one party to another. The interests and rights of the various parties in a particular parcel of land must be recorded so that such rights are legally effective against third parties who do not have knowledge or notice of the rights. If a transfer of real estate title is taking place, any provision in the transfer documents intended to prevent recording is void.

Possession of real estate is generally interpreted as constructive notice of the rights of the person in possession. Actual notice is knowledge acquired directly and personally, such as by visiting the property.

Title evidence shows whether a seller conveys marketable title. A deed of conveyance is evidence that a grantor has conveyed his or her interest in land, but it is not evidence of the title's kind or condition. A marketable title is generally one that is so free from significant defects that the purchaser can be insured against having to defend the title.

Three forms of providing title evidence are commonly used throughout the United States: abstract and attorney's opinion of title, certificate of title, and title insurance policy. Each form reveals the history of a title. Title evidence must be revisited or dated as a continuation whenever title evidence is reissued.

| In Illinois | In Illinois, the title insurance policy is the most commonly used indication of ownership and clear title. ■ |

Title searches prior to closing are done in some detail to assure the new homeowner that title was clear at time of conveyance. A deed shows that the previous owner's interest was conveyed, but it does not by itself provide assurance of the condition of the title.

QUESTIONS

1. A title search in the public records may be conducted by
   a. anyone.
   b. attorneys and abstractors only.
   c. attorneys, abstractors, and real estate licensees only.
   d. anyone who obtains a court order under the *Freedom of Information Act.*

2. Which of the following statements best explains why instruments affecting real estate are recorded?
   a. Recording gives constructive notice to the world of the rights and interests of a party in a particular parcel of real estate.
   b. Failing to record will void the transfer.
   c. The instruments must be recorded to comply with the terms of the statute of frauds.
   d. Recording proves the execution of the instrument.

3. A purchaser went to the county building to check the recorder's records. She found that the seller was the grantee in the last recorded deed and that no mortgage was on record against the property. The purchaser may assume which of the following?
   a. All taxes are paid, and no judgments are outstanding.
   b. The seller has good title.
   c. The seller did not mortgage the property.
   d. No one else is occupying the property.

4. The date and time a document was recorded establish which of the following?
   a. Priority
   b. Abstract of title
   c. Subrogation
   d. Marketable title

5. Pam bought Laura's house, received a deed, and moved into the residence but neglected to record the document. One week later, Laura died, and her heirs in another city, unaware that the property had been sold, conveyed title to Michael, who recorded the deed. Who owns the property?
   a. Pam
   b. Michael
   c. Laura's heirs
   d. Both Pam and Michael

6. A property has encumbrances. Can it be sold?
   a. No, a property cannot be sold if it has any encumbrances.
   b. No, not unless the seller secures title insurance.
   c. Yes, if title insurance can be purchased by the buyer covering the encumbrances.
   d. Yes, if the buyer agrees to buy it subject to the encumbrances.

7. Which would *NOT* be an acceptable proof of ownership?
   a. ALTA policy
   b. Title insurance policy
   c. Abstract and attorney's opinion
   d. Deed signed by the last seller

8. Chain of title refers to which of the following?
   a. Summary or history of all documents and legal proceedings affecting a specific parcel of land
   b. Report of the contents of the public record regarding a particular property
   c. Instrument or document that protects the insured parties (subject to specific exceptions) against defects in the examination of the record and hidden risks such as forgeries, undisclosed heirs, and errors in the public records
   d. Record of a property's ownership

9. Bill, the seller, delivered a deed to the buyer at the closing. A title search disclosed no serious defects, and the title did not appear to be based on doubtful questions of law or fact or to expose the buyer to possible litigation. Bill's title did not appear to present a threat to the buyer's quiet enjoyment, and the title policy was sufficient to convince a reasonably well-informed person that the property could be resold. The title conveyed would commonly be referred to as a(n)

    a. certificate of title.
    b. abstract of title.
    c. marketable title.
    d. attorney's opinion of title.

10. The person who prepares an abstract of title for a parcel of real estate

    a. searches the public records and then summarizes the events and proceedings that affect title.
    b. insures the condition of the title.
    c. inspects the property.
    d. issues a certificate of title.

11. Susan is frantic because she cannot find her deed and now wants to sell the property. She

    a. may need a suit to quiet title.
    b. must buy title insurance.
    c. does not need the deed to sell if it was recorded.
    d. should execute a replacement deed to herself.

12. Which statement is *TRUE* regarding the lender's title insurance?

    a. The lender's protection increases with each principal payment that is made.
    b. The seller is usually required to purchase the lender's policy.
    c. The mortgagee's policy covers only the mortgagee.
    d. The mortgagee's premium is paid monthly with the mortgage payment.

13. Which of the following are traditionally covered by a standard title insurance policy?

    a. Unrecorded rights of persons in possession
    b. Improperly delivered deeds
    c. Changes in land use due to zoning ordinances
    d. Unrecorded liens not known of by the policyholder

14. General Title Company settled a claim against its insured, Robert. General Title made a substantial payment to the person who sued Robert. Now, General Title may seek damages from Sam, who originally gave Robert a general warranty deed. Through what right can General Title recover the amount it paid out in the settlement?

    a. Escrow
    b. Encumbrance
    c. Subordination
    d. Subrogation

15. The documents referred to as title evidence include

    a. title insurance.
    b. warranty deeds.
    c. security agreements.
    d. a deed.

16. The legal presumption that information can be obtained through diligent inquiry is referred to as

    a. actual notice.
    b. constructive notice.
    c. priority.
    d. subrogation.

17. Karen sells a portion of her property to Linda. Linda promptly records the deed in the appropriate county office. If Karen tries to sell the same portion of her property to Mark, which of the following statements is *TRUE*?
    a. Mark has been given constructive notice of the prior sale because Linda promptly recorded it.
    b. Mark has been given actual notice of the prior sale because Linda promptly recorded it.
    c. Because Mark's purchase of the portion of Karen's property is the more recent, it will have priority over Linda's interest, regardless of when Linda recorded the deed.
    d. Because Linda recorded the deed, Mark is presumed by law to have actual knowledge of Linda's interest.

18. Adam sold a house to Brian, who immediately occupied it. Brian neglected to have the deed recorded. Adam, who is somewhat absentminded but of sound mind, later sold the same house to Candace, who recorded the deed but did not make any prior inspection of the property. Based on these facts, which of the following would be the most likely finding of a court in this case?
    a. Brian owns the house, because Candace had constructive notice of Brian's interest.
    b. Candace owns the property, because Brian failed to record his interest.
    c. Adam is still the owner of the property until such time as Brian records; the conveyance to Candace is invalid due to Brian's possessory interest.
    d. Brian and Candace own the property as tenants in common.

In Illinois

---

19. For a deed to be recorded in Illinois, what is necessary?
    a. The names of the grantor and grantee typed or printed below their signatures
    b. The past address of the grantee
    c. An escrow exemption statement
    d. Permanent tax index number

20. Which of the following statements correctly describes the requirements for recording a tax deed?
    a. A tax deed must be recorded within 30 days after expiration of the redemption period.
    b. A tax deed may be recorded at any time before or after the redemption period.
    c. Tax deeds are specifically exempted from recording deadlines and are effective regardless of whether or not they have been recorded.
    d. A tax deed must be recorded within one year after expiration of the redemption period or it will become null and void.

21. Seth, a Chicago resident, purchases farmland in southern Illinois as an investment. The deed to Seth should be recorded
    a. in the county recorder's office of Cook County, where Seth's permanent residence is located.
    b. in the statewide land registry located in Springfield.
    c. in the recorder's office of the county in which the farm is located.
    d. in the tax records of the city of Chicago.

22. The population of Outlet County is 54,000. In Outlet County, the recorder of deeds
    a. must be elected.
    b. is the county clerk.
    c. is the county treasurer.
    d. is appointed by the secretary of state.

23. Nathan conveyed Halfacre Farm to Marlon. While both Nathan and Marlon are Illinois residents, the transfer was conducted entirely in their native Urdu language. The deed was written in Urdu so that both parties could read and understand it. Based on these facts, which of the following statements is true of this deed?

a. The deed is invalid between the parties, because deeds in Illinois must be in English.

b. The deed gives constructive notice by its existence in the public records, regardless of whether the details of the conveyance can be immediately read by non-Urdu-speakers.

c. The deed does not give constructive notice unless an English translation is attached at the time of recording.

d. The deed may not be recorded, because Illinois law prohibits deeds in foreign languages.

24. What would be found in a title insurance policy?

a. The premium amount

b. The estate covered

c. The type of policy issued

d. An abstract of title

CHAPTER 14

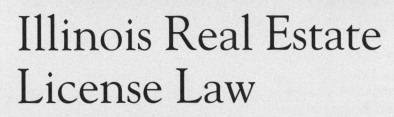

Illinois Real Estate License Law

■ **LEARNING OBJECTIVES** *When you've finished reading this chapter, you should be able to*

■ **identify** the various categories of licensure.

■ **describe** the actions which result in discipline against a licensee.

■ **explain** the statutory duties of the agency relationship.

■ **distinguish** the processes involved in sponsoring and terminating a license.

■ **define** the following key terms:

affinity relationships
blind ads
branch office license
broker
Bureau of Real Estate Professions (BRE)
business offense
Class A misdemeanor
Class C misdemeanor
Class 4 felony
criminal prosecution
designated agency
disciplinary consent order

disclosure of agency
disclosure of compensation
Division of Professional Regulation
Illinois Department of Financial and Professional Regulation (IDFPR)
informed written consent
inoperative status
laws of agency
leasing agent license
licenses

pocket card
Real Estate Administration and Disciplinary Board
Real Estate Education Advisory Council
Real Estate License Administration Fund
Real Estate Recovery Fund
Real Estate Research and Education Fund
referral fees
salesperson
sponsor card

Since 1921, Illinois has had a real estate license law. This body of law is intended to regulate the real estate industry for the *protection of the public*. Today, the law is called the *Real Estate License Act of 2000*.

In 2004, as a result of a government agency consolidation, the **Illinois Department of Financial and Professional Regulation (IDFPR)** was created. Under the IDFPR is the Division of Professional Regulation. Within the Division of Professional Regulation is the Bureau of Real Estate Professions (BRE).

The BRE is responsible for administering and enforcing the Illinois Real Estate License Act of 2000. In addition, the BRE administers all licenses for Illinois real estate brokers, salespersons, leasing agents, real estate corporations, partnerships, limited liability companies, real estate branch offices, real estate schools, and real estate instructors.

The IDFPR through the BRE promulgates rules for the License Act's implementation and enforcement. These are often referred to as "the Rules" and they supply explanatory detail and guidelines for the Act. The Act, Rules, and other significant legislation are available online at *www.ilga.gov* (click on Illinois Compiled Statutes, Chapter 225; ILCS 454).

The Act and the Rules implementing it are essential knowledge for any real estate licensee. To approach this large body of law in a way that is meaningful, this chapter is arranged in the order that the Real Estate License Act is likely to have an impact on a licensee's life.

References to article and section numbers in the *Real Estate License Act of 2000* will be displayed throughout so that you can reference the Act itself for more detail on any topic.

In general, the Illinois *Real Estate License Act of 2000* is one of the strongest and most complete licensing laws in the country. Knowing the law well will strengthen and safeguard your real estate career.

■ ADMINISTRATION OF THE ILLINOIS REAL ESTATE LICENSE ACT

Directly under the **IDFPR's Division of Professional Regulation** is the **Bureau of Real Estate Professions (BRE)**, which is responsible for administering the *Real Estate License Act of 2000*.

The BRE oversees the Real Estate Administration and Disciplinary Board and the Real Estate Education Advisory Council and both boards report to the Director of Real Estate.

There are four major funds administered through BRE: the **Real Estate License Administration Fund** (to which license fees and other funds initially go), the **Real Estate Research and Education Fund** (for research and scholarships), the **Real Estate Recovery Fund** (a consumer-oriented fund for compensating consumers harmed by licensees' actions), and the **Real Estate Audit Fund** (for conducting audits of special accounts).

The Bureau of Real Estate Professions

The Bureau of Real Estate Professions (BRE), pursuant to the powers and duties of the *Civil Administrative Code of Illinois*, has primary authority to administer the Act. It is also empowered to issue rules and regulations that implement and interpret the act. The Rules accompanying the Act are important to a full understanding of the Act's implications and applications. BRE has the authority to contract with third parties for any services deemed necessary for proper administration of the Act, such as the AMP testing service for Illinois state testing.

BRE is responsible for administrative activities such as these:

- *Conducting license examinations*
- *Issuing and renewing licenses*
- *Preparing all forms*, including applications, licenses, and sponsor cards and
- *Collecting fees* from applicants and licensees

BRE has the following additional functions, which may be exercised only on the initiative and approval of the Real Estate Administration and Disciplinary Board:

- *Conducting hearings* that may result in the revocation or suspension of licenses or in refusal to issue or renew licenses
- *Imposing penalties* for violations of the Act
- *Restoring* suspended or revoked licenses

Director of Real Estate

A licensed broker is appointed to the position of Director of Real Estate after the recommendations of real estate professionals and organizations are considered. This individual's license is surrendered to IDFPR during his or her term.

The Director of Real Estate's duties include

- acting as ex officio Chairperson of the Real Estate Administration and Disciplinary Board (without a vote);
- being the direct liaison between IDFPR, the real estate profession, and real estate organizations and associations;
- preparing and circulating educational material for licensees;
- appointing any committees necessary to assist IDFPR in carrying out its duties;
- supervising real estate activities; and
- serving as Chairman of the Real Estate Education Advisory Council.

Real Estate Administration and Disciplinary Board (Section 25-10)

The Real Estate Administration and Disciplinary Board ("the Board") acts in an advisory capacity to the Director of Real Estate regarding matters involving standards of professional conduct, discipline, and examination. In addition to its advisory functions, the Board conducts hearings on disciplinary actions against persons accused of violating the Act or the Rules.

Composition of the Board. The Board is composed of *nine members* appointed by the governor, all of whom must have been residents and citizens of Illinois for at least six years before their appointment date. Six of the nine must have been active brokers or salespeople for at least ten years. The remaining three must be unlicensed, unconnected with the real estate profession, and clearly represent the interests of consumers. None of the consumer members (or their spouses) may hold licenses. The Board itself should reasonably reflect representation from all the various geographic areas of Illinois.

Members are appointed to four-year staggered terms. Appointments to fill vacancies are for the unexpired portion of the replaced member's term. Board members may be reappointed, but no individual may serve more than a total of eight years. Missing more than four Board meetings annually is grounds for termination. The governor may also terminate Board members on the basis of his or her own judgment if there is cause. The Real Estate Director is the nonvoting, ex officio Board chairperson.

Real Estate Education Advisory Council (Section 30-10)

Matters related to real estate education are handled by the Real Estate Education Advisory Council, another governor-appointed body. This seven-member council is charged with considering applications for real estate licensing schools and instructors. Prelicensing and continuing education (CE) course content is also supervised by this body. Members are appointed for four years, with an eight-year lifetime limit.

The purpose of the Real Estate Education Advisory Council is to approve and regulate schools, curricula, sponsors, and programs and to suggest administrative rules to the IDFPR (Bureau of Real Estate Professions). Three members of the seven must be current members of the Real Estate Administration and Disciplinary Board, one must be a representative of an Illinois real estate trade organization (someone who is not a member of the disciplinary board), one must be a representative of an approved real estate school or CE sponsor, and one must be from an institution of higher education that offers prelicense and CE courses. The Real Estate Director serves as the ex officio chair of the Advisory Council—without a vote.

The Real Estate Research and Education Fund (Section 25-25)

This fund was created to advance education in the field of real estate. It is run by the Real Estate Education Advisory Council, and it is supported by annual funds of $125,000 transferred from the Real Estate License Administration Fund each September 15. Of this money, $15,000 is used for scholarships for minorities seeking an education in real estate, and other portions of the funds go to real estate education research.

■ OBTAINING AND KEEPING A REAL ESTATE LICENSE

Determining who can obtain a real estate license, the purposes of a license, and the types of licenses available are all covered in Article 5 of the Real Estate License Act, with supportive definitions found in Article 1. Educational requirements such as the prelicensing coursework needed, testing requirements, and continuing education requirements for an Illinois license are clearly stated in the Act.

Who Needs to Be Licensed?

It is illegal for anyone to act as a broker or salesperson without a properly issued sponsor card or real estate license issued by the IDFPR. Any person (or business entity) who performs any of the following services for another and for compensation must have a license (1-10):

■ Sells, exchanges, purchases, rents, or leases real estate
■ Offers to sell, exchange, purchase, rent, or lease real estate
■ Negotiates, offers, attempts, or agrees to negotiate the sale, exchange, purchase, rental, or leasing of real estate
■ Lists, offers, attempts, or agrees to list real estate for sale, lease, or exchange

- Buys, sells, offers to buy or sell, or otherwise deals in options on real estate or improvements
- Supervises the collection, offers, attempts, or agrees to collect rent for the use of real estate
- Advertises or represents himself or herself as being engaged in the business of buying, selling, exchanging, renting, or leasing real estate
- Assists or directs in the procuring or referring of prospects intended to result in the sale, exchange, lease, or rental of real estate
- Assists or directs in the negotiation of any transaction intended to result in the sale, exchange, lease, or rental of real estate
- Opens real estate to the public for marketing purposes
- Sells, leases, or offers for sale or lease real estate at auction

Exempt Persons and Entities (5-20)

The requirement for holding a broker, salesperson, or leasing agent license does not apply to the following:

- Owners or lessors (whether individuals or business entities) or their regular employees who sell, lease, or otherwise deal with *their own property* in the ways described under Article 1 definitions. This applies in the course of the management, the sale, or other disposition of their own [or their employer's] property.
- Attorneys-in-fact acting under duly executed and recorded power of attorney to convey real estate from the owner or lessor
- The services rendered by an attorney at law in the performance of his or her duties as an attorney at law
- Any person acting as receiver, trustee in bankruptcy, administrator, executor, or guardian, or while acting under a court order or under the authority of a will or a testamentary trust
- A resident apartment manager working for an owner or working for a broker managing the property, if the apartment is his or her primary residence and if he or she is engaged in leasing activities of the managed property
- State and federal officers and employees, or state government or political subdivision representatives performing official duties
- Multiple-listing services
- Railroads and other public utilities regulated by the state of Illinois or their subsidiaries or affiliates and the employees of such organizations
- Any advertising medium that routinely sells or publishes real estate advertising but provides no other real estate-related services
- Any tenant of a residential dwelling unit who refers no more than three tenants in any 12-month period, and who receives no more than $1,000 or one month's rent (whichever is less) in total yearly compensation, and who does not engage in actually showing the properties or discussing terms
- An exchange company and its regular employees registered under the Real Estate Timeshare Act of 1999 only when conducting an exchange program as defined in the Act
- An existing time-share owner who, for compensation, refers prospective purchasers, but only if the existing time-share owner refers no more than 20 prospective purchasers in any calendar year, receives no more than $1,000 for referrals in any calendar year, and limits activities to referring prospective purchasers of time-share interests to the developer

- Any person who is licensed without examination under Section 10-25 of the Auction License Act for the limited purpose of selling or leasing real estate at auction
- A hotel operator who is registered with the Illinois Department of Revenue and pays taxes under the Hotel Operator's Occupation Tax Act and rents rooms for a period of not more than 30 consecutive days and not more than 60 days in a calendar year

Civil Penalty for the Unlicensed Practice of Real Estate (20-10)

It is illegal in Illinois for any person to practice, offer, or attempt to practice, or to hold himself or herself out to practice as a real estate broker, salesperson, or leasing agent without being licensed. Anyone who does so is subject to a civil fine (in addition to any other penalties provided by law) of up to $25,000 *per offense*. The civil fine is assessed by and payable to IDFPR after a disciplinary hearing. The IDFPR has the authority to investigate any alleged unlicensed activity. The civil fine must be paid within 60 days after the effective date of the order. The order constitutes a judgment.

■ LICENSE CATEGORIES AND REQUIREMENTS (ARTICLE 5)

The *Real Estate License Act of 2000* designates three categories of real estate licensees: *brokers*, *salespeople*, and *leasing agents*. The law provides requirements and limitations specific to each type of licensee.

General requirements. All individual license applicants must pass a written examination administered by an independent testing service, Applied Measurement Professionals, Inc. (AMP). Anyone who wishes to take the exam must apply to AMP. AMP acts as the agent of IDFPR (Bureau of Real Estate Professions) and is empowered to screen potential license candidates to ensure that they meet the statutory requirements of brokers and salespersons as established in the License Act and the Rules. For a detailed content outline of the AMP examination, visit the AMP Web site at *www.goamp.com*.

Section 5-50 stipulates that, once licensed, each licensee must carry a pocket card indicating the license held. This pocket card must be shown to anyone requesting it. IDFPR maintains a list of all active licensees. Should a sponsoring broker's license be revoked or rendered inoperative, all licensees under that sponsoring broker must cease real estate activities immediately. Expiration dates for individual licenses are set by rule and can be renewed within 90 days prior to expiration. If a license expires, renewal is possible only for a period of two years. After that, the original requirements for a license must be met.

Broker's License (Article 5, Sections 25, 30, 35)

A **broker** is defined as any individual, partnership, limited liability company (LLC), corporation, or registered limited liability partnership other than a salesperson or leasing agent, who for another and for compensation, or with the intention or expectation of receiving compensation, either directly or indirectly, any of the services for which a real estate license is required (1-10).

Broker requirements. Applicants for a broker's license must meet the following requirements, as discussed throughout Sections 5-25 and 5-30:

- Be at least 21 years of age and willing to supply a Social Security number (Exception: 18 years with four semesters of college credit emphasizing real estate completed)
- Be of good moral character
- Have graduated from high school or obtained the equivalent of a high school diploma
- Have successfully completed 120 *classroom hours* of real estate courses approved by the Advisory Council if not currently a licensed salesperson (If currently a licensed salesperson, 75 additional hours of approved real estate courses.)
- Have completed a minimum of 15 of the above required hours of prelicense education in Brokerage Administration
- Satisfactorily pass a state-sponsored written examination. New broker licensees will be required to complete a 6-hour broker management course within 180 days of initial licensure

Education exemptions: broker and salesperson. The following educational exemption applies to both the broker and the salesperson:

- *If an applicant for a broker's or salesperson's license is currently an attorney admitted to the practice of law by the Illinois Supreme Court, he or she is exempt from the education requirements. The attorney still must take and pass the state exam (5-30, 2C-1).*

Salesperson's License (Article 5, Sections 25, 30, 35)

A **salesperson** is defined as anyone, other than a broker or leasing agent, who engages in the activities for which a license is required and "who is employed by or is associated by written agreement with a real estate broker as an independent contractor" (1-10).

Salesperson requirements. All applicants for a salesperson's license must meet the following requirements, as noted throughout Sections 5-25 and 5-30. The applicant must meet the following requirements:

- Be at least 21 years of age and willing to show a Social Security number (Exception: 18 years with four semesters of college credit emphasizing real estate completed)
- Be of good moral character
- Have graduated from high school or obtained the equivalent of a high school diploma
- Have successfully completed at least 45 *classroom hours* of real estate courses approved by the Advisory Council
- Have completed a minimum of 15 of the above required hours of prelicense education in courses related to *"Article 15 of this Act [which concerns agency], disclosure and environmental issues, or any other currently topical areas that are determined by the Advisory Council"* (5-30, 2d) and must
- Satisfactorily pass a state-sponsored written examination

Continued eligibility—brokers and salespersons (Section 5-35). Approved education for potential salespersons and brokers is valid for purposes of licensure for *three years from course completion dates.* An official uniform transcript is needed for taking the state exam except for persons exempt from the educational requirements.

The salesperson or broker's license must be applied for within one year of passing the state test. Failure to do so means retaking the test. Failing the state test (either broker's or salesperson's) three (3) times requires one to retake the educational course work.

Corporations, Limited Liability Companies, and Partnerships (Section 5-15)

A corporation, partnership, or limited liability company (LLC) may receive a broker's license under the following conditions:

- In a *corporation*, every corporate officer who actively participates in the organization's real estate activities must hold a broker's license. In addition, every employee of the corporation who acts as a salesperson or leasing agent on the corporation's behalf also must hold a license as a real estate broker, salesperson, or leasing agent.
- In a *partnership*, every general partner must hold a broker's license. Every employee of the partnership who acts as a salesperson or leasing agent on the partnership's behalf also must hold a license as a real estate broker, salesperson, or leasing agent.
- In a *limited liability company* (LLC) or *limited liability partnership* (LLP), every manager must hold a real estate broker's license. Additionally, every employee of the LLC/LLP who acts as a salesperson or leasing agent on the LLC/LLP's behalf also must hold a license as a broker, salesperson, or leasing agent.

No corporation, partnership, LLC, or LLP may be licensed to conduct a brokerage business if any individual salesperson, leasing agent, or group of salespeople and/or leasing agents owns—or directly or indirectly controls—more than 49 percent of the shares of stock or ownership interest in the business entity.

Leasing Agent's License (Section 5-5, 5-10)

The *Real Estate License Act of 2000* provides for a limited scope **leasing agent license** for persons who wish to engage only in activities related to the leasing of residential real property for which a license is required. This license allows such activities as "leasing or renting residential real property; attempting, offering, or negotiating to lease or rent residential real property; or supervising the collection, offer, attempt, or agreement to collect rent for the use of residential real property." Licensed brokers and salespersons do not need a leasing agent license for these activities.

A limited leasing agent license applicant must meet the following requirements:

- Be at least 18 years of age
- Be of good moral character
- Have a high school diploma or its equivalent
- Successfully complete a 15-hour leasing agent prelicense course and
- Pass the state's written leasing license examination

Persons who hold leasing agent licenses must comply with qualification requirements, standards of practice, and disciplinary guidelines established and enforced by the Real Estate Administration and Disciplinary Board and IDFPR. A licensed leasing agent must be sponsored by a licensed real estate broker.

Note: *A person may engage in residential leasing activities for up to 120 consecutive days without a license, so long as the person is acting under the supervision of a licensed real estate broker and the broker has notified IDFPR that the person is pursuing licensure.*

■ THE LICENSING EXAMINATION (ARTICLE 5, SECTION 35)

Anyone applying for a first-time broker's or salesperson's license must receive a passing score on a written exam at established test centers throughout Illinois. The questions are designed to demonstrate *"the applicant's competency to transact the business of a broker or salesperson, in such a manner as to safeguard the interests of the public"* (Section 5-35a).

Candidates must call, fax, or mail their registration forms to the testing service (AMP) in advance of the test, along with any fees to be paid to reserve a spot at one of many locations on a day that is convenient to them.

All candidates must bring to the testing center two pieces of current identification. The first MUST be a driver's license with photograph, a passport or military identification with photograph, or an official state identification card with photograph. The second form of identification must display the name and signature of the candidate for signature verification. All examinations are given on a computer that displays all the test questions on a monitor and records all the answers. *No special knowledge of computers is necessary.*

After completing the test, candidates are immediately informed if they passed or failed. Passing candidates will be given a *score report*, which will let them know they passed, but will not be given an *actual score* unless they fail. Passing candidates also receive a license application, including directions for applying for a real estate license, and an applicant sponsor card. *Passing candidates have one year in which to apply for a license, after which time a new examination will be required.*

Candidates who fail the examination will be told their score and be given diagnostic information in addition to directions on how to apply for a future test. Candidates who fail only one portion (either the state or national portion) of the exam are required to retake only the failed portion.

After three failures, the applicant must successfully *repeat all prelicense education* before further testing. The fourth attempt to pass the exam is then treated by IDFPR as if it were a first attempt (Section 5-35c).

■ THE REAL ESTATE LICENSE (ARTICLE 5, SECTIONS 40–85)

After passing the state exam, a formal application for licensure needs to be made to the state.

Prior to receiving the actual license and pocket card in the mail, a person who has just passed the licensing exam still may practice real estate with a sponsor card. After passing the state exam, he or she is given a blank **sponsor card** with his or her picture on it at the testing site. When completed by a broker, this sponsor card is valid while the new licensee and pocket card are being processed.

Once a workplace has been selected, the sponsoring broker signs the card, makes a copy for the new licensee and for office records, and sends the original to the IDFPR within 24 hours. *Completed sponsor cards are required for all new active salespeople and broker associates and leasing agents who are working as either employees or independent contractors.* The sponsor card certifies the bearer's relationship with the sponsoring broker and serves as a temporary permit to practice real estate.

Completed sponsor cards are valid for a *maximum of 45 days* or until the licensee receives his or her license from IDFPR.

Those approved will receive their **licenses** from IDFPR. The license will specify whether the individual is authorized to act as a broker, a salesperson, or a leasing agent. *This license is to be displayed conspicuously in the licensee's place of business.* In addition to the license, IDFPR issues a **pocket card** to each licensee. This card authorizes the bearer to engage in appropriate licensed activities for the current license period. *Licensees must carry this card when engaging in any of the activities for which a license is required by Illinois law.* The pocket card must be displayed on request.

What Happens to Your License When You Change or Leave Firms? (Section 5-40)

If a salesperson, broker, or leasing agent terminates employment with a broker for any reason, the licensee must obtain his or her license from the employing broker at whose firm it has been hanging. The employing broker signs the license, which indicates that the relationship has been terminated. The broker must send IDFPR a copy of the signed license *within two days.* The signed license automatically becomes *inoperative,* as does the licensee's ability to practice real estate, unless he or she accepts employment with a new sponsoring broker. If the licensee is simply changing brokers, the new sponsoring broker will immediately complete a sponsor card for the licensee to carry until a new license and pocket card (with the new firm's name indicated as sponsor) arrives. The broker prepares and sends a duplicate sponsor card to IDFPR for this transition period, along with the original signed or terminated license from the previous broker and the required fee within 24 hours of sponsorship.

Change of Address, Name, or Business Information (Rules, Section 1450.110)

It is the licensee's responsibility to promptly notify IDFPR of any change of name, address, or office location. When a licensee acquires or transfers any interest in a corporation, LLC, partnership, or LLP that is licensed under the Real Estate Act, appropriate change of business information must be filed with IDFPR. Additionally, any changes in managing brokers, branch managers, or principal officers must be reported in writing to IDFPR within 15 days after the change.

Inoperative or Expired Status (Section 5-50 and 5-55)

Inoperative status describes a licensee who has qualified for current licensure but is prohibited from engaging in the real estate business because he or she is unsponsored. **One must have a licensed sponsoring broker to practice real estate.** Inoperative status can result if a licensee terminates employment with a broker and fails to become immediately associated with a new sponsoring broker. Inoperative status also occurs when the sponsoring broker's license is itself revoked, suspended, or otherwise invalidated because the licensee fails to pay renewal fees or complete necessary CE courses. Renewal or reinstatement of a license remains possible with appropriate fees and any needed CE courses for up to two years after termination or expiration. After that time, full requirements for licensure must again be met.

Nonresidents and License by Reciprocity (Section 5-60)

A broker or salesperson who lives in a state that has a reciprocal licensing agreement with Illinois may be issued an Illinois license if the following conditions are met:

For a reciprocal broker's license:

- The broker holds a *broker's license* in his or her home state.
- The licensing standards of that state are *substantially equivalent* to or greater than the minimum standards required in Illinois.
- The broker has been actively practicing as a broker for at least two years immediately prior to the application date.
- The broker furnishes IDFPR with an official statement, under seal, from his or her home state's licensing authority that the broker has an active broker's license, is in good standing, and has no complaints pending.
- The broker's home state grants reciprocal privileges to Illinois licensees.
- The broker completes a course of education and passes a test on Illinois-specific real estate brokerage laws.

The issuance of a nonresident salesperson's license is at the discretion of IDFPR. For a nonresident salesperson to qualify for a nonresident license to practice real estate in Illinois (but still under the umbrella of a nonresident broker), the following conditions must be met:

- The salesperson's home state must have entered into a *reciprocal licensing agreement* with IDFPR.
- The salesperson must maintain an *active license* in his or her home state.
- The salesperson must *reside in the same state as the nonresident sponsoring broker*, who also must hold an Illinois license, as stated above.
- The salesperson must pass a test on *Illinois-specific real estate* brokerage laws.
- The nonresident sponsoring broker of the salesperson, *who must also be licensed in Illinois*, will issue a *sponsor card* to the salesperson in compliance with Illinois law using an IDFPR form.

Currently Illinois has reciprocity with the following states under the *Real Estate License Act of 2000*: *Kentucky, Nebraska, South Dakota, Colorado, Connecticut, Indiana, Iowa, Georgia, and Wisconsin.* Always check the IDFPR Web site for the latest update on reciprocal states.

Before a nonresident broker or salesperson will be issued a license, the applicant must file a designation in writing to act as his or her agent in Illinois. Additionally, he or she must agree that all judicial or other process or legal notices directed to the nonresident may be served on the designee. Service upon the agent so designated is equivalent to personal service on the nonresident licensee.

Nonresidents applying for an Illinois license must furnish the IDFPR with proof of active licensure in their home state. They also must pay the same license fees that are required of resident brokers and salespeople. Prospective nonresident licensees must agree in writing to abide by all provisions of the Act and to submit to IDFPR's jurisdiction.

However, once acquired, the reciprocal license allows a new resident who has recently been working under such a license to obtain a valid resident's license without examination. Licenses previously granted under reciprocal agreements with other states shall remain in force "so long as IDFPR has a reciprocal agreement with that state."

Renewal of Expired Licenses (Rules, Section 1450.105)

Licenses under the jurisdiction of the Act that have been expired for less than two years may be renewed by paying all lapsed renewal fees plus a reinstatement fee and completion of any needed CE. *A license that has been expired for over two years cannot be renewed.*

Renewal without Fee (Rules, Section 1450.105g)

Licensees whose licenses have expired may renew without paying any lapsed renewal or reinstatement fees if the license expired while the licensee was performing any of the following functions:

- On active duty with the U.S. armed services or called into the service or training of the United States
- Engaged in training or education under supervision of the United States prior to induction into military service
- Serving as Real Estate Director in Illinois or as an employee of IDFPR

■ LICENSE FEES (SECTION 1450.95 OF THE RULES)

Licensing Fees [Rules, 1450.95(h)]

Applicants for real estate licenses are subject to appropriate fees in addition to the testing fee paid to AMP when applying for the examination. The Act provides for predetermined licensing fees.

A leasing license initial fee is $75. When applying for a broker or salesperson license, the applicant must submit an initial license fee of $125. The initial broker's license fee for a partnership, LLC, or corporation is $125. Included in the initial license fees are a Real Estate Recovery Fund fee of $10 and a Real Estate Research and Education fee of $5. Other licensing fees are indicated in the Rules.

Other fees are set according to actual cost incurred by IDFPR and may vary.

Returned check penalties and failure to pay (the Act, Section 20-25). Anyone who delivers a check or other payment to IDFPR that is returned for insufficient funds must pay a returned check fine of $50, plus the amount originally owed. If the licensee fails to make full payment of all fees and fines owed within 30 calendar days of the notification that payment is due, IDFPR will automatically terminate his or her license without a hearing. The licensee may apply for reinstatement of the license and pay all fees, fines, and any other fees IDFPR may impose.

Expiration and Renewal of Licenses (Rules, Sections 1450.95 and 1450.105)

Broker's licenses expire on *April 30 of every even-numbered year.* Licensees may renew their licenses preceding the expiration date by paying the renewal fee of $150. Sponsoring brokers will also submit a completed "consent to audit and examine special accounts" form.

Salespersons' licenses in Illinois expire on *April 30 of each odd-numbered year.* Salespersons may renew their licenses preceding the expiration date by paying the renewal fee of $100. Every *leasing agent license* expires on *July 31 of each even-numbered year.* A leasing agent license is renewable by paying the renewal fee of $100. Licenses issued to *business entities or branch offices expire on October 31 of every even-numbered year.*

■ CONTINUING EDUCATION

Each broker and salesperson who applies for renewal of his or her license must successfully complete six hours *per year* (or its equivalent) of real estate continuing education (CE) courses approved by the Real Estate Education Advisory Council. Salespersons must complete 12 hours of CE in any normal two-year license renewal period. In addition, brokers must complete the 6 hours of Broker Management for a total of 18 hours for the two year renewal period.

Only CE schools approved by the Advisory Council may provide real estate CE courses. Instructors and course materials also must be approved, for both the pre-licensing schools and the CE schools. The license law includes strict criteria for obtaining and renewing approvals.

Course Content (Rules, Section 1450.115)

The CE requirement may be satisfied by successfully completing coursework consisting of six hours from "core courses" and six hours of electives. The Education Advisory Council determines the core areas, and they are subject to change.

Core requirements. The core CE requirement, now the same for both brokers and salespersons, required three hours in each of the following mandatory topic areas:

- Core A, which consists of License Law and Escrow
- Core B, which consists of Agency and Fair Housing

Electives. A maximum of six hours of course work also must be completed from among such *elective topics* as appraisal; property management; residential brokerage; farm property management; rights and duties of sellers, buyers, and brokers; commercial brokerage and leasing; financing; or any other currently approved CE courses.

Courses that may *not* be used for CE. Exam-prep courses; courses such as speed reading, memory improvement, advertising, or sales psychology; sales marketing; time management; or standard real estate company training will not satisfy CE requirements.

Instructors. Real estate CE credit may be earned by serving as an approved instructor in an approved course. The amount of credit earned matches the amount of credit given to the course.

For purposes of CE credit, one course hour must include at least *50 minutes of classroom instruction* exclusive of time spent taking an examination, *unless the course is specifically designated "self-study."* Credit also may be earned by means of state-approved self-study or computer-based programs.

No more than six hours of courses may be taken in any one day. Courses must be for a minimum of three CE credit hours and must be offered in three-hour or six-hour increments. For any course—on-site, online, or home study—the examination must be *proctored* and given *at the sponsor's site. A score of at least 70 percent on*

License Renewals

Broker: April 30, even years

Salesperson: April 30, odd years

Leasing Agent: July 31, even years

Real Estate Businesses: October 31, even years

the final exam is required for the successful completion of a CE course and the crediting of CE hours.

All CE courses must contribute to the advancement, integrity, extension, and enhancement of a licensee's professional skills. Courses must provide relevant experiences and be developed and presented by qualified instructors with expertise in the field being taught.

CE Exemptions and Waivers (the Act— Section 5-70; Rules, Section 1450.115a, 2)

A person who is issued an initial license as a real estate salesperson less than one year prior to the expiration date of that license is exempt. A person who is issued an initial license as a real estate broker less than one year prior to the expiration date of that license and who has not been licensed as a real estate salesperson during the prerenewal period is exempt. Brokers receiving an initial broker license 90 days or less before the renewal date do not have to take the additional 6 hours for that renewal period. The law also allows a broker to change their license status to "salesperson" at any renewal date. Also exempt from the CE requirement are licensees who, during the prerenewal period, served in the armed services of the United States or as elected state or federal officials served as a full-time employee of IDFPR, and licensees who are licensed attorneys admitted to practice law in Illinois.

If a renewal applicant has earned CE hours in another state, the Education Advisory Council may approve the credit at its discretion based upon whether the course is one that would be approved under the Act.

■ YOUR REAL ESTATE BUSINESS AND THE ACT

Place of Business (Section 5-45)

Any sponsoring broker actively engaged in the real estate business must maintain a definite office or place of business within Illinois. The broker must display a visible, conspicuous identification sign outside the office. Inside, the broker must conspicuously display his or her own license certificate along with those of any licensees he or she employs or is associated with by way of independent contractor agreements.

The broker's office or place of business may not be located in any retail or financial establishment, unless it is set apart as a clearly separate and distinct area within that establishment.

Branch offices.   Any sponsoring broker who wants to establish branch offices must apply for a **branch office license** for each branch office maintained. The sponsoring broker names a managing broker for each branch office and is responsible for supervising all managing brokers. The managing broker, who must be a licensed Illinois broker, oversees the branch's operations. A managing broker may now manage more than one branch.

The name of the branch office must be the same as the primary real estate office or closely linked to it. IDFPR must be notified immediately in writing of any change of a primary or branch office location and within 15 days of a change of a managing broker for any branch.

Exceptions to required place of business. A broker licensed in Illinois by reciprocity with another state may be exempt from the requirement of maintaining a definite place of business in Illinois if the broker

- maintains an active broker's license in the home state;
- maintains an office in that home state; and
- has filed a written statement with IDFPR appointing a designee as his or her agent for service of process and other legal notices, agreeing to abide by all the provisions of the Illinois Real Estate License Act and submitting to the jurisdiction of IDFPR.

Loss of a Branch Office Manager or Death of Proprietor (Section 5-45e)

In the event a sponsoring broker dies or a managing broker leaves a branch office unexpectedly, a request may be made to IDFPR within 15 days of this development to grant an extension for continued office operations. The extension may be granted for up to 60 days. In most cases of loss of a sponsoring or managing broker, a licensed real estate broker assumes the management of the office. He or she must sign a written promise to personally supervise the office operations and accept responsibility for the office until a permanent replacement is located.

Employment Agreements (Section 10-20)

Who Needs a Written Agreement with Their Sponsoring Brokers?

All salespersons, brokers, or leasing agents
All licensed personal assistants in the firm

A licensee must have only one sponsoring broker at any given time and may perform real estate activities only for that sponsoring broker. In turn, a broker must have a written agreement with any salespersons or brokers he or she employs or with any other licensees working as independent contractors. The agreement must describe the significant aspects of their professional relationship, such as supervision, duties, compensation, and grounds for termination. Section 1450.160 of the 2000 Rules amplifies this. *The Rules note that the sponsoring broker must provide any employee or independent contractor with a written copy of the "employment" (or independent contractor) agreement.*

A sponsoring broker must also have a written agreement with any licensed personal assistants of licensees sponsored by the broker.

Agency Relationships (Article 15)

Once a relationship has been formed between a licensee and a sponsoring broker, the next set of relationships that dominate the real estate business falls under **law of agency.** Article 15 deals with the licensee's relationships with the public. This article indicates specific standards to be held to in agency relationships. It clearly indicates that *"the law of agency under this Act . . . primarily governs the actions of licensees, not common law."*

Note that Article 15 of the *Real Estate License Act of 2000* is the only section of the Act that has private right of action.

Who Is a Client?

Any consumer with whom a licensee works is presumed to be a client unless parties agree in writing.

Section 15-10 sets out the basic relationship with consumers by saying "licensees shall be considered to be *representing the consumer they are working with as a designated agent for the consumer* unless (1) there is a written agreement between the sponsoring broker and the consumer providing that there is a different relationship or (2) the licensee is performing only ministerial acts [see earlier definition] on behalf of the consumer."

Replacing common law, **Section 15-15** notes the statutory duties a licensee has toward his or her client.

The statutory duties are fulfilled by

■ performing the terms of the brokerage agreement between a broker and a client;

■ promoting the best interest of the client (e.g., timely offer presentation, material facts disclosure, best interests of the client prevail over any self-interest);

■ obeying any directions that are not contrary to public policy or law;

■ exercising skill and care in performing brokerage services;

■ timely accounting for all money and property received in which the client has, may have, or should have had an interest;

■ keeping confidential information confidential; and

■ complying with the Act and applicable statutes.

The Act also clarifies certain often misunderstood situations that occur when one is an agent. Under the Act the following apply:

■ It is considered reasonable to show available properties to various prospects, without being viewed as breaching duty to a given client.

■ It is *not* considered a conflict for a buyer's agent to show homes wherein the commission is based on the ultimate sales price (in other words, where a higher price creates a higher commission).

■ *Unless a licensee "knew or should have known the information was false,"* a licensee is not considered responsible or liable for false information passed on to the client from a customer via the licensee, or vice versa.

■ The licensee remains responsible under common law "for negligent or fraudulent misrepresentation of material information."

Section 15-25 deals with a licensee's treatment of *customers*. A licensee shall "treat all customers honestly and shall not negligently or knowingly give them false information." Ministerial acts are permitted.

Section 15-40 clearly states that *compensation does not determine agency*.

Informed written consent is required of both buyer and seller for dual agency under Section 15-45 of the Act. Also, a licensee may not serve as dual agent in any transaction in which he or she has an ownership interest, whether direct or indirect. (Rules, Section 1450.215).

Designated agency is highlighted in **Section 15-50**. This system allows the broker to appoint or designate one agent for the buyer and one agent for the seller, even within the same firm, without legally being construed as a dual agent. The broker is obligated to protect any confidential information. Because of this, *"a designated agent may disclose to his or her sponsoring broker (or persons specified by the sponsoring broker) confidential information of a client for the purpose of seeking advice or assistance for the benefit of the client in regard to a possible transaction."*

Article 15 (Agency) also clearly notes the following:

■ *Offers of subagency through the multiple listing service (MLS) are not permitted* in Illinois. The MLS now offers cooperative commissions, not subagency.

- *A consumer cannot be held "vicariously liable"* for his or her agent's actions on the consumer's supposed behalf *unless* those actions were specifically directed by the consumer/client.
- *IDFPR may further amplify anything in Article 15 by way of promulgating additional rules at any time.*
- *There is a time limit on legal actions.* Legal actions under Article 15 may be forever barred *"unless commenced within two years* after the person bringing the action knew or should reasonably have known of such act or omission." In no case may actions be brought after more than five years.

Disclosure

What Must Be Disclosed:

- Material facts of a property
- Known latent physical defects
- Agency relationships
- Designated agency
- Dual agency
- Lack of agency (to a purchasing customer)
- Compensation sources

Disclosure issues go hand in hand with agency, and consequently, they are heavily addressed in **Article 15.** Real estate disclosure means an acknowledgment, stated clearly and usually in writing, of certain key facts that the law holds might, if left unknown or if unclear, unfairly influence the course of events. Disclosures have to do with who has clear and full representation in a transaction and who does not. They may have to do with one's interest as a licensee in a property that one is selling. Matters of structure, surroundings, client representation, dual agency, previous agency, or agent interest in a property all may demand disclosure. Failure to disclose is an increasingly serious issue in a consumer-based society and under consumer-driven laws.

Article 15, material facts disclosure. A licensee must disclose to the client "material facts concerning the transaction of which the licensee has actual knowledge, unless that information is confidential information. Material facts do not include physical conditions with little or no adverse effect on the value of the real estate."

Material facts must also be disclosed to customers. A listing agent must disclose to prospective buyer customers "all latent, material, adverse facts pertaining to the physical condition of the property that are actually known by the licensee and that could not be discovered by a reasonably diligent inspection of the property by the customer." A licensee is not to be held liable for false information provided to the customer that the licensee did not actually know was false (15-25a).

Not-required disclosure items are HIV, AIDS, or "any other medical condition"; the fact that a property was "the site of an act or occurrence that had no effect on the physical condition of the property or its environment or the structures located thereon"; factual situations for properties other than the "subject of the transaction"; and physical conditions on nearby properties that "do not have a substantial adverse effect on the value of the real estate that is the subject of the transaction." (*It is illegal under federal law to disclose that a property's occupant has or had HIV or AIDS.*)

Section 15-35, agency relationship disclosure. Before a listing agreement, buyer agency agreement, or any other brokerage agreement may be created, a consumer must be told

- whom the broker has appointed for the consumer as designated agent, and if there is a designated agency.
- the sponsoring broker's compensation policy insofar as cooperating with brokers who represent other parties in a transaction.

- if he or she does not have client status and how to acquire it if desired. This information should be presented well in advance of but "in no event later than the preparation of an offer to purchase or lease real property." However, Section 15-35b says that residential leases do not require this disclosure, unless an option to purchase is attached to the lease.
- of *any dual agency situation*, in writing, using the dual agency consent form. This is reinforced with a second written confirmation of consent at contract signing.

Section 10-5, disclosure of compensation.   The Act holds that clients must be made aware of compensation, source of compensation, and the broker policy on sharing commission with cooperating brokers.

Handling Client Funds (Section 20-20h(8); Rule 1450.175)

A critical area of the real estate business involves handling the funds of others. Salespersons and "nonsponsoring" brokers should immediately provide any earnest money checks to their sponsoring broker for proper deposit in a special account. The Act states that the broker's escrow account is to be *noninterest bearing*, "unless the character of the deposit is such that payment of interest thereon is otherwise required by law or unless the principals to the transaction specifically require, in writing, that the deposit be placed in an interest bearing account and who the recipient of the interest is."

The broker must "maintain and deposit in a special account, separate and apart from personal and other business accounts, all escrow monies belonging to others entrusted to a licensee while acting as a real estate broker, escrow agent, or temporary custodian of the funds of others." Receipts must be made and a duplicate kept by the broker for any escrow monies received. Earnest money and security deposits must be deposited within *one day* of contract or lease acceptance or, if a holiday, the next available business day. The escrow must be in a federally insured depository. The Act does not limit the number of escrow accounts one broker may maintain. Commingling of personal and business funds is strictly prohibited.

If there should be disputes between parties regarding escrow money, *the broker "shall continue to hold the deposit."* The broker must wait for all parties to signal agreement on the escrow disposition by signing a definite agreement; otherwise he or she should not disburse funds until such an agreement or a court decision is reached. The Rules also list provisions for making *"payment into court"* in the event of a civil action or to turn monies over to the State Treasurer in the event of unclaimed property *[Rules, Section 1450.175 (h), Special Accounts]*.

Each sponsoring broker who accepts earnest money shall maintain, in his or her office or place of business, a bookkeeping system in accordance with sound accounting principles, and such system shall consist of at least the following escrow records:

1. **Journal.** A journal must be maintained for each escrow account. The journal shall show the chronological sequence in which funds are received and disbursed. For funds received, the journal shall include the date the funds were received, the name of the person on whose behalf the funds are delivered to that broker, and the amount of the funds delivered. For fund disbursement, the journal shall include the date, the payee, the check number, and

the amount disbursed. A running balance shall be shown after each entry (receipt of disbursement).

2. **Ledger.** A ledger shall be maintained for each transaction. The ledger shall show the receipt and the disbursement of funds affecting a single particular transaction such as between buyer and seller, or landlord and tenant, or the respective parties to any other relationship. The ledger shall include the names of all parties to a transaction, the amount of such funds received by the broker and the date of such receipt. The ledger shall show, in connection with the disbursements of such funds, the date, the payee, the check number, and the amount disbursed. The ledger shall segregate one transaction from another transaction. There shall be a separate ledger or separate section of each ledger, as the broker shall elect, for each of the various kinds of real estate transactions. If the ledger is computer generated, the broker must maintain copies of the bank deposit slips, bank disbursement slips, or other bank receipts to account for the data on the ledger.

3. **Monthly Reconciliation Statement.** Each broker shall reconcile, within ten days after receipt of the monthly bank statement, each escrow account maintained by the broker except where there has been no transactional activity during the previous month. Such reconciliation shall include a written work sheet comparing the balances as shown on the bank statement, the journal and the ledger, respectively, in order to insure agreement between the escrow account and the journal and the ledger entries with respect to such escrow account. Each reconciliation shall be kept for at least five years from the last day of the month covered by the reconciliation.

4. **Master Escrow Account Log.** Each broker shall maintain a Master Escrow Account Log identifying all escrow bank account numbers, and the name and address of the bank where the escrow accounts are located. The Master Escrow Account Log must specifically include all bank account numbers opened for the individual transactions, even if such account numbers fall under another umbrella account number.

The broker must always be able to account for client or escrow funds and any pertinent documents. If IDFPR requests to view or audit escrow records, they must be supplied *within 24 hours* of the request to IDFPR personnel. Escrow records must be maintained for five years. The escrow records for the immediate prior two years shall be maintained in the office location and the balance of the records can be maintained at another location.

The License Act and Personal Assistants (Sections 1-10, 10-5, 10-20)

As a real estate business grows, it is not uncommon for a licensee to hire a personal assistant. The *Real Estate License Act of 2000* has addressed this issue.

Illinois provides that *personal assistants either may be licensed* as real estate salespersons (1-10), *or may be unlicensed.*

Unlicensed assistants can legally perform only limited tasks (typing, filing, answering phones). However, the actual employment agreement for a licensed assistant is made with the sponsoring broker of the firm.

This same pattern applies to compensation. "Any person who is a licensed personal assistant for another licensee may only be compensated in his or her capacity as a personal assistant by the sponsoring broker for that licensed personal assistant"

(10-5c). This may seem awkward, but it is designed to keep a clear money trail focused in one location—the sponsoring broker. (Additional detail on personal assistant duties is found in 1450.165 of the Rules.)

Advertising Regulations (Section 10-30 and Rules 1450.140-1450.145)

A broker must include his or her business name and franchise affiliation in all advertisements. **Blind ads** are prohibited (that is, those not indicating the brokerage firm name; not indicating that the advertiser is a licensee; and offering only a box number, street address, or telephone number for responses). *No blind advertisements may be used by a licensee* regarding the sale or lease of any real estate, other real estate activities, or the hiring of other licensees.

Ads prepared by licensees should at least include

- licensee name,
- company name (as registered with IDFPR) and company city/state, and
- the city or area of the advertised property.

> A licensee must
> - NEVER advertise in only his or her name
> - ALWAYS include the firm's name
> - NEVER advertise another sponsoring broker's listings without permission
> - ALWAYS keep advertisements up-to-date and clear

Advertising on the Internet (Rule 1450.145).   Ads prepared for the Internet must adhere to the following:

- An Internet ad must include proper identification—licensee name, company name, company location, geographic location of property.
- Additionally, e-correspondence, bulletin boards, or e-commerce discussion groups require licensee name, company name, and company location.
- Links to listing information from other Internet sites are *permitted without approval* unless the Web site owner requires approval for links to be added. Any such link must not "mislead or deceive the public as to the ownership of any listing information."
- As with other advertising, Internet sites are to be updated periodically and kept current.

In Internet advertising situations, the Rules do not allow

- "advertising a property that is subject to an exclusive listing agreement with a sponsoring broker other than the licensee's own without the permission of and identifying that listing broker," and
- "failing to remove advertising of a listed property within a reasonable time, given the nature of the advertising, after the earlier of the closing of a sale on the listed property or the expiration or termination of the listing agreement."

Advertising must contain all the information necessary to communicate to the public in an accurate, direct, and readily comprehensible manner. It is specifically indicated that any portions of the Act and Rules that apply to advertising are intended to include "farming" (marketing to a small group), unsolicited marketing of services, and all Internet materials.

> A licensee must
> - ALWAYS disclose "agent-owned"
> - Place "agent-owned" on the sign if FSBO

Selling your own property.   *Selling or leasing your own property* or a property in which you have an interest means you, as a licensee, must use the term "broker-owned" or "agent-owned" in all advertising and on listing sheets.

If the real estate firm's sign is used in the yard, and the firm's services are being used, then having the "agent-owned" or "broker-owned" notation on the sign itself is deemed not necessary. However, all written materials (listing sheets, ads, Internet ads) still must carry the "broker-owned" or "agent-owned" notation. The Act provides that no matter how one lists an agent-owned property—by owner or through a real estate firm—the agent must take care not to confuse the public.

Finally, it *is* possible and permitted by IDFPR to list your own personal real estate with a firm other than the one at which you work if you so desire and if your sponsoring broker approves.

If a licensee advertises to personally purchase or lease real estate, disclosure of licensee status is required.

Phone book listings.   Licensees must not place their own names under the heading "Real Estate" in a telephone directory or otherwise advertise their services to the public through any media without also listing the business name of the broker with whom they are affiliated. This rule is consistent throughout all advertising media.

Print size restriction changes.   *There no longer is a print size restriction "as between the broker's business name and the name of the licensee" [Article 10, Section 30 (f)].*

Collecting Your Paycheck

While collecting your paycheck may seem like a simple proposition, experience has proven that issues surrounding compensation can become confusing and sometimes may pose ethical questions. Compensation procedures therefore are strictly covered by the Act. Real estate checks always go to and come from the sponsoring broker. The check at the closing will be in the broker's name only.

Compensation and Business Practice (Article 10)

- **Section 10-5**—*A licensee may not receive compensation from anyone other than his or her sponsoring broker.* In turn, brokers may compensate only licensees whom they personally sponsor (including licensed personal assistants). The one exception is a former licensee now working for another broker but who is due a commission from work completed while still at the first firm.

Sponsoring brokers may directly compensate other sponsoring brokers (as in a co-op commission arrangement for the listing broker to pay commission to the firm with the buyer).

- **Section 10-10**—Disclosure of compensation is a significant issue. The Act holds that clients must be made aware of compensation, source of compensation, and the broker's policy on sharing commission with cooperating brokers.

If compensation is being issued to an agent from both buyer and seller in one transaction, this must be disclosed. Any third-party compensation must also be disclosed.

If a licensee refers a client to a service in which the licensee has greater than 1 percent interest (title, legal, mortgage), the interest must be disclosed.

- **Section 10-15**—It is illegal to compensate unlicensed persons or anyone being held in violation of the Act.

To sue for commission in Illinois, one must be a licensed real estate sponsoring broker.

Funds from sellers or buyers always go through the sponsoring broker. He or she is the only one who issues compensation to salespersons, brokers, leasing agents, or licensed personal assistants working under him or her.

Rule 1450.205 addresses **referral fees** and **"affinity relationships."** No licensee may pay a referral fee to an unlicensed person who is not a principal to the transaction. Nor may a licensee request a referral fee unless *reasonable cause* for payment of the fee exists (a contractual referral fee arrangement).

- **Section 10-15**—also states that a licensee "may offer cash, gifts, prizes, awards, coupons, merchandise, rebates or chances to win a game of chance, if not prohibited by any other law" to consumers as a legitimate approach to garnering business. Additionally, it is perfectly legal to share commission compensation with a principal to a given transaction.
- It now is legal for a broker to pay a corporation set up by the licensee, rather than the licensee directly, if desired.

■ DISCIPLINARY PROVISIONS AND LOSS OF LICENSE (ARTICLE 20)

The *Real Estate License Act of 2000* lists specific violations for which licensees may be subject to discipline. The IDFPR is authorized to impose the following disciplinary penalties:

- Refuse to issue or renew any license
- Suspend or revoke any license
- Censure or reprimand a licensee
- Place a licensee on probation
- Impose a civil penalty of not more than $25,000 for any one cause or any combination of causes

Causes for Discipline

IDFPR may take disciplinary action against a licensee for any one cause or a combination of causes. Specifically, a licensee may be subject to disciplinary action or fines if the licensee

- makes a false or fraudulent representation in attempting to obtain a license;
- has been convicted of a felony or of a crime involving dishonesty, fraud, larceny, embezzlement, or obtaining money, property, or credit by false pretenses or by means of a confidence game;
- has been convicted in Illinois or any other state of a crime that constitutes a felony under Illinois law;
- has been convicted of a felony in a federal court;
- has been found by a court to be a person under legal disability or subject to voluntary or judicial admission under the *Illinois Mental Health and Developmental Disabilities Code*;
- performs or attempts to perform any act as a broker or salesperson in a retail sales establishment from an office, desk, or space that is not separated from the main retail business and in a separate and distinct area;
- has been subjected to disciplinary action by another state, the District of Columbia, a territory, a foreign nation, a government agency, or any other

entity authorized to impose discipline if at least one of the grounds for that discipline is the same as or equivalent to a cause for discipline in Illinois;

■ has engaged in real estate activity without a license or with an expired or inoperative license; or

■ attempts to subvert or cheat on the licensing exam or assists someone else in doing so.

A licensee also is subject to disciplinary action if, in performing or attempting to perform any act as a broker or salesperson *or in handling his or her own property* (whether held by deed, option, or otherwise), the licensee is found guilty of any of the following activities:

■ Making any substantial misrepresentation or untruthful advertising

■ Making any false promises to influence, persuade, or induce

■ Pursuing a continued and flagrant course of misrepresentation or making false promises through agents, salespeople, advertising, or otherwise

■ Using any misleading or untruthful advertising

■ Using any trade name or insignia of membership in any real estate organization of which the licensee is not a member

■ Acting for more than one party in a transaction without providing written agency disclosure

■ Representing or attempting to represent a broker other than the sponsoring broker

■ Failing to account for or to remit any monies or documents belonging to others that come into the licensee's possession

■ Failing to properly maintain and deposit escrow monies in a separate account

■ Failing to make all escrow records maintained in connection with the practice of real estate available during normal business hours and within 24 hours of submitted request

■ Failing to furnish on request copies of all documents relating to a real estate transaction to all parties executing them

■ Failure of the sponsoring broker to provide appropriate licensing documents (sponsor cards, license termination information) in a timely way

■ Engaging in dishonorable, unethical, or unprofessional conduct of a character likely to deceive, defraud, or harm the public

■ Commingling the money or property of others with one's own

■ Employing any person on a purely temporary or single-deal basis as a means of evading the law regarding illegal payment of fees to nonlicensees

■ Permitting the use of one's license by another person in order to operate a real estate office

■ Engaging in any dishonest dealing, whether specifically mentioned by the Act or not

■ Displaying a For Rent or For Sale sign on any property without the written consent of the owner or advertising in any fashion without consent of the owner

■ Failing to provide information requested within 30 days of the request, as related to audits or complaints made against the licensee based on the Act

■ Utilizing blind advertising

■ Offering an improperly constructed guaranteed sales plan, one that does not meet the Act's requirements for such plans

- Intending to promote racial or religious segregation by use of actions or words or behaving or speaking in such a way as to discourage integration
- Violating the Illinois Human Rights Act
- Inducing any individual to break out of an existing contract to enter into a new one, whether a sales contract or a listing contract
- Negotiating directly with the client of another agent
- Acting as an attorney in the same transaction in which one acts as a real estate licensee
- If merchandise or services are advertised for free, any conditions or obligations necessary for receiving the merchandise or services must appear in the same ad or offer
- Disregarding or violating any provisions of the Land Sales Registration Act or the Time-Share Act
- Violating a disciplinary order
- Paying out any compensation that violates the Act
- Disregarding or violating any provision of this Act or the published Rules or any regulations promulgated to enforce the Act
- Assisting any individual or business entity in disregarding the Act or Rules
- Violating the terms of a disciplinary order issued by IDFPR
- Forcing any party to a transaction to compensate the licensee as a requirement for releasing earnest money

Nonpayment of child support, income tax, student loans (Sections 20-35 and 20-45).   Specifically highlighted in the Act, IDFPR will refuse to issue or renew (or may revoke or suspend) the licenses of individuals who are more than 30 days delinquent in child support payments (Article 20, Section 45).

Anyone who fails to file a tax return or to pay any tax, penalty, interest, or final assessment required by the Illinois Department of Revenue may have his or her license withheld or suspended until any such tax requirements are met (Section 20-35).

Failure to repay Illinois student loans is also emphasized. If student loans were provided or guaranteed by the Illinois Student Assistance Commission or any governmental agency of the state, and not paid back, IDFPR will not grant a real estate license to that individual. For an existent licensee, a hearing is made available, after which, if no satisfactory repayment plan has been made, the license may be suspended or revoked (Section 20-40).

> To keep your license, be sure to pay
> - all Illinois taxes,
> - student loans, and
> - child support.

Licensee guilty of discrimination (Section 20-50).   Civil rights violations are taken as seriously by IDFPR as they are by the federal government. If there has been a civil or criminal trial in which a licensee has been found to have engaged in illegal discrimination in the course of a licensed activity, IDFPR must suspend or revoke the licensee's license unless the adjudication is in appeal. Similarly, if an administrative agency finds that a licensee has engaged in illegal discriminatory activities, IDFPR must take disciplinary action against the licensee unless the administrative order is in appeal.

Guaranteed sales plans.   One of the areas noted for discipline is the offering of an *improperly constructed* guaranteed sales plan. A licensee is subject to disciplinary action if he or she offers a guaranteed sales plan without complying with the Act's strict requirements for such agreements. A *guaranteed sales plan* is any real estate purchase or sales plan in which a broker enters into an unconditional written contract with a seller, promising to purchase the seller's property for a specified price if the property has not sold within an agreed period of time on terms acceptable to the seller.

The Act indicates how such a plan can be constructed *so as to comply with Illinois law*. An Illinois broker who offers a guaranteed sales plan in compliance with the Act must

- provide the details and conditions of the plan in writing to the seller;
- offer evidence of sufficient financial resources to satisfy the agreement's purchase commitment; and
- market the listing in the same manner in which he or she would market any other property, unless the agreement with the seller provides otherwise.

A broker who fails to perform on a guaranteed sales plan in strict accordance with its terms is subject to all the penalties for violating the Act, plus a civil penalty of up to $25,000, payable to the injured party.

NOT Subject to Discipline

Multiple-client transactions within designated agency (Section 15-50). Sometimes situations can be construed as involving multiple interests and conflicting representation when they really do not. To avoid the appearance of impropriety, **disclosure of agency** and **designated agency** are key. A broker may specifically designate the salespersons employed by or affiliated with the broker who will be acting as legal agents for the represented parties in a given transaction. Such designated agencies "will be to the exclusion of all other salespersons employed by or affiliated with the broker."

A broker who enters into such an agreement is not considered to be acting for more than one party in a transaction if the salespersons designated as legal agents are not representing more than one party in any single transaction. The Act provides that no licensee will be considered a dual agent, or be liable for acting as an undisclosed dual agent, merely for performing the services as described in Article 15, Section 50.

Unlawful actions by associates if no broker knowledge [Section 20-60(f)]. A broker will not have his or her license revoked because of an unlawful act or violation by any salesperson or broker employed by or associated with the broker, or by any unlicensed employee, *unless the broker had knowledge of the unlawful act or violation*. The broker could possibly be held liable for the employee's actions under *vicarious responsibility*.

Procedure for Disciplinary Hearings (Section 20-60)

The Real Estate Administration and Disciplinary Board will initiate an investigation of anyone regulated by the License Act of 2000 based on (1) its own initiative; (2) the motion of IDFPR; or (3) a written, verified complaint that would constitute grounds for disciplinary action and is submitted by any person.

Prior to a disciplinary hearing, the matter must be reviewed by a subcommittee of the Board. If the complaint has merit and is not frivolous, the subcommittee will make a recommendation of its validity and the Board will schedule a hearing. The accused must be notified of the charges in writing at least 30 days prior to the hearing. He or she must be told that if no answer is filed, action can nevertheless be taken against him or her. If the accused still fails to file an answer, the Board will enter a judgment by default against the accused. A licensee's practice may be decreased in nature or scope, or his or her license may be suspended or revoked altogether in addition to other disciplinary actions deemed appropriate. A 30-day continuance may be granted "for good cause" at IDFPR's discretion.

At the hearing, the accused and the complainant are given the opportunity to appear before the Board in person or by counsel to present statements, testimony, evidence, and argument. IDFPR and the Board have the power to subpoena witnesses, documents, and evidence and to administer oaths. A record of the proceedings must be kept. Both IDFPR and the accused are entitled to have a court reporter present to transcribe the proceedings or prehearing conference at their own expense. If a transcript is produced, a copy must be provided to the other party at cost.

At the conclusion of the hearing, the Board will present to the Director of Real Estate a written report of its findings and recommendations. Within 20 days after receiving a copy of the report, the accused may request a rehearing by submitting a written motion describing the grounds for the request.

If the Director is not satisfied that substantial justice has been done, he or she may order a rehearing. The Director is required to give the Board and the Illinois Secretary of State a written statement detailing his or her reasons for disagreeing with the findings within 20 days of the Board's recommendations and prior to any contrary action. After the 20-day period has passed, the Director has the right to take the action recommended by the Board.

IDFPR is entitled to seize the license of any person whose license has been suspended or revoked and who has failed to surrender his or her license to IDFPR. At any time after the suspension or revocation of a license, IDFPR may reinstate the license, without examination, on the written recommendation of the Board.

Disciplinary Consent Orders [Section 20-60 (m)]

IDFPR may bypass the hearing process and negotiate a **disciplinary consent order** directly with the accused. A disciplinary consent order may provide for any of the permitted forms of disciplinary action. The order must include a statement that it was not entered into as a result of any coercion of the accused. The order is filed with the Director along with the Board's disciplinary recommendation. The Director may accept or reject the order within 60 days.

Right to Petition Administrative/Judicial Review (Section 20-75)

All final administrative decisions are subject to judicial review under the provisions of the *Administrative Review Law*. The accused may request a judicial review by petitioning the circuit court of the county of his or her residence. The circuit court's decision may, in turn, be appealed directly to the Illinois Supreme Court.

Criminal Prosecution and Penalties (Section 20-80)

In addition to the administrative penalties and procedures, the License Act permits **criminal prosecution** of individuals and business entities as well. The state's attorney of the county in which the offense was committed prosecutes violations. (The Act specifically excludes misleading and untruthful advertising and improper use of trade names or insignia from the possible criminal prosecution noted for other offenses.)

General violations.   Any person convicted by a court of violating the *Real Estate License Act of 2000* is guilty of a **Class C misdemeanor** for a first offense and a **Class A misdemeanor** for any second or subsequent offense. An *LLC or corporation* convicted of a first-time violation is guilty of a business offense and is subject to a fine not to exceed $2,000. A second or subsequent business offense results in a fine of not less than $2,000 and not more than $5,000.

Officers, members, and agents of corporations, partnerships, or LLCs who personally participate in or were accessories to the business entity's violation may be prosecuted as individuals and are subject to the prescribed criminal penalties for individuals.

Practicing real estate without a license.   Individuals, LLCs, LLPs, or corporations that engage in real estate business activities without a license are singled out for especially harsh penalties. For an individual, conviction for a first offense constitutes a **Class A misdemeanor** (a fine of up to $2,500 and imprisonment for up to one year). For a corporation, LLC, or LLP, such a violation constitutes a **business offense** and carries a fine of *up to $10,000.*

A second or subsequent violation of the law against practicing real estate without a license is a Class 4 felony for individual licensees. A **Class 4 felony** in Illinois carries a *fine of up to $25,000 and imprisonment for one to three years* for individuals. LLCs, LLPs, and corporations convicted of a second or subsequent violation must pay a fine of between $10,000 and $25,000.

Practicing without a License

First individual offense
- Class A misdemeanor (Fines to $2,500 and up to one year in jail)
- Up to $25,000 fine to IDFPR

Second individual offense
- Class 4 felony (Fines up to $25,000 and up to three years in jail)
- Up to $25,000 fine to IDFPR.

Corporation penalties are equally severe.

Injunctions

In addition to criminal prosecutions, IDFPR has the duty and authority to originate an injunction to prevent or stop a violation or to prevent an unlicensed person from acting as a broker, a salesperson, or leasing agent.

A violation of the License Act is specifically declared to be harmful to the public welfare and a public nuisance. The Attorney General of Illinois, a county state's attorney, the IDFPR, and even private citizens may seek an injunction to stop or prevent a violation. However, administration and enforcement of the License Act is the responsibility of the BRE.

Disciplinary Statute of Limitations (Section 20-115)

IDFPR may not take disciplinary action against any licensee for a violation of the License Act or its rules unless the action is commenced within five years after the alleged violation occurred. A violation that is continuing will be deemed to have occurred on the date when the circumstances that gave rise to the violation last existed. Article 15 (agency) has a two-year statute of limitations for civil actions after the person knew or should have known of the violation (15-70b), and in no case more than five years.

Index of Decisions (Section 20-5)

IDFPR is required to maintain an index of all of its licensee-related formal decisions. This includes all refusals to issue, all renewals or refusals to renew, all revocations or suspensions of licenses, and all probationary and other disciplinary actions. The decisions must be indexed according to the relevant sections of statutes and rules that form the basis for each. The index is available for public inspection during normal business hours.

In addition, IDFPR is required to prepare a summary report at least every other month of all final disciplinary actions it has taken since the last report. The summary must include a brief description of the facts of each case and the final disciplinary action taken.

■ THE REAL ESTATE RECOVERY FUND (SECTION 20-85)

The Real Estate Recovery Fund provides a means of compensation for actual monetary losses (as opposed to losses in market value) suffered by any person as a result of

■ a violation of the Real Estate License Act of 2000, its rules and regulations; or

■ an act of embezzlement of money or property, obtaining money or property by false pretenses, artifice, trickery, forgery, fraud, misrepresentation, deceit, or discrimination by a licensee or a licensee's unlicensed employee.

Maximum Liability Against the Fund

For one act = $10,000

Combined acts of any one licensee = $50,000

Maximum to attorneys = 15 percent of award

Aggrieved persons may recover from the fund only for damages resulting from the act or omission of a licensed broker, salesperson, or unlicensed employee who was, at the time of the act or omission, apparently acting in a business capacity. The person who was wronged also must have acquired a valid judgment confirming the wrongful act, as provided in Section 20-90 of the Act. *This fund is not intended to cover violations of the* Time-Share Act *or the* Land Sales Registration Act.

An aggrieved person may recover up to $10,000 in actual damages together with court costs, costs of suit, and attorney's fees, with the latter not to exceed 15 percent of the amount recovered from the fund. The maximum total amount that will be paid for any single act is $10,000, to be spread equitably among all co-owners and aggrieved persons. The maximum liability against the fund arising from several acts of any single licensee or unlicensed employee is $50,000. The courts may not award interest. The circuit court of the county in which the violation occurred has jurisdiction to order recovery of damages from the fund.

Collection from the Recovery Fund (Article 20, Sections 90–100)

When a lawsuit may result in a claim against the Real Estate Recovery Fund, IDFPR must be notified in writing by the aggrieved person at the time the action is commenced—specifically, within seven days of filing. Failure to notify IDFPR of the potential liability precludes any recovery from the fund. If the plaintiff is unable to serve the defendant with a summons, the Director may be served instead, and this service will be valid and binding on the defendant. Additionally, legal action must have commenced no later than two years after the aggrieved person knew of the acts or omissions that gave rise to possible right of recovery from the fund.

If a claimant recovers a valid judgment in any court against any licensee or unlicensed employee for damages resulting from an act or omission qualifying for coverage under the fund, IDFPR must receive written notice of the judgment within 30 days. IDFPR is also entitled to 20 days' written notice of any supplementary proceedings, to permit it to participate in all efforts to collect on the judgment.

For a claimant to obtain recovery from the fund, all proceedings (including all reviews and appeals) must be completed. In addition, the claimant must show that he or she has attempted to recover the judgment amount from the licensee or unlicensed employee's real or personal property or other assets and was either unable to do so or the amount recovered was insufficient to satisfy the judgment. The names of all licensees and other parties that are in *any way responsible for the loss* must have been named in the suit; if they were not, it may preclude recovery from the fund. Finally, the claimant must show that the amount of attorney's fees being sought is reasonable.

When a judgment amount is paid from the Recovery Fund, IDFPR takes over the rights of the aggrieved party on this issue. He or she is required to assign all right, title, and interest in judgment to the IDFPR. By this *subrogation*, any funds recovered on the judgment will be deposited back in the Recovery Fund.

Fund Losses Held Against the Licensee (Sections 20–110 and 20–125)

When payment is made from the Recovery Fund to settle a claim or satisfy a judgment against a licensed broker, salesperson, or unlicensed employee, the license of the offending broker or salesperson is automatically terminated. The broker or salesperson may not petition for the restoration of his or her license until he or she has made *repayment in full to the Recovery Fund of all awards made due to his or her actions*, plus interest at the statutory annual rate. A *discharge in bankruptcy does not relieve a person from the liabilities and penalties provided for in the Act.*

Statute of Limitations (Sections 20–90 and 20–115)

A suit that may ultimately result in collection from the fund must be commenced within two years after the date the alleged violation occurred. IDFPR must initiate any action it plans to take against an individual licensee within five years of the violation.

Financing the Recovery Fund (Sections 25–35)

If at any time during the year the fund slips below $750,000, The Real Estate License Administration Fund is utilized to upgrade the level to a minimum balance of $800,000.

All Recovery Fund monies received from applications, renewals, and other sources are deposited into the Real Estate Recovery Fund and its sums may be invested and reinvested. Any interest or dividends returned from the investment efforts are deposited into the Real Estate Research and Education Fund.

■ SUMMARY

The Illinois Department of Financial and Professional Regulation (IDFPR) was created in 2004. It is the key governing authority for real estate activity in Illinois. The IDFPR, through the Bureau of Real Estate Professions (BRE), has responsibility for administering and enforcing the Illinois Real Estate License Act of 2000 and its Rules.

It is vital that all licensees and prospective licensees have a clear understanding of all facets of the Act and Rules to ensure that their activities are ethical, legal, and responsible. No summary of reasonable length could do justice to the critical details of the Act. The Illinois *Real Estate License Act of 2000* also lists a long series of specific definitions designed to give a clear understanding of real estate as it is practiced in Illinois and as legally defined by the Act. These can be found in *Article 1 General Provisions.*

You can reach IDFPR directly at:

Springfield
500 E. Monroe
Springfield, IL 62701
217-785-3000

Chicago
100 W. Randolph
Suite 9-300
Chicago, IL 60601
312-793-8704

QUESTIONS

1. In Illinois, which of the following would need to be a licensed broker?

   a. A person who employs fewer than three apartment leasing agents

   b. A licensed attorney acting under a power of attorney to convey real estate

   c. A resident apartment manager working for an owner, if the manager's primary residence is the apartment building being managed

   d. A partnership selling a building owned by the partners

2. An unlicensed individual who has been found twice to be engaging in activities for which a real estate license is required is subject to which of the following penalties?

   a. A fine not to exceed $1,000

   b. A fine not to exceed $5,000 and one year imprisonment

   c. A civil penalty not to exceed $25,000 in addition to other penalties provided by law

   d. A civil penalty not to exceed $25,000 and a mandatory prison term not to exceed five years

3. Which statement is *TRUE* of a corporation that wishes to receive a broker's license in Illinois?

   a. Every officer actively engaged in the real estate business must hold at a minimum a salesperson's license.

   b. No more than 50 percent of the shares of the company may be held by salespeople.

   c. The initial license fee is $125.

   d. The business must submit a $55 license processing fee.

4. To meet the continuing education requirement in Illinois, salespersons must obtain how many hours of continuing education per year?

   a. 4

   b. 6

   c. 10

   d. 12

5. The IDFPR has revoked broker Barry's license for commingling earnest money with his own personal funds. Based on these facts, which of the following is a correct statement?

   a. Barry may appeal the license revocation to the local circuit court.

   b. Barry may have the license reinstated by signing an irrevocable release of liability and filing it within 60 days of the disciplinary action.

   c. Barry may continue to conduct business for 90 days after the revocation by posting a bond with the Recovery Fund.

   d. Barry's employees may continue in business for 90 days because they were not found guilty of any offense.

6. If an aggrieved person is awarded a judgment against a real estate licensee for violations of the Illinois *Real Estate License Act of 2000*, which of the following correctly states the aggrieved party's rights regarding the Recovery Fund?

   a. He or she has the right, under the license law, to immediately apply for payment from the Recovery Fund for the full judgment amount, plus court costs and attorney's fees.

   b. He or she has the right to a maximum award amount of $50,000 from the Recovery Fund, including court costs and attorney's fees.

   c. He or she has the right to seek satisfaction from the licensee in a private civil action after being compensated from the Recovery Fund.

   d. He or she has the right to a $10,000 maximum recovery from the Recovery Fund, plus limited court costs and attorney's fees.

7. Tanya's broker's license expired three years ago, but she placed ads in the newspaper seeking listings and continued to act as a broker. If found guilty, and it's a first offense, Tanya's maximum penalty from IDFPR will be a(n)

    a. prison term of five to ten years.
    b. fine of up to $10,000.
    c. fine of up to $25,000.
    d. injunction, plus a fine appropriate for a Class C misdemeanor.

8. A broker who lives in a state that has a reciprocal licensing agreement with Illinois may be issued an Illinois license if

    a. the broker maintains an office in Illinois.
    b. the broker passes the Illinois broker's license exam.
    c. the broker's home state has a reciprocal licensing agreement with Illinois.
    d. the broker's sponsored salespeople have reciprocal licenses in Illinois.

9. When a salesperson passes the license examination, the first proof of eligibility to engage in real estate activities in Illinois is a

    a. sponsor card.   c. license.
    b. pocket card.   d. pass card.

10. A broker licensed in Illinois by reciprocity with another state may be exempt from the requirement of maintaining a definite place of business in Illinois if the broker

    a. employs no sales agents.
    b. has been licensed for at least ten years.
    c. does not plan on engaging in any real estate activities.
    d. maintains an office in his or her home state.

11. The fee to apply for a salesperson's license is
    a. $15.   c. $125.
    b. $50.   d. $500.

12. If a salesperson is found guilty of violating the Act, his or her employing broker also may be disciplined if the

    a. salesperson was a convicted criminal.
    b. broker had prior knowledge of the violation.
    c. broker failed to conduct the four-step pre-employment investigation of the salesperson's background and character required by the license law.
    d. broker failed to keep all local business licenses current.

13. Which of the following activities requires a real estate license?

    a. A resident manager who collects rent on behalf of a building owner
    b. A service that, for a fee (not a commission), matches individuals from different parts of the country who want to exchange properties and that assists them in doing so
    c. A multiple listing service providing listing information to members
    d. An executor selling a descendent's building

14. An Illinois real estate broker's license can be revoked for which cause?

    a. Agreeing with a seller to accept a listing for more than the normal commission rate
    b. Disclosing his or her agency relationship
    c. Showing buyers with the same specifications the same properties
    d. Depositing escrow money in his or her personal checking account

15. If a broker violates the license law, resulting in monetary damages to a consumer, what is the latest date on which the injured party may file a lawsuit that may result in a collection from the Real Estate Recovery Fund?

    a. One year after the alleged violation occurred
    b. Two years after the alleged violation occurred
    c. Three years after the alleged violation occurred
    d. Three years after the date on which a professional relationship of trust and accountability commenced

16. Broker Norman wants to list a property but is getting a lot of competition from other brokers who also would like to list it. Norman offers the seller the following inducement to sign his listing agreement: "I'll buy your property if it doesn't sell in 90 days." Under these facts, Norman may *NOT*

    a. buy the property at the agreed figure at any time during the 90 days.

    b. market the property as if no special agreement existed.

    c. show the seller evidence of Norman's financial ability to buy the property.

    d. show the seller written details of the plan before any contract of guaranty is executed.

17. Which action will *NOT* violate Illinois law?

    a. Encouraging a seller to reject an offer because the prospective buyer is a Methodist

    b. Placing a For Sale sign in front of a house after asking the seller's permission and receiving written permission to do so

    c. Advertising that individuals who attend a promotional presentation will receive a prize without mentioning that they will also have to take a day trip to a new subdivision site

    d. Standing in the hallway outside the testing room and offering employment to new licensees as soon as they receive their passing score at the testing center

18. Salesperson Jana placed the following order with the telephone company: "List my name in the directory under the heading 'Real Estate,' as 'Jana Hall, Real Estate Salesperson, Residential Property My Specialty.'" Jana is also required to include

    a. her license number.

    b. the expiration date of her license.

    c. her street address.

    d. the name of her employing broker.

19. In Illinois, all real estate salespersons' licenses expire on the same date. What is that date?

    a. April 30 of every odd-numbered year

    b. March 31 of every even-numbered year

    c. January 31 of every odd-numbered year

    d. January 31 of every even-numbered year

20. Victor owns an apartment building in Chicago. He offers to give existing tenants a "finder's fee" if they find a tenant for any vacant apartment. This year, Cindy, a longtime tenant, has helped Victor fill three vacant units. If apartments in Victor's building rent for $1,200 per month, and Cindy is not a real estate licensee, which of the following statements is *TRUE*?

    a. Under these facts, Cindy must have a valid Illinois real estate license to legally collect any compensation.

    b. In this situation, if Victor fails to pay Cindy the finder's fee, Cindy is entitled to bring a lawsuit as a private citizen under the Illinois Real Estate License Act's provisions for recovering a commission of $3,600.

    c. Cindy is entitled to the finder's fee but only in the amount of $3,000.

    d. If Cindy's activities are limited to finding prospective tenants, and if Cindy finds no more tenants this year, Cindy is entitled to legally collect a finder's fee of $1,000 without having a real estate license.

21. In Illinois, which of the following is true of an individual who wishes to engage only in activities related to the leasing of residential real property?

    a. He or she must obtain a salesperson's license and associate with a broker who specializes in residential leases.

    b. He or she may obtain a certified leasing agent designation by completing a 20-hour training course and passing a written examination.

    c. He or she may obtain a limited leasing agent license by completing 15 hours of instruction and passing a written examination.

    d. He or she may engage in residential leasing activities without obtaining a license or other certification.

22. Luke, Manny, and Ned are licensees who obtained their licenses in 1994. Luke takes a 12-hour course on using spreadsheet programs effectively in a real estate office, offered by a local community college. Manny takes a six-hour course on managing agricultural property, offered by an approved CE sponsor. Ned teaches a pre-license real estate class several evenings a week, and also has taught two three-hour continuing education classes. Based on these facts, which (if any) of these licensees has satisfied the annual CE requirements in Illinois?

    a. None of them
    b. Manny only
    c. Luke and Ned only
    d. Manny and Ned only

23. What is the purpose of the Illinois Real Estate Recovery Fund?

    a. To ensure that Illinois real estate licensees have adequate funds available to pay their licensing and continuing education fees
    b. To provide a means of compensation for actual monetary losses suffered by individuals as a result of the acts of a licensee who violated the license law or committed other illegal acts related to a real estate transaction
    c. To protect the IDFPR from claims by individuals that they have suffered a monetary loss as the result of the action of a licensee who violated the license law or committed other illegal acts related to a real estate transaction
    d. To provide an interest-generating source of revenue to fund the activities of the IDFPR

24. Under what circumstances can a limited liability company obtain a real estate broker's license?

    a. Only if every managing member holds a broker's license
    b. Only if at least 50 percent of the ownership interest in the LLC is controlled by individuals who are licensed real estate salespersons
    c. Only if no licensed salesperson holds stock or any other ownership interest in the entity
    d. Only if the LLC has engaged in real estate sales activities for three of the past five years

15

Real Estate Financing: Principles

LEARNING OBJECTIVES *When you've finished reading this chapter, you should be able to*

- **identify** the basic provisions of security and debt instruments: promissory notes, mortgage documents, deeds of trust, and land contracts.

- **describe** the effect of discount points on yield.

- **explain** the procedures involved in a foreclosure.

- **distinguish** between lien, title, and intermediate theories.

- **define** the following *key terms:*

acceleration	foreclosure	note
acceleration clause	hypothecation	prepayment penalty
alienation clause	impound account	promissory note
beneficiary	interest	release deed
certificate of sale	intermediate theory	satisfaction of mortgage
deed in lieu of foreclosure	judicial foreclosure	sheriff's deed
deed of reconveyance	judicial sale	sheriff's sale
deed of trust	land contract	statutory right of redemption
defeasance clause	lien theory	statutory right of reinstatement
deficiency judgment	loan amount	strict foreclosure
discount points	loan origination fee	title theory
equitable right of redemption	mortgage	trust account
escrow account	mortgagee	usury
equitable title	mortgagor	
	negotiable instrument	
	non-judicial foreclosure	

■ MORTGAGE LAW

A **mortgage** is a *voluntary lien* on real estate. The person who borrows money to buy a piece of property voluntarily gives the lender the right to take that property if the borrower fails to repay the loan. The borrower, or **mortgagor,** pledges the land to the lender, or **mortgagee,** as security for the debt. Exactly what rights the mortgagor gives the mortgagee vary from state to state.

In **title-theory** states, *legal title* is actually held by the mortgagee (the lending institution or some private financer), while the borrower holds **equitable title.** Legal title is returned to the mortgagor when the debt is paid in full (or some other obligation is performed). In theory, *the lender actually owns the property until the debt is paid.* The lender allows the borrower all the usual rights of ownership, such as possession and use. Because the lender holds legal title, the lender has the right to immediate possession of the real estate and rents from the mortgaged property if the mortgagor defaults.

> The *mortgagor* is the *borrower*.
> The *mortgagee* is the *lender*.

In **lien-theory** states, *the mortgagor/borrower holds both legal and equitable title.* The mortgagee/lender simply has a lien on the property as security for the mortgage debt. The mortgage is nothing more than collateral for the loan. If the mortgagor defaults, the mortgagee must go through a formal *foreclosure* proceeding to obtain legal title. The property is offered for sale, and sale proceeds are used to pay all or part of the remaining debt. In many states, a defaulting mortgagor may redeem the property during a certain period after the sale. A borrower who fails to redeem the property during that time loses the property irrevocably.

A number of states have adopted an **intermediate theory** based on the principles of title theory states but still requiring the mortgagee to formally foreclose to obtain legal title.

> **In Illinois**

Illinois does not adhere strictly to either the title or lien theory. As a result, Illinois often is referred to as an *intermediate-theory state.* Mortgages and deeds of trust in Illinois convey only qualified title to the lender as security for the loan during the existence of the debt. The mortgagor/borrower remains the owner of the mortgaged property for all beneficial purposes, subject to the lien created by the mortgage or deed of trust. The qualified title held by the lender is subject to the **defeasance clause,** which stipulates that such title must be fully reconveyed, or released back, to the mortgagor at the time the debt is repaid in full. ■

In reality, the differences between the parties' rights in a lien-theory state and those in a title-theory state are more technical than actual. A typical procedure before any foreclosure is to *accelerate* the loan based on the original agreement made with the borrower. **Acceleration** means asking for the loan to be paid in full based on the borrower's having broken the original promise to repay with regular payments.

■ SECURITY AND DEBT

A basic principle of property law is that no one can convey more than he or she actually owns. This principle also applies to mortgages. The owner of a fee simple estate can mortgage the fee. The owner of a leasehold or subleasehold can mortgage that leasehold interest. The owner of a condominium unit can mortgage the fee interest in the condominium. The owner of a cooperative interest may be able to offer that personal property *interest* as collateral for a loan.

Mortgage Loan Instruments

There are two parts to a mortgage loan: the debt itself and the security for the debt. When a property is to be mortgaged, the new owner must execute (sign) two separate instruments:

1. The **promissory note,** also referred to simply as the *note* or *financing instrument,* is the borrower's personal *promise to repay a debt* according to agreed-on terms. The mortgagor/buyer executes one or more promissory notes to total the amount of the debt.
2. The **mortgage,** also known as the *security instrument,* creates the lien on the property. The mortgage allows the lender the right to sue for foreclosure in the event the borrower defaults.

Hypothecation is the term used to describe the pledging of property (*collateral*) as security for payment of a loan without actually surrendering possession of the property. Hypothecation is the pledge itself; *collateralizing* is the entire process of using real or personal property for loan acquisition.

A pledge of security—a mortgage or deed of trust—cannot be legally effective unless there is a debt to secure. Both a note and mortgage are executed to create a secured loan.

Deed of trust.   In some situations, lenders may prefer to use a three-party instrument known as a **deed of trust,** or trust deed, rather than a mortgage. A deed of trust conveys naked title or bare legal title—that is, title without the right of possession. The deed is given as security for the loan to a third party, called the trustee. The trustee holds title on behalf of the lender, who is known as the **beneficiary.** The beneficiary is the holder of the note. The conveyance establishes the actions that the trustee may take if the borrower (the *trustor*) defaults under any

FIGURE   15.1

Mortgages

Mortgage—Two Parties

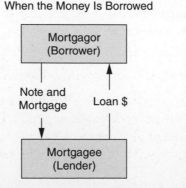

| When the Money Is Borrowed | When the Money Is Repaid |

Mortgagor (Borrower)

Note and Mortgage   Loan $

Mortgagee (Lender)

Mortgagor (Borrower)

Pays the Loan $ Satisfaction of Mortgage

Mortgagee (Lender)

FIGURE   **15.2**

Deeds of Trust

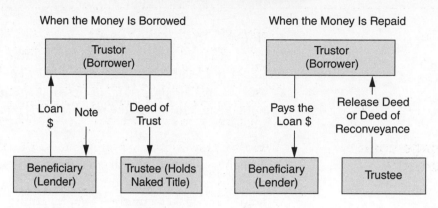

of the deed of trust terms. (See Figure 15.1 and Figure 15.2 for a comparison of mortgages and deeds of trust.) In states where a deed of trust is generally preferred, foreclosure procedures for default are *usually* simpler and faster than for mortgage loans.

In Illinois

In Illinois, a deed of trust is treated like a mortgage and is subject to the same rules including foreclosure. In Illinois, the trustor (borrower) in a deed of trust holds the title to the real estate. ■

Usually, the lender chooses the trustee and reserves the right to substitute trustees in the event of death or dismissal. State law usually dictates who may serve as trustee. Although the deed of trust is particularly popular in certain states, it is used all over the country. For example, in the financing of commercial and industrial real estate ventures that involve a large loan and several lenders, the borrower generally executes a single deed of trust to secure as many notes as necessary.

■ PROVISIONS OF THE NOTE

The promissory note is the borrower's promise to pay. It is the primary evidence of the debt. A **promissory note** executed by a borrower (known as the *maker* or *payor*) generally states the *amount of the debt*, the *time and method of payment*, and the *rate of interest*. The note, like the mortgage or deed of trust, should be signed by all parties who have an interest in the property.

A note is a **negotiable instrument** like a check or bank draft. The lender who holds the note is referred to as the *payee* and transfers the right to receive payment to a third party in one of two ways:

1. By signing the instrument over (that is, by *assigning* it) to the third party
2. By *delivering* the instrument to the third party

Interest

A charge for using money is called **interest.** Interest may be due at either the end or the beginning of each payment period. Payment made at the beginning of each period is payment in advance. When payments are made at the end of a period, it is known as *payment in arrears*. Whether interest is charged *in arrears or in advance* is specified in the note. This distinction is important if the property is sold before the debt is repaid in full. Most mortgages have interest in arrears.

Usury. To protect consumers from unscrupulous lenders, many states have enacted laws limiting the interest rate that may be charged on loans. In some states, the legal maximum rate is a fixed amount. In others, it is a floating interest rate that is adjusted up or down at specific intervals based on a certain economic standard such as the prime lending rate or the rate of return on government bonds.

Whichever approach is taken, charging interest in excess of the maximum rate is called **usury,** and lenders are penalized for making usurious loans. In some states, a lender that makes a usurious loan is permitted to collect the borrowed money but only at the legal rate of interest. In others, a usurious lender may lose the right to collect any interest or may lose the entire amount of the loan in addition to the interest.

| In Illinois | Technically, there is no legal limit specifically imposed by Illinois on the rate of interest that a lender may charge a borrower *when the loan is secured by real estate.* |

There is, however, exemption from these state laws. *Residential first mortgage loans made by federally chartered institutions, or loans made by lenders insured or guaranteed by federal agencies, are exempt from state interest regulations,* and consequently are subject to federal limits. National Banks may only charge interest that is 1 percent greater than the 90-day discount rate in the Federal Reserve District in which the bank is located.

Included in the federal law's definition of "residential loans" are loans for purchasing houses, condominiums, manufactured housing, and loans to buy stock in a cooperative. *The overall effect in Illinois is to apply federal usury limits to many if not most residential loans, thereby protecting the consumer.* ■

Loan origination fee. The processing of a mortgage application is known as *loan origination.* When a mortgage loan is originated, a **loan origination fee** is charged by most lenders to cover the expenses involved in generating the loan. These include the loan officer's salary, paperwork, and the lender's other costs of doing business. A loan origination fee is not prepaid interest; rather, it is a charge that must be paid to the lender. While a loan origination fee serves a different purpose from discount points, both increase the lender's yield. Therefore, the federal government treats the fee like discount points. It is included in the annual percentage rate of *Regulation* Z, and the IRS lets a buyer deduct the loan origination fee as interest paid up front.

| A point is 1 percent of the loan amount. | **Discount points.** A lender may sell a mortgage to investors (discussed later in this chapter). However, the interest rate that a lender charges the borrower for a loan might be less than the yield (true rate of return) an investor demands. To make up the difference, the lender charges the borrower **discount points.** The number of points charged depends on two factors: |

1. The difference between the interest rate and the required investor yield
2. How long the lender expects it will take the borrower to pay off the loan

For the borrowers, one discount point equals 1 percent of the **loan amount** and is charged as prepaid interest at the closing. For instance, three discount points charged on a $100,000 loan would be $3,000 ($100,000 × 3%, or .03). If a house sells for $100,000 and the borrower seeks an $80,000 loan, each point would be $800. In some cases, however, the points in a new acquisition may be paid in cash at closing rather than being financed as part of the total loan amount.

■ **FOR EXAMPLE** To determine how many points are charged on a loan, divide the total dollar amount of the points by the amount of the loan. For example, if the loan amount is $350,000 and the charge for points is $9,275, how many points are being charged?

$9,275 ÷ $350,000 = 0.0265 or 2.65% or 2.65 points

Prepayment

Most mortgage loans are paid in installments over a long period of time. As a result, the total interest paid by the borrower can add up to more than the principal amount of the loan. That does not come as a surprise to the lender; the total amount of accrued interest is carefully calculated during the origination phase to determine the profitability of each loan. If the borrower repays the loan before the end of the term, the lender collects less than the anticipated interest. For this reason, some mortgage notes contain a prepayment clause. This clause requires that the borrower pay a **prepayment penalty** against the unearned portion of the interest for any payments made ahead of schedule.

The penalty may be as little as 1 percent of the balance due at the time of prepayment or as much as all the interest due for the first ten years of the loan. Some lenders allow the borrower to pay off a certain percentage of the original loan without paying a penalty. However, if the loan is paid off in full, the borrower may be charged a percentage of the principal paid in excess of that allowance. **Note:** *Lenders may not charge prepayment penalties on mortgage loans insured or guaranteed by the federal government or on those loans that have been sold to Fannie Mae or Freddie Mac.*

In Illinois

Lenders in Illinois are prohibited from charging a borrower a *prepayment penalty* on a fixed rate loan secured by residential real estate when the loan's interest rate is greater than 8 percent per year. However, they can charge a prepayment penalty on an adjustable rate loan. ■

■ PROVISIONS OF THE MORTGAGE DOCUMENT OR DEED OF TRUST

The mortgage document or deed of trust clearly establishes that the property is security for a debt, identifies the lender and the borrower, and includes an accurate legal description of the property. Both the mortgage document and deed of trust incorporate the terms of the note by reference. They should be signed by all parties who have an interest in the real estate. Common provisions of both instruments are discussed below.

Duties of the Mortgagor or Trustor

The borrower is required to fulfill certain obligations. These usually include the following:

■ Payment of the debt in accordance with the terms of the note

- Payment of all real estate taxes on the property given as security
- Maintenance of adequate insurance to protect the lender if the property is destroyed or damaged by fire, windstorm, or other hazard
- Maintenance of the property in good repair at all times
- Receipt of lender authorization before making any major alterations on the property

Failure to meet any of these obligations can result in a borrower's default. The loan documents may, however, provide for a grace period (such as 30 days) during which the borrower can meet the obligation and cure the default. If the borrower does not do so, the lender has the right to foreclose on the mortgage or deed of trust and collect on the note.

Provisions for Default

The mortgage or deed of trust typically includes an **acceleration clause** to assist the lender in foreclosure. If a borrower defaults, the lender has the right to "accelerate the maturity of the debt." This means the lender may declare the entire debt due and payable immediately. Without an acceleration clause, the lender would have to sue the borrower every time a payment was overdue.

Other clauses in a mortgage or deed of trust enable the lender to *take care of the property in the event of the borrower's negligence or default.* If the borrower does not pay taxes or insurance premiums or fails to make necessary repairs on the property, the lender may step in and do so. The lender has the power to *protect the security* (the real estate). Any money advanced by the lender to cure a default may be either added to the unpaid debt or declared immediately due from the borrower.

MATH CONCEPTS

DISCOUNT POINTS AND INVESTOR YIELD

Lenders use computers or prepared tables to determine the number of discount points that must be paid. However, as a general guideline, each discount point paid to the lender will increase the lender's yield (return) by approximately ⅛ of 1 percent (.00125). In using the guideline, for each discount point charged by a lender, add ⅛ to the stated (contract) mortgage interest rate to estimate the lender's real return (and cost to the borrower) from the loan.

Note: This guideline calculation is designed to estimate the real (or effective) mortgage interest rate expressed as an annual percentage rate (APR), not as a dollar amount. The stated interest rate, as such, will not change.

To determine the actual cost, in dollars, added by discount points, each discount point is equal to 1% of the mortgage balance (1 point = 1%). The mortgage balance (loan amount) is multiplied by this discount percent to find the dollar amount of the discount being charged.

For example, assume the market rate of interest is 10¼% and the FHA rate of interest is 9½%. The following steps should be used to approximate the discount points required to equal the market rate of interest and determine the amount of discount charged on a $60,000 FHA mortgage.

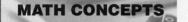

MATH CONCEPTS

DISCOUNT POINTS AND INVESTOR YIELD (CONTINUED)

A. Estimating the discount points required to raise the yield to the lender's required return:

1. Calculate the difference in the two rates.

   Current market rate – Stated (contract) interest rate = Difference

   10¼%   – 9½%   = ¾%

2. Convert the difference to eighths of a percent.

   ¾% = ⁶⁄₈%

3. Convert the eighths into discount points.

   ⁶⁄₈% ÷ ⅛% = 6 discount points required

B. Amount of discount charged

1. Convert discount points to discount rate.

   6 points × 1% per point = 6%

2. Calculate the amount of discount.

   Total loan amount × Discount rate = Amount of discount

   $60,000   × .06   = $3,600 (cost of discount)

With most loans, a borrower usually is not familiar with the above information. Commonly, the borrower or his or her agent is told that a loan will require payment of 4 discount points, or 3, or 5, and so forth. The problem then is not only to calculate the amount of discount cost (step B above) but also to determine the real yield to the lender.

For example, using the same situation as above, assume that the need is to find the amount of yield to the lender if 6 discount points are charged for an FHA loan showing a contract rate of 9½% interest.

1. Convert discount points to percent of increase (1 point results in ⅛ of 1% increase)

   6 points × ⅛% per point = ⁶⁄₈% increase

2. Add to the contract rate the percent of increase

   9½% + ⁶⁄₈% = 10¼% (approximate yield to lender)

When solving mortgage discount problems, remember that the cost of discount points is figured on the amount of the loan (1 discount point = 1% of the loan amount).

Assignment of the Mortgage

As mentioned previously, a note may be sold to a third party, such as an investor or another mortgage company. The original mortgagee endorses the note to the third party and executes an assignment of mortgage. The assignee becomes the new owner of the debt and security instrument. When the debt is paid in full (or satisfied), the assignee is required to execute the *satisfaction* (or release) of the security instrument.

Release of the Mortgage Lien

When all mortgage loan payments have been made and the note has been paid in full, the mortgagor will want the public record to show that the debt has been satisfied and that the mortgagee is divested of all rights conveyed under the mortgage. By the provisions of the *defeasance clause* in most mortgage documents, the mortgagee is required to execute a **satisfaction of mortgage** (also known as a *release of mortgage* or *mortgage discharge*) when the note has been fully paid. This document returns to the mortgagor all interest in the real estate originally conveyed to the mortgagee. Entering this release in the public record shows that the mortgage lien has been removed from the property.

If a mortgage has been assigned by a recorded assignment, the release must be executed by the assignee or mortgagee.

When a real estate loan secured by a deed of trust has been completely repaid, the beneficiary must make a written request that the *trustee* convey the property back to the *grantor*. The trustee executes and delivers a **release deed,** sometimes called a **deed of reconveyance,** to the trustor. The release deed conveys the same rights and powers that the trustee was given under the deed of trust. The release deed should be acknowledged and recorded in the public records of the county in which the property is located.

In Illinois

Any mortgagee, or his or her assigns or agents, who fails to deliver a release to the mortgagor or the grantor of a deed of trust within one month after full payment and satisfaction will be liable to pay the mortgagor or grantor a $200 penalty. The release also must state the following on its face in bold letters: **FOR THE PROTECTION OF THE OWNER, THIS RELEASE SHALL BE FILED WITH THE RECORDER OR THE REGISTRAR OF TITLES IN WHOSE OFFICE THE MORTGAGE OR DEED OF TRUST WAS FILED.** It is then the mortgagor's responsibility to record the release. ■

Tax and Insurance Reserves

> The basic recurring components of a borrower's monthly loan payment may be remembered as **PITI:** *Principal, Interest, Taxes, and Insurance*

Many lenders require that borrowers provide a reserve fund to meet future real estate taxes and property insurance premiums. This fund is called an **impound account**, a **trust account,** or an **escrow account**. When the mortgage or deed of trust loan is made, the borrower starts the reserve by depositing funds to cover the amount of unpaid real estate taxes. If a new insurance policy has just been purchased, the insurance premium reserve will be started with the deposit of one-twelfth of the insurance premium liability. The borrower's monthly loan payments will include principal, interest, tax, and insurance reserves, and other costs such as flood insurance or homeowners' association dues. RESPA, the federal *Real Estate Settlement Procedures Act*, limits the total amount of reserves that a lender may require.

In Illinois

Illinois law prescribes additional guidelines that must be followed by lenders who require escrow accounts for mortgage loans on single-family, owner-occupied residential properties. The Illinois *Mortgage Escrow Account Act at 765 ILCS 915/* provides that except during the first year of the loan, a lender may not require an escrow accumulation of more than 150 percent of the previous year's real estate taxes. Lenders must give borrowers written notice of the Act's provisions at closing. When the principal loan balance has been reduced to 65 percent of its original amount, the borrower may terminate his or her escrow account. The latter does not apply to loans insured, guaranteed, supplemented, or assisted by the state of Illinois or agencies of the federal government such as FHA and VA.

Also, borrowers have the right to pledge an interest-bearing deposit in an amount sufficient to cover the entire amount of anticipated future tax bills and insurance premiums instead of establishing an escrow account. ∎

Flood insurance reserves. The *National Flood Insurance Reform Act of 1994* imposes certain mandatory obligations on lenders and loan servicers to set aside (escrow) funds for flood insurance on new loans. However, the act also applies to any loan still outstanding on September 23, 1994. This means that if a lender or servicer discovers that a secured property is in a flood hazard area, it must notify the borrower. The borrower then has 45 days to purchase flood insurance. If the borrower fails to procure flood insurance, the lender will purchase the insurance on the borrower's behalf. The cost of the insurance may be charged to the borrower.

Assignment of Rents

If the property involved includes rental units, the borrower may provide for rents to be assigned to the lender in the event of the borrower's default. The assignment may be included in the mortgage or deed of trust, or it may be a separate document. In either case, the assignment should clearly indicate that the borrower intends to assign the rents, not merely pledge them as security for the loan. In title-theory states, lenders are automatically entitled to any rents if the borrower defaults.

Buying Property "Subject to" or "Assuming" Existing Financing

When a person purchases real estate that is subject to an outstanding mortgage or deed of trust, the buyer may take the property in one of two ways. The property may be purchased *subject to* the mortgage or the buyer may *assume* the mortgage and agree to pay the debt. This technical distinction becomes important if the buyer defaults and the mortgage or deed of trust is foreclosed.

When the property is sold *subject to* the mortgage, the buyer is not personally obligated to pay the debt in full. The buyer takes title to the real estate knowing that he or she must make payments on the existing loan. On default, the lender forecloses and the property is sold by court order to pay the debt. If the sale does not pay off the entire debt, the purchaser is not liable for the difference. In some circumstances, however, the original seller might continue to be liable.

∎ **FOR EXAMPLE** Robert owns an investment rental property that is mortgaged. For health reasons, he wants to sell the property to Janet who has been managing the property and who also wants to use the rental property as an investment. Robert sells the property to Janet *subject to* the mortgage. In the sale, Janet takes title and assumes responsibilities for the loan, but after two months she can no longer make payments on the loan. There is a foreclosure sale and because Robert sold the property *subject to* the mortgage, Robert (not Janet) is personally liable if proceeds from the foreclosure sale do not meet the obligations.

In contrast, a buyer who purchases the property and *assumes* the seller's debt becomes *personally obligated* for the payment of the entire debt and the seller (original mortgagor) is still liable until the mortgagee releases the seller. This release generally occurs when the buyer establishes a seasoned payment history (a stable and consistent history of payments under the terms of the loan). If the mortgage is foreclosed and the court sale does not bring enough money to pay the debt in full, a deficiency judgment against the assumer and the original borrower may be obtained for the unpaid balance of the note. If the original borrower has been released by the lender, only the assumer is liable.

In many cases, a mortgage loan may not be assumed without lender approval. The lending institution requires that the assumer qualify financially, and many lending institutions charge a transfer fee to cover the costs of changing the records. This charge usually is paid by the purchaser.

Alienation clause. The lender may want to prevent a future purchaser of the property from being able to assume the loan, particularly if the original interest rate is low. For this reason, some lenders include an **alienation clause,** also known as a *resale clause, due-on-sale clause,* or *call clause,* in the note. An alienation clause provides that when the property is sold, the lender may either declare the entire debt due immediately or permit the buyer to assume the loan at the current market interest rate.

Recording a Mortgage or Deed of Trust

The mortgage document or deed of trust must be recorded in the recorder's office of the county in which the real estate is located. Recording gives constructive notice to the world of the borrower's obligations. Recording also establishes the lien's priority.

Priority of a Mortgage or Deed of Trust

Priority of mortgages and other liens normally is determined by the order in which they were recorded. A mortgage or deed of trust on land that has no prior mortgage lien is a *first mortgage* or *deed of trust.* If the owner later executes another loan for additional funds, the new loan becomes a *second mortgage* or *deed of trust* (or a *junior lien*) when it is recorded. The second lien is *subject to* the first lien; the first has prior claim to the value of the land pledged as security. Because second loans represent greater risk to the lender, they are usually issued at higher interest rates.

The priority of mortgage or deed of trust liens may be changed by a *subordination agreement,* in which the first lender *subordinates* its lien to that of the second lender. To be valid, such an agreement must be signed by both lenders.

■ PROVISIONS OF LAND CONTRACTS

Under a **land contract,** the buyer (called the *vendee*) agrees to make a down payment and a monthly loan payment that includes interest and principal directly to the seller. The payment also may include real estate tax and insurance reserves. The seller (called the *vendor*) retains legal title to the property during the contract term, and the buyer is granted *equitable title* and possession. At the end of the loan term, the seller delivers clear title. In the event the seller fails to deliver clear title, the buyer (vendee) would file a vendee's lien. The contract usually permits the seller to evict the buyer in the event of default. In that case, the seller may keep any money the buyer has already paid. If, however, the buyer has 20 percent equity in the property and a contract in excess of five years, judicial foreclosure would be necessary.

■ FORECLOSURE

When a borrower defaults on the payments or fails to fulfill any of the other obligations set forth in the mortgage or deed of trust, the lender's rights can be enforced through foreclosure. **Foreclosure** is a legal procedure in which property pledged as security is sold to satisfy the debt. The foreclosure procedure brings the rights of the parties and all junior lienholders to a conclusion. It passes title either to the person holding the mortgage document or deed of trust or to a third party who purchases the realty at a *foreclosure sale*. The purchaser could be the mortgagee. At the foreclosure sale, the property is sold *free of the foreclosing mortgage and all junior liens*.

Methods of Foreclosure

There are three general types of foreclosure proceedings—nonjudicial, judicial, and strict. One, two, or all three may be available. The specific provisions and procedures for each vary from state to state.

Nonjudicial foreclosure.   Some states allow **nonjudicial foreclosure** procedures to be used when the security instrument contains a *power-of-sale* clause. In nonjudicial foreclosure, no court action is required.

Judicial foreclosure.   **Judicial foreclosure** allows the property to be sold by court order after the mortgagee has given sufficient public notice. When a borrower defaults, the lender may accelerate the due date of the remaining principal balance, along with all overdue interest, penalties, and administrative costs. The lender's attorney then can file a suit to foreclose the lien. After presentation of the facts in court, the property is ordered sold. A public sale is advertised and held, and the real estate is sold to the highest bidder.

| In Illinois |

By statute, mortgage foreclosures may be brought about only through a court proceeding. As a result, Illinois is classified as a *judicial foreclosure state*. Under the Illinois 1987 *Mortgage Foreclosure Law*, the term *mortgage* includes

- deeds of trust,
- installment contracts payable over a period in *excess* of five years (when the unpaid balance is less than 80 percent of the purchase price),
- certain collateral assignments of the beneficial interest in land trusts used as security for lenders, and
- traditional mortgage instruments. ■

Strict foreclosure.   Although judicial foreclosure is the prevalent practice, it is still possible in some states for a lender to acquire mortgaged property through a **strict foreclosure** process. First, appropriate notice must be given to the delinquent borrower. Second, once the proper papers have been prepared and recorded, the court establishes a deadline by which time the balance of the defaulted debt must be paid in full. If the borrower does not pay off the loan by that date, the court simply awards full legal title to the lender. No sale takes place.

Deed in Lieu of Foreclosure

As an alternative to foreclosure, a lender may accept a **deed in lieu of foreclosure** from the borrower. This is sometimes known as a *friendly foreclosure* because it is carried out by mutual agreement, rather than by lawsuit. The major disadvantage of the "deed in lieu" is that the mortgagee takes the real estate *subject to all junior* *liens.* In a foreclosure action, all junior liens are eliminated. Also, by accepting a deed in lieu of foreclosure, the lender usually loses any rights pertaining to FHA or private mortgage insurance or VA guarantees. Finally, a deed in lieu of foreclosure is still considered an adverse element in the borrower's credit history.

Redemption

Most states give defaulting borrowers a chance to redeem their property through the **equitable right of redemption**. If, after default but *before* the foreclosure sale, the borrower (or any other person who has an interest in the real estate, such as another creditor) pays the lender the amount in default, plus costs, the debt will be reinstated and regular payments may be resumed. In some cases, the person who redeems may be required to repay the accelerated loan in full. If some person other than the mortgagor or trustor redeems the real estate, the borrower becomes responsible to that person for the amount of the redemption.

Some states also allow defaulted borrowers a period in which to redeem their real estate after the sale. During this period (which may be as long as one year), the borrower has a **statutory right of redemption.** The mortgagor who can raise the necessary funds to redeem the property within the statutory period pays the redemption money to the court. Because the debt was paid from the proceeds of the sale, the borrower can take possession free and clear of the former defaulted loan. The court may appoint a receiver to take charge of the property, collect rents, and pay operating expenses during the redemption period.

In Illinois

There is no statutory right of redemption in Illinois. In Illinois, a mortgagor in default who wishes to exercise the *equitable right of redemption* to avoid loss of the mortgaged real estate may do so for a period of *seven months after the date of service* on the mortgagor or after first publication date, whichever is later. This time period can currently be *shortened to as little as 30 days after a judgment is entered if the property has been abandoned or is vacant.* When a property is redeemed in this way, the foreclosure sale does not occur. Otherwise, the foreclosure sale is held as soon as possible after the equitable right of redemption expires.

The mortgagor generally has a right to remain in possession of the property from the time of service of summons until the entry of a judgment of foreclosure. After judgment and through the 30th day after confirmation of the sale, the mortgagor can still retain possession, but he or she must pay rent to the holder of the certificate of sale. Thirty-one days after judgment, the mortgagor must have vacated the property or be subject to eviction. The owner of the certificate of sale receives a **sheriff's deed** and gains the right to possession.

While Illinois does not have statutory right of redemption, it does offer **statutory right of reinstatement.** This option is applicable when the defaulting mortgagor wishes to cure the default and reinstate the loan as if no acceleration had occurred. The mortgagor has the right to exercise this statutory right *for a period of 90 days after service of summons or publication date.* At the lender's discretion, expressed through an attorney, the right of reinstatement may be extended to run as long as the equitable right of redemption.

The reinstatement right usually may be exercised only *once every five years.* After reinstatement occurs, the suit must be dismissed by the lender, and the mortgage loan remains in effect just as before. (See the *Illinois Code of Civil Procedure, Article 15; 735 ILCS 5/.*)

When a default is not cured by redemption or reinstatement, the entry of a decree of foreclosure will lead to a **judicial sale** of the property, usually called a **sheriff's sale**. Each defendant to the suit must be given written personal notice of the sale, and public notice of the sale must be published in a newspaper of general circulation. The successful bidder at the sale receives a **certificate of sale**, not a deed. Only after the sale is confirmed by the court will the certificate holder receive a *sheriff's deed.* ■

Deficiency Judgment

The foreclosure sale may not produce enough cash to pay the loan balance in full after deducting expenses and accrued unpaid interest. In this case, where permitted by law, the mortgagee may be entitled to a *personal judgment* against the borrower for the unpaid balance. Such a judgment is a **deficiency judgment.** It also may be obtained against any endorsers or guarantors of the note and against any owners of the mortgaged property who assumed the debt by written agreement. However, if any money remains from the foreclosure sale after paying the debt and any other liens (such as a second mortgage or mechanic's lien), expenses, and interest, these proceeds are paid to the borrower. Strict foreclosure does not always provide for a deficiency judgment.

■ SUMMARY

Some states, known as title-theory states, recognize the lender as the owner of mortgaged property. Others, known as lien-theory states, recognize the borrower as the primary owner of mortgaged property.

In Illinois

A few intermediate-theory states, such as Illinois, recognize modified, compromise versions of these theories. In Illinois, required court procedures protect consumers in the event of possible foreclosure. ■

Mortgage and deed of trust loans provide the principal sources of financing for real estate operations. Mortgage loans involve a borrower (the mortgagor) and a lender (the mortgagee). Deed of trust loans involve a third party "manager" (the trustee), in addition to a borrower (the trustor) and a lender (the beneficiary). Often the trustee/manager and the beneficiary in this type of loan have close interaction.

After a lending institution has received, investigated, and approved a loan application, it issues a commitment to make the mortgage loan. The borrower is required to execute a note agreeing to repay the debt and a mortgage or deed of trust placing a lien on the real estate to secure the note. The security instrument is recorded to give constructive notice to the world of the lender's interest.

The mortgage document or deed of trust secures the debt and sets forth the obligations of the borrower and the rights of the lender. Full payment of the note by its terms entitles the borrower to a satisfaction, or release, which is recorded to clear the lien from the public records. Default by the borrower may result in acceleration of payments, a foreclosure sale, and, after the redemption period (if provided by state law), loss of title.

In Illinois

Illinois is an intermediate-theory state. There is no state-imposed usury limit in Illinois on the rate that may be charged for a loan secured by real estate and made by private lenders. However, federal antiusury laws supersede state laws on first-time residential mortgages and on federally insured or guaranteed loans. The *Illinois Mortgage Escrow Account Act* gives borrowers certain protections by limiting the size of escrow accounts and permitting alternatives to escrow.

Illinois is also classified as a judicial foreclosure state. There is no statutory right of redemption in Illinois, but there is equitable right of redemption and statutory right of reinstatement. When property is purchased at a sheriff's sale, the successful bidder receives a certificate of sale until the sale is confirmed by a court. After confirmation, the certificate holder receives a quitclaim deed, which in this situation is also called a sheriff's deed. ■

QUESTIONS

1. A charge of three discount points on a $120,000 loan equals
   a. $450.
   b. $3,600.
   c. $4,500.
   d. $116,400.

2. Nancy wants to buy a house but needs to borrow money to do so. She applies for and obtains a real estate loan from the First National Loan Company. Nancy signs a note and a mortgage. In this example, Nancy is referred to as the
   a. mortgagor.
   b. beneficiary.
   c. mortgagee.
   d. vendor.

3. In the previous question, First National Loan is the
   a. mortgagor.
   b. beneficiary.
   c. mortgagee.
   d. vendor.

4. The borrower under a deed of trust is known as the
   a. trustor.
   b. trustee.
   c. beneficiary.
   d. vendee.

5. In a land contract the vendee
   a. is not responsible for the real estate taxes on the property.
   b. does not pay interest and principal.
   c. obtains legal title at closing.
   d. has possession during the term of the contract.

6. The law of the state of New Sagebrush provides that lenders cannot charge more than 18 percent interest on any loan. This kind of law is called
   a. a truth-in-lending law.
   b. a usury law.
   c. the statute of frauds.
   d. RESPA.

7. In some states, a borrower who has defaulted on a loan may seek to pay off the debt plus any accrued interest and costs after the foreclosure sale under what right?
   a. Equitable redemption
   b. Defeasance
   c. Usury
   d. Statutory redemption

8. A borrower has defaulted on a loan. Which of the following would best describe the rights of the lender in this situation?
   a. The escalation clause in the note allows the lender to collect all future interest due on the loan should a buyer default.
   b. The defeasance clause in the note stipulates that the lender may begin foreclosure proceedings to collect the remaining mortgage balance.
   c. The alienation clause in the note allows the lender to convey the mortgage to a buyer at the foreclosure sale.
   d. The acceleration clause in the note gives the lender the right to have all future installments due and payable immediately on default.

9. A mortgagor has just made her final payment to the mortgagee. Which of the following would *MOST LIKELY* occur?
   a. The mortgagee would give the mortgagor a satisfaction of mortgage.
   b. The mortgagee would give the mortgagor a release deed.
   c. The mortgagee would give the mortgagor a deed of trust.
   d. The mortgagee would give the mortgagor a mortgage estoppel.

10. Under a typical land contract, when does the vendor give the deed to the vendee?
   a. When the contract is fulfilled
   b. At the closing
   c. When the contract for deed is approved by the parties
   d. After the first year's real estate taxes are paid

11. If a borrower must pay $2,700 for points on a $90,000 loan, how many points is the lender charging for this loan?

   a. 2
   b. 3
   c. 5
   d. 6

12. Lee buys property from Renee in a transaction involving a land contract. The vendee would do which of the following?

   a. Provide financing for the vendor
   b. Be liable for any senior financing
   c. Retain legal title.
   d. Retain possession of the property

13. Which of the following allows a mortgagee to proceed to a foreclosure sale without having to go to court first?

   a. Waiver of redemption right
   b. Power of sale
   c. Alienation clause
   d. Hypothecation

14. Pledging property for a loan without giving up possession of the property itself is referred to as

   a. hypothecation.
   b. defeasance.
   c. alienation.
   d. novation.

15. Discount points on a mortgage are computed as a percentage of the

   a. selling price.
   b. amount borrowed.
   c. closing costs.
   d. down payment.

16. What do the terms *alienation clause*, *resale clause*, *due-on-sale clause*, and *call clause* have in common?

   a. They are all names for clauses found in mortgages that stipulate that should the borrower default, the lender may declare the entire unpaid balance on the note due and payable.
   b. They are all names for clauses found in mortgages that stipulate that a note may be prepaid at any time without penalty.
   c. They are all names for clauses found in land contracts that stipulate that the vendor must convey the title to the vendee when the final payment is made.
   d. They are all names for clauses found in mortgages that stipulate that when a property is sold, the lender may either declare the entire debt due immediately or permit the buyer to assume the loan at the current market interest rate.

In Illinois

17. In Illinois, mortgage foreclosures may be obtained only through a court proceeding. This means Illinois is characterized as a

   a. strict foreclosure state.
   b. judicial foreclosure state.
   c. foreclosure-by-lawsuit state.
   d. sheriff's foreclosure state.

18. Hal purchased a home in Cairo, Illinois, and financed the purchase with a loan secured by a deed of trust. If Hal defaults on the loan, what must the lender do?

   a. It need not file a foreclosure suit but need only direct the trustee to sell the property.
   b. It must wait for the statutory reinstatement period to expire before proceeding with any legal action.
   c. It must proceed with a foreclosure action just as if the security were a mortgage.
   d. It need not notify Hal of any legal action because the breach of the loan agreement waives all notification rights.

19. Illinois real estate financed by a mortgage loan that is in default may be redeemed by the mortgagor

   a. at any time between the entry of a judgment of foreclosure and the foreclosure sale.

   b. up to six months after the property is sold at the foreclosure sale.

   c. by notifying the mortgagee in writing of his or her intent to pay the current market value of the property, and doing so within 90 days of notification.

   d. by paying the current market value to the highest bidder at the sale.

20. In Illinois, a mortgagor in default may exercise his or her *right of reinstatement*

   a. at any time prior to the foreclosure sale.

   b. up to six months after the foreclosure sale.

   c. up to 90 days after service of summons.

   d. up to 90 days after the payments become delinquent but before summons.

21. In Illinois, when must a release be delivered to a mortgagor or trustor once the mortgage or deed of trust has been fully satisfied?

   a. Within 48 hours of full payment and satisfaction

   b. Within five business days after full payment and satisfaction

   c. Within one month after full payment and satisfaction

   d. Within 90 days after full payment and satisfaction

22. The successful bidder at a foreclosure sale in Illinois immediately receives a

   a. sheriff's deed.

   b. certificate of sale.

   c. deed of foreclosure.

   d. certificate of foreclosure.

23. According to the Illinois Mortgage Escrow Act, an individual who has owned his or her home for 12 years and reduced his or her mortgage balance to 65 percent of its original amount may

   a. receive a 50 percent rebate from the lender on his or her escrow account.

   b. earn the statutory interest rate on his or her escrow account deposit.

   c. terminate his or her escrow account.

   d. obtain a second loan with only a token down payment.

24. What is the Illinois usury ceiling for loans secured by real property?

   a. 8 percent

   b. 9½ percent

   c. A fluctuating rate based on the quarterly federal reserve rate

   d. There is no usury ceiling for such loans in Illinois.

25. Which of the following is included in the definition of mortgage contained in the Illinois Mortgage Foreclosure Law?

   a. Installment contracts payable over a maximum of five years

   b. Assignments of beneficial interests in living trusts

   c. Deeds in trust

   d. Installment contracts payable over at least five years, with a 20 percent down payment

26. Which of the following describes the theory of the mortgagor/mortgagee relationship in Illinois?

   a. Title theory

   b. Lien theory

   c. Intermediate theory

   d. Conventional theory

Real Estate Financing: Practice

■ **LEARNING OBJECTIVES** *When you've finished reading this chapter, you should be able to*

■ **identify** the types of institutions in the primary and secondary mortgage markets.

■ **describe** the various types of financing techniques available to real estate purchasers and the role of government financing regulations.

■ **explain** the requirements and qualifications for conventional, FHA, and VA loan programs.

■ **distinguish** among the different types of financing techniques.

■ **define** the following *key terms:*

adjustable-rate mortgage	Fannie Mae	home equity loan
amortized loans	Farm Credit System	Homeowners Protection Act of 1998
balloon payment	Farmer Mac	loan-to-value ratios
blanket loan	Farm Service Agency	Office of Thrift Supervision
buydown	Federal Deposit Insurance Corporation	open-end loan
certificate of eligibility		package loan
Community Reinvestment Act	Federal Open Market Committee	primary mortgage market
computerized loan origination	Federal Reserve System	private mortgage insurance
construction loan	FHA loan	purchase-money mortgage
conventional loans	Freddie Mac	
Equal Credit Opportunity Act	Ginnie Mae	
entitlement	growing-equity mortgage	

Real Estate Settlement
    Procedures Act
Regulation Z
reverse-annuity
    mortgage

sale-leaseback
secondary mortgage
    market
Truth-in-Lending Act
VA loan

Veterans Millennium
    Health Care and
    Benefits Act of 1999
wraparound loan

■ INTRODUCTION TO THE REAL ESTATE FINANCING MARKET

The real estate financing market has the following three basic components:

1. Government influences, primarily the Federal Reserve System, but also the Home Loan Bank System and the Office of Thrift Supervision
2. The primary mortgage market
3. The secondary mortgage market

Under the umbrella of the financial policies set by the Federal Reserve System, the primary mortgage market originates loans that are bought, sold, and traded in the secondary mortgage market. Before turning to the specific types of mortgage options available to consumers, it is important to have a clear understanding of the bigger picture: the market in which those mortgages exist.

The Federal Reserve System

The role of the **Federal Reserve System** (also known as "the Fed") is to maintain sound credit conditions, help counteract inflationary and deflationary trends, and create a favorable economic climate. The Federal Reserve System divides the country into 12 federal reserve districts, each served by a federal reserve bank. All nationally chartered banks must join the Fed and purchase stock in its district reserve banks.

The Federal Reserve System regulates the flow of money and interest rates in the marketplace through its member banks by controlling *reserve requirements* and *discount rates*. The Federal Reserve can also regulate the money supply through the **Federal Open Market Committee (FOMC),** which buys and sells U.S. government securities on the open market. When the FOMC sells securities, it effectively removes from circulation the money paid by buyers. When it buys them, it infuses its own reserves back into the general supply.

Reserve requirements.   The Federal Reserve System requires that each member bank keep a certain level of assets on hand as reserve funds. These reserves are unavailable for loans or any other use. This requirement not only protects customer deposits but also provides a means of manipulating the flow of cash in the money market.

Fed Controls

Decreasing reserve requirements lowers rates
- Increases money for loans
- Stimulates market
- Increases inflation

Increasing reserve requirements raises rates
- Decreases money flow
- Slows economy and purchases
- Slows inflation

By increasing its reserve requirements, the Federal Reserve System in effect limits the amount of money that member banks can use to make loans. When the amount of money available for lending decreases, interest rates (the amount lenders charge for the use of their money) rise. By causing interest rates to rise, the Fed can slow down an overactive economy; higher rates limit the number of loans that would have been directed toward major purchases of goods and services. The opposite is also true: By decreasing the reserve requirements, the Fed can encourage more lending. Increased lending causes the amount of money circulated in the marketplace to rise while simultaneously causing interest rates to drop.

Discount rate. Federal Reserve member banks are permitted to borrow money from the district reserve banks to expand their lending operations. The discount rate is the rate charged by the Federal Reserve when it lends money to its member banks. The federal funds rate is the rate recommended by the Federal Reserve for the member banks to charge each other on short-term loans. These rates form the basis on which the banks determine the rate of interest they will charge their loan customers. The *prime rate* (the short-term interest rate charged to a bank's largest, most creditworthy customers) is strongly influenced by the Fed's discount rate. In turn, the prime rate is often the basis for determining a bank's interest rate on other loans, including home mortgages. In theory, when the Federal Reserve System discount rate is high, bank interest rates are high. When bank interest rates are high, fewer loans are made and less money circulates in the marketplace. On the other hand, a lower discount rate results in lower interest rates, more bank loans, and more money in circulation.

The Primary Mortgage Market

The **primary mortgage market** is made up of the lenders that originate mortgage loans. These lenders make money available directly to borrowers. From a borrower's point of view, a loan is a means of financing an expenditure; from a lender's point of view, a loan is an investment. All investors look for profitable returns on their investments. For a lender, a loan must generate enough income to be attractive as an investment. Income on the loan is realized from two sources:

1. *Finance charges*—collected at closing, such as loan origination fees and discount points
2. *Recurring income*—that is, the interest collected during the term of the loan

Primary Mortgage Market

- Thrifts
- Savings associations
- Commercial banks
- Insurance companies
- Credit unions
- Pension funds
- Endowment funds
- Investment group financing
- Mortgage banking companies
- Mortgage brokers

An increasing number of lenders look at the income generated from the fees charged in originating loans as their primary investment objective. Once the loans are made, they are sold to investors. By selling loans to investors in the secondary mortgage market, lenders generate funds with which to originate additional loans.

In addition to the income directly related to loans, some lenders derive income from *servicing* loans for other mortgage lenders or the investors who have purchased the loans. Servicing loans involves such activities as

- collecting payments (including insurance and taxes),
- accounting,
- bookkeeping,
- preparing insurance and tax records,
- processing payments of taxes and insurance, and
- following up on loan payment and delinquency.

The terms of the servicing agreement stipulate the responsibilities and fees for the service. Some of the sources for mortgage funds in the primary market include the following:

- *Thrifts, savings associations, and commercial banks:* These institutions are known as *fiduciary lenders* because of their fiduciary obligations to protect and preserve their depositors' funds. Mortgage loans are perceived as secure investments for generating income and enable these institutions to pay interest to their depositors. Fiduciary lenders are subject to standards and regulations established by government agencies, strengthened to protect depositors against the reckless lending that characterized the savings and loan industry in the 1980s.

- **Insurance companies:** Insurance companies accumulate large sums of money from the premiums paid by their policyholders. While part of this money is held in reserve to satisfy claims and cover operating expenses, much of it is free to be invested in profit-earning enterprises such as long-term real estate loans. Although insurance companies are considered primary lenders, they tend to invest their money in large, long-term loans that finance commercial and industrial properties rather than single-family home mortgages.

- **Credit unions:** Credit unions are cooperative organizations whose members place money in savings accounts. In the past, credit unions made only short-term consumer and home improvement loans. Recently, however, they have branched out to originating longer-term first and second mortgage and deed of trust loans.

- **Pension funds:** Pension funds usually have large amounts of money available for investment. Because of the comparatively high yields and low risks offered by mortgages, pension funds have begun to participate actively in financing real estate projects. Most real estate activities for pension funds are handled through mortgage bankers and mortgage brokers.

- **Endowment funds:** Many commercial banks and mortgage bankers handle investments for endowment funds. The endowments of hospitals, universities, colleges, charitable foundations, and other institutions provide a good source of financing for low-risk commercial and industrial properties.

- **Investment group financing:** Large real estate projects, such as highrise apartment buildings, office complexes, and shopping centers, are often financed as joint ventures through group financing arrangements like syndicates, limited partnerships, and real estate investment trusts.

- **Mortgage banking companies:** Mortgage banking companies originate mortgage loans with money belonging to insurance companies, pension funds, and individuals with funds of their own. They make real estate loans with the intention of selling them to investors and receiving a fee for servicing the loans. Mortgage banking companies generally are organized as stock companies. As a source of real estate financing, they are subject to fewer lending restrictions than are commercial banks or savings associations. Mortgage banking companies often are involved in all types of real estate loan activities and often serve as intermediaries between investors and borrowers. They are not mortgage brokers.

- **Mortgage brokers:** Mortgage brokers are not lenders. They are intermediaries who bring borrowers and lenders together. Mortgage brokers locate potential borrowers, process preliminary loan applications, and submit the applications to lenders for final approval. Frequently, they work with and for mortgage banking companies. They do not service loans once they are made. Mortgage brokers also may be real estate brokers who offer these financing services in addition to their regular brokerage activities. Many state governments are establishing separate licensure requirements for mortgage brokers to regulate their activities.

A growing number of consumers apply for mortgage loans via the Internet. Many major lenders have Web sites that offer information to potential borrowers regarding their current loan programs and requirements. In addition, online brokerage or match-making organizations link lenders with potential borrowers. Some borrowers prefer the Internet for its convenience in shopping for the best rates and terms, accessing a wide variety of loan programs, and speeding up the loan approval process.

Information on the Internet regarding lenders and their programs is constantly changing. Consider using a search engine such as *www.altavista.com*, *www.excite.com*, *www.google.com*, *www.lycos.com*, or *www.yahoo.com* to search for terms such as *real estate*, *financing*, *lending programs*, and *home mortgages*.

The Secondary Mortgage Market

In addition to the primary mortgage market, where loans are originated, there is a **secondary mortgage market.** Here, loans are bought and sold only after they have been funded. Lenders routinely sell loans to avoid interest rate risks and to realize profits on the sales. This secondary market activity helps lenders raise capital to continue making mortgage loans. Secondary market activity is especially desirable when money is in short supply. Such activity stimulates both the housing construction market and the mortgage market by expanding the types of loans available.

When a loan is sold, the original lender may continue to collect the payments from the borrower. The lender then passes the payments along to the investor who purchased the loan. The investor is charged a fee for servicing the loan. Loans are sold in packages by the lenders through warehousing agencies.

Warehousing agencies purchase a number of mortgage loans and package them into what are called *pools.* Securities that represent shares in these pooled mortgages are then sold to investors. Loans are eligible for sale to the secondary market only when the collateral, borrower, and documentation meet certain requirements to provide a degree of safety for the investors. The major warehousing agencies are noted below.

Fannie Mae.   **Fannie Mae**, or FNMA (formerly the *Federal National Mortgage Association*), is a quasi-governmental agency. It is organized as a privately owned corporation that issues its own common stock and provides a secondary market for mortgage loans. Fannie Mae deals in conventional, FHA, and VA loans. Fannie Mae buys a block or pool of mortgages from a lender in exchange for *mortgage-backed securities* that are sold on the global market. The Fannie Mae loan limits shown in Table 16.1 define loans that are conforming, that is, fall within the limit set by Fannie Mae. Non-conforming loans are called jumbo loans.

Ginnie Mae.   Unlike Fannie Mae, **Ginnie Mae** (formerly the *Government National Mortgage Association*) is entirely a governmental agency. Ginnie Mae is a division of the Department of Housing and Urban Development (HUD), organized as a corporation without capital stock. Ginnie Mae administers special-assistance programs and guarantees mortgage backed securities using FHA and VA loans as collateral.

Ginnie Mae guarantees investment securities issued by private offerors (such as banks, mortgage companies, and savings and loan associations) and backed by

TABLE 16.1

Fannie Mae/Freddie Mac Conforming Loan Limits (2008)

Fannie Mae/Freddie Mac Conforming Loan Limits (2008)	
One-family unit	$417,000
Two-family unit	$533,850
Three-family unit	$645,300
Four-family unit	$801,950
Second mortgages	$208,500
Maximum loan limits are 50 percent higher in Alaska, Hawaii, the U.S. Virgin Islands, and Guam.	

pools of FHA and VA mortgage loans. The Ginnie Mae *passthrough certificate* is a security interest in a pool of mortgages that provides for a monthly passthrough of principal and interest payments directly to the certificate holder. Such certificates are guaranteed by Ginnie Mae.

Freddie Mac. Freddie Mac, or FHLMC (formerly the *Federal Home Loan Mortgage Corporation*), provides a secondary market for mortgage loans, primarily conventional loans. Freddie Mac has the authority to purchase mortgages, pool them, and sell bonds in the open market with the mortgages as security. However, FHLMC does not guarantee payment of Freddie Mac mortgages.

Many lenders use the standardized forms and follow the guidelines issued by Fannie Mae and Freddie Mac. In fact, the use of such forms is mandatory for lenders wishing to sell mortgages in the agencies' secondary mortgage market. The standardized documents include loan applications, credit reports, and appraisal forms.

IN PRACTICE

Because Fannie Mae's and Freddie Mac's involvement in the secondary market is so pervasive, many underwriting guidelines are written to comply with their regulations. Bank statements, tax returns, verifications of employment, and child support statements—in short, most of the paperwork a potential borrower must deal with—may be tied to Fannie Mae and Freddie Mac requirements.

■ FINANCING TECHNIQUES

Now that you understand *where* real estate financing comes from, we'll turn to the *what*: the types of financing available. Real estate financing comes in a wide variety of forms. While the payment plans described in the following sections are commonly referred to as *mortgages*, they are really loans secured by either a mortgage or a deed of trust.

Interest-Only Loans

An **interest-only mortgage** (also known as a **sraight loan**, *term loan*, or *nonamortized loan*) is a mortgage that requires the payment of interest only for a stated period of time with the principal balance due at the end of the term. In the past, interest-only mortgages were used for short-term financing. In the early years of the first decade of this century, there was significant growth in interest-only loans and other affordable lending products. This pushed homeownership to new levels. However, as the housing market began to slow, there was no longer equity in the homes to support refinancing, and selling a home became more difficult as the number of home sales decreased. Now consumers are being cautioned to consider all risks before entering into an interest-only mortgage, as with any product.

Amortized Loans

The word *amortize* literally means "to kill off slowly, over time." Most mortgage and deed of trust loans are **amortized loans.** The amount of money needed to meet the periodic payments of principal and interest on a loan that is being amortized is called debt service. If the periodic payments are constant, in equal amounts, then a portion will pay off accrued interest with the remainder reducing principal. The most common periods are 15 years or 30 years, although 40 and 50 year mortgages are also available.

MATH CONCEPTS

INTEREST AND PRINCIPAL CREDITED FROM AMORTIZED PAYMENTS

Lenders charge borrowers a certain percentage of the principal as interest for each year a debt is outstanding. The amount of interest due on any one payment date is calculated by computing the total yearly interest (based on the unpaid balance) and dividing that figure by the number of payments made each year.

For example, assume the current outstanding balance of a loan is $70,000. The interest rate is 7.5 percent per year, and the monthly payment is $489.30. Based on these facts, the interest and principal due on the next payment would be computed as shown:

$70,000 loan balance x .075 annual interest rate = $5,250 annual interest

$5,250 annual interest ÷ 12 months = $437.50 monthly interest

$489.30 monthly payment − $437.50 monthly interest = $51.80 monthly principal

$70,000 loan balance − $51.80 monthly principal = $69,948.20

This process is followed with each payment over the term of the loan. The same calculations are made each month, starting with the declining new balance figure from the previous month.

At the end of the term, the full amount of the principal and all interest due is reduced to zero. Such loans are also called *direct reduction loans*. Most amortized mortgage and deed of trust loans are paid in monthly installments.

Different payment plans tend alternately to gain and lose favor with lenders and borrowers as the cost and availability of mortgage money fluctuate. The most frequently used plan is the *fully amortized loan*, or *level-payment loan*. The mortgagor pays a constant amount, usually monthly. The lender credits each payment first to the interest due, then to the principal amount of the loan. As a result, while each payment remains the same, the portion applied to repayment of the principal grows and the interest due declines as the unpaid balance of the loan is reduced. (See Figure 16.1.) If the borrower pays additional amounts that are applied directly to the principal, the loan will amortize more quickly. This benefits the borrower because he or she will pay less interest if the loan is paid off before the end of its term. Of course, lenders are aware of this, too, and may guard against unprofitable loans by including penalties for early payment.

FIGURE 16.1

Level-Payment Amortized Loan

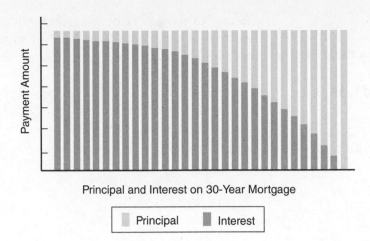

Principal and Interest on 30-Year Mortgage

Principal   Interest

The amount of the constant payment is determined from a prepared mortgage payment book or a mortgage factor chart. (See Table 16.2.) The mortgage factor chart indicates the amount of monthly payment per $1,000 of loan, depending on the term and interest rate. The factor is multiplied by the number of thousands (and fractions of thousands) of the amount borrowed.

IN PRACTICE

Of course, there are relatively inexpensive calculators that will accurately perform most of the standard mortgage lending calculations. Also, most commercial lenders provide mortgage calculators on their Web sites. Nonetheless, it's valuable both to know what the calculator is doing and to be able to perform the calculations manually if the calculator breaks or no calculator is available.

Adjustable-Rate Mortgages (ARMs)

An **adjustable-rate mortgage** (ARM) is generally originated at one rate of interest that fluctuates up or down during the loan term based on some objective economic indicator. Because the interest rate on ARMs may change, the mortgagor's loan repayments also may change. Details of how and when the interest rate will change are included in the note. Common components of an ARM include the following:

- The interest rate is tied to the movement of an objective economic indicator called an *index. Some common indexes* are U.S. Treasury bills, LIBOR, and 11th District Cost of Funds index.
- Usually, the interest rate is the index rate plus a premium, called the *margin.* The margin represents the lender's cost of doing business. For example, the loan rate may be 2 percent over the U.S. Treasury bill rate.
- *Rate caps* limit the amount the interest rate may change. Most ARMs have two types of rate caps—periodic and aggregate. A *periodic rate cap* limits the amount the rate may increase at any one time. An *aggregate rate cap* limits the amount the rate may increase over the entire life of the loan.
- The mortgagor is protected from unaffordable individual payments by the *payment cap.* The payment cap sets a limit on the amount of increase in the borrower's monthly principal and interest at the payment adjustment date. This takes effect if the principal and interest called for by the interest rate increase exceeds the payment cap percentage. This limitation may result in negative amortization (the loan balance increases rather than decreases due to an interest shortage which gets added back to the loan and is payable at maturity).

T A B L E   16.2

Mortgage Rate Factor Chart

Rate	Term 10 Years	Term 15 Years	Term 20 Years	Term 25 Years	Term 30 Years
6	11.10	8.44	7.16	6.44	6.00
6⅛	11.16	8.51	7.24	6.52	6.08
6¼	11.23	8.57	7.31	6.60	6.16
6⅜	11.29	8.64	7.38	6.67	6.24
6½	11.35	8.71	7.46	6.75	6.32
6⅝	11.42	8.78	7.53	6.83	6.40
6¾	11.48	8.85	7.60	6.91	6.49
6⅞	11.55	8.92	7.68	6.99	6.57
7	11.61	8.98	7.75	7.06	6.65
7⅛	11.68	9.06	7.83	7.15	6.74
7¼	11.74	9.12	7.90	7.22	6.82
7⅜	11.81	9.20	7.98	7.31	6.91
7½	11.87	9.27	8.05	7.38	6.99
7⅝	11.94	9.34	8.13	7.47	7.08
7¾	12.00	9.41	8.20	7.55	7.16
7⅞	12.07	9.48	8.29	7.64	7.25
8	12.14	9.56	8.37	7.72	7.34
8⅛	12.20	9.63	8.45	7.81	7.43
8¼	12.27	9.71	8.53	7.89	7.52
8⅜	12.34	9.78	8.60	7.97	7.61
8½	12.40	9.85	8.68	8.06	7.69
8⅝	12.47	9.93	8.76	8.14	7.78
8¾	12.54	10.00	8.84	8.23	7.87
8⅞	12.61	10.07	8.92	8.31	7.96
9	12.67	10.15	9.00	8.40	8.05

How to Use This Chart

To use this chart, start by finding the appropriate interest rate. Then follow that row over to the column for the appropriate loan term. This number is the *interest rate factor* required each month to amortize a $1,000 loan. To calculate the principal and interest (P&I) payment, multiply the interest rate factor by the number of 1,000s in the total loan.

For example, if the interest rate is 8 percent for a term of 30 years, the interest rate factor is 7.34. If the total loan is $100,000, the loan contains 100 1,000s. Therefore, 100 × 7.34 = $743 PI only.

- The adjustment period establishes how often the rate may be changed. For instance, the adjustment period may be monthly, quarterly, or annually.
- Lenders may offer a conversion option, which permits the mortgagor to convert from an adjustable-rate to a fixed-rate loan at certain intervals during the life of the mortgage. The option is subject to certain terms and conditions for the conversion.

Figure 16.2 illustrates the effect interest rate fluctuations and periodic caps have on an adjustable-rate mortgage. Obviously, without rate caps and payment caps, a single mortgage's interest rate could fluctuate wildly over several adjustment periods, depending on the behavior of the index to which it is tied. In Figure 16.2, the borrower's rate changes from a low of 5.9 percent to a high of 9.5 percent. Such unpredictability makes personal financial planning difficult. On the other hand, if the loan had a periodic rate cap of 7.5 percent, the borrower's rate would never go above that level, regardless of the index's behavior. Similarly, a lender would

FIGURE 16.2

Adjustable-Rate Mortgage

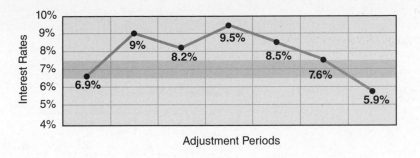

want a floor to keep the rate from falling below a certain rate (here, 6.5 percent). The shaded area in the figure shows how caps and floors protect against dramatic changes in interest rates.

Balloon Payment Loan

When the periodic payments are not enough to fully amortize the loan by the time the final payment is due, the final payment is larger than the others. This is called a **balloon payment.** A balloon loan is a *partially amortized loan* because principal is still owed at the end of the term. It is frequently assumed that if payments are made promptly, the lender will extend the balloon payment for another limited term. The lender, however, is not legally obligated to grant this extension and can require payment in full when the note is due.

Growing-Equity Mortgage (GEM)

A **growing-equity mortgage** (GEM) is also known as a *rapid-payoff mortgage*. The GEM uses a fixed interest rate, but payments of principal are increased according to an index or a schedule. Thus, the total payment increases, and the loan is paid off more quickly. A GEM is most frequently used when the borrower's income is expected to keep pace with the increasing loan payments.

Reverse-Annuity Mortgage (RAM)

A **reverse-annuity mortgage** (RAM) is one in which payments are made by the lender to the borrower. The payments are based on the equity the homeowner has invested in the property given as security for the loan. This loan allows senior citizens on fixed incomes to use the equity they have built up in their homes without having to sell. The borrower is charged a fixed rate of interest, and the loan eventually is repaid from the sale of the property or from the borrower's estate after his or her death.

Nonrecourse Loan

A *nonrecourse loan* is one in which the borrower is not held personally responsible for the loan. The lender has no recourse against the borrower personally in the event of a default. Nonrecourse loans are common in those situations in which the lender is highly confident that the value of the property involved is itself sufficient security. Nonrecourse loans are more common in commercial and investment real estate transactions than in residential situations.

■ LOAN PROGRAMS

Mortgage loans are generally classified based on their **loan-to-value ratios,** or *LTVs.* The LTV is the ratio of debt to value of the property. *Value* is the sale price or the appraisal value, whichever is less. The *lower* the ratio of debt to value, the *higher* the down payment by the borrower. For the lender, the higher down payment means a more secure loan, which minimizes the lender's risk.

MATH CONCEPTS

DETERMINING LTV

If a property has an appraised value of $100,000, secured by a $90,000 loan, the LTV is 90 percent:

$$\$90,000 \div \$100,000 = 90\%$$

Conventional Loans

Low LTV = *High* down payment, Small loan *High* down payment = *Low* lender risk

Conventional loans are viewed as the most secure loans because their loan-to-value ratios are lowest. Usually, the ratio is 80 percent of the value of the property or less, because the borrower makes a down payment of at least 20 percent. The security for the loan is provided solely by the mortgage; the payment of the debt rests on the ability of the borrower to pay. In making such a loan, the lender relies primarily on its appraisal of the security (the real estate). Information from credit reports that indicates the reliability of the prospective borrower is also important. No additional insurance or guarantee on the loan is necessary to protect the lender's interest. In conventional loans the government is not involved.

Lenders can set criteria by which a borrower and the collateral are evaluated to qualify for a loan. However, in recent years the secondary mortgage market has had a significant impact on borrower qualifications, standards for the collateral, and documentation procedures followed by lenders. Loans must meet strict criteria to be sold to Fannie Mae and Freddie Mac. *Lenders still can be flexible in their lending decisions, but they may not be able to sell unusual loans in the secondary market.*

To qualify for a conventional loan under Fannie Mae guidelines, for instance, the borrower's monthly housing expenses, including PITI, must not exceed 28 percent of total monthly gross income. Also, the borrower's total monthly obligations, including housing costs plus other regular monthly payments, must not exceed 36 percent of his or her total monthly gross income (33 percent in the case of 95 percent LTV loans). Loans that meet these criteria are called conforming loans and are eligible to be sold in the secondary market. Loans that exceed the limits are referred to as nonconforming loans and are not marketable in the secondary market but, instead, are generally held in the lender's investment portfolio.

Conforming loans with larger ratios may be available in certain situations. Both Fannie Mae and Freddie Mac currently have a variety of conforming affordable loan products with qualifying ratios of 33 percent for housing expense and up to 38 percent for total debt. These loans only require a 3 percent down payment but are subject to certain income limitations and may require the borrowers to attend homeownership classes.

Private Mortgage Insurance

One way a borrower can obtain a mortgage loan with a lower down payment is by obtaining **private mortgage insurance** (PMI). Because the loan-to-value ratio is *higher* than for other conventional loans (meaning a lower down payment), the lender requires additional security to minimize its risk. The borrower purchases insurance from a private mortgage insurance company as additional security to insure the lender against borrower default. LTVs of up to 95 percent of the appraised value of the property are allowable with mortgage insurance. PMI is usually required when a down payment is less than 20 percent.

PMI protects the top 20 percent to 30 percent of the loan against borrower default. Normally, the borrower pays a monthly fee while the insurance is in force. Because only a portion of the loan is insured, the lender must allow the borrower to terminate the coverage once the loan is repaid to a certain level.

Under the **Homeowners' Protection Act of 1998** (implemented in 1999) PMI must terminate automatically when the borrower reaches a 22 percent equity position based on the original value of the property at the time the loan was originated with no allowance for appreciation or depreciation if the loan was written after July 29, 1999.

FHA-Insured Loans

The Federal Housing Administration (FHA) operates under the control of HUD and has the primary responsibility for administering the government home loan insurance program. This program allows buyers who might not otherwise qualify for a home loan to obtain one because the risk is removed from the lender by the FHA.

The most popular FHA program is Title II, Section 203(b), fixed-interest rate loans for 10 years to 30 years on one-family to four-family residences. Rates are competitive with other types of loans, even though they are high-LTV loans. Certain technical requirements must be met before the FHA will insure the loans. These requirements include the following:

- The borrower is charged a percentage of the loan as a premium for the FHA insurance. The *up-front premium* is paid at closing by the borrower or some other party. It also may be financed along with the total loan amount. The up-front premium is charged on all loans except those for the purchase of a condominium. All FHA loans will have the monthly premium charged. Insurance premiums vary for new loans, refinancing, and condominiums.
- FHA regulations set standards for type and construction of buildings, quality of neighborhood, and credit requirements for borrowers.
- The mortgaged real estate must be appraised by an *approved FHA appraiser*. The loan amount generally cannot exceed either of the following:

  1. 98.75 percent for loans over $50,000 with 1.25 percent down (for loans less than $50,000, the buyer must contribute 3 percent of the sales price to the down payment and closing costs).
  2. 97.75 percent of the sales price or appraised value for loans over $50,000 with 2.25 percent down.

     If the purchase price exceeds the FHA-appraised value, the buyer may pay the difference in cash as part of the down payment. In addition, the FHA has set maximum loan amounts for various regions of the country. In all cases, the purchaser must contribute 3 percent of the sales price to the transaction, either in down payment or closing costs.

Other types of FHA loans are available, including one-year adjustable-rate mortgages, home improvement and rehabilitation loans, and loans for the purchase of condominiums. Specific standards for condominium complexes and the ratio of owner-occupants to renters must be met for a loan on a condominium unit to be financed through the FHA insurance programs.

Although lenders can charge interest until the next payment due date on an FHA payoff, lenders may not deny the assumption of the mortgage by a qualified buyer even if the interest rates have skyrocketed.

IN PRACTICE

The FHA sets lending limits for single-unit and multiple-unit properties. The limits vary significantly, depending on the average cost of housing in different regions of the country. In addition, the FHA changes its regulations for various programs from time to time. Contact your local FHA office or mortgage lender for loan amounts in your area and for specific loan requirements, or visit *www.hud.gov/offices/hsg/index.cfm.*

Prepayment privileges. A borrower may repay an FHA-insured loan on a one-family to four-family residence without penalty. For loans made *before* August 2, 1985, the borrower must give the lender written notice of intention to exercise the prepayment privilege at least 30 days before prepayment. If the borrower fails to provide the required notice, the lender has the option of charging up to 30 days' interest. For loans initiated *after* August 2, 1985, no written notice of prepayment is required.

Assumption rules. The assumption rules for FHA-insured loans vary, depending on the dates the loans were originated, as follows:

- FHA loans originating before December 1986 generally have no restrictions on their assumptions.
- For an FHA loan originating between December 1, 1986, and December 15, 1989, a creditworthiness review of the prospective assumer is required. If the original loan was for the purchase of a principal residence, this review is required during the first 12 months of the loan's existence. If the original loan was for the purchase of an investment property, the review is required during the first 24 months of the loan.
- For FHA loans originating on December 15, 1989, and later, no assumptions are permitted without complete buyer qualification.

Discount points. The lender of an FHA-insured loan may charge discount points in addition to a loan origination fee. The payment of points is a matter of negotiation between the seller and the buyer. However, if the seller pays more than 6 percent of the costs normally paid by the buyer (such as discount points, the loan origination fee, the mortgage insurance premium, buydown fees, prepaid items, and impound or escrow amounts), the lender will treat the payments as a reduction in sales price and recalculate the mortgage amount accordingly.

VA-Guaranteed Loans

The Department of Veterans Affairs (VA) is authorized to guarantee loans to purchase or construct homes for eligible veterans and their spouses (including unremarried spouses of veterans whose deaths were service-related). The VA also guarantees loans to purchase mobile homes and plots on which to place them. A veteran who meets any of the following time-in-service criteria is eligible for a **VA loan:**

- 90 days of active service for veterans of World War II, the Korean War, the Vietnam conflict, and the Persian Gulf War
- A minimum of 181 days of active service during peacetime periods between July 26, 1947, and September 6, 1980 (or to 10/16/81 if an officer)
- Two full years of service during any peacetime period after September 7, 1980 (or after 10/16/81 if an officer), or if called to active service for at least 181 days after that date
- Six or more years of continuous duty as a reservist in the U.S. Army, Navy, Air Force, Marine Corps, or Coast Guard or as a member of the Army or Air National Guard

The VA assists veterans in financing the purchase of homes with little or no down payments at market interest rates. The VA issues rules and regulations that set forth the qualifications, limitations, and conditions under which a loan may be guaranteed.

Like the term *FHA loan*, **VA loan** is something of a misnomer. The VA does not normally lend money; it guarantees loans made by lending institutions approved by the agency. The term *VA loan* refers to a loan that is not made by the agency but is guaranteed by it.

There is no VA dollar limit on the amount of the loan a veteran can obtain; this limit is determined by the lender and qualification of the buyer. The VA limits the amount of the loan it will guarantee.

IN PRACTICE

The VA loan guarantee is tied to the current conforming loan limit for Fannie Mae and Freddie Mac. Typically, lenders will loan four times the guarantee (for example, a conforming loan of $417,000 ÷ 4 = $104,250 VA guarantee).

To determine what portion of a mortgage loan the VA will guarantee, the veteran must apply for a *certificate of eligibility*. This certificate does not mean that the veteran automatically receives a mortgage. It merely sets forth the maximum guarantee to which the veteran is entitled. For individuals with full eligibility, no down payment is required for a loan up to the maximum guarantee limit.

The VA also issues a *certificate of reasonable value* (CRV) for the property being purchased. The CRV states the property's current market value based on a VA-approved appraisal. The CRV places a ceiling on the amount of a VA loan allowed for the property. If the purchase price is greater than the amount cited in the CRV, the veteran may pay the difference in cash. The CRV is based on an appraisal. New VA regulations allow only one active VA loan at a time, and a veteran may own only two properties acquired using VA loan benefits. However, a veteran may use his or her VA benefits as many times as he or she chooses, as long as the previous benefit use has been paid.

The VA borrower pays a loan origination fee to the lender, as well as a funding fee (2 percent to 3 percent, depending on the down payment amount) to the Department of Veterans Affairs. The funding fee depends on whether it is first time use (2 percent) or a subsequent use (3 percent). Reservists and National Guard veterans pay higher funding fees. Reasonable discount points may be charged on a VA-guaranteed loan, and either the veteran or the seller may pay them.

Prepayment privileges.   As with an FHA loan, the borrower under a VA loan can prepay the debt at any time without penalty.

Assumption rules.   VA loans made before March 1, 1988, are freely assumable, although an assumption processing fee will be charged. For loans made on or after March 1, 1988, the VA must approve the buyer and assumption agreement. The original veteran borrower remains personally liable for the repayment of the loan unless the VA approves a *release of liability*. The release of liability will be issued by the VA only if

- the buyer assumes all of the veteran's liabilities on the loan, and
- the VA or the lender approves both the buyer and the assumption agreement.

A release also would be possible if another veteran used his or her own entitlement in assuming the loan.

IN PRACTICE

A release of liability issued by the VA does not release the veteran's liability to the lender. This must be obtained separately from the lender. Real estate licensees should contact their local VA offices or mortgage lenders for specific requirements for obtaining or assuming VA-insured loans. The programs change from time to time.

VA legislation.   The **Veterans Millennium Health Care and Benefits Act of 1999**, Public Law 106-117, authorized VA to restore the home loan eligibility of surviving spouses who lost such eligibility as a result of remarriage if the remarriage has been terminated by death or divorce. More on eligibility, including that of individuals who are not otherwise eligible and who have completed a total of at least six years of honorable service in the Selected Reserves, including the National Guard, is available on the VA's Internet loan information site.

Agricultural Loan Programs

The **Farm Service Agency** (FSA), formerly the Farmers Home Administration, is a federal agency of the Department of Agriculture. The FSA offers programs to help families purchase or operate family farms. Through the Rural Housing and Community Development Service, it also provides loans to help families purchase or improve single-family homes in rural areas. Loans are made to low-income and moderate-income families, and the interest rate charged can be as low as 1 percent, depending on the borrower's income. The FSA provides assistance to rural and agricultural businesses and industry through the Rural Business and Cooperative Development Service (RBCDS).

FSA loan programs fall into two categories: guaranteed loans, made and serviced by private lenders and guaranteed for a specific percentage by the FSA, and loans made directly by the FSA.

The **Farm Credit System (Farm Credit)** provides loans to more than 500,000 borrowers, including farmers, ranchers, rural homeowners, agricultural cooperatives, rural utility systems, and agribusinesses. Unlike commercial banks, Farm Credit System banks and associations do not take deposits. Instead, loanable funds are raised through the system-wide sale of bonds and notes in the nation's capital markets.

Farmer Mac (formerly the Federal Agricultural Mortgage Corporation, or FAMC), is another government-sponsored enterprise (GSE) that operates similarly to Fannie Mae and Freddie Mac but in a context of agricultural loans. It was created to improve the availability of long-term credit at stable interest rates to America's farmers, ranchers, and rural homeowners, businesses, and communities. Farmer Mac pools or bundles agricultural loans from lenders for sale as mortgage-backed securities.

IN PRACTICE There have been many changes in all of the agricultural lending programs. Since 1994, the Farmer's Home Administration, the Rural Development Administration, the Rural Electrification Administration, and the Agricultural Cooperative Service have been combined into the USDA Rural Development Agency.

■ OTHER FINANCING TECHNIQUES

Because borrowers often have different needs, a variety of other financing techniques have been created.

Purchase-Money Mortgages

A **purchase-money mortgage** is a note and mortgage created at the time of purchase. Its purpose is to make the sale possible. It may refer to any security instrument that originates at the time of sale. More often, it refers to the instrument given by the purchaser to the seller (vendor). It can be a first or second mortgage, depending on whether prior liens exist.

■ **FOR EXAMPLE** Ben wants to buy Brownacre for $200,000. Ben has a $40,000 down payment and agrees to assume an existing mortgage of $80,000. Because Ben might not qualify for a new mortgage under the circumstances, the owner agrees to take back a purchase-money second mortgage in the amount of $80,000. At the closing, Ben will execute a mortgage and note in favor of the owner, who will convey title to Ben.

Package Loans

A **package loan** includes not only the real estate but also all personal property and appliances installed on the premises. In recent years, this kind of loan has been used extensively to finance furnished condominium units. Package loans usually include furniture, drapes, and carpets as well as kitchen range, refrigerator, dishwasher, garbage disposal, washer, dryer, food freezer, and other appliances as part of the sales price of the home.

Blanket Loans

A **blanket loan** covers more than one parcel or lot. It is usually used to finance subdivision developments. However, it can be used to finance the purchase of improved properties or to consolidate loans as well. A blanket loan usually includes a provision known as a *partial release clause*. This clause permits the borrower to obtain the release of any one lot or parcel from the lien by repaying a certain amount of the loan. The lender issues a partial release for each parcel released from the mortgage lien. The release form includes a provision that the lien will continue to cover all other unreleased lots.

Wraparound Loans

A **wraparound loan** enables a borrower with an existing mortgage or deed of trust loan to obtain additional financing from a second lender *without paying off the first loan*. The second lender gives the borrower a new, increased loan at a higher interest rate and *assumes payment of the existing loan*. The total amount of the new loan includes the existing loan as well as the additional loan taken out by the borrower. The borrower makes payments to the new lender based on the total amount, and the new lender in turn makes payments on the original loan out of the borrowers' payments.

Another common use of wraparound financing is to facilitate the purchase of real property when an existing mortgage cannot be paid off or a seller's current loan vehicle offers especially good terms. In this case the buyer may execute a wraparound mortgage to the seller, who collects payments based on the terms of the new, seller-financed loan. The seller then uses that regular monthly cash, or part of it, to make payments on the old bank loan. Wraparounds also can finance the sale of real estate when the buyer wishes to invest a minimum amount of initial cash.

Wraparound loans that are intended to place a new owner in a house are possible *only if the original lender and loan vehicle permit it.* An **alienation clause** or a **due-on-sale clause** in the original loan documents may prevent a sale under a wraparound loan. *Due-on-sale* means that if a property is sold, full payment must be made to the lender and the loan ends.

IN PRACTICE

To protect themselves against a seller's default on a previous loan, buyers should require protective clauses to be included in any wraparound document to grant them the right to make payments directly to the original lender.

Open-End Loans

An **open-end loan** secures a note executed by the borrower to the lender. It also secures any *future advances of funds* made by the lender to the borrower. The interest rate on the initial amount borrowed is fixed, but interest on future advances may be charged at the market rate in effect. An open-end loan is often a less costly alternative to a home improvement loan. It allows the borrower to "open" the mortgage or deed of trust to increase the debt to its original amount, or the amount stated in the note, after the debt has been reduced by payments over a period of time. The mortgage usually states a maximum amount that can be secured, the terms and conditions under which the loan can be opened, and the provisions for repayment.

Construction Loans (Interim Financing)

A **construction loan** is made to finance the construction of improvements on real estate such as homes, apartments, and office buildings. The lender commits to the full amount of the loan but disburses the funds in payments during construction. These payments also are known as *draws*. Draws are made to the general contractor for that part of the construction work that has been completed since the previous payment. Before each payment, the lender has the right to inspect the work. The general contractor must provide the lender with adequate waivers that release all mechanic's lien rights for the work covered by the payment.

This kind of loan generally bears a higher-than-market interest rate because of the risks assumed by the lender. These risks include the inadequate releasing of mechanics' liens, possible delays in completing the construction, or the financial failure of the contractor or subcontractors. Construction loans are generally short-term or interim financing. The borrower pays interest only on the monies that have actually been disbursed. The borrower is expected to arrange for a permanent loan, also known as an *end loan* or *take-out loan*, that will repay or "take out" the construction financing lender when the work is completed. Some lenders now offer construction-to-permanent programs in which a single loan carries throughout the construction, automatically becoming a mortgage loan when the work is finished. *Participation financing* occurs when a lender (perhaps a private lender) demands an equity position in the project as a requirement for making the loan.

Sale-Leaseback

Sale-leaseback arrangements are used to finance large commercial or industrial properties. The land and building, usually used by the seller for business purposes, are sold to an investor. The real estate is then leased back by the investor to the seller, who continues to conduct business on the property as a tenant. The buyer becomes the lessor, and the original owner becomes the lessee. This enables a business to free money tied up in real estate to use it as working capital.

Sale-leaseback arrangements involve complicated legal procedures, and their success is usually related to the effects the transaction has on the firm's tax situation. Legal and tax experts should be involved in this type of transaction.

Buydowns

A **buydown** is a way to temporarily lower the initial interest rate on a mortgage or deed of trust loan. In a buydown, cash funds for an agreed-on amount are paid to the lender at the closing. This payment offsets the interest rate and monthly payments during the mortgage's first few years. Typical buydown arrangements reduce the interest rate by 1 percent to 2 percent over the first one to two years of the loan term, after which it rises. The assumption is that the borrower's income also will increase and that the borrower will be better able to absorb the increased monthly payments. In a permanent buydown, a larger up-front payment reduces the effective interest rate for the life of the loan.

Home Equity Loans

Using the equity buildup in a home to finance other purchases is an alternative to refinancing. **Home equity loans** are a source of funds that homeowners use for a variety of financial needs:

- To finance the purchase of expensive items
- To consolidate existing installment loans on credit card debt
- To pay medical, education, home improvement, or other expenses

The original mortgage loan remains in place, and the home equity loan is junior to the original lien. If the homeowner refinances, the original mortgage loan is paid off and replaced by a new loan.

A home equity loan can be taken out as a fixed loan amount or as an equity line of credit. With the home equity line of credit, referred to as a HELOC, lenders extend a line of credit that borrowers can use whenever they want. Borrowers receive their money by checks sent to them, deposits made in checking or savings accounts, or a book of drafts they can use up to their credit limits.

IN PRACTICE

The homeowner must consider a number of factors before deciding to secure a home equity loan. The costs involved in obtaining a new mortgage loan or a home equity loan, current interest rates, total monthly payments, and income tax consequences are all important issues to be examined.

■ FINANCING LEGISLATION

The federal government regulates the lending practices of mortgage lenders through the Truth-in-Lending Act, the Equal Credit Opportunity Act, the Community Reinvestment Act of 1977, and the Real Estate Settlement Procedures Act.

Truth-in-Lending Act and Regulation Z

Regulation Z, which was promulgated pursuant to the **Truth-in-Lending Act,** requires that credit institutions inform borrowers of the *true cost of obtaining credit.* Its purpose is to enable borrowers to compare the costs of various lenders and avoid the uninformed use of credit. *Regulation Z applies when a credit transaction is secured by a residence.* The regulation does *not* apply to business or commercial loans or to agricultural loans of more than $25,000, nor to personal, family, or household loans *over* $25,000.

Under the *Truth-in-Lending Act, Regulation Z,* a consumer must be fully informed of all finance charges and the true interest rate before a transaction is completed. The finance charge disclosure must include any loan fees, finder's fees, service charges, and points, as well as interest. In the case of a mortgage loan made to finance the purchase of a dwelling, the lender must compute and disclose the *annual percentage rate* (APR). However, the lender does not have to indicate the total interest payable during the term of the loan. Also, the lender does not have to include actual costs such as title fees, legal fees, appraisal fees, credit reports, survey fees, and closing expenses as part of the finance charge.

Creditor. A *creditor,* for purposes of *Regulation Z,* is any person who extends consumer credit more than 25 times each year or more than 5 times each year if the transactions involve dwellings as security. The credit must be subject to a finance charge or payable in more than four installments by written agreement.

Three-day right of rescission. In the case of many consumer credit transactions covered by *Regulation Z,* the borrower has three days in which to rescind the transaction by merely notifying the lender. *However, this right of rescission does not apply to residential purchase-money or first mortgage or deed of trust loans.*

Advertising. *Regulation Z* provides strict regulation of real estate advertisements that include mortgage financing terms. General phrases like "liberal terms available" may be used, but if details are given, they must comply with the Act.

Advertisements for buydowns or reduced-interest rate mortgages must show both the limited term to which the interest rate applies and the annual percentage rate. If a variable-rate mortgage is advertised, the advertisement must include

■ the number and timing of payments;
■ the amount of the largest and smallest payments; and
■ a statement of the fact that the actual payments will vary between these two extremes.

Specific credit terms, such as down payment, monthly payment, dollar amount of the finance charge, or term of the loan may not be advertised unless the advertisement includes the following information:

- Cash price
- Required down payment
- Number, amounts, and due dates of all payments
- Annual percentage rate
- Total of all payments to be made over the term of the mortgage (unless the advertised credit refers to a first mortgage or deed of trust to finance the acquisition of a dwelling)

Penalties.   *Regulation Z* provides penalties for noncompliance. The penalty for violation of an administrative order enforcing *Regulation Z* is $10,000 for each day the violation continues. A fine of up to $10,000 may be imposed for engaging in an unfair or a deceptive practice. In addition, a creditor may be liable to a consumer for twice the amount of the finance charge, for a minimum of $100 and a maximum of $1,000, plus court costs, attorneys' fees, and any actual damages. Willful violation is a misdemeanor punishable by a fine of up to $5,000, one year's imprisonment, or both.

Equal Credit Opportunity Act (ECOA)

The federal **Equal Credit Opportunity Act** (ECOA) prohibits lenders and others who grant or arrange credit to consumers from discriminating against credit applicants on the basis of

- race,
- color,
- religion,
- national origin,
- sex,
- marital status,
- age (provided the applicant is of legal age), or
- dependence on public assistance.

In addition, lenders and other creditors must inform all rejected credit applicants of the principal reasons for the denial or termination of credit. The notice must be provided in writing, within 30 days. The ECOA also provides that a borrower is entitled to a copy of the appraisal report if the borrower paid for the appraisal.

Community Reinvestment Act (CRA)

Community reinvestment refers to the responsibility of financial institutions to help meet their communities' needs for low-income and moderate-income housing. In 1977, Congress passed the **Community Reinvestment Act** (CRA). Under the CRA, financial institutions are expected to meet the deposit and credit needs of their communities; participate and invest in local community development and rehabilitation projects; and participate in loan programs for housing, small businesses, and small farms.

The law requires any federally supervised financial institution to prepare a statement containing

- a definition of the geographic boundaries of its community;
- an identification of the types of community reinvestment credit offered (such as residential housing loans, housing rehabilitation loans, small-business loans, commercial loans, and consumer loans); and
- comments from the public about the institution's performance in meeting its community's needs.

Financial institutions are periodically reviewed by one of four federal financial supervisory agencies: the Comptroller of the Currency, the Federal Reserve's Board of Governors, the **Federal Deposit Insurance Corporation** (FDIC), and the **Office of Thrift Supervision** (OTS). The institutions must post a public notice that their community reinvestment activities are subject to federal review, and they must make the results of these reviews public.

Real Estate Settlement Procedures Act

The federal **Real Estate Settlement Procedures Act** (RESPA) applies to any residential real estate transaction involving a new first mortgage loan. RESPA is designed to ensure that buyer and seller are fully informed of all settlement costs. At time of loan application, the lender *must* supply the borrower with a good-faith estimate (GFE) of settlement costs payable by the buyer. The lender must also give the buyer a special settlement information booklet, *Settlement Costs and You,* to inform consumers of their rights and what they can expect to happen during the loan process and at closing. If this information is not supplied immediately at loan application, it must be mailed to the applicant within three business days. Bank regulators may impose stiff penalties on lenders who fail to comply with this federal law.

RESPA also governs the open disclosure of any bonuses or referrals involved in the transactions, and imposes sanctions against any possible *kickbacks.* (Refer to Chapter 23.)

■ COMPUTERIZED LOAN ORIGINATION AND AUTOMATED UNDERWRITING

A **computerized loan origination** (CLO) system is an electronic network for handling loan applications through remote computer terminals linked to several lenders' computers. With a CLO system, a real estate broker or salesperson can call up a menu of mortgage lenders, interest rates, and loan terms, then help a buyer select a lender and apply for a loan right from the brokerage office.

Under federal regulations, licensees may assist applicants in answering the on-screen questions and in understanding the services offered. The broker in whose office the terminal is located may earn fees. The borrower, not the mortgage broker or lender, must pay the fee. The fee amount may be financed, however. While multiple lenders may be represented on an office's CLO computer, consumers must be informed that other lenders and lending services are available outside the office. An applicant's ability to comparison shop for a loan may be enhanced by a CLO system, but the full range of options still must be indicated.

On the lender's side, new automated underwriting procedures can shorten loan approvals from weeks to minutes. Automated underwriting using desktop or portable computers also tends to lower the cost of loan application and approval by as much as 60 percent. Freddie Mac uses a system called *Loan Prospector.* Fannie Mae has a system called *Desktop Underwriter* that reduces approval time to minutes, based on the borrower's credit report, a paycheck stub, and a drive-by appraisal of the property. Even complex mortgages can be processed in less than 72 hours. In addition, a prospective buyer can now strengthen his or her purchase offer by including proof of loan *preapproval* with the offer itself prior to negotiating.

This is usually called a written preapproval. Preapproval usually enhances an offer because it means the buyer will get the loan, barring unusual circumstances. A strong financial picture at offer time is critical to the seller and may result in the seller agreeing to a lower price because he or she knows the buyer is likely to perform on the contract.

■ SUMMARY

The federal government affects real estate financing money and interest rates through the Federal Reserve Board's discount rate and reserve requirements; it also participates in the secondary mortgage market. The secondary market generally is composed of the investors who ultimately purchase and hold the loans as investments. These include insurance companies, investment funds, and pension plans.

Types of loans available are almost infinite with today's creative lenders. The common ones include fully amortized and straight loans as well as adjustable-rate mortgages, growing-equity mortgages (GEMS), balloon payment mortgages, and reverse-annuity (RAM) mortgages.

Many mortgage and deed of trust loan programs exist, including conventional loans and those insured by the FHA or private mortgage insurance companies or guaranteed by the VA. FHA and VA loans must meet certain requirements for the borrower to obtain the benefits of government backing. It is this backing that induces the lender to lend its funds at the good rates FHA and VA purchasers typically enjoy. The interest rates for these loans are often lower than those charged for conventional loans, and other requirements may be less stringent. Consequently, FHA and VA loans are usually very advantageous for those who qualify.

Agricultural loan programs are available through the Farm Service Agency, Farm Credit System, and Farmer Mac. The Farm Service Agency offers programs to help families purchase or operate family farms. The Farm Credit System provides loans to farmers, ranchers, rural homeowners, agricultural cooperatives, rural utility systems, and agribusiness. Farmer Mac operates similarly to Fannie Mae and Freddie Mac but in the context of agricultural loans.

Other types of real estate financing include seller-financed purchase-money mortgages or deeds of trust, blanket mortgages, package mortgages, wraparound mortgages, open-end mortgages, construction loans, sale-leasebacks, and home equity loans.

Regulation Z implements the federal *Truth-in-Lending Act*. This Act requires that lenders inform prospective borrowers of all finance charges involved in a loan if real estate is the security. Severe penalties are provided for noncompliance. The federal *Equal Credit Opportunity Act* prohibits creditors from discriminating against credit applicants on the basis of race, color, religion, national origin, sex, marital status, age, or dependence on public assistance. The *Real Estate Settlement Procedures Act* requires that lenders inform both buyers and sellers in advance of all fees and charges required for the settlement or closing of residential real estate transactions, and it also prohibits kickbacks.

QUESTIONS

1. The buyers purchased a residence for $95,000. They made a down payment of $15,000 and agreed to assume the seller's existing mortgage, which had a current balance of $23,000. The buyers financed the remaining $57,000 of the purchase price by executing a mortgage and note to the seller. This type of loan, by which the seller becomes the mortgagee, is called a
   a. wraparound mortgage.
   b. package mortgage.
   c. balloon note.
   d. purchase-money mortgage.

2. Tammy purchased a new residence for $175,000. She made a down payment of $15,000 and obtained a $160,000 mortgage loan. The builder of Tammy's house paid the lender 3 percent of the loan balance for the first year and 2 percent for the second year. This represented a total savings for Tammy of $8,000. What type of arrangement does this represent?
   a. Wraparound mortgage
   b. Package mortgage
   c. Blanket mortgage
   d. Buydown mortgage

3. Which of the following is not a participant in the secondary market?
   a. Fannie Mae
   b. Ginnie Mae
   c. RESPA
   d. Freddie Mac

4. Fatima purchased her home for cash 30 years ago. Today, Fatima receives monthly checks from the bank that supplement her income. Fatima most likely has obtained a(n)
   a. shared-appreciation mortgage.
   b. adjustable-rate mortgage.
   c. reverse-annuity mortgage.
   d. overriding deed of trust.

5. If buyers seek a mortgage on a single-family house, they would be LEAST likely to obtain the mortgage from a
   a. thrift.
   b. college endowment fund.
   c. credit union.
   d. commercial bank.

6. A purchaser obtains a fixed-rate loan to finance a home. Which of the following characteristics is TRUE of this type of loan?
   a. The amount of interest to be paid is predetermined.
   b. The loan cannot be sold in the secondary market.
   c. The monthly payment amount will fluctuate each month.
   d. The interest rate change may be based on an index.

7. When the Federal Reserve Board raises its discount rate, which is likely to happen?
   a. The buyer's points will decrease.
   b. Interest rates will rise.
   c. Mortgage money will become plentiful.
   d. The percentage of ARMs will decrease.

8. In a loan that requires periodic payments that do not fully amortize the loan balance by the final payment, what term BEST describes the final payment?
   a. Adjustment
   b. Acceleration
   c. Balloon
   d. Variable

9. A developer received a loan that covers five parcels of real estate and provides for the release of the mortgage lien on each parcel when certain payments are made on the loan. This type of loan arrangement is called a
   a. purchase-money loan.
   b. blanket loan.
   c. package loan.
   d. wraparound loan.

10. Funds for Federal Housing Administration loans are usually provided by
    a. the Federal Housing Administration.
    b. the Federal Reserve System.
    c. qualified lenders.
    d. the seller.

11. Under the provisions of the Truth-in-Lending Act (Regulation Z), the annual percentage rate (APR) of a finance charge includes which component?
    a. Mortgage principal
    b. Discount points
    c. Real estate taxes
    d. Property insurance

12. A home is purchased using a fixed-rate, fully amortized mortgage loan. Which of the following statements is *TRUE* regarding this mortgage?
    a. A balloon payment will be made at the end of the loan.
    b. Each payment amount is the same.
    c. Each payment reduces the principal by the same amount.
    d. The principal amount in each payment is greater than the interest amount.

13. Which of the following best defines the secondary market?
    a. Lenders who deal exclusively in second mortgages
    b. Where loans are bought and sold after they have been originated
    c. The major lender of residential mortgages and deeds of trust
    d. The major lender of FHA and VA loans

14. With a fully amortized mortgage or deed of trust loan
    a. interest may be charged in arrears—that is, at the end of each period for which interest is due.
    b. the interest portion of each payment increases throughout the term of the loan.
    c. interest only is paid each period.
    d. a portion of the principal will be owed after the last payment is made.

15. What does Freddie Mac do?
    a. Guarantees mortgages by the full faith and credit of the federal government
    b. Buys and pools blocks of conventional mortgages, selling bonds with such mortgages as security
    c. Acts in tandem with Ginnie Mae to provide special assistance in times of tight money
    d. Buys and sells VA and FHA mortgages

16. A borrower obtains a $100,000 mortgage loan for 30 years at 7.5 percent interest. If the monthly payments of $902.77 are credited first to interest and then to principal, what will be the balance of the principal after the borrower makes the first payment?
    a. $99,772.00
    b. $99,722.23
    c. $99,097.32
    d. $100,000.00

17. Using Table 16.2 on page 312, what is the monthly interest rate factor required to amortize a loan at 8⅛, percent over a term of 25 years?
    a. 7.72
    b. 7.81
    c. 7.89
    d. 8.06

18. Using Table 16.2 on page 312, calculate the principal and interest payment necessary to amortize a loan of $135,000 at 7¾ percent interest over 15 years.
    a. $1,111.85
    b. $1,270.35
    c. $1,279.80
    d. $1,639.16

19. Henry borrowed $85,000, to be repaid in monthly installments of $823.76 at 11½ percent annual interest. How much of Henry's first month's payment was applied to reducing the principal amount of the loan?
    a. $8.15
    b. $9.18
    c. $91.80
    d. $814.58

20. If a lender agrees to make a loan based on an 80 percent LTV, what is the amount of the loan if the property appraises for $114,500 and the sales price is $116,900?
    a. $83,200
    b. $91,300
    c. $91,600
    d. $92,900

21. A lender has agreed to negotiate a loan on the following terms: 90 percent of the first $50,000 of the appraised value, 95 percent of the next $25,000, and 97 percent of the remaining amount. If a property is appraised for $129,000, how much can he borrow?
    a. $118,750
    b. $120,121
    c. $120,380
    d. $121,130

22. A borrower wanted to negotiate a $113,000 loan. Different lenders in his town offered him the following loans. Which loan would he need to accept to pay the least amount of interest over the life of the loan?
    a. 7 percent amortized over a period of 30 years
    b. 8 percent amortized over a period of 20 years
    c. 9 percent amortized over a period of 15 years
    d. 10 percent amortized over a period of 25 years

23. The difference between the market value and any mortgages the borrower has on the property is BEST described by the word
    a. equity.
    b. equitable interest.
    c. equitable title.
    d. equitable lien.

24. Which law requires that all advertising that references mortgage financing terms contain certain disclosures?
    a. Equal Credit Opportunity Act
    b. Truth-in-Lending Act (Regulation Z)
    c. Community Reinvestment Act
    d. Fair Housing Act

25. Which of the following is NOT associated with a mortgage/note?
    a. Alienation clause/acceleration clause
    b. Pledge of property/evidence of debt
    c. Hypothecation/annual percentage rate
    d. Defeasible fee/indefeasible fee

26. Which statement is TRUE regarding Truth-in-lending (Regulation Z)?
    a. Finance charges that must be disclosed include loan fees, service charges, and discount points.
    b. If a borrower is refinancing, Regulation Z states that the borrower has five days to rescind the transaction by merely notifying the lender.
    c. If an advertisement discloses the interest rate, then it has met Truth-in-Lending requirements.
    d. For the purposes of Regulation Z, a creditor is a person who extends consumer credit more than five times each year.

27. Which of the following does NOT act as a warehousing agency?
    a. Federal National Mortgage Association
    b. Federal Housing Administration
    c. Federal Home Loan Mortgage Corporation
    d. Government National Mortgage Association

28. In order to assist a prospective buyer who lacked a down payment on their property, Mr. and Mrs. Seller agreed to "take back paper" at the closing for a part of the purchase price. The document MOST LIKELY used would be a
    a. reverse annuity mortgage.
    b. package mortgage.
    c. purchase-money mortgage.
    d. shared appreciation mortgage.

CHAPTER 17

Leases

■ **LEARNING OBJECTIVES** *When you've finished reading this chapter, you should be able to*

■ **identify** the four types of leasehold estates.

■ **describe** the requirements and general conditions of a valid lease and how a lease may be discharged.

■ **explain** the rights of landlords and tenants in an eviction proceeding and the effect of protenant legislation and civil rights laws on the landlord-tenant relationship.

■ **distinguish** the various types of leases.

■ **define** the following *key terms:*

actual eviction	ground lease	net lease
assignment	holdover tenancy	percentage lease
cash rent	implied warranty of	rental-finding service
constructive eviction	habitability	reversionary right
estate at sufferance	lease	security deposit
estate at will	leasehold estate	sharecropping
estate for years	lease purchase	subleasing
estate from period to	lessee	triple-net lease
period	lessor	
gross lease	month-to-month tenancy	

■ LEASING REAL ESTATE

A **lease** is a contract between an owner of real estate, the **lessor,** and a tenant, the **lessee.** It is a contract to transfer the lessor's rights to exclusive possession and use of the property to the tenant for a specified period of time. The lease establishes the length of time the contract is to run and the amount the lessee is to pay for use of the property. Other rights and obligations of the parties may be set forth as well.

In effect, the lease agreement combines two contracts. It is a conveyance of an interest in the real estate and a contract to pay rent and assume other obligations. The lessor grants the lessee the right to occupy the real estate and use it for purposes stated in the lease. In return, the landlord receives payment for use of the premises and retains a **reversionary right** to possession after the lease term expires. The lessor's interest is called a *leased fee estate plus reversionary right.*

In Illinois

The statute of frauds in Illinois requires that lease agreements be in writing to be enforceable if they are for *more than one year.* The written rule also applies to leases for one year or less that will not be performed within one year of the contract date. Verbal leases for one year or less that *can* be performed within a year of their making are enforceable. Written leases always should be signed by both lessor and lessee. ■

■ LEASEHOLD ESTATES

A tenant's right to possess real estate for the term of the lease is called a **leasehold** (less-than-freehold) **estate.** A leasehold is generally considered personal property. Just as there are several types of freehold (ownership) estates, there are different kinds of leasehold estates. (See Figure 17.1.)

Estate for Years

An **estate** (tenancy) **for years** is a leasehold estate that continues for a *definite period of time.* That period may be years, months, weeks, or even days. An estate for years (sometimes referred to as an *estate for term*) always has specific starting and ending dates.

When the estate expires, the lessee is required to vacate the premises and surrender possession to the lessor. No notice is required to terminate the estate for years. This is because the lease agreement states a specific expiration date. *When the expiration date comes, the lease expires, and the tenant's rights are extinguished.*

Tenancy for years = Any definite period

If both parties agree, the estate for years may be terminated before the expiration date. Otherwise, neither party may terminate without showing that the lease agreement has been breached. Any extension of the tenancy requires that a new contract be negotiated.

As is characteristic of all leases, a tenancy for years gives the lessee the right to occupy and use the leased property according to the terms and covenants contained in the lease agreement. It must be remembered that a lessee has the right to use the premises for the entire lease term. That right is unaffected by the original

FIGURE   17.1

Leasehold Estates

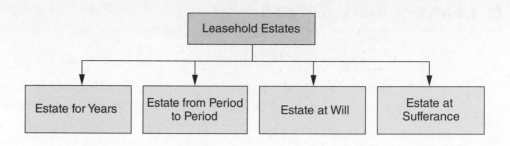

lessor's death or sale of the property unless the lease states otherwise. If the original lease provides for an option to renew, no further negotiation is required; the tenant merely exercises his or her option.

Estate from Period to Period

An **estate from period to period,** or *periodic tenancy*, is created when the landlord and tenant enter into an agreement for an indefinite time. That is, the lease does not contain a specific expiration date. Such a tenancy is created for a specific payment period—for instance, month to month, week to week, or year to year—but continues *indefinitely* until proper notice of termination is given. Rent is payable at *definite* intervals. A periodic tenancy is characterized by continuity because it is *automatically renewable under the original terms of the agreement until one of the parties gives notice to terminate.* In effect, the payment and acceptance of rent extend the lease for another period. A **month-to-month tenancy,** for example, is created when a tenant takes possession with no definite termination date and pays monthly rent.

If the original agreement provides for the conversion from an estate for years to a periodic tenancy, no negotiations are necessary; the tenant simply exercises his or her option.

> **Periodic tenancy =** *Indefinite term; automatically renewing*

An estate from period to period also might be created when a tenant with an estate for years remains in possession, or holds over, after the lease term expires. If no new lease agreement has been made, a **holdover tenancy** is created. The landlord may evict the tenant or treat the holdover tenant as one who holds a periodic tenancy. The landlord's acceptance of rent usually is considered conclusive proof of acceptance of the periodic tenancy. The courts customarily rule that a tenant who holds over can do so for a term equal to the term of the original lease, provided the period is for one year or less. For example, a tenant with a lease for six months would be entitled to a new six-month tenancy. However, if the original lease were for five years, the holdover tenancy could not exceed one year. Some leases stipulate that in the absence of a renewal agreement, a tenant who holds over does so as a month-to-month tenant.

> **In Illinois**

In Illinois, a holdover tenancy is for the same term as the estate from period to period. ■

To terminate a periodic estate, either the landlord or the tenant must give proper notice. The form and timing of the notice are usually established by state statute. Normally, the notice must be given *one period in advance.* That is, to terminate an estate from week to week, one week's notice is required; to terminate an estate from month to month, one month's notice is required. For an estate from year to year, however, the requirements vary from two to six months' notice.

In Illinois The following notices are required by Illinois statute:

- *Tenancy from year to year*—At least 60 days' written notice is required at any time within the four-month period prior to the last 60 days of the lease period.
- *Tenancy from month to month*—In any periodic estate having a term of less than year to year but greater than week to week, 30 days' written notice is required.
- *Tenancy from week to week*—Seven days' written notice is required.
- *Farm tenancies from year to year*—Parties must give at least four months' written notice to terminate and may do so only at the end of the period. To vacate March 1, farm tenancy notice must be given by November 1. ■

Estate at Will

An **estate** (tenancy) **at will** gives the tenant the right to possess property *with the landlord's consent* for an unspecified or uncertain term. *An estate at will is a tenancy of indefinite duration.* It continues until it is terminated by either party's giving proper notice. No definite initial period is specified, as is the case in a periodic tenancy. An estate at will is automatically terminated by the death of either the landlord or the tenant. It may be created by express agreement or by operation of law. During the existence of a tenancy at will, the tenant has all the rights and obligations of a lessor-lessee relationship, including the duty to pay rent at regular intervals.

> **Tenancy at will** = *Indefinite term; possession with landord's consent*

As a practical matter, tenancy at will is rarely used in a written agreement and is viewed skeptically by the courts. It is usually interpreted as a periodic tenancy, with the period being defined by the interval of rental payments.

Estate at Sufferance

An **estate** (tenancy) **at sufferance** arises when a tenant who lawfully possessed real property continues in possession of the premises *without the landlord's consent* after the rights expire. This estate can arise when a tenant for years fails to surrender possession at the lease's expiration or when a tenant is in breach of the lease. A tenancy at sufferance also can occur by operation of law when a borrower continues in possession after a foreclosure sale and beyond the redemption period's expiration.

> **Tenancy at sufferance** = *Tenant's previously lawful possession continued without landlord's consent*

In Illinois A landlord has the option of considering a holdover tenant's action as being a *willful withholding of possession*, in which case the landlord is entitled to charge double rent. ■

■ LEASE AGREEMENTS

Most states require no special wording to establish the landlord-tenant relationship. The lease may be written, oral, or implied, depending on the circumstances and the requirements of the statute of frauds. The law of the state where the real estate is located must be followed to ensure the validity of the lease.

Requirements of a Valid Lease

A lease is a form of contract. To be valid, a lease must meet essentially the same requirements as any other contract:

■ *Capacity to contract*—The parties must have the legal capacity to contract.
■ *Legal objectives*—The objectives of the lease must be legal.
■ *Offer and acceptance*—The parties must reach a mutual agreement on all the terms of the contract.
■ *Consideration*—The lease must be supported by valid consideration. Rent is the normal consideration given for the right to occupy the leased premises. However, the payment of rent is not essential as long as consideration was granted in creating the lease itself. Sometimes, for instance, this consideration is labor performed on the property. Because a lease is a contract, it is not subject to subsequent changes in the rent or other terms unless these changes are in writing and executed in the same manner as the original lease.

> The elements of a valid lease can be remembered by the acronym **CLOAC:** *Capacity, Legal objective, Offer and Acceptance, and Consideration*

The leased premises should be clearly described. The legal description of the real estate should be used if the lease covers land, such as a ground lease. If the lease is for a part of a building, such as an apartment, the space itself or the apartment designation should be described specifically. If supplemental space is to be included, the lease should clearly identify it.

IN PRACTICE

Preprinted lease agreements are usually better suited to residential leases. Commercial leases are generally more complex, have different legal requirements, and may include complicated calculations of rent and maintenance costs. Drafting a commercial lease or a complex residential lease should be done by a licensed attorney.

Possession of Premises

The lessor, as the owner of the real estate, is usually bound by the implied covenant of quiet enjoyment. Quiet enjoyment does not have anything to do with barking dogs or late-night motorcycles. The covenant of quiet enjoyment is a presumed promise by the lessor that the lessee may take possession of the premises. The landlord further guarantees that he or she will not interfere in the tenant's possession or use of the property.

The lease may allow the landlord to enter the property to perform maintenance, to make repairs, or for other stated purposes. The tenant's permission is usually required.

If the premises are occupied by a holdover tenant or an adverse claimant at the beginning of the new lease period, most states require that the landlord take whatever measures are necessary to recover actual possession. In a few states, however, the landlord is bound to give the tenant only the right of possession; it is the tenant who must bring a court action to secure actual possession.

Use of Premises

A lessor may restrict a lessee's use of the premises through provisions included in the lease.

Use restrictions are particularly common in leases for stores or commercial space. For example, a lease may provide that the leased premises are to be used "only as a real estate office and for no other purpose." In the absence of such clear limitations, a lessee may use the premises for any lawful purpose.

Term of Lease

The term of a lease is the period for which the lease will run. It should be stated precisely, including the beginning and ending dates, together with a statement of the total period of the lease. For instance, a lease might run "for a term of 30 years beginning June 1, 2008, and ending May 31, 2038." A perpetual lease for an inordinate amount of time or an indefinite term usually will be ruled invalid. However, if the language of the lease and the surrounding circumstances clearly indicate that the parties intended such a term, the lease will be binding on the parties. Some states prohibit leases that run for 100 years or more.

Security Deposit

Most leases require that the tenant provide some form of **security deposit** to be held by the landlord during the lease term. If the tenant defaults on payment of rent or destroys the premises, the lessor may keep all or part of the deposit to compensate for the loss. Some state laws set maximum amounts for security deposits and specify how they must be handled. Some prohibit security deposits from being used for both nonpayment of rent and property damage. Some require that lessees receive annual interest on their security deposits.

Other safeguards against nonpayment of rent may include an advance rental payment, contracting for a lien on the tenant's property, or requiring that the tenant have a third person guarantee payment.

In Illinois

Landlords who receive security deposits on residential leases of units in properties containing *five or more units* may not withhold any part of a security deposit as compensation for property damage unless they give the tenant an itemized statement listing the alleged damage. This statement must be delivered within 30 days of the date on which the premises are vacated, and copies of repair receipts must be furnished 30 days after the statement is delivered. If the statement or receipts are not furnished, the landlord must return the entire security deposit within 45 days of the premises being vacated. Any landlord who is found by a court to have failed to comply with these requirements, or who has done so in bad faith, must pay the tenant double the security deposit due plus court costs and attorney's fees.

Illinois lessees are entitled to receive annual interest on their security deposits. Landlords who receive security deposits on residential leases of units in properties of 25 or more units, on deposits held for more than six months, are required to pay interest from the date of the deposit at a rate equal to the interest paid on a minimum deposit passbook savings account of the state's largest commercial bank (measured by total assets) with its main banking facilities located in Illinois. Any landlord who is found by a court to have willfully withheld interest on a tenant's security deposit must pay the tenant an amount equal to the security deposit plus the tenant's court costs and attorney's fees. Professional property managers must put security deposits in special escrow accounts. ■

IN PRACTICE

A lease should specify whether a payment is a security deposit or an advance rental. If it is a security deposit, the tenant is usually not entitled to apply it to the final month's rent. If it is an advance rental, the landlord must treat it as income for tax purposes.

Improvements

Neither the landlord nor the tenant is required to make any improvements to the leased property. The tenant may, however, make improvements with the landlord's permission. Any alterations generally become the landlord's property; that is, they become fixtures. However, the lease may give the tenant the right to install trade fixtures. Trade fixtures may be removed before the lease expires, provided the tenant restores the premises to their previous condition, with allowance for the wear and tear of normal use.

Accessibility.   The federal *Fair Housing Act* makes it illegal to discriminate against prospective tenants on the basis of physical disability. Tenants with disabilities must be permitted to make reasonable modifications to a property at their own expense. However, if the modifications would interfere with a future tenant's use, the landlord may require that the premises be restored to their original condition at the end of the lease term.

IN   PRACTICE

The *Americans with Disabilities Act* (ADA) applies to commercial, nonresidential property in which public goods or services are provided. The ADA requires that such properties either be free of architectural barriers or provide reasonable accommodations for people with disabilities.

Maintenance of Premises

Many states require that a residential lessor maintain dwelling units in a habitable condition. Landlords must make any necessary repairs to common areas such as hallways, stairs, and elevators, and they must maintain safety features such as fire sprinklers and smoke alarms. The tenant does not have to make any repairs but must return the premises in the same condition they were received, with allowances for ordinary wear and tear.

In Illinois

The Illinois Supreme Court first confirmed the concept of an **implied warranty of habitability** in residential tenancies in 1972. Since then, Illinois courts have repeatedly confirmed and amplified the warranty. A landlord must deliver and maintain any residential leasehold free from defects that would render the use of the dwelling "unsafe or unsanitary" and unfit for human occupancy. Nothing may be present on the premises that could seriously endanger the life, health, or safety of the tenant.

There are no precisely defined standards; each alleged breach is considered on a case-by-case basis. Not every little defect constitutes a breach of the implied warranty of habitability. A tenant must give the landlord notice of the defect and reasonable time in which to cure it. As a remedy, the tenant may choose to

- move out,
- stay and repair the problem himself or herself, or
- terminate the tenancy and claim constructive eviction (discussed later in this chapter).

The tenant may sue for any damages resulting from the defective condition. Damages are measured by the decreased rental value of the premises due to the defect or by the reasonable cost incurred to repair the deficiency. The tenant also may use the breach as a defense to a *suit for possession* brought by the landlord. ■

Destruction of Premises

In leases involving agricultural land, the courts have held that when improvements are damaged or destroyed, the tenant is obligated to pay rent to the end of the term. The tenant's liability does not depend on whether the damage was his or her fault. This ruling has been extended in most states to include ground leases for land on which the tenant has constructed a building. In many instances, it also includes leases that give possession of an entire building to the tenant. In this

F I G U R E **17.2**

Assignment versus Subletting

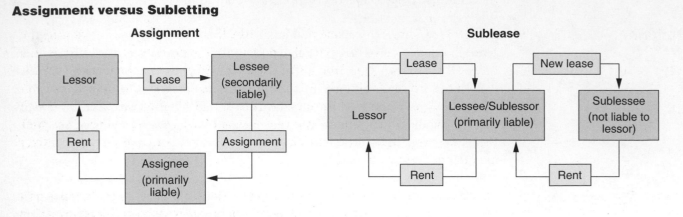

case, the tenant leases the land on which that building is located, as well as the structure itself. Insurance is available to cover such contingencies.

A tenant who leases only *part of a building*, such as office or commercial space or a residential apartment, is not required to continue to pay rent after the leased premises are destroyed. In some states, if the property was destroyed as a result of the landlord's negligence, the tenant can even recover damages.

Assignment and Subleasing

When a tenant transfers all of his or her leasehold interests to another person, the lease has been *assigned*. On the other hand, when a tenant transfers less than all the leasehold interests by leasing them to a new tenant, he or she has **subleased** (or sublet) the property. **Assignment** and **subleasing** are permitted whenever a lease does not prohibit them.

In most cases, the sublease or assignment of a lease does not relieve the original lessee of the obligation to pay rent. The landlord may, however, agree to waive the former tenant's liability. Most leases prohibit a lessee from assigning or subletting without the lessor's consent. This permits the lessor to retain control over the occupancy of the leased premises. As a rule, the lessor must not unreasonably withhold consent. The sublessor's (original lessee's) interest in the real estate is known as a *sandwich lease*. (See Figure 17.2.)

Recording a Lease

Possession of leased premises is considered constructive notice to the world of the lessee's leasehold interests. Anyone who inspects the property receives actual notice. For these reasons, it is usually considered unnecessary to record a lease. However, most states do allow a lease to be recorded in the county in which the property is located. Furthermore, leases of three years or longer often are recorded as a matter of course. Some states require that long-term leases be recorded, especially when the lessee intends to mortgage the leasehold interest.

In some states, only a memorandum of lease is filed. A *memorandum of lease* gives notice of the interest but does not disclose the terms of the lease. Only the names of the parties and a description of the property are included.

Creditors of the property owner and purchasers who do not have actual notice of a leasehold interest are considered to have legal notice of a lease if the lease, or a memorandum of it, is recorded with the recorder or registrar of the county in which the property is located.

Options

A lease may contain an *option* that grants the lessee the privilege of renewing the lease. The lessee must, however, give notice of his or her intention to exercise the option. Some leases grant the lessee the option to purchase the leased premises. This option normally allows the tenant the right to purchase the property at a predetermined price within a certain time period, possibly the lease term. Although it is not required, the owner may give the tenant credit toward the purchase price for some percentage of the rent paid. The lease agreement is a primary contract over the option to purchase.

IN   PRACTICE

All of these general statements concerning provisions of a lease are controlled largely by the terms of the agreement and state law. Great care must be exercised in reading the entire lease document before signing it because every clause in the lease has an economic and a legal impact on either the landlord or the tenant. While preprinted lease forms are available, there is no such thing as a standard lease. When complicated lease situations arise, legal counsel should be sought.

■ TYPES OF LEASES

The manner in which rent is determined indicates the type of lease that exists. (See Table 17.1.)

Gross Lease

In a **gross lease**, the tenant pays a fixed rent, and the landlord pays all taxes, insurance, repairs, utilities, and the like connected with the property (usually called *property charges* or *operating expenses*). This is typically the type of rent structure involved in apartment rentals.

Net Lease

In a **net lease,** the tenant pays *all or some of the property charges* in addition to the rent. Leases for entire commercial or industrial buildings and the land on which they are located, ground leases, and long-term leases, are usually net leases.

In a **triple-net lease,** or *net-net-net lease*, the tenant pays *all operating and other expenses* in addition to rent. These expenses include taxes, insurance, assessments, maintenance, utilities, and other charges related to the premises.

Percentage Lease

Either a gross lease or a net lease may be a **percentage lease.** The rent is based on a minimum fixed rental fee plus a *percentage of the gross income received by the tenant doing business on the leased property*. This type of lease is usually used for retail businesses and restaurants. The percentage charged is negotiable and varies depending on the nature of the business, the location of the property, and general economic conditions.

Variable Lease

Several types of leases allow for increases in the rental charges during the lease periods. One of the more common is the *graduated lease*. A **graduated lease** provides for specified rent increases at set future dates. Another is the **index lease** that allows rent to be increased or decreased periodically, based on changes in the consumer price index or some other indicator.

TABLE 17.1

Types of Leases

Type of Lease	Lessee
Gross lease	Pays basic rent
Net lease	Pays basic rent plus all or some property charges
Percentage lease	Pays basic rent plus percent of gross sales (may pay property charges)

Ground Lease

When a landowner leases unimproved land to a tenant who agrees to erect a building on the land, the lease is usually referred to as a **ground lease**. Ground leases usually involve *separate ownership of the land and buildings*. These leases must be for a long enough term to make the transaction desirable to the tenant investing in the building. They often run for terms of 50 years up to 99 years. Ground leases are generally net leases. The lessee must pay rent on the ground, as well as real estate taxes, insurance, upkeep, and repairs.

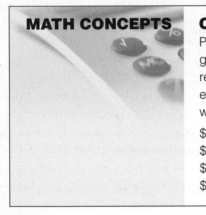

MATH CONCEPTS

CALCULATING PERCENTAGE LEASE RENTS

Percentage leases usually call for a minimum monthly rent plus a percentage of gross sales income exceeding a stated annual amount. For example, a lease might require minimum rent of $1,300 per month plus 5 percent of the business's sales exceeding $160,000. On an annual sales volume of $250,000, the annual rent would be calculated as follows:

$1,300 per month	× 12 months	=	$15,600
$250,000	− $160,000	=	$90,000
$90,000	× .05 (5%)	=	$4,500
$15,600 base rent	+ $4,500 percentage rent	=	$20,100 total rent

Oil and Gas Lease

When an oil company leases land to explore for oil and gas, a special lease agreement must be negotiated. Usually, the landowner receives a cash payment for executing the lease. If no well is drilled within the period stated in the lease, the lease expires. However, most oil and gas leases permit the oil company to continue its rights for another year by paying another flat rental fee. Such rentals may be paid annually until a well is produced. If oil or gas is found, the landowner usually receives a percentage of its value as a royalty. As long as oil or gas is obtained in significant quantities, the lease continues indefinitely.

Lease Purchase

A **lease purchase** is used when a tenant wants to purchase the property, but is unable to do so. Perhaps the tenant cannot obtain favorable financing or clear title, or the tax consequences of a current purchase would be unfavorable. In this arrangement, the purchase agreement is the primary consideration, and the lease is secondary. Part of the periodic rent is applied toward the purchase price of the property until that price is reduced to an amount for which the tenant can obtain financing or purchase the property outright, depending on the terms of the lease-purchase agreement.

Agricultural landowners often lease their land to tenant farmers, who provide the labor to produce and bring in the crop. An owner can be paid by a tenant in one of two ways: as an agreed-on rental amount in cash in advance, **cash rents,** or as a percentage of the profits from the sale of the crop when it is sold, **sharecropping.** (Any losses would be split as well.)

■ DISCHARGE OF LEASES

As with any contract, a lease is discharged when the contract terminates. Termination can occur when all parties have fully performed their obligations under the agreement. In addition, the parties may agree to cancel the lease. If the tenant, for instance, offers to surrender the leasehold interest and the landlord accepts the tenant's offer, the lease is terminated. A tenant who simply abandons leased property remains liable for the terms of the lease—including the rent. The terms of the lease will usually indicate whether the landlord is obligated to try to rerent the space. If the landlord intends to sue for unpaid rent, most states require an attempt to mitigate damages by rerenting the premises to limit the amount owed.

The lease does not terminate if the parties die or if the property is sold. *There are two exceptions to this general rule:*

1. A lease from the owner of a *life estate* ends when the life tenant dies.
2. The death of either party terminates a *tenancy at will.*

If leased real estate is sold or otherwise conveyed, the new landlord takes the property subject to the rights of the tenants. A lease agreement may, however, contain language that permits a new landlord to terminate existing leases. The clause, commonly known as a *sale clause,* requires that the tenants be given some period of notice before the termination. Because the new owner has taken title subject to the rights of the tenants, the sale clause enables the new landlord to claim possession and negotiate new leases under his or her own terms and conditions.

A tenancy may also be terminated by operation of law, as in a bankruptcy or condemnation proceeding.

Breach of Lease

When a tenant breaches any lease provision, the landlord may sue the tenant to obtain a judgment to cover past-due rent, damages to the premises, or other defaults. Likewise, when a landlord breaches any lease provision, the tenant is entitled to certain remedies. The rights and responsibilities of the landlord-tenant relationship are usually governed by state law.

If a tenant defaults on the payment of rent, the landlord has two options:

1. He or she may elect to serve the tenant with five days' written notice, demanding payment of the delinquent rent within five days after the notice is received. If the tenant fails to pay the rent, the landlord may terminate the lease automatically and sue for possession without further notice. *If the tenant pays the past-due rent, the lease continues in full force.*
2. Alternatively (and in cases in which the tenant's breach is other than nonpayment of rent), the landlord may terminate the tenancy by serving the tenant with ten days' written notice, including a demand for possession. After the ten-day period expires, the landlord may sue for possession without further notice, *even if the default is cured.*

Landlord's remedies—actual eviction. When a tenant breaches a lease or improperly retains leased premises, the landlord may regain possession through a legal process known as **actual eviction.** The landlord must serve notice on the tenant before commencing the lawsuit. Most lease terms require at least a ten-day notice in the case of default. In many states, however, only a five-day notice is necessary when the tenant defaults in the payment of rent. When a court issues a judgment for possession to a landlord, the tenant must vacate the property. If the tenant fails to leave, the landlord can have the judgment enforced by a court officer, who forcibly removes the tenant and the tenant's possessions. The landlord then has the right to re-enter and regain possession of the property.

| In Illinois | In Illinois, a landlord seeking actual eviction of a tenant must file an action called a *forcible entry and detainer*. It can be used when a tenancy has expired by default, by its terms, by operation of law, or by proper notice. The suit should be filed in the circuit court of the county in which the property is located. |

In Illinois, a landlord seeking actual eviction of a tenant must file an action called a *forcible entry and detainer*. It can be used when a tenancy has expired by default, by its terms, by operation of law, or by proper notice. The suit should be filed in the circuit court of the county in which the property is located.

If the court rules in favor of the landlord, a *judgment for possession* (and money damages) will be entered, and an *order of possession* will be issued by the clerk of the court. The tenant must then leave peaceably, removing all of his or her property from the premises. Traditionally, however, if a residential tenant personally appears in court and the landlord prevails, the court will delay issuing the order for a reasonable period of time, to allow the tenant to find alternative housing.

When a tenant refuses to vacate peaceably after a judgment for possession has been entered, the landlord must deliver the order to the sheriff, who will forcibly evict the tenant. The landlord then has the right to re-enter and regain possession of the property.

Until a judgment for possession is issued, the landlord must be careful not to harass the tenant in any manner, such as locking the tenant out of the property, impounding the tenant's possessions, or disconnecting the unit's utilities (such as electricity and natural gas). Illinois landlords have no right to *self-help*; that is, they may not forcibly remove a tenant without following the proper legal procedures. ∎

Tenants' remedies—constructive eviction. If a landlord breaches any clause of a lease agreement, the tenant has the right to sue and recover damages against the landlord. If the leased premises become unusable for the purpose stated in the lease, the tenant may have the right to abandon them. This action, called **constructive eviction,** terminates the lease agreement. The tenant must prove that the premises have become unusable because of the conscious neglect of the landlord. To claim constructive eviction, the tenant must leave the premises while the conditions that made the premises uninhabitable exist.

■ CIVIL RIGHTS LAWS

The fair housing laws affect landlords and tenants just as they do sellers and purchasers. All persons must have access to housing of their choice without any differentiation in the terms and conditions because of their race, color, religion, familial status (the presence of children under the age of 18), disability, or gender. State and local municipalities may have their own fair housing laws that add protected classes such as age and sexual orientation. Withholding an apartment that is available for rent, segregating certain persons in separate sections of an apartment complex or parts of a building, and charging different amounts for rent or security deposits to persons in the protected classes all constitute violations of the law.

| In Illinois |

The *Illinois Human Rights Act* extends the list of protected classes for Illinois. It states as the public policy of Illinois and purpose of the act: "Freedom from unlawful discrimination. To secure for all individuals within Illinois the freedom from discrimination against an individual because of his or her race, color, religion, sex, national origin, ancestry, age, marital status, physical or mental disability, familial status, military status, unfavorable discharge from military service, or sexual orientation and/or preference in connection with employment, real estate transactions, access to financial credit, and the availability of public accommodations." Article 3 of this act deals with real estate transactions. ■

■ LEAD-BASED PAINT

The 1996 federal *Lead-Based Paint Hazard Reduction Act—Title X* focused more strongly on disclosure and REALTOR® liability. This federal law supersedes any state laws that are not as strong. Real estate agents leasing properties built before 1978 must ensure that landlords disclose any possible lead-based paint or related hazards. *This disclosure form must be completed even in the case of an oral lease agreement.* Once an offer for lease is received, the agent representing the lessor (landlord) must make certain a completed *Disclosure of Information* (from landlord) and *Acknowledgment Form* (from tenant) are attached, showing that the disclosure requirements were met. Finally, a federal lead hazard information pamphlet, obtained through the *National Lead Information Clearinghouse* at 800-526-5456 must be distributed before leasing the property.

| In Illinois |

The *Illinois Lead Poisoning Prevention Act* requires that the owner of any residential building cited by the state as a lead paint hazard give prospective tenants written notice of the danger unless the owners have a certificate of compliance. This act is bolstered in its scope by the federal legislation noted earlier. When a *mitigation order* is issued to an owner of a building containing lead hazards, the owner has 90 days to eliminate the hazard in a manner prescribed by state law, or 30 days if occupied by a child under age six or by a pregnant woman. ■

■ REGULATION OF THE RENTAL INDUSTRY

Rental-Finding Services

Because of the nationwide demand for rental housing, caused in part by the increased mobility of the U.S. population, there has been a rapid growth in the rental-finding service industry.

| In Illinois |

A **rental-finding service** is any business that finds, attempts to find, or offers to find for any person for consideration a unit of rental real estate or a lessee for a unit of rental real estate not owned or leased by the business. Any person or business entity that operates a rental-finding service must obtain a real estate license and comply with all provisions of the *Illinois Real Estate License Act of 2000*. General-circulation newspapers that advertise rental property and listing contracts between owners or lessors of real estate and registrants are exempt from this requirement.

Rental-finding services are required to enter into written contracts with the parties for whom their services are to be performed. The contract must clearly disclose

- the term of the contract;
- the total amount to be paid for the services;
- the service's policy regarding the refunding of fees paid in advance, and the conditions under which refunds may or may not be paid (printed in a larger typeface than the rest of the contract);
- the type of rental unit, geographic area, and price range the prospective tenant desires;
- a detailed statement of the services to be performed;
- a statement that the contract shall be void, and all fees paid in advance shall be refunded, if the information provided regarding possible rental units available is not current or accurate (that is, if a rental unit is listed that has not been available for more than two days); and
- a disclosure that information regarding possible rental units may be up to two days old.

With regard to any individual rental unit, a prospective tenant must be provided with the name, address, and telephone number of the owner; a description of the unit, monthly rent, and security deposit required; a description of the utilities available and included in the rent; the occupancy date and lease term; a statement describing the source of the information; and any other information the prospective tenant may reasonably be expected to need.

A rental-finding service may not list or advertise any rental unit without the express written authority of the unit's owner or agent.

A licensee who violates any of these requirements will be construed to have demonstrated unworthiness or incompetence and will be subject to the appropriate disciplinary measures.

Leasing Agents

The *Illinois Real Estate License Act of 2000* (Section 5-5 through Section 5-10) provides for a limited-scope license for individuals who wish to engage *solely* in activities related to the leasing of residential real property. For instance, the following activities would appropriately fall under this limited license, if the licensee did not engage in any other real estate activities (such as marketing single-family homes):

- Leasing or renting residential real property
- Collecting rent for residential real property
- Attempting, offering, or negotiating to lease, rent, or collect rent for the use of residential real property

The act establishes specific qualifications and educational requirements for leasing agents, including a written examination. (See Chapter 14 for requirements.)

Referral Fees

The *Illinois Real Estate License Act of 2000* (Section 5-5 through Section 5-10) allows landlords to pay a referral fee to tenants. A resident tenant of a unit who refers a prospective tenant for a unit in the same building or complex may be paid a referral fee if he or she

1. refers no more than three prospective lessees in any 12-month period;
2. receives compensation of no more than $1,000 or the equivalent of one month's rent, whichever is less, for any 12-month period; and
3. limits his or her activities to referring prospective lessees to the owner (or the owner's agent) and does not show units, discuss lease terms, or otherwise participate in the negotiation of a lease. ∎

■ SUMMARY

A lease is an agreement that grants one person the right to use the property of another in return for consideration.

A leasehold estate that runs for a specific length of time creates an estate for years; one that runs for an indefinite period creates an estate from period to period (year to year, month to month). An estate at will runs as long as the landlord permits; and an estate at sufferance is possession without the consent of the landlord. A leasehold estate is classified as a personal property interest.

The requirements of a valid lease include capacity to contract, legal objectives, offer and acceptance, and consideration. In addition, state statutes of frauds generally require that any lease that will not be completed within one year of the date of its making must be in writing to be enforceable in court. Most leases also include clauses relating to rights and obligations of the landlord and tenant, such as the use of the premises, subletting, judgments, maintenance of the premises, and termination of the lease period.

A lease may be terminated by the expiration of the lease period, the mutual agreement of the parties, or a breach of the lease by either the landlord or tenant. In most cases, neither the death of the tenant nor the landlord's sale of the rental property terminates a lease.

If a tenant defaults on any lease provision, the landlord may sue for a money judgment, actual eviction, or both. If the premises have become uninhabitable due to the landlord's negligence or failure to correct within a reasonable time, the tenant may have the remedy of constructive eviction—that is, the right to abandon the premises and refuse to pay rent until the premises are repaired.

The rental industry is highly regulated. The fair housing laws protect the rights of tenants. Besides prohibiting discrimination based on race, color, religion, familial status, national origin, and sex, the laws address the rights of individuals with disabilities and families with children.

In Illinois

The Illinois *Real Estate License Act of 2000* (Section 5-5 through Section 5-10) provides for a limited-scope license for individuals who wish to engage solely in activities related to the leasing of residential real property. Article 5 contains particulars on the leasing agent license.

The *Illinois Human Rights Act* defines fair housing in this state as including freedom from discrimination against an individual due to race, color, religion, sex, national origin, ancestry, age, marital status, physical or mental disability, familial status, military status, unfavorable discharge from military service, or sexual orientation and/or preference in connection with employment, real estate transactions, access to financial credit, and the availability of public accommodations.

The Illinois *Statute of Frauds* requires that leases for more than one year or that cannot be performed within one year be in writing to be enforceable. Oral leases for less than one year are enforceable. Illinois law establishes specific notice requirements for termination of leases and for the withholding or payment of interest on security deposits. Lead-based-paint laws are strictly enforced in Illinois. Even a short oral lease requires that a lead-paint disclosure be supplied. ∎

QUESTIONS

1. A ground lease is usually
   a. short term.
   b. for 100 years or longer.
   c. long term.
   d. a gross lease.

2. Jane and Yolanda enter into a commercial lease that requires a monthly rent based on a minimum set amount plus an additional amount determined by the tenant's gross receipts exceeding $5,000. This type of lease is called a
   a. standard lease.
   b. gross lease.
   c. percentage lease.
   d. net lease.

3. If a tenant moved out of a rented store building because access to the building was blocked as a result of the landlord's negligence
   a. the tenant would have no legal recourse against the landlord.
   b. the landlord would be liable for the rent until the expiration date of the lease.
   c. the landlord would have to provide substitute space.
   d. the tenant would be entitled to recover damages from the landlord.

4. In June, Vince signs a one-year lease and moves into Streetview Apartments. Vince deposits the required security deposit with the landlord. Six months later, Vince pays the January rent and mysteriously moves out. Vince does not arrange for a sublease or an assignment and makes no further rent payments. The apartment is still in good condition. What is Vince's liability to the landlord in these circumstances?
   a. Because half the rental amount has been paid and the apartment is in good condition, Vince has no further liability.
   b. Vince is liable for the balance of the rent, plus forfeiture of the security deposit.
   c. Vince is liable for the balance of the rent only.
   d. Vince is liable for the balance of the rent, plus the security deposit and any marketing costs the landlord incurs.

5. Katy still has five months remaining on a one-year apartment lease. When Katy moves to another city, she transfers possession of the apartment to Lynn for the entire remaining term of the lease. Lynn pays rent directly to Katy. Under these facts, Katy is a(n)
   a. assignor.
   b. sublessor.
   c. sublessee.
   d. lessor.

6. A tenant's lease has expired. The tenant has neither vacated nor negotiated a renewal lease, and the landlord has declared that she does not want the tenant to remain in the building. This form of possession is called a(n)
   a. estate for years.
   b. periodic estate.
   c. estate at will.
   d. estate at sufferance.

7. Phil's tenancy for years will expire in two weeks. Phil plans to move to a larger apartment across town when the current tenancy expires. What must Phil do to terminate this agreement?
   a. Phil must give the landlord two weeks' prior notice.
   b. Phil must give the landlord one week's prior notice.
   c. Phil needs to do nothing; the agreement will terminate automatically.
   d. The agreement will terminate only after Phil signs a lease for the new apartment.

8. When a tenant holds possession of a landlord's property without a current lease agreement and without the landlord's approval
   a. the tenant is maintaining a gross lease.
   b. the landlord can file suit for possession.
   c. the tenant has no obligation to pay rent.
   d. the landlord may be subject to a constructive eviction.

9. Under the terms of a residential lease, the lessor is required to maintain the water heater. If a lessee is unable to get hot water because of a faulty water heater that the lessor has failed to repair, which remedy would be available to the lessee?
   a. Suing the tenant for damages
   b. Abandoning the premises under constructive eviction
   c. Refunding the tenant back rent
   d. Assigning the lease agreement

10. Jon has a one-year leasehold interest in Blackacre. The interest automatically renews itself at the end of each year. Jon's interest is referred to as a tenancy
    a. for years.
    b. from period to period.
    c. at will.
    d. at sufferance.

11. Which of the following describes a net lease?
    a. An agreement in which the tenant pays a fixed rent and the landlord pays all taxes, insurance, and other charges on the property
    b. A lease in which the tenant pays rent plus maintenance and property charges
    c. A lease in which the tenant pays the landlord a percentage of the monthly profits derived from the tenant's commercial use of the property
    d. A lease-purchase agreement in which the landlord agrees to apply part of the monthly rent toward the ultimate purchase price of the property

12. A tenancy in which the tenant continues in possession after the lease has expired, with the landlord's permission, is a tenancy
    a. for years.
    b. by the entireties.
    c. at will.
    d. at sufferance.

13. A commercial lease calls for a minimum rent of $1,200 per month plus 4 percent of the annual gross business exceeding $150,000. If the total rent paid at the end of one year was $19,200, how much business did the tenant do during the year?
    a. $159,800
    b. $250,200
    c. $270,000
    d. $279,200

14. Which of the following would be associated with leases?
    a. Joint tenancy
    b. Tenancy in common
    c. Estate for years
    d. Community possession

In Illinois

15. In Illinois, which of the following statements is true regarding a lease for more than one year?
    a. The lease must be in writing and signed to be enforceable in court.
    b. The lease must include a provision for interest to be paid on all security deposits.
    c. The lease must be recorded to give actual notice of the resident tenant's right of possession.
    d. The lease may be terminated only by written notice to the tenant, even if it contains a definite expiration date.

16. Tami rents an apartment in a 100-unit high-rise in Chicago for $900 per month. Tami decides to move when she learns that her rent will be raised by 25 percent at the expiration of her one-year lease. When she moved in, Tami deposited $1,200 as a security deposit. How will the interest paid on Tami's deposit be determined?

    a. The interest paid should be based on the prime rate as of December 31 of the calendar year preceding the rental agreement.

    b. The interest paid should be 5 percent per year, from the date of deposit.

    c. The interest rate should be computed at a rate equal to that paid on a minimum deposit passbook savings account at the state's largest commercial bank.

    d. Under these facts, Tami is not entitled to receive interest on her security deposit.

17. How many days' advance notice is required to terminate a month-to-month tenancy in Illinois?

    a. 5
    b. 15
    c. 30
    d. 60

18. Ursula, who owns a 20-unit apartment building in Decatur, Illinois, has held tenant Jerry's security deposit for three months. Jerry, who is on a month-to-month lease, informs Ursula that he will be vacating the apartment in 30 days. Based on these facts, which of the following statements is *TRUE*?

    a. Ursula must pay Jerry four months' interest on the security deposit.

    b. Ursula owes Jerry no interest on the security deposit.

    c. Jerry is entitled to three months' interest on the security deposit.

    d. If Jerry vacates the premises in these circumstances, Ursula is entitled to retain the security deposit as statutory damages.

19. Chuck has a one-year lease on an apartment in Chicago. If Chuck fails to pay his rent when it is due, the landlord may

    a. serve notice on Chuck to pay the delinquent rent within five days.

    b. terminate Chuck's lease without notice when the rent is more than ten days past due.

    c. hire a moving company to remove Chuck's furniture and personal property from the premises.

    d. serve notice on Chuck to pay the rent within five days and proceed with a suit for possession regardless of whether or not Chuck pays the past-due rent.

20. In Illinois, a landlord must give a tenant at least 60 days' written notice to terminate which of the following tenancies?

    a. Tenancy at will
    b. Tenancy for years
    c. Tenancy from year to year
    d. Tenancy at sufferance

21. Efficient Efficiencies is a rental-finding service specializing in efficiency apartments in Champaign-Urbana. Before entering into a service relationship with a prospective tenant, Efficient Efficiencies must provide him or her with a written contract that discloses what information?

    a. The total amount to be paid over the lease term

    b. A statement that the contract will be invalid if information about a rental unit is provided when the unit has been unavailable for more than five days

    c. A statement that information about rental units may be up to two days old

    d. A copy of the brokerage agreement between the owner and the broker

CHAPTER 18

Property Management

■ **LEARNING OBJECTIVES** *When you've finished reading this chapter, you should be able to*

- ■ **identify** the basic elements of a management agreement.

- ■ **describe** a property manager's functions.

- ■ **explain** the role of environmental regulations and the Americans with Disabilities Act in the property manager's job.

- ■ **distinguish** the various types of insurance alternatives.

- ■ **define** the following *key terms:*

Americans with Disabilities Act	management agreement	surety bonds
	multiperil policies	tenant improvements
construction	property manager	workers' compensation
life cycle costing	risk management	acts

■ THE PROPERTY MANAGER

Property management is a real estate specialization. It involves the leasing, managing, marketing, and overall maintenance of real estate owned by others, usually rental property. The **property manager** has three principal responsibilities:

1. Financial management
2. Physical management (structure and grounds)
3. Administrative management (files and records)

A *property manager*
- maintains the owner's investment, and
- ensures that the property produces income.

The property manager is responsible for maintaining the owner's investment and making sure the property earns income. This can be done in several ways. The physical property must be maintained in good condition. Suitable tenants must be found, rent must be collected, and employees must be hired and supervised. The property manager is responsible for budgeting and controlling expenses, keeping proper accounts, and making periodic reports to the owner. In all of these activities, the manager's primary goal is to operate and maintain the physical property in such a way as to preserve and enhance the owner's capital investment.

Some property managers work for property management companies. These firms manage properties for a number of owners under management agreements (discussed later). Other property managers are independent. The property manager has an agency relationship with the owner, which involves greater authority and discretion over management decisions than an employee would have. A property manager or an owner may employ building managers to supervise the daily operations of a building. In some cases, these individuals may be residents of the building.

In Illinois

Illinois property managers must be licensed real estate brokers because they engage in collecting rent, negotiating leases and rentals, and procuring tenants, among other functions. However, the Illinois *Real Estate License Act of 2000* specifically exempts resident managers of apartment buildings, duplexes, and apartment complexes from licensure requirements when their primary residence is on the premises being managed.

Illinois permits individuals whose real estate practice is limited to leasing or renting residential property, collecting rent, negotiating leases, and similar activities to obtain a limited scope leasing-agent license instead of the broader-scope broker or salesperson license. An individual with a limited scope license must be sponsored by a licensed real estate broker. ■

The Management Agreement

The first step in taking over the management of any property is to enter into a **management agreement** with the owner. This agreement creates an *agency relationship* between the owner and the property manager. The property manager usually is considered to be the owner's general agent. In all activities, the manager's first responsibility is to realize the highest return on the property in a manner consistent with the owner's instructions.

Like any other contract involving real estate, the management agreement should be in writing. It should include:

- *Description* of the property.
- *Time period* the agreement covers.
- Definition of the *management's responsibilities*. All the manager's duties should be specifically stated in the contract. Any limitations or restrictions on what the manager may do should be included.
- Statement of the *owner's purpose*. The owner should state clearly what he or she wants the manager to accomplish. One owner may want to maximize net income, while another will want to increase the capital value of the investment. Long-term goals are often key.
- Extent of the *manager's authority*. This provision should state what authority the manager is to have in matters such as hiring, firing, and supervising

employees; fixing rental rates for space; and making expenditures and authorizing repairs. Repairs that exceed a certain expense limit may require the owner's written approval.

■ *Reporting*. The frequency and detail of the manager's periodic reports on operations and financial position should be agreed on. These reports serve as a means for the owner to monitor the manager's work and operational trends; they form a basis for shaping management policy.

■ *Management fee*. The fee may be based on a percentage of gross or net income, a fixed fee, or some combination of these and other factors. Management fees are subject to the same antitrust considerations as sales commissions and cannot be standardized in the marketplace (e.g., price-fixing). The fee must be negotiated between the agent and the principal. In addition, the property manager may be entitled to a commission on new rentals and renewed leases.

■ *Allocation of costs*. The agreement should state which of the property manager's expenses—such as office rent, office help, telephone, advertising, and association fees—will be paid by the manager. Other costs will be paid by the owner.

■ *Antitrust provisions*. Management fees are subject to the same antitrust considerations as sales commissions.

■ *Equal opportunity statement*. Residential property management agreements should include a statement that the property will be shown, rented, and otherwise made available to all persons protected by state or federal law.

■ MANAGEMENT FUNCTIONS

A property manager's specific responsibilities are determined by the management agreement. Certain duties, however, are found in most agreements. Basic management duties include budgeting, capital expenditures, setting rental rates, selecting tenants, collecting rent, maintaining the property, and complying with legal requirements.

Budgeting Expenses

Before attempting to rent any property, the property manager should develop an operating budget based on anticipated revenues and expenses. In addition, the budget must reflect the owner's long-term goals. In preparing a fiscal plan, the manager considers such fixed expenses as employees' salaries, property taxes, and insurance premiums.

MATH CONCEPTS   **RENTAL COMMISSIONS**

Residential property managers often earn commissions when they find tenants for a property. *Rental commissions usually are based on the annual rent from a property.* For example, if an apartment unit rents for $1,200 per month and the commission payable is 8 percent, the commission is calculated as follows:

$1,200 per month × 12 months = $14,400
$14,400 × .08 (8%) = $1,152

Next, the manager should establish a cash reserve fund for variable expenses such as repairs, decorating, and supplies. The amount allocated for the reserve fund can be computed from the previous yearly costs of the variable expenses.

Capital expenditures.   A capital expenditure is the cost of a capital improvement that extends the life of the asset and/or adds to the value of the property. Typical capital improvements include boiler replacement, a paved driveway, roof replacement, and landscaping. In depreciable property, a capital expenditure usually must be amortized over the life of the property or that portion of the property to which the improvement belongs. The expense is not currently tax deductible as are repairs.

The owner and the property manager may decide that modernization or renovation of a property will enhance its value. In this case, the manager should budget money to cover the costs of remodeling. The property manager should either be thoroughly familiar with the *principle of contribution* or seek expert advice when estimating any expected increase in value. In the case of capital expenditures, the expenses charged against the property's income can be spread over several years.

The cost of equipment to be installed in a modernization or renovation must be evaluated over its entire useful life. This is called **life cycle costing.** This term simply means that both the initial and the operating costs of equipment over its expected life must be measured to compare the total cost of one type of equipment with that of another.

Renting the Property

Effective rental of the property is essential. However, the role of the property manager in managing a property should not be confused with that of a broker who acts as a leasing agent. The manager must be concerned with the long-term financial health of the property; the broker is concerned solely with renting space. The property manager sometimes makes use of a leasing agent as one part of property management.

Setting rental rates.   Rental rates are influenced primarily by supply and demand. The property manager should conduct a detailed survey of the competitive space available in the neighborhood, emphasizing similar properties. In establishing rental rates, the property manager has four long-term considerations:

1. The rental income must be *sufficient to cover the property's fixed charges and operating expenses.*
2. The rental income must *provide a fair return on the owner's investment.*
3. The rental rate should be *in line with prevailing rates in comparable buildings.* It may be slightly higher or slightly lower, depending on the strength of the property.
4. The *current vacancy rate in the property* is a good indicator of how much of a rent increase is advisable. A building with a low vacancy rate is a better candidate for an increase than one with a high vacancy rate.

A rental rate for residential space is usually stated as the monthly rate per unit. Commercial leases—including office, retail, and industrial space rentals—are usually stated according to either annual or monthly rates *per square foot.*

If the vacancy level is high, the manager should attempt to determine why. An elevated level of vacancy does not necessarily indicate that rents are too high. Instead, the problem may be poor management or a defective or an undesirable property. The manager should attempt to identify and correct the problems first rather than immediately lower rents. *On the other hand, a high occupancy rate may mean that rental rates are too low.* Whenever the occupancy level of an apartment house or office building exceeds 95 percent, serious consideration should be given to raising rents. First, however, the manager should investigate the rental market to determine whether a rent increase is warranted.

Selecting Tenants

A building manager's success depends on establishing and maintaining sound, long-term relationships with his or her tenants. The first and most important step is selection. The manager should be sure that the premises are suitable for a tenant in size, location, and amenities. Most important, the manager should be sure that the tenant is able to pay for the space. This may include a credit check through one of the three main companies involved in credit checks: Equifax, Trans Union, or Experian. See their Internet sites in the Appendix of Web Addresses.

Such a credit check may be at the prospective tenant's cost. Occasionally tenants with borderline credit or those who have endured a recent bankruptcy but have good income may be accepted, *provided* a significant amount of rent can be paid in advance to reduce risk.

A commercial tenant's business should be compatible with the building and the other tenants. The manager must consider how all tenants mesh. The types of businesses or services should be complementary, and the introduction of competitors (sometimes precluded in the lease) should be undertaken only with care. This not only pleases existing tenants but helps diversify the owner's investment and makes profitability more likely.

If a commercial tenant is likely to expand in the future, the manager should consider the property's potential for expansion.

The residential property manager must always comply with fair housing laws in selecting tenants. *Although fair housing laws do not apply to commercial properties, commercial property managers need to be aware of federal, state, and local antidiscrimination and equal opportunity laws that may govern industrial or retail properties.*

Collecting rents. A property manager should accept only those tenants who can be expected to meet their financial obligations. In addition to contacting credit bureaus, the process involves calling financial references and, if possible, interviewing the former landlord.

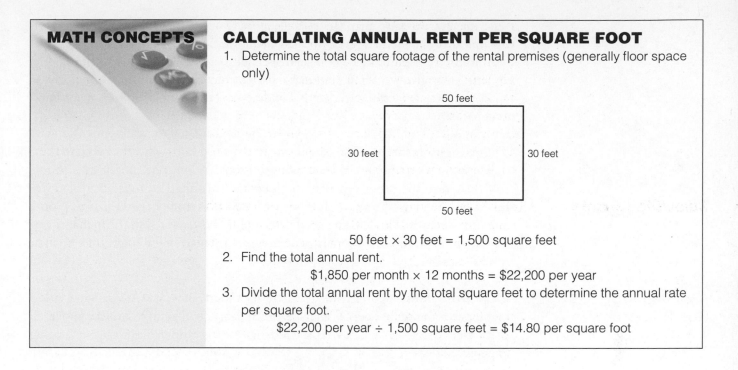

MATH CONCEPTS

CALCULATING ANNUAL RENT PER SQUARE FOOT

1. Determine the total square footage of the rental premises (generally floor space only)

50 feet

30 feet   30 feet

50 feet

$$50 \text{ feet} \times 30 \text{ feet} = 1,500 \text{ square feet}$$

2. Find the total annual rent.

$$\$1,850 \text{ per month} \times 12 \text{ months} = \$22,200 \text{ per year}$$

3. Divide the total annual rent by the total square feet to determine the annual rate per square foot.

$$\$22,200 \text{ per year} \div 1,500 \text{ square feet} = \$14.80 \text{ per square foot}$$

The terms of rental payment should be spelled out in the lease agreement, including

■ time and place of payment,

■ provisions and penalties for late payment, and

■ provisions for cancellation and damages in case of nonpayment.

The property manager should establish a firm and consistent collection plan. The plan should include a system of notices and records that complies with state and local law.

Every attempt must be made to collect rent without resorting to legal action. Legal action is costly and time-consuming and does not contribute to good tenant relations. When it is unavoidable, legal action must be taken in cooperation with the property owner's or management firm's legal counsel.

In Illinois

Specific legal procedures must be followed in taking legal action against a tenant. In addition, Illinois law has specific provisions regarding the maintenance and payment of interest on security deposits. *Property managers (who must have brokers' licenses) must put security deposits in a special escrow account, in the same way that brokers must handle earnest money.* The security deposits must be deposited in the escrow account by the *next business day* after a lease is signed, and this must be recorded in the journal and ledger. This escrow account is a non-interest-bearing account, unless the property is residential with *25* or more units, in which case interest must be paid to the tenants. Sole owners of income property do *not* have to have escrow accounts for their tenants' security deposits, even if the owner has a broker's license. ■

Maintaining Good Relations with Tenants

The ultimate success of a property manager depends on the ability of the manager to maintain good relations with tenants. Dissatisfied tenants eventually vacate the property. A high tenant turnover rate results in greater expenses for advertising and redecorating as well as lowered profits from rents.

An effective property manager establishes a good communication system with tenants. Regular newsletters or posted memoranda help keep tenants informed and involved. Maintenance and service requests must be attended to promptly, and all lease terms and building rules must be enforced consistently and fairly. A good manager is tactful and decisive and acts to the benefit of both owner and occupants.

The property manager must be able to handle residents who do not pay their rents on time or who break building regulations. When one tenant fails to follow the rules, the other tenants often become frustrated and dissatisfied. Careful record keeping shows whether rent is remitted promptly and in the proper amount. Records of all lease renewal dates should be kept so that the manager can anticipate expiration and retain good tenants who otherwise might move when their leases end.

Maintaining the Property

One of the most important functions of a property manager is the supervision of property maintenance. A manager must learn to balance services provided with their costs—that is, to satisfy tenants' needs while minimizing operating expenses.

To maintain the property efficiently, the manager must be able to assess the building's needs and how best to meet them. Staffing requirements vary with the type, size, and geographic location of the property, so the owner and manager usually agree in advance on maintenance objectives. In some cases, the best plan may be to operate a low-rental property with minimal expenditures for services and maintenance. Another property may be more lucrative if kept in top condition and operated with all possible tenant services. A well-maintained, high-service property can command premium rental rates.

A primary maintenance objective is to protect the physical integrity of the property over the long term. For example, preserving the property by repainting the exterior or replacing the heating system helps decrease long-term maintenance costs. Keeping the property in good condition involves the following four types of maintenance:

1. Preventive maintenance
2. Repair or corrective maintenance
3. Routine maintenance
4. Construction

Preventive maintenance helps prevent problems and expenses.

Corrective maintenance corrects problems after they've occurred.

Routine maintenance keeps up with everyday wear and tear.

Preventive maintenance includes regularly scheduled activities such as painting and seasonal servicing of appliances and systems. Preventive maintenance preserves the long-range value and physical integrity of the building. This is both the most critical and the most neglected maintenance responsibility. Failure to perform preventive maintenance invariably leads to greater expense in other areas of maintenance.

Repair or *corrective maintenance* involves the actual repairs that keep the building's equipment, utilities, and amenities functioning. Repairing a boiler, fixing a leaky faucet, or mending a broken air-conditioning unit are acts of corrective maintenance.

A property manager must also supervise the *routine maintenance* of the building. Routine maintenance includes such day-to-day duties as cleaning common areas, performing minor carpentry and plumbing adjustments, and providing regularly scheduled upkeep of landscaping. Good routine maintenance is similar to good preventive maintenance. Both head off problems before they become expensive.

IN PRACTICE

One of the major decisions a property manager faces is whether to contract for maintenance services from an outside firm or hire on-site employees to perform such tasks. This decision should be based on a number of factors, including

■ size of the building,

■ complexity of the tenants' requirements, and

■ availability of suitable labor.

> **Construction** involves making a property meet a tenant's needs.

A commercial or an industrial property manager often is called on to make **tenant improvements.** These are alterations to the interior of the building to meet a tenant's particular space needs. Such *construction* alterations range from simply repainting or recarpeting to completely gutting the interior and redesigning the space by erecting new walls, adding partitions, and revamping electrical systems. In new construction, especially, the interiors are usually left incomplete so that they can be adapted to the needs of individual tenants. One matter that must be clarified is which improvements will be considered *trade fixtures* (personal property belonging to the tenant) and which will belong to the owner of the real estate.

Modernization or renovation of buildings that have become functionally obsolete and thus unsuited to today's building needs is also important. The renovation of a building often enhances marketability and potential income.

Handling Environmental Concerns

Property managers must be able to respond to a variety of environmental problems, because they have become increasingly important issues. Managers may manage structures containing asbestos or radon or be called on to arrange an environmental audit of a property. Managers must see that any hazardous wastes produced by their employers or tenants are properly disposed of. Even nonhazardous waste of an office building must be controlled to avoid violation of laws requiring segregation and recycling of types of wastes. Of course, property managers may want to provide recycling facilities for tenants even if not required by law to do so. On-site recycling creates an image of good citizenship that enhances the reputation (and value) of a commercial or residential property.

Air quality issues are a key concern for those involved in property management and design.

The Americans with Disabilities Act

The **Americans with Disabilities Act** (ADA) has had a significant impact on the responsibilities of the property manager, both in building amenities and in employment issues.

Title I of the ADA provides for the employment of qualified job applicants regardless of their disability. Any employer with 15 or more employees must adopt nondiscriminatory employment procedures. In addition, employers must make reasonable accommodations to enable individuals with disabilities to perform essential job functions.

FIGURE **18.1**

FIGURE 18.1

Reasonable Modifications to Public Facilities or Services

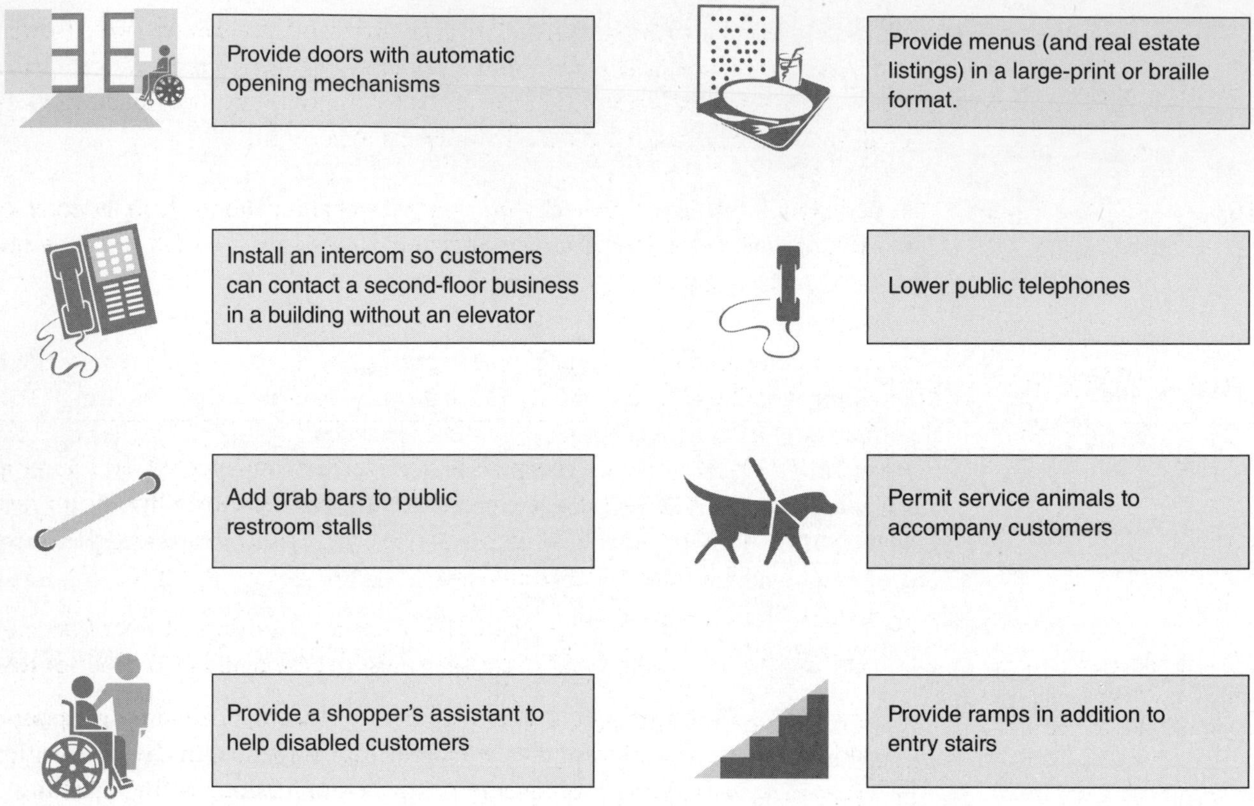

Provide doors with automatic opening mechanisms	Provide menus (and real estate listings) in a large-print or braille format.
Install an intercom so customers can contact a second-floor business in a building without an elevator	Lower public telephones
Add grab bars to public restroom stalls	Permit service animals to accompany customers
Provide a shopper's assistant to help disabled customers	Provide ramps in addition to entry stairs

Property managers must also be familiar with Title III of the ADA, which prohibits discrimination in commercial properties. The ADA requires that managers ensure that people with disabilities have full and equal access to facilities and services. The property manager typically is responsible for determining whether a building meets the ADA's accessibility requirements. The property manager must also prepare and execute a plan for restructuring or retrofitting a building that is not in compliance. ADA experts and architectural designers may need to be consulted.

To protect owners of existing structures from the massive expense of extensive remodeling, the ADA recommends *reasonably achievable accommodations* to provide access to the facilities and services. New construction and remodeling, however, must meet higher standards because new design costs less than retrofitting. An unexpected benefit to new owners is that many of the accessible design features and accommodations benefit everyone.

Existing barriers must be removed when this can be accomplished in a readily achievable manner—that is, with little difficulty and at low cost. (See Figure 18.1.) The following are typical examples of readily achievable modifications:

- Ramping or removing an obstacle from an otherwise accessible entrance
- Lowering wall-mounted public telephones
- Adding raised letters and braille markings on elevator buttons

- Installing auditory signals in elevators
- Reversing the direction in which doors open (for wheelchair accessibility)
- Providing doors that have mechanisms that will open and close the doors automatically

Alternative methods can be used to provide reasonable accommodations if extensive restructuring is impractical or if retrofitting is unduly expensive. For instance, installing a cup dispenser at a water fountain that is too high for an individual in a wheelchair may be more practical than installing a lower unit.

IN PRACTICE   Federal, state, and local laws may provide additional requirements for accommodating people with disabilities. Licensees should be aware of the full range of laws to ensure that their practices are in compliance.

■ RISK MANAGEMENT

Enormous monetary losses can result from certain unexpected or catastrophic events. As a result, one of the most critical areas of responsibility for a property manager is risk management. **Risk management** involves answering the question "What happens if something goes wrong?"

The perils of any risk must be evaluated in terms of options. In considering the possibility of a loss, the property manager must decide whether it is better to

> The four alternative risk management techniques may be remembered by the acronym **ACTOR:** *Avoid, Control, Transfer,* or *Retain.*

- *avoid* risk, by removing the source of risk (for instance, a swimming pool may pose an unacceptable risk if a day-care center is located in the building);
- *control* it, by preparing for an emergency before it happens (by installing sprinklers, fire doors, and security systems, for example);
- *transfer* it, by shifting the risk onto another party (that is, by taking out an insurance policy); or
- *retain* it, by deciding that the chances of the event occurring are too small to justify the expense of any other response (an alternative might be to take out an insurance policy with a large deductible, which is usually considerably less expensive).

Security of Tenants

The physical safety of tenants of the leased premises is an important issue for property managers and owners. Recent court decisions in several parts of the country have held owners and their agents responsible for physical harm that was inflicted on tenants by intruders. These decisions have prompted property managers and owners to think about how to protect tenants and secure apartments from intruders.

Types of Insurance

Insurance is one way to protect against losses. Many types of insurance are available. An insurance audit should be performed by a competent, reliable insurance agent who is familiar with insurance issues for the type of property involved. The audit will indicate areas in which greater or lesser coverage is recommended and will highlight particular risks. The final decision, however, must be made by the property owner.

Some common types of coverage available to income property owners and managers include the following:

■ *Fire and hazard:* Fire insurance policies provide coverage against direct loss or damage to property from a fire on the premises. Standard fire coverage can be extended to include other hazards such as windstorm, hail, smoke damage, or civil insurrection.

■ *Consequential loss, use, and occupancy:* Consequential loss insurance covers the results, or consequences, of a disaster. Consequential loss can include the loss of rent or revenue to a business that occurs if the business's property cannot be used.

■ *Contents and personal property:* This type of insurance covers building contents and personal property during periods when they are not actually located on the business premises.

■ *Liability:* Public liability insurance covers the risks an owner assumes whenever the public enters the building. A claim paid under this coverage is used for medical expenses by a person who is injured in the building as a result of the owner's negligence. Claims for those hurt in the course of their employment are covered by state laws known as **workers' compensation acts.** (A building owner who is an employer must obtain a workers' compensation policy from a private insurance company.)

■ *Casualty:* Casualty insurance policies include coverage against theft, burglary, vandalism, and machinery damage as well as health and accident insurance. Casualty policies are usually written on specific risks, such as theft, rather than being all-inclusive.

■ *Surety bonds:* **Surety bonds** cover an owner against financial losses resulting from an employee's criminal acts or negligence while performing assigned duties.

Many insurance companies offer **multiperil policies** for apartment and commercial buildings. Such a policy offers the property manager a "package" of standard commercial coverages, such as fire, hazard, public liability, and casualty. Special coverage for earthquakes and floods is also available.

Insurance for the personal property of tenants is also available to tenants. Many tenants do not realize that if a property burns, their personal property is usually not covered by the landlord's policy. (In Illinois, the policy type tenants should ask for is HO4, designed specifically to cover renters' personal property.)

Claims

Two possible methods can be used to determine the amount of a claim under an insurance policy. One is the *depreciated,* or *actual cash, value* of the damaged property. That is, the property is not insured for what it would cost to replace it, but rather for what it was originally worth, *less the depreciation in value* that results from use and the passage of time. The other method is *current replacement cost.* In this sort of policy, the building or property is insured for what it would cost to rebuild or replace it today.

When purchasing insurance, a manager must decide whether a property should be insured at full replacement cost or at a depreciated cost. Full replacement cost coverage is generally more expensive than depreciated cost. As with homeowners' policies, commercial policies include coinsurance clauses that require the insured to carry fire coverage, usually in an amount equal to 80 percent of a building's replacement value. If the coinsured amount is met on a policy *guaranteeing* replacement cost, it may mean that if a property is destroyed, the insured can collect more than the stated appraised value on the property.

▪ THE MANAGEMENT PROFESSION

Most metropolitan areas have local associations of building and property owners and managers that are affiliates of regional and national associations. The Institute of Real Estate Management (IREM) is one of the affiliates of the National Association of REALTORS®. It awards the Certified Property Manager (CPM) designation. The Building Owners and Managers Association (BOMA) International is a federation of local associations of building owners and managers. The Building Owners and Managers Institute (BOMI) International, an independent institute affiliated with BOMA, offers training courses leading to several designations: Real Property Administrator (RPA), Systems Maintenance Administrator (SMA), and Facilities Management Administrator (FMA). In addition, many specialized professional organizations provide information and contacts for apartment and condominium association managers, shopping center managers, and others. Find more information on the Internet. Addresses for these associations are located in the Web Link Appendix.

▪ SUMMARY

Property management is a specialized service provided to owners of income-producing properties. The owner's managerial function may be delegated to an individual or a firm with particular expertise in the field. The manager, as agent of the owner, becomes the administrator of the project and assumes the executive functions required for the care and operation of the property.

A management agreement establishes the agency relationship between owner and manager. It must be prepared carefully to define and authorize the manager's duties and responsibilities, and it should be in writing.

Projected expenses, the manager's analysis of the building's condition, and local rent patterns form the basis for determining rental rates for the property. Once a rent schedule is established, the property manager is responsible for soliciting financially solid tenants whose needs are suited to the available space. The manager collects rents, maintains the building, hires necessary employees, pays taxes for the building, and deals with tenant problems.

Maintenance includes safeguarding the physical integrity of the property and performing routine cleaning and repairs. It also includes making tenant improvements, such as adapting the interior space and overall design of the property to suit tenants' needs.

The manager is expected to secure adequate insurance coverage for the premises. Fire and hazard insurance cover the property and fixtures against catastrophes. Consequential loss, use, and occupancy insurance protects the owner against revenue losses. Casualty insurance provides coverage against losses such as theft, vandalism, and destruction of machinery. The manager should also secure public liability insurance to insure the owner against claims made by people injured on the premises. Workers' compensation policies cover the claims of employees injured on the job.

Increasing needs for safety and security awareness, knowledge of environmental issues, and concern for the federal and state fair housing laws round out the potpourri of issues that a property manager must often address.

This growing real estate specialty is supported by many regional and national organizations that help property managers maintain high professional standards. A few of the important ones are The Building Owners and Managers Association (BOMA), The Building Owners and Managers Institute (BOMI), and the Institute of Real Estate Management (IREM).

In Illinois   Property managers must be licensed real estate brokers. Resident managers are exempt under certain circumstances. ■

QUESTIONS

1. Ken is an employee who is injured on the job. Which of the following types of insurance coverage insures Ken's employer against most claims for job-related injuries?
   a. Consequential loss
   b. Workers' compensation
   c. Casualty
   d. Surety bond

2. Apartment rental rates are usually expressed in what way?
   a. In monthly amounts
   b. On a per-room basis
   c. In square feet per month
   d. In square feet per year

3. From a management point of view, apartment building occupancy that reaches as high as 98 percent would tend to indicate that
   a. the building is poorly managed.
   b. the building has reached its maximum potential.
   c. the building is a desirable place to live.
   d. rents could be raised.

4. A guest slips on an icy apartment building stair and is hospitalized. A claim against the building owner for medical expenses may be paid under which of the following policies held by the owner?
   a. Workers' compensation
   b. Casualty
   c. Liability
   d. Fire and hazard

5. When a property manager is establishing a budget for the building, what should be included as an operating expenses?
   a. Replacement reserves
   b. Debt service
   c. Utilities
   d. Depreciation

6. A property manager is offered a choice of three insurance policies: one has a $500 deductible, one has a $1,000 deductible, and the third has a $5,000 deductible. If the property manager selects the policy with the highest deductible, which risk management approach is illustrated?
   a. Avoiding risk
   b. Retaining risk
   c. Controlling risk
   d. Transferring risk

7. Contaminated groundwater, toxic fumes from paint and carpeting, and lack of proper ventilation are all examples of
   a. issues beyond the scope of a property manager's job description.
   b. problems faced only in newly constructed properties.
   c. issues that arise under the Americans with Disabilities Act.
   d. environmental concerns that a property manager may have to address.

8. Tenant improvements are
   a. always construed to be fixtures.
   b. adaptations of space to suit tenants' needs.
   c. removable by the tenant.
   d. paid for by the landlord.

9. In preparing a budget, a property manager should set up which of the following for variable expenses?
   a. Control account
   b. Floating allocation
   c. Cash reserve fund
   d. Asset account

10. Rents should be determined by
    a. supply-and-demand factors.
    b. the local apartment owners' association.
    c. HUD's annually published rental guidelines.
    d. a tenants' union.

11. Whittaker Towers, a highrise apartment building, burns to the ground. What type of insurance covers the landlord against the resulting loss of rent?

    a. Fire and hazard
    b. Liability
    c. Consequential loss, use, and occupancy
    d. Casualty

12. Property manager Janet hires Walter as the full-time maintenance person for one of the buildings she manages. While repairing a faucet in one of the apartments, Walter steals a television set. Janet could protect the owner against this type of loss by obtaining

    a. liability insurance.
    b. workers' compensation insurance.
    c. a surety bond.
    d. casualty insurance.

13. Which of the following might indicate rents are too low?

    a. A poorly maintained building
    b. Many For Lease signs in the area
    c. High building occupancy
    d. High tenant turnover rates

14. Jin repairs a malfunctioning boiler in the building she manages. This is classified as which type of maintenance?

    a. Preventive
    b. Corrective
    c. Routine
    d. Construction

15. An owner has just entered into a property management agreement with a licensee. In regard to this situation, has an agency relationship been formed, and, if so, which of the following would BEST describe the relationship?

    a. Yes, an agency relationship has been created, and the licensee would be best described as a special agent.
    b. Yes, an agency relationship has been created, and the licensee would be best described as a general agent.
    c. No, an agency relationship cannot be created between owners and property managers.
    d. No, an agency relationship can only be created by an executed power of attorney between the property manager and the licensee.

16. Which action by a property manager would be a breach of her or his fiduciary relationship to the owner?

    a. Checking the credit history of minority applicants only
    b. Generating a high net operating income by maintaining the property
    c. Maintaining good relations with the tenants
    d. Scrutinizing property expenses.

17. Fred is the manager of an apartment building in central Illinois. Fred's total compensation consists of a monthly salary, a 12 percent commission based on annual rental for each vacant unit Fred fills, and the free use of one of the apartments as Fred's personal primary residence. Based on these facts, is Fred required by Illinois law to obtain a real estate broker's license?

    a. Yes. Any person who is compensated for performing real estate activities for a commission must have a broker's license, regardless of any other form of compensation.

    b. Yes. Because Fred's compensation is based in part on recruiting new tenants, rather than simply collecting rents, Fred must have a broker's license.

    c. No. Property managers are not required to have real estate licenses in Illinois.

    d. No. Persons acting as resident managers, who live in the managed property, are specifically exempt from the general licensing requirements.

CHAPTER

Real Estate Appraisal

■ **identify** the different types and basic principles of value.

■ **describe** the three basic valuation approaches used by appraisers.

■ **explain** the steps in the appraisal process.

■ **distinguish** the four methods of determining reproduction or replacement cost.

■ **define** the following *key terms:*

anticipation	Financial Institutions	progression
appraisal	Reform, Recovery, and	quantity-survey method
appraiser	Enforcement Act	reconciliation
assemblage	functional obsolescence	regression
capitalization rate	gross income multiplier	replacement cost
change	gross rent multiplier	reproduction cost
competition	highest and best use	sales comparison
conformity	income approach	approach
contribution	increasing returns	square-foot method
cost approach	index method	straight-line method
depreciation	law of diminishing returns	substitution
economic life	market value	supply and demand
external obsolescence	physical deterioration	unit-in-place method
	plottage	value

■ APPRAISING

<table>
<tr><td>

Regulation of Appraisal Activities

</td><td>

An **appraisal** is an opinion of value based on supportable evidence and approved methods. An **appraiser** is an independent person trained to provide an *unbiased* opinion of value. Appraising is a professional service performed for a fee.

Title XI of the federal **Financial Institutions Reform, Recovery, and Enforcement Act of 1989 (FIRREA)** requires that most appraisals used in connection with a federally related transaction must be performed by someone licensed or certified by law. A *federally related transaction* is any real estate-related financial transaction in which a federal financial institution or regulatory agency—the Department of Housing and Urban Development, Fannie Mae, Freddie Mac, or the National Credit Union Administration—engages in, contracts for, or regulates and requires the services of an appraiser. This includes transactions involving the sale, lease, purchase, investment, or exchange of real property. It also includes the financing, refinancing, or the use of real property as security for a loan or an investment, including mortgage-backed securities.

</td></tr>
</table>

In Illinois   The *Real Estate Appraiser Licensing Act of 2002* provides for the licensure and certification of Illinois appraisers. It is located under Illinois Compiled Statutes, Chapter 225, 225 ILCS 458, at *www.ilga.gov*.

Illinois recognizes three categories of appraisers:

1. *Associate real estate appraiser*—entry level appraiser limited to appraisal of non-complex property having a transaction value under $1 million; all reports must be cosigned by a state certified residential real estate appraiser or state certified general real estate appraiser.
2. *Certified residential real estate appraiser*—qualified to appraise residential property of one unit to four units without regard to transaction value or complexity, but with restrictions in accordance with Title XI, USPAP, and criteria established by the Appraisal Qualifications Board (AQB).
3. *Certified general real estate appraiser*—qualified to appraise all types of real property without restrictions as to the scope of practice.

Only individuals (not corporations, partnerships, firms, or groups) may be certified as appraisers, or act as associate real estate appraisers. A certified appraiser may, however, sign appraisal reports on behalf of a business entity.

An appraisal report prepared by an appraiser recognized under the act must identify on the report by name the individual who ordered or originated the appraisal assignment. The appraiser must retain the original copy of all contracts engaging his or her services as an appraiser and all appraisal reports, including any supporting data used to develop the appraisal report, for a period of five years, or two years after the final disposition of any judicial proceeding in which testimony was given, whichever is longer. In addition, the appraiser must retain contracts, logs, and appraisal reports used in meeting prelicense experience requirements for a period of five years.

An individual appraiser may *not* use the titles "state certified" or "associate real estate appraiser" unless he or she is recognized as such by the state. On the other hand, nothing in the *Real Estate Appraiser Licensing Act of 2002* prohibits a non-recognized individual from appraising real estate for compensation in transactions that are not federally related.

The *Real Estate Appraiser Licensing Act of 2002* establishes a fee structure and disciplinary and enforcement mechanism for appraisers. Appraisal certification and associate candidates also must meet strict educational, qualification, examination, and experience requirements. The profession itself maintains rigorous standards, and most Illinois appraisers become associate appraisers or certified appraisers and undergo demanding apprenticeships.

Comparative Market Analysis

Not all estimates of value are made by professional appraisers. A salesperson often must help a seller arrive at a listing price or assist a buyer in determining an offering price for property without the aid of a formal appraisal report. In such a case, the salesperson prepares a report compiled from research of the marketplace, primarily similar properties that have been sold, known as a *comparative market analysis (CMA)*. The salesperson must be knowledgeable about the fundamentals of valuation to compile the market data. The comparative market analysis is not as comprehensive or as technical as an appraisal and should not be represented as an appraisal.

■ VALUE

To have **value** in the real estate market—that is, to have monetary worth based on desirability—a property must have the following four characteristics:

> **Memory Tip**
>
> The four characteristics of value can be remembered by the acronym **DUST**: *Demand, Utility, Scarcity, and Transferability.*

- *Demand*—The need or desire for possession or ownership backed by the financial means to satisfy that need
- *Utility*—The property's usefulness for its intended purposes
- *Scarcity*—A finite supply
- *Transferability*—The relative ease with which ownership rights are transferred from one person to another

Market Value

Generally, the goal of an appraiser is to render an opinion of value.

The **market value** of real estate is the most probable price that a property should bring in a fair sale. This definition makes three assumptions. First, it presumes a competitive and open market. Second, the buyer and seller are both assumed to be acting prudently and knowledgeably. Finally, market value depends on the price not being affected by unusual circumstances.

The following are essential factors in rendering an opinion of value:

- The transaction is an arm's-length transaction.
- The most probable price is *not* the average or highest price.
- The buyer and seller must be unrelated and acting without undue pressure.
- Both buyer and seller must be well informed about the property's use and potential, including both its defects and its advantages.
- A reasonable time must be allowed for exposure in the open market.
- Payment must be made in cash or its equivalent.

■ The price must represent a normal consideration for the property sold, unaffected by special financing amounts or terms, services, fees, costs, or credits incurred in the market transaction.

Market value versus market price.   *Market value* is an opinion of value based on an analysis of data. The data may include not only an analysis of comparable sales but also an analysis of potential income, expenses, and replacement costs (less any depreciation). *Market price*, on the other hand, is what a property *actually* sells for—its sales price. In theory, market price should be the same as market value. Market price can be taken as accurate evidence of current market value. However, that is true only if the conditions essential to market value exist. Sometimes, property may be sold below market value—for instance, when the seller is forced to sell quickly or when a sale is arranged between relatives.

> *Market value* is a reasonable opinion of a property's value; *market price* is the actual selling price of a property; *cost* may not equal either market value or market price.

Market value versus cost.   An important distinction can be made between market value and *cost*. One of the most common misconceptions about valuing property is that cost represents market value. Cost and market value may be the same. In fact, when the improvements on a property are new, cost and value are likely to be equal. But more often, cost does not equal market value. For example, a homeowner may install a swimming pool for a cost of $15,000; however, the cost of the improvement may not add $15,000 to the value of the property.

Basic Principles of Value

A number of economic principles can affect the value of real estate. The most important are defined in the text that follows.

Anticipation.   According to the principle of **anticipation,** value is created by the expectation that certain events will occur. Value can increase or decrease in anticipation of some future benefit or detriment. For instance, the value of a house may be affected if rumors circulate that an adjacent property may be converted to commercial use in the near future. If the property has been a vacant eyesore, it is possible that the neighboring home's value will increase. On the other hand, if the vacant property was perceived as a park or playground that added to the neighborhood's quiet atmosphere, the news of commercial use might cause the home's value to decline.

Change.   No physical or economic condition remains constant. This is the principle of **change.** Real estate is subject to natural phenomena such as tornadoes, fires, and routine wear and tear. The real estate business is subject to market demands, as is any other business. An appraiser must be knowledgeable about both the past and perhaps the predictable future effects of natural phenomena, and the changeable behavior of the marketplace.

Competition.   **Competition** is the *interaction* of supply and demand. Excess profits tend to attract competition. For example, the success of a retail store may cause investors to open similar stores in the area. This tends to mean less profit for all the stores concerned unless the purchasing power in the area increases substantially.

Conformity.   The principle of **conformity** says that maximum value is created when a property is in harmony with its surroundings. Maximum value is realized if the use of land conforms to existing neighborhood standards. In single-family residential neighborhoods, for instance, buildings should be similar in design, construction, size, and age.

Contribution.   Under the principle of **contribution,** the value of any part of a property is measured by its effect on the value of the whole. Installing a swimming pool, greenhouse, or private bowling alley may not add value to the property equal to the cost. On the other hand, remodeling an outdated kitchen or bathroom probably would.

Highest and best use.   The most profitable single use to which a property may be put, or the use that is most likely to be in demand in the near future, is the property's **highest and best use.** The use must be

- legally permitted,
- financially feasible,
- physically possible, and
- maximally productive.

The highest and best use of a site can change with social, political, and economic forces. For instance, a parking lot in a busy downtown area may not maximize the land's profitability to the same extent an office building might. Highest and best use is noted in every appraisal.

Increasing and diminishing returns.   The addition of more improvements to land and structures increases total value only to the asset's *maximum value.* Beyond that point, additional improvements no longer affect a property's value. As long as money spent on improvements produces an increase in income or value, the **law of increasing returns** applies. At the point where additional improvements do not increase income or value, the **law of diminishing returns** applies. No matter how much money is spent on the property, the property's value will not keep pace with the expenditures.

Plottage: The total value of two adjacent properties may be greater if they are combined than the sum of their individual values if each is sold separately.

Plottage.   The principle of **plottage** holds that merging or consolidating adjacent lots into a single larger one produces a greater total land value than the sum of the two sites valued separately. For example, two adjacent lots valued at $35,000 each might have a combined value of $90,000 if consolidated. The process of merging two separately owned lots under one owner is known as **assemblage.**

Regression: The lowering of a property's value due to its neighbors.

Progression: The increasing of a property's value due to its neighbors.

Regression and progression.   In general, the worth of a better-quality property is adversely affected by the presence of a lesser-quality property. This is known as the principle of **regression.** Thus, in a neighborhood of modest homes, a structure that is larger, better maintained, or more luxurious would tend to be valued in the same range as the less-lavish homes. Conversely, under the principle of **progression,** the value of a modest home would be higher if it were located among larger, fancier properties.

Substitution.   Under the principle of **substitution,** the maximum value of a property tends to be set by how much it would cost to purchase an equally desirable and valuable substitute property.

Supply and demand. The principle of **supply and demand** holds that the value of a property depends on the number of properties available in the marketplace—the supply of the product. Other factors include the prices of other properties, the number of prospective purchasers, and the price buyers will pay.

■ THE THREE APPROACHES TO VALUE

To arrive at an accurate opinion of value, appraisers traditionally use three basic valuation techniques: the *sales comparison approach*, the *cost approach*, and the *income approach*. The three methods serve as checks against each other. Using them narrows the range within which the final estimate of value falls. Each method is generally considered most reliable for specific types of property.

The Sales Comparison Approach

In the **sales comparison approach** (also known as the *market data approach* or *direct market comparison approach*), an estimate of value is obtained by comparing the property being appraised (the *subject property*) with recently sold *comparable properties* (properties similar to the subject, called *comps*). Because no two parcels of real estate are exactly alike, each comparable property must be analyzed for differences and similarities between it and the subject property. This approach is a good example of the principle of substitution, discussed previously. The sales prices *of the comparables* must be adjusted for any dissimilarities.

Memory Tip

Take the selling price of the comp and add or subtract for any differences, one at a time, from the subject property. The rules are CBS and CPA. **CBS** = if the **C**omp is **B**etter, **S**ubtract. **CPA** = if the **C**omp is **P**oorer, **A**dd.

■ **FOR EXAMPLE** Two condos in the same neighborhood, one that sold and one that is the subject of an appraisal, are very similar. The comp sold for $145,000 and has a garage valued at $9,000. The subject property has no garage, but it has a fireplace valued at $5,000. What is the indicated value of the property?

$145,000	The comp sale price
−9,000	(The Comp is Better, Subtract—CBS)
+5,000	(The Comp is Poorer, Add—CPA)
$141,000	The indicated value of the subject property

The principal factors for which adjustments must be made include the following:

■ *Property rights:* An adjustment must be made when less than fee simple, the full legal bundle of rights, is involved. This includes land leases, ground rents, life estates, easements, deed restrictions, and encroachments.

■ *Financing concessions:* The financing terms must be considered, including adjustments for differences such as mortgage loan terms and owner financing.

■ *Conditions of sale:* Adjustments must be made for motivational factors that would affect the sale, such as foreclosure, a sale between family members, or some nonmonetary incentive.

■ *Date of sale:* An adjustment must be made if economic changes occur between the date of sale of the comparable property and the date of the appraisal.

■ *Location:* Similar properties might differ in price from neighborhood to neighborhood or even between locations within the same neighborhood.

■ *Physical features and amenities:* Physical features, such as the structure's age, size, and condition, may require adjustments.

TABLE 19.1

Sales Comparison Approach to Value

	Subject Property: 155 Potter Drive	Comparables		
		A	B	C
Sales price		**$260,000**	**$252,000**	**$265,000**
Financing concessions	none	none	none	none
Date of sale		current	current	current
Location	good	same	poorer +6,500	same
Age	6 years	same	same	same
Size of lot	60' × 135'	same	same	larger –5,000
Landscaping	good	same	same	same
Construction	brick	same	same	same
Style	ranch	same	same	same
No. of rooms	6	same	same	same
No. of bedrooms	3	same	poorer +500	same
No. of baths	1½	same	same	better –500
Sq. ft. of living space	1,500	same	same	better –1,000
Other space (basement)	full basement	same	same	same
Condition—exterior	average	better –1,500	poorer +1,000	better –1,500
Condition—interior	good	same	same	better –500
Garage	2-car attached	same	same	same
Other improvements	none	none	none	none
Net adjustments		–1,500	+8,000	–8,500
Adjusted value		**$258,500**	**$260,000**	**$256,500**

Note: The value of a feature that is present in the subject but not in the comparable property is *added* to the sales price of the comparable. Likewise, the value of a feature that is present in the comparable but not in the subject property is *subtracted*. A good way to remember this is: CBS stands for "comp better subtract"; and CPA stands for "comp poor add." The adjusted sales prices of the comparables represent the probable range of value of the subject property. From this range, a single market value estimate can be selected.

The sales comparison approach is considered the most reliable of the three approaches in appraising single-family homes, where the intangible benefits might be difficult to measure otherwise. Most appraisals include a minimum of three comparable sales reflective of the subject property. An example of the sales comparison approach is shown in Table 19.1.

The Cost Approach

The **cost approach** to value also is based on the principle of substitution. The cost approach consists of five steps:

1. Estimate the *current cost* of constructing the buildings and improvements.
2. Estimate the amount of *accrued depreciation* resulting from the property's physical deterioration, functional obsolescence, and external depreciation.
3. *Deduct* the accrued depreciation (Step 2) from the current construction cost (Step 1).
4. Estimate the *value of the land* as if it were vacant and available to be put to its highest and best use.
5. *Add* the estimated land value (Step 4) to the depreciated cost of the building and site improvements (Step 3) to arrive at the total property value.

TABLE 19.2

Cost Approach to Value

Subject Property: 155 Potter Drive

Land Valuation: Size 60' × 135' @ $450 per front foot	= $27,000
Plus site improvements: driveway, walks, landscaping, etc.	= 8,000
Total	$35,000

Building Valuation: Replacement Cost
  1,500 sq. ft. @ $85 per sq. ft.   = $127,500

Less Depreciation:
Physical depreciation
  Curable
    (items of deferred maintenance)

exterior painting	$4,000
Incurable (structural deterioration)	9,750
Functional obsolescence	2,000
External depreciation	-0-
Total Depreciation	$15,750

Depreciated Value of Building	$111,750
Indicated Value by Cost Approach	$146,750

■ **FOR EXAMPLE**

Current cost of construction	=	$185,000
Accrued depreciation	=	$30,000
Value of the land	=	$55,000
$185,000 – $30,000 + 55,000	=	$210,000

In this example, the total property value is $210,000.

There are two ways to look at the construction cost of a building for appraisal purposes: reproduction cost and replacement cost. **Reproduction cost** is the construction cost at current prices of an exact duplicate of the subject improvement, including both the benefits and the drawbacks of the property. **Replacement cost** new is the cost to construct an improvement similar to the subject property using current construction methods and materials, but not necessarily an exact duplicate. **Replacement cost** new is more frequently used in appraising older structures because it eliminates obsolete features and takes advantage of current construction materials and techniques.

An example of the cost approach to value, applied to the same property as in Table 19.1, is shown in Table 19.2.

Determining reproduction or replacement cost new.   An appraiser using the cost approach computes the reproduction or replacement cost of a building using one of the following four methods:

1. **Square-foot method.** The cost per square foot of a recently built comparable structure is multiplied by the number of square feet (using exterior dimensions) in the subject building. This is the most common and easiest method of cost estimation. Table 19.2 uses the square-foot method, also referred to as the *comparison method*. For some properties, the cost per cubic foot of a

recently built comparable structure is multiplied by the number of cubic feet in the subject structure.

2. **Unit-in-place method.** In the unit-in-place method, the replacement cost of a structure is estimated based on the construction cost per unit of measure of individual building components, including material, labor, overhead, and builder's profit. Most components are measured in square feet, although items such as plumbing fixtures are estimated by cost. The sum of the components is the cost of the new structure.

3. **Quantity-survey method.** The quantity and quality of all materials (such as lumber, brick, and plaster) and the labor are estimated on a unit cost basis. These factors are added to indirect costs (e.g., building permit, survey, payroll, taxes, and builder's profit) to arrive at the total cost of the structure. Because it is so detailed and time-consuming, this method is usually used only in appraising historical properties. It is, however, the most accurate method of appraising new construction.

4. **Index method.** A factor representing the percentage increase of construction costs up to the present time is applied to the original cost of the subject property. Because it fails to take into account individual property variables, this method is useful only as a check of the estimate reached by one of the other methods.

Depreciation. In a real estate appraisal, **depreciation** is a loss in value due to any cause compared with today's cost of replacement. It refers to a condition that adversely affects the value of an improvement to real property. *Land does not depreciate*—it retains its value indefinitely, except in such rare cases as downzoned urban parcels, improperly developed land, or misused farmland.

Depreciation is considered to be *curable* or *incurable*, depending on the contribution of the expenditure to the value of the property. For appraisal purposes, depreciation is divided into three classes, according to its cause:

1. **Physical deterioration.** *Curable:* An item in need of repair, such as painting (deferred maintenance), that is economically feasible and would result in an increase in value equal to or exceeding the cost. *Incurable:* A defect caused by physical wear and tear if its correction would not be economically feasible or contribute a comparable value to the building. The cost of a major repair may not warrant the financial investment.

2. **Functional obsolescence.** *Curable:* Outmoded or unacceptable physical or design features that are no longer considered desirable by purchasers. Such features, however, could be replaced or redesigned at a cost that would be offset by the anticipated increase in ultimate value. Outmoded plumbing, for instance, is usually easily replaced. Room function may be redefined at no cost if the basic room layout allows for it. A bedroom adjacent to a kitchen, for example, may be converted to a family room. *Incurable:* Currently undesirable physical or design features that could not be easily remedied because the cost of cure would be greater than its resulting increase in value. An office building that cannot be economically air-conditioned, for example, suffers from incurable functional obsolescence if the cost of adding air-conditioning is greater than its contribution to the building's value.

3. **External obsolescence.** *Incurable:* Caused by negative factors not on the subject property, such as zoning, environmental, social, or economic forces. This type of depreciation is always incurable. The loss in value cannot be reversed

TABLE 19.3

Income Capitalization Approach to Value

Potential Gross Annual Income		$60,000
Market rent (100% capacity)		
Income from other sources (vending machines and pay phones)		+ 600
		$60,600
Less vacancy and collection losses (estimated) @4%		−2,424
Effective Gross Income		$58,176
Expenses:		
Real estate taxes	$9,000	
Insurance	1,000	
Heat	2,500	
Maintenance	6,400	
Utilities	800	
Repairs	1,200	
Decorating	1,400	
Replacement of equipment	800	
Legal and accounting	600	
Advertising	300	
Management	3,000	
Total		$27,000
Annual Net Operating Income		$31,176

Capitalization rate = 10% (overall rate)

Capitalization of annual net income: $31,176 ÷ .10 = $311,760

Indicated Value by Income Approach = $311,760

by spending money on the property. For example, proximity to a nuisance, such as a polluting factory or a deteriorating neighborhood, is one factor that could not be cured by the owner of the subject property.

The easiest but least precise way to determine depreciation is the **straight-line method,** also called the *economic age-life method.* Depreciation is assumed to occur at an even rate over a structure's **economic life,** the period during which it is expected to remain useful for its original intended purpose. The property's cost is divided by the number of years of its expected economic life to derive the amount of annual depreciation.

■ **FOR EXAMPLE** A $300,000 property may have a land value of $75,000 and an improvement value of $225,000. If the improvement is expected to last 60 years, the annual straight-line depreciation would be $3,750 ($225,000 divided by 60 years). Such depreciation can be calculated as an annual dollar amount or as a percentage of a property's improvements.

The cost approach is most helpful in the appraisal of newer or special-purpose buildings such as schools, churches, and public buildings. Such properties are difficult to appraise using other methods because there are seldom enough local sales to use as comparables and because the properties do not ordinarily generate income.

Much of the functional obsolescence and all of the external depreciation can be evaluated by considering the actions of buyers in the marketplace.

The Income Approach

The **income approach** to value is based on the present value of the rights to future income. It assumes that the income generated by a property will determine the property's value. The income approach is used for valuation of income-producing properties such as apartment buildings, office buildings, and shopping centers. In estimating value using the income approach, an appraiser must take five steps, illustrated in Table 19.3.

1. Estimate annual *potential gross income*. An estimate of economic rental income must be made based on market studies. Current rental income may not reflect the current market rental rates, especially in the case of short-term leases or leases about to terminate. Potential income includes other income to the property from such sources as vending machines, parking fees, and laundry machines.
2. Deduct an appropriate allowance for vacancy and rent loss, based on the appraiser's experience, and arrive at *effective gross income*.
3. Deduct the annual operating expenses, enumerated in Table 19.3, from the effective gross income to arrive at the annual *net operating income* (NOI). Management costs are always included, even if the current owner manages the property. Mortgage payments (principal and interest) are *debt service* and not considered operating expenses.
4. Estimate the price a typical investor would pay for the income produced by this particular type and class of property. This is done by estimating the rate of return (or yield) that an investor will demand for the investment of capital in this type of building. This rate of return is called the **capitalization** (or "cap") **rate** and is determined by comparing the relationship of net operating income to the sales prices of similar properties that have sold in the current market. For example, a comparable property that is producing an annual net income of $15,000 is sold for $187,500. The capitalization rate is $15,000 divided by $187,500, or 8 percent. If other comparable properties sold at prices that yielded substantially the same rate, it may be concluded that 8 percent is the rate that the appraiser should apply to the subject property.
5. Apply the capitalization rate to the property's annual net operating income to arrive at the estimate of the property's value.

With the appropriate capitalization rate and the projected annual net operating income, the appraiser can obtain an indication of value by the income approach.

This formula and its variations are important in dealing with income property:

$$\text{Income} \div \text{Rate} = \text{Value} \quad \text{Income} \div \text{Value} = \text{Rate} \quad \text{Value} \times \text{Rate} = \text{Income}$$

These formulas may be illustrated graphically as

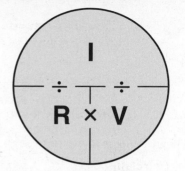

Annual net operating income ÷ Capitalization rate = Value

Example: $72,000 income ÷ 9% cap rate = $800,000 value or
$72,000 income ÷ 8% cap rate = $900,000 value

Note the relationship between the rate and value. As the rate goes down, the value increases.

A very simplified version of the computations used in applying the income approach is illustrated in Table 19.3.

Gross rent or gross income multipliers.   Certain properties, such as single-family homes and two-unit buildings, are not purchased primarily for income. As a substitute for a more elaborate income capitalization analysis, the **gross rent multiplier** (GRM) and **gross income multiplier** (GIM) are often used in the appraisal process. Each relates the sales price of a property to its rental income.

Because single-family residences usually produce only rental incomes, the gross rent multiplier is used. This relates a sales price to monthly rental income. However, commercial and industrial properties generate income from many other sources (rent, concessions, escalator clause income, and so forth), and they are valued using their annual income from all sources.

The formulas are as follows:

> For five or more residential units, commercial or industrial property:
> Sales Price ÷ Gross Annual Income = Gross Income Multiplier (GIM)

> or

> For one to four residential units:
> Sales Price ÷ Gross Monthly Rent = Gross Rent Multiplier (GRM)

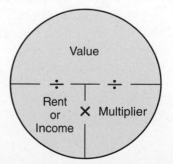

	Comparable No.	Sales Price	Monthly Rent	GRM
TABLE 19.4	1	$193,600	$1,650	117
	2	178,500	1,450	123
Gross Rent Multiplier	3	195,500	1,675	117
	4	182,000	1,565	116
	Subject	?	1,625	?

Note: Based on an analysis of these comparisons, a GRM of 117 seems reasonable for homes in this area. In the opinion of an appraiser, then, the estimated value of the subject property would be $1,625 × 117, or $190,125.

■ **FOR EXAMPLE** If a home recently sold for $382,000 and its monthly rental income was $2,650, the GRM for the property would be computed

$$\$382,000 \div \$2,650 = 144.15 \text{ GRM}$$

To establish an accurate GRM, an appraiser must have recent sales and rental data from at least four properties that are similar to the subject property. The resulting GRM then can be applied to the estimated fair market rental of the subject property to arrive at its market value. The formula would be

$$\text{Rental Income} \times \text{GRM} = \text{Estimated Market Value}$$

Table 19.4 shows some examples of GRM comparisons.

Reconciliation

When the three approaches to value are applied to the same property, they normally produce three separate indications of value. (For instance, compare Table 19.1 with Table 19.2.) **Reconciliation** is the art of analyzing and effectively weighing the findings from the three approaches. It is an ongoing process, culminating in the final reconciliation where the three approaches to value are weighed and a final opinion of value determined.

The process of reconciliation is more complicated than simply taking the average of the three estimates of value. An average implies that the data and logic applied in each of the approaches are equally valid and reliable and should therefore be given equal weight. In fact, however, certain approaches are more valid and reliable with some kinds of properties than with others. However, data must be verified by an independent source.

■ **FOR EXAMPLE** In appraising a home, the income approach is rarely valid, and the cost approach is of limited value unless the home is relatively new. Therefore, the sales comparison approach is usually given greatest weight in valuing single-family residences. In the appraisal of income or investment property, the income approach normally is given the greatest weight. In the appraisal of churches, libraries, museums, schools, and other special-use properties, where little or no income or sales revenue is generated, the cost approach usually is assigned the greatest weight. From this analysis, or reconciliation, a single estimate of market value is produced.

FIGURE 19.1

The Appraisal Process

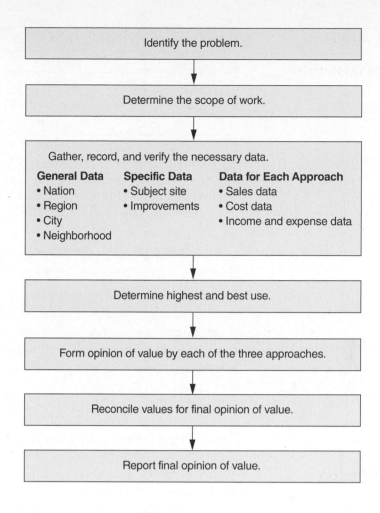

Identify the problem.

Determine the scope of work.

Gather, record, and verify the necessary data.

General Data	Specific Data	Data for Each Approach
• Nation	• Subject site	• Sales data
• Region	• Improvements	• Cost data
• City		• Income and expense data
• Neighborhood		

Determine highest and best use.

Form opinion of value by each of the three approaches.

Reconcile values for final opinion of value.

Report final opinion of value.

■ THE APPRAISAL PROCESS

Although appraising is not an exact or a precise science, the key to an accurate appraisal lies in the methodical collection and analysis of data. The appraisal process is an orderly set of procedures used to collect and analyze data to arrive at an ultimate value conclusion. The data are divided into two basic classes:

1. *General data,* covering the nation, region, city, and neighborhood. Of particular importance is the neighborhood, where an appraiser finds the physical, economic, social, and political influences that directly affect the value and potential of the subject property.
2. *Specific data,* covering details of the subject property as well as comparative data relating to costs, sales, and income and expenses of properties similar to and competitive with the subject property.

Figure 19.1 outlines the steps an appraiser takes in carrying out an appraisal assignment.

Once the approaches have been reconciled and an opinion of value has been reached, the appraiser prepares a report for the client. The report should

■ identify the real estate and real property interest being appraised;
■ state the purpose and intended use of the appraisal;
■ define the value to be estimated;
■ state the effective date of the value and the date of the report;

- state the extent of the process of collecting, confirming, and reporting the data;
- list all assumptions and limiting conditions that affect the analysis, opinion, and conclusions of value;
- describe the information considered, the appraisal procedures followed, and the reasoning that supports the report's conclusions; if an approach was excluded, the report should explain why;
- describe (if necessary or appropriate) the appraiser's opinion of the highest and best use of the real estate;
- describe any additional information that may be appropriate to show compliance with the specific guidelines established in the Uniform Standards of Professional Appraisal Practice (USPAP) or to clearly identify and explain any departures from these guidelines; and
- include signed certification, as required by the Uniform Standards.

Figure 19.2 shows the Uniform Residential Appraisal Report, the form required by many government agencies. It illustrates the types of detailed information required of an appraisal of residential property.

IN PRACTICE

The appraiser relies on experience and expertise in valuation theories to evaluate market data. The appraiser does not establish the property's worth; instead, he or she verifies what the market indicates. This is important particularly when dealing with a property owner who may lack objectivity about the realistic value of his or her property. The lack of objectivity also can complicate a salesperson's ability to list the property within the most probable range of market value. An appraiser supplies a supportable and objective report about value and the market creating it.

■ SUMMARY

To appraise real estate means to estimate its value. Although many types of value exist, the most common objective of an appraisal is to estimate market value—the most probable sales price of a property. Basic to appraising are certain underlying economic principles, such as highest and best use, substitution, supply and demand, conformity, anticipation, increasing and diminishing returns, regression, progression, plottage, contribution, competition, and change.

Value is an estimate of future benefits, cost represents a measure of past expenditures, and price reflects the actual amount of money paid for a property.

In the sales comparison approach, the value of the subject property is compared with the values of others like it that have sold recently. Because no two properties are exactly alike, adjustments must be made to account for any differences. With the cost approach, an appraiser calculates the cost of building a similar structure on a similar site. The appraiser then subtracts depreciation (losses in value), which reflects the differences between new properties of this type and the present condition of the subject property. The income approach is an analysis based on the relationship between the rate of return that an investor requires and the net income that a property produces.

An informal version of the income approach, called the gross rent multiplier (GRM), may be used to estimate the value of single-family residential properties that are not usually rented, but could be. The GRM is computed by dividing the sales price of a property by its gross monthly rent. For commercial or industrial property, a gross income multiplier (GIM), based on gross annual income from all sources, may be used. In the process of reconciliation, the validity and reliability of each approach are weighed objectively to arrive at the single best and most supportable estimate of value.

In Illinois   The Illinois *Real Estate Appraiser Licensing Act of 2002* requires licensure and certification of Illinois appraisers in federally related transactions. Only individuals (not corporations, partnerships, firms, or groups) may be certified as appraisers or act as associate real estate appraisers. ■

F I G U R E 19.2

Uniform Residential Appraisal Report

Uniform Residential Appraisal Report
File #

The purpose of this summary appraisal report is to provide the lender/client with an accurate, and adequately supported, opinion of the market value of the subject property.

SUBJECT

Property Address		City		State	Zip Code
Borrower	Owner of Public Record			County	

Legal Description

Assessor's Parcel #		Tax Year	R.E. Taxes $
Neighborhood Name		Map Reference	Census Tract

Occupant ☐ Owner ☐ Tenant ☐ Vacant   Special Assessments $ ☐ PUD HOA $ ☐ per year ☐ per month

Property Rights Appraised ☐ Fee Simple ☐ Leasehold ☐ Other (describe)

Assignment Type ☐ Purchase Transaction ☐ Refinance Transaction ☐ Other (describe)

Lender/Client   Address

Is the subject property currently offered for sale or has it been offered for sale in the twelve months prior to the effective date of this appraisal? ☐ Yes ☐ No

Report data source(s) used, offering price(s), and date(s).

CONTRACT

I ☐ did ☐ did not analyze the contract for sale for the subject purchase transaction. Explain the results of the analysis of the contract for sale or why the analysis was not performed.

Contract Price $ Date of Contract   Is the property seller the owner of public record? ☐ Yes ☐ No Data Source(s)

Is there any financial assistance (loan charges, sale concessions, gift or downpayment assistance, etc.) to be paid by any party on behalf of the borrower? ☐ Yes ☐ No
If Yes, report the total dollar amount and describe the items to be paid.

NEIGHBORHOOD

Note: Race and the racial composition of the neighborhood are not appraisal factors.

Neighborhood Characteristics			One-Unit Housing Trends			One-Unit Housing		Present Land Use %	
Location ☐ Urban ☐ Suburban ☐ Rural			Property Values ☐ Increasing ☐ Stable ☐ Declining			PRICE	AGE	One-Unit	%
Built-Up ☐ Over 75% ☐ 25–75% ☐ Under 25%			Demand/Supply ☐ Shortage ☐ In Balance ☐ Over Supply			$ (000)	(yrs)	2-4 Unit	%
Growth ☐ Rapid ☐ Stable ☐ Slow			Marketing Time ☐ Under 3 mths ☐ 3–6 mths ☐ Over 6 mths			Low		Multi-Family	%
Neighborhood Boundaries						High		Commercial	%
						Pred.		Other	%

Neighborhood Description

Market Conditions (including support for the above conclusions)

SITE

Dimensions		Area	Shape		View	

Specific Zoning Classification   Zoning Description

Zoning Compliance ☐ Legal ☐ Legal Nonconforming (Grandfathered Use) ☐ No Zoning ☐ Illegal (describe)

Is the highest and best use of the subject property as improved (or as proposed per plans and specifications) the present use? ☐ Yes ☐ No If No, describe

Utilities	Public	Other (describe)		Public	Other (describe)	Off-site Improvements—Type	Public	Private
Electricity	☐	☐	Water	☐	☐	Street	☐	☐
Gas	☐	☐	Sanitary Sewer	☐	☐	Alley	☐	☐

FEMA Special Flood Hazard Area ☐ Yes ☐ No FEMA Flood Zone   FEMA Map #   FEMA Map Date

Are the utilities and off-site improvements typical for the market area? ☐ Yes ☐ No If No, describe

Are there any adverse site conditions or external factors (easements, encroachments, environmental conditions, land uses, etc.)? ☐ Yes ☐ No If Yes, describe

IMPROVEMENTS

General Description		Foundation		Exterior Description	materials/condition	Interior	materials/condition
Units ☐ One ☐ One with Accessory Unit		☐ Concrete Slab ☐ Crawl Space		Foundation Walls		Floors	
# of Stories		☐ Full Basement ☐ Partial Basement		Exterior Walls		Walls	
Type ☐ Det. ☐ Att. ☐ S-Det./End Unit		Basement Area sq. ft.		Roof Surface		Trim/Finish	
☐ Existing ☐ Proposed ☐ Under Const.		Basement Finish %		Gutters & Downspouts		Bath Floor	
Design (Style)		☐ Outside Entry/Exit ☐ Sump Pump		Window Type		Bath Wainscot	
Year Built		Evidence of ☐ Infestation		Storm Sash/Insulated		Car Storage ☐ None	
Effective Age (Yrs)		☐ Dampness ☐ Settlement		Screens		☐ Driveway # of Cars	
Attic ☐ None		Heating ☐ FWA ☐ HWBB ☐ Radiant		Amenities ☐ Woodstove(s) #		Driveway Surface	
☐ Drop Stair ☐ Stairs		☐ Other Fuel		☐ Fireplace(s) # ☐ Fence		☐ Garage # of Cars	
☐ Floor ☐ Scuttle		Cooling ☐ Central Air Conditioning		☐ Patio/Deck ☐ Porch		☐ Carport # of Cars	
☐ Finished ☐ Heated		☐ Individual ☐ Other		☐ Pool ☐ Other		☐ Att. ☐ Det. ☐ Built-in	

Appliances ☐ Refrigerator ☐ Range/Oven ☐ Dishwasher ☐ Disposal ☐ Microwave ☐ Washer/Dryer ☐ Other (describe)

Finished area **above** grade contains: Rooms   Bedrooms   Bath(s)   Square Feet of Gross Living Area Above Grade

Additional features (special energy efficient items, etc.)

Describe the condition of the property (including needed repairs, deterioration, renovations, remodeling, etc.).

Are there any physical deficiencies or adverse conditions that affect the livability, soundness, or structural integrity of the property? ☐ Yes ☐ No If Yes, describe

Does the property generally conform to the neighborhood (functional utility, style, condition, use, construction, etc.)? ☐ Yes ☐ No If No, describe

F I G U R E 19.2 (CONTINUED)

Uniform Residential Appraisal Report

Uniform Residential Appraisal Report   File

There are	comparable properties currently offered for sale in the subject neighborhood ranging in price from $		to $	
There are	comparable sales in the subject neighborhood within the past twelve months ranging in sale price from $		to $	

FEATURE	SUBJECT	COMPARABLE SALE # 1	COMPARABLE SALE # 2	COMPARABLE SALE # 3
Address				
Proximity to Subject				
Sale Price	$	$	$	$
Sale Price/Gross Liv. Area	$ sq. ft.	$ sq. ft.	$ sq. ft.	$ sq. ft.
Data Source(s)				
Verification Source(s)				

VALUE ADJUSTMENTS	DESCRIPTION	DESCRIPTION	+(-) $ Adjustment	DESCRIPTION	+(-) $ Adjustment	DESCRIPTION	+(-) $ Adjustment
Sale or Financing Concessions							
Date of Sale/Time							
Location							
Leasehold/Fee Simple							
Site							
View							
Design (Style)							
Quality of Construction							
Actual Age							
Condition							
Above Grade	Total Bdrms. Baths	Total Bdrms. Baths		Total Bdrms. Baths		Total Bdrms. Baths	
Room Count							
Gross Living Area	sq. ft.	sq. ft.		sq. ft.		sq. ft.	
Basement & Finished Rooms Below Grade							
Functional Utility							
Heating/Cooling							
Energy Efficient Items							
Garage/Carport							
Porch/Patio/Deck							
Net Adjustment (Total)		☐ + ☐ - $		☐ + ☐ - $		☐ + ☐ - $	
Adjusted Sale Price of Comparables		Net Adj. % Gross Adj. % $		Net Adj. % Gross Adj. % $		Net Adj. % Gross Adj. % $	

I ☐ did ☐ did not research the sale or transfer history of the subject property and comparable sales. If not, explain

My research ☐ did ☐ did not reveal any prior sales or transfers of the subject property for the three years prior to the effective date of this appraisal.

Data source(s)

My research ☐ did ☐ did not reveal any prior sales or transfers of the comparable sales for the year prior to the date of sale of the comparable sale.

Data source(s)

Report the results of the research and analysis of the prior sale or transfer history of the subject property and comparable sales (report additional prior sales on page 3).

ITEM	SUBJECT	COMPARABLE SALE # 1	COMPARABLE SALE # 2	COMPARABLE SALE # 3
Date of Prior Sale/Transfer				
Price of Prior Sale/Transfer				
Data Source(s)				
Effective Date of Data Source(s)				

Analysis of prior sale or transfer history of the subject property and comparable sales

Summary of Sales Comparison Approach

Indicated Value by Sales Comparison Approach $

Indicated Value by: Sales Comparison Approach $ Cost Approach (if developed) $ Income Approach (if developed) $

This appraisal is made ☐ "as is", ☐ subject to completion per plans and specifications on the basis of a hypothetical condition that the improvements have been completed, ☐ subject to the following repairs or alterations on the basis of a hypothetical condition that the repairs or alterations have been completed, or ☐ subject to the following required inspection based on the extraordinary assumption that the condition or deficiency does not require alteration or repair:

Based on a complete visual inspection of the interior and exterior areas of the subject property, defined scope of work, statement of assumptions and limiting conditions, and appraiser's certification, my (our) opinion of the market value, as defined, of the real property that is the subject of this report is $, as of   , which is the date of inspection and the effective date of this appraisal.

F I G U R E 19.2 (CONTINUED)

Uniform Residential Appraisal Report

Uniform Residential Appraisal Report   File

ADDITIONAL COMMENTS

COST APPROACH TO VALUE (not required by Fannie Mae)

Provide adequate information for the lender/client to replicate the below cost figures and calculations.

Support for the opinion of site value (summary of comparable land sales or other methods for estimating site value)

COST APPROACH

ESTIMATED ☐ REPRODUCTION OR ☐ REPLACEMENT COST NEW   OPINION OF SITE VALUE .... = $

Source of cost data   Dwelling   Sq. Ft. @ $ .... = $

Quality rating from cost service   Effective date of cost data   Sq. Ft. @ $ .... = $

Comments on Cost Approach (gross living area calculations, depreciation, etc.)

Garage/Carport   Sq. Ft. @ $ .... = $

Total Estimate of Cost-New .... = $

Less   Physical   Functional   External

Depreciation   =$(   )

Depreciated Cost of Improvements .... = $

"As-Is" Value of Site Improvements .... = $

Estimated Remaining Economic Life (HUD and VA only)   Years   Indicated Value By Cost Approach .... = $

INCOME APPROACH TO VALUE (not required by Fannie Mae)

INCOME

Estimated Monthly Market Rent $ X Gross Rent Multiplier   = $ Indicated Value by Income Approach

Summary of Income Approach (including support for market rent and GRM)

PROJECT INFORMATION FOR PUDs (if applicable)

PUD INFORMATION

Is the developer/builder in control of the Homeowners' Association (HOA)? ☐ Yes ☐ No   Unit type(s) ☐ Detached ☐ Attached

Provide the following information for PUDs ONLY if the developer/builder is in control of the HOA and the subject property is an attached dwelling unit.

Legal name of project

Total number of phases   Total number of units   Total number of units sold

Total number of units rented   Total number of units for sale   Data source(s)

Was the project created by the conversion of an existing building(s) into a PUD? ☐ Yes ☐ No   If Yes, date of conversion

Does the project contain any multi-dwelling units? ☐ Yes ☐ No   Data source(s)

Are the units, common elements, and recreation facilities complete? ☐ Yes ☐ No   If No, describe the status of completion.

Are the common elements leased to or by the Homeowners' Association? ☐ Yes ☐ No   If Yes, describe the rental terms and options.

Describe common elements and recreational facilities

Freddie Mac Form 70   March 2005   Page 3 of 6   Fannie Mae Form 1004   March 2005

F I G U R E 19.2 (CONTINUED)

Uniform Residential Appraisal Report

Uniform Residential Appraisal Report   File #

This report form is designed to report an appraisal of a one-unit property or a one-unit property with an accessory unit; including a unit in a planned unit development (PUD). This report form is not designed to report an appraisal of a manufactured home or a unit in a condominium or cooperative project.

This appraisal report is subject to the following scope of work, intended use, intended user, definition of market value, statement of assumptions and limiting conditions, and certifications. Modifications, additions, or deletions to the intended use, intended user, definition of market value, or assumptions and limiting conditions are not permitted. The appraiser may expand the scope of work to include any additional research or analysis necessary based on the complexity of this appraisal assignment. Modifications or deletions to the certifications are also not permitted. However, additional certifications that do not constitute material alterations to this appraisal report, such as those required by law or those related to the appraiser's continuing education or membership in an appraisal organization, are permitted.

SCOPE OF WORK: The scope of work for this appraisal is defined by the complexity of this appraisal assignment and the reporting requirements of this appraisal report form, including the following definition of market value, statement of assumptions and limiting conditions, and certifications. The appraiser must, at a minimum: (1) perform a complete visual inspection of the interior and exterior areas of the subject property, (2) inspect the neighborhood, (3) inspect each of the comparable sales from at least the street, (4) research, verify, and analyze data from reliable public and/or private sources, and (5) report his or her analysis, opinions, and conclusions in this appraisal report.

INTENDED USE: The intended use of this appraisal report is for the lender/client to evaluate the property that is the subject of this appraisal for a mortgage finance transaction.

INTENDED USER: The intended user of this appraisal report is the lender/client.

DEFINITION OF MARKET VALUE: The most probable price which a property should bring in a competitive and open market under all conditions requisite to a fair sale, the buyer and seller, each acting prudently, knowledgeably and assuming the price is not affected by undue stimulus. Implicit in this definition is the consummation of a sale as of a specified date and the passing of title from seller to buyer under conditions whereby: (1) buyer and seller are typically motivated; (2) both parties are well informed or well advised, and each acting in what he or she considers his or her own best interest; (3) a reasonable time is allowed for exposure in the open market; (4) payment is made in terms of cash in U. S. dollars or in terms of financial arrangements comparable thereto; and (5) the price represents the normal consideration for the property sold unaffected by special or creative financing or sales concessions* granted by anyone associated with the sale.

*Adjustments to the comparables must be made for special or creative financing or sales concessions. No adjustments are necessary for those costs which are normally paid by sellers as a result of tradition or law in a market area; these costs are readily identifiable since the seller pays these costs in virtually all sales transactions. Special or creative financing adjustments can be made to the comparable property by comparisons to financing terms offered by a third party institutional lender that is not already involved in the property or transaction. Any adjustment should not be calculated on a mechanical dollar for dollar cost of the financing or concession but the dollar amount of any adjustment should approximate the market's reaction to the financing or concessions based on the appraiser's judgment.

STATEMENT OF ASSUMPTIONS AND LIMITING CONDITIONS: The appraiser's certification in this report is subject to the following assumptions and limiting conditions:

1. The appraiser will not be responsible for matters of a legal nature that affect either the property being appraised or the title to it, except for information that he or she became aware of during the research involved in performing this appraisal. The appraiser assumes that the title is good and marketable and will not render any opinions about the title.

2. The appraiser has provided a sketch in this appraisal report to show the approximate dimensions of the improvements. The sketch is included only to assist the reader in visualizing the property and understanding the appraiser's determination of its size.

3. The appraiser has examined the available flood maps that are provided by the Federal Emergency Management Agency (or other data sources) and has noted in this appraisal report whether any portion of the subject site is located in an identified Special Flood Hazard Area. Because the appraiser is not a surveyor, he or she makes no guarantees, express or implied, regarding this determination.

4. The appraiser will not give testimony or appear in court because he or she made an appraisal of the property in question, unless specific arrangements to do so have been made beforehand, or as otherwise required by law.

5. The appraiser has noted in this appraisal report any adverse conditions (such as needed repairs, deterioration, the presence of hazardous wastes, toxic substances, etc.) observed during the inspection of the subject property or that he or she became aware of during the research involved in performing this appraisal. Unless otherwise stated in this appraisal report, the appraiser has no knowledge of any hidden or unapparent physical deficiencies or adverse conditions of the property (such as, but not limited to, needed repairs, deterioration, the presence of hazardous wastes, toxic substances, adverse environmental conditions, etc.) that would make the property less valuable, and has assumed that there are no such conditions and makes no guarantees or warranties, express or implied. The appraiser will not be responsible for any such conditions that do exist or for any engineering or testing that might be required to discover whether such conditions exist. Because the appraiser is not an expert in the field of environmental hazards, this appraisal report must not be considered as an environmental assessment of the property.

6. The appraiser has based his or her appraisal report and valuation conclusion for an appraisal that is subject to satisfactory completion, repairs, or alterations on the assumption that the completion, repairs, or alterations of the subject property will be performed in a professional manner.

F I G U R E 19.2 (CONTINUED)

Uniform Residential Appraisal Report

Uniform Residential Appraisal Report
File #

APPRAISER'S CERTIFICATION: The Appraiser certifies and agrees that:

1. I have, at a minimum, developed and reported this appraisal in accordance with the scope of work requirements stated in this appraisal report.

2. I performed a complete visual inspection of the interior and exterior areas of the subject property. I reported the condition of the improvements in factual, specific terms. I identified and reported the physical deficiencies that could affect the livability, soundness, or structural integrity of the property.

3. I performed this appraisal in accordance with the requirements of the Uniform Standards of Professional Appraisal Practice that were adopted and promulgated by the Appraisal Standards Board of The Appraisal Foundation and that were in place at the time this appraisal report was prepared.

4. I developed my opinion of the market value of the real property that is the subject of this report based on the sales comparison approach to value. I have adequate comparable market data to develop a reliable sales comparison approach for this appraisal assignment. I further certify that I considered the cost and income approaches to value but did not develop them, unless otherwise indicated in this report.

5. I researched, verified, analyzed, and reported on any current agreement for sale for the subject property, any offering for sale of the subject property in the twelve months prior to the effective date of this appraisal, and the prior sales of the subject property for a minimum of three years prior to the effective date of this appraisal, unless otherwise indicated in this report.

6. I researched, verified, analyzed, and reported on the prior sales of the comparable sales for a minimum of one year prior to the date of sale of the comparable sale, unless otherwise indicated in this report.

7. I selected and used comparable sales that are locationally, physically, and functionally the most similar to the subject property.

8. I have not used comparable sales that were the result of combining a land sale with the contract purchase price of a home that has been built or will be built on the land.

9. I have reported adjustments to the comparable sales that reflect the market's reaction to the differences between the subject property and the comparable sales.

10. I verified, from a disinterested source, all information in this report that was provided by parties who have a financial interest in the sale or financing of the subject property.

11. I have knowledge and experience in appraising this type of property in this market area.

12. I am aware of, and have access to, the necessary and appropriate public and private data sources, such as multiple listing services, tax assessment records, public land records and other such data sources for the area in which the property is located.

13. I obtained the information, estimates, and opinions furnished by other parties and expressed in this appraisal report from reliable sources that I believe to be true and correct.

14. I have taken into consideration the factors that have an impact on value with respect to the subject neighborhood, subject property, and the proximity of the subject property to adverse influences in the development of my opinion of market value. I have noted in this appraisal report any adverse conditions (such as, but not limited to, needed repairs, deterioration, the presence of hazardous wastes, toxic substances, adverse environmental conditions, etc.) observed during the inspection of the subject property or that I became aware of during the research involved in performing this appraisal. I have considered these adverse conditions in my analysis of the property value, and have reported on the effect of the conditions on the value and marketability of the subject property.

15. I have not knowingly withheld any significant information from this appraisal report and, to the best of my knowledge, all statements and information in this appraisal report are true and correct.

16. I stated in this appraisal report my own personal, unbiased, and professional analysis, opinions, and conclusions, which are subject only to the assumptions and limiting conditions in this appraisal report.

17. I have no present or prospective interest in the property that is the subject of this report, and I have no present or prospective personal interest or bias with respect to the participants in the transaction. I did not base, either partially or completely, my analysis and/or opinion of market value in this appraisal report on the race, color, religion, sex, age, marital status, handicap, familial status, or national origin of either the prospective owners or occupants of the subject property or of the present owners or occupants of the properties in the vicinity of the subject property or on any other basis prohibited by law.

18. My employment and/or compensation for performing this appraisal or any future or anticipated appraisals was not conditioned on any agreement or understanding, written or otherwise, that I would report (or present analysis supporting) a predetermined specific value, a predetermined minimum value, a range or direction in value, a value that favors the cause of any party, or the attainment of a specific result or occurrence of a specific subsequent event (such as approval of a pending mortgage loan application).

19. I personally prepared all conclusions and opinions about the real estate that were set forth in this appraisal report. If I relied on significant real property appraisal assistance from any individual or individuals in the performance of this appraisal or the preparation of this appraisal report, I have named such individual(s) and disclosed the specific tasks performed in this appraisal report. I certify that any individual so named is qualified to perform the tasks. I have not authorized anyone to make a change to any item in this appraisal report; therefore, any change made to this appraisal is unauthorized and I will take no responsibility for it.

20. I identified the lender/client in this appraisal report who is the individual, organization, or agent for the organization that ordered and will receive this appraisal report.

Freddie Mac Form 70 March 2005   Page 5 of 6   Fannie Mae Form 1004 March 2005

F I G U R E 19.2 (CONTINUED)

Uniform Residential Appraisal Report

Uniform Residential Appraisal Report   File #

21. The lender/client may disclose or distribute this appraisal report to: the borrower; another lender at the request of the borrower; the mortgagee or its successors and assigns; mortgage insurers; government sponsored enterprises; other secondary market participants; data collection or reporting services; professional appraisal organizations; any department, agency, or instrumentality of the United States; and any state, the District of Columbia, or other jurisdictions; without having to obtain the appraiser's or supervisory appraiser's (if applicable) consent. Such consent must be obtained before this appraisal report may be disclosed or distributed to any other party (including, but not limited to, the public through advertising, public relations, news, sales, or other media).

22. I am aware that any disclosure or distribution of this appraisal report by me or the lender/client may be subject to certain laws and regulations. Further, I am also subject to the provisions of the Uniform Standards of Professional Appraisal Practice that pertain to disclosure or distribution by me.

23. The borrower, another lender at the request of the borrower, the mortgagee or its successors and assigns, mortgage insurers, government sponsored enterprises, and other secondary market participants may rely on this appraisal report as part of any mortgage finance transaction that involves any one or more of these parties.

24. If this appraisal report was transmitted as an "electronic record" containing my "electronic signature," as those terms are defined in applicable federal and/or state laws (excluding audio and video recordings), or a facsimile transmission of this appraisal report containing a copy or representation of my signature, the appraisal report shall be as effective, enforceable and valid as if a paper version of this appraisal report were delivered containing my original hand written signature.

25. Any intentional or negligent misrepresentation(s) contained in this appraisal report may result in civil liability and/or criminal penalties including, but not limited to, fine or imprisonment or both under the provisions of Title 18, United States Code, Section 1001, et seq., or similar state laws.

SUPERVISORY APPRAISER'S CERTIFICATION: The Supervisory Appraiser certifies and agrees that:

1. I directly supervised the appraiser for this appraisal assignment, have read the appraisal report, and agree with the appraiser's analysis, opinions, statements, conclusions, and the appraiser's certification.

2. I accept full responsibility for the contents of this appraisal report including, but not limited to, the appraiser's analysis, opinions, statements, conclusions, and the appraiser's certification.

3. The appraiser identified in this appraisal report is either a sub-contractor or an employee of the supervisory appraiser (or the appraisal firm), is qualified to perform this appraisal, and is acceptable to perform this appraisal under the applicable state law.

4. This appraisal report complies with the Uniform Standards of Professional Appraisal Practice that were adopted and promulgated by the Appraisal Standards Board of The Appraisal Foundation and that were in place at the time this appraisal report was prepared.

5. If this appraisal report was transmitted as an "electronic record" containing my "electronic signature," as those terms are defined in applicable federal and/or state laws (excluding audio and video recordings), or a facsimile transmission of this appraisal report containing a copy or representation of my signature, the appraisal report shall be as effective, enforceable and valid as if a paper version of this appraisal report were delivered containing my original hand written signature.

APPRAISER

Signature_____

Name _____

Company Name _____

Company Address_____

_____

Telephone Number _____

Email Address_____

Date of Signature and Report_____

Effective Date of Appraisal _____

State Certification #_____

or State License #_____

or Other (describe) _____ State #_____

State _____

Expiration Date of Certification or License _____

ADDRESS OF PROPERTY APPRAISED

_____

APPRAISED VALUE OF SUBJECT PROPERTY $ _____

LENDER/CLIENT

Name _____

Company Name _____

Company Address_____

_____

Email Address_____

SUPERVISORY APPRAISER (ONLY IF REQUIRED)

Signature_____

Name _____

Company Name _____

Company Address_____

_____

Telephone Number _____

Email Address_____

Date of Signature _____

State Certification #_____

or State License #_____

State _____

Expiration Date of Certification or License _____

SUBJECT PROPERTY

☐ Did not inspect subject property

☐ Did inspect exterior of subject property from street
    Date of Inspection _____

☐ Did inspect interior and exterior of subject property
    Date of Inspection _____

COMPARABLE SALES

☐ Did not inspect exterior of comparable sales from street

☐ Did inspect exterior of comparable sales from street
    Date of Inspection _____

Freddie Mac Form 70   March 2005   Page 6 of 6   Fannie Mae Form 1004   March 2005

QUESTIONS

1. Which of the following appraisal methods uses a rate of investment return?
   a. Sales comparison approach
   b. Cost approach
   c. Income approach
   d. Gross income multiplier method

2. The characteristics of value include which of the following?
   a. Competition
   b. Scarcity
   c. Anticipation
   d. Balance

3. We know that 457 and 459 Tarpepper Street are adjacent vacant lots, each worth approximately $50,000. If their owner sells them as a single lot, however, the combined parcel will be worth $120,000. What principle does this illustrate?
   a. Substitution
   b. Plottage
   c. Regression
   d. Progression

4. The amount of money a property commands in the marketplace is its
   a. intrinsic value.
   b. market value.
   c. subjective value.
   d. book value.

5. Evan constructs an eight-bedroom brick house with a tennis court, a greenhouse, and an indoor pool in a neighborhood of modest two-bedroom and three-bedroom frame houses on narrow lots. The value of Evan's house is likely to be affected by what principle?
   a. Progression
   b. Assemblage
   c. Change
   d. Regression

6. In question 5, the owners of the lesser-valued houses in Evan's immediate area may find that the values of their homes are affected by what principle?
   a. Progression
   b. Increasing returns
   c. Competition
   d. Regression

7. For appraisal purposes, depreciation is NOT caused by
   a. functional obsolescence.
   b. physical deterioration.
   c. external obsolescence.
   d. accelerated capitalization.

8. *Reconciliation* refers to which of the following?
   a. Loss of value due to any cause
   b. Separating the value of the land from the total value of the property to compute depreciation
   c. Analyzing the results obtained by the different approaches to value to determine a final estimate of value
   d. The process by which an appraiser determines the highest and best use for a parcel of land

9. If a property's annual net income is $24,000 and it is valued at $300,000, what is its capitalization rate?
   a. 8 percent
   b. 10.5 percent
   c. 12.5 percent
   d. 15 percent

10. Certain figures must be determined by an appraiser before value can be computed by the income approach. Which is NOT required for this process?
    a. Annual net operating income
    b. Capitalization rate
    c. Accrued depreciation
    d. Annual gross income

11. Janet, an appraiser, is asked to determine the value of an existing strip shopping center. To which approach to value will Janet probably give the MOST weight?
    a. Cost approach
    b. Sales comparison approach
    c. Income approach
    d. Index method

12. The market value of a parcel of real estate is
    a. an estimate of its future benefits.
    b. the amount of money paid for the property.
    c. an estimate of the most probable price it should bring.
    d. its value without improvements.

13. Capitalization is the process by which annual net operating income is used to
    a. determine cost.
    b. estimate value.
    c. establish depreciation.
    d. determine potential tax value.

14. From the reproduction or replacement cost of a building, the appraiser deducts depreciation, which represents
    a. the remaining economic life of the building.
    b. remodeling costs to increase rentals.
    c. loss of value due to any cause.
    d. costs to modernize the building.

15. The effective gross annual income from a property is $112,000. Total expenses for this year are $53,700. What capitalization rate was used to obtain a valuation of $542,325?
    a. 9.75 percent
    b. 10.25 percent
    c. 10.50 percent
    d. 10.75 percent

16. Which factor would be important in comparing properties under the sales comparison approach to value?
    a. Active listings
    b. Property rent roll
    c. Depreciation
    d. Date of sale

17. Trendsetter Terrace cost $240,000. The building is currently 5 years old and has an estimated remaining useful life of 60 years. Using straight-line depreciation, what is the property's total depreciation to date?
    a. $14,364
    b. $18,462
    c. $20,000
    d. $54,000

18. In question 17, what is the current value of Trendsetter Terrace?
    a. $235,636
    b. $221,538
    c. $220,000
    d. $186,000

19. The appraised value of a residence with four bedrooms and one bathroom would probably be reduced because of
    a. external obsolescence.
    b. functional obsolescence.
    c. curable physical deterioration.
    d. incurable physical deterioration.

20. Ignacio, an appraiser, estimates that it would require 4,000 square feet of concrete, 10,000 square feet of lumber, and $15,000 worth of copper pipe to replace a structure. Ignacio also estimates other factors, such as material, labor, overhead, and builder's profit. Which method of determining reproduction or replacement cost is Ignacio using?
    a. Square-foot method
    b. Quantity-survey method
    c. Index method
    d. Unit-in-place method

21. An appraiser has been hired to determine the value of a vacant city lot. Which of the following would he consider in determining the value of the property?
    a. Topography
    b. Physical depreciation
    c. Assemblage
    d. Utilization of the land

22. If a factory opens or closes in a community, the appraiser would *MOST LIKELY* consider which of the following principles of appraising in determining the value of property in the community?

   a. Substitution

   b. Regression

   c. Progression

   d. Supply and demand

23. What data must be determined by an appraiser in computing value by the income approach?

   a. Appropriate gross income multiplier

   b. Depreciation

   c. Debt service

   d. Annual operating expenses

24. Which of the following is true regarding gross rent multipliers?

   a. An appraiser would use this method to appraise a vacant city lot.

   b. This method of appraising would be used to find the value of a single-family home used for investment purposes.

   c. The first step to computing the gross rent multiplier is to subtract expenses from the rent.

   d. This method of appraising is also known as the *sales comparison approach.*

25. A 35-year-old property has been poorly maintained over the years. It is *MOST LIKELY* to be suffering from

   a. physical deterioration.

   b. external obsolescence.

   c. functional obsolescence.

   d. highest and best use.

In Illinois

26. Amanda wants to be an appraiser in the northwest suburbs of Chicago. While Amanda would be willing to appraise residential properties, her real interest is in appraising commercial properties. If Amanda wants to be qualified to conduct appraisals under FIRREA, what must she do?

   a. Amanda must become a licensed real estate appraiser.

   b. Amanda must become a certified appraiser.

   c. Amanda must become a certified general appraiser.

   d. Amanda must do nothing because individuals who wish to conduct appraisals under FIRREA must receive federal appraisal certification rather than state licensing.

CHAPTER

20

Land-Use Controls and Property Development

■ **LEARNING OBJECTIVES** *When you've finished reading this chapter, you should be able to*

■ **identify** the various types of public and private land-use controls.

■ **describe** how a comprehensive plan influences local real estate development.

■ **explain** the various issues involved in subdivision.

■ **distinguish** the function and characteristics of building codes and zoning ordinances.

■ **define** the following *key terms:*

buffer zones	enabling acts	nonconforming use
building codes	gridiron	plat
clustering	Illinois Human Rights Act	restrictive covenants
comprehensive plan	Illinois Land Sales	subdivider
conditional-use permit	Registration Act	subdivision
deed restriction	Interstate Land Sales Full	taking
density zoning	Disclosure Act	variance
developer	master plan	zoning ordinances

■ **LAND-USE CONTROLS**

Broad though they may be, the rights of real estate ownership are not absolute. Land use is regulated by public and private restrictions and through the public ownership of land by federal, state, and local governments.

Over the years, the government's policy has been to encourage private ownership of land in keeping with "the American Dream." It is necessary, however, for a certain amount of land to be owned by the government for such uses as municipal buildings, state legislative houses, schools, and military stations. In addition, government ownership may serve the public interest through urban renewal efforts, public housing, and streets and highways. Land is also set aside for recreational and conservation purposes in the form of national and state parks and forest preserves.

Many controls on property are instituted at the local level. States delegate to counties and local municipalities the authority to enact ordinances in keeping with general laws. The laws have accumulated over time so that many locations now have controls over noise, air, and water pollution as well as population density.

In Illinois *Article VII of the Illinois Constitution* allows for *home rule* units of government. Any municipality with a population in excess of 25,000 and any county that has a chief executive officer elected by the people are automatically home rule units. However, a home rule unit may elect by referendum not to be one. On the other hand, a municipality of fewer than 25,000 people may elect by referendum to become a home rule unit of government. *Townships are not allowed to be home rule units.*

Constitutionally, a home rule unit of government may exercise any power and perform any function pertaining to its government, including the exercise of *police power* by way of laws that control the use of land. Home rule units also have greater freedom to enforce their laws, including the power to jail offenders for up to six months. Nonhome rule units derive their authority to pass land-use controls from the state government, through *enabling statutes*.

Occasionally, the laws of one unit of government conflict with another's. If any ordinance of a home rule county conflicts with any ordinance of a home rule municipality, the *municipal ordinance prevails*. Township zoning ordinances must give way to county zoning ordinances, and townships are not empowered to pass subdivision controls or building codes. ■

■ THE COMPREHENSIVE PLAN

Local governments establish development goals by creating a **comprehensive plan.** This is also referred to as a **master plan**. The plan includes the municipality's objectives for the future and the strategies and timing for those objectives to be implemented. For instance, a community may want to ensure that social and economic needs are balanced with environmental and aesthetic concerns. The comprehensive plan usually includes the following basic elements:

■ Land use—that is, a determination of how much land may be proposed for residence, industry, business, agriculture, traffic and transit facilities, utilities, community facilities, parks and recreational facilities, floodplains, and areas of special hazards

■ Housing needs of present and anticipated residents, including rehabilitation of declining neighborhoods as well as new residential developments

■ Movement of people and goods, including highways and public transit, parking facilities, and pedestrian and bikeway systems

- Community facilities and utilities, such as schools, libraries, hospitals, recreational facilities, fire and police stations, water resources, sewage and waste treatment and disposal, storm drainage, and flood management
- Energy conservation to reduce energy consumption and promote the use of renewable energy sources

The preparation of a comprehensive plan involves surveys, studies, and analyses of housing, demographic, and economic characteristics and trends. A given municipality's planning activities may be coordinated with other government bodies and private interests to achieve orderly growth and development.

■ **FOR EXAMPLE** After the Great Chicago Fire of 1871 reduced most of the city's downtown to rubble and ash, the city engaged planner Daniel Burnham to lay out a design for Chicago's future. The resulting Burnham Plan of orderly boulevards linking a park along Lake Michigan with other large parks and public spaces throughout the city established an ideal urban space. This master plan is still being implemented today.

■ ZONING

Zoning ordinances are local laws that implement the comprehensive plan and regulate and control the use of land and structures within designated land-use districts. If the comprehensive or master plan is the big picture, zoning makes up the details. Zoning affects such matters as

- permitted uses of each parcel of land,
- lot sizes,
- types of structures,
- building heights,
- setbacks (the minimum distance away from streets or sidewalks that structures may be built),
- style and appearance of structures,
- density (the ratio of land area to structure area), and
- protection of natural resources.

Zoning ordinances cannot be static; they must remain flexible to meet the changing needs of society.

■ **FOR EXAMPLE** In many cities, factories and warehouses sit empty. Some cities have begun changing the zoning ordinances for such properties to permit new residential or commercial developments in areas once zoned strictly for heavy industrial use. Coupled with tax incentives, the changes lure developers back into the cities. The resulting housing is modern, conveniently located, and affordable. Simple zoning changes can help revitalize whole neighborhoods in big cities.

No nationwide or statewide zoning ordinances exist. Rather, zoning powers are conferred on municipal governments by state **enabling acts.** State and federal governments may, however, regulate land use through special legislation, such as scenic easement, coastal management, and environmental laws.

Zoning Objectives

Zoning ordinances have traditionally classified land use into residential, commercial, industrial, and agricultural. These land-use areas are further divided into subclasses. For example, residential areas may be subdivided to provide for detached single-family dwellings, semidetached structures containing not more than four dwelling units, walk-up apartments, highrise apartments, and so forth.

To meet both the growing demand for a variety of housing types and the need for innovative residential and nonresidential development, municipalities are adopting ordinances for subdivisions and planned residential developments. Some municipalities also use **buffer zones,** such as landscaped parks and playgrounds, to screen residential areas from nonresidential zones. Certain types of zoning that focus on special land-use objectives are used in some areas. These include

- *bulk zoning* (or *density zoning)* to control density and avoid overcrowding by imposing restrictions such as setbacks, building heights, and percentage of open area or by restricting new construction projects;
- *aesthetic zoning* to specify certain types of architecture for new buildings; and
- *incentive zoning* to ensure that certain uses are incorporated into developments, such as requiring the street floor of an office building to house retail establishments.

Taking.   The concept of **taking** comes from the takings clause of the Fifth Amendment to the U.S. Constitution. The clause reads, "nor shall private property be taken for public use, without just compensation." This means that when land is taken for public use through the government's power of eminent domain or condemnation, the owner must be compensated. This payment is referred to as *just compensation*—compensation that is just and fair. The compensation may be negotiated between the owner and the government, or the owner may seek a court judgment setting an amount based on appraisals.

Zoning Permits

Zoning laws are generally enforced through the use of permits. Compliance with zoning can be monitored by requiring that property owners obtain permits before they begin any development. A permit will not be issued unless a proposed development conforms to the permitted zoning, among other requirements. *Zoning permits* are usually required before building permits can be issued.

Zoning hearing board.   Zoning hearing boards (or zoning boards of appeal) have been established in most communities to hear complaints about the effects a zoning ordinance may have on specific parcels of property. Petitions for variances or exceptions to the zoning law may be presented to an appeal board.

Nonconforming use.   Frequently, a lot or an improvement does not conform to the zoning law because it existed before the enactment or amendment of the zoning ordinance. Such a **nonconforming use** may be allowed to continue legally as long as it complies with the regulations governing nonconformities in the local ordinance or until the improvement is destroyed or torn down or the current use is abandoned. If the nonconforming use is allowed to continue indefinitely, it is grandfathered into the new zoning.

■ **FOR EXAMPLE** Under Pleasantville's old zoning ordinances, the C&E Store was well within a commercial zone. When the zoning map was changed to accommodate an increased need for residential housing in Pleasantville, C&E was *grandfathered* into the new zoning; that is, it was allowed to continue its successful operations, even though it did not fit the new zoning rules.

Variances and conditional-use permits.   Each time a plan or zoning ordinance is enacted, some property owners are inconvenienced and want to change the use of their property. Generally, these owners may appeal for either a conditional-use permit or a variance to allow a use that does not meet current zoning requirements.

Conditional-use permits allow nonconforming but related land uses.

Variances permit prohibited land uses to avoid undue hardship.

A **conditional-use permit** (also known as a *special-use permit*) is usually granted to a property owner to allow a special use of property, defined as an *allowable conditional use*, within that zone, such as a house of worship or day-care center in a residential district. For a conditional-use permit to be appropriate, the intended use must meet certain standards set by the municipality.

A **variance** (or *exception*), on the other hand, permits a landowner to use his or her property in a manner that is strictly prohibited by the existing zoning. To qualify for a variance, the owner must demonstrate the unique circumstances that make the variance necessary. In addition, the owner must prove that he or she is harmed and burdened by the regulations. Any such variance is said to "run with the land," meaning the exception is passed on to any later owners after a change has been made.

Both variances and conditional-use permits are issued by zoning boards only after public hearings. The neighbors of a proposed use must be given an opportunity to voice their opinions.

A property owner also can seek a complete change in the zoning classification of a parcel of real estate, by obtaining an amendment to the district map or a zoning ordinance for that area, but this is significantly more involved and requires approval by the governing body of the community. Local zoning laws and maps are increasingly available on the Internet for the specific communities involved (*keyword: zoning, paired with the community name*).

■ BUILDING CODES

Most municipalities have enacted ordinances to specify construction standards that must be met when repairing or erecting buildings. These are called **building codes,** and they set the requirements for kinds of materials and standards of workmanship, sanitary equipment, electrical wiring, fire prevention, and similar issues. The International Code Council (ICC) offers Internet support to professionals in keeping track of these numerous codes.

In addition to adhering to building codes, a property owner who wants to build a structure or alter or repair an existing building usually must obtain a *building permit* (costs vary by location and project). Through the permit requirement, municipal officials are made aware of new construction or alterations and can verify compliance with building codes and zoning ordinances. Inspectors will closely examine the plans and conduct periodic inspections of the work. Once the completed structure has been inspected and found satisfactory, the municipal inspector issues a *certificate of occupancy* or *occupancy permit*.

Similarly, communities with historic districts, or those that are interested in maintaining a particular "look" or character, may have aesthetic ordinances. These laws require that all new construction or restorations be approved by a special board. The board ensures that the new structures will "blend in" with existing building styles.

<table>
<tr><td>

IN PRACTICE

</td><td>

The subject of planning, zoning, and restricting the use of real estate is extremely technical, and the interpretation of the law is not always clear. Questions concerning any of these subjects in relation to real estate transactions should be referred to legal counsel. Furthermore, the landowner should be aware of the costs for various permits.

</td></tr>
</table>

■ SUBDIVISION

Subdividers split up land into parcels.

Developers construct improvements on the subdivided parcels.

Most communities have adopted subdivision and land development ordinances as part of their comprehensive plans. An ordinance includes provisions for submitting and processing *subdivision plats*. A major advantage of subdivision ordinances is that they encourage flexibility, economy, and ingenuity in the use of land. A **subdivider** is a person who buys undeveloped acreage and divides it into smaller lots for sale to individuals or developers or for the subdivider's own use. A **developer** (who also may be a subdivider) improves the land, constructs homes or other buildings on the lots, and sells them. *Developing is generally a much more extensive activity than subdividing.*

Regulation of Land Development

There is no national planning and land development legislation that consistently affects the whole country. Laws governing subdividing and land planning are controlled by the state and local governing bodies where the land is located. Many local governments have established standards that are higher than minimum standards set by government agencies.

Land development plan.   Before the actual subdividing can begin, the subdivider must go through the process of *land planning*. The resulting *land development plan* must comply with the municipality's comprehensive plan. Although comprehensive plans and zoning ordinances are not necessarily inflexible, a plan that requires them to be changed must undergo more complicated hearings.

Plats.   From the land development and subdivision plans, the subdivider draws plats. A **plat** is a detailed map that illustrates the geographic boundaries of individual lots. It shows the blocks, sections, streets, public easements, and monuments in the prospective subdivision. A plat also may include engineering data and restrictive covenants. Plat maps are increasingly available for viewing on the Internet.

Subdivision Plans

In plotting out a **subdivision** according to local planning and zoning controls, a subdivider usually determines the size as well as the location of the individual lots. The maximum or minimum size of a lot generally is regulated by local ordinances and must be considered carefully.

The land itself must be studied, usually in cooperation with a surveyor, so that the subdivision takes advantage of natural drainage and land contours. In addition,

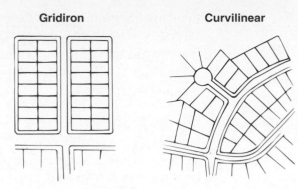

Gridiron   Curvilinear

a percolation test of the soil is done to determine the ability of the ground to absorb and drain water. This information helps to determine the suitability of a site for certain kinds of development and for the installation of septic tanks or injection wells for sewage treatment plants. A subdivider registering his or her development with HUD must include a percolation report in the application. A subdivider should provide for utility easements as well as easements for water and sewer mains.

Many local governments strictly regulate nearly all aspects of subdivision development.

Subdivision Density

Zoning controls often include minimum lot sizes and population density requirements for subdivisions. For example, a typical zoning restriction may set the minimum lot area on which a subdivider can build a single-family housing unit at 10,000 square feet. This means that the subdivider can build four houses per acre. **Density zoning** (or *bulk zoning*) ordinances restrict the average maximum number of houses per acre that may be built within a particular subdivision. In such cases, the subdivider may choose to cluster building lots to achieve an open effect. Regardless of lot size or number of units, the subdivider will be consistent with the ordinance as long as the average number of units in the development remains at or below the maximum density. This average is called *gross density*.

Street patterns.   By varying street patterns and clustering housing units, a subdivider can dramatically increase the amount of open or recreational space in a development. Two possible patterns are the *gridiron* and *curvilinear* patterns. (See Figure 20.1.)

The gridiron pattern evolved out of the government rectangular survey system. Curvilinear developments avoid the uniformity of the gridiron and are quieter and more secure. However, getting from place to place may be more challenging.

Clustering for open space.   By slightly reducing lot sizes and **clustering** them around varying street patterns, a divider can house as many people in the same area as could be done using traditional subdividing plans but with substantially increased tracts of open space.

For example, compare the two subdivisions illustrated in Figure 20.2. Both subdivisions are equal in size and terrain. But when lots are reduced in size and clustered

FIGURE 20.2

Subdivision Styles

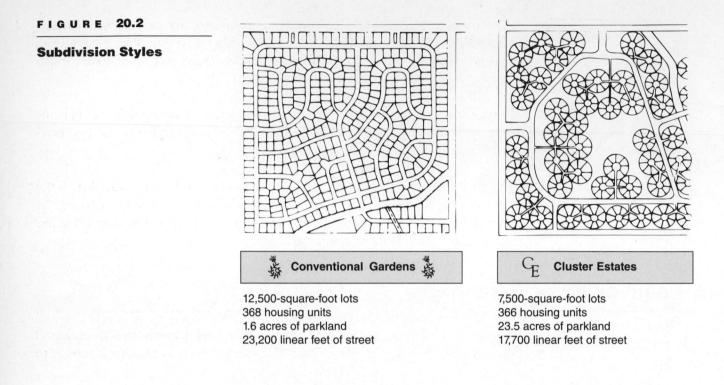

Conventional Gardens

12,500-square-foot lots
368 housing units
1.6 acres of parkland
23,200 linear feet of street

Cluster Estates

7,500-square-foot lots
366 housing units
23.5 acres of parkland
17,700 linear feet of street

around limited-access cul-de-sacs, the number of housing units remains nearly the same (366), with less street area (17,700 linear feet) and dramatically increased open space (23.5 acres).

■ PRIVATE LAND-USE CONTROLS

Certain restrictions to control and to maintain the desirable quality and character of a property or subdivision may be created by private entities, including the property owners themselves. However, no private restriction can violate a local, state, or federal law.

Restrictive covenants. **Restrictive covenants** set standards for all the parcels within a defined subdivision. They usually govern the type, height, and size of buildings that individual owners can erect, as well as land use, architectural style, construction methods, setbacks, and square footage. The deed conveying a particular lot in the subdivision will refer to the plat or declaration of restrictions, thus limiting the title conveyed and binding all grantees. These are known as **deed restrictions** (sometimes called *CC&Rs*), which may even have specific time frames after which they expire.

Restrictive covenants are usually considered valid if they are reasonable restraints that benefit all property owners in the subdivision—for instance, to protect property values or safety. Restrictive covenants can never be for illegal purposes, such as for the exclusion of members of certain races, nationalities, or religions, and are enforced by court injuctions.

| In Illinois | Any restrictive covenant that forbids or restricts conveyance, encumbrance, occupancy, or lease on the basis of race, color, religion, or national origin is void. Exceptions to this section of the **Illinois Human Rights Act** are allowed for religious and charitable organizations. ∎ |

Private land-use controls are often more restrictive of an owner's use than the local zoning ordinances. The rule is that the more restrictive of the two takes precedence.

Private restrictions can be enforced in court when one lot owner applies to the court for an *injunction* to prevent a neighboring lot owner from violating the recorded restrictions. However, rights in this regard may be lost through undue delay or failure to assert them (called *laches*).

∎ REGULATION OF LAND SALES

Just as the sale and use of property within a state are controlled by state and local governments, the sale of property in one state to buyers in another is subject to strict federal and state regulations.

Interstate Land Sales Full Disclosure Act

The federal **Interstate Land Sales Full Disclosure Act** regulates the interstate sale of unimproved lots. The act is administered by the Secretary of Housing and Urban Development (HUD) through the office of Interstate Land Sales Registration. It is designed to prevent fraudulent marketing schemes that may arise when land is sold without being seen by the purchasers. (You may be familiar with stories about gullible buyers whose land purchases were based on glossy brochures shown by smooth-talking salespersons. When the buyers finally went to visit the "pieces of paradise" they'd purchased, they frequently found worthless swampland or barren desert.)

The act with HUD offers unimproved lots in interstate commerce by telephone or through the mail. The statements of record must contain numerous disclosures about the properties.

Developers also are required to provide each purchaser or lessee of property with a printed report before the purchaser or lessee signs a purchase contract or lease. The report must disclose:

- the type of title being transferred to the buyer,
- the number of homes currently occupied on the site,
- the availability of recreation facilities,
- the distance to nearby communities,
- utility services and charges, and
- soil conditions and foundation or construction problems.

Under the act, the purchaser has the right to revoke any contract to purchase a regulated lot until midnight on the seventh day after the contract was signed. If the purchaser or lessee does not receive a copy of the property report before signing the purchase contract or lease, he or she may bring an action to void the contract within two years after signing it.

The act does not apply to subdivisions consisting of fewer than 25 lots or to those in which the lots are of 20 acres or more. Lots offered for sale solely to developers also are exempt from the act's requirements, as are lots on which buildings exist or where a seller is obligated to construct a building within two years. Misrepresentation or failure to comply with the act's requirements subjects a seller to criminal penalties (fines and imprisonment) as well as to civil damages.

State "Subdivided Land" Sales Laws

Many state legislatures have enacted their own subdivided-land sales laws. Some affect only the sale of land located outside the state to state residents. Other states' laws regulate sales of land located both inside and outside the states. These state land sales laws tend to be stricter and more detailed than the federal law. Licensees should be aware of the laws in their state and how they compare with federal law.

In Illinois

The sale or promotion within Illinois of subdivided land is regulated by the **Illinois Land Sales Registration Act** of 1999. This act regulates the offering, sale, lease, or assignment of any improved or unimproved land divided into 25 or more lots and offered as a part of a common promotional plan.

Under this legislation, subdividers must register with the state and file a full disclosure report containing information on the land, location, tax status, financial arrangements, and liens associated with the offering. *A purchaser who does not receive a copy of the public property report at least 48 hours before signing a binding contract of sale has the option of voiding the contract within 48 hours after signing.* Every subdivision submitted for registration must be held open for on-site inspection at the expense of the applicant or for searches of records held by other state or federal agencies. ∎

■ SUMMARY

The control of land use is exercised through public controls, private (or nongovernmental) controls, and direct public ownership of land.

Through power conferred by state enabling acts, local governments exercise public controls based on the states' police powers to protect the public health, safety, and welfare.

A comprehensive plan or master plan sets forth the development goals and objectives for the community. Zoning ordinances carrying out the provisions of the plan and control the use of land and structures within designated land-use districts. Zoning enforcement problems involve zoning hearing boards, conditional-use permits, variances, and exceptions, as well as nonconforming uses. Subdivision and land development regulations are adopted to maintain control of the development of expanding community areas so that growth is harmonious with community standards.

Building codes specify standards for construction, plumbing, sewers, electrical wiring, and fire prevention equipment.

Public ownership is a means of land-use control that provides land for such public benefits as parks, highways, schools, and municipal buildings.

A subdivider buys undeveloped acreage, divides it into smaller parcels, and develops or sells it. A developer builds homes on the lots and sells them through the developer's own sales organization or through local real estate brokerage firms. City planners and land developers, working together, plan whole communities that are later incorporated into cities, towns, or villages.

Land development must comply with the master plans adopted by counties, cities, villages, or towns. This may entail approval of land-use plans by local planning committees or commissioners.

The process of subdivision includes dividing the tract of land into lots and blocks and providing for utility easements, as well as laying out street patterns and widths. A subdivider generally must record a completed plat of subdivision (including the necessary approvals from public officials) in the county where the land is located. Subdividers usually place restrictions on the use of all lots in a subdivision as a general plan for the benefit of all future owners.

By varying street patterns and housing density and clustering housing units, a subdivider can dramatically increase the amount of open and recreational space within a development.

Private land-use controls are exercised by owners through deed restrictions and restrictive covenants. These private restrictions may be enforced by obtaining a court injunction to stop a violator.

Subdivided land sales are regulated on the federal level by *the Interstate Land Sales Full Disclosure Act.* This law requires that developers engaged in certain interstate land sales or leases register the details of the land with HUD. Developers also must provide prospective purchasers or lessees with property reports containing all essential information about the property in any development that exceeds 25 lots.

In Illinois

The Illinois Constitution provides for certain units of government to exercise home rule authority. When a county's ordinance conflicts with a municipality's, the municipal ordinance prevails.

The *Illinois Human Rights Act* prohibits restrictive covenants that discriminate on the basis of race, color, religion, or national origin.

The sale or promotion within Illinois of subdivided land is regulated by the *Illinois Land Sales Registration Act* of 1999. Additional property-related statutes are located in Chapter 765 of the Illinois Compiled Statutes. ∎

QUESTIONS

1. A subdivision declaration reads, "No property within this subdivision may be further subdivided for sale or otherwise, and no property may be used for other than single-family housing." This is an example of
   a. a restrictive covenant.
   b. an illegal reverter clause.
   c. R-1 zoning.
   d. a conditional-use clause.

2. A landowner who wants to use property in a manner that is prohibited by a local zoning ordinance but that would benefit the community can apply for which of the following?
   a. Conditional-use permit
   b. Down zoning
   c. Occupancy permit
   d. Dezoning

3. What is NOT included in public land use controls?
   a. Subdivision regulations
   b. Restrictive covenants
   c. Environmental protection laws
   d. Comprehensive plan specifications

4. Under its zoning, the town of New Pompeii may legally regulate which of the following?
   a. Building ownership
   b. Business ownership
   c. The number of buildings
   d. Enabling acts

5. The purpose of a building permit is to
   a. override a deed's restrictive covenant.
   b. maintain municipal control over the volume of building.
   c. provide evidence of compliance with municipal regulations.
   d. show compliance with restrictive covenants.

6. Zoning powers would MOST LIKELY be conferred on municipal governments in which of the following ways?
   a. By state enabling acts
   b. Through the master plan
   c. By eminent domain
   d. Through escheat

7. The town of East Westchester enacts a new zoning code. Under the new code, commercial buildings are not permitted within 1,000 feet of Lake Westchester. A commercial building that is permitted to continue in its former use even though it is built on the lakeshore is an example of
   a. a nonconforming use.
   b. a variance.
   c. a special use.
   d. inverse condemnation.

8. To determine whether a location can be put to future use as a retail store, one would examine the
   a. building code.
   b. list of permitted nonconforming uses.
   c. housing code.
   d. zoning ordinance.

9. Which would NOT be properly included in a list of deed restrictions?
   a. Types of buildings that may be constructed
   b. Allowable ethnic origins of purchasers
   c. Activities that are not to be conducted at the site
   d. Minimum size of buildings to be constructed

10. A restriction in a seller's deed may be enforced by which of the following?
    a. Court injunction
    b. Zoning board of appeal
    c. City building commission
    d. State legislature

11. George owns a large tract of land. After an adequate study of all the relevant facts, George legally divides the land into 30 lots suitable for the construction of residences. George is a(n)

    a. subdivider.
    b. developer.
    c. land planner.
    d. urban planner.

12. A map illustrating the sizes and locations of streets and lots in a subdivision is called a

    a. gridiron plan.
    b. survey.
    c. plat of subdivision.
    d. property report.

13. In Glendale, subdivision developers are limited by law to constructing no more than an average of three houses per acre in any subdivision. To what does this restriction refer?

    a. Clustering
    b. Density
    c. Out-lots
    d. Covenants

14. The city of Northbend is laid out in a pattern of intersecting streets and avenues. All streets run north and south; all avenues run east and west. Northbend is an example of which street pattern style?

    a. Block plan
    b. Gridiron system
    c. Radial streets plan
    d. Intersecting system

15. Permitted land uses and set-asides, housing projections, transportation issues, and objectives for implementing future controlled development would all be found in a community's

    a. zoning ordinance.
    b. comprehensive plan.
    c. enabling act.
    d. land-control law.

16. Which would NOT usually be shown on the plat for a new subdivision?

    a. Easements for sewer and water mains
    b. Land to be used for streets
    c. Numbered lots and blocks
    d. Prices of residential and commercial lots

17. Acorn Acres is a subdivision featuring spacious homes grouped on large cul-de-sac blocks connected to a central winding road and surrounded by large landscaped common areas. This is an example of which type of subdivision plan?

    a. Cluster plan
    b. Curvilinear system
    c. Rectangular street system
    d. Gridiron system

18. A subdivider can increase the amount of open or recreational space in a development by

    a. varying street patterns.
    b. meeting local housing standards.
    c. scattering housing units.
    d. eliminating multistory dwellings.

19. Under the federal law designed to protect the public from fraudulent interstate land sales, a developer involved in interstate land sales of 25 or more lots must

    a. provide each purchaser with a printed report disclosing details of the property.
    b. pay the prospective buyer's expenses to see the property involved.
    c. provide preferential financing.
    d. allow a 30-day cancellation period.

In Illinois

20. Which of the following statements BEST describes enabling statutes in Illinois?

    a. They grant counties, cities, and villages the power to make and enforce local zoning ordinances.
    b. They make all counties, cities, and villages subject to Illinois state zoning laws.
    c. They require all Illinois counties, cities, and villages to adopt the requirements of the federal municipal planning commission.
    d. They set environmental controls on current land use.

21. Sharon lives in River City, Illinois. She thinks that video-game arcades are a bad influence on the city's young people and wants River City zoned to prohibit all arcades and other public video-gaming facilities. Which of the following would be Sharon's *BEST* course of action?

    a. Try to get the Illinois legislature to amend the state zoning laws

    b. File suit to force River City to conform with existing Illinois zoning laws

    c. Try to persuade the River City town government to change the local zoning laws

    d. Ask the U.S. Department of Housing and Urban Development to force River City to zone against video arcades under its Fifth Amendment powers

22. A zoning law passed by the Village of Blackhawk conflicts with an existing county zoning law. Both the village and the county are home rule units of government. In this situation, which of the following statements is *TRUE*?

    a. Under the Illinois constitution, the county law will prevail, because its zoning laws affect a larger geographic area.

    b. The Village of Blackhawk's law will prevail, because municipal ordinances supersede county ordinances under the Illinois Constitution.

    c. The Illinois Constitution provides that a conflict between the laws of two home rule units must be resolved in the appropriate circuit court.

    d. Whichever law is most restrictive will prevail, unless the issue involves a constitutional question, in which case the law least restrictive of private property rights will supersede the more restrictive law.

21

Fair Housing and Ethical Practices

■ **LEARNING OBJECTIVES** *When you've finished reading this chapter, you should be able to*

■ **identify** the classes of people who are protected against discrimination in housing by various laws.

■ **describe** how the *Fair Housing Act* is enforced.

■ **explain** how fair housing laws address a variety of discriminatory practices and regulate real estate advertising.

■ **distinguish** the protections offered by the *Fair Housing Act*, the *Housing and Community Development Act*, the *Fair Housing Amendments Act*, the *Equal Credit Opportunity Act*, and the *Americans with Disabilities Act*.

■ **define** the following *key terms*:

Americans with Disabilities Act	Equal Credit Opportunity Act	steering
blockbusting	ethics	U.S. Administrative Law Judge
Civil Rights Act of 1866	Fair Housing Act	U.S. District Court Judge
Code of Ethics	Home Mortgage Disclosure Act	Title VIII of the Civil Rights Act of 1968
Department of Housing and Urban Development	redlining	

■ EQUAL OPPORTUNITY IN HOUSING

The purpose of civil rights laws within the real estate industry is to create a marketplace in which all persons of similar financial means are shown the same range of homes in the location of their choice. The goal is to ensure that everyone has the opportunity to live where he or she chooses. Owners, real estate licensees, apartment management companies, real estate groups, lenders, builders, and developers must all take a part in creating this open housing market. Federal, state, and local fair housing or equal opportunity laws affect every phase of a real estate transaction, from listing to closing.

> "All citizens of the United States shall have the same right in every state and territory as is enjoyed by white citizens thereof to inherit, purchase, lease, sell, hold, and convey real and personal property."
> —Civil Rights Act of 1866

The U.S. Congress and the Supreme Court have created a legal framework that preserves the constitutional rights of all citizens. However, while the passage of laws may establish a code for public conduct, damaging attitudes reinforced by centuries of discrimination are not so easily eliminated. Real estate licensees *must* eliminate actions or words that create discrimination (or the appearance of discrimination) if they wish to conduct an ethical and legal business. Similarly, any discriminatory attitudes of property owners or property seekers *must* be addressed by the licensee if these attitudes affect compliance with fair housing laws.

Working with clients who may have discriminatory attitudes is not easy, and the pressure to avoid offending a seller client or buyer client can be intense. However, ethics and the law demand that licensees comply with fair housing laws. *Failure to comply with fair housing laws is both a civil and criminal violation and constitutes grounds for disciplinary action against a licensee.*

The Illinois *Real Estate License Act of 2000* and the *General Rules* require that licensees fully adhere to the principles of equal housing opportunity. A licensed broker or salesperson is prohibited from taking any listing or participating in any transaction in which the property owner seeks to discriminate based on race, color, ancestry, religion, national origin, sex, handicap, or familial status. Breaking fair housing laws in Illinois is a criminal act and grounds for discipline. Violating provisions or restrictions of the Illinois *Real Estate License Act of 2000* (or the *Rules*) can result in suspension, nonrenewal, or revocation of the violator's license or censure, reprimand, or fine imposed by IDFPR.

In Illinois

The *Real Estate License Act of 2000* requires that when a judgment in either a civil or criminal proceeding has been made against a licensee for illegally discriminating, his or her license must be suspended or revoked, unless an appeal is active. Finally, if there has already been an order by an administrative agency finding discrimination by a licensee, the board *must* penalize the licensee.

In addition to state and federal laws, many cities and villages in Illinois have their own fair housing laws. These laws are enforced on the local level and may take precedence over federal laws when the local law has been ruled substantially equivalent to the federal statute. Many local fair housing laws are stricter than state or federal laws. Licensees should familiarize themselves with local regulations as well as with state and federal law. ■

Federal Laws

The federal government's effort to guarantee equal housing opportunities to all U.S. citizens began with the passage of the **Civil Rights Act of 1866.** This law prohibits discrimination based on race.

The U.S. Supreme Court's 1896 decision in *Plessy v. Ferguson* established the "separate but equal" doctrine of "legalized" racial segregation. A series of court

FIGURE 21.1

Federal and State Fair Housing Laws

Legislation	Race	Color	Religion	National Origin	Sex	Age	Marital Status	Disability	Familial Status	Public Assistance Income
Civil Rights Act of 1866	•									
Fair Housing Act of 1968 (Title VIII)	•	•	•	•						
Housing and Community Development Act of 1774					•					
Fair Housing Amendments Act of 1988								•	•	
Equal Credit Opportunity Act of 1974 (lending)	•	•	•	•	•	•	•			•
* Illinois Human Rights Act	•	•	•	•	•	•	•	•	•	

* **Note:** The *Illinois Human Rights Act* specifies both "physical and mental" disability. It also adds as a protected class: ancestry, military status, unfavorable military discharge, and sexual orientation and/or preference as it impacts employment, real estate transactions, financial credit, or availability of public accommodations.

decisions and federal laws in the 20 years between 1948 and 1968 attempted to address housing inequities resulting from *Plessy*. Those efforts, however, often addressed only specific aspects of the housing market (such as federally funded housing programs). As a result, their impact was limited. *Title VIII of the Civil Rights Act of 1968*, however, prohibited specific discriminatory practices throughout the real estate industry.

■ FAIR HOUSING ACT

The *Fair Housing Act* prohibits discrimination based on
■ race,
■ color,
■ religion,
■ sex,
■ disability,
■ familial status, and
■ national origin.

Title VIII of the Civil Rights Act of 1968 prohibited discrimination in housing based on race, color, religion, and national origin. In 1974, the *Housing and Community Development Act* added sex to the list of protected classes. In 1988, the *Fair Housing Amendments Act* added disability and familial status (that is, the presence of children). Today, these laws together are known as the federal **Fair Housing Act.** (See Figure 21.1.) The Fair Housing Act prohibits discrimination on the basis of race, color, religion, sex, disability, familial status, or national origin.

The act also makes it illegal to discriminate against individuals due to their association with persons in the protected classes. The **Department of Housing and Urban Development (HUD)** administers this law. HUD has established rules and regulations that further interpret impacted housing practices. In addition,

FIGURE 21.2

Equal Opportunity Housing Poster

U.S. Department of Housing and Urban Development

EQUAL HOUSING
OPPORTUNITY

We Do Business in Accordance With the Federal Fair Housing Law

(The Fair Housing Amendments Act of 1988)

It is Illegal to Discriminate Against Any Person Because of Race, Color, Religion, Sex, Handicap, Familial Status, or National Origin

---

- In the sale or rental of housing or residential lots
- In advertising the sale or rental of housing
- In the financing of housing

- In the provision of real estate brokerage services
- In the appraisal of housing
- Blockbusting is also illegal

Anyone who feels he or she has been discriminated against may file a complaint of housing discrimination:
    1-800-669-9777 (Toll Free)
    1-800-927-9275 (TDD)

**U.S. Department of Housing and Urban Development
Assistant Secretary for Fair Housing and Equal Opportunity
Washington, D.C. 20410**

Previous editions are obsolete

form HUD-928.1A (2/2003)

HUD distributes the equal housing opportunity poster. (See Figure 21.2.) This poster declares that the office in which it is displayed promises to adhere to the *Fair Housing Act* and pledges support for affirmative marketing and advertising programs. The fair housing poster should be displayed in every real estate office.

IN PRACTICE   When HUD investigates a broker for discriminatory practices, it may consider failure to prominently display the equal housing opportunity poster in the broker's place of business as evidence of discrimination.

In 1988, Congress passed the Fair Housing Amendments Act that expanded federal civil rights protections. In addition to race, color, religion, and national origin being protected classes, the act extended coverage to include families with children and persons with physical or mental disabilities. The act also made the penalties more severe and added damages for noneconomic injuries.

Definitions

HUD's regulations provide specific definitions that clarify the scope of the Fair Housing Act.

Housing.   Housing is defined as a "dwelling" that includes any building or part of a building designed for occupancy as a residence by one or more families. A single-family house, condominium, cooperative, or manufactured housing (mobile home) as well as vacant land on which any of these structures will be located—qualifies under this definition.

Familial status.   *Familial status* refers to the presence of one or more individuals who have not reached the age of 18 and who live with either a parent or guardian. In effect, the familial status reference means that the act's protections extend to families with children. The term includes a woman who is pregnant. Unless a property qualifies as housing for older persons, all properties must be made available to families with children under the same terms and conditions as to anyone else. It is illegal to advertise properties as being for "adults only" or to indicate preferred number of children. Occupancy standards (the number of persons permitted to reside in a property) must be based on objective factors such as sanitation or safety. Landlords cannot restrict the number of occupants to eliminate families with children.

■ **FOR EXAMPLE** Grant owned an apartment building. One of his elderly tenants, Paula, was terminally ill. Paula requested that no children be allowed in the vacant apartment next door because the noise would be difficult for her to bear. Grant agreed and refused to rent to families with children. Even though Grant only wanted to make things easier for a dying tenant, he was nonetheless found to have violated the *Fair Housing Act* by discriminating on the basis of familial status.

Disability.   A *disability* is a physical or mental impairment. The term includes having a history of, or being regarded as having, an impairment that limits one or more of an individual's major life activities. Persons who have AIDS are protected by the fair housing laws under this classification.

Prohibited by Federal Fair Housing Act	Example
Refusing to sell, rent, or negotiate the sale or rental of housing	K owns an apartment building with several vacant units. When an Asian family asks to see one of the units, K tells them to go away.
Changing terms, conditions, or services for different individuals as a means of discriminating	S, a Roman Catholic, calls on a duplex, and the landlord tells her the rent is $400 per month. When she talks to the other tenants, she learns that all the Lutherans in the complex pay only $325 per month.
Advertising any discriminatory preference or limitation in housing or making any inquiry or reference that is discriminatory in nature	A real estate agent places the following advertisement in a newspaper: "Just Listed! Perfect home for white family, near excellent parochial school!" A developer places this ad in an urban newspaper: "Sunset River Hollow—Dream Homes Just For You!" The ad is accompanied by a photo of several African-American families.
Representing that a property is not available for sale or rent when in fact it is	J, who uses a wheelchair, is told that the house J wants to rent is no longer available. The next day, however, the For Rent sign is still in the window.
Profiting by inducing property owners to sell or rent on the basis of the prospective entry into the neighborhood of persons of a protected class	N, a real estate agent, sends brochures to homeowners in the predominantly white Ridgewood neighborhood. The brochures, which feature N's past success selling homes, include photos of racial minorities, population statistics, and the caption, "The Changing Face of Ridgewood."
Altering the terms or conditions of a home loan, or denying a loan, as a means of discrimination	A lender requires M, a divorced mother of two young children, to pay for a credit report. In addition, her father must cosign her application. After talking to a single male friend, M learns that he was not required to do either of those things, despite his lower income and poor credit history.
Denying membership or participation in a multiple listing service, a real estate organization, or another facility related to the sale or rental of housing as a means of discrimination	The Topper County Real Estate Practitioners' Association meets every week to discuss available properties and buyers. None of Topper County's black or female agents is allowed to be a member of the association.

IN PRACTICE

The federal fair housing laws do not extend to defining current users of illegal or controlled substances as persons with disabilities. Nor is anyone who has been convicted of the illegal manufacture or distribution of a controlled substance protected under this law. However, the law does prohibit discrimination against those who are participating in addiction recovery programs. For instance, a landlord could lawfully discriminate against a cocaine addict but not against a member of Alcoholics Anonymous.

It is unlawful to discriminate against prospective buyers or tenants on the basis of disability. Landlords must make reasonable accommodations to existing policies, practices, or services to permit persons with disabilities to have equal enjoyment of the premises. For instance, it would be reasonable for a landlord to permit service animals (such as guide dogs) in a normally "no-pets" building or to provide designated parking spaces for persons with disabilities.

People with disabilities must be permitted to make reasonable modifications to the premises at their own expense. Such modifications might include lowering door handles or installing bath rails for a person in a wheelchair. **Failure to permit reasonable modification constitutes discrimination.** However, the law recognizes that certain reasonable modifications might make a rental property undesirable to the general population. In such a case, the landlord is allowed to require that the property be restored to its previous condition when the lease period ends.

The landlord may not increase for handicapped persons any customarily required security deposit. However, where it is necessary in order to ensure with reasonable certainty that funds will be available to pay for the restorations at the end of the tenancy, the landlord may negotiate as part of such a restoration agreement a provision requiring that the tenant pay into an interest bearing escrow account, over a reasonable period, a reasonable amount of money not to exceed the cost of the restorations. The interest shall accrue to the benefit of the tenant. A landlord may condition permission for a modification on the renter providing a reasonable description of the proposed modifications as well as reasonable assurances that the work will be done in a workmanlike manner and that any required building permits will be obtained.

The law does not prohibit restricting occupancy to persons with disabilities in dwellings that are designed specifically for their accommodation.

For new construction of certain multifamily properties, a number of accessibility and usability requirements must be met under federal law. Access is specified for public-use and common-use portions of the buildings, and adaptive and accessible design must be implemented for the interior of the dwelling units. (Some local areas have additional guidelines and regulations.)

Exemptions to the Fair Housing Act

The federal *Fair Housing Act* provides for certain exemptions. It is important for licensees to know in what situations the exemptions apply. However, licensees should be aware that *no exemptions involve race and no exemptions apply when a real estate licensee is involved in a transaction* (including when selling or leasing his or her own property).

The *Fair Housing Act* exempts:

- owner-occupied buildings with no more than four units,
- single-family housing sold or rented without the use of a broker, and
- housing operated by organizations and private clubs that limit occupancy to members.

The sale or rental of a single-family home is exempt when

- the home is owned by an individual who does not own more than three such homes at one time (and who does not sell more than one every two years),
- a real estate broker or salesperson is *not* involved in the transaction, and
- discriminatory advertising is not used.

The rental of rooms or units is exempt in an owner-occupied one-family to four-family dwelling.

Note that dwelling units owned by religious organizations may be restricted to people of the same religion if membership in the organization is not restricted on the basis of race, color, or national origin. A private club that is not open to the public may restrict the rental or occupancy of lodgings that it owns to its members as long as the lodgings are not operated commercially.

The *Fair Housing Act* does not require that housing be made available to any individual whose tenancy would constitute a direct threat to the health or safety of other individuals or that would result in substantial physical damage to the property of others.

Housing for older persons. While the *Fair Housing Act* protects families with children, certain properties can be restricted to occupancy by elderly persons. Housing intended for persons age 62 or older or housing occupied by at least one person 55 years of age or older (where 80 percent of the units are occupied by individuals 55 or older) is exempt from the familial status protection.

Jones v. Mayer. In 1968, the Supreme Court heard the case of *Jones v. Alfred H. Mayer Company*, 392 U.S. 409 (1968). In its decision, the court upheld the *Civil Rights Act of 1866*. This decision is important because although the federal law exempts individual homeowners and certain groups, the 1866 law prohibits all racial discrimination without exception. A person who is discriminated against on the basis of race may still recover damages under the 1866 law. Where race is involved, no exceptions apply.

The U.S. Supreme Court has expanded the definition of the term *race* to include ancestral and ethnic characteristics, including certain physical, cultural, or linguistic characteristics that are shared by a group with a common national origin. These rulings are significant because discrimination on the basis of race, as it is now defined, affords due process of complaints under the provisions of the *Civil Rights Act of 1866*.

> The *Equal Credit Opportunity Act* prohibits discrimination in granting credit based on
> - race,
> - color,
> - religion,
> - national origin,
> - sex,
> - marital status,
> - age, and
> - public assistance.

Equal Credit Opportunity Act

The federal **Equal Credit Opportunity Act** (ECOA) prohibits discrimination based on race, color, religion, national origin, sex, marital status, or age in the granting of credit. Note that ECOA protects more classes of persons than the *Fair Housing Act*. The ECOA bars discrimination on the basis of marital status and age. It also prevents lenders from discriminating against recipients of public assistance programs, food stamps, or Social Security. The ECOA requires that credit applications be considered only on the basis of income, net worth, job stability, and credit rating.

Americans with Disabilities Act

Although the **Americans with Disabilities Act** (ADA) is not a housing or credit law, it still has a significant effect on the real estate industry. The ADA is important to licensees because it addresses the rights of individuals with disabilities in employment and public accommodations. Real estate brokers are often employers, and real estate brokerage offices are public spaces. The ADA's goal is to enable individuals with disabilities to become part of the economic and social mainstream of society.

The *Americans with Disabilities Act* requires reasonable *accommodations* in employment and access to goods, services, and public buildings.

Title 1 of the ADA requires that employers (including real estate offices) make reasonable accommodations that enable an individual with a disability to perform essential job functions. *Reasonable accommodations* include making the work site accessible, restructuring a job, providing part-time or flexible work schedules, and modifying equipment used on the job. The provisions of ADA apply to any employer with 15 or more employees.

ADA's *Title III* provides for accessibility to goods and services for individuals with disabilities. While the federal civil rights laws have traditionally been seen as focused on residential housing, business and commercial real estate are fully covered by Title III. Because people with disabilities have the right to full and equal access to businesses and public services under the ADA, building owners and managers must ensure that any obstacle restricting this right is eliminated. The *Americans with Disabilities Act Accessibility Guidelines* (ADAAG) contain detailed specifications for designing parking spaces, curb ramps, elevators, drinking fountains, toilet facilities, and directional signs to ensure maximum accessibility.

IN   PRACTICE

Real estate agents need a general knowledge of the ADA's provisions. It is necessary for a broker's workplace and employment policies to comply with the law. Also, licensees who are building managers must ensure that the properties are legally accessible. ADA compliance questions may arise with regard to a client's property, too. Unless the agent is a qualified ADA expert, it is best to advise commercial clients to seek the services of an attorney, an architect, or a consultant who specializes in ADA issues. *Note for future appraisers: It is possible that an appraiser may be liable for failing to identify and account for a property's noncompliance.*

■ FAIR HOUSING PRACTICES

For the civil rights laws to accomplish their goal of eliminating discrimination, licensees must apply them routinely. Of course, compliance also means that licensees consistently represent the ethical standards of the profession. The following discussion examines certain ethical and legal issues that may confront real estate licensees in their day-to-day practice.

Blockbusting

Blockbusting: encouraging the sale or renting of property by claiming that the entry of a protected class of people into the neighborhood will negatively affect property values.asdf

Blockbusting is the act of encouraging people to sell or rent their homes by claiming that the entry of a protected class of people into the neighborhood will have some sort of negative impact on property values. Blockbusting was a common practice during the 1950s and 1960s, when some unscrupulous real estate agents profited by fueling so-called white flight from cities to suburbs. Any message, however subtle or accidental, that property should be sold or rented because the neighborhood is "undergoing changes" is considered blockbusting. *It is illegal to suggest that the presence of certain persons will cause property values to decline, crime or antisocial behavior to increase, or the quality of schools to suffer.*

A critical element in defining blockbusting, according to HUD, is the profit motive. A property owner may be intimidated into selling his or her property at a depressed price to the blockbuster, who in turn sells the property to another person at a higher price. Blockbusting is also called *panic selling*. To avoid accusations of blockbusting, licensees should use good judgment when choosing locations and methods for marketing their services and soliciting listings.

Steering

> *Steering:* channeling homebuyers to particular neighborhoods based on race, religion, nationality, or other consideration.

Steering is the channeling of homebuyers to particular neighborhoods. It also includes discouraging potential buyers from considering some areas. In either case, it is an illegal limitation of a purchaser's options. Many cases of steering are subtle, motivated by assumptions or perceptions about a homebuyer's preferences, based on some stereotype. Such assumptions about a buyer's preferences may be legally dangerous. The licensee should never assume that prospective buyers "expect" to be directed to neighborhoods or properties. Steering anyone is illegal.

> **In Illinois**

The Illinois *Real Estate License Act of 2000* expressly prohibits "Influencing or attempting to influence by any words or acts a prospective seller, purchaser, occupant, landlord, or tenant of real estate, in connection with viewing, buying or leasing of real estate, so as to promote, or tend to promote, the continuance or maintenance of racially and religiously segregated housing, or so as to retard, obstruct or discourage racially integrated housing on or in any street, block, neighborhood, or community." ■

Advertising

No advertisement of property for sale or rent may include language indicating a preference or limitation. No exception to this rule exists, regardless of subtle or "accidental" wordings. HUD's regulations cite numerous examples that are considered discriminatory. (See Figure 21.3.) Promotions of property or real estate services must not target any one population to the exclusion of others. The use of media that targets only certain groups based on, for example, language or geography, is also viewed as being potentially discriminatory. For instance, limiting advertising to a cable television channel viewed mostly by one demographic group might be construed as discriminatory. The best rule is never to advertise using only one group of narrowly focused media. Running ads in several locales *or* in general-circulation media as a standard rule is good practice.

Positive language in the ads, too, may be a factor in determining the legitimacy of a discrimination charge. Many agents choose to run a small version of the equal housing opportunity symbol in all of the materials that represent them, along with the words "equal housing opportunity" underneath. Or repeating the HUD poster statement, *"We do business in accordance with the Federal Fair Housing Law"* may go a long way toward assisting a licensee whose integrity on such issues is ever incorrectly questioned. The fair housing symbol signals the world that one is open for business to anyone who is of age and financially able to purchase real estate.

Appraising

Those who prepare appraisals or any statements of valuation, whether they are formal or informal, oral or written (including a competitive market analysis), may consider any normal qualifying factors that affect value. However, race, color, religion, national origin, sex, disability, and familial status are *not* factors that may be considered.

Redlining

The practice of refusing to make mortgage loans or issue insurance policies in specific areas for reasons other than the applicant's financial qualifications is known as **redlining**. Redlining refers to literally or figuratively drawing a line around particular areas. Such practices contribute to the deterioration of older neighborhoods. Redlining is often based on racial grounds rather than on any real objection to an applicant's creditworthiness. Redlining means that the lender has made a policy

FIGURE 21.3

HUD's Advertising Guidelines

Category	Rule	Permitted	Not Permitted
Race Color National Origin	No discrimination limitation/preference may be expressed	"master bedroom" "good neighborhood"	"white neighborhood "no French"
Religion	No religious preference/limitation	"chapel on premises" "kosher meals available" "Merry Christmas"	"no Muslims" "nice Christian family" "near great Catholic school"
Sex	No explicit preference based on sex	"mother-in-law suite" "master bedroom" "female roommate sought"	"great house for a man" "wife's dream kitchen"
Disability	No exclusions or limitations based on disability	"wheelchair ramp" "walk to shopping"	"no wheelchairs" "able-bodied tenants only"
Familial Status	No preference or limitations based on family size or nature	"two-bedroom" "family room" "quiet neighborhood"	"married couple only" "no more than two children" "retiree's dream house"
Photographs or Illustrations of People	People should be clearly representative and nonexclusive	Illustrations showing ethnic races, family groups, singles, etc.	Illustrations showing *only* singles, African American families, elderly white adults, etc.

decision that *no* property in a certain area will qualify for a loan, no matter who wants to buy it. The federal *Fair Housing Act* prohibits discrimination in mortgage lending and covers not only the actions of primary lenders but also activities in the secondary mortgage market. (A lending institution can, however, refuse a loan solely on sound, documentable financial grounds.)

The **Home Mortgage Disclosure Act** requires that all institutional mortgage lenders with assets in excess of $36 million and one or more offices in a given geographic area make annual reports. The reports must detail all mortgage loans the institution has made or purchased, broken down by census tract. This law enables the government to detect patterns of lending behavior that might constitute redlining.

Intent and Effect

If an owner or real estate licensee *purposely* sets out to engage in blockbusting, steering, or other unfair activities, the *intent* to discriminate is obvious. However, owners and licensees must examine their activities and policies carefully to determine whether they *unintentionally* appear to engage in discriminatory actions. *When policies or practices result in unequal treatment of persons in a protected class, they are considered discriminatory, regardless of intent.* This "effects test" is applied by regulatory agencies to determine whether discrimination has occurred.

■ ENFORCEMENT OF THE FAIR HOUSING ACT

The federal *Fair Housing Act* is administered by the Office of Fair Housing and Equal Opportunity (OFHEO) under the direction of the Secretary of HUD. Any aggrieved person who believes illegal discrimination has occurred may file a complaint with HUD within one year of the alleged act. HUD may also initiate its own complaint. Complaints may be reported to the Office of Fair Housing and Equal Opportunity, Department of Housing and Urban Development, Washington, DC 20410, or to the Office of Fair Housing and Equal Opportunity in care of the nearest HUD regional office.

On receiving a complaint, HUD initiates an investigation. Within 100 days of the filing of the complaint, HUD either determines that reasonable cause exists to bring a charge of illegal discrimination or dismisses the complaint. During this investigation period, HUD can attempt to resolve the dispute informally through conciliation. *Conciliation* is the resolution of a complaint by obtaining assurance that the person against whom the complaint was filed (the respondent) will remedy any violation that may have occurred. The respondent further agrees to take steps to eliminate or prevent discriminatory practices in the future. If necessary, these agreements can be enforced through civil action.

Once a formal charge of discrimination has been filed, a *formal hearing* is required. Either the complainant or the respondent may force the hearing to District Court by means of what is called an *election*, which must be made within 20 days after charges are issued. If no election is made, the case will be heard before a **U.S. Administrative Law Judge (ALJ)** who is an expert in housing discrimination. If either party prefers, then by election the case goes to a **U.S. District Court Judge** (no fair housing specialization, under the Department of Justice, and a jury trial may be requested). Cases under the ALJs normally proceed much more quickly than if they were heard in District Court, and the fair housing expertise may be higher. The judge has the authority to award actual damages to the aggrieved person or persons and, if it is believed the public interest will be served, to impose monetary penalties. The penalties range from up to $11,000 for the first offense to $27,500 for a second violation within five years and $55,000 for further violations within seven years. An ALJ also has the authority to issue an injunction to order the offender to either take action (such as rent an apartment to the complaining party) or refrain from an action (such as continuing to rent to only one group).

E & O Insurance

May not cover fair housing violations!

The parties may elect civil action in federal court at any time within two years of the discriminatory act. For cases heard in federal court, unlimited punitive damages can be awarded in addition to actual damages. The court also can issue injunctions. *Errors and omissions insurance carried by licensees may not cover violations of the fair housing laws.*

Whenever the attorney general has reasonable cause to believe that any person or group is engaged in a pattern or practice of resistance to the full enjoyment of any of the rights granted by the federal fair housing laws, he or she may file a civil action in any federal district court. Civil penalties may result in an amount not to exceed $50,000 for a first violation and an amount not to exceed $100,000 for second and subsequent violations.

Complaints brought under the Civil Rights Act of 1866 are taken directly to federal courts. The only time limit for action is a state's statute of limitations for torts— injuries one individual inflicts on another.

In Illinois

The Illinois Human Rights Act.   The Illinois *Real Estate License Act of 2000* prohibits any action that constitutes a violation of the *Illinois Human Rights Act*. This is true regardless of whether a complaint has been filed with or adjudicated by the Human Rights Commission. The *Illinois Human Rights Act* includes some prohibitions that also are specifically addressed by the *Real Estate License Act of 2000* as well.

Under the *Illinois Human Rights Act*, it is a civil rights violation for any licensee to engage in any of the following acts of discrimination based on race, color, religion, national origin, ancestry, age, sex, marital status, physical or mental disability, military service or unfavorable discharge from military service, familial status, or sexual orientation and/or preference:

- Refuse to engage in a real estate transaction with a person
- Alter the terms, conditions, or privileges of a real estate transaction
- Refuse to receive or fail to transmit an offer
- Refuse to negotiate
- Represent that real property is not available for inspection, sale, rental, or lease when in fact it is available; or fail to bring a property listing to an individual's attention; or refuse to permit him or her to inspect real estate
- Publicize, through any means or use, an application form that indicates an intent to engage in unlawful discrimination
- Offer, solicit, accept, use, or retain a listing of real property with knowledge that unlawful discrimination is intended

It is a civil rights violation for the owner or agent of any housing accommodation to engage in any of the following discriminatory acts *against children*:

- Require, as a condition to the rental of a housing accommodation, that the prospective tenant shall not have one or more children under 18 residing in his or her family at the time the application for rental is made
- Insert in any lease a condition that terminates the lease if one or more children younger than age 18 are ever in the family occupying the housing

Any agreement or lease that contains a condition such as the above is legally "void as to that condition." The lease itself remains in force, but the clause is void and unenforceable.

It is also a civil rights violation in Illinois to discriminate against any person who is blind, hearing-impaired, or physically disabled in the terms, conditions, or privileges of sale or rental property. Similarly, it is a civil rights violation to refuse to sell or rent to a prospective buyer or tenant because he or she has a service animal. Neither may a seller or landlord require the inclusion of any additional charge in a lease, rental agreement, or contract of purchase or sale because a person who is blind, hearing-impaired, or physically disabled has a service animal. Of course, the tenant may be liable for any actual damage done to the premises by the animal.

Note: The *Illinois Human Rights Act* defines an elderly person as anyone over the age of 40.

Exemptions.   Certain individuals, property types, and transactions are exempt from the antidiscriminatory provisions of the *Illinois Human Rights Act*:

- Private owners of single-family homes are exempt if (1) they own *fewer than three single-family homes* (including beneficial interests); (2) they were (or a member of their family was) the *last current resident of the home*; (3) the home was sold *without the use of a real estate salesperson or broker*; and (4) the home was sold *without the use of discriminatory advertising.*
- Owner-occupied apartment buildings of five units or less are exempt.
- Private rooms in a private home occupied by an owner or owner's family member are exempt.
- Reasonable local, state, or federal restrictions regarding the maximum number of occupants permitted to occupy a dwelling.
- A religious organization, association, or society (or any nonprofit institution or organization operated, controlled, or supervised by or in conjunction with a religious organization, association, or society) may limit the sale, rental, or occupancy of dwellings owned or operated by it (for other than commercial reasons) to persons of the same religion or give preference to persons of the same religion. This exemption is limited: It does not apply if membership in the religion is restricted on account of race, color, or national origin.
- Restricting the rental of rooms in a housing accommodation to persons of one sex.
- Appraisers may take into consideration any factors *other than those based on unlawful discrimination or familial status* in furnishing appraisals.
- Individuals who have been convicted by any court of illegally manufacturing or distributing controlled substances are not protected by the *Illinois Human Rights Act's* antidiscrimination provisions.
- Housing for older persons is exempt from the act's provisions regarding nondiscrimination against individuals on the basis of familial status. "Housing for older persons" means housing that is (1) intended for and occupied solely by persons 62 years of age or older or (2) intended and operated for occupancy by persons 55 years of age or older and at least 80 percent of the occupied units are occupied by at least one person who is 55 or older. ■

Coercion and Threats

It is possible that licensees may find themselves the targets of threats, verbal abuse, or intimidation merely for complying with fair housing laws. The federal *Fair Housing Act of 1968* protects the rights of those who seek the benefits of the open housing law. It also protects owners, brokers, and salespersons who aid or encourage the enjoyment of open housing rights. Threats or coercion are punishable as criminal actions. *In such a case, or if a licensee ever feels in danger, the individual should file a report immediately with the local police, notify his or her sponsoring broker, and report the situation to the nearest office of the Federal Bureau of Investigation.*

■ IMPLICATIONS FOR BROKERS AND SALESPEOPLE

The real estate industry is largely responsible for creating and maintaining an open housing market. Brokers and salespersons are a community's real estate experts. Along with the privilege of profiting from real estate transactions come the social and legal responsibilities to ensure that everyone's civil rights are protected. The reputation of the industry cannot afford any appearance that its licensees are committed to any less than fair and open housing opportunities. Licensees and the industry must be publicly conspicuous in their equal opportunity efforts. Establishing relationships with community and fair housing groups to discuss common concerns and develop solutions to problems is a constructive activity. Moreover, a licensee who is active in helping to improve his or her community will earn a reputation for being a concerned citizen, which may well translate into a larger client base.

Fair housing is the law. The consequences for anyone who violates the law are serious. In addition to the financial penalties, a real estate broker's or salesperson's livelihood will be in danger if his or her license is suspended or revoked. That the offense was unintentional is no defense. Licensees must scrutinize their practices with care and not fall victim to clients or customers who maneuver to discriminate.

All parties deserve the same standard of service. Every future homeowner has the right to expect fair and equal treatment, with house showings based only on his or her stated needs and financial capability. A good test is to answer the question, "Are we providing this service for everyone?" If an act is not performed consistently, or if an act affects individuals in a less than standard way, it could be construed as discriminatory. Standardized inventories of property listings, standardized criteria for financial qualification, and written documentation of activities and conversations (especially if the licensee senses a client wishes to act in a discriminatory way) are three effective means of self-protection for licensees.

HUD requires that its fair housing posters be displayed in any place of business where real estate is offered for sale or rent. Following HUD's advertising procedures and using the fair housing slogan and logo bolsters public awareness of the broker's commitment to equal opportunity.

Beyond being the law, fair housing is good business. It ensures the greatest number of properties available for sale and rent and the largest possible pool of potential purchasers and tenants.

■ PROFESSIONAL ETHICS

Professional conduct involves more than compliance with federal laws or the state licensing laws that are so crucial to full understanding. The letter of the law is not always enough: every day licensees perform legally but *unethically*.

Ethics refers to a high moral system of principles, rules, and standards based on conduct and values. The ethical system of a profession establishes guidelines that reach to the higher principles of what is "right." Those principles may form the law, but they exist apart from the law. Professional ethics in business usually focus on two main aspects of the profession:

1. They establish standards for integrity and competence in dealing with consumers of an industry's services.
2. They define a code of conduct for relations within the industry and among its professionals.

Code of Ethics

One way that many organizations address ethics among their members or in their respective businesses is by adopting specific, written codes of ethical conduct. A code of ethics is a written system of standards for professional, values-based conduct. The code contains statements designed to advise, guide, and regulate job behavior. To be effective, a code of ethics must be specific by creating rules that either prohibit or encourage certain behaviors. By including sanctions for violators, a code of ethics becomes more effective.

The National Association of REALTORS® (NAR), the largest trade association in the country, adopted a *Code of Ethics and Standards of Practice* for its members in 1913. REALTORS® are expected to subscribe to this strict code of conduct. Not all licensees are REALTORS®, only those who are members of NAR.

NAR has established procedures for professional standards committees at the local, state, and national levels of the organization to administer compliance. Interpretations of the code are known as *Standards of Practice*. The NAR *Code of Ethics* has proven especially helpful to practicing professionals because it contains practical applications of business ethics. Many smaller professional organizations within the real estate industry also promote and subscribe to codes of ethics.

In Illinois

In the Rules for the Administration of the Act, Section 1450.220 Unprofessional Conduct states that "IDFPR may suspend, revoke, or take other disciplinary action based upon its finding that the licensee or applicant has engaged in dishonorable, unethical, or unprofessional conduct of a character likely to deceive, defraud, or harm the public." ■

> A copy of the *Code of Ethics and Standards of Practice* may be obtained by writing the National Association of REALTORS® at 430 North Michigan Avenue, Chicago, Illinois 60611, or on the Internet at *www.realtor.org*.

■ SUMMARY

The federal regulations regarding equal opportunity in housing are contained principally in two laws. The *Civil Rights Act of 1866* prohibits all racial discrimination, and the *Fair Housing Act (Title VIII of the Civil Rights Act of 1968)*, as amended, prohibits discrimination on the basis of race, color, religion, sex, disability, familial status, or national origin in the sale, rental, or financing of residential property. Discriminatory actions include refusing to deal with an individual or a specific group, changing any terms of a real estate or loan transaction, changing the services offered for any individual or group, creating statements or advertisements that indicate discriminatory restrictions, or otherwise attempting to make a dwelling unavailable to any person or group because of race, color, religion, sex, disability, familial status, or national origin. The law also prohibits steering, blockbusting, and redlining.

Complaints under the *Fair Housing Act* may be reported to and investigated by the Department of Housing and Urban Development (HUD). Such complaints also may be taken directly to U.S. district courts. In states and localities that have enacted fair housing legislation that is substantially equivalent to the federal law, complaints are handled by state and local agencies and state courts. Complaints under the *Civil Rights Act of 1866* must be taken to federal courts.

A real estate business is only as good as its reputation. Real estate licensees can maintain good reputations by demonstrating good business ability and adhering to ethical standards of business practices. Many licensees subscribe to a code of ethics as members of professional real estate organizations, such as the National Association of REALTORS®, with its various state and local chapters.

| In Illinois | Licensees are required by various statutes and the *Real Estate License Act of 2000* to adhere to all principles of equal opportunity in housing. *Failure to comply with state and federal equal housing laws is grounds for license revocation in addition to other civil or criminal penalties.*

The *Illinois Human Rights Act* amplifies federal legislation for Illinois. It bars discrimination on the basis of race, color, religion, national origin, ancestry, age, sex, marital status, physical and mental disability, military service, unfavorable discharge, familial status, or sexual orientation and/or preference. ■

QUESTIONS

1. Which of the following actions is legally permitted?
   a. Advertising property for sale only to a special group
   b. Altering the terms of a loan for a member of a minority group
   c. Refusing to make a mortgage loan to a minority individual because of a poor credit history
   d. Telling a minority individual that an apartment has been rented when in fact it has not

2. Which of the following statements is *TRUE* of complaints relating to the *Civil Rights Act of 1866*?
   a. They must be taken directly to federal courts.
   b. They are no longer reviewed in the courts.
   c. They are handled by HUD.
   d. They are handled by state enforcement agencies.

3. Why is the *Civil Rights Act of 1866* unique?
   a. It has been broadened to protect the aged.
   b. It adds welfare recipients as a protected class.
   c. It contains "choose your neighbor" provisions.
   d. It provides no exceptions that would permit racial discrimination.

4. On a listing presentation a real estate agent said to the seller, who owned two residential properties, "I hear they are moving in, and you'd better put your house on the market before values drop!" Has the agent violated fair housing law?
   a. Yes, and this example represents steering.
   b. Yes, and this example represents blockbusting.
   c. No, because the seller owns fewer than three houses.
   d. No, because the agent does not intend to publicly advertise the property.

5. A licensee entered into a buyer agency agreement with a person from Japan who was moving to America. The agent showed him only properties where it was obvious that other Japanese people lived. Has the agent violated fair housing law?
   a. Yes, and this example represents blockbusting.
   b. Yes, and this example represents steering.
   c. No, because a buyer from Japan would want to live in a Japanese neighborhood.
   d. No, because as a buyer agent it is the agent's responsibility to make decisions for the buyer.

6. A lender's refusal to lend money to potential homeowners attempting to purchase properties located in predominantly African American neighborhoods is known as
   a. redlining.
   b. blockbusting.
   c. steering.
   d. qualifying.

7. Which of the following would *NOT* be permitted under the federal Fair Housing Act?
   a. The Harvard Club in New York rents rooms only to graduates of Harvard who belong to the club.
   b. The owner of a 20-unit residential apartment building rents to white men only.
   c. A Catholic convent refuses to furnish housing for a Jewish man.
   d. An owner refuses to rent the other side of her duplex to a family with children.

8. Nathan, a real estate broker, wants to end racial segregation. As an office policy, Nathan requires that salespersons show prospective buyers from racial or ethnic minority groups only properties that are in certain areas of town where few members of their groups currently live. Nathan prepares a map illustrating the appropriate neighborhoods for each racial or ethnic group. Through this policy, Nathan hopes to achieve racial balance in residential housing. Which of the following statements is *TRUE* regarding Nathan's policy?

    a. While Nathan's policy may appear to constitute blockbusting, application of the effects test proves its legality.

    b. Because the effect of Nathan's policy is discriminatory, it constitutes illegal steering regardless of his intentions.

    c. Nathan's policy clearly shows the intent to discriminate.

    d. While Nathan's policy may appear to constitute steering, application of the intent test proves its legality.

9. If a mortgage lender discriminates against a loan applicant on the basis of marital status, it violates what law?

    a. ADA

    b. *Civil Rights Act of 1866*

    c. ECOA

    d. *Fair Housing Act*

10. A Lithuanian American real estate broker offers a special discount to Lithuanian American clients. This practice is

    a. legal in certain circumstances.

    b. illegal.

    c. legal but ill-advised.

    d. an example of steering.

11. Which of the following statements describes the Supreme Court's decision in the case of *Jones v. Alfred H. Mayer Company*?

    a. Racial discrimination is prohibited by any party in the sale or rental of real estate.

    b. Sales by individual residential homeowners are exempted, provided the owners do not use brokers.

    c. Laws against discrimination apply only to federally related transactions.

    d. Persons with disabilities are a protected class.

12. After a broker takes a listing of a residence, the owner specifies that he will not sell his home to any Asian family. The broker should do which of the following?

    a. Advertise the property exclusively in Asian-language newspapers

    b. Explain to the owner that the instruction violates federal law and that the broker cannot comply with it

    c. Abide by the principal's directions despite the fact that they conflict with the fair housing laws

    d. Require that the owner sign a separate legal document stating the additional instruction as an amendment to the listing agreement

13. The fine for a first violation of the federal Fair Housing Act could be as much as

    a. $8,000.

    b. $9,500.

    c. $10,000.

    d. $11,000.

14. A single man with two small children has been told by a real estate salesperson that homes for sale in a condominium complex are available only to married couples with no children. Which of the following statements is *TRUE*?

    a. Because a single-parent family can be disruptive if the parent provides little supervision of the children, the condominium is permitted to discriminate against the family under the principle of rational basis.

    b. Condominium complexes are exempt from the fair housing laws and can therefore restrict children.

    c. The man may file a complaint alleging discrimination on the basis of familial status.

    d. Restrictive covenants in a condominium take precedence over the fair housing laws.

15. The following ad appeared in the newspaper: "For sale: 4 BR brick home; Redwood School District; excellent Elm Street location; next door to St. John's Church and right on the bus line. Move-in condition; priced to sell." Which of the following statements is *TRUE*?

    a. The ad describes the property for sale and is very appropriate.

    b. The fair housing laws do not apply to newspaper advertising.

    c. The ad should state that the property is available to families with children.

    d. The ad should not mention St. John's Church.

16. A landlord rented an apartment to a handicapped person. The tenant wants to make certain changes to the unit to accommodate her disability. Which of the following would *NOT* constitute a reasonable modification?

    a. Widen the doorways.

    b. Lower the kitchen cabinets.

    c. Lower the light switches.

    d. Equip the elevator lobby with a dog run.

17. The *Illinois Human Rights Act* defines an elderly person as being how old?

    a. 40

    b. 65

    c. 68

    d. 70

18. When landlord Robert rented an apartment in his six-unit building to Charlotte and Len, he didn't notice that Charlotte was pregnant. After the baby was born, Robert canceled their lease, citing the no-children clause that had been inserted in it. Based on these facts, which of the following statements is *TRUE*?

    a. Robert is violating the *Illinois Human Rights Act* regarding the exclusion of children.

    b. Robert is acting legally under an exemption to the *Illinois Human Rights Act*.

    c. Robert must give Charlotte and Len 60 days in which to find a new apartment.

    d. Robert may refuse to rent to families with children only if he lives in the building.

19. Lydia owns two multiunit apartment buildings, a two-flat on Oak Street and a 12-unit building on Main Street. She lives in an apartment in the Main Street property. Which of Lydia's properties, if any, is exempt from the *Illinois Human Rights Act*?

    a. The Oak Street property only

    b. The Main Street property only

    c. Neither property

    d. Both properties

CHAPTER 22

Environmental Issues and the Real Estate Transaction

■ **LEARNING OBJECTIVES** *When you've finished reading this chapter, you should be able to*

■ **identify** the basic environmental hazards an agent should be aware of in order to protect his or her client's interests.

■ **describe** the warning signs, characteristics, causes, and solutions for the various environmental hazards most commonly found in real estate transactions.

■ **explain** the fundamental liability issues arising under environmental protection laws.

■ **distinguish** lead-based paint issues from other environmental issues.

■ **define** the following *key terms:*

asbestos	groundwater	polychlorinated biphenyls
Brownfields Legislation	innocent landowner immunity	radon
capping	joint and several liability	retroactive liability
carbon monoxide	landfill	strict liability
CERCLA	lead	underground storage tanks
chlorofluorocarbons	mold	urea-formaldehyde
electromagnetic fields	MTBE	water table
encapsulation		

■ ENVIRONMENTAL ISSUES

Most states, including Illinois, have recognized the need to balance commercial use of land with the need to preserve vital resources and to protect our air, water, and soil. A growing number of homebuyers base their decisions in part on the desire for fresh air, clean water, and outdoor recreational opportunities. Preservation of a state's environment both enhances the quality of life and helps strengthen property values. Preventing environmental problems and cleaning up existent pollutants revitalizes the land while creating greater opportunities for responsible development.

In Illinois

The Illinois Environmental Protection Agency (IEPA) is charged with maintaining and enhancing the state's air, land, and water quality through education, inspection, regulation, enforcement, recycling, and prevention activities. The Pollution Control Board and Hazardous Waste Advisory Council are two of the many bodies created to assist the IEPA in specific areas. *Most Illinois environmental regulations are required by statute to be "identical in substance" to environmental protection regulations established by the U.S. Environmental Protection Agency (EPA).* ■

Environmental issues are health issues, and health issues based on environmental hazards have become real estate issues. For this reason, it is extremely important that licensees not only make property disclosures but also see that prospective purchasers get authoritative information about hazardous substances so that they can make informed decisions.

It is important that licensees keep up on environmental issues and practice proper disclosure, encouraging buyer clients to seek outside expertise for testing and information whenever appropriate. Agents must also encourage their seller clients to make full, honest disclosures, and assist any buyer clients to locate authoritative information about hazardous substances. Licensees are expected to be aware of environmental issues and to ensure that the safety interests of all parties involved in real estate transactions are protected.

Licensees should be familiar with state and federal environmental laws and the regulatory agencies that enforce them.

■ HAZARDOUS SUBSTANCES

Pollution and hazardous substances in the environment can affect the desirability and market value of entire neighborhoods and towns. A toxic environment is not a place where anyone would want to live. When showing properties, each possible living structure should be studied with an eye to red flags that may suggest problems. (See Figure 22.1.)

Asbestos

Asbestos is a mineral that once was used as insulation because it was resistant to fire and contained heat effectively. Before 1978 (the year when the use of asbestos insulation was banned), asbestos was found in most residential construction. It was a component of more than 3,000 types of building materials. *The EPA*

FIGURE   22.1

Environmental Hazards

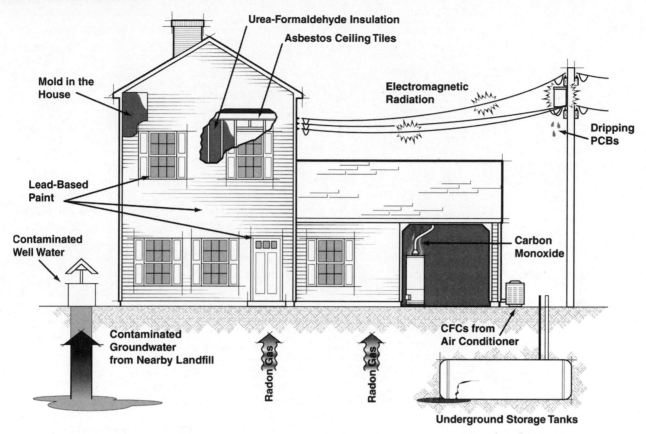

estimates that about 20 percent of the nation's commercial and public buildings built before 1978 contain asbestos.

Today, we know that inhaling microscopic asbestos fibers can result in a variety of respiratory diseases. The presence of asbestos insulation alone is not necessarily a health hazard. Asbestos is harmful only if it is disturbed or exposed, as often occurs during renovation or remodeling. *Asbestos is highly friable.* This means that as it ages, asbestos fibers break down easily into tiny filaments and particles. When these particles become airborne, they pose a risk to humans. Airborne asbestos contamination is most prevalent in public and commercial buildings, including schools. If the asbestos fibers in the indoor air of a building reach a dangerous level, the building becomes difficult to lease, finance, or insure.

Asbestos contamination also can be found in residential properties. It was used to cover pipes, ducts, and heating and hot water units. Its fire-resistant properties made it a popular material for use in floor tile, exterior siding, and roofing products. Though it may be easy to identify some asbestos contaminating materials, for instance, insulation wrapped around heating and water pipes, identification may be more difficult when it is behind walls or under floors.

Asbestos insulation can create airborne contaminants that may result in respiratory diseases.

Asbestos is costly to remove because the process requires state-licensed technicians and specially sealed environments. Removal itself may be dangerous. The waste generated should be disposed of at a licensed facility, which further adds to the cost of removal. **Encapsulation,** or the sealing off of disintegrating asbestos, is an alternate method of asbestos control that is often preferable to removal. However, an owner must periodically monitor the condition of the encapsulated asbestos to make sure it is not disintegrating.

A certified asbestos inspector can perform an asbestos inspection of a structure to identify which building materials may contain asbestos. The inspector can also provide recommendations and costs associated with remediation. It is vital that a buyer knows where asbestos-containing materials are located so that they are not disturbed during any repair, remodeling, demolition, or even routine use. Appraisers also should be aware of the possible presence of asbestos.

More information on asbestos-related issues is available from the EPA. In addition, the EPA has numerous publications that provide guidance, information, and assistance with asbestos issues.

Lead-Based Paint and Other Lead Hazards

Lead was used as a pigment and drying agent in alkyd oil-based paint. Lead-based paint may be on any interior or exterior surface, but it is particularly common on doors, windows, and other woodwork. The federal government estimates that lead is present in about 75 percent of all private housing built before 1978, or approximately 57 million homes, ranging from low-income apartments to million-dollar mansions.

Lead from paint or other sources can result in damage to the brain, nervous system, kidneys, and blood.

An elevated level of lead in the body can cause serious damage to the brain, kidneys, nervous system, and red blood cells. The degree of harm is related to the amount of exposure and the age at which a person is exposed. Children under the age of six are particularly vulnerable.

Lead dust can be ingested from the hands, for example, a crawling infant; inhaled by any occupant of a structure, or ingested from the water supply because of lead pipes or lead solder. In fact, lead particles can be present elsewhere, too. Soil and groundwater may be contaminated by everything from lead plumbing in leaking landfills to discarded lead buckshot at skeet shooting areas and bullets from an old shooting range. High levels of lead have been found in soil located near waste-to-energy incinerators. The air or soil may be contaminated by leaded gasoline fumes from gas stations or automobile exhaust.

The use of lead-based paint was banned in 1978. Licensees who are involved in the sale, management, financing, or appraisal of properties constructed before 1978 face potential liability for any personal injury that might be suffered by an occupant if proper disclosure is not made. The law puts the burden of compliance on sellers and lessors, requiring them to disclose any prior test results or any actual knowledge of lead-based paint hazards. The listing agent must advise sellers of their obligations to make the required disclosures. There is a variety of opinion as to whether the Lead-based Paint Hazard Reduction Act applies to buyer's agents. The act clearly applies to seller's agents; however, court decisions have differed as to whether buyer's agents can also be held liable. It is important for buyer's agents to be proactive and either provide or ensure that seller's agents have given buyers all the necessary forms, pamphlets, and disclosures required under the act before a contract is signed. Records should be kept for a minimum of three years for completed transactions.

No federal law requires that homeowners test for the presence of lead-based paint. However, known lead-based paint hazards must be disclosed. In 1996, the EPA and the Department of Housing and Urban Development (HUD) issued final regulations requiring disclosure of the presence of any known lead-based paint hazards to potential buyers or renters. Under the *Residential Lead-Based Paint Hazard Reduction Act*, persons selling or leasing residential housing constructed before 1978 must disclose the presence of known lead-based paint and provide purchasers or tenants with any relevant records or reports. *A lead-based paint disclosure statement must be attached to all sales contracts and leases regarding residential properties built before 1978, and a lead hazard pamphlet must be distributed to all buyers and tenants.* (See Figure 22.2.) Purchasers must be given ten days in which to conduct risk assessments or inspections for lead-based paint or lead-based paint hazards. Purchasers are not bound by any real estate contract until the ten-day period has expired.

The regulations apply to housing built prior to 1978 with the following six exceptions:

1. Property sold at foreclosure, although the disclosure must be made at resale time
2. Rental property that is certified "lead-based paint free" by an inspector who is certified under a federal program or federally authorized state certification program
3. Property leased for 100 days or less, with no lease renewal or extension
4. Renewals of existing leases if disclosure was made at the time of the initial lease
5. Units with no bedrooms, or with no separation between sleeping and living areas
6. Housing for the elderly or disabled if children under the age of six are not expected to live there

1978 is a year to remember. Lead paint AND asbestos were both banned.

There is considerable controversy about practical approaches for handling the presence of lead-based paint. Removal or encapsulation are sometimes utilized. Federal law requires that only licensed lead inspectors, abatement contractors, risk assessors, abatement project designers, and abatement workers may deal with the removal or encapsulation of lead in a structure.

In Illinois

Anyone who performs lead abatement or mitigation activities without a license is guilty of a Class A misdemeanor. The Department of Public Health (DPH) oversees the qualifying, training, and licensing of lead abatement contractors and lead abatement workers in Illinois.

EPA guidance pamphlets and other information about lead-based hazards are available from the National Lead Information Center at (800) 424-5323.

The *Illinois Lead Poisoning Prevention Act* (410 ILCS 45) requires that physicians screen children younger than six years old for lead poisoning when the child lives in an area considered by the state to be at "high risk" for lead exposure. *High-risk areas* include slum and blighted housing; proximity to highway or heavy local traffic; proximity to a lead-using or lead-generating industry; and incidence of elevated blood lead levels, poverty, and the number of young children in the area.

F I G U R E   22.2

Disclosure of Lead-Based Paint and Lead-Based Paint Hazards Form

CHICAGO ASSOCIATION OF REALTORS©
DISCLOSURE OF INFORMATION AND ACKNOWLEDGEMENT
LEAD-BASED PAINT AND/OR LEAD-BASED PAINT HAZARDS

Lead Warning Statement

Every purchaser of any interest in residential real property on which a residential dwelling was built prior to 1978 is notified that such property may present exposure to lead from lead-based paint that may place young children at risk of developing lead poisoning. Lead poisoning in young children may produce permanent neurological damage, including learning disabilities, reduced intelligence quotient, behavioral problems, and impaired memory. Lead poisoning also poses a particular risk to pregnant women. The seller of any interest in residential real property is required to provide the buyer with any information on lead-based paint hazards from risk assessments or inspections in the seller's possession and notify the buyer of any known lead-based paint hazards. A risk assessment or inspection for possible lead-based paint hazards is recommended prior to purchase.

Seller's Disclosure (initial) (All Sellers should initial)

_____ (a) Presence of lead-based paint and/or lead-based paint hazards (check one below):

_____ ☐ Known lead-based paint and/or lead-based paint hazards are present in the housing (explain):
_____
_____

☐ Seller has no knowledge of lead-based paint and/or lead-based paint hazards in the housing.

_____ (b) Records and Reports available to the seller (check one below):

_____ ☐ Seller has provided the purchaser with all available records and reports pertaining to lead-based paint and/or lead-based hazards in the housing (list documents below):
_____
_____

☐ Seller has no reports or records pertaining to lead-based paint and/or lead-based paint hazards in the housing.

Purchaser's Acknowledgement (initial) (All Purchasers should initial)

_____ (c) Purchaser has received copies of all information listed above.

_____ (d) Purchaser has received the pamphlet *Protect Your Family From Lead in Your Home.*

_____ (e) Purchaser has (check one below):

☐ Received a 10-day opportunity (or mutually agreed upon period) to conduct a risk assessment or inspection of the presence of lead-based paint or lead-based paint hazards, or

☐ Waived the opportunity to conduct a risk assessment or inspection for the presence of lead-based paint and/or lead-based paint hazards.

Agent's Acknowledgement (initial) (Seller's Designated Agent)

_____ (f) Agent has informed the seller of the seller's obligations under 42 U.S.C. 4852 d and is aware of his/her responsibility to ensure compliance.

Certification of Accuracy

The following parties have reviewed the information above and certify, to the best of their knowledge, that the information they have provided is true and accurate.

Seller _____ Date _____ Seller _____ Date _____

Purchaser _____ Date _____ Purchaser _____ Date _____

Agent _____ Date _____ Agent _____ Date _____

Location of Property _____ City _____ State ____ Zip Code _____

Keep a fully executed copy of this document for three (3) years from the date hereof.
This Disclosure From should be attached to the Real Estate Sale Contract.

Source: Published with permission, Chicago Association of REALTORS®

When a child is diagnosed as having an elevated level of lead in his or her bloodstream, the physician must report the condition to the Department of Public Health (DPH). After notification, the DPH may inspect the child's residence for the existence of exposed lead-bearing substances (including dust, paint, and lead pipes). If the inspection identifies a lead hazard, the property owner is required to mitigate the condition within 90 days (30 days if a child under six or a pregnant woman is at risk). Licensed lead abatement contractors must be used for lead removal. The owner will receive a certificate of compliance once the DPH is satisfied that the lead hazard has been removed.

An owner who has received a lead mitigation notice must provide any prospective lessees for the affected unit with a written notice of the existence of an identified lead hazard. In addition, *all owners of residential buildings or units must give current and prospective lessees information on the potential health hazards posed by lead and a copy of an informational brochure.* ■

Radon

Radon is a naturally occurring, odorless, colorless, radioactive gas produced by the natural decay of other uranium and radium that can be produced in many different types of soils and rocks. Because radon is chemically inactive and not bound to other materials, it can move easily through pores or voids in soil, including soils found beneath homes. Although radon can occur anywhere, some areas are known to have abnormally high amounts. The northeastern United States is especially rich in radon, but deposits can occur anywhere.

If radon dissipates into the outside air from the soil, it is not likely to cause harm. *However, when radon enters buildings and is trapped in high concentrations (usually in basements with inadequate ventilation), it often causes health problems.* For these reasons, many real estate purchasers wish to have their prospective property tested for radon. Currently, the EPA *suggests an action level of 4 pCi/L; in other words, if a reading of four or higher is obtained, mitigation is suggested.*

> *Radon* is a naturally occurring gas that is a suspected cause of lung cancer.

Opinions differ as to minimum "safe" levels of radon. But *growing evidence suggests that radon may be the single most underestimated cause of lung cancer,* particularly as it affects children, individuals who smoke, and those who spend considerable time indoors.

Because radon is odorless and tasteless, it is impossible to detect without testing. The modern practice of creating energy-efficient homes and buildings with practically airtight walls and windows may increase the potential for radon gas accumulation in these homes. On the plus side, home radon-detection kits are available as a first step for homeowners. Radon contamination can usually be easily decreased to acceptable levels. The EPA's pamphlet, *A Citizen's Guide to Radon,* is available from any local EPA office, or on the Internet.

In Illinois

The Illinois Radon Awareness Act, effective January 1, 2008, requires a seller to provide to a buyer, before the buyer is obligated under any contract to purchase residential real property, a Disclosure of Information on Radon Hazards along with a pamphlet entitled "Radon Testing Guidelines for Real Estate Transactions" stating that the property may present the potential for exposure to radon. (See Figure 22.3.)

In short, the act requires a separate disclosure document for radon to be included in the majority of residential real estate transactions. The disclosure document

- has a Radon Warning Statement advising buyers that the home may pose a threat to their health if it has elevated levels of radon and that all homes should be tested for radon;
- requires that a seller provide an Illinois Emergency Management Agency (IEMA) approved pamphlet about general radon information to a buyer and disclose all information along with any available documentation of the radon levels in the home;
- requires that real estate agents sign the disclosure to confirm that seller has been made aware of his or her obligations; and
- requires that all parties involved sign the disclosure acknowledging the transfer of the above information.

The act does not require that all homes in a real estate transaction be tested or that the home be mitigated if the test results are elevated.

If any of the disclosures required occurs after the buyer has made an offer to purchase the residential real property, the seller shall complete the required disclosure activities prior to accepting the buyer's offer and allow the buyer an opportunity to review the information and possibly amend the offer.

The provisions of this Act do not apply to:

1. Transfers pursuant to court order
2. Transfers from a mortgagor to a mortgagee by deed in lieu of foreclosure or consent judgment, transfer by judicial deed issued pursuant to a foreclosure sale, transfer by a collateral assignment of a beneficial interest of a land trust, or a transfer by a mortgagee or a successor in interest to the mortgagee's secured position.
3. Transfers by a fiduciary in the course of the administration of a decedent's estate, guardianship, conservatorship, or trust.
4. Transfers from one co-owner to one or more other co-owners.
5. Transfers pursuant to testate or intestate succession.
6. Transfers made to a spouse, or to a person or persons in the lineal line of consanguinity of one or more of the sellers.
7. Transfers from an entity that has taken title to residential real property from a seller for the purpose of assisting in the relocation of the seller, so long as the entity makes available to all prospective buyers a copy of the disclosure form furnished to the entity by the seller.
8. Transfers to or from any governmental entity.

Urea-Formaldehyde

Urea-formaldehyde was first used in building materials, particularly insulation, in the 1970s. Gases leak out of urea-formaldehyde foam insulation (UFFI) as it hardens, and the gases become trapped in the interior of a building. In 1982, the Consumer Product Safety Commission banned the use of UFFI. The ban was reduced to a warning after courts determined that there was insufficient evidence to support a ban. Urea-formaldehyde is known to cause cancer in animals, but *the evidence of its effect on humans is still inconclusive*, and urea formaldehyde is classed as a *probable carcinogen*. Formaldehyde does cause some individuals to suffer respiratory problems as well as eye and skin irritations.

FIGURE 22.3

Radon Disclosure Form

Illinois Association of REALTORS

DISCLOSURE OF INFORMATION ON RADON HAZARDS
(For Residential Real Property Sales or Purchases)

Radon Warning Statement

Every buyer of any interest in residential real property is notified that the property may present exposure to dangerous levels of indoor radon gas that may place the occupants at risk of developing radon-induced lung cancer. Radon, a Class-A human carcinogen, is the leading cause of lung cancer in non-smokers and the second leading cause overall. The seller of any interest in residential real property is required to provide the buyer with any information on radon test results of the dwelling showing elevated levels of radon in the seller's possession.

The Illinois Emergency Management Agency (IEMA) strongly recommends ALL homebuyers have an indoor radon test performed prior to purchase or taking occupancy, and mitigated if elevated levels are found. Elevated radon concentrations can easily be reduced by a qualified, licensed radon mitigator.

Seller's Disclosure (initial each of the following which applies)

_____ (a) Elevated radon concentrations (above EPA or IEMA recommended Radon Action Level) are known to be present within the dwelling. (Explain).

_____ (b) Seller has provided the purchaser with all available records and reports pertaining to elevated radon concentrations within the dwelling.

_____ (c) Seller has no knowledge of elevated radon concentrations in the dwelling.

_____ (d) Seller has no records or reports pertaining to elevated radon concentrations within the dwelling.

Purchaser's Acknowledgment (initial each of the following which applies)

_____ (e) Purchaser has received copies of all information listed above.

_____ (f) Purchaser has received the IEMA approved Radon Disclosure Pamphlet.

Agent's Acknowledgement (initial if applicable)

_____ (g) Agent has informed the seller of the seller's obligations under Illinois law.

Certification of Accuracy

The following parties have reviewed the information above and each party certifies, to the best of his or her knowledge, that the information he or she has provided is true and accurate.

Seller _____   Date_____

Seller _____   Date_____

Purchaser _____   Date _____

Purchaser _____   Date _____

Agent _____   Date _____

Agent_____   Date_____

Property Address _____   City, State, Zip Code _____

FORM 422   COPYRIGHT ILLINOIS ASSOCIATION OF REALTORS

Source: Published with permission, Illinois Association of REALTORS®

UFFI is an insulating foam that can release harmful formaldehyde gases.

Because UFFI and *formaldehyde gas* have received considerable adverse publicity, many buyers express justified concern about them. Tests can be conducted to determine the level of formaldehyde gas in a house. Pressed wood products, especially new ones, can also emit these fumes. Care should be exercised to ensure that the results of the tests are accurate and that the source of the gases is properly identified.

Licensees should be careful that any conditions in an agreement of sale that require tests for formaldehyde are worded properly to identify the purpose for which the tests are being conducted, such as to determine the presence of the insulation or to identify some other source. Appraisers should also be aware of the presence of UFFI.

Carbon Monoxide

Carbon monoxide is a by-product of fuel combustion that may result in death in poorly ventilated areas.

Carbon monoxide (CO) is a colorless, odorless gas that occurs due to incomplete combustion as a by-product of burning such fuels as wood, oil, and natural gas. Furnaces, water heaters, space heaters, fireplaces, and wood stoves all produce CO as a natural result of combustion. When these appliances function properly and are properly ventilated, CO emissions are not a problem. However, when improper ventilation or equipment malfunctions permit large quantities of CO to be released into a residence or commercial structure, it poses a significant health hazard. The effects of CO are compounded by the fact that it is so difficult to detect. CO is quickly absorbed by the body. It inhibits the blood's ability to transport oxygen and results in dizziness and nausea. As the concentrations of CO increase, the symptoms become more severe. A number of deaths from CO poisoning occur each year.

CO detectors are available, and their use is mandatory in some areas. Annual maintenance of heating systems also helps avoid CO exposure.

In Illinois

Illinois requires that all residences be equipped with working carbon monoxide detectors. ■

Polychlorinated Biphenyls

Polychlorinated biphenyls (PCBs) linger in the environment for long periods of time and can cause health problems.

Polychlorinated biphenyls (PCBs) were often used as an insulating material in dielectric oil. PCBs may be present in electrical equipment, such as transformers, fluorescent light ballasts, and hydraulic oil in older equipment. PCBs are suspected of causing health problems and are known to linger in the environment for long periods of time. For example, in tests conducted on offspring of fish who were exposed to PCBs, the offspring also had elevated levels of PCBs.

In January 1978, the manufacture, processing, commercial distribution, and use of PCB materials was prohibited, except when contained in a *totally enclosed manner*. The EPA, however, made case-by-case exceptions to these limitations if it determined that an unreasonable risk of injury to public health or the environment was not present. On January 1, 1979, the manufacture of PCBs was completely banned; commercial distribution of PCBs was banned on July 1, 1979.

Chlorofluorocarbons

Chlorofluorocarbons (CFCs) are nontoxic, nonflammable chemicals containing atoms of carbon, chlorine, and fluorine. CFCs are most often used in air conditioners, refrigerators, aerosol sprays, paints, solvents, and foam blowing applications. CFCs are safe in most applications and are inert in the lower atmosphere, but once CFC vapors rise to the upper atmosphere, they are broken down by ultraviolet light into chemicals that deplete the ozone layer.

Global treaties have sought to reduce the production levels of CFCs. The manufacture of these chemicals ended for the most part in 1996, with exceptions for production in developing countries, medical products (for example, asthma inhalers), and research.

IN PRACTICE

Licensees need to be aware that homes may have products, especially air conditioners and refrigerators, that contain CFCs. Licensees may want to advise consumers to consider upgrading to newer, environmentally friendly appliances. Consumers should also be aware of safe CFC disposal procedures.

Electromagnetic Fields

Electromagnetic fields (EMFs) are generated by the movement of electrical currents. The use of any electrical appliance creates a small field of electromagnetic radiation; clock radios, blow-dryers, televisions, and computers all produce EMFs. The major concern regarding EMFs involves high-tension power lines. The EMFs produced by these high-voltage lines, as well as by secondary distribution lines and transformers, are suspected of causing cancer, hormonal changes, and behavioral abnormalities. There is considerable controversy (and much conflicting evidence) about whether EMFs pose a health hazard. The most recent studies suggest that only very high levels pose any possible danger.

EMFs are produced by electrical currents and may be related to a variety of health complaints.

As research into EMFs continues, real estate licensees should stay informed about current findings.

Mold

Mold has become the latest environmental scare to hit the real estate industry. The disclosure responsibilities and liability of real estate agents is currently evolving; real estate professionals need to be aware of the growing problems concerning mold and take necessary steps to protect themselves from liability.

Mold can be found almost anywhere and can grow on almost any organic substance, so long as moisture, oxygen, and an organic food source are present. Moisture feeds mold growth. If a moisture problem is not discovered or addressed, mold growth can gradually destroy what it is growing on.

In addition, some molds can cause serious health problems. They can trigger allergic reactions and asthma attacks. Some molds are known to produce potent toxins and/or irritants.

Some moisture problems in homes and buildings have been directly linked to recent changes in construction practices. Some of these practices have resulted in buildings that are too tightly sealed, preventing adequate ventilation. Building materials, such as drywall, may not allow moisture to escape easily. The material used in dry walls *wick* moisture to the nutrition source of glue and paper. Vinyl wallpaper and exterior insulation finish system (EIFS), that is, synthetic stucco, do not allow moisture to escape. Other moisture problems include roof leaks, unvented combustion appliances, and landscaping or gutters that direct water to the building.

The EPA has published guidelines for the remediation and/or cleanup of mold and moisture problems in schools and commercial buildings.

IN PRACTICE

Mold is an increasingly important issue for licensees. Initially, lawsuits were brought against construction and insurance companies. But then insurance companies started amending their homeowner's insurance policies to exclude mold from coverage. Now, plaintiffs name sellers, landlords, property management companies, and real estate licensees as defendants, in addition to construction and insurance companies.

■ **FOR EXAMPLE** In a 2005 case, *Eddy v. B.S.T.V., Inc*, a couple sued a real estate company for failing to disclose mold contamination in the home they purchased. The real estate company's insurers refused to provide coverage stating that the insurance policies had specific exclusion clauses that would not cover property damage arising out of a real estate agent's failure to render professional services. The issue in the case was whether the professional-services exclusion clause in the insurance policy issued to the real estate company applied to the couple's claims. The couple alleged that the real estate agents breached the real estate company's professional-service responsibilities and that, therefore, the exclusions applied. The real estate company tried to argue that because its real estate agents were trained in identifying mold-related hazards, the claim did not fit the exclusion clause. The court did not agree, and the real estate company was held liable. The court held the exclusion clauses in the policies prevented insurance coverage for the injuries.

In light of this case and other court decisions on this topic, it can be difficult for real estate companies and licensees to know what to do when mold is suspected or found on a property. There are no federal requirements to disclose mold contamination at this time, and only a few states require disclosure. Licensees should remind buyers that sellers cannot disclose what they do not know. Also, licensees should advise buyers that they not only have the right but the burden to discover.

Licensees may need to take extra steps to protect themselves from liability. When a licensee suspects mold is present in a home, the licensee should ask many questions about leaks, floods, and prior damage. There are also mold testing services that can be hired, usually at an expensive cost, but well worth the cost if it saves problems down the road.

The EPA has a publication entitled *A Brief Guide to Mold, Moisture, and Your Home*. The guide provides information and guidance for homeowners and renters on how to clean up residential mold problems and how to prevent mold growth. There is no practical way to eliminate all mold and mold spores in the indoor environment. The key to mold control is moisture control. It is important to dry water-damaged areas and items within 24 to 48 hours to prevent mold growth.

Statutory, regulatory, and case law addressing the duties of real estate professionals regarding mold concerns is currently evolving. Real estate licensees should consider adopting practices intended to help their clients and customers become aware of and familiar with mold concerns.

IN PRACTICE

HUD now requires mold disclosure on all HUD sales contracts. Mold disclosure forms are available through your state or local REALTOR® association. (See Figure 22.4.)

■ GROUNDWATER PROTECTION

Groundwater is the water that exists under the earth's surface within the tiny spaces or crevices in geological formations. Groundwater forms the **water table,** the natural level at which the ground is saturated. This may be near the surface (in areas where the water table is very high) or several hundred feet underground. Surface water also can be absorbed into the groundwater.

Any contamination of the underground water can threaten the supply of pure, clean water for private wells or public water systems. If groundwater is not protected from contamination, the earth's natural filtering systems may be inadequate to ensure the availability of pure water. Numerous state and federal laws have been enacted to preserve and protect the water supply, led by the *Safe Drinking Water Act* and its 1996 and 2000 amendments. The 1996 amendment enhanced existing law by recognizing source water protection operator training, funding for water system improvements, and public information. In 2000, the EPA required that water suppliers report any health risk situation within 24 hours.

Water can be contaminated from a number of sources. Runoff from waste disposal sites, leaking underground storage tanks, and pesticides and herbicides are some of the main culprits. Because water flows naturally, contamination can spread far from its source. Once contamination has been identified, its source can usually be eliminated, and the water may eventually become or be made clean. However, the process can be time-consuming and expensive.

IN PRACTICE   Real estate agents need to be aware of potential groundwater contamination sources on or near a property. These include storage tanks, septic systems, holding ponds, drywells, buried materials, and surface spills. Because groundwater flows over wide areas, the source of contamination may not be nearby.

■ UNDERGROUND STORAGE TANKS

Approximately 3 million to 5 million **underground storage tanks** (USTs) exist in the United States. Underground storage tanks are commonly found on sites where petroleum products are used or where gas stations and auto repair shops are located. They also may be found in a number of other commercial and industrial establishments—including printing and chemical plants, wood treatment plants, paper mills, paint manufacturers, dry cleaners, and food-processing plants—for storing chemicals or process wastes. Military bases and airports are also common sites for underground tanks. In residential areas, they are used to store heating oil.

Some of these tanks may be active, but many were long ago abandoned. It is an unfortunate fact that it was once common to dispose of toxic wastes by simple burial: out of sight, out of mind. Over time, however, neglected tanks may leach hazardous substances into the environment. This permits contaminants to pollute not only the soil around the tank but also adjacent parcels and groundwater. Licensees should be particularly alert to the presence of fill pipes, vent lines, stained soil, and fumes or odors, any of which may indicate the presence of a

FIGURE 22.4

Mold Disclosure Form

MOLD DISCLOSURE
(Buyer and Seller)

Printed Name(s) of Seller(s): _____

Printed Name(s) of Buyer(s): _____

Property Address: _____

1. <u>Seller's Disclosure</u>: To the best of Seller's actual knowledge, Seller represents:

   A. The Property described above _____ has _____ has not been previously tested for molds:

   (If the answer for 1.A. is "has not", then skip 1.B and 1.C and go to Section 2.)

   B. The molds found _____ were _____ were not identified as toxic molds;

   C. With regard to any molds that were found, measures _____ were _____ were not taken to remove those molds.

2. <u>Mold Inspection</u>: Molds, fungus, mildew, and similar organisms ("Mold Conditions") may exist in the Property of which the Seller is unaware and has not actual knowledge. The Mold Conditions generally grow in places where there is excessive moisture, such as where leakage may have occurred in roofs, pipes, walls, plant pots, or where there has been flooding. A professional home inspection may not disclose Mold Conditions. As a result, Buyer may wish to obtain an inspection specifically for Mold Conditions to more fully determine the condition of the Property and this environmental status. Neither Seller's nor Buyer's agents are experts in the field of Mold Conditions and other related conditions and Buyer and Seller shall not rely on Broker or it's agents for information relating to such conditions. Buyer is strongly encouraged to satisfy itself as to the condition of the property.

3. <u>Hold Harmless</u>: Buyer's decision to purchase the Property is independent of representation of the Broker or Broker's agents involved in the transaction regarding Mold Conditions. Accordingly, Buyer agrees to indemnify and hold _____

   _____ (print name of Broker(s) and Designated Agent(s)) harmless in the event any Mold Conditions are present on the Property.

4. <u>Receipt of Copy</u>: Seller and Buyer have read and acknowledge receipt of a copy of this Mold Disclosure.

<u>Professional Advice</u>: Seller and Buyer acknowledge that they have been advised to consult with a professional of their choice regarding any questions or concerns relating to Mold Conditions or this Mold Disclosure.

_____   _____
Buyer   Date   Seller   Date

_____   _____
Buyer   Date   Seller   Date

REV 01/03

UST. Detection, removal, and cleanup of surrounding contaminated soil can be an expensive operation.

State and federal laws impose strict requirements on landowners to detect and correct leaks in an effort to protect the groundwater. The federal UST program is regulated by the EPA. The regulations apply to tanks that contain hazardous substances or liquid petroleum products and that store at least 10 percent of their volume underground. UST owners are required to register their tanks and adhere to strict technical and administrative requirements that govern

■ installation,
■ maintenance,
■ corrosion prevention,
■ overspill prevention,
■ monitoring, and
■ record keeping.

Owners also are required to demonstrate that they have sufficient financial resources to cover any damage that might result from leaks.

The following types of tanks are among those that are exempt from the federal regulations:

■ Tanks that hold less than 110 gallons
■ Farm and residential tanks that hold 1,100 gallons or less of motor fuel used for noncommercial purposes
■ Tanks that store heating oil burned on the premises
■ Tanks on or above the floor of underground areas such as basements or tunnels
■ Septic tanks and systems for collecting stormwater and wastewater

Some states have adopted laws regulating underground storage tanks that are more stringent than the federal laws.

In addition to being aware of possible noncompliance with state and federal regulations, the parties to a real estate transaction should be aware that many older tanks have never been registered. There may be no visible sign of their presence.

In Illinois *The Leaking Underground Storage Tank (LUST) program governs the detection, identification, monitoring, mitigation, and removal of buried underground storage tanks (particularly those containing petroleum products). The program is administered by the state fire marshal and the IEPA and is authorized to disburse money from a special fund to assist property owners in complying with mandatory remediation activities. The fund derives from permit fees, fines, and payments required under such acts as the Motor Fuel Tax Law and the Environmental Impact Fee Law. Illinois is one of the states under watch with regard to MTBE, the latest water contaminant from gasoline. Real estate professionals may wish to encourage their clients to have their water tested for the presence of MTBE and other contaminants.* ■

MTBE A recent and highly problematic water problem has been triggered by the groundwater spread of methyl-t-butyl ether fuel oxygenates or **MTBE**. These were added to gasoline beginning in 1979 to enhance octane, to reduce CO and ozone emissions, and to replace lead. Now MTBE has been found to present a difficult water pollution challenge. Entire towns in the western and southwestern United States have had to cut off their natural water supply because of the leaching of this contaminant into groundwater from gas stations, from lakes or rivers where water vehicles utilize gasoline, and from leaking gasoline pipelines. Foul-tasting, foul-smelling, and clammy-feeling water is associated with the presence of MTBE. While health reports are not yet in, few consumers whose water supply is affected wish to continue using the water, nor are they advised to do so. The EPA has classed MTBE as a "potential carcinogen," and the government has put MTBE health impact research on a special fast-track plan. *MTBE spreads farther and faster than any other water pollutant known to date, and no workable means for cleaning it up currently exists.*

Consumers and real estate professionals should be vigilant in locating any underground storage tanks that might be leaking MTBE or other pollutants. *The EPA Safe Drinking Water Hotline can be reached at 800-426-4791.*

■ WASTE DISPOSAL SITES

Americans produce vast quantities of garbage every day. Despite public and private recycling and composting efforts, huge piles of waste materials—beer cans, junk mail, diapers, paint, and toxic chemicals—continue to grow in size and impact. Landfill operations have become the main receptacles for garbage and refuse, and many of these are overloaded. Special hazardous waste disposal sites have been established to contain radioactive waste from nuclear power plants, toxic chemicals, and waste materials produced by medical, scientific, and industrial processes, but political battles rage over just where the many new disposal sites needed should be located.

Perhaps the most prevalent method of common waste disposal is simply to bury it. A **landfill** is an enormous hole, either excavated for the purpose of waste disposal or left over from surface mining operations. The hole is lined with clay or a synthetic liner to prevent leakage of waste material into the water supply. A system of underground drainage pipes permits monitoring of leaks and leaching. Waste is laid on the liner at the bottom of the excavation, and a layer of topsoil is then compacted onto the waste. The layering procedure is repeated again and again until the landfill is full, the layers mounded up sometimes as high as several hundred feet over the surrounding landscape. **Capping** is the process of laying two feet to four feet of soil over the top of the site and then planting grass or some other vegetation to enhance the landfill's aesthetic value and to prevent erosion. A ventilation pipe runs from the landfill's base through the cap to vent off accumulated natural gases created by the decomposing waste.

Federal, state, and local regulations govern the location, construction, content, and maintenance of landfill sites. Test wells around landfill operations are installed to constantly monitor the groundwater in the surrounding area, and soil analyses can be used to test for contamination. Capped landfills have been used for such purposes as parks and golf courses.

■ **FOR EXAMPLE** A suburban office building constructed on an old landfill site was very popular until its parking lot began to sink. While the structure itself was supported by pilings driven deep into the ground, the parking lot was unsupported. As the landfill beneath it compacted, the concrete lot sank lower and lower around the building. Each year, the building's management had to relandscape to cover the exposed foundations. The sinking parking lot eventually severed underground phone and power lines and water mains, causing the tenants considerable inconvenience. Computers were offline for hours, and flooding was frequent on the ground floor. Finally, leaking gases from the landfill began causing unpleasant odors. The tenants moved out, and the building was left vacant, a victim of poorly conceived landfill design.

Hazardous and radioactive waste disposal sites are subject to strict state and federal regulation to prevent the escape of toxic substances into the surrounding environment. Some materials, such as radioactive waste, are sealed in containers and placed in "tombs" buried deep underground. The tombs are designed to last thousands of years and are built according to strict federal and state regulations in remote locations.

The Midwest Interstate Compact on Low-Level Radioactive Waste is one example of a regional approach to the disposal of hazardous materials. The states of Delaware, Illinois, Indiana, Iowa, Kansas, Kentucky, Maryland, Michigan, Minnesota, Missouri, Nebraska, North Dakota, Ohio, South Dakota, Virginia, and Wisconsin have agreed to cooperate in establishing and managing regional low-level radioactive waste sites. This approach allows the participants to share the costs, benefits, obligations, and inconveniences of radioactive waste disposal in a fair and reasonable way.

| In Illinois |

The construction and maintenance of waste disposal sites in Illinois are regulated by statute (415 ILCS 5/20 et seq.). ■

IN PRACTICE

Environmental issues have a significant impact on the real estate industry. In 1995, a jury awarded $6.7 million to homeowners whose property values had been lowered because of a defendant tire company's negligent operation and maintenance of a hazardous waste dump site. The 1,713 plaintiffs relied on testimony from economists and a real estate appraiser to demonstrate how news stories about the site had lowered the market values of their homes. Nationwide, some landfill operators now offer price guarantees to purchasers of homes near waste disposal sites. Similarly, a recent university study found that a home's value increases by more than $6,000 for each mile of its distance from a garbage incinerator.

■ BROWNFIELDS

For decades, old industrial sites have plagued communities as eyesores and as potentially dangerous and hazardous property. These old industrial sites are known as **brownfields** and are defined as defunct, derelict, or abandoned commercial or industrial sites. Many of the sites have toxic wastes. According to the U.S. General Accounting Office, there may be more than 500,000 brownfields across the country.

In 2002, the **Brownfields Legislation** became law. The law gives states and localities up to $250 million a year for five years to clean up polluted industrial sites. The law is also important for property owners and developers because it shields innocent developers from liability for toxic wastes that existed at a site prior to the purchase of property. In effect, if a property owner neither caused nor contributed to the contamination, the property owner is not liable for the cleanup.

Significantly, the law encourages the development of abandoned properties, some of which are located in prime real estate areas.

■ ENVIRONMENTAL PROTECTION

The majority of legislation dealing with environmental problems has been enacted within the past two decades. Although the EPA was created at the federal level to oversee such problems, several other federal agencies' areas of concern generally overlap. The federal laws were created to encourage state and local governments to enact their own legislation.

CERCLA

The **Comprehensive Environmental Response, Compensation, and Liability Act** (CERCLA) was created in 1980. It established a fund of $9 billion, called the Superfund, to clean up uncontrolled hazardous waste sites and to respond to spills. It created a process for identifying *potentially responsible parties* (PRPs) and ordering them to take responsibility for the cleanup action. CERCLA is administered and enforced by the EPA.

Liability.   A landowner is liable under CERCLA when a release of a hazardous substance has taken place on his or her property. Regardless of whether the contamination is the result of the landowner's actions or those of others, *the owner can be held responsible for the cleanup. This liability includes the cleanup not only of the landowner's property but also of any neighboring property that has been contaminated.* A landowner who is not responsible for the contamination can seek recovery reimbursement for the cleanup cost from previous landowners, any other responsible party, or the Superfund. However, if other parties are not available, *even a landowner who did not cause the problem could be solely responsible for the costs.*

Once the EPA determines that hazardous material has been released into the environment, it is authorized to begin remedial action. First, it attempts to identify the PRPs. If the PRPs agree to cooperate in the cleanup, they must agree about how to divide the cost. If the PRPs do not voluntarily undertake the cleanup, the EPA may hire its own contractors to do the necessary work. The EPA then bills the PRPs for the cost. If the PRPs refuse to pay, the EPA can seek damages in court for up to three times the actual cost of the cleanup.

Liability under the Superfund is considered to be strict, joint and several, and retroactive. **Strict liability** means that the owner is responsible to the injured party without excuse. **Joint and several liability** means that each of the individual owners is personally responsible for the total damages. If only one of the owners is financially able to handle the total damages, that owner must pay the total and collect the proportionate shares from the other owners whenever possible.

Retroactive liability means that the liability is not limited to the current owner but includes people who have owned the site in the past.

Superfund Amendments and Reauthorization Act

In 1986, the U.S. Congress reauthorized the *Superfund Amendments and Reauthorization Act* (SARA). The amended statute contains stronger cleanup standards for contaminated sites and five times the funding of the original Superfund, which expired in September 1985.

The amended act also sought to clarify the obligations of lenders. As mentioned, liability under the Superfund extends to both the present and all previous owners of the contaminated site. Real estate lenders found themselves either as present owners or somewhere in the chain of ownership through foreclosure proceedings.

The amendments created a concept called **innocent landowner immunity.** It was recognized that *in certain cases, a landowner in the chain of ownership was completely innocent of all wrongdoing and therefore should not be held liable.* The innocent landowner immunity clause established the criteria by which to judge whether a person or business could be exempted from liability. The criteria included the following:

- The pollution was caused by a third party.
- The property was acquired after the fact.
- The landowner had no actual or constructive knowledge of the damage.
- Due care was exercised when the property was purchased (the landowner made a reasonable search, called an *environmental site assessment*) to determine that no damage to the property existed.
- Reasonable precautions were taken in the exercise of ownership rights.

■ LIABILITY OF REAL ESTATE PROFESSIONALS

Real estate licensees can avoid liability with environmental issues by

- becoming familiar with common environmental problems in their area;
- looking for signs of environmental contamination;
- advising (and including as a contingency) an environmental audit if you suspect contamination; and
- not giving advice on environmental issues.

Environmental law is a relatively new phenomenon. Although federal and state laws have defined many of the liabilities involved, common law is being used for further interpretation. The real estate professional and all others involved in a real estate transaction must be aware of both actual and potential liability.

Sellers, as mentioned earlier, often carry the most legal liability exposure. Innocent landowners might be held responsible, even though they did not know about the presence of environmental hazards. Purchasers may be held liable, even if they didn't cause the contamination. *Lenders may end up owning worthless assets if owners default on the loans rather than undertaking expensive cleanup efforts. Real estate licensees could be held liable for improper disclosure; therefore, it is necessary to be aware of the potential environmental risks from neighboring properties such as gas stations, manufacturing plants, or even funeral homes.*

Additional exposure is created for individuals involved in other aspects of real estate transactions. For example, real estate appraisers must identify and adjust for environmental problems. Adjustments to market value typically reflect the cleanup cost plus a factor of the degree of panic and suspicion that exist in the current market. Although the sales price can be affected dramatically, it is possible that the underlying market value would remain relatively equal to others in the neighborhood. The real estate appraiser's greatest responsibility is to the lender, who depends on the appraiser to identify environmental hazards. Although the lender may be protected under certain conditions through the 1986 amendments to the Superfund Act, the lender must be aware of any potential problems and may require additional environmental reports.

Insurance carriers also might be affected in the transactions. Mortgage insurance companies protect lenders' mortgage investments and might be required to carry part of the ultimate responsibility in cases of loss. More important, hazard insurance carriers might be directly responsible for damages if such coverage was included in the initial policy.

Discovery of Environmental Hazards

Real estate licensees are not expected to have the technical expertise necessary to discover the presence of environmental hazards. However, because they are presumed by the public to have special knowledge about real estate, licensees must be aware both of possible hazards and of where to seek professional help.

Obviously, the first step for a licensee is to ask the owner. He or she already may have conducted tests for CO or radon. The owner also may be aware of a potential hazardous condition. An environmental hazard actually can be turned into a marketing plus if the owner has already done the detection and abatement work. If a seller is willing to put in the necessary work ahead of time, potential buyers can then be assured that an older home is no longer a lead-based paint or an asbestos risk.

The most appropriate people on whom a licensee can rely for sound environmental information are scientific or technical experts. Environmental auditors can provide the most comprehensive studies. Their services usually are relied on by developers and purchasers of commercial and industrial properties. An environmental audit includes the property's history of use and the results of extensive and complex tests of the soil, water, air, and structures. Trained inspectors conduct air-sampling tests to detect radon, asbestos, or EMFs. They can test soil and water quality and can inspect for lead-based paints. (Lead inspections required by the *Residential Lead-Based Paint Hazard Reduction Act* must be conducted by certified inspectors.) While environmental auditors may be called on at any stage in a transaction, they are most frequently brought in as a condition of closing. Not only can such experts detect environmental problems, they usually can offer guidance about how best to resolve the conditions.

IN PRACTICE

Environmental assessments and tests conducted by environmental consultants can take time. Licensees should be aware of the time involved and contact environmental consultants as soon as they know such tests are needed in order to prevent delays in closing a transaction.

■ ENVIRONMENTAL SITE ASSESSMENTS

An *environmental site assessment* is often performed on a property to show that due care was exercised in determining if any environmental impairments exist. The assessment can help prevent parties from becoming involved in contaminated property and work as a defense to liability. It is often requested by a lending institution, developer, or a potential buyer. The assessment is commonly performed in phases, such as Phase 1 or Phase 2. A Phase 1 Environmental Report is requested first to determine if any potential environmental problems exist at or near the subject property that may cause impairment. Additional phases are performed, as warranted and requested.

There are no federal regulations that define what an environmental assessment must include. However, one of the most accepted industry standards is provided by the American Society for Testing Materials International.

A federally funded project requires that an environmental impact statement (EIS) be performed. These statements detail the impact the project will have on the environment. They can include information about air quality, noise, public health and safety, energy consumption, population density, wildlife, vegetation, and need for sewer and water facilities. Increasingly, these statements are also being required for private development.

Disclosure of Environmental Hazards

State laws address the issue of disclosure of known material facts regarding a property's condition. These same rules apply to the presence of environmental hazards. *A real estate licensee may be liable if he or she should have known about a condition, even if the seller neglected to disclose it.*

■ SUMMARY

Environmental issues are important to real estate licensees because they have an impact on our clients. They may affect real estate transactions by raising issues of health risks or cleanup costs. Some of the principal environmental toxins include asbestos, lead, radon, urea-formaldehyde insulation, formaldehyde gas, and mold.

Asbestos is a friable carcinogen that is less dangerous when left intact or handled by a professional than if an amateur tries to remove it. Small particles in the air are its danger. Encapsulation and professional removal are solutions. Lead is found in paint dust, paint chips, and lead pipes, and also may be present in soil or groundwater. Eating or ingesting the chips or dust of lead paint (or drinking water that has passed through lead pipes) can lead to serious health problems, especially mental diminishment and kidney difficulties. The effects are hardest on small children. Painting over lead paint is of some use, especially if no children are present. Lead pipes should be removed, and sometimes paint is best totally removed also, but by qualified professionals. Licensees should be aware of the significance of 1978 for lead and asbestos, after which these materials were not legally used in construction.

Radon is a possible carcinogenic danger above 4 pCi/L, as measured by radon canisters or electronic measurement devices. This odorless gas from the ground is easily sealed out or vented to an acceptable level, which is at or near the level we usually breathe outdoors. Sealing crawl spaces, sealing sump pumps, or filling basement floor cracks to the ground may solve the problem. If not, fans and venting installed by professionals may be needed. Formaldehyde gas, which leaks out of urea-formaldehyde products such as insulation, can cause respiratory problems and eye and skin irritation. Urea-formaldehyde products are less of a problem with age once the fumes have escaped.

| In Illinois | The Illinois Radon Awareness Act requires sellers to provide buyers of residential real estate an IEMA pamphlet entitled "Radon Testing Guidelines for Real Estate Transactions" along with the Illinois Disclosure of Information on Radon Hazards form stating that the property may present the potential for exposure to radon. A seller is not required to test or mitigate if test results are elevated. ■ |

Water pollutants, many from gasoline, can often be filtered out if they are identified. The source of the problem—such as leaking pipes or underground storage tanks—should always be addressed and, ideally, removed.

There is no known filtering system yet developed for MTBE, the latest significant "possible carcinogen" found in gasoline leaks. Currently there is no way to clean up water that is polluted in this way. Agents, consumers, and clients should know that leaching into groundwater may begin some distance from the final dispersal site of polluted water, especially with MTBE.

Mold can be found anywhere and can grow on almost any organic substance, as long as moisture, oxygen, and an organic food source are present. If a moisture problem is not discovered or addressed, mold growth can gradually destroy what it is growing on.

EMFs are generated by the movement of electrical currents.

Improperly constructed or maintained landfills may also present a danger to ground water that exists under the earth's surface.

CERCLA established the Superfund to finance the cleanup of hazardous waste disposal sites. Liability can be retroactive. The government deals more reasonably with persons who report their own situation as opposed to waiting to be turned in. This is especially true with underground storage tanks, where all or a large part of accumulated fines may be eliminated for citizens who "self-report" and seek assistance in cleanup of a leaking tank.

Licensees and their clients should be aware and on the watch for any possible environmental contamination sources.

QUESTIONS

1. Asbestos is MOST dangerous when it
   a. is used as insulation.
   b. crumbles and becomes airborne.
   c. gets wet.
   d. is wrapped around heating and water pipes.

2. *Encapsulation* refers to the
   a. process of sealing a landfill with three to four feet of topsoil.
   b. way in which asbestos insulation is applied to pipes and wiring systems.
   c. method of sealing disintegrating asbestos.
   d. way in which asbestos becomes airborne.

3. Jerry is a real estate salesman. He shows a pre-World War I house to Aruna, a prospective buyer. Aruna has two toddlers and is worried about potential health hazards. Which of the following is *TRUE*?
   a. There is a risk that urea-foam insulation was used in the original construction.
   b. Because Jerry is a licensed real estate salesman, he can offer to inspect for lead and remove any lead risks.
   c. Because the house was built before 1978, there is a good likelihood of the presence of lead-based paint.
   d. Lead poisoning occurs only when lead paint chips are chewed and swallowed.

4. Which of the following is *TRUE* regarding asbestos?
   a. The removal of asbestos can cause further contamination of a building.
   b. Asbestos causes health problems only when it is eaten.
   c. The level of asbestos in a building is affected by weather conditions.
   d. HUD requires all asbestos-containing materials to be removed from all residential buildings.

5. Which of the following *BEST* describes the water table?
   a. Natural level at which the ground is saturated
   b. Level at which underground storage tanks may be safely buried
   c. Measuring device used by specialists to measure groundwater contamination
   d. Always underground

6. Radon poses the greatest potential health risk to humans when it is
   a. contained in insulation material used in residential properties during the 1970s.
   b. found in high concentrations in unimproved land.
   c. trapped and concentrates in inadequately ventilated areas.
   d. emitted by malfunctioning or inadequately ventilated appliances.

7. Which of the following describes the process of creating a landfill site?
   a. Waste is liquefied, treated, and pumped through pipes to "tombs" under the water table.
   b. Waste and topsoil are layered in a pit, mounded up, then covered with dirt and plants.
   c. Waste is compacted and sealed into a container, then placed in a "tomb" designed to last several thousand years.
   d. Waste is buried in an underground concrete vault.

8. Liability under the Superfund is
   a. limited to the owner of record.
   b. joint and several and retroactive, but not strict.
   c. voluntary.
   d. strict, joint and several, and retroactive.

9. All of the following have been proven to pose health hazards *EXCEPT*

   a. asbestos fibers.
   b. carbon monoxide.
   c. electromagnetic fields.
   d. lead-based paint.

10. Which of the following environmental hazards poses a risk due to particles or fibers in the air?

   a. Carbon monoxide
   b. Radon
   c. UFFI
   d. Asbestos

11. The *Residential Lead-Based Paint Hazard Reduction Act* sets forth procedures for disclosing the presence of lead in

   a. all residential properties offered for sale.
   b. new residential construction only.
   c. residential properties built prior to 1978.
   d. residential properties built prior to 1990.

12. Which of the following is *NOT* exempt from disclosure regulations of the *Residential Lead-Based Hazard Reduction Act*?

   a. A duplex built before 1978
   b. Studio apartments where the living area is not separated from the sleeping area
   c. Senior-citizen housing
   d. Residences for the disabled

13. The segment of the population that is most likely to obtain lead poisoning from paint is

   a. the elderly.
   b. children.
   c. teenagers.
   d. All groups

14. Mold and mildew found in the home fall into which category of pollutants?

   a. Pesticides
   b. Formaldehyde
   c. Biological
   d. Hazardous waste

15. Suggestions on making your home less mold friendly include

   a. maintaining indoor humidity below 50 percent.
   b. using air conditioners.
   c. maintaining adequate ventilation.
   d. All of the above

In Illinois

16. The agency primarily responsible for protecting Illinois's natural resources against pollution and other hazards is the

   a. Pollution Control Board of Illinois (PCB).
   b. Illinois Department of Environmental Affairs (IDEA).
   c. Illinois Environmental Protection Agency (IEPA).
   d. Illinois Department of Environmental Regulation (IDER).

17. Environmental regulations in Illinois are

   a. all more stringent than federal regulations.
   b. substantially equivalent to federal regulations.
   c. less restrictive than federal regulations.
   d. not subject to federal regulations.

18. Which are exempt from radon disclosure under the *Illinois Radon Awareness Act*?

   a. Residential rentals
   b. Properties with six or more units
   c. Transfers between co-owners
   d. Transfers between neighbors

CHAPTER

23

Closing the Real Estate Transaction

■ **LEARNING OBJECTIVES** *When you've finished reading this chapter, you should be able to*

■ **identify** the issues of particular interest to the buyer and the seller as a real estate transaction closes.

■ **describe** the steps involved in preparing a closing statement.

■ **explain** the general rules for prorating.

■ **distinguish** the procedures involved in face-to-face closings from those in escrow closings.

■ **define** the following *key terms*:

accrued item	credit	Real Estate Settlement
closing	debit	Procedures Act
closing statement	escrow	Uniform Settlement
controlled business	prepaid items	Statement
arrangement	prorations	

■ PRECLOSING PROCEDURES

Everything a licensee does in the course of a real estate transaction, from garnering clients to presenting offers and coordinating inspections, leads to one final event—closing. Closing is the consummation of the real estate transaction. Closing actually involves two events: (1) the promises made in the sales contract are fulfilled and (2) the mortgage loan funds (if any) are distributed to the buyer. It is the time when the title to the real estate is transferred in exchange for payment of the purchase price. Closing marks the end of any real estate transaction. Before the property changes hands, however, important issues must be resolved.

Buyer's Issues

The buyer wants to be sure that the seller delivers title. The buyer also should ensure that the property is in the promised condition. This involves inspecting

- the title evidence;
- the seller's deed;
- any documents demonstrating the removal of undesired liens and encumbrances;
- the survey;
- the results of any required inspections, such as termite or structural inspections, or required repairs; and
- any leases if tenants reside on the premises.

Final property inspection. Shortly before the closing takes place, the buyer usually makes a final inspection of the property with the broker (often called the *walk-through*). Through this inspection, the buyer makes sure that necessary repairs have been made, that the property has been well maintained, that all fixtures are in place, and that there has been no unauthorized removal or alteration of any part of the improvements.

Survey. A *survey* gives information about the exact location and size of the property. The sales contract specifies who will pay for the survey. It is usual for the survey to "spot" the location of all buildings, driveways, fences, and other improvements located primarily on the premises being purchased. Any improvements located on adjoining property that may encroach on the premises being bought also will be noted. The survey should set out, in full, any existing easements and encroachments. Whether or not the sales contract calls for a survey, lenders frequently require one.

IN PRACTICE

One of the most frequent causes of lawsuits against licensees is inaccurate lot lines. Buyers want to be confident that the properties they purchase are in fact what they believe they are paying for. Relying on old surveys is not necessarily a good idea; the property should be resurveyed by a competent surveyor, whether or not the title company or lender requires it.

Seller's Issues

Obviously, the seller's main interest is in receiving payment for the property. He or she will want to be sure that the buyer has obtained the necessary financing and has sufficient funds to complete the sale. The seller also will want to be certain that he or she has complied with all the buyer's requirements so the transaction will be completed.

Both parties will want to inspect the closing statement to make sure that all monies involved in the transaction have been accounted for properly. The parties may be accompanied by their attorneys.

IN PRACTICE

Licensees may discuss with clients the approximate expenses involved in closing at the time the listing agreement or buyer agency agreement is entered into but not later than the time when the sales contract is signed.

Title Procedures

Both the buyer and the buyer's lender will want assurance that the seller's title complies with the requirements of the sales contract. Additionally, lenders require title insurance in the event any "clouds" on the title (encumbrances on the real estate or claims on the title) should come up during the course of ownership. The title insurance is not issued until it is clear that such encumbrances from the past are unlikely. A major goal of title procedures is for the new owner to obtain a clear and valid "owner's title policy." Such a policy comes as close as any document can to providing evidence of ownership of a property that is unencumbered by any past liens or potential claims.

As a first step toward a new owner's title policy, prior to closing and establishment of the new owner's title, the seller usually is required to produce a current abstract of title or title commitment from the title insurance company. When an abstract of title is used, the purchaser's attorney examines it and issues an opinion of title. This opinion, like the title commitment, is a statement of the status of the seller's title. It discloses all liens, encumbrances, easements, conditions, or restrictions that appear on the record and to which the seller's title is subject.

On the date when the sale is actually completed (the date of delivery of the deed), the buyer has a title commitment or an abstract that was issued several days or weeks before the closing. For this reason, there usually are two searches of the public records. The first shows the status of the seller's title on the date of the first search. Usually, the seller pays for this search. The second search, known as a *bring-down*, is made after the closing and generally paid for by the purchaser. The abstract should be reviewed before closing to resolve any problems that might cause delays or threaten the transaction.

As part of this later search, the seller may be required to execute an *affidavit of title*. This is a sworn statement in which the seller assures the title insurance company (and the buyer) that there have been no judgments, bankruptcies, or divorces involving the seller since the date of the title examination. The affidavit promises that no unrecorded deeds or contracts have been made, no repairs or improvements have gone unpaid, and no defects in the title have arisen that the seller knows of. The seller also affirms that he or she is in possession of the premises. In some areas, this form is required before the title insurance company will issue an owner's policy to the buyer. The affidavit gives the title insurance company the right to sue the seller if his or her statements in the affidavit are incorrect.

When the purchaser pays cash or obtains a new loan to purchase the property, the seller's existing loan is paid in full and satisfied on record. The exact amount required to pay the existing loan is provided in a current payoff statement from the lender, effective on the date of closing. This payoff statement (also called an estoppel certificate or certificate of no defense) notes the unpaid amount of principal, the interest due through the date of payment, the fee for issuing the certificate of satisfaction or release deed, credits (if any) for tax and insurance reserves, and the amount of any prepayment penalties. Once the borrower has executed the estoppel certificate, the borrower cannot thereafter claim that he or she did not owe the amount indicated in the payoff or estoppel certificate. The same procedure would be followed for any other liens that must be released before the buyer takes title.

In a transaction in which the buyer assumes the seller's existing mortgage loan, the buyer will want to know the exact balance of the loan as of the closing date. In some areas, it is customary for the buyer to obtain a mortgage reduction certificate from the lender that certifies the amount owed on the mortgage loan, the interest rate, and the last interest payment made.

In some areas, real estate sales transactions customarily are closed through an escrow (discussed below). In these areas, the escrow instructions usually provide for an extended coverage policy to be issued to the buyer as of the date of closing. The seller has no need to execute an affidavit of title.

■ CONDUCTING THE CLOSING

Closing is the point at which ownership of a property is transferred in exchange for the selling price.

Closing is known by many names. For instance, in some areas closing is called *settlement* and *transfer*. In other parts of the country, the parties to the transaction sit around a single table and exchange copies of documents, a process known as *passing papers*. In still other regions, the buyer and seller may never meet at all; the paperwork is handled by an escrow agent. This process is known as *closing escrow*. Whether the closing occurs face-to-face or through escrow, the main concerns are that the buyer receives marketable title, the seller receives the purchase price, and certain other items are adjusted properly between the two.

In Illinois

In Illinois, the closing statement is customarily prepared by the buyer's lender, the lender's agent (usually a title insurance company), or the seller's lawyer. Although real estate licensees are prohibited by the Illinois Supreme Court's decision in *Chicago Bar Association, et al., v. Quinlan and Tyson, Inc.* from completing formal closing statements, estimated statements are often needed when preparing a CMA, when filling out an offer for a buyer, or when presenting an offer to a seller. For this reason, licensees must understand the preparation of a closing statement, which includes the expenses and prorations of costs to close the transaction. In addition, the Illinois licensing examination for broker candidates includes specific questions regarding closing statement calculations. ■

Face-to-Face Closing

A *face-to-face closing* involves the resolution of two issues. First, the promises made in the sales contract are fulfilled. Second, the buyer's loan is finalized, and the mortgage lender disburses the loan funds. The difference between a face-to-face closing and an escrow closing is that in a face-to-face closing, these two issues are resolved during a single meeting of all the parties and their attorneys. As discussed earlier, the parties in an escrow closing may never meet. The phrase "passing papers" vividly describes a face-to-face closing.

In a *face-to-face closing*, the parties meet face-to-face.

Face-to-face closings may be held at a number of locations, including the offices of the title company, the lending institution, one of the parties' attorneys, the broker, the county recorder, or the escrow company. Those attending a closing may include

- the buyer or the buyer's duly authorized agent;
- the seller or the seller's duly authorized agent;
- the real estate salespersons or brokers (both the buyer's and the seller's agents);
- the seller's and the buyer's attorneys;

- representatives of the lending institutions involved with the buyer's new mortgage loan, the buyer's assumption of the seller's existing loan, or the seller's payoff of an existing loan; and
- a representative of the title insurance company.

In Illinois The *Real Estate License Act of 2000* defines duly authorized agent to mean "an attorney-in-fact, an attorney-at-law who represents that he or she is acting on behalf of one of the principals to the transaction, or any other person the licensee can prove was authorized to act on behalf of a principal to the transaction." ■

Closing agent or closing officer. One person usually conducts the proceedings at a closing and calculates the division of income and expenses between the parties (called *settlement*). The closing agent can be the buyer's or seller's attorney, a representative of the lender, or a representative of the title company. Some title companies and law firms employ paralegal assistants who conduct closings for their firms.

Preparation for closing involves ordering and reviewing an array of documents, such as the title insurance policy or title certificate, surveys, property insurance policies, and other items. Arrangements must be made with the parties for the time and place of closing. Closing statements and other documents must be prepared.

The exchange. When the parties are satisfied that everything is in order, the exchange is made. All pertinent documents are then recorded in the correct order to ensure continuity of title. For instance, if the seller pays off an existing loan and the buyer obtains a new loan, the seller's satisfaction of mortgage must be recorded *before* the seller's deed to the buyer. The buyer's new mortgage or deed of trust must be recorded *after* the deed because the buyer cannot pledge the property as security for the loan until he or she owns it.

Closing in Escrow

Although a few states prohibit transactions that are closed in escrow, escrow closings are used to some extent in most states.

In an *escrow closing*, a third party coordinates the closing activities on behalf of the buyer and seller.

An **escrow** is a method of closing in which a disinterested third party is authorized to act as escrow agent and to coordinate the closing activities. The escrow agent also may be called the *escrow holder*. The escrow agent may be an attorney, a title company, a trust company, an escrow company, or the escrow department of a lending institution. Many real estate firms offer escrow services. However, a broker cannot be a disinterested party in a transaction from which he or she expects to collect a commission. Because the escrow agent is placed in a position of great trust, many states have laws regulating escrow agents and limiting who may serve in this capacity.

Escrow procedure. When a transaction will close in escrow, the buyer and seller execute escrow instructions to the escrow agent after the sales contract is signed. One of the parties selects an escrow agent. Which party selects the agent is determined either by negotiation or by state law. Once the contract is signed, the broker turns over the earnest money to the escrow agent, who deposits it in a special trust, or escrow, account.

Buyer and seller deposit all pertinent documents and other items with the escrow agent before the specified date of closing. The seller usually deposits

- the deed conveying the property to the buyer;
- title evidence;
- existing hazard insurance policies;
- a letter or mortgage reduction certificate from the lender stating the exact principal remaining (if the buyer assumes the seller's loan);
- affidavits of title (if required);
- a payoff statement (if the seller's loan is to be paid off);
- bill of sale;
- survey;
- transfer tax declarations;
- paid water bill; and
- other instruments or documents necessary to clear the title or to complete the transaction.

The buyer deposits

- the balance of the cash needed to complete the purchase in certified check form;
- loan documents (if the buyer secures a new loan);
- proof of hazard insurance and flood insurance (if required);
- other necessary documents, such as inspection reports required by the lender.

The escrow agent has the authority to examine the title evidence. When marketable title is shown in the name of the buyer and all other conditions of the escrow agreement have been met, the agent is authorized to disburse the purchase price to the seller, minus all charges and expenses. The agent then records the deed and mortgage or deed of trust (if a new loan has been obtained by the purchaser).

If the escrow agent's examination of the title discloses liens, a portion of the purchase price can be withheld from the seller. The withheld portion is used to pay the liens to clear the title.

If the seller cannot clear the title, or if for any reason the sale cannot be consummated, the escrow instructions usually provide that the parties be returned to their former statuses, as if no sale occurred. The escrow agent reconveys title to the seller and returns the purchase money to the buyer. If the seller dies prior to the closing date, but after having given a signed deed to the escrow agent, the closing still may proceed, with the escrow agent transferring title to the buyer and turning the purchase price over to the seller's estate.

IRS Reporting Requirements

Every real estate transaction must be reported to the IRS by the closing agent on a Form 1099-S. Information includes the sales price, the amount of property tax reimbursement credited to the seller, and the seller's Social Security number. If the closing agent does not notify the IRS, the responsibility for filing the form falls on the mortgage lender, although the brokers or the parties to the transaction ultimately could be held liable. Also, all cash payments over $10,000 must be reported to the federal government, using Form 8300.

Broker's Role at Closing

Depending on local practice, the broker's role at closing can vary from simply collecting the commission to conducting the proceedings. Real estate brokers are not authorized to give legal advice or otherwise engage in the practice of law. This means that in some states, a broker's job is essentially finished as soon as the sales contract is signed. After the contract is signed, the attorneys take over. Even so, a broker's service generally continues all the way through closing. The broker makes sure all the details are taken care of so that the closing can proceed smoothly. This means making arrangements for title evidence, surveys, appraisals, and inspections or repairs for structural conditions, water supplies, sewage facilities, or toxic substances.

Though real estate licensees do not always conduct closing proceedings, they usually attend. Often, the parties look to their agents for guidance, assistance, and information during what can be a stressful experience. Licensees need to be thoroughly familiar with the process and procedures involved in preparing a closing statement, which includes the expenses and prorations of costs to close the transaction. It is also in the brokers' best interests that the transactions move successfully and smoothly to a conclusion. The brokers' commissions are generally paid out of the proceeds at closing.

IN PRACTICE

Licensees should avoid recommending sources for any inspection or testing services. If a buyer suffers any injury as a result of a provider's negligence, the licensee also may be liable. The better practice is to give clients the names of several professionals who offer high-quality services.

Lender's Interest at Closing

Whether a buyer obtains new financing or assumes the seller's existing loan, the lender wants to protect its security interest in the property. The lender has an interest in making sure the buyer gets good, marketable title and that tax and insurance payments are maintained. Lenders want their mortgage lien to have priority over other liens. They also want to ensure that insurance is kept up-to-date in case property is damaged or destroyed. For this reason, a lender generally requires a title insurance policy and a fire and hazard insurance policy (along with a receipt for the premium). In addition, a lender may require other information: a survey, a termite or another inspection report, or a certificate of occupancy (for a newly constructed building). A lender also may request that a reserve account be established for tax and insurance payments.

■ RESPA REQUIREMENTS

The federal **Real Estate Settlement Procedures Act** (RESPA) was enacted to protect consumers from abusive lending practices. RESPA also aids consumers during the mortgage loan settlement process. It ensures that consumers are provided with important, accurate, and timely information about the actual costs of settling or closing a transaction. It also eliminates kickbacks and other referral fees that tend to inflate the costs of settlement unnecessarily. RESPA prohibits lenders from requiring excessive escrow account deposits.

RESPA requirements apply when a purchase is financed by a federally related mortgage loan. *Federally related loans* means loans made by banks, savings associations, or other lenders whose deposits are insured by federal agencies. It also includes loans insured by the FHA and guaranteed by the VA; loans administered by HUD; and loans intended to be sold by the lenders to Fannie Mae, Ginnie Mae, or Freddie Mac. RESPA is administered by HUD.

FIGURE 23.1

Affiliated Business Arrangement Disclosure

Affiliated Business Arrangement Disclosure

This is to give you notice that _____ (referring Party) has a business relationship with _____ as a loan originator/solicitor. Because of this relationship, this referral may provide (referring party) a financial or other benefit.

[A.] Set forth below is the estimated charge or range of charges for the settlement services listed.

You are **NOT** required to use the listed provider as a condition for settlement of your loan on, or purchase, sale, or refinance of, the subject property. **THERE ARE FREQUENTLY OTHER SETTLEMENT SERVICE PROVIDERS AVAILABLE WITH SIMILAR SERVICES. YOU ARE FREE TO SHOP AROUND TO DETERMINE THAT YOU ARE RECEIVING THE BEST SERVICES AND THE BEST RATE FOR THESE SERVICES.**

[provider] [charge or range of charges]

_____

_____

[B.] Set forth below is the estimated charge or range of charges for the settlement services of an attorney, credit reporting agency, or real estate appraiser that we, as your lender, will require you to use, as a condition of your loan on this property, to represent our interests in the transaction.

[provider and settlement service] [charge or range of charges]

_____

_____

ACKNOWLEDGMENT:

l/we have read this disclosure form, and understand that _____ (referring party) is referring me/us to purchase from the above-described settlement service provider and may receive a financial or other benefit as the result of this referral.

Borrower's Signature   Date

_____   _____

Borrower's Signature   Date

_____   _____

RESPA regulations apply to first-lien residential mortgage loans made to finance the purchases of one-family to four-family homes, cooperatives, and condominiums, for either investment or occupancy. RESPA also governs second or subordinate liens for home equity loans. A transaction financed solely by a purchase-money mortgage taken back by the seller, an installment contract (contract for deed), or a buyer's assumption of a seller's existing loan are not covered by RESPA. However, if the terms of the assumed loan are modified, or if the lender charges more than $50 for the assumption, the transaction is subject to RESPA regulations.

IN PRACTICE

While RESPA's requirements are aimed primarily at lenders, some provisions of the act affect real estate brokers and agents as well. Real estate licensees fall under RESPA when they refer buyers to particular lenders, title companies, attorneys, or other providers of settlement services. Licensees who offer *computerized loan origination* (CLO) services also are subject to regulation. Remember: Buyers have the right to select their own providers of settlement services.

Controlled Business Arrangements

A consumer service that is increasing in popularity is one-stop shopping for real estate services. A real estate firm, title insurance company, mortgage broker, home inspection company, or even a moving company may agree to offer a package of services to consumers. RESPA permits a **controlled business arrangement** (CBA), as long as a consumer is clearly informed of the relationship among the service providers and that other providers are available. Fees may not be exchanged among the affiliated companies simply for referring business to one another. (See Figure 23.1.)

Disclosure Requirements

Lenders and settlement agents have certain disclosure obligations at the time of loan application and loan closing:

RESPA's Consumer Protections:
- CLO regulation
- CBA disclosure
- Settlement cost booklet
- Good-faith estimate of settlement costs
- Uniform Settlement Statement
- Prohibition of kickbacks and unearned fees

- *Special information booklet*—Lenders must provide a copy of a special informational HUD booklet to every person from whom they receive or for whom they prepare a loan application (except for refinancing). The HUD booklet must be given at the time the application is received or within three business days afterward. The booklet provides the borrower with general information about settlement (closing) costs. It also explains the various provisions of RESPA, including a line-by-line description of the Uniform Settlement Statement.
- *Good-faith estimate of settlement costs*—No later than three business days after receiving a loan application, the lender must provide to the borrower a good-faith estimate of the settlement costs the borrower is likely to incur. This estimate may be either a specific figure or a range of costs based on comparable past transactions in the area. In addition, if the lender requires use of a particular attorney or title company to conduct the closing, the lender must state whether it has any business relationship with that firm and must estimate the charges for this service.
- *Uniform Settlement Statement (HUD-1 Form)*—RESPA requires that a special HUD form be completed to itemize all charges to be paid by a borrower and seller in connection with settlement. The **Uniform Settlement Statement** includes all charges that will be collected at closing, whether required by the lender or a third party. Items paid by the borrower and seller outside closing, not required by the lender, are not included on the HUD-1 form. Charges required by the lender that are paid for before closing are indicated as "paid outside of closing" (POC). RESPA prohibits lenders from requiring that borrowers deposit amounts in escrow accounts for taxes and insurance that exceed certain limits, thus preventing the lenders from taking advantage of the borrowers. Sellers are also prohibited from requiring, as a condition of a sale, that the buyer purchase title insurance from a particular company. A copy of the HUD-1 form is illustrated later in this chapter as Figure 23.4.

The settlement statement must be made available for inspection by the borrower at or before settlement. Borrowers have the right to inspect a completed HUD-1, to the extent that the figures are available, one business day before the closing. (Sellers are not entitled to this privilege.)

FIGURE 23.2

Allocation of Expenses

Item	Paid by Seller	Paid by Buyer
Broker's commission	✗ by agreement	✗ by agreement
Attorney's fees	✗ by agreement	✗ by agreement
Recording expenses	✗ to clear title	✗ transfer charges
Transfer tax	✗ state and county	✗ some municipal taxes
Title expenses	✗ title search	✗ attorney inspection, title insurance
Loan fees	✗ prepayment penalty	✗ origination fee
Tax and insurance reserves (escrow or impound accounts)		✗
Appraisal fees		✗
Survey fees	✗ if required to pay by sales contract	✗ new mortgage financing

* This chart is based on generally applicable practices. Please note that closing practices may be different in your state.

Lenders must retain these statements for two years after the date of closing. In addition, state laws generally require that licensees retain all records of a transaction for a specific period. The Uniform Settlement Statement may be altered to allow for local custom, and certain lines may be deleted if they do not apply in an area.

Kickbacks and referral fees. RESPA prohibits the payment of kickbacks, or unearned fees, in any real estate settlement service. It prohibits referral fees when no services are actually rendered. The payment or receipt of a fee, a kickback, or anything of value for referrals for settlement services includes activities such as mortgage loans, title searches, title insurance, attorney services, surveys, credit reports, and appraisals.

IN PRACTICE

Under HUD regulations, employers may not pay referral fees to employees who steer customers to the brokerage's ancillary businesses. However, employees who generate business *for the brokerage itself* (not for any ancillary) may be paid a referral fee. Management-level employees may be paid bonuses for performance but may not be paid individual referral fees.

■ PREPARATION OF CLOSING STATEMENTS

The purpose of a closing statement is to determine how much money the buyer must bring to the closing and how much the seller will net after the closing. A typical real estate transaction involves, in addition to the purchase price, expenses for both parties. These include items prepaid by the seller for which he or she must be reimbursed and items of expense the seller has incurred but for which the buyer will be billed. The financial responsibility for these items must be prorated (or divided) between the buyer and the seller. All expenses and prorated items are

FIGURE 23.3

Credits and Debits

Item	Credit to Buyer	Debit to Buyer	Credit to Seller	Debit to Seller	Prorated
Principal amount of new mortgage	X				
Payoff of existing mortgage				X	
Unpaid principal balance if assumed mortgage	X			X	
Accrued interest on existing assumed mortgage	X			X	X
Tenant's security deposit	X			X	
Purchase-money mortgage	X			X	
Unpaid water and other utility bills	X			X	X
Buyer's earnest money	X				
Selling price of property		X	X		
Fuel oil on hand (valued at current market price)		X	X		X
Prepaid insurance and tax reserve for mortgage assumed by buyer		X	X		X
Refund to seller of prepaid water charges and similar utility expenses		X	X		X
Accrued general real estate taxes	X			X	X

* This chart is based on generally applicable practices. Please note that closing practices may be different in your state.

accounted for on the settlement statement. This is how the exact amount of cash required from the buyer and the net proceeds to the seller are determined. (See Figure 23.2.)

How the Closing Statement Works

The completion of a **closing statement** involves an accounting of the parties' debits and credits. A **debit** is a charge, an amount that a party owes and must pay at closing. A **credit** is an amount entered in a person's favor—an amount that has already been paid, an amount being reimbursed, or an amount the buyer promises to pay in the form of a loan.

> A *debit* is an amount *to be paid* by the buyer or seller; a *credit* is an amount *payable to* the buyer or seller.

To determine the amount a buyer needs at closing, the buyer's debits are totaled. Any expenses and prorated amounts for items prepaid by the seller are added to the purchase price. Then the buyer's credits are totaled. These include the earnest money (already paid), the balance of the loan the buyer obtains or assumes, and the seller's share of any prorated items the buyer will pay in the future. (See Figure 23.3.) Finally, the total of the buyer's credits is subtracted from the total debits to arrive at the actual amount of cash the buyer must bring to closing. Usually, the buyer brings a cashier's or certified check.

A similar procedure is followed to determine how much money the seller actually will receive. The seller's debits and credits are each totaled. The credits include the purchase price plus the buyer's share of any prorated items that the seller has prepaid. The seller's debits include expenses, the seller's share of prorated items to be paid later by the buyer, and the balance of any mortgage loan or other lien that the seller pays off. Finally, the total of the seller's debits is subtracted from the total credits to arrive at the amount the seller will receive.

Broker's commission.   The responsibility for paying the broker's commission will have been determined by previous agreement. If the broker is the agent for the seller, the seller normally is responsible for paying the commission. If an agency agreement exists between a broker and the buyer, or if two agents are involved, one for the seller and one for the buyer, the commission may be apportioned as an expense between both parties or according to some other arrangement.

Attorney's fees.   If either of the parties' attorneys will be paid from the closing proceeds, that party will be charged with the expense in the closing statement. This expense may include fees for the preparation or review of documents or for representing the parties at settlement.

Recording expenses.   The seller usually pays for recording charges (filing fees) necessary to clear all defects and furnish the purchaser with a marketable title. Items customarily charged to the seller include the recording of release deeds or satisfaction of mortgages, quitclaim deeds, affidavits, and satisfaction of mechanics' liens. The purchaser pays for recording charges that arise from the actual transfer of title. Usually, such items include recording the deed that conveys title to the purchaser and a mortgage or deed of trust executed by the purchaser.

Transfer tax.   Most states require some form of transfer tax, conveyance fee, or tax stamps on real estate conveyances. This expense is most often borne by the seller, although customs vary. In addition, many cities and local municipalities charge transfer taxes. Responsibility for these charges varies according to local practice.

> **In Illinois**

In Illinois, state and county transfer taxes are usually paid by the seller in accordance with most sales contracts. Local ordinances usually establish which party is responsible for paying municipal transfer taxes. ■

Title expenses.   Responsibility for title expenses varies according to local custom. In most areas, the seller is required to furnish evidence of good title and pay for the title search. If the buyer's attorney inspects the evidence or if the buyer purchases a title insurance policy, the buyer is charged for the expense.

| In Illinois | Because the seller usually is required by the contract to furnish evidence of good title, the seller customarily pays for the owner's title insurance policy. The buyer customarily pays for the lender's policy, which ensures that the lender has a valid first lien. ■ |

Loan fees.   When the buyer secures a new loan to finance the purchase, the lender ordinarily charges a loan origination fee of 1 percent to 2 percent of the loan. The fee is usually paid by the purchaser at the time the transaction closes. The lender also may charge discount points. If the buyer assumes the seller's existing financing, the buyer may pay an assumption fee. Also, under the terms of some mortgage loans, the seller may be required to pay a prepayment charge or penalty for paying off the mortgage loan before its due date.

Tax reserves and insurance reserves (escrow or impound accounts). Most mortgage lenders require that borrowers provide reserve funds or escrow accounts to pay future real estate taxes and insurance premiums. A borrower starts the account at closing by depositing funds to cover at least the amount of unpaid real estate taxes from the date of lien to the end of the current month. (The buyer receives a credit from the seller at closing for any unpaid taxes.) Afterward, an amount equal to one month's portion of the estimated taxes is included in the borrower's monthly mortgage payment.

The borrower is responsible for maintaining adequate fire or hazard insurance as a condition of the mortgage loan. Generally, the first year's premium is paid in full at closing. An amount equal to one month's premium is paid after that. The borrower's monthly loan payment includes the principal and interest on the loan, plus one-twelfth of the estimated taxes and insurance (PITI). The taxes and insurance are held by the lender in the escrow or impound account until the bills are due.

Appraisal fees.   The purchaser usually pays the appraisal fees. When the buyer obtains a mortgage, it is customary for the lender to require an appraisal, and the buyer bears the cost. If the fee is paid at the time of the loan application, it is reflected on the closing statement as already having been paid.

Survey fees.   The purchaser who obtains new mortgage financing customarily pays the survey fees. The sales contract may require the seller to furnish a survey.

| In Illinois | Most real estate contracts in Illinois require that the seller furnish a current survey to the buyer. As a result, the expense of preparing a survey usually is borne by the seller. ■ |

Additional fees.   An FHA borrower owes a lump sum for payment of the *mortgage insurance premium* (MIP) if it is not financed as part of the loan. A VA mortgagor pays a funding fee directly to the VA at closing. If a conventional loan carries private mortgage insurance, the buyer prepays one year's insurance premium at closing.

Accounting for Expenses

Expenses paid out of the closing proceeds are debited only to the party making the payment. Occasionally, an expense item, such as an escrow fee, a settlement fee, or a transfer tax, may be shared by the buyer and the seller. In this case, each party is debited for his or her share of the expense.

■ PRORATIONS

Most closings involve the division of financial responsibility between the buyer and seller for such items as loan interest, taxes, rents, fuel, and utility bills. These allowances are called **prorations.** Prorations are necessary to ensure that expenses are divided fairly between the seller and the buyer. For example, the seller may owe current taxes that have not been billed; the buyer would want this settled at the closing. Where taxes must be paid in advance, the seller is entitled to a rebate at the closing. If the buyer assumes the seller's existing mortgage or deed of trust, the seller usually owes the buyer an allowance for accrued interest through the date of closing.

Accrued items = buyer credits
Prepaid items = seller credits

Accrued items such as water bills, Illinois real estate taxes, and interest on an assumed mortgage that is paid in arrears are expenses to be prorated that are owed by the seller but later will be paid by the buyer. The seller therefore pays for these items by giving the buyer credits for them at closing.

Prepaid items such as fuel oil in a tank are expenses to be prorated that have been *prepaid by the seller but not fully used up.* They are therefore credits to the seller.

The Arithmetic of Prorating

Accurate prorating involves four considerations:

1. Nature of the item being prorated
2. Whether it is an accrued item that requires the determination of an earned amount
3. Whether it is a prepaid item that requires the determination of an unearned amount (that is, a refund to the seller)
4. What arithmetic processes must be used

The computation of a proration involves identifying a yearly charge for the item to be prorated, then dividing by 12 to determine a monthly charge for the item. Usually, it is also necessary to identify a daily charge for the item by dividing the monthly charge by the number of days in the month. These smaller portions then are multiplied by the number of months or days in the prorated time period to determine the accrued or unearned amount that will be figured in the settlement.

Using this general principle, there are two methods of calculating prorations:

1. The yearly charge is divided by a *360-day year* (commonly called a *statutory,* or *banking, year*), or 12 months of 30 days each.
2. The yearly charge is divided by 365 (366 in a leap year) to determine the daily charge. Then the actual number of days in the proration period is determined, and this number is multiplied by the daily charge.

In Illinois

A third method, the *statutory month variation,* is also acceptable in Illinois. In this method, the yearly charge is divided by 12 to determine a monthly amount. The monthly charge then is divided by the actual number of days in the month in which the closing occurs. This final number is the daily charge for that month. ■

The final proration figure will vary slightly, depending on which computation method is used. The final figure also varies according to the number of decimal places to which the division is carried. All of the computations in this chapter are computed by carrying the division to three decimal places. The third decimal place is rounded off to cents only after the final proration figure is determined.

Accrued Items

When the real estate tax is levied for the calendar year and is payable during that year or in the following year, the accrued portion is for the period from January 1 through the date of closing. If the current tax bill has not yet been issued, the parties must agree on an estimated amount based on the previous year's bill and any known changes in assessment or tax levy for the current year.

Sample proration calculation.   Assume a sale is to be closed on September 17. Current real estate taxes of $1,200 are to be prorated. A 360-day year is used. The accrued period, then, is 8 months and 17 days. First determine the prorated cost of the real estate tax per month and day:

$$\frac{\$100 \text{ per month}}{12)\$1,200} \qquad \frac{\$3.333 \text{ per day}}{30)\$100.000}$$
$$\text{months} \qquad\qquad \text{days}$$

Next, multiply these figures by the accrued period, and add the totals to determine the prorated real estate tax:

$100	$ 3.333	$800.000
× 8 months	× 17 days	+ 56.661
$800	$56.661	$856.661

Thus, the accrued real estate tax for 8 months and 17 days is $856.66 (rounded off to two decimal places after the final computation). This amount represents the seller's accrued earned tax. It will be a credit to the buyer and a debit to the seller on the closing statement.

To compute this proration using the actual number of days in the accrued period, the following method is used: The accrued period from January 1 to September 17 runs 260 days (January's 31 days plus February's 28 days and so on, plus the 17 days of September).

$1,200 tax bill ÷ 365 days = $3.288 per day
$3.288 × 260 days = $854.880, or $854.88

While these examples show proration as of the date of settlement, the agreement of sale may require otherwise. For instance, a buyer's possession date may not coincide with the settlement date. In this case, the parties could prorate according to the date of possession.

IN PRACTICE   On state licensing examinations, tax prorations are usually based on a 30-day month (360-day year), unless specified otherwise. This may differ from local customs regarding tax prorations. Many title insurance companies provide proration charts that detail tax factors for each day in the year. To determine a tax proration using one of these charts, multiply the factor given for the closing date by the annual real estate tax.

Prepaid Items

A tax proration could be a prepaid item in some locations. Because real estate taxes may be paid in the early part of the year, a tax proration calculated for a closing that takes place later in the year must reflect that the seller has already paid the tax. For example, in the preceding problem, suppose that all taxes had been paid. The buyer, then, would have to reimburse the seller; the proration would be credited to the seller and debited to the buyer.

In figuring the tax proration, it is necessary to ascertain the number of future days, months, and years for which taxes have been paid. The formula commonly used for this purpose is as follows:

	Years	Months	Days
Taxes paid to (Dec. 31, end of tax year)	2008	12	30
Date of closing (Sept. 17, 2008)	2008	−9	−17
Period for which tax must be returned to seller (in "prepay" locale)		3	13

With this formula (using the statutory-month method), we can find the amount the buyer will reimburse the seller for the portion of the real estate tax already paid for time the buyer will live in the house. The prepaid period, as determined using the formula for prepaid items, is 3 months and 13 days. Three months at $100 per month equals $300, and 13 days at $3.333 per day equals $43.329. Add days and months to arrive at $343.329, or $343.33 credited to the seller and debited to the buyer. *Where taxes are paid in arrears (2008 is paid in 2009), as in Illinois, the roles reverse (buyer credit, seller debit), but the math is essentially the same.*

Sample prepaid item calculation. One example of a prepaid item is a water bill. Assume that the water is billed in advance by the city without using a meter. The six months' billing is $60 for the period ending October 31. The sale is to be closed on August 3. Because the water bill is paid to October 31, the prepaid time must be computed. Using a 30-day basis, the time period is the 27 days left in August plus 2 full months: $60 ÷ 6 = $10 per month. For one day, divide $10 by 30, which equals $0.333 per day. The prepaid period is 2 months and 27 days, so

$$
\begin{array}{ll}
27 \text{ days} \quad \times \; \$ \; 0.333 \text{ per day} = \$8.991 \\
2 \text{ months} \times \$10 \qquad\qquad = \underline{\$20} \\
\qquad\qquad\qquad\qquad\qquad\quad \$28.991, \text{ or } \$28.99
\end{array}
$$

This is a prepaid item; it is credited to the seller and debited to the buyer on the closing statement.

To figure this based on the actual days in the month of closing, the following process would be used:

$$\begin{array}{rcl}
\$10 \text{ per month} \div 31 \text{ days in August} & = & \$0.323 \text{ per day} \\
\text{August 4 through August 31} & = & 28 \text{ days} \\
28 \text{ days} \times \$0.323 & = & \$9.044 \\
2 \text{ months} \times \$10 & = & \$20 \\
\$9.044 + \$20 & = & \$29.044, \text{ or } \$29.04
\end{array}$$

General Rules for Prorating

The rules or customs governing the computation of prorations for the closing of a real estate sale vary greatly from state to state. The following are some general guidelines for preparing the closing statement:

- In most states, the seller owns the property on the day of closing, and prorations or apportionments usually are made to and including the day of closing. In a few states, however, it is provided specifically that the buyer owns the property on the closing date. In that case, adjustments are made as of the day preceding the day on which title is closed.

- Mortgage interest, general real estate taxes, water taxes, insurance premiums, and similar expenses usually are computed by using 360 days in a year and 30 days in a month. However, the rules in some areas provide for computing prorations on the basis of the actual number of days in the calendar month of closing. The agreement of sale should specify which method will be used.

- Accrued general real estate taxes usually are prorated at the closing. When the amount of the current real estate tax cannot be determined definitely, the proration is usually based on the last obtainable tax bill.

- Special assessments for municipal improvements such as sewers, water mains, or streets usually are paid in annual installments over several years, with annual interest charged on the outstanding balance of future installments. The seller normally pays the current installment, and the buyer assumes all future installments. The special assessment installment generally is not prorated at the closing. A buyer may insist that the seller allow the buyer a credit for the seller's share of the interest to the closing date. The agreement of sale may address the manner in which special assessments will be handled at settlement.

- Rents are usually adjusted on the basis of the actual number of days in the month of closing. It is customary for the seller to receive the rents for the day of closing and to pay all expenses for that day. If any rents for the current month are uncollected when the sale is closed, the buyer often agrees by a separate letter to collect the rents if possible and remit the pro rata share to the seller.

- Security deposits made by tenants to cover the last month's rent of the lease or to cover the cost of repairing damage caused by the tenant generally are transferred by the seller to the buyer.

Real estate taxes.   Proration of real estate taxes varies, depending on how the taxes are paid in the area where the real estate is located. In some states, real estate taxes are paid in advance; that is, if the tax year runs from January 1 to December 31, taxes for the coming year are due on January 1. In this case, the seller, who has prepaid a year's taxes, should be reimbursed for the portion of the year remaining after the buyer takes ownership of the property. In other areas, taxes are paid in arrears, on December 31 for the year just ended. In this case, the buyer should be credited by the seller for the time the seller occupied the property. Sometimes, taxes are due during the tax year, partly in arrears and partly in advance; sometimes they are payable in installments. It gets even more complicated: city, state, school, and other property taxes may start their tax years in different months. Whatever the case may be in a particular transaction, the licensee should understand how the taxes will be prorated.

> **In Illinois**

Taxes in Illinois are paid in the *year after they become a lien (i.e., "paid in arrears")*. The buyer must be credited for any taxes that still will be paid in the future for time in the "past" (i.e., up until closing) when the seller occupied the property. If an unpaid installment based on last year has been billed, this specific amount is credited to the buyer and debited to the seller. The buyer must be credited with the current year's taxes to time of closing, because those taxes will not be paid until *next* year (again by the buyer/new owner). Consequently, the seller is debited accordingly, to the date of close, and a proration (and often a tax estimate based on last year's tax) is necessary for this latter figure.

The following formula may be used in Illinois:

Last annual tax bill ÷ 360 × Number of days from January 1 to closing date = Tax proration: the amount *seller owes buyer.* ∎

Mortgage loan interest.   On almost every mortgage loan the interest is paid in arrears, so buyer and seller must understand that the mortgage payment due on June 1, for example, includes interest due for the month of May. Thus, the buyer who assumes a mortgage on May 31 and makes the June payment pays for the time the seller occupied the property and should be credited with a month's interest. On the other hand, the buyer who places a new mortgage loan on May 31 may be pleasantly surprised to hear that he or she will not need to make a mortgage payment until a month later.

> **In Illinois**

The terms of some assumed mortgage loans provide that interest is charged at the beginning of the month (in advance); without this provision, interest is always charged at the end of the month (in arrears). When the interest on the existing mortgage to be assumed by the buyer is charged at the beginning of the month, the *unearned portion* (that is, the part that is prepaid from the date of closing to the end of the month) must be credited to the seller and debited to the buyer. When the mortgage interest is charged at the end of the month, the *earned portion* of the mortgage interest through the date of closing is an accrued expense, debited to the seller and credited to the buyer. ∎

∎ SAMPLE CLOSING STATEMENT

Settlement computations take many possible formats. The remaining portion of this chapter illustrates a sample transaction using the HUD-1 form (Uniform Settlement Statement), Figure 23.4.

Basic Information of Offer and Sale

John and Joanne Iuro list their home at 3045 North Racine Avenue in Riverdale with the Open Door Real Estate Company. The listing price is $118,500, and possession can be given within two weeks after all parties have signed the contract. Under the terms of the listing agreement, the sellers agree to pay the broker a commission of 6 percent of the sales price.

On May 18, the Open Door Real Estate Company submits a contract offer to the Iuros from Brook Redemann, a bachelor residing at 22 King Court, Riverdale. Redemann offers $115,000, with earnest money and down payment of $23,000 and the remaining $92,000 of the purchase price to be obtained through a new conventional loan. No private mortgage insurance is necessary because the loan-to-value ratio does not exceed 80 percent. The Iuros sign the contract on May 29. Closing is set for June 15 at the office of the Open Door Real Estate Company, 720 Main Street, Riverdale.

The unpaid balance of the Iuros' mortgage as of June 1, 2009, will be $57,700. Payments are $680 per month, with interest at 11 percent per annum on the unpaid balance.

The sellers submit evidence of title in the form of a title insurance binder at a cost of $10. The title insurance policy, to be paid by the sellers at the time of closing, costs an additional $540, including $395 for lender's coverage and $145 for homeowner's coverage. Recording charges of $20 are paid for the recording of two instruments to clear defects in the sellers' title. State transfer tax stamps in the amount of $115 ($.50 per $500 of the sales price or fraction thereof) are affixed to the deed. In addition, the sellers must pay an attorney's fee of $400 for preparing the deed and for legal representation. This amount will be paid from the closing proceeds.

The buyer must pay an attorney's fee of $300 for examining the title evidence and for legal representation. He also must pay $10 to record the deed. These amounts also will be paid from the closing proceeds.

Real estate taxes in Riverdale are paid in arrears. Taxes for this year, estimated at last year's figure of $1,725, have not been paid. According to the contract, prorations will be made on the basis of 30 days in a month.

Computing the prorations and charges. The following list illustrates the various steps in computing the prorations and other amounts to be included in the settlement to this point:

- Closing date: June 15, 2008
- Commission: 6% (.06) × $115,000 sales price = $6,900
- Seller's mortgage interest: 11% (.11) × $57,700 principal due after June 1 payment = $6,347 interest per year; $6,347 ÷ 360 days = $17.631 interest per day; 15 days of accrued interest to be paid by the seller × $17.631 = $264.465 interest owed by the seller; $57,700 + $264.465 = $57,964.465, or $57,964.47 payoff of seller's mortgage
- Real estate taxes (estimated at $1,725): $1,725 ÷ 12 months = $143.75 per month; $143.75 ÷ 30 days = $4.792 per day
- The earned period, from January 1 to and including June 15, equals 5 months and 15 days: $143.75 × 5 months = $718.75; $4.792 × 15 days = $71.88; $718.75 + $71.88 = $790.63 seller owes buyer
- Transfer tax ($.50 per $500 of consideration or fraction thereof): $115,000 ÷ $500 = 230; 230 × $.50 = $115 transfer tax owed by seller

FIGURE 23.4

HUD-1

A. **Settlement Statement**	U.S. Department of Housing and Urban Development	OMB Approval No. 2502-0265

B. Type of Loan

1. ☐ FHA	2. ☐ FmHA	3. ☒ Conv. Unins.	6. File Number:	7. Loan Number:	8. Mortgage Insurance Case Number:
4. ☐ VA	5. ☐ Conv. Ins.				

C. Note: This form is furnished to give you a statement of actual settlement costs. Amounts paid to and by the settlement agent are shown. Items marked "(p.o.c.)" were paid outside the closing; they are shown here for informational purposes and are not included in the totals.

D. Name & Address of Borrower:	E. Name & Address of Seller:	F. Name & Address of Lender:
Brook Redemann 22 King Court Riverdale, ED 00000	John Iuro and Joanne Iuro 3045 North Racine Avenue Riverdale, ED 00000	Thrift Federal Savings 1100 Fountain Plaza Riverdale, ED 00000

G. Property Location:	H. Settlement Agent:
3045 North Racine Avenue Riverdale, ED 00000	Open Door Real Estate Co.

	Place of Settlement:	I. Settlement Date:
	720 Main Street Riverdale, ED 00000	June 15, 200-

J. Summary of Borrower's Transaction		K. Summary of Seller's Transaction	
100. Gross Amount Due From Borrower		**400. Gross Amount Due To Seller**	
101. Contract sales price	$115,000.00	401. Contract sales price	$115,000.00
102. Personal property		402. Personal property	
103. Settlement charges to borrower (line 1400)	4,892.09	403.	
104.		404.	
105.		405.	
Adjustments for items paid by seller in advance		Adjustments for items paid by seller in advance	
106. City/town taxes to		406. City/town taxes to	
107. County taxes to		407. County taxes to	
108. Assessments to		408. Assessments to	
109.		409.	
110.		410.	
111.		411.	
112.		412.	
120. Gross Amount Due From Borrower	119,892.09	**420. Gross Amount Due To Seller**	$115,000.00
200. Amounts Paid By Or In Behalf Of Borrower		**500. Reductions In Amount Due To Seller**	
201. Deposit or earnest money	23,000.00	501. Excess deposit (see instructions)	
202. Principal amount of new loan(s)	92,000.00	502. Settlement charges to seller (line 1400)	8,285.00
203. Existing loan(s) taken subject to		503. Existing loan(s) taken subject to	
204.		504. Payoff of first mortgage loan	57,964.47
205.		505. Payoff of second mortgage loan	
206.		506.	
207.		507.	
208.		508.	
209.		509.	
Adjustments for items unpaid by seller		Adjustments for items unpaid by seller	
210. City/town taxes to		510. City/town taxes to	
211. County taxes 1/1 to 6/15	790.63	511. County taxes 1/1 to 6/15	790.63
212. Assessments to		512. Assessments to	
213.		513.	
214.		514.	
215.		515.	
216.		516.	
217.		517.	
218.		518.	
219.		519.	
220. Total Paid By/For Borrower	115,790.63	**520. Total Reduction Amount Due Seller**	67,040.10
300. Cash At Settlement From/To Borrower		**600. Cash At Settlement To/From Seller**	
301. Gross Amount due from borrower (line 120)	119,892.09	601. Gross amount due to seller (line 420)	115,000.00
302. Less amounts paid by/for borrower (line 220)	(115,790.63)	602. Less reductions in amt. due seller (line 520)	(67,040.10)
303. Cash ☒ From ☐ To Borrower	$ 4,101.46	**603. Cash** ☒ To ☐ From Seller	$ 47,959.90

Section 5 of the Real Estate Settlement Procedures Act (RESPA) requires the following: • HUD must develop a Special Information Booklet to help persons borrowing money to finance the purchase of residential real estate to better understand the nature and costs of real estate settlement services; • Each lender must provide the booklet to all applicants from whom it receives or for whom it prepares a written application to borrow money to finance the purchase of residential real estate; • Lenders must prepare and distribute with the Booklet a Good Faith Estimate of the settlement costs that the borrower is likely to incur in connection with the settlement. These disclosures are manadatory.

Section 4(a) of RESPA mandates that HUD develop and prescribe this standard form to be used at the time of loan settlement to provide full disclosure of all charges imposed upon the borrower and seller. These are third party disclosures that are designed to provide the borrower with pertinent information during the settlement process in order to be a better shopper.

The Public Reporting Burden for this collection of information is estimated to average one hour per response, including the time for reviewing instructions, searching existing data sources, gathering and maintaining the data needed, and completing and reviewing the collection of information.

This agency may not collect this information, and you are not required to complete this form, unless it displays a currently valid OMB control number.

The information requested does not lend itself to confidentiality.

F I G U R E 23.4 (CONTINUED)

HUD-1

L. Settlement Charges

			Paid From Borrowers Funds at Settlement	Paid From Seller's Funds at Settlement
700. Total Sales/Broker's Commission based on price $ 115,000.00 @ 6 % = 6,900.00				
Division of Commission (line 700) as follows:				
701. $	to			
702. $	to			
703. Commission paid at Settlement				$ 6,900.00
704.				
800. Items Payable In Connection With Loan				
801. Loan Origination Fee	%		$ 920.00	
802. Loan Discount	%		1,840.00	
803. Appraisal Fee 250.00	to Swift Appraisal		POC	
804. Credit Report 60.00	to Amce Credit Bureau		POC	
805. Lender's Inspection Fee				
806. Mortgage Insurance Application Fee to				
807. Assumption Fee				
808.				
809.				
810.				
811.				
900. Items Required By Lender To Be Paid In Advance				
901. Interest from 6/16 to 6/30 @$25.556 /day			383.34	
902. Mortgage Insurance Premium for		months to		
903. Hazard Insurance Premium for	1 years to Hite Insurance Co.		345.00	
904.	years to			
905.				
1000. Reserves Deposited With Lender				
1001. Hazard insurance	2 months@$ 28.75	per month	57.50	
1002. Mortgage insurance	months@$	per month		
1003. City property taxes	months@$	per month		
1004. County property taxes	7 months@$ 143.75	per month	1,006.25	
1005. Annual assessments	months@$	per month		
1006.	months@$	per month		
1007.	months@$	per month		
1008.	months@$	per month		
1100. Title Charges				
1101. Settlement or closing fee	to			
1102. Abstract or title search	to			
1103. Title examination	to			
1104. Title insurance binder	to			10.00
1105. Document preparation	to			
1106. Notary fees	to			
1107. Attorney's fees	to		300.00	400.00
(includes above items numbers:				
1108. Title insurance	to			540.00
(includes above items numbers:				
1109. Lender's coverage	$ 395.00			
1110. Owner's coverage	$ 145.00			
1111.				
1112.				
1113.				
1200. Government Recording and Transfer Charges				
1201. Recording fees: Deed $ 20.00 ; Mortgage $ 20.00 ; Releases $ 20.00			40.00	20.00
1202. City/county tax/stamps: Deed $; Mortgage $				
1203. State tax/stamps: Deed $; Mortgage $				115.00
1204. Record 2 documents to clear title				40.00
1205.				
1300. Additional Settlement Charges				
1301. Survey	to			175.00
1302. Pest inspection to				85.00
1303.				
1304.				
1305.				
1400. Total Settlement Charges (enter on lines 103, Section J and 502, Section K)			$ 4,892.09	$ 8,285.00

The sellers' loan payoff is $57,964.47. They must pay an additional $10 to record the mortgage release, as well as $85 for a pest inspection. The buyer's new loan is from Thrift Federal Savings, 1100 Fountain Plaza, Riverdale, in the amount of $92,000 at 10 percent interest. In connection with this loan, Redemann will be charged $125 to have the property appraised by Swift Appraisal. Acme Credit Bureau will charge $60 for a credit report. (Because appraisal and credit reports are performed before loan approval, they are paid at the time of loan application, whether or not the transaction eventually closes. These items are noted as POC— paid outside closing—on the settlement statement.) In addition, Redemann will pay for interest on his loan for the remainder of the month of closing: 15 days at $25.556 per day, or $383.34. His first full payment (including July's interest) will be due on August 1. He must deposit $1,006.25 into a tax reserve account. That's seven-twelfths of the anticipated county real estate tax of $1,725. A one-year hazard insurance premium at $3 per $1,000 of appraised value ($115,000 ÷ 1,000 × 3 = $345) is paid in advance to Hite Insurance Company. An insurance reserve to cover the premium for three months is deposited with the lender. Redemann will have to pay an additional $10 to record the mortgage, a loan origination fee of $920, and two discount points. The sellers will pay $175 for a survey.

The Uniform Settlement Statement

HUD-1 is divided into 12 sections. Sections J, K, and L contain particularly important information. The borrower's and seller's summaries (J and K) are very similar. In Section J, the buyer-borrower's debits are listed on lines 100 through 112. They are totaled on line 120 (gross amount due from borrower). The total of the settlement costs itemized in Section L of the statement is entered on line 103 as one of the buyer's charges. The buyer's credits are listed on lines 201 through 219 and totaled on line 220 (total paid by or for borrower). Then the buyer's credits are subtracted from the charges to arrive at the cash due from the borrower to close (line 303).

In Section K, the seller's credits are entered on lines 400 through 412 and totaled on line 420 (gross amount due to seller). The seller's debits are entered on lines 501 through 519 and totaled on line 520 (total reductions in amount due seller). The total of the seller's settlement charges is on line 502. Then the debits are subtracted from the credits to arrive at the cash due to the seller at closing (line 603).

Section L summarizes all the settlement charges for the transaction; the buyer's expenses are listed in one column and the seller's expenses in the other. If an attorney's fee is listed as a lump sum in line 1107, the settlement should list by line number the services that were included in that total fee.

■ SUMMARY

Closing a real estate sale involves both title procedures and financial matters. The real estate salesperson or broker is often present at the closing to see that the sale is actually concluded, to lend support to valued clients, and to account for the earnest money deposit (which has normally been held in escrow by the real estate office).

Closings must be reported to the IRS on Form 1099-S.

The federal *Real Estate Settlement Procedures Act* (RESPA) requires disclosure of all settlement costs when a residential real estate purchase is financed by a federally related mortgage loan. RESPA requires lenders to use a Uniform Settlement Statement to detail the financial particulars of a transaction.

The actual amount to be paid by a buyer at closing is computed on a closing statement form or settlement statement. This lists the sales price, earnest money deposit, and all adjustments and prorations due between buyer and seller. The purpose of this statement is to determine the net amount due the seller at closing. The buyer reimburses the seller for prepaid items like unused taxes or fuel oil. The seller credits the buyer for bills the seller owes, but the buyer will have to pay accrued items such as unpaid water bills.

The closing statement is customarily prepared by the buyer's lender, the lender's agent, or the seller's lawyer. State and county transfer taxes are usually paid by the seller, who also customarily pays for the survey and the owner's title insurance policy. The buyer usually pays for the lender's title insurance policy.

| In Illinois | Illinois permits proration by the statutory month variation method.

Real estate taxes in Illinois are paid in arrears; in other words, in the year after they become a lien. ∎

QUESTIONS

1. Which of the following statements is *TRUE* of real estate closings in most states?
   a. Closings are generally conducted by real estate salespersons.
   b. The buyer usually receives the rents for the day of closing.
   c. The buyer must reimburse the seller for any title evidence provided by the seller.
   d. The seller usually pays the expenses for the day of closing.

2. All encumbrances and liens shown on the report of title other than those waived or agreed to by the purchaser and listed in the contract must be removed so that the title can be delivered free and clear. The removal of such encumbrances is the duty of the
   a. buyer.
   b. seller.
   c. broker.
   d. title company.

3. Generally, legal title passes from seller to buyer
   a. on the date of execution of the deed.
   b. when the closing statement has been signed.
   c. when the deed is placed in escrow.
   d. when the deed is delivered.

4. Which of the following would a lender generally require at the closing?
   a. Title insurance binder
   b. Market value appraisal
   c. Application
   d. Credit report

5. Juan is buying a house. In Juan's area, closings are traditionally conducted in escrow. Which of the following items will Juan deposit with the escrow agent before the closing date?
   a. Deed to the property
   b. Title evidence
   c. Estoppel certificate
   d. Cash needed to complete the purchase

6. The RESPA Uniform Settlement Statement (HUD-1) must be used to illustrate all settlement charges for
   a. every real estate transaction.
   b. transactions financed by VA and FHA loans only.
   c. residential transactions financed by federally related mortgage loans.
   d. all transactions involving commercial property.

7. A mortgage reduction certificate is executed by a(n)
   a. abstract company.
   b. attorney.
   c. lending institution.
   d. grantor.

8. The principal amount of a purchaser's new mortgage loan is a
   a. credit to the seller.
   b. credit to the buyer.
   c. debit to the seller.
   d. debit to the buyer.

9. The earnest money left on deposit with the broker is a
   a. credit to the seller.
   b. credit to the buyer.
   c. balancing factor.
   d. debit to the buyer.

10. The annual real estate taxes on a property amount to $1,800. The seller has paid the taxes in advance for the calendar year. If closing is set for June 15, which of the following is *TRUE*?
    a. Credit seller $825; debit buyer $975
    b. Credit seller $1,800; debit buyer $825
    c. Credit buyer $975; debit seller $975
    d. Credit seller $975; debit buyer $975

11. If a seller collected rent of $1,400, payable in advance, from an attic tenant on August 1, which of the following is *TRUE* at the closing on August 15?
    a. Seller owes buyer $1,400
    b. Buyer owes seller $1,400
    c. Seller owes buyer $700
    d. Buyer owes seller $700

12. Security deposits should be listed on a closing statement as a credit to the
    a. buyer.
    b. seller.
    c. lender.
    d. broker.

13. A building was purchased for $285,000, with 10 percent down and a loan for the balance. If the lender charged the buyer two discount points, how much cash did the buyer need to come up with at closing if the buyer incurred no other costs?
    a. $31,700
    b. $28,500
    c. $33,630
    d. $30,200

14. A buyer of a $300,000 home has paid $22,000 as earnest money and has a loan commitment for 70 percent of the purchase price. How much more cash does the buyer need to bring to the closing, provided the buyer has no closing costs?
    a. $68,000
    b. $30,000
    c. $58,000
    d. $61,600

15. At closing, the listing broker's commission usually is shown as a
    a. credit to the seller.
    b. credit to the buyer.
    c. debit to the seller.
    d. debit to the buyer.

16. At the closing of a real estate transaction, the seller's attorney gave the buyer a credit for certain accrued items. These items were
    a. bills relating to the property that have already been paid by the seller.
    b. bills relating to the property that will have to be paid by the buyer.
    c. all of the seller's real estate bills.
    d. all of the buyer's real estate bills.

17. The *Real Estate Settlement Procedures Act* (RESPA) applies to the activities of
    a. brokers selling commercial office buildings.
    b. security salespersons selling limited partnerships.
    c. Ginnie Mae or Fannie Mae when purchasing mortgages.
    d. lenders financing the purchases of borrowers' residences.

18. The purpose of RESPA is to
    a. make sure buyers do not borrow more than they can repay.
    b. make real estate brokers more responsive to buyers' needs.
    c. help buyers know how much money is required.
    d. see that buyers know all settlement costs.

19. The document that provides borrowers with general information about settlement costs, RESPA provisions, and the Uniform Settlement Statement is the
    a. HUD-1 Form.
    b. special information booklet.
    c. good-faith estimate of settlement costs.
    d. closing statement.

20. Which of the following statements is *TRUE* of a computerized loan origination (CLO) system?

    a. The mortgage broker or lender may pay any fee charged by the real estate broker in whose office the CLO terminal is located.

    b. The borrower must pay the fee charged by the real estate broker in whose office the CLO terminal is located.

    c. The real estate broker in whose office the CLO terminal is located may charge a fee of up to two points for the use of the system.

    d. The fee charged by the real estate broker for using the CLO terminal may not be financed as part of the loan.

21. Which of the following is *TRUE* regarding the *Real Estate Settlement Procedures Act* (RESPA)?

    a. The purpose of RESPA is to assist lenders in determining their settlement charges on a local level.

    b. If a borrower is negotiating a loan on a six-unit apartment building, RESPA regulations must be followed.

    c. RESPA is a federal law enacted so buyers and sellers will be informed of settlement costs in residential real estate transactions.

    d. RESPA is a federal law enacted to regulate the settlement procedures on agricultural properties.

22. A real estate agent negotiated a contract for deed for a buyer and seller on a single-family residential property. A HUD-1 settlement sheet was not used in the transaction. Must the agent use a HUD-1 settlement sheet in this transaction?

    a. Yes; because it is a single-family residential property, a HUD-1 settlement sheet must be used.

    b. Yes; if a real estate agent is involved in a transaction, RESPA requires a HUD-1 settlement sheet.

    c. No, because RESPA does not regulate contract for deeds.

    d. No, because RESPA regulates only commercial properties.

23. If the annual real estate taxes on a property were $2,129 last year, what would be the per diem amount for prorations this year using the actual-number-of-days method?

    a. $4.90

    b. $5.83

    c. $5.86

    d. $5.98

24. In Illinois, the closing statement is customarily prepared by which party?

    a. Buyer's attorney

    b. Listing broker

    c. Buyer's lender

    d. Seller's lender

25. Which of the following formulas *BEST* expresses the statutory month variation method of calculating a daily prorated charge for an annual prepaid expense?

    a. (Total charge ÷ 12) ÷ Actual days in month of closing = Daily prorated charge

    b. (Total charge ÷ 360) × 12 = Daily prorated charge

    c. (Total charge ÷ 360) × Actual days in month of closing = Daily prorated charge

    d. (Total charge ÷ 365 = y) (y ÷ 12) × Actual days in closing month = Daily prorated charge

26. In Illinois, which party usually pays the state and county transfer taxes?

    a. Buyer

    b. Buyer pays state taxes; seller pays county and municipal taxes

    c. Whichever party is specified in the local ordinance

    d. Seller

MATH FAQs

Answers to Your Most Frequently
Asked Real Estate Math Questions

SECTION

Fractions, Decimals, and Percentages

■ WHAT ARE THE PARTS OF A FRACTION?

The **denominator** shows the number of equal parts in the whole or total. The **numerator** shows the number of those parts with which you are working. In the example below, the whole or total has been divided into eight equal parts, and you have seven of those equal parts.

$$\frac{7}{8} \qquad \frac{\text{Numerator}}{\text{Denominator}} \qquad \frac{\text{(Top Number)}}{\text{(Bottom Number)}}$$

■ WHAT IS MEANT BY A "PROPER FRACTION"?

⅞ is an example of a **proper fraction.** In a proper fraction the numerator is less than the whole or less than 1.

■ WHAT IS AN "IMPROPER FRACTION"?

$$\frac{11}{8} \qquad \frac{\text{Numerator}}{\text{Denominator}}$$

This is an example of an **improper fraction.** In an improper fraction, the numerator is greater than the whole or greater than 1.

■ WHAT IS A MIXED NUMBER?

11½ is a **mixed number.** You have a whole number plus a fraction. A mixed number is greater than the whole or greater than 1.

■ HOW DO I MULTIPLY FRACTIONS?

When multiplying fractions, the numerator is multiplied by the numerator, and the denominator by the denominator. Let's start with an easy question. What is ½ × ¾?

First multiply the numerators (top numbers) 1 × 3 = 3; then the denominators (bottom numbers) 2 × 4 = 8. Thus, ½ × ¾ = ⅜.

475

What is 4⅔ × 10⅝? The first step is to convert the whole number 4 into thirds. This is done by multiplying 4 × 3 = 12. (Multiply the whole number, 4, by the denominator of the fraction, 3.) Thus, the whole number 4 is equal to ¹²⁄₃.

4⅔ is equal to ¹²⁄₃ + ⅔ = ¹⁴⁄₃.

The next step is to convert the whole number 10 into eighths. This is done by multiplying 10 × 8 = 80. (Multiply the whole number, 10, by the denominator of the fraction, 8.) Thus, the whole number 10 is equal to ⁸⁰⁄₈. ⁸⁰⁄₈ + ⅝ = ⁸⁵⁄₈.

So, what is ¹⁴⁄₃ × ⁸⁵⁄₈? First multiply 14 × 85 = 1,190. Then, 3 × 8 = 24. ¹,¹⁹⁰⁄₂₄ = 49.58. (That is, 1,190 ÷ 24 = 49.58.)

An easier way to work the question is to convert the fractions to decimals.

⅔ is equal to 2 ÷ 3 or .67.

⅝ is equal to 5 ÷ 8 or .625.

4.67 × 10.625 = 49.62.

Whenever working with fractions or decimals equivalents, the answers will be close but not exact.

■ HOW DO I DIVIDE BY FRACTIONS?

Dividing by fractions is a two-step process. What is ¾ ÷ ¼?

First, invert the ¼ to ⁴⁄₁. Then, multiply ¾ × ⁴⁄₁ = ¹²⁄₄. Finally, 12 ÷ 4 = 3.

You may also convert ¾ to the decimal .75 and ¼ to the decimal .25.

.75 ÷ .25 = 3. (There are three .25 in .75.)

What is 100⅞ ÷ ¾?

100 × 8 = 800.

800 + 7 = ⁸⁰⁷⁄₈.

¾ is inverted to ⁴⁄₃.

⁸⁰⁷⁄₈ × ⁴⁄₃ = 807 × 4 = 3,228; 8 × 3 = 24. ³,²²⁸⁄₂₄ = 3,228 ÷ 24 = 134.5

Or 7 ÷ 8 = .875 and 3 ÷ 4 = .75.

100.875 ÷ .75 = 134.50.

■ HOW DO I CONVERT FRACTIONS TO DECIMALS?

Fractions will sometimes be used in real estate math problems. Since calculators may be used on most licensing examinations, it is best to convert fractions to decimals.

M A T H ✓ T I P To convert a fraction to a decimal, the top number, called the numerator, is divided by the bottom number, the denominator.

For example:

$$\tfrac{7}{8} = 7 \div 8 = \mathbf{0.875}$$
$$1\tfrac{1}{8} = 11 \div 8 = \mathbf{1.375}$$
$$11\tfrac{1}{2} = 1 \div 2 = 0.5 + 11 = \mathbf{11.5}$$

Once fractions have been converted to decimals, other calculations can be easily completed using the calculator. Note that many calculators automatically add the zero before the decimal point as in the first two examples above.

■ HOW DO I ADD OR SUBTRACT DECIMALS?

Line up the decimals, add or subtract, and bring the decimal down in the answer. You may add zeros if necessary as place holders. For example, 0.5 is the same as 0.50, or .5.

$$\begin{array}{r} 0.50 \\ +3.25 \\ \hline \mathbf{3.75} \end{array} \qquad \begin{array}{r} 8.20 \\ -0.75 \\ \hline \mathbf{7.45} \end{array}$$

M A T H ✓ T I P When you use a calculator, the decimal will be in the correct place in the answer.

0.5 + 3.25 = 3.75, and 8.2 – 0.75 = 7.45

■ HOW DO I MULTIPLY DECIMALS?

Multiply the numbers, then count the number of decimal places in each number. Next, start with the last number on the right and move the decimal the total number of decimal places to the left in the answer.

Multiply as you normally would to get the 1,500, then count the four decimal places in the numbers (.20 and .75). In the 1,500, start at the last zero on the right, and count four decimal places to the left. The decimal is placed to the left of the **1**.

$$\begin{array}{r} 0.20 \\ \times 0.75 \\ \hline 100 \\ 140 \\ \hline \mathbf{.1500} \text{ or } \mathbf{.15} \end{array}$$

Note: When you use a calculator, the decimal will be in the correct place in the answer (0.2 × 0.75 = **0.15**).

■ HOW DO I DIVIDE DECIMALS?

Divide the **dividend** (the number being divided) by the **divisor** (the number you are dividing by) and bring the decimal in the dividend straight up in the **quotient** (answer). If the divisor has a decimal, move the decimal to the right of the divisor and move the decimal the same number of places to the right in the dividend. Now divide as stated above.

$$
\begin{array}{r} = 0.75 \\ 2\overline{)1.5} \\ \underline{1.4} \\ 10 \\ \underline{10} \\ 0 \end{array}
\qquad
0.5\overline{)15.5} \quad = \quad
\begin{array}{r} = 31 \\ 5\overline{)155.} \\ \underline{15} \\ 05 \\ \underline{5} \\ 0 \end{array}
$$

M A T H ✓ T I P   When you use a calculator, you can have a decimal in the divisor and the decimal will be in the correct place in the answer.

$1.5 ÷ 2 = 0.75$, and $15.5 ÷ 0.5 = 31$

■ WHAT IS A PERCENTAGE?

Percent (%) means *per hundred* or *per hundred parts*. The whole or total always represents 100 percent.

$$5\% = 5 \text{ parts of } 100 \text{ parts, or } 5 ÷ 100 = 0.05 \text{ or } \tfrac{1}{20}$$
$$75\% = 75 \text{ parts of } 100 \text{ parts, or } 75 ÷ 100 = 0.75 \text{ or } \tfrac{3}{4}$$
$$120\% = 120 \text{ parts of } 100 \text{ parts, or } 120 ÷ 100 = 1.2 \text{ or } 1\tfrac{1}{5}$$

■ HOW CAN I CONVERT A PERCENTAGE TO A DECIMAL?

Move the decimal *two places* to the *left* and *drop* the % sign.

$$20\% = 2 ÷ 100 = 0.20 \text{ or } \mathbf{0.2}$$
$$1\% = 1 ÷ 100 = \mathbf{0.01}$$
$$12\tfrac{1}{4}\% = 12.25\%, \quad 12.25 ÷ 100 = \mathbf{0.1225}$$

See Figure 1.1.

■ HOW CAN I CONVERT A DECIMAL TO A PERCENTAGE?

Move the decimal *two places* to the *right* and *add* the % sign.

$$0.25 = \mathbf{25\%}$$
$$0.9 = \mathbf{90\%}$$
$$0.0875 = \mathbf{8.75\%} \text{ or } 8\tfrac{3}{4}\%$$

See Figure 1.1.

F I G U R E   **1.1**

**Converting Decimal
to Percentage and
Percentage to Decimal**

Decimal to Percentage

.10 ⟹ 10%

Move decimal **two places right**
to find the percentage

Percentage to Decimal

.10 ⟸ 10%

Move percentage **two places left**
to find the decimal

■ HOW DO I MULTIPLY BY PERCENTAGES?

$500 \times 25\% = 500 \times {}^{25}/_{100} = {}^{12,500}/_{100} = $ **125**

or

$500 \times 25\% = $ **125**, or $500 \times .25 = $ **125**

■ HOW DO I DIVIDE BY PERCENTAGES?

$100 \div 5\% = 100 \div 5/100 = 100 \times {}^{100}/_{5} = {}^{10,000}/_{5} = $ **2,000**

or

$100 \div 5\% = $ **2,000**, or $100 \div .05 = $ **2,000**

■ IS THERE ANY EASY WAY TO REMEMBER HOW TO SOLVE PERCENTAGE PROBLEMS?

The following three formulas are important for solving all percentage problems:

$$\text{TOTAL} \times \text{RATE} = \text{PART}$$
$$\text{PART} \div \text{RATE} = \text{TOTAL}$$
$$\text{PART} \div \text{TOTAL} = \text{RATE}$$

There is a simple way to remember how to use these formulas:

- *MULTIPLY* when PART is UNKNOWN.
- *DIVIDE* when PART is KNOWN.
- When you divide, always enter PART into the calculator first.

■ WHAT IS THE "T-BAR" METHOD?

The T-Bar is another tool to use to solve percentage problems. For some people, the "three-formula method" is more difficult to remember than the visual image of a *T*.

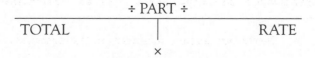

FIGURE 1.2

Using the T-Bar

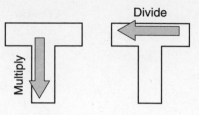

■ HOW DO I USE THE T-BAR?

The procedure for using the T-Bar is as follows:

1. Enter the two *known* items in the correct places.
2. If the line between the two items is *vertical*, you *multiply* to equal the missing item.
3. If the line between the two items is *horizontal*, you *divide* to equal the missing item. When you divide, the top **(Part)** always goes into the calculator first and is divided by the bottom **(Total** or **Rate).**

See Figure 1.2.

The following examples show how the T-Bar can be used to solve percentage problems. These examples deal with discounts because everyone can relate to buying an item that is on sale. Later we will see how the T-Bar can be used for many types of real estate problems.

■ **FOR EXAMPLE** John purchased a new suit that was marked $500. How much did John save if it was on sale for 20 percent off?

= ? ($100)		$100 Saved
$500		20%
Total Price		0.2
	×	

$500 × 20% (.20) = $100

How much did John pay for the suit?

$500 Total Price – $100 Discount   **$400 Paid**
or
100% Total Price – 20% Discount = 80% Paid

= ? ($400)		$400 Paid
$500		80%
Total Price		0.8
	×	

$500 × 80% (.80) = $400

■ **FOR EXAMPLE** Susie paid $112.50 for a dress that was reduced 25 percent. How much was it originally marked?

100% Original Price – 25% Discount = 75% Paid

$112.50 ÷ 75% (.75) = $150

■ **FOR EXAMPLE** Chris paid $127.50 for a coat that was marked down from the original price of $150. What percent of discount did Chris receive?

$150 Original Price – $127.50 Discount Price = $22.50 Discount

÷ 22.50 Discount		
$150 Original Price	= ? (0.15 = 15%)	15% Discount

$22.50 ÷ $150 = .15 or 15%

or

÷ $127.50 Paid		
$150	= ? (0.85 = 85%)	85% of Original Price Paid

$127.50 ÷ $150 = .85 or 85%

85% was the percent paid; therefore

100% Original Price – 85% Paid = **15% Discount**

■ WORD PROBLEMS CAN BE TRICKY. HOW SHOULD I DEAL WITH THEM?

There are five important steps that must be taken to solve word problems.

1. **Read** the problem carefully and completely. Never touch the calculator until you have read the entire problem.
2. **Analyze** the problem to determine what is being asked, what facts are given that *will* be needed to solve for the answer, and what facts are given that *will not* be needed to solve for the answer. Eliminate any information and/or numbers given that are not needed to solve the problem. Take the remaining information and/or numbers and determine which will be needed first, second, etc., depending on the number of steps it will take to solve the problem.
3. **Choose** the proper formula(s) and steps it will take to solve the problem.
4. **Insert** the known elements and calculate the answer.
5. **Check** your answer to be sure you keyed in the numbers and functions properly on your calculator. Be sure you finished the problem. For example, when the problem asks for the salesperson's share of the commission, do not stop at the broker's share of the commission and mark that answer just because it is one of the choices.

Percentage Problems

■ HOW DO I WORK COMMISSION PROBLEMS?

The full **commission** is a percentage of the sales price unless stated differently in the problem. Remember that full commission rates, commission splits between brokers, and commission splits between the broker and salespersons are always negotiable. Always read a problem carefully to determine the correct rate(s).

÷ Full Commission ÷

Sales Price	Full Commission Rate

×

Sales Price × Full Commission Rate = **Full Commission**
Full Commission ÷ Full Commission Rate = **Sales Price**
Full Commission ÷ Sales Price = **Full Commission Rate**

÷ Broker's Share of the Commission ÷

Full Commission	% of Full Commission to the Broker

×

Full Commission	×	% of Full Commission to the Broker	=	**Broker's Share of the Commission**
Broker's Share of the Commission	÷	% of Full Commission to the Broker	=	**Full Commission**
Broker's Share of the Commission	÷	Full Commission	=	**% of Full Commission to the Broker**

÷ Salesperson's Share of the Commission ÷

Broker's Share of the Commission	Salesperson's % of the Broker's Share

×

| Broker's Share of the Commission | × | Salesperson's % of the Broker's Share | = | **Salesperson's Share of the Commission** |

| Salesperson's Share of the Commission | ÷ | Salesperson's % of the Broker's Share | = | **Broker's Share of the Commission** |

| Salesperson's Share of the Commission | ÷ | Broker's Share of the Commission | = | **Salesperson's % of the Broker's Share** |

■ **FOR EXAMPLE** A seller listed a home for $200,000 and agreed to pay a full commission rate of 5 percent. The home sold four weeks later for 90 percent of the list price. The listing broker agreed to give the selling broker 50 percent of the commission. The listing broker paid the listing salesperson 50 percent of her share of the commission, and the selling broker paid the selling salesperson 60 percent of his share of the commission. How much commission did the selling salesperson receive?

= $180,000 Sales Price	
$200,000 List Price	90% or 0.9

×

$200,000 × 90% (.90) = $180,000

= $9,000 Full Commission	
$180,000 Sales Price	5% or 0.05

×

$180,000 × 5% (.05) = $9,000

= $4,500 Broker's Share of the Commission	
$9,000 Full Commission	50% or 0.5

×

$9,000 × 50% (.50) = $4,500

= $2,700 Selling Salesperson's Commission	
$4,500 Broker's Share of Comm.	60% or 0.6

×

4,500 × 60% (.60) = $2,700

$2,700 Selling Salesperson's Commission is the answer.

■ WHAT IS MEANT BY "SELLER'S DOLLARS AFTER COMMISSION"?

The first deduction from the sales price is the real estate commission. For example, if a house sold for $100,000 and a 7% commission was paid, that means $7,000 was paid in commissions. The seller still has 93% or $93,000. The seller's dollars after commission will be used to pay the seller's other expenses and hopefully will leave some money for the seller.

÷ Seller's Dollars after Commission ÷	
Sales Price	Percent after Commission

×

Remember, the sales price is 100%. Thus 100% – Commission % = Percent after Commission.

Sales Price	×	Percent after Commission	=	**Seller's Dollars after Commission**
Seller's Dollars after Commission	÷	Percent after Commission	=	**Sales Price**
Seller's Dollars after Commission	÷	Sales Price	=	**Percent after Commission**

■ **FOR EXAMPLE** After deducting $5,850 in closing costs and a 5 percent broker's commission, the sellers received their original cost of $175,000 plus a $4,400 profit. What was the sales price of the property?

$5,850 Closing Costs + $175,000 Original Cost + $4,400 Profit = $185,250 Seller's Dollars after Commission

100% Sales Price – 5% Commission = 95% Percent after Commission

$185,250 Seller's Dollars after Commission ÷	
= $195,000 Sales Price	95% or 0.95

$185,250 ÷ 95% (.95) = $195,000

$195,000 **Sales Price** is the answer.

■ HOW DO I DETERMINE INTEREST?

Interest is the cost of using money. The amount of interest paid is determined by the agreed-on annual interest rate, the amount of money borrowed (loan amount) or amount of money still owed (loan balance), and the period of time the money is held. When a lender grants a loan for real estate, the loan-to-value (LTV) ratio is the percentage of the sales price or appraised value, whichever is less, that the lender is willing to lend.

÷ Loan Amount ÷

Sales Price or Appraised Value (whichever is less)	Loan-to-Value Ratio (LTV)

×

Sales Price or Appraised Value (whichever is less)	×	Loan-to-Value Ratio (LTV)	=	**Loan Amount**

Loan Amount	÷	Loan-to-Value Ratio (LTV)	=	**Sales Price or Appraised Value** (whichever is less)

Loan Amount	÷	Sales Price or Appraised Value (whichever is less)	=	**Loan-to-Value Ratio (LTV)**

÷ Annual Interest ÷

Loan Amount (Principal)	Annual Interest Rate

×

Loan Amount	×	Annual Interest Rate	=	**Annual Interest**

Annual Interest	÷	Annual Interest Rate	=	**Loan Amount**

Annual Interest	÷	Loan Amount	=	**Annual Interest Rate**

■ **FOR EXAMPLE** A parcel of real estate sold for $335,200. The lender granted a 90 percent loan at 7.5 percent for 30 years. The appraised value on this parcel was $335,500. How much interest is paid to the lender in the first monthly payment?

= $301,680 Loan Amount

$335,200 Sales Price	90% or 0.9

×

$335,200 × 90% (.90) = $301,680 Loan

= $22,626 Annual Interest

$301,680 Loan Amount	7.5% or 0.075

×

$301,680 × 7.5% (.075) = $22,626

$22,626 Annual Interest ÷ 12 Months = $1,885.50 Monthly Interest

$1,885.50 Interest in the First Monthly Payment is the answer.

■ HOW DO I DETERMINE MONTHLY PRINCIPAL AND INTEREST PAYMENTS?

A **loan payment factor** can be used to calculate the monthly principal and interest (PI) payment on a loan. The factor represents the monthly principal and interest payment to amortize a $1,000 loan and is based on the annual interest rate and the term of the loan.

See Table 16.2 for a loan factor chart found on page 312.

Loan Amount ÷ $1,000 × Loan Payment Factor = **Monthly PI Payment**
Monthly PI Payment ÷ Loan Payment Factor = **Loan Amount**

■ **FOR EXAMPLE** If the lender in the previous example uses a loan payment factor of $6.99 per $1,000 of loan amount, what will be the monthly PI (principal and interest) payment?

$301,680 Loan Amount ÷ $1,000 × $6.99 = $2,108.74 Monthly PI Payment

$2,108.74 Monthly PI Payment is the answer.

■ HOW DO I WORK PROBLEMS ABOUT POINTS?

One **point** equals 1 percent of the loan amount.

÷ Amount for Points ÷	
Loan Amount	Points Converted to a Percent

×

Loan Amount	×	Points Converted to a Percent	= **Amount for Points**
Amount of Points	÷	Points Converted to a Percent	= **Loan Amount**
Amount of Points	÷	Loan Amount	= **Points Converted to a Percent**

■ **FOR EXAMPLE** The lender will charge 3½ loan discount points on an $80,000 loan. What will be the total amount due?

= $2,800 for Points	
$80,000 Loan Amount	3.5% or 0.035

×

$80,000 × 3.5% (.035) = $2,800

$2,800 for Points is the answer.

■ HOW DO I DETERMINE PROFIT?

A **profit** is made when we sell something for more than we paid for it. If we sell something for less than we paid, we have suffered a **loss.**

Sales Price – Cost = Profit

÷ Profit ÷	
Cost	Percent of Profit
×	

Cost	×	Percent of Profit	=	**Profit**
Profit	÷	Percent of Profit	=	**Cost**
Profit	÷	Cost	=	**Percent of Profit**
Cost	+	Profit	=	**Sales Price**

÷ Sales Price ÷	
Cost	Percent Sold of Cost
×	

(100% Cost + % Profit = % Sales Price)

Cost	×	Percent Sold of Cost	=	**Sales Price**
Sales Price	÷	Percent Sold of Cost	=	**Cost**
Sales Price	÷	Cost	=	**Percent Sold of Cost**

■ **FOR EXAMPLE** Your home listed for $285,000 and sold for $275,000, which gave you a 10 percent profit over the original cost. What was the original cost?

100% Original Cost + 10% Profit = 110% Sales Price

$275,000 Sales Price	
= $250,000 Original Cost	110% or 1.1
×	

$275,000 ÷ 110% (1.1) = $250,000

$250,000 Original Cost is the answer.

■ WHAT IS THE DIFFERENCE BETWEEN APPRECIATION AND DEPRECIATION?

Appreciation is increase in value. **Depreciation** is decrease in value. Both are based on the original cost. We only will cover the **straight-line method,** which is what should be used in math problems unless you are told differently. The straight-line method means that the value is increasing (appreciating) or decreasing (depreciating) the same amount each year. The amount of appreciation or depreciation is based on the original cost.

■ HOW DO I SOLVE APPRECIATION PROBLEMS?

$$\div \text{ Annual Appreciation } \div$$

Cost	Annual Appreciation Rate
×	

Cost	×	Annual Appreciation Rate	=	**Annual Appreciation**

Annual Appreciation	÷	Annual Appreciation Rate	=	**Cost**

Annual Appreciation	÷	Cost	=	**Annual Appreciation Rate**

Annual Appreciation Rate × Number of Years = **Total Appreciation Rate**
100% Cost + Total Appreciation Rate = **Today's Value as a Percent**

$$\div \text{ Today's Value (Appreciated Value) } \div$$

Cost	Today's Value as a Percent
×	

Cost	×	Today's Value as a Percent	=	**Today's Value (Appreciated Value)**

Today's Value (Appreciated Value)	÷	Today's Value as a Percent	=	**Cost**

Today's Value (Appreciated Value)	÷	Cost	=	**Today's Value as a Percent**

■ HOW DO I SOLVE DEPRECIATION PROBLEMS?

$$\frac{\div \text{ Annual Depreciation } \div}{\text{Cost} \quad | \quad \text{Annual Depreciation Rate}}$$
$$\times$$

| Cost | × | Annual Depreciation Rate | = | **Annual Depreciation** |

| Annual Depreciation | × | Annual Depreciation Rate | = | **Cost** |

| Annual Depreciation | ÷ | Cost | = | **Annual Depreciation Rate** |

Annual Depreciation Rate × Number of Years = **Total Depreciation Rate**
100% Cost ÷ Total Depreciation Rate = **Today's Value as a Percent**

$$\frac{\div \text{ Today's Value (Depreciated Value) } \div}{\text{Cost} \quad | \quad \text{Today's Value as a Percent}}$$
$$\times$$

| Cost | × | Today's Value as a Percent | = | **Today's Value (Depreciated Value)** |

| Today's Value (Depreciated Value) | ÷ | Today's Value as a Percent | = | **Cost** |

| Today's Value (Depreciated Value) | ÷ | Cost | = | **Today's Value as a Percent** |

■ **FOR EXAMPLE** Seven years ago you purchased a piece of real estate for $93,700, including the original cost of the land, which was $6,700. What is the total value of the land today using an appreciation rate of 8 percent per year?

8% Appreciation per Year × 7 Years = 56% Total Appreciation Rate
100% cost + 56% Appreciation = 156% Today's Value

$$\frac{= \$10,452 \text{ Today's Value}}{\begin{array}{c|c} \$6,700 & 156\% \\ \text{Original Cost} & \text{or } 1.56 \end{array}}$$
$$\times$$

$6,700 × 156% (1.56) = $10,452

$10,452 Today's Value is the answer.

■ **FOR EXAMPLE** The value of a house without the lot at the end of four years is $132,300. What was the original cost of the house if the yearly rate of depreciation was 2.5 percent?

2.5% depreciation per year × 4 years = 10% total depreciation rate

100% cost − 10% depreciation = 90% today's value

$132,300 Today's Value ÷

$147,000	90%
Original Cost	or 0.9

×

$132,300 ÷ 90% (.90) = $147,000

$147,000 Original Cost is the answer.

■ HOW DO I ESTIMATE VALUE FOR INCOME-PRODUCING PROPERTIES?

When appraising income-producing property, the value is estimated by using the annual net operating income (NOI) and the current market rate of return or capitalization rate. Annual scheduled gross income is adjusted for vacancies and credit losses to arrive at the annual effective gross income. The annual operating expenses are deducted from the annual effective gross income to arrive at the annual NOI. Vacancy/credit loss is usually expressed as a percentage of the scheduled gross.

Annual Scheduled Gross Income − Vacancies and Credit Losses = **Annual Effective Gross Income**

Annual Effective Gross Income − Annual Operating Expenses = **Annual NOI**

÷ Annual NOI ÷

Value	Annual Rate of Return or Annual Capitalization Rate

×

Annual NOI ÷ Annual Rate of Return = **Value**

Value × Annual Rate of Return = **Annual NOI**

Annual NOI ÷ Value = **Annual Rate of Return**

■ **FOR EXAMPLE** An office building produces $132,600 annual gross income. If the annual expenses are $30,600 and the appraiser estimates the value using an 8.5 percent rate of return, what is the estimated value?

$132,600 Annual Gross Income – $30,600 Annual Expenses = $102,000 Annual NOI

$102,000 Annual NOI ÷	
= $1,200,000 Value	8.5% or 0.085
×	

$102,000 ÷ 8.5% = $1,200,000

$1,200,000 Value is the answer.

The above formulas also can be used for investment problems. The total becomes *original cost* or *investment* instead of value.

■ **FOR EXAMPLE** You invest $335,000 in a property that should produce a 9 percent rate of return. What monthly NOI will you receive?

= $30,150 Annual NOI	
$335,000 Investment	9% or 0.09
×	

$335,000 × 9% (.09) = $30,150

$30,150 Annual NOI ÷ 12 Months = $2,512.50

$2,512.50 Monthly NOI is the answer.

■ HOW DO I SOLVE PROBLEMS INVOLVING PERCENTAGE LEASES?

When establishing the rent to be charged in a lease for retail space, the lease may be a **percentage lease** instead of a lease based on dollars per square foot. In the percentage lease, there is normally a base or minimum monthly rent plus a percentage of the gross sales in excess of an amount set in the lease. The percentage lease also can be set up as a percentage of the total gross sales or of the base/minimum rent, whichever is larger. We shall look at the minimum plus percentage lease only.

Gross Sales	–	Gross Sales Not Subject to the Percentage	=	**Gross Sales Subject to the Percentage**

÷ Percentage Rent ÷

Gross Sales Subject to the Percentage		% in the Lease

×

Gross Sales Subject to the Percentage	×	% in the Lease	=	**Percentage Rent**

Percentage Rent	÷	% in the Lease	=	**Gross Sales Subject to the Percentage**

Percentage Rent	÷	Gross Sales Subject to the Percentage	=	**% in the Lease**

Percentage Rent	+	Base/Minimum Rent	=	**Total Rent**

■ **FOR EXAMPLE** A lease calls for monthly minimum rent of $900 plus 3 percent of annual gross sales in excess of $270,000. What was the annual rent in a year when the annual gross sales were $350,600?

$900 Monthly Minimum Rent × 12 Months = $10,800 Annual Minimum Rent

$350,600 Annual Gross Sales – $270,000 Annual Gross Sales Not Subject to the Percentage = $80,600 Annual Gross Sales Subject to the Percentage

= $2,418 Annual Percentage Rent

$80,600 Annual Gross Subject to the Percentage		3% or 0.03

×

$80,600 × 3% = $2,418 Annual Percentage Rent
$10,800 Annual Minimum Rent + $2,418 Annual Percentage Rent = $13,218
$13,218 Total Annual Rent is the answer.

Measurement Problems

■ WHAT ARE LINEAR MEASUREMENTS?

Linear measurement is line measurement. When the terms

- *per foot,*
- *per linear foot,*
- *per running foot, or*
- *per front foot*

are used, you are being asked to determine the *total length* of the object whether measured in a straight line, crooked line, or curved line. The abbreviation for feet is '. Thus, 12 feet could be written as 12'. The abbreviation for inches is ". Thus, 12 inches could be written as 12".

■ WHAT DOES THE PHRASE "FRONT FOOT" REFER TO?

When the term *per front foot* is used, you are dealing with the number of units on the **frontage** of a lot. The frontage is normally the street frontage, but it could be the water frontage if the lot is on a river, lake, or ocean. If two dimensions are given for a tract of land, the first dimension given is the frontage if the dimensions are not labeled.

■ HOW DO I CONVERT ONE KIND OF LINEAR MEASUREMENT TO ANOTHER?

12 inches = 1 foot

Inches ÷ 12 = Feet (144 inches ÷ 12 = 12 feet)
Feet × 12 = Inches (12 feet × 12 = 144 inches)

36 inches = 1 yard

Inches ÷ 36 = Yards (144 inches ÷ 36 = 4 yards)
Yards × 36 = Inches (4 yards × 36 = 144 Inches)

3 feet = 1 yard

Feet ÷ 3 = Yards (12 feet ÷ 3 = 4 yards)
Yards × 3 = Feet (4 yards × 3 = 12 feet)

5,280 feet = 1 mile

> Feet ÷ 5,280 = Miles (10,560 feet ÷ 5,280 = 2 miles)
> Miles × 5,280 = Feet (2 miles × 5,280 = 10,560 feet)

16½ feet = 1 rod

> Feet ÷ 16.5 = Rods (82.5 feet ÷ 16.5 = 5 rods)
> Rods × 16.5 = Feet (5 rods × 16.5 = 82.5 feet)

320 rods = 1 mile

> Rods ÷ 320 = Miles (640 rods ÷ 320 = 2 miles)
> Miles × 320 = Rods (2 miles × 320 = 640 rods)

■ **FOR EXAMPLE** A rectangular lot is 50 feet × 150 feet. The cost to fence this lot is priced per linear/running foot. How many linear/running feet will be used to calculate the price of the fence?

```
                    150'

50'                                        50'

                    150'
```

50 Feet + 150 Feet + 50 Feet + 150 Feet = 400 Linear/Running Feet

400 Linear/Running Feet is the answer.

■ **FOR EXAMPLE** A parcel of land that fronts on Interstate 90 in Elgin, Illinois, is for sale at $5,000 per front foot. What will it cost to purchase this parcel of land if the dimensions are 150' by 100'?

150 is the frontage because it is the first dimension given.
150 Front Feet × $5,000 = $750,000 Cost

$750,000 Cost is the answer.

■ HOW DO I SOLVE FOR AREA MEASUREMENT?

Area is the two-dimensional surface of an object. Area is quoted in *square units* or in *acres*. We will look at calculating the area of squares, rectangles, and triangles. Squares and rectangles are four-sided objects. All four sides of a square are the same. Opposite sides of a rectangle are the same. A triangle is a three-sided object. The three sides of a triangle can be the same dimension or three different dimensions.

MATH TIP

When two dimensions are given, we assume it to be a rectangle unless told otherwise.

■ HOW DO I CONVERT ONE KIND OF AREA MEASUREMENT TO ANOTHER?

144 square inches = 1 square foot

Square Inches ÷ 144 = Square Feet (14,400 square inches ÷ 144 = 100 square feet)
Square Feet × 144 = Square Inches ÷ (100 square feet × 144 = 14,400 square inches)

1,296 square inches = 1 square yard

Square Inches ÷ 1,296 = Square Yards (12,960 ÷ 1,296 = 10 square yards)
Square Yards × 1,296 = Square Inches (10 square yards × 1,296 = 12,960 square yards)

9 square feet = 1 square yard

Square Feet ÷ 9 = Square Yards (90 square feet ÷ 9 = 10 square yards)
Square Yards × 9 = Square Feet (10 square yards × 9 = 90 square feet)

43,560 square feet = 1 acre

Square Feet ÷ 43,560 = Acres (87,120 ÷ 43,560 = 2 acres)
Acres × 43,560 = Square Feet (2 acres × 43,560 = 87,120 square feet)

640 acres = 1 section = 1 square mile

Acres ÷ 640 = Sections (Square Miles) (1,280 acres ÷ 640 = 2 sections)
Sections (Square Miles) × 640 = Acres (2 sections × 640 = 1,280 acres)

■ HOW DO I DETERMINE THE AREA OF A SQUARE OR RECTANGLE?

Length   ×   Width   =   **Area of a Square or Rectangle**

■ **FOR EXAMPLE** How many square feet are in a room 15'6" × 30'9"?

Remember, we must use like dimensions, so the inches must be converted to feet.

6" ÷ 12 = 0.5' + 15' = 15.5' wide
9" ÷ 12 = 0.75' + 30' = 30.75' long
30.75' × 15.5' = 476.625 Square Feet

476.625 Square Feet is the answer.

■ **FOR EXAMPLE** If carpet costs $63 per square yard to install, what would it cost to carpet the room in the previous example?

476.625 Square Feet ÷ 9 = 52.958333 Square Yards × $63 per Square Yard = $3,336.375 or $3,336.38 rounded

$3,336.38 Carpet Cost is the answer.

■ **FOR EXAMPLE** How many acres are there in a parcel of land that measures 450' × 484'?

484' × 450' = 217,800 Square Feet ÷ 43,560 = 5 Acres

5 Acres of Land is the answer.

■ HOW DO I DETERMINE THE AREA OF A TRIANGLE?

½ Base   ×   Height   =   **Area of a Triangle**

or

Base   ×   Height   ÷   2   =   **Area of a Triangle**

■ **FOR EXAMPLE** How many square feet are contained in a triangular parcel of land that is 400 feet on the base and 200 feet high?

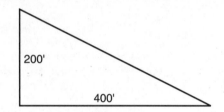

200'

400'

400' × 200' ÷ 2 = 40,000 Square Feet

40,000 Square Feet is the answer.

■ **FOR EXAMPLE** How many acres are in a three-sided tract of land that is 300' on the base and 400' high?

300' × 400' ÷ 2 = 60,000 Square Feet ÷ 43,560 = 1.377 Acres

1.377 Acres is the answer.

■ HOW DO I SOLVE FOR VOLUME?

Volume is the space inside a three-dimensional object. Volume is quoted in cubic units. We will look at calculating the volume of boxes and triangular prisms.

■ HOW DO I CONVERT FROM ONE KIND OF VOLUME MEASUREMENT TO ANOTHER?

1,728 cubic inches = 1 cubic foot

Cubic Inches ÷ 1,728 = Cubic Feet
(17,280 cubic inches ÷ 1,728 = 10 cubic feet)

Cubic Feet × 1,728 = Cubic Inches
(10 cubic feet × 1,728 = 17,280 cubic inches)

46,656 cubic inches = 1 cubic yard

Cubic Inches ÷ 46,656 = Cubic Yards
(93,312 cubic inches ÷ 46,656 = 2 cubic yards)

Cubic Yards × 46,656 = Cubic Inches
(2 cubic yards × 46,656 = 93,312 cubic inches)

27 cubic feet = 1 cubic yard

Cubic Feet ÷ 27 = Cubic Yards (270 cubic feet ÷ 27 = 10 cubic yards)
Cubic Yards × 27 = Cubic Feet (10 cubic yards × 27 = 270 cubic feet)

■ HOW DO I DETERMINE THE VOLUME OF A ROOM?

For purposes of determining volume, think of a room as if it were a box.

$$\text{Length} \quad \times \quad \text{Width} \quad \times \quad \text{Height} \quad = \quad \textbf{Volume of a Box}$$

■ **FOR EXAMPLE** A building is 500 feet long, 400 feet wide, and 25 feet high. How many cubic feet of space are in this building?

500' × 400' × 25' = 5,000,000 Cubic Feet

5,000,000 Cubic Feet is the answer.

■ **FOR EXAMPLE** How many cubic yards of concrete would it take to build a sidewalk measuring 120 feet long; 2 feet, 6 inches wide; and 3 inches thick?

6" ÷ 12' = .5' + 2' = 2.5' Wide
3" ÷ 12' = .25' Thick
120' × 2.5' × .25' = 75 Cubic Feet ÷ 27 = 2.778 Cubic Yards (rounded)
2.778 Cubic Yards is the answer.

■ HOW DO I DETERMINE THE VOLUME OF A TRIANGULAR PRISM?

The terms *A-frame*, *A-shaped*, or *gable roof* on an exam describe a triangular prism.

$$\tfrac{1}{2}\,\text{Base} \quad \times \quad \text{Height} \quad \times \quad \text{Width} \quad = \quad \textbf{Volume of a Triangular Prism}$$

or

$$\text{Base} \quad \times \quad \text{Height} \quad \times \quad \text{Width} \quad \div \quad 2 \quad = \quad \textbf{Volume of a Triangular Prism}$$

■ **FOR EXAMPLE** An A-frame cabin in the mountains is 50 feet long and 30 feet wide. The cabin is 25 feet high from the base to the highest point. How many cubic feet of space does this A-frame cabin contain?

50' × 30' × 25' ÷ 2 = 18,750 Cubic Feet

18,750 Cubic Feet is the answer.

■ **FOR EXAMPLE** A building is 40 feet by 25 feet with a 10-foot-high ceiling. The building has a gable roof that is 8 feet high at the tallest point. How many cubic feet are in this structure, including the roof?

40' × 25' × 10' = 10,000 Cubic Feet in the Building
40' × 25' × 8' ÷ 2 = 4,000 Cubic Feet in the Gable Roof
10,000 Cubic Feet + 4,000 Cubic Feet = 14,000 Total Cubic Feet

14,000 Cubic Feet is the answer.

Real Estate Math Practice Problems

1. The value of your house, not including the lot, is $91,000 today. What was the original cost if it has depreciated 5 percent per year for the past seven years?
   - a. $67,407.41
   - b. $95,789.47
   - c. $122,850.00
   - d. $140,000.00

2. What did the owners originally pay for their home if they sold it for $98,672, which gave them a 12 percent profit over their original cost?
   - a. $86,830
   - b. $88,100
   - c. $89,700
   - d. $110,510

3. What would you pay for a building producing $11,250 annual net income and showing a minimum rate of return of 9 percent?
   - a. $125,000
   - b. $123,626
   - c. $101,250
   - d. $122,625

4. An owner agrees to list his property on the condition that he will receive at least $47,300 after paying a 5 percent broker's commission and paying $1,150 in closing costs. At what price must it sell?
   - a. $48,450
   - b. $50,815
   - c. $50,875
   - d. $51,000

5. The Loving Gift Shop pays rent of $600 per month plus 2.5 percent of gross annual sales in excess of $50,000. What was the average monthly rent last year if gross annual sales were $75,000?
   - a. $1,125.00
   - b. $756.25
   - c. $600.00
   - d. $652.08

6. If your monthly rent is $1,050, what percent would this be of an annual income of $42,000?
   - a. 25 percent
   - b. 30 percent
   - c. 33 percent
   - d. 40 percent

7. Two brokers split the 6 percent commission on a $73,000 home. The selling salesperson, Joe, was paid 70 percent of his broker's share. The listing salesperson, Janice, was paid 30 percent of her broker's share. How much did Janice receive?
   - a. $657
   - b. $4,380
   - c. $1,533
   - d. $1,314

8. The buyer has agreed to pay $175,000 in sales price, 2.5 loan discount points, and a 1 percent origination fee. If the buyer receives a 90 percent loan-to-value ratio, how much will the buyer owe at closing for points and the origination fee?
   - a. $1,575.00
   - b. $3,937.50
   - c. $5,512.50
   - d. $6,125.00

9. Calculate eight months' interest on a $5,000 interest-only loan at 9.5 percent.
   - a. $475.00
   - b. $316.67
   - c. $237.50
   - d. $39.58

10. A 100-acre farm is divided into lots for homes. The streets require ⅛ of the whole farm, and there are 140 lots. How many square feet are in each lot?
    - a. 43,560
    - b. 35,004
    - c. 31,114
    - d. 27,225

11. What is the monthly net income on an investment of $115,000 if the rate of return is 12.5 percent?
    - a. $1,150.00
    - b. $1,197.92
    - c. $7,666.67
    - d. $14,375.00

12. A salesperson sells a property for $58,500. The contract he has with his broker is 40 percent of the full commission earned. The commission due the broker is 6 percent. What is the salesperson's share of the commission?
    - a. $2,106
    - b. $1,404
    - c. $3,510
    - d. $2,340

13. What is the interest rate on a $10,000 loan with semiannual interest of $450?
    - a. 7%
    - b. 9%
    - c. 11%
    - d. 13.5%

14. A warehouse is 80' wide and 120' long with ceilings 14' high. If 1,200 square feet of floor surface has been partitioned off, floor to ceiling, for an office, how many cubic feet of space will be left in the warehouse?
    - a. 151,200
    - b. 134,400
    - c. 133,200
    - d. 117,600

15. The lot you purchased five years ago for $30,000 has appreciated 3.5 percent per year. What is it worth today?
    a. $30,375
    b. $33,525
    c. $34,500
    d. $35,250

16. A lease calls for $1,000 per month minimum plus 2 percent of annual sales in excess of $100,000. What is the annual rent if the annual sales were $150,000?
    a. $12,000
    b. $13,000
    c. $14,000
    d. $15,000

17. There is a tract of land that is 1.25 acres. The lot is 150 feet deep. How much will the lot sell for at $65 per front foot?
    a. $9,750
    b. $8,125
    c. $23,595
    d. $8,725

18. Sue earns $20,000 per year and can qualify for a monthly PITI payment equal to 25 percent of her monthly salary. If the annual tax and insurance is $678.24, what is the loan amount she will qualify for if the monthly PI payment factor is $10.29 per $1,000 of loan amount?
    a. $66,000
    b. $43,000
    c. $40,500
    d. $35,000

19. You pay $65.53 monthly interest on a loan bearing 9.25 percent annual interest. What is the loan amount rounded to the nearest hundred dollars?
    a. $1,400
    b. $2,800
    c. $6,300
    d. $8,500

20. What percentage of profit would you make if you paid $10,500 for a lot, built a home on the lot that cost $93,000, and then sold the lot and house together for $134,550?
    a. 13 percent
    b. 23 percent
    c. 30 percent
    d. 45 percent

21. An income-producing property has $62,500 annual gross income and monthly expenses of $1,530. What is the appraised value if the appraiser uses a 10 percent capitalization rate?
    a. $441,400
    b. $625,000
    c. $183,600
    d. $609,700

22. Alfred pays $2,500 each for four parcels of land. He subdivides them into six parcels and sells each of the six parcels for $1,950. What was Alfred's percentage of profit?
    a. 14.5 percent
    b. 17 percent
    c. 52 percent
    d. 78 percent

23. A property sells for $96,000. If it has appreciated 4 percent per year straight line for the past five years, what did the owner pay for the property five years ago?
    a. $76,800
    b. $80,000
    c. $92,300
    d. $115,200

24. If you purchase a lot that is 125' ×150' for $6,468.75, what price did you pay per front foot?
    a. $23.52
    b. $43.13
    c. $51.75
    d. $64.69

25. Calculate the amount of commission earned by a broker on a property selling for $61,000 if 6 percent is paid on the first $50,000 and 3 percent on the remaining balance.
    a. $3,330
    b. $3,830
    c. $3,600
    d. $3,930

Answer Key for Real Estate Math Practice Problems

1. d   **$140,000.00 Original Cost**

   5% Depreciation per Year × 7 Years = 35% Total Depreciation
   100% Original Cost – 35% Total Depreciation = 65% Today's Value

   $91,000 Today's Value ÷

= $140,000 Original Cost	65% or 0.65

   $91,000 ÷ 65% (.65) = **$140,000 Original Cost**

2. b   **$88,100 Original Cost**

   100% Original Cost + 12% Profit = 112% Sales Price

   $98,672 Sales Price ÷

= $88,100 Original Cost	112% or 1.12

   $98,672 ÷ 112% (1.12) = **$88,100 Original Cost**

3. a   **$125,000 Price**

   $11,250 Annual Net Income ÷

= $125,000 Price	9% or 0.09

   $11,250 ÷ 9% (.09) = **$125,000 Price**

4. d   **$51,000 Sales Price**

   $47,300 Net to Seller + $1,150 Closing Costs =
   $48,450 Seller's Dollars after Commission
   100% Sales Price – 5% Commission = 95% Seller's Percent after Commission

   $48,450 Seller's Dollars after Commission ÷

= $51,000 Sales Price	95% or 0.95

   $48,450 ÷ 95% (0.95) = **$51,000 Sales Price**

5. d $652.08 Average Monthly Rent

$75,000 Gross Annual Sales − $50,000 =
$25,000 Gross Annual Sales Subject to 2.5%

= $625 Annual Percentage Rent	
$25,000 Gross Annual Sales	2.5% or 0.025

×

$25,000 × 2.5% (.025) = $625

$625 Annual Percentage Rent ÷ 12 Months =
$52.08 Monthly Percentage Rent
$600 Monthly Minimum Rent + $52.08 Monthly Percentage Rent =
$652.08 Average Monthly Rent

6. b 30%

$1,050 Monthly Rent × 12 Months = $12,600 Annual Rent

÷ $12,600 Annual Rent	
$42,000 Annual Income	**= 0.3 or 30%**

$12,600 ÷ $42,000 = .30 or **30%**

7. a $657 Commission to Janice

= $4,380 Full Commission	
$73,000 Sales Price	6% 0.06

×

$73,000 × 6% (.06) = $4,380
$4,380 Full Commission ÷ 2 Brokers =
$2,190 Broker's Share of the Commission

= $657 Janice's Commission	
$2,190 Broker's Share of the Commission	30% 0.3

×

$2,190 × 30% (.30) = **$657 Commission**

8. c $5,512.50 for Points and the Origination Fee

2.5 Points Loan Discount + 1 Point Origination Fee = 3.5 Points

= $157,500 Loan	
$175,000 Sales Price	90% or 0.9

×

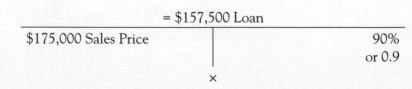

$175,000 \times 90\%$ or $(.90) = \$157,500$

$5,512.50 for Points and Origination Fees

$157,500 Loan	3.5% or 0.035

×

$157,500 \times 3.5\%$ $(.035) = **\$5,512.50 for Points and Origination Fees**

9. b **\$316.67 Interest**

= \$475 Annual Interest

$5,000 Loan	9.5% or 0.095

×

$5,000 \times 9.5\%$ $(.095) = \$475$
$475 Annual Interest ÷ 12 Months × 8 Months = **$316.67 Interest**

10. d **27,225 Square Feet per Lot**

⅛ = 1 ÷ 8 = 0.125 for Streets
100 Acres × 0.125 = 12.5 Acres for Streets
100 Acres − 12.5 Acres for Streets = 87.5 Acres for Lots × 43,560 =
3,811,500 Square Feet ÷ 140 Lots = **27,225 Square Feet per Lot**

11. b **$1,197.92 Monthly Net Operating Income**

= $14,375 Annual Net Operating Income

$115,000 Investment	12.5% or 0.125

×

$115,000 \times 12.5\%$ $(.125) = \$14,375$
$14,375 Annual Net Operating Income ÷ 12 Months =
$1,197.92 Monthly Net Operating Income

12. b **$1,404 Salesperson's Commission**

= $3,510 Full Commission

$58,500 Sales Price	6% or 0.06

×

$58,500 \times 6\%$ $(.06) = \$3,510$

= $1,404 Salesperson's Commission

$3,510 Full Commission	40% or 0.4

×

$3,510 \times 40\%$ $(.40) = **\$1,404 Salesperson's Commission**

13. b   9% Annual Interest Rate

$450 × 2 = $900 Annual Interest

÷ $900 Annual Interest	
$10,000 Loan	= 0.09 or 9%

×

$900 ÷ $10,000 = **0.09 or 9% Interest Rate**

14. d   117,600 Cubic Feet

120' × 80' = 9,600 Square Feet in Building – 1,200 Square Feet for Office = 8,400 Square Feet Left in Warehouse × 14' Ceiling = **117,600 Cubic Feet Left in Warehouse**

15. d $35,250 Today's Value

3.5% Appreciation per Year × 5 Years = 17.5% Total Appreciation
100% Cost + 17.5% Total Appreciation = 117.5% Today's Value

= $35,250 Today's Value	
$30,000 Original Cost	117.5% or 1.175

×

$30,000 × 117.5% (1.175) = **$35,250 Today's Value**

16. b $13,000 Annual Rent

$1,000 Monthly Minimum Rent × 12 Months =
$12,000 Annual Minimum Rent
$150,000 Annual Sales – $100,000 = $50,000 Annual Sales Subject to 2%

= $1,000 Annual Percentage Rent	
$50,000 Annual Sales Subject to 2%	2% or 0.02

×

$50,000 × 2% (.02) = $1,000

$12,000 Annual Minimum Rent + $1,000 Annual Percentage Rent = **$13,000 Annual Rent**

17. c $23,595 Sales Price

1.25 Acres × 43,560 = 54,450 Square Feet ÷ 150' Deep = 363' Frontage × $65 per Front Foot = **$23,595 Sales Price**

18. d $35,000 Loan

$20,000 Annual Salary ÷ 12 Months = $1,666.67 Monthly Salary

= $416.67 Monthly PITI Payment

$1,666.67 Monthly Salary	25% or 0.25

×

$1,666.67 × 25% = $416.67

$678.24 Annual Tax and Insurance ÷ 12 Months =
$56.52 Monthly Tax and Insurance
$416.67 Monthly PITI Payment − $56.52 Monthly TI =
$360.15 Monthly PI Payment
$360.15 Monthly PI Payment ÷ $10.29 × $1,000 = **$35,000 Loan**

19. d **$8,500 Loan**

$65.53 Monthly Interest × 12 Months = $786.36 Annual Interest

$786.36 Annual Interest ÷	
= 8,501.19 **or $8,500 Loan**	9.25% or 0.0925

$786.36 ÷ 9.25% (.0925) = **$8501.19 Loan**

20. c **30%**

$10,500 Cost of Lot + $93,000 Cost of Home = $103,500 Total Cost
$134,550 Sales Price − $103,500 Total Cost = $31,050 Profit

÷ $31,050 Profit	
$103,500 Total Cost	**= 0.3 or 30%**

$31,050 ÷ $103,500 = **0.3 or 30%**

21. a **$441,400 Value**

$1,530 Monthly Expenses × 12 Months = $18,360 Annual Expenses
$62,500 Annual Gross Income − $18,360 Annual Expenses =
$44,140 Annual Net Operating Income

$44,140 Annual Net Operating Income ÷	
= $441,400 Value	10% or 0.1

$44,140 ÷ 10% (.10) = **$441,400 Value**

22. b **17% Profit**

$2,500 Cost × 4 Parcels = $10,000 Total Cost
$1,950 Sales Price × 6 Parcels = $11,700 Sales Price
$11,700 Sales Price − $10,000 Cost = $1,700 Profit

÷ $1,700 Profit	
$10,000 Cost	**= 0.17 or 17% Profit**

$1,700 ÷ $10,000 Cost = 0.17 or **17% Profit**

23. b $80,000 Original Cost

4% Annual Appreciation × 5 Years = 20% Total Appreciation
100% Cost + 20% Total Appreciation = 120% Today's Value

$96,000 Today's Value ÷	
= **$80,000 Original Cost**	120% 1.2

$96,000 ÷ 120% (1.20) = **$80,000 Original Cost**

24. c $51.75 per Front Foot

$6,468.75 Price ÷ 125 Front Feet = **$51.75 per Front Foot**

25. a $3,330 Total Commission

= $3,000 Commission	
$50,000 Sales Price	6% or 0.06
×	

$50,000 × 6% (.06) = $3,000

$61,000 Total Sales Price − $50,000 Sales Price at 6% =
$11,000 Sales Price at 3%

= $330 Commission	
$11,000 Sales Price	3% or 0.03
×	

$11,000 × 3% (.03) = $330
$3,000 Commission + $330 Commission = **$3,330 Total Commission**

Sample Illinois Real Estate Licensing Examinations

Modern Real Estate Practice in Illinois, Sixth Edition, is designed to prepare you for a career in real estate. However, before you can become a broker, a salesperson, a leasing agent, or an instructor, you must, under Illinois law, obtain a license. Passing the real estate licensing examination plays a large part in determining your eligibility to become licensed. The examination is designed to test your knowledge of real estate laws, principles, and practices.

The state test is currently prepared and administered by Applied Measurement Professionals, Inc. (AMP), an independent testing company under the sanction of IDFPR/BRE. You can contact AMP to determine the right test site and time for you. The site also provides current, *in-depth* topic outlines, exact procedures for establishing an examination appointment, and rules for the examination. Sample AMP-designed questions are available at *www.goAMP.com.*

■ WHAT TO EXPECT FROM THE EXAM

Illinois salesperson, broker, leasing agent, and instructor candidates are given separate examinations. Questions for the exams involve two broad areas: knowledge of material and application of knowledge in the real estate professions. The broker's examination places the greater emphasis on broker-specified areas, such as brokerage practice, escrow accounts, record keeping, business entities, and commercial brokerage.

Both salesperson and broker exams consist of 140 questions: 100 questions devoted to general knowledge (national real estate practices and principles that apply everywhere in the United States), and 40 questions devoted to the state (Illinois-specific practice and licensing issues). At least 10 percent of the questions involve some sort of mathematical calculations. The questions are multiple-choice in format, with four answer choices for each question.

Remember that the rules for taking the exam are set by IDFPR/BRE and the AMP testing service and are detailed in the *AMP Illinois Candidate Handbook*. The state exam must be completed within the allotted time, which currently is 3½ hours for brokers' and salespersons' exams. AMP provides computer monitors equipped with a clock that shows you exactly how much time you have left to complete the exam. You are given an opportunity to take a practice exam before beginning the actual exam. Once the test begins, you are not allowed to leave the test site until you have completed the exam. *Guessing is not penalized; be sure to answer every question.* You are allowed to leave questions blank and return to them later if you wish.

You must pass *both* the national and state sections of the exam to qualify for your real estate license. While national and Illinois questions are mixed together in the testing, they are scored separately.

Candidates who pass only one portion must retake and pass the other portion within one year of passing the first portion. Failure to do so will result in having to take the entire examination again. Candidates need a score of 75 percent on each portion of the examination.

Candidates are allowed up to three attempts to pass the examination. After the third attempt, you are required to retake the education coursework. Candidates also must not let their coursework lapse for more than three years before taking the examination or they will need to retake the education coursework.

Salesperson Examination

Approximately 70 percent of the questions in the salesperson's exam are devoted to national real estate topics, and the remainder are devoted to Illinois-specific real estate topics. Like the broker's exam, the state test may include questions based on closing statement prorations and computations. However, salesperson candidates are also expected to solve basic problems in real estate mathematics related to such topics as commissions, interest, and square footage. When you review the *AMP Illinois Candidate Handbook*, it will include an outline of the subject areas that are tested on the national section of the test and the approximate number of questions coming from each area.

Examination Outlines

The following is the most recent AMP Detailed National Content Outline, along with the chapters of *Modern Real Estate Practice in Illinois*, Sixth Edition, in which the subjects are covered:

Topic Headings–National Portion   **Chapter**
(topics in italics appear on the Broker Examination only)

1. **Listing Property**
   A. Listing
      1. Legal description   9
      2. Lot size   9
      3. Physical dimensions of structure   9
      4. Appurtenances (for example, easements and water rights)   7
      5. Utilities   7
      6. Type of construction   8
      7. Encumbrances (for example, liens, encroachments, restrictions) 6, 7
      8. Compliance with building codes   20
      9. Ownership of record   13
      10. Homeowners association documents and expenses   8
      11. Brokerage fee   5
      12. Property taxes   10
   B. Assessment of Property Value
      1. Location   2
      2. Anticipated changes (for example, zoning and use)   20
      3. Depreciation   19
      4. Deterioration (for example, physical)   2
      5. Obsolescence (for example, usefulness, outdated characteristics) 19

4. **Settlement/Transfer of Ownership**
   A. Tax Issues
      1. Tax implications of interest expenses 3
      2. Real property taxes 10
      3. Tax shelters 3
      4. Capital improvements 3
      5. Property taxation (for example, ad valorem, ... 10
         special assessments)
      6. Tax-deferred exchanges 3
   B. Titles
      1. Need for title search 13
      2. Title insurance (for example, owner and mortgagee) 13
      3. Title problems 13
      4. Legal procedures (for example, quiet title, foreclosure, ... 13
         bankruptcy, declaratory judgment)
      5. Preparation of title abstracts 13
      6. Liens and order of priority (for example, judgments by court) 13
      7. Importance of recording 13
   C. Settlement Procedures
      1. Purposes and procedures of settlement 23
      2. Obligations of settlement agent 23
      3. Calculations regarding proration/prepayment 23
      4. Warranties associated with deeds (for example, grant, ... 12
         quitclaim)
      5. Settlement statement (HUD-1 form) 23
      6. Other settlement statement documents 23
         (for example, deed, bill of sale, note, deed of trust)
      7. Real Estate Settlement Procedures Act 23
      8. Transfer tax 12
   D. Completion of the Transaction
      1. Negotiations between buyers and sellers 11, 23
         leading to an agreement
      2. Contract requirements and fulfillment of contingencies 23
         leading to closing
      3. Federal statutory requirements 4, 23
      4. Rights of home ownership (for example, homestead, ... 8
         rights of husband and wife)
      5. Rights of others related to property 8, 9
         (for example, adverse possession, adjoining owners,
         encroachments)
      6. Nature and types of common interest ownership 8
         (for example, condominium, planned unit development,
         cooperative, townhouse)
      7. Eminent domain proceedings 20
      8. Legal proceedings against property 13
         (for example, attachments and notice of pending legal action)
      9. Securities law application and referral 23
      10. Situations where experts are required 5
          (for example, financial planning and legal advice)
      11. Closing statements (for example, calculate amount 23
          owed by buyer and net to seller)

5. **Financing**
   A. Sources of Financing
      1. Institutional (for example, savings and loans, banks, mortgage brokers) — 16
      2. Seller financing (for example, land contract, purchase money mortgage) — 16
      3. Assumption of financing — 16
      4. Other sources of financing — 16
   B. Types of Loans
      1. Security for loans (for example, land contracts, mortgages) — 16
      2. Repayment methods (for example, adjustable rate mortgage, fully/partially/nonamortized, renegotiated rate) — 16
      3. Forms of financing (such as FHA, VA, FmHA, conventional loan) — 16
      4. Secondary mortgage markets (for example, Fannie Mae, FHLMC, GNMA) — 16
      5. Other types of mortgage loans (for example, wraparound, blanket, package) — 16
      6. Down payment assistance programs — 16
   C. Terms and Conditions
      1. Compliance with provisions of federal regulations (for example, Truth-in-Lending Act, Equal Credit Opportunity Act) — 15, 23
      2. Loan origination costs (for example, appraisal fee, credit reports, points) — 15
      3. Lender requirements (for example, property insurance, escrow, deposits, underwriting criteria) — 15
      4. Conditional approval — 15
      5. Default — 15
      6. Foreclosure and redemption rights — 15
      7. Nonrecourse provision — 15
   D. Common Clauses and Terms in Mortgage Instruments
      1. Clauses and terms in mortgage (for example, prepayment, interest rates, release, due-on-sale, subordination) — 15
      2. Escalation — 15
      3. Acceleration — 15

6. **Professional Responsibilities/Fair Practice/Administrative**
      1. *Terms of contract between salesperson and broker (for example, employee, independent contractor)* — 5
      2. *Trust accounts* — 12, 18
      3. Complete and accurate records of business transactions — 5
      4. *Required notifications and reports to real estate regulatory* — 5
      5. *Company policies, procedures, and standards* — 5
      6. Market trends, availability of financing, rates, and conditions of obtaining credit — 15
      7. Resolving misunderstandings among parties to real estate transactions — 23
      8. *Sales force training* — 5
      9. *Sales force supervision* — 5
      10. Commission from sales of real estate — 5

11. *Appropriate distribution of commissions*   5

12. *Accounting procedures in the office*   5

Illinois-Specific Topics

The following is the most recent AMP Detailed Content Outline for the Illinois-specific portion of the examination, along with the chapters of *Modern Real Estate Practice in Illinois*, Sixth Edition, in which the subjects are covered.

Topic Headings	Chapter
1. Licensing Requirements	
A. License exemptions	14
B. Activities requiring a license	14
C. Types of licenses	14
1. Salesperson	14
2. Broker	14
3. Leasing Agent	14
D. Personal assistants	5, 14
E. Eligibility for licensing, including sponsor card	14
F. Examination	14
G. License renewal	14
H. Continuing education	14
I. Change in licensee information	14
J. Reciprocity	14
K. Real Estate Recovery Fund	14
2. Laws and Rules Regulating Real Estate Practice	
A. Purpose of license law	14
B. Advertising (other than disclosure)	14
C. Broker/salesperson relationship	4, 14
D. Commissions	
1. Finder's fee/referral fee	14
2. Rental finding services	14, 17
E. Ownership issues	
1. Land trust	8
2. Homestead	8
3. Land Sales Registration Act/Time share	8
F. Handling of monies	
1. Special accounts	14
2. Security deposits	17
G. Handling of documents	5, 14
H. Performing activities exceeding scope of real estate licensing	
1. Law	14
2. Securities	14
I. Transfer tax stamps/affordable housing	12
J. Intestacy	12
K. Legal description/Plat Act	9
L. Real estate taxes and exemptions	3, 10, 11, 23
M. Illinois Human Rights Act	21
N. Interference with contracts or listings	14

3. **Disclosures**
   A. Agency
      1. Designated agencies
         a. seller   4, 14
         b. buyer   4, 14
         c. dual   4, 14
   B. Ministerial activities   4, 14
   C. Advertising   14
   D. Property disclosures
      1. Residential Real Property Disclosure Act   4
      2. AIDS (HIV)   4
      3. Stigmatized property   4
      4. Material defects   4

4. **Broker Topics**
   A. *Broker responsibilities*   14
   B. *Special accounts*   14
   C. *Examination of records*   14
   D. *Corporation/partnership/limited liability company licensure*   8, 14
   E. *Commercial Broker Lien Act*   10

Broker Examination

Approximately 70 percent of the questions in the Illinois real estate broker's exam are devoted to national real estate topics and the remainder to Illinois real estate topics. The broker's outline is the same as the salesperson's; however, the allocation of questions in the topic areas varies.

Broker candidates are expected to be familiar with all areas of Illinois real estate law and practice covered in this book. For study purposes, brokers should be particularly aware of the following topics, in addition to those listed for the salesperson's exam:

- Broker responsibilities
- Special accounts
- Examination of records
- Corporation/partnership/limited liability company licensure
- Commercial Broker Lien Act

■ MULTIPLE-CHOICE QUESTIONS: TEST-TAKING STRATEGIES

There are as many different ways to prepare for and take multiple-choice examinations as there are test takers. Before you try the following sample exams, take some time to read this brief overview of test-taking strategies. While no one can tell you which method will work best for you, it's always a good idea to think about what you're going to do before you do it.

One of the most important things to remember about multiple-choice test questions is this: *They always give you the correct answer.* You don't have to remember how things are spelled, and you don't have to try to guess what the question is about. The answer is always there, right in front of you.

Of course, if it were as easy as that, it wouldn't be much of a test. The key to success in taking multiple-choice examinations is actually twofold: First, *know the correct answer.* You do that by going to class, paying attention, taking good notes, and studying the material. Then, if you don't know the correct answer, be able to analyze the questions and answers effectively, so you can apply the second key: *Be able to make a reasonable guess.* Even if you don't know the answer, you will probably know which answers are clearly wrong and which ones are more likely than the others to be right.

If you can eliminate one answer as wrong, you have improved your odds of "guessing correctly" by 25 percent, from 4-to-1 to 3-to-1. If you can eliminate two wrong answers, you have a 50/50 shot at a correct guess. Of course, if you can eliminate *three* wrong answers, your chance of a correct response is 100 percent. In any case, there is no secret formula: *The only sure way to improve your odds of a correct answer is to study and learn the material.*

Structure of the Question

A multiple-choice question has a basic structure. It starts with what test writers call the *stem.* That's the text of the question that sets up the need for an answer. The stem may be an incomplete statement that is finished by the correct answer; it may be a story problem or hypothetical example (called a *fact-pattern*) about which you will be asked a question. Or it may be a math problem, in which you are given basic information and asked to solve a mathematical issue, such as the amount of a commission or capital gain.

The stem is always followed by *options:* four possible answers to the question presented by the stem. Depending on the structure and content of the stem, the options may be single words or numbers, phrases or complete sentences. Three of the options are *distractors:* incorrect answers intended to "distract" you from the correct choice. One of the options is the correct answer, called the *key.*

Reading a Multiple-Choice Question

Here are three suggestions for how to read a multiple-choice test question.

1. The Traditional Method.   Read the question through from start to finish, then read the options. When you get to the correct answer, mark it and move on. This method works best for short questions, such as those that require completion or simply define a term. For long, more-complicated questions or those that are not quite so clear, however, you may miss important information.

2. The Focus Method.   As we've seen, multiple-choice questions have different parts. In longer math or story-type questions, the last line of the stem will contain the question's *focus:* the basic issue the item asks you to address. That is, *the question is always in the last line of the stem.* In the focus method, when you come to a longer item, read the last line of the stem first. This will clue you in to what the question is about. Then go back and read the stem from beginning to end. The advantage is this: While you are reading the complicated facts or math elements, you know what to look for. You can watch for important items and disregard unnecessary information. It's a sad fact of multiple-choice exams that sometimes test writers include distracting elements in the stem itself. If you check for the question's focus first, you'll spot the test-writer's tricks right away.

3. The Upside-Down Method. This technique takes the focus method one step further. Here, you do just what the name implies: You start reading the question from the bottom up. By reading the four options first, you can learn exactly what the test writer wants you to focus on. For instance, a fact-pattern problem might include several dollar values in the stem, leading you to believe you're going to have to do a math calculation. You'll be trying to recall all the equations you've memorized, only to find at the end of the stem that you're only expected to define a term. If you've read the options first, you would have known what to look for.

■ TAKING THE SAMPLE EXAMINATIONS

The following three sample examinations have been designed to help you prepare for the actual licensing exam. The first two exams are in two parts: 90 questions on general, national, real estate principles and 60 covering Illinois-specific law and practice. On your actual exam, 5 questions in each section are "pretest" items, used for statistical purposes only. They do not factor into your final score. For our review purposes here, however, there are no pretest-type items: every question counts. Note that proration calculations are based on a 30-day month unless otherwise specified.

The third practice exam consists of 100 Illinois-specific questions, with emphasis on the Illinois *Real Estate License Act of 2000*.

EXAM ONE PART ONE—GENERAL REAL ESTATE PRACTICE AND PRINCIPLES

1. Which of the following is a lien on real estate?
   a. Recorded easement
   b. Recorded mortgage
   c. Encroachment
   d. Deed restriction

2. A sales contract was signed under duress. Which of the following describes this contract?
   a. Voidable
   b. Breached
   c. Discharged
   d. Void

3. A broker receives a check for earnest money from a buyer and deposits the money in the broker's personal interest-bearing checking account over the weekend. This action exposes the broker to a charge of
   a. commingling.
   b. novation.
   c. subrogation.
   d. accretion.

4. A borrower takes out a mortgage loan that requires monthly payments of $875.70 for 20 years and a final payment of $24,095. This is what type of loan?
   a. Wraparound
   b. Accelerated
   c. Balloon
   d. Variable

5. If a borrower computed the interest charged for the previous month on his $60,000 loan balance as $412.50, what is the borrower's interest rate?
   a. 7.5 percent
   b. 7.75 percent
   c. 8.25 percent
   d. 8.5 percent

6. A broker signs a contract with a buyer. Under the contract, the broker agrees to help the buyer find a suitable property and to represent the buyer in negotiations with the seller. Although the buyer may not sign an agreement with any other broker, she may look for properties on her own. The broker is entitled to payment only if the broker locates the property that is purchased. What kind of agreement has this broker signed?
   a. Exclusive buyer agency agreement
   b. Exclusive-agency buyer agency agreement
   c. Open buyer agency agreement
   d. Option contract

7. Talia conveys property to Nicholas by delivering a deed. The deed contains five covenants. This is MOST LIKELY a
   a. warranty deed.
   b. quitclaim deed.
   c. grant deed.
   d. deed in trust.

8. Pamela, a real estate broker, does not show non-Asian clients any properties in several traditionally Asian neighborhoods. She bases this practice on the need to preserve the valuable cultural integrity of Asian immigrant communities. Which of the following statements is TRUE regarding Pamela's policy?
   a. Pamela's policy is steering and violates the fair housing laws regardless of her motivation.
   b. Because Pamela is not attempting to restrict the rights of any single minority group, the practice does not constitute steering.
   c. Pamela's policy is steering, but it does not violate the fair housing laws because she is motivated by cultural preservation, not by exclusion or discrimination.
   d. Pamela's policy has the effect, but not the intent, of steering.

9. Helene grants a life estate to her grandson and stipulates that on the grandson's death, the title to the property will pass to her son-in-law. This second estate is known as a(n)

    a. remainder.
    b. reversion.
    c. estate at sufferance.
    d. estate for years.

10. When property is held in joint tenancy

    a. a maximum of two people can own the real estate.
    b. the fractional interests of the owners can be different.
    c. additional owners may be added later.
    d. there is always the right of survivorship.

11. A real estate salesperson who has a written contract with his broker that specifies that he will not be treated as an employee, and whose entire income is from sales commissions rather than an hourly wage, is probably a(n)

    a. real estate assistant.
    b. employee.
    c. subagent.
    d. independent contractor.

12. The states in which the lender holds title to mortgaged real estate are known as

    a. title-theory states.
    b. lien-theory states.
    c. statutory title states.
    d. strict title forfeiture states.

13. The form of tenancy that expires on a specific date is a

    a. joint tenancy.
    b. tenancy for years.
    c. tenancy in common.
    d. tenancy by the entirety.

14. A suburban home that lacks indoor plumbing suffers from which of the following?

    a. Functional obsolescence
    b. Curable physical deterioration
    c. Incurable physical deterioration
    d. External obsolescence

15. If a developer wants to build a commercial building closer to the street than is permitted by the local zoning ordinance because the shape of the lot makes a standard setback impossible, she or he should seek a

    a. variance.
    b. nonconforming use permit.
    c. conditional use permit.
    d. density zoning permit.

16. Assuming that the listing broker and the selling broker in a transaction split their commission equally, what was the sales price of the property if the commission rate was 6.5 percent and the listing broker, after paying the selling broker, kept $2,593.50?

    a. $39,900   c. $79,800
    b. $56,200   d. $88,400

17. Karl, a real estate broker, specializes in helping both buyers and sellers with the necessary paperwork involved in transferring property. While Karl is not an agent of either party, he may not disclose either party's confidential information to the other. Karl is a(n)

    a. buyer's agent.
    b. independent contractor.
    c. dual agent.
    d. transactional broker.

18. A mortgage lender intends to lend money at 9¾ percent on a 30-year loan. If the loan yields 10⅜ percent, how many discount points must be charged on this loan?

    a. ½   c. 5
    b. 4   d. 8

19. In a 28/36 ratio, the 36 means

    a. recurring long-term debts and housing payment combined may not exceed 36 percent of gross monthly income.
    b. recurring long-term debts and housing payment combined may not exceed 36 percent of net monthly income.
    c. housing payment may not exceed 36 percent of net income.
    d. credit card debt and other monthly (non-house) payments may not exceed 36 percent of gross monthly income.

20. Police powers include which of the following?
    a. Deed restrictions
    b. Zoning
    c. Restrictive covenants
    d. Taxation

21. A seller wants to net $65,000 from the sale of her house after paying the broker's fee of 6 percent. The seller's gross sales price will be
    a. $61,100.
    b. $64,752.
    c. $68,900.
    d. $69,149.

22. How many square feet are in three acres?
    a. 43,560
    b. 130,680
    c. 156,840
    d. 27,878,400

23. Wendy is purchasing a condominium unit in a subdivision and obtains financing from a local savings association. In this situation, which of the following BEST describes Wendy?
    a. Vendor
    b. Mortgagor
    c. Grantor
    d. Lessor

24. The current value of a property is $40,000. The property is assessed at 40 percent of its current value for real estate tax purposes, with an equalization factor of 1.5 applied to the assessed value. If the tax rate is $4 per $100 of assessed valuation, what is the amount of tax due on the property?
    a. $640
    b. $960
    c. $1,600
    d. $2,400

25. A building was sold for $60,000, with the purchaser putting 10 percent down and obtaining a loan for the balance. The lending institution charged a 1 percent loan origination fee. What was the total cash used for the purchase?
    a. $540
    b. $6,000
    c. $6,540
    d. $6,600

26. A parcel of vacant land has an assessed valuation of $274,550. If the assessment is 85 percent of market value, what is the market value?
    a. $315,732.50
    b. $320,000.00
    c. $323,000.00
    d. $830,333.33

27. What is a capitalization rate?
    a. Amount determined by the gross rent multiplier
    b. Rate of return a property will produce
    c. Mathematical value determined by a sales price
    d. Rate at which the amount of depreciation in a property is measured

28. A parcel of land described as "the NW¼ and the SW¼ of Section 6, T4N, R8W of the Third Principal Meridian" was sold for $875 per acre. The listing broker will receive a 5 percent commission on the total sales price. How much will the broker receive?
    a. $1,750
    b. $5,040
    c. $14,000
    d. $15,040

29. If a house was sold for $40,000 and the buyer obtained an FHA-insured mortgage loan for $38,500, how much money would the buyer pay in discount points if the lender charged four points?
    a. $385
    b. $1,500
    c. $1,540
    d. $1,600

30. The commission rate is 7¾ percent on a sale of $50,000. What is the dollar amount of the commission?
    a. $3,500
    b. $3,875
    c. $4,085
    d. $4,585

31. A buyer makes an offer on a property and the seller accepts. Three weeks later, the buyer announces that "the deal's off" and refuses to go through with the sale. If the seller is entitled to keep the buyer's earnest money deposit, it is MOST LIKELY because there is what kind of clause in the sales contract?

    a. Liquidated damages clause
    b. Contingent damages clause
    c. Actual damages clause
    d. Revocation clause

32. Garrett purchases a home under a land contract. Until the contract is paid in full, what is the status of Garrett's interest in the property?

    a. Garrett holds legal title to the premises.
    b. Garrett has no legal interest in the property.
    c. Garrett possesses a legal life estate in the premises.
    d. Garrett has equitable title in the property.

33. Fred and Karen enter into an agreement. Karen will mow Fred's lawn every week during the summer. Later, Karen decides to go into a different business. Valerie would like to assume Karen's obligation to mow Fred's lawn. Fred agrees and enters into a new contract with Valerie. Fred and Karen tear up their original agreement. This is known as

    a. assignment.
    b. novation.
    c. substitution.
    d. rescission.

34. Using the services of a mortgage broker, Gerald borrowed $4,000 from a private lender. After deducting the loan costs, Gerald received $3,747. What is the face amount of the note?

    a. $3,747
    b. $4,000
    c. $4,253
    d. $7,747

35. Whose signature is necessary for an offer to purchase real estate to become a contract?

    a. Buyer's only
    b. Buyer's and seller's
    c. Seller's only
    d. Seller's and seller's broker's

36. A borrower has just made the final payment on a mortgage loan. Regardless of this fact, the records will still show a lien on the mortgaged property until which of the following events occurs?

    a. A satisfaction of the mortgage document is recorded.
    b. A reconveyance of the mortgage document is delivered to the mortgage holder.
    c. A novation of the mortgage document takes place.
    d. An estoppel of the mortgage document is filed with the clerk of the county in which the mortgagee is located.

37. If the annual net income from a commercial property is $22,000 and the capitalization rate is 8 percent, what is the value of the property using the income approach?

    a. $176,000   c. $200,000
    b. $183,000   d. $275,000

38. A broker enters into a listing agreement with a seller in which the seller will receive $120,000 from the sale of a vacant lot and the broker will receive any sale proceeds exceeding that amount. This is what type of listing?

    a. Exclusive-agency
    b. Net
    c. Exclusive-right-to-sell
    d. Multiple

39. An individual sold her house and moved into a cooperative apartment. Under the cooperative form of ownership, the individual will

    a. become a shareholder in the corporation.
    b. not lose her apartment if she pays her share of the expenses.
    c. have to take out a new mortgage loan on her unit.
    d. receive a fixed-term lease for her unit.

40. A defect or a cloud on title to property may be cured by

    a. obtaining quitclaim deeds from all appropriate parties.
    b. bringing an action to register the title.
    c. paying cash for the property at the settlement.
    d. bringing an action to repudiate the title.

41. A buyer signed an exclusive-agency buyer agency agreement with a broker. If the buyer finds a suitable property with no assistance from any broker, the broker is entitled to
    a. full compensation from the buyer, regardless of who found the property.
    b. full compensation from the seller.
    c. partial compensation as generally required under this type of agreement.
    d. no compensation under the terms of this type of agreement.

42. Under the terms of a net lease, a commercial tenant usually would be responsible for paying
    a. principle debt service.
    b. real estate taxes.
    c. income tax payments.
    d. mortgage interest expense.

43. The *Civil Rights Act of 1866* prohibits discrimination based on
    a. sex.
    b. religion.
    c. race.
    d. familial status.

44. If a borrower must pay $6,000 for points on a $150,000 loan, how many points is the lender charging for this loan?
    a. 3
    b. 4
    c. 5
    d. 6

45. What is the difference between a general lien and a specific lien?
    a. A general lien cannot be enforced in court, while a specific lien can.
    b. A specific lien is held by only one person, while a general lien must be held by two or more.
    c. A general lien is a lien against personal property, while a specific lien is a lien against real estate.
    d. A specific lien is a lien against a certain parcel of real estate, while a general lien covers all of a debtor's property.

46. In an option to purchase real estate, which of the following statements is *TRUE* of the optionee?
    a. The optionee must purchase the property but may do so at any time within the option period.
    b. The optionee is limited to a refund of the option consideration if the option is exercised.
    c. The optionee cannot obtain third-party financing on the property until after the option has expired.
    d. The optionee has no obligation to purchase the property during the option period.

47. In 1991, an owner constructed a building that was eight stories high. In 2008, the municipality changed the zoning ordinance and prohibited buildings taller than six stories. Which of the following statements is *TRUE* regarding the existing eight-story building?
    a. The building must be demolished.
    b. The building is a conditional use.
    c. The building is a nonconforming use.
    d. The owner must obtain a variance.

48. How many acres are there in the N½ of the SW¼ and the NE¼ of the SE¼ of a section?
    a. 20
    b. 40
    c. 80
    d. 120

49. Branca's home is the smallest in a neighborhood of large, expensive houses. The effect of the other houses on the value of Branca's home is known as
    a. regression.
    b. progression.
    c. substitution.
    d. contribution.

50. A lien that arises as a result of a judgment, estate or inheritance taxes, the decedent's debts, or federal taxes is what sort of lien?
    a. Specific
    b. General
    c. Voluntary
    d. Equitable

51. A broker received a deposit, along with a written offer from a buyer. The offer stated "The offeror will leave this offer open for the seller's acceptance for a period of ten days." On the fifth day, and before acceptance by the seller, the offeror notified the broker that the offer was withdrawn and demanded the return of the deposit. Which of the following statements is *TRUE* in this situation?

    a. The offeror cannot withdraw the offer; it must be held open for the full ten-day period, as promised.
    b. The offeror has the right to withdraw the offer and secure the return of the deposit any time before being notified of the seller's acceptance.
    c. The offeror can withdraw the offer, and the seller and the broker will each retain one-half of the forfeited deposit.
    d. While the offeror can withdraw the offer, the broker is legally entitled to declare the deposit forfeited and retain all of it in lieu of the lost commission.

52. Charles and Linda are joint tenants. Linda sells her interest to Francine. What is the relationship between Charles and Francine regarding the property?

    a. Joint tenants
    b. Tenants in common
    c. Tenants by the entirety
    d. No relationship exists because Linda cannot sell her joint tenancy interest

53. Sam and Wally orally enter into a six-month lease. If Wally defaults, which of the following statements is *TRUE?*

    a. Sam may not bring a court action because six-month leases must be in writing under the parol evidence rule.
    b. Sam may not bring a court action because the statute of frauds governs six-month leases.
    c. Sam may bring a court action because six-month leases need not be in writing to be enforceable.
    d. Sam may bring a court action because the statute of limitations does not apply to oral leases, regardless of their term.

54. On Monday, Tom offers to sell his vacant lot to Kent for $12,000. On Tuesday, Kent counteroffers to buy the lot for $10,500. On Friday, Kent withdraws his counteroffer and accepts Tom's original price of $12,000. Under these circumstances

    a. a valid agreement exists because Kent accepted Tom's offer exactly as it was made, regardless of the fact that it was not accepted immediately.
    b. a valid agreement exists because Kent accepted before Tom advised him that the offer was withdrawn.
    c. no valid agreement exists because Tom's offer was not accepted within 72 hours of its having been made.
    d. no valid agreement exists because Kent's counteroffer was a rejection of Tom's offer, and once rejected, it cannot be accepted later.

55. Yvette's neighbors use her driveway to reach their garage, which is on their property. Yvette's attorney explains that the neighbors have an easement appurtenant that gives them the right to use her driveway. Yvette's property is the

    a. dominant tenement.
    b. servient tenement.
    c. prescriptive tenement.
    d. appurtenant tenement.

56. If the quarterly interest at 7.5 percent is $562.50, what is the principal amount of the loan?

    a. $7,500   c. $30,000
    b. $15,000   d. $75,000

57. A deed conveys ownership to the grantee "as long as the existing building is not torn down." What type of estate does this deed create?

    a. Determinable fee estate
    b. Fee simple absolute estate
    c. Nondestructible estate
    d. Life estate *pur autre vie*, with the measuring life being the building's

58. If the mortgage loan is 80 percent of the appraised value of a house and the interest rate of 8 percent amounts to $460 for the first month, what is the appraised value of the house?

    a. $69,000   c. $86,250
    b. $71,875   d. $92,875

59. Local zoning ordinances may regulate
    a. environmental penalties.
    b. deed restrictions.
    c. restrictive covenants.
    d. permitted land uses.

60. A broker took a listing and later discovered that the client had been declared incompetent by a court. What is the current status of the listing?
    a. The listing is unaffected because the broker acted in good faith as the owner's agent.
    b. The listing is of no value to the broker because the contract is void.
    c. The listing is the basis for recovery of a commission from the client's guardian or trustee if the broker produces a buyer.
    d. The listing may be renegotiated between the broker and the client, based on the new information.

61. A borrower defaulted on his home mortgage loan payments, and the lender obtained a court order to foreclose on the property. At the foreclosure sale, the property sold for $64,000; the unpaid balance on the loan at the time of foreclosure was $78,000. What must the lender do to recover the $14,000 that the borrower still owes?
    a. Sue for specific performance
    b. Sue for damages
    c. Seek a deficiency judgment
    d. Seek a judgment by default

62. All of the following are exemptions to the federal *Fair Housing Act of 1968 EXCEPT*
    a. the sale of a single-family home where the listing broker does not advertise the property.
    b. the restriction of noncommercial lodgings by a private club to members of the club.
    c. the rental of a unit in an owner-occupied three-family dwelling where an advertisement is placed in the paper.
    d. the restriction of noncommercial housing in a convent where a certified statement has not been filed with the government.

63. Greg purchases a $37,000 property, depositing $3,000 as earnest money. If Greg obtains a 75 percent loan-to-value loan on the property, no additional items are prorated and there are no closing costs to Greg, how much more cash will Greg need at the settlement?
    a. $3,250
    b. $3,500
    c. $5,250
    d. $6,250

64. Broker Kyra arrives to present a purchase offer to Don, who is seriously ill, and finds Don's son and daughter-in-law also present. The son and daughter-in-law angrily urge Don to accept the offer, even though it is much less than the asking price for the property. If Don accepts the offer, Don may later claim that
    a. Kyra improperly presented an offer that was less than the asking price.
    b. Kyra's failure to protect Don from the son and daughter-in-law constituted a violation of Kyra's fiduciary duties.
    c. Don's rights under the ADA have been violated by the son and daughter-in-law.
    d. Don was under undue influence from the son and daughter-in-law, so the contract is voidable.

65. Pat sold his property to Wallace. The deed of conveyance contained only the following guarantee: "This property was not encumbered during the time Pat owned it except as noted in this deed." What type of deed did Pat give to Wallace?
    a. General warranty
    b. Special warranty
    c. Bargain and sale
    d. Quitclaim

66. Steve and Teri, who are not married, own a parcel of real estate. Each owns an undivided interest, with Steve owning one-third and Teri owning two-thirds. The form of ownership under which Steve and Teri own their property is
    a. severalty.
    b. joint tenancy.
    c. tenancy at will.
    d. tenancy in common.

67. Tyrone agrees to purchase a house for $84,500. Tyrone pays $2,000 as earnest money and obtains a new mortgage loan for $67,600. The purchase contract provides for a March 15 settlement. Tyrone and the sellers prorate the present year's real estate taxes of $1,880.96, which have been prepaid. Tyrone has additional closing costs of $1,250, and the sellers have other closing costs of $850. Using the actual number of days method, how much cash must Tyrone bring to the settlement?

    a. $16,389
    b. $17,650
    c. $17,840
    d. $19,639

68. A broker advertised a house he had listed for sale at the price of $47,900. Jon, a member of a racial minority group, saw the house and was interested in it. When Jon asked the broker the price of the house, the broker told Jon $53,000. Under the federal *Fair Housing Act of 1968*, such a statement is

    a. legal because the law requires only that Jon be given the opportunity to buy the house.
    b. legal because the representation was made by the broker and not directly by the owner.
    c. illegal because the difference in the offering price and the quoted price was greater than 10 percent.
    d. illegal because the terms of the potential sale were changed for Jon.

69. Linda placed Blackacre in a trust, naming herself as the beneficiary. When Linda died, her will directed the trustee to sell Blackacre and distribute the proceeds of the sale to her heirs. The trustee sold Blackacre in accordance with the will. What type of deed was delivered at settlement?

    a. Trustee's deed
    b. Trustor's deed
    c. Deed in trust
    d. Reconveyance deed

70. An appraiser has been hired to prepare an appraisal report of a property for loan purposes. The property is an elegant old mansion that is now leased out as a restaurant. To which approach to value should the appraiser probably give the greatest weight when making this appraisal?

    a. Income
    b. Sales comparison
    c. Replacement cost
    d. Reproduction cost

71. Catherine applies for a mortgage, and the loan officer suggests that she might consider a term mortgage loan. Which of the following statements *BEST* explains what the loan officer means?

    a. All of the interest is paid at the end of the term.
    b. The debt is partially amortized over the life of the loan.
    c. The length of the term is limited by state law.
    d. The entire principal amount is due at the end of the term.

72. Valley Place is a condominium community with a swimming pool, tennis courts, and a biking trail. These facilities are most likely owned by the

    a. Valley Place condominium board.
    b. corporation in which the unit owners hold stock.
    c. unit owners in the form of proportional divided interests.
    d. unit owners in the form of percentage undivided interests.

73. On a closing statement in a typical real estate transaction, the buyer's earnest money deposit is reflected as a

    a. credit to buyer only.
    b. credit to seller, debit to buyer.
    c. credit to buyer and seller.
    d. debit to buyer only.

74. Prepaid insurance and tax reserves, where the buyer assumes the mortgage, will appear on a typical closing statement as a

    a. credit to buyer, debit to seller.
    b. credit to seller only.
    c. debit to seller only.
    d. debit to buyer, credit to seller.

75. Real property can become personal property by the process known as
   a. attachment.
   b. severance.
   c. hypothecation.
   d. accretion.

76. Jack and Sal are next-door neighbors. Sal gives Jack permission to park a camper in Sal's yard for a few weeks. Sal does not charge Jack rent for the use of the yard. Sal has given Jack a(n)
   a. easement.
   b. estate for years.
   c. license.
   d. permissive encroachment.

77. What is the cost of constructing a fence 6 feet, 6 inches high around a lot measuring 90 feet by 175 feet if the cost of erecting the fence is $1.25 per linear foot and the cost of materials is $.825 per square foot of fence?
   a. $1,752
   b. $2,054
   c. $2,084
   d. $3,505

78. Ken signs a listing agreement with broker Elaine. Broker Nancy obtains a buyer for the house, and Elaine does not receive a commission. *Elaine does not sue Ken.* The listing agreement between Ken and Elaine was probably which of the following?
   a. Exclusive-right-to-sell
   b. Open
   c. Exclusive-agency
   d. Dual agency

79. A broker has established the following office policy: "All listings taken by any salesperson associated with this real estate brokerage must include compensation based on a 7 percent commission. No lower commission rate is acceptable." If the broker attempts to impose this uniform commission requirement, which of the following statements is *TRUE?*
   a. A homeowner may sue the broker for violating the antitrust law's prohibition against price-fixing.
   b. The salespersons associated with the brokerage will not be bound by the requirement and may negotiate any commission rate they choose.
   c. The broker must present the uniform commission policy to the local professional association for approval.
   d. The broker may, as a matter of office policy, legally set the minimum commission rate acceptable for the firm.

80. Tina leased an apartment from Lou. Because Lou failed to perform routine maintenance, the apartment building's central heating plant broke down in the fall. Lou neglected to have the heating system repaired, and Tina had no heat in her apartment for the first six weeks of winter. Although eight months remained on Tina's lease, she moved out of the apartment and refused to pay any rent. If Lou sues to recover the outstanding rent, which of the following would be Tina's *BEST* defense?
   a. Because Tina lived in the apartment for more than 25 percent of the lease term, she was entitled to move out at any time without penalty.
   b. Tina was entitled to vacate the premises because the landlord's failure to repair the heating system constituted abandonment.
   c. Because the apartment was made uninhabitable, the landlord's actions constituted actual eviction.
   d. The landlord's actions constituted constructive eviction.

81. A buyer purchased a parcel of land and immediately sold the mineral rights to an oil company. The buyer gave up which of the following?
    a. Air rights
    b. Surface rights
    c. Subsurface rights
    d. Occupancy rights

82. A developer built a structure that has six stories. Several years later, an ordinance was passed in that area banning any building six stories or higher. This building is a
    a. nonconforming use.
    b. situation in which the structure would have to be demolished.
    c. conditional use.
    d. violation of the zoning laws.

83. What is the maximum capital gains tax exclusion allowable for a married couple, filing jointly, who have lived in their home for the past 3½ years?
    a. $100,000
    b. $250,000
    c. $500,000
    d. $750,000

84. Statements by a real estate licensee that somewhat exaggerate the intangibles of a property without committing fraud are called
    a. polishing.
    b. puffing.
    c. prospecting.
    d. marketing.

85. A building sold for $157,000. The broker divided the 6 percent commission as follows: 10 percent to the listing salesperson; one-half of the balance to the selling salesperson. What was the listing salesperson's commission?
    a. $239
    b. $942
    c. $1,570
    d. $4,239

86. Which of the following is TRUE regarding condominiums?
    a. if a unit owner does not pay his or her monthly maintenance fee the entire community will be foreclosed.
    b. the covenants and restrictions define the responsibilities of the owners and declare how the homeowner's association will operate the condo community.
    c. balconies and assigned parking spaces are examples of limited fee simple interests.
    d. they are a blend of severalty and tenancy in common ownership.

87. Which of the following is NOT an unlawful practice?
    a. To refuse to sell, rent, or negotiate with a person because of race
    b. As a property manager, to check the credit of females only
    c. To display the Equal Housing Opportunity poster
    d. To refuse to let handicapped persons, at their expense, modify a dwelling

88. All of the following are voidable contracts EXCEPT a contract entered into
    a. with contingencies.
    b. under duress.
    c. under fraud.
    d. by a minor.

89. An owner has entered into a three-month listing agreement with a broker. Last week, the owner also entered into the same three-month listing agreement with two separate brokers. The owner has negotiated
    a. exclusive-right-to-sell listings.
    b. exclusive agency listings.
    c. open listings.
    d. net listings.

90. All of the following would be associated with depreciation EXCEPT
    a. a neighbor who does not maintain his property.
    b. a house without enough electrical outlets.
    c. shutters that need to be painted.
    d. the square foot method.

EXAM ONE PART TWO—ILLINOIS REAL ESTATE LAW AND PRACTICE

1. A large manufacturing company agrees to relocate to an economically depressed neighborhood of Chicago if the city can provide suitable property in a short period of time. The property needed is a large vacant lot owned by an investment partnership that refuses to sell. If the City of Chicago wants to relieve unemployment in the neighborhood and improve commercial conditions in the city by bringing in the manufacturer immediately, what can the city legally do?

   a. Nothing: Private real property is exempt from the power of eminent domain.

   b. Obtain title to the property by escheat through the provisions of Article I, Section 15, of the Illinois Constitution.

   c. Obtain title to the property through a court action seeking condemnation of the property.

   d. Obtain immediate rights of possession and use by depositing a sum of money that a court preliminarily considers to be just compensation with the county treasurer through a process known as a *quick-take*.

2. Illinois law requires that a preprinted offer to purchase that is intended to become a binding contract have which of the following headings?

   a. Real Estate Sales Contract

   b. Offer to Purchase

   c. Standard Purchase Offer and Contract

   d. Purchase Offer Form

3. In 1968, James (an Illinois resident) granted Rolling Acre to Brian "on condition that no liquor is ever served on the property." The conveyance provided that if liquor was served on Rolling Acre, ownership would revert to James. In 2008, Brian sold Rolling Acre to Charles. Based on these facts, which statement is *TRUE*?

   a. The sale of Rolling Acre in 2008 extinguished James's right of reverter.

   b. Both James's right of reverter and the condition expired by operation of Illinois statute in 1990; Charles is free to sell Rolling Acre without condition.

   c. While the condition continues forever, James's right of reverter automatically expired in 2008.

   d. Both the condition and James's right of reverter automatically expired in 1995.

4. Chris and Debbie are married Illinois residents. If their co-owned home is sold to satisfy their unpaid credit card debts, what is the maximum the creditors will receive if the property sells for $165,000?

   a. Nothing. By statute, an Illinois resident's home may not be sold except to satisfy a mortgage debt or real estate taxes.

   b. $135,000

   c. $157,500

   d. $163,600

5. Which of the following statements in a deed would establish a valid tenancy by the entirety in Illinois?

   a. "To Ken and Helen, a lawfully married couple, as tenants by the entirety"

   b. "To Ken and Helen, husband and wife, not as joint tenants or tenants in common but as tenants by the entirety"

   c. "To Ken and Helen jointly, as married tenants by the entirety"

   d. "To Ken and Helen as tenants by the entirety in accordance with Illinois law"

6. An ownership arrangement in which the purchaser receives a fee simple ownership in real property for longer than three years but the right to actually use the property for a specific period of less than one year (on a recurring basis) is a

   a. time-share use.
   b. time-share estate.
   c. public offering statement.
   d. membership camp.

7. Which of the following would be required to be surveyed and have a plat recorded under the Illinois Plat Act?

   a. An owner divides a 30-acre parcel into five equal lots.
   b. An owner divides a 20-acre parcel into five equal lots.
   c. An owner conveys a single 20-acre parcel.
   d. An owner divides a single 20-acre parcel into two 6-acre lots and an 8-acre lot.

8. The general datum plane referred to by surveyors throughout Illinois is the

   a. Chicago City Datum.
   b. New York Harbor Datum.
   c. United States Geological Survey Datum.
   d. Centralia Datum.

9. While the identity of the beneficiary of a land trust is not usually disclosed without the beneficiary's written permission, the trustee may be compelled to do so in all the following situations *EXCEPT*

   a. when the information is demanded by the Internal Revenue Service.
   b. during the discovery process of a lawsuit or criminal action involving the property.
   c. when applying to a state agency for a license or permit affecting the property.
   d. when a private request is filed in the public records office.

10. An owner paid the first installment of her Illinois general real estate tax on July 1. The amount due was $2,380. If the county assessor issued the owner's bill 30 days before the penalty date of June 1, does the owner owe any penalty?

    a. No: The penalty date for the payment of all Illinois general real estate taxes is September 1.
    b. Yes: The owner will have to pay $35.70 as a penalty in addition to the real estate tax owed.
    c. No: The assessor is required by statute to issue tax bills 60 days before any penalty date.
    d. Yes: The owner will have to pay $71.40 as a penalty in addition to the real estate tax owed.

11. A judgment issued by an Illinois court is a

    a. general, involuntary legal lien on all of a debtor's real property and an equitable, specific lien on the debtor's personal property.
    b. general, involuntary, equitable lien on both real and personal property owned by the debtor.
    c. specific lien on the debtor's real and personal property, effective for a nonrenewable period of five years.
    d. general, involuntary, equitable lien on both real and personal property, effective for renewable five-year periods.

12. The property at 614 Stevenson Street in Peoria is owned by Walter, who is married to Hanna. Walter bought the property before he married Hanna. Hanna has no ownership interest in the property. Walter and Hanna live in Chicago, and the house in Peoria is occupied by a tenant, Tia. If Walter wants to sell the property, who is required by law to sign the listing agreement?

    a. Both Walter and Hanna, because they are a married couple
    b. Walter only, because Walter and Hanna do not live in the house
    c. Walter as owner and Tia as tenant in possession
    d. Walter, Hanna, and Tia

13. A common item appearing in an Illinois listing agreement is
    a. a statement that the property must be shown only to certain prospective buyers because of race, color, religion, national origin, sex, handicap, or familial status.
    b. the time duration of the listing.
    c. the complete legal description of the property being sold.
    d. the proposed net sales price of the property.

14. In Illinois, which agency is responsible for licensing leasing agents?
    a. Department of Professional Regulation
    b. Department of Financial Institutions
    c. Illinois Department of Financial and Professional Regulation
    d. Department of Insurance Registration

15. In Illinois, if a broker is taking a listing and asks the seller to complete a disclosure of property conditions, which of the following statements is TRUE?
    a. The disclosures are optional, and the seller may avoid liability by refusing to make any disclosures about the condition of the property.
    b. The standard disclosures cover a narrow range of structural conditions only.
    c. An agent should give the seller advice regarding which property conditions to disclose and which to ignore.
    d. Seller disclosure of known property conditions is required by Illinois statute.

16. How long must a claimant hold adverse, exclusive, continuous, and uninterrupted use of a property under claim of right in Illinois in order to obtain a prescriptive easement in Illinois?
    a. 10 years
    b. 17 years
    c. 20 years
    d. 30 years

17. Keri is an Illinois real estate licensee and the listing agent for a home. After one month of the three-month listing has gone by without any offers on the property, Keri becomes concerned. At the time the listing agreement was signed, Keri and the sellers orally agreed that if no offers were received after one month, the price of the property would be reduced by 10 percent. Because the sellers are out of town, Keri crosses out the old listing price, writes in the new one, and then updates the information on the computerized listing service. Three days later, a prospective buyer comes into Keri's office to make an offer on the property. Based on these facts, which of the following statements is TRUE?
    a. Illinois licensees are prohibited by law from making any addition to, deletion from, or other alteration of a written listing agreement without the written consent of the principal.
    b. While alteration of a written listing agreement is usually prohibited by Illinois law, Keri acted properly in this situation because the sellers were out of town.
    c. Changing the listing price of a property is a matter of professional discretion, and Illinois licensees are permitted to make alterations to only that aspect of a listing agreement without the written consent of the principal.
    d. While alteration of a written listing agreement is usually prohibited by Illinois law, Keri acted properly in this situation because of the prior oral agreement with the sellers.

18. Martin, a broker, signs a listing agreement with a seller. The agreement contains the following clause: "If the Property has not been sold after three months from the date of this signing, this agreement will automatically continue for additional three-month periods thereafter until the property is sold." Based on these facts, which of the following statements is *TRUE*?

    a. The agreement is legal under Illinois law, because it contains a reference to a specific time limit.

    b. This agreement is illegal in Illinois.

    c. Illinois law will automatically apply a statutory six-month listing period to this open listing.

    d. This agreement is legal under Illinois law, because the time periods are for less than six months each.

19. Under a land contract in Illinois, what type of title does the purchaser have until the "final" closing when the obligation to seller is paid in full?

    a. Equitable title

    b. Full legal title

    c. Land title

    d. No title

20. How are members of the Illinois Real Estate Disciplinary Board selected?

    a. Appointed by the governor

    b. Appointed by the Commissioner of Real Estate

    c. Elected by licensees

    d. Elected in statewide elections every six years

21. What is the advantage of seeking an injunction against a licensee who is violating the act?

    a. The statute of limitations no longer applies.

    b. When the injunction is granted, it doubles the penalty for violations of the act.

    c. It increases the offense to a felony.

    d. It stops the violation from continuing.

22. An Illinois licensee may have his or her license suspended or revoked for which of the following actions?

    a. Giving earnest money to his or her sponsoring broker rather than depositing it directly

    b. Being declared mentally incompetent

    c. Disclosing agency

    d. Displaying a For Sale sign on a property with the owner's consent

23. In Illinois, which of the following is a required element of a valid deed?

    a. Specifically identified grantee

    b. Notarization of grantees' signature

    c. Hold harmless clause

    d. Name of the lender

24. An approximately straight line (except for corrections) connecting Rockford and Cairo is the

    a. Second Principal Meridian.

    b. Third Principal Meridian.

    c. Fourth Principal Meridian.

    d. Centralia Base Line.

25. Sponsoring Broker Greg received an earnest money deposit along with a sales contract from a buyer. Under Illinois law, what must Greg do with the money?

    a. Open a special, separate escrow account that will contain funds for this transaction only, separate from funds received in any other transaction

    b. Deposit the money in an existing special noninterest-bearing escrow account in which all earnest money received from buyers may be held at the same time

    c. Immediately (or by the next business day) commingle the funds by depositing the earnest money in his personal interest-bearing checking or savings account

    d. Hold the earnest money deposit in a secure place in his real estate brokerage office until the offer is accepted

26. *Chicago Bar Association, et al. v. Quinlan and Tyson, Inc.* established what principle in Illinois real estate law?

    a. Real estate brokers must establish a special escrow account for earnest money deposits.

    b. The seller must bear any losses that occur before title to property passes or before the buyer takes possession.

    c. Brokers and salespersons may only fill in blanks and make appropriate deletions on preprinted standard form contracts.

    d. Once a contract is signed, a broker or salesperson may not make any additions, deletions, or insertions without the written consent of the parties.

27. Under Illinois law, what is the statutory usury ceiling on loans secured by real estate?

    a. 10 percent
    b. 15 percent
    c. 22 percent
    d. There is none

28. Derek, a real estate broker, is aware that certain areas of the city are particularly unfriendly to members of certain minority groups. For these groups' own protection, Derek shows members of such groups homes for sale only in "friendly" neighborhoods into which members of their minority group have moved in the past. Based on these facts, which of the following statements is *TRUE?*

    a. The *Real Estate License Act of 2000* would not prohibit Derek's actions, because Derek is being protective rather than discriminatory.

    b. The critical element in this type of activity is profit motive; if Derek's actions are not driven by increased profits, Derek will not be subject to discipline under the *Real Estate License Act of 2000*.

    c. While Derek's actions are clearly prohibited by Illinois statute, the *Real Estate License Act of 2000* does not address blockbusting or steering.

    d. Derek's actions are expressly prohibited by the *Real Estate License Act of 2000*.

29. Ben conveys real property to Chris. The sale price of the property is $250,000. What is the Illinois state transfer tax on this transaction?

    a. $125
    b. $250
    c. $500
    d. $1,250

30. In the previous question, how much of the state transfer tax payable will go to fund affordable housing under the *Illinois Affordable Housing Act?*

    a. 10 percent
    b. 25 percent
    c. 50 percent
    d. None

31. In Illinois, how must the real property transfer tax be paid?

    a. By personal check, made out to the Illinois Department of Revenue

    b. By certified check, made out to the Illinois Housing Development Authority

    c. By purchasing transfer tax stamps from the county recorder or appropriate local authority

    d. In monthly payments to the lender during the first five years of ownership

32. In Illinois, which property is totally exempt from paying general real estate taxes?

    a. Retirement housing for the elderly
    b. Properties financed with FHA funds
    c. Private schools
    d. Housing owned by a disabled veteran

33. Tom, a landlord, has a "no pets" policy in his apartment building. If a visually impaired person wants to rent an apartment from Tom, but owns a guide dog, which of the following statements is *TRUE?*

    a. If Tom's "no pets" policy is applied uniformly, in a nondiscriminatory manner, it may be legally applied to the guide dog as well.

    b. The *Illinois Human Rights Act* specifically prohibits Tom from refusing to rent the apartment to the visually impaired person on the basis of Tom's "no pets" policy.

    c. Under the *Illinois Human Rights Act*, Tom may not discriminate against the visually impaired person on the basis of a "no pets" policy, but Tom may require the tenant to pay an additional damage fee.

    d. The *Illinois Human Rights Act* does not address the issue of guide, hearing, or support dogs.

34. Marta conveys real property to Noelle for $185,000. What amount will have to be paid in county transfer tax?

  a. $37.00
  b. $92.50
  c. $185.00
  d. $1,850.00

35. Which of the following statements is *TRUE* of an Illinois county having fewer than 60,000 residents?

  a. The recorder of deeds must be elected.
  b. Deeds are recorded by the elected recorder of deeds in the nearest county having a population over 60,000.
  c. The city clerk of the largest population center acts as recorder of deeds.
  d. The county clerk also serves as recorder of deeds.

36. Which is a requirement for a deed to be recorded in Illinois?

  a. The name of the grantee must be typed or printed below her or his signature
  b. Payment of required tax stamps
  c. A blank page for use by the recorder
  d. The name, address, and age of the grantee

37. The purpose of the Real Estate Recovery Fund is to

  a. permit licensees to reestablish their businesses after a natural or financial disaster.
  b. reward consumers for identifying licensees who are engaged in violations of the real estate license law or other wrongful acts.
  c. compensate individuals who suffer losses due to the wrongful acts of a licensee.
  d. pay for the court costs and legal fees required to defend licensees against accusations of wrongdoing.

38. Which activity requires a real estate license?

  a. MLS providing listing information to members
  b. A resident manager who collects rent on behalf of a building owner
  c. A service that, for a fee, matches individuals who want to buy and sell properties
  d. An executor selling a decedent's building

39. Lynn is an Illinois real estate broker and also a part-owner of LMN Title, a title insurance company. Lynn has registered with the appropriate state agency and has disclosed the relationship to the owner of Blackacre. Under these facts, can Lynn recommend that LMN produce the title insurance policy when Blackacre sells?

  a. Yes: Lynn has fully complied with the requirements of the Illinois Title Insurance Act.
  b. No: Lynn also must obtain the written permission of her client.
  c. Yes: Because Lynn is only a part owner of LMN Title, the provisions of the Illinois Title Insurance Act do not apply.
  d. Yes, if Lynn also fills out and provides state disclosure forms to both her clients.

40. What is the name of the act that requires that Illinois developers file statements of record with HUD before they offer unimproved lots for sale in interstate commerce via telephone?

  a. *HUD Registration Act*
  b. *Interstate Land Sales Full Disclosure Act*
  c. *Interstate Undeveloped Land Act*
  d. NAFA

41. In Illinois, if an owner defaults on his or her mortgage loan and the property is ordered sold at a foreclosure sale, the owner may redeem the property

  a. prior to the sale, under the statutory right of redemption.
  b. prior to the sale, under the equitable right of redemption.
  c. after the sale, under the statutory right of redemption.
  d. after the sale, under the statutory right of reinstatement.

42. For three days, Manuel watched from his kitchen window as a small construction crew built an attractive gazebo in his backyard. Manuel had not contracted with anyone to build a gazebo and in fact had never given much thought to having one. But Manuel liked what he saw. When the contractor presented Manuel with a bill for the work, Manuel refused to pay, pointing out that he'd never signed a contract to have the work done. Can the contractor impose a mechanic's lien on Manuel's property under Illinois law?

   a. No: In Illinois a mechanic's lien attaches on the date the contract is signed or the work is ordered, and neither event occured here.
   b. No: Manuel cannot be forced to pay for the contractor's mistake.
   c. Yes: Where a landowner knows of work being done on his or her property and does not object or disclaim responsibility, a mechanic's lien may be created.
   d. Yes: Manuel should have mailed a notice of nonresponsibility to the contractor's main place of business.

43. Penny's property in Peoria has an assessed value of $175,000. The local tax rate is 30 mills, and no equalization factor is used. If the tax was levied in April 2007, Penny had to pay

   a. $5,250 on June 1, 2007.
   b. $2,625 on September 1, 2007.
   c. $2,625 on January 1, 2008.
   d. $2,625 on June 1, 2008.

44. In Illinois, brokers and salespeople may do which of the following?

   a. Complete a bill of sale after a sales contract has been signed
   b. Fill in blanks on preprinted form contracts customarily used in their community
   c. Suggest additional language to be added to a preprinted sales contract by a buyer or seller
   d. Explain the legal significance of specific preprinted contract clauses to a buyer or seller

45. For which of the following acts is the IDFPR required to suspend or revoke a licensee's license?

   a. Failing to perform as promised in a guaranteed sales plan
   b. Having been found liable in a civil trial for illegal discrimination
   c. Commingling others' money or property with her or his own
   d. Failing to provide information requested by the IDFPR within 30 days of the request as part of a complaint or audit procedure

46. Three weeks before Nate begins his Illinois real estate prelicense class, he offers to help his neighbor sell her house. The neighbor agrees to pay Nate a 5 percent commission. An offer is accepted while Nate is taking the class and closes the day before Nate passes the examination and receives his salesperson's license. The neighbor refuses to pay Nate the agreed commission. Can Nate sue to recover payment?

   a. Yes: Because Nate was formally enrolled in a course of study intended to result in a real estate license at the time an offer was procured and accepted, the commission agreement is binding.
   b. No: In Illinois, a real estate salesperson must have a permanent office in which his or her license is displayed in order to collect a commission from a seller.
   c. Yes: While the statute of frauds forbids recovery on an oral agreement for the conveyance of real property, Illinois law permits enforcement of an oral commission contract under these facts.
   d. No: Illinois law prohibits lawsuits to collect commissions unless the injured party is a licensed broker and the license was in effect before the agreement was reached.

47. An Illinois real estate salesperson may lawfully collect compensation from

   a. either a buyer or a seller.
   b. his or her sponsoring broker only.
   c. any party to the transaction or the party's representative.
   d. a licensed real estate broker only.

48. Pat has a mortgage loan secured by real property. Under recent law, Pat may terminate the loan's escrow account when the remaining balance is equal to or less than what percentage of the original amount?

    a. 35 percent
    b. 50 percent
    c. 65 percent
    d. 75 percent

49. The JKL Partnership was established to buy and sell real estate. Of the three general partners, only Janet and Kallie will be actively involved in real estate transactions. Janet plans to specialize in commercial properties and Kallie in residential. The third general partner, Laura, is responsible only for supervising the partnership's office decor and planning holiday parties. Under these facts, which of the general partners needs to be licensed for JKL to qualify for a broker's license in Illinois?

    a. None: Under Illinois law, a partnership is an independent entity that may obtain a broker's license regardless of the status of any individual partner.
    b. Either Janet or Kallie, depending on whether the partnership's emphasis will be residential or commercial properties.
    c. Both Janet and Kallie must be licensed salespersons, but Laura need not be licensed.
    d. Janet, Kallie, and Laura must all be licensed real estate brokers.

50. With regard to mortgages, Illinois is most accurately described as a(n)

    a. intermediate-theory state.
    b. lien-theory state.
    c. title-theory state.
    d. equitable-theory state.

51. Which of the following is perfectly legal in Illinois?

    a. Offering finder's fees to consumers
    b. Giving referral fees to other licensees (which do not need to be disclosed)
    c. Offering merchandise incentives to potential buyers or sellers
    d. Indicating a "standard commission" when asked

52. Theo is the landlord of a three-unit apartment building. Dane is the landlord of a 30-unit apartment building. Based on these facts, which of the following is TRUE of security deposits under Illinois law?

    a. Both Theo and Dane must give tenants an itemized statement of alleged damages before they can withhold any part of the security deposit as compensation.
    b. Only Dane is required to pay interest on security deposits.
    c. Only Theo is required to give tenants an itemized statement of alleged damages before any part of the security deposit may be withheld as compensation.
    d. Both Theo and Dane are required to pay interest on security deposits at a rate linked to minimum deposit passbook savings accounts at Illinois's largest commercial bank.

53. How many members are on the Illinois Real Estate Administration and Disciplinary Board?

    a. 6
    b. 8
    c. 9
    d. 12

54. In Illinois, how much written notice is a landlord required to give a tenant to pay overdue rent prior to terminating the lease, when the tenant is in default only for failing to pay rent on time?

    a. 0 days
    b. 3 days
    c. 5 days
    d. 10 days

55. In Illinois, if a home rule county has an ordinance that conflicts with that of a home rule city, whose ordinance will prevail?

    a. The county's ordinance
    b. The city's ordinance
    c. The relevant township ordinance
    d. The dispute is constitutional in nature and so may be resolved only by the Illinois Supreme Court.

56. Which of the following is *NOT* a requirement for a valid lease?
   a. An option agreement
   b. Description of the leased premises
   c. Signatures of the parties
   d. Consideration

57. Jean Marie is a broker for XYZ Realty. When Jean Marie is representing her client, she is *MOST LIKELY* acting as a(n)
   a. universal agent.
   b. ostensible agent.
   c. special agent.
   d. double agent.

58. Which of the following is *NOT* necessary to create a fiduciary relationship?
   a. A listing agreement
   b. A buyer agency agreement
   c. A contractual agreement to represent another
   d. The payment of the commission

59. Which of the following statements are *TRUE* regarding severance and attachment?
   a. Attachment is associated with real property, while severance is associated with personal property.
   b. Attachment means to add to the land, while severance means to separate from the land.
   c. Attachment means to separate from the land, while severance means to add to the land.
   d. Attachment is associated with condominiums, while severance is associated with cooperatives.

60. Which is *TRUE* regarding fee simple absolute estates?
   a. They are based on calendar time.
   b. They are not inheritable.
   c. They are the highest level of ownership recognized by law.
   d. They are represent a defeasible title.

EXAM TWO PART ONE—GENERAL REAL ESTATE PRACTICE AND PRINCIPLES

1. Tenant Dennis's landlord has sold the building where Dennis lives to the state so that a freeway can be built. Dennis's lease has expired, but the landlord permits him to stay in the apartment until the building is torn down. Dennis continues to pay the rent as prescribed in the lease. What kind of tenancy does Dennis have?

   a. Holdover tenancy
   b. Month-to-month tenancy
   c. Tenancy at sufferance
   d. Tenancy at will

2. The owner of a house wants to fence the yard for her dog. When the fence is erected, the fencing materials are converted to real estate by

   a. severance.
   b. subrogation.
   c. adaptation.
   d. attachment.

3. George is interested in selling his house as quickly as possible and believes that the best way to do this is to have several brokers compete against each other for the commission. George's listing agreements with four different brokers specifically promise that if one of them finds a buyer for his property, George will be obligated to pay a commission to that broker. What type of agreement has George entered into?

   a. Executed
   b. Discharged
   c. Unilateral
   d. Bilateral

4. In some states, by paying the debt after a foreclosure sale, a borrower has the right to regain the property under which of the following?

   a. Novation
   b. Redemption
   c. Reversion
   d. Recovery

5. Wendy enters into a sale-leaseback agreement with Jerry, under which Jerry will become the owner of Wendy's ranch. Which of the following statements is *TRUE* of this arrangement?

   a. Wendy retains title to the ranch.
   b. Jerry receives possession of the property.
   c. Jerry is the lessor.
   d. Wendy is the lessor.

6. Tammy is a real estate broker employed by Milos. When Tammy finds a property that Milos might be interested in buying, she is careful to find out as much as possible about the property's owners and why their property is on the market. Tammy's efforts to keep Milos informed of all facts that could affect a transaction is the common-law duty of

   a. care.   c. obedience.
   b. loyalty.   d. disclosure.

7. A parcel of vacant land 80 feet wide and 200 feet deep was sold for $200 per front foot. How much money would a salesperson receive for her 60 percent share in the 10 percent commission?

   a. $640
   b. $960
   c. $1,600
   d. $2,400

8. Which situation violates the federal *Fair Housing Act of 1968*?

   a. The refusal of a property manager to rent an apartment to a Catholic couple who are not otherwise qualified
   b. The general policy of a loan company to grant home improvement loans to qualified individuals living in transitional neighborhoods
   c. A widowed woman's insistence on renting her spare bedroom only to another widowed woman
   d. The intentional neglect of a broker to show an Asian family any property listings in all-white neighborhoods

9. If a storage tank that measures 12 feet by 9 feet by 8 feet is designed to store a gas that costs $1.82 per cubic foot, what does it cost to fill the tank to one-half of its capacity?

   a. $685   c. $864
   b. $786   d. $1,572

10. Roland bought a condo for $125,000. It appraised for $120,500 and previously sold for $118,250. Based on these facts, if Roland applies for an 80 percent mortgage, what will be the amount of the loan Roland will receive?

    a. $94,600   c. $100,000
    b. $96,400   d. $106,750

11. Karen offers to buy Laura's property by signing a purchase contract. Laura accepts Karen's offer. What kind of title interest does Karen have in the property at this point?

    a. Legal
    b. Equitable
    c. Defeasible
    d. Karen has no title interest at this point.

12. Which of the following federal laws requires that finance charges be stated as an annual percentage rate?

    a. *Truth-in-Lending Act*
    b. *Real Estate Settlement Procedures Act (RESPA)*
    c. *Equal Credit Opportunity Act (ECOA)*
    d. *Federal Fair Housing Act*

13. Fran signed a 90-day listing agreement with a broker. Two weeks later, Fran was killed in an accident. What is the present status of the listing?

    a. The listing agreement is binding on Fran's estate for the remainder of the 90 days.
    b. Because Fran's intention to sell was clearly defined, the listing agreement is still in effect and the broker may proceed to market the property on behalf of Fran's estate.
    c. The listing agreement is binding on Fran's estate only if the broker can produce an offer to purchase the property within the remainder of the listing period.
    d. The listing agreement was terminated automatically when Fran died.

14. Maria conveys the ownership of an office building to a nursing home. The nursing home agrees that the rental income will pay for the expenses of caring for Maria's parents. When Maria's parents die, ownership of the office building will revert to Maria. The estate held by the nursing home is a

    a. remainder life estate.
    b. legal life estate.
    c. life estate *pur autre vie*.
    d. temporary leasehold estate.

15. Henry is a real estate broker. Stan signs a buyer's brokerage agreement under which Henry will help Stan find a three-bedroom house in the $285,000 to $300,000 price range. James comes into Henry's office and signs a listing agreement to sell James's two-bedroom condominium for $170,000. Based on these facts, which of the following statements is *TRUE*?

    a. Stan is Henry's client; James is Henry's customer.
    b. Stan is Henry's customer; James is Henry's client.
    c. While both Stan and James are clients, Henry owes the fiduciary duties of an agent only to James.
    d. Because both Stan and James are Henry's clients, Henry owes the fiduciary duties of an agent to both.

16. In a township of 36 sections, which of the following statements is *TRUE*?

    a. Section 31 lies to the east of Section 32.
    b. Section 18 is by law set aside for school purposes.
    c. Section 6 lies in the northeast corner of the township.
    d. Section 16 lies to the north of Section 21.

17. Lawyer Sara represented the seller in a transaction. Her client informed her that he did not want to recite the actual consideration that was paid for the house. In this situation, which of the following statements is *TRUE?*

   a. Sara must inform her client that only the actual price of the real estate may appear on the deed.

   b. Sara may prepare a deed that shows only nominal consideration of $10.

   c. Sara should inform the seller that either the full price should be stated in the deed or all references to consideration should be removed from it.

   d. Sara may show a price on the deed other than the actual price, provided that the variance is not greater than 10 percent of the purchase price.

18. Broker Bess obtained a listing agreement to act as the agent in the sale of Geri's house. A buyer has been found for the property, and all agreements have been signed. As an agent for Geri, the broker is responsible for which of the following?

   a. Completing the buyer's loan application

   b. Making sure that the buyer receives copies of all documents the seller is required to deliver to the buyer

   c. Ensuring that the buyer is qualified for the new mortgage loan

   d. Scheduling the buyer's inspection of the property

19. Jeff is a real estate salesperson employed by broker Tim. What is Jeff's share of the commission when the sales price of a property was $195,000 and Jeff is entitled to 65 percent of the 7.5 percent commission?

   a. $950.63

   b. $8,872.50

   c. $9,506.25

   d. $95,062.50

20. Quinn, an appraiser, estimates the value of a property using the cost approach. Which of the following describes what Quinn should do?

   a. Estimate the replacement cost of the improvements

   b. Deduct the depreciation of the land and buildings

   c. Determine the original cost and adjust for depreciation

   d. Review the sales prices of comparable properties

21. Tonya is a mortgage lender. Before the closing of a real estate transaction, Tonya provides the buyer and seller with statements of all fees and charges they will incur. In doing this, Tonya complies with the

   a. *Equal Credit Opportunity Act (ECOA).*

   b. *Truth-in-Lending Act (Regulation Z).*

   c. *Real Estate Settlement Procedures Act (RESPA).*

   d. *Fair Housing Act.*

22. The landlord of an apartment building neglected to repair the building's plumbing system. As a result, the apartments did not receive water, as provided by the leases. If a tenant's unit becomes uninhabitable, which of the following would *MOST LIKELY* result?

   a. Suit for possession

   b. Claim of constructive eviction

   c. Tenancy at sufferance

   d. Suit for negligence

23. Philip conveys a life estate to Mary. Under the terms of Philip's conveyance, the property will pass to Terrence upon Mary's death. Which of the following *BEST* describes Terrence's interest in the property during Mary's lifetime?

   a. Remainder

   b. Reversion

   c. Life estate *pur autre vie*

   d. Redemption

24. On a settlement statement, prorations for real estate taxes paid in arrears are shown as a
    a. credit to the seller and a debit to the buyer.
    b. debit to the seller and a credit to the buyer.
    c. credit to both the seller and the buyer.
    d. debit to both the seller and the buyer.

25. What type of lease establishes a rental payment and requires that the lessor pay for the taxes, insurance, and maintenance on the property?
    a. Percentage
    b. Net
    c. Expense only
    d. Gross

26. A conventional loan was closed on July 1 for $57,200 at 13.5 percent interest amortized over 25 years at $666.75 per month. On August 1, what would the principal amount be after the monthly payment was made?
    a. $56,533.25   c. $57,065.35
    b. $56,556.50   d. $57,176.75

27. In the preceding question, what would the interest portion of the payment be?
    a. $610.65   c. $643.50
    b. $620.25   d. $666.75

28. Rebecca listed her home with broker Kent for $190,000. Rebecca told Kent, "I have to sell quickly because of a job transfer. If necessary, I can accept a price as low as $175,000." Kent tells a prospective buyer to offer $180,000 "because Rebecca is desperate to sell." Rebecca accepts the buyer's offer. In this situation, which of the following statements is *TRUE?*
    a. Kent's action did not violate his agency relationship with Rebecca because Kent did not reveal Rebecca's lowest acceptable price.
    b. Kent violated his agency relationship with Rebecca.
    c. Kent acted properly to obtain a quick offer on Rebecca's property, in accordance with Rebecca's instructions.
    d. Kent violated his duties toward the buyer by failing to disclose that Rebecca would accept a lower price than the buyer offered.

29. Which of the following *BEST* describes the capitalization rate under the income approach to estimating the value of real estate?
    a. Rate at which a property increases in value
    b. Rate of return a property earns as an investment
    c. Rate of capital required to keep a property operating most efficiently
    d. Maximum rate of return allowed by law on an investment

30. On a settlement statement, the cost of the lender's title insurance policy required for a new loan is usually shown as which of the following?
    a. Credit to the seller
    b. Credit to the buyer
    c. Debit to the seller
    d. Debit to the buyer

31. An FHA-insured loan for $57,500 at 8.5 percent for 30 years was closed on July 17, 2001. The first monthly payment is due on September 1. Because interest is paid monthly in arrears, what was the amount of the interest adjustment the buyer owes at the settlement, using the statutory method?
    a. $190.07
    b. $230.80
    c. $407.29
    d. $4,887.50

32. If a home that originally cost $142,500 three years ago is now valued at 127 percent of its original cost, what is its current market value?
    a. $164,025
    b. $172,205
    c. $174,310
    d. $180,975

33. Carol has a contract to paint Otto's garage door for $1200. Before starting the project, Carol has a skiing accident and breaks both arms. Carol asks another painter, Jamie, to take over the job. Jamie paints Otto's garage door, and Otto pays Jamie $1200 for the work. This scenario is an example of
    a. assignment.
    b. acceptance.
    c. novation.
    d. revocation.

34. Whitney searches the public record regarding title to Brownacre. Which of the following is Whitney *MOST LIKELY* to discover?

    a. Encroachments
    b. Rights of parties in possession
    c. Inaccurate survey
    d. Judgments

35. A rectangular lot is worth $193,600. This value is the equivalent of $4.40 per square foot. If one lot dimension is 200 feet, what is the other dimension?

    a. 110 feet
    b. 220 feet
    c. 400 feet
    d. 880 feet

36. Broker Bart listed Kendra's property at an 8 percent commission rate. After the property was sold and the settlement had taken place, Kendra discovered that the broker had been listing similar properties at 6 percent commission rates. Based on this information alone, which of the following statements is *TRUE*?

    a. Bart has done nothing wrong because a commission rate is always negotiable between the parties.
    b. If Bart inflated the usual commission rate for the area, Bart may be subject to discipline by the state real estate commission.
    c. Kendra is entitled to rescind the transaction based on the principle of lack of reality of consent.
    d. Kendra is entitled to a refund from Bart of 2 percent of the commission.

37. Melanie has six months remaining on her apartment lease. Melanie's monthly rent is $875. Melanie moves out of the apartment, and Teresa moves in. Teresa pays Melanie a monthly rental of $700, and Melanie continues paying the full rental amount under her lease to the landlord. When Melanie's lease term expires, Teresa will either move out or sign a new lease with the landlord. This is an example of

    a. assignment.
    b. subletting.
    c. rescission and renewal.
    d. surrender.

38. One broker asked another, "Will I have to prove that I was the procuring cause if my seller sells the property himself?" The other broker answers, "No, not if you have an

    a. option listing."
    b. open listing."
    c. exclusive-agency listing."
    d. exclusive-right-to-sell listing."

39. The capitalization rate on a property reflects which of the following factors?

    a. Risk of the investment
    b. Replacement cost of the improvements
    c. Real estate taxes
    d. Debt service

40. An investment property worth $180,000 was purchased seven years ago for $142,000. At the time of the purchase, the land was valued at $18,000. Assuming a 31½-year life for straight-line depreciation purposes, what is the present book value of the property?

    a. $95,071
    b. $113,071
    c. $114,444
    d. $126,000

41. A person who dies without having made a will is said to be

    a. a testate.
    b. a testator.
    c. in probate.
    d. intestate.

42. A farmer owns the W½ of the NW¼ of the NW¼ of a section. The remainder of the NW¼ can be purchased for $300 per acre. Owning all of the NW¼ of the section would cost the farmer

    a. $6,000.
    b. $12,000.
    c. $42,000.
    d. $48,000.

43. In a standard sales contract, several words were crossed out or inserted by the parties. To eliminate future controversy as to whether the changes were made before or after the contract was signed, the usual procedure is to

a. write a letter to each party listing the changes.
b. have each party write a letter to the other approving the changes.
c. redraw the entire contract.
d. have both parties initial or sign in the margin near each change.

44. Pablo is the manager of the Bellevue Terrace apartments. For each new tenant that Pablo signs, the owner pays him an 8½ percent commission, based on the unit's annualized rent. In one year, Pablo signed five new tenants. Three of the apartments rented for $795 per month; one rented for $1,200 per month; and one rented for $900 per month. What was the total amount of Pablo's new-tenant commissions for that year?

a. $381.23
b. $2,952.90
c. $3,685.47
d. $4,574.70

45. The monthly rent on a warehouse is $1 per cubic yard. Assuming the warehouse is 36 feet by 200 feet by 12 feet high, what would the annual rent be?

a. $3,200
b. $9,600
c. $38,400
d. $115,200

46. A veteran wishes to refinance his home with a VA-guaranteed loan. The lender is willing, but insists on 3½ discount points. In this situation, the veteran can

a. refinance with a VA loan, provided the lender charges no discount points.
b. refinance with a VA loan, provided the lender charges no more than two discount points.
c. be required to pay a maximum of 1 percent of the loan as an origination fee.
d. proceed with the refinance loan and pay the discount points.

47. Grant owns two properties: Redacre and Brownacre. He conveys Redacre to Sharon with no restrictions; Sharon holds all rights to Redacre forever. Grant then conveys Brownacre to Tim "so long as no real estate broker or salesperson ever sets foot on the property." If a broker or salesperson visits Brownacre, ownership will revert to Grant. Based on these two conveyances, which of the following statements is true?

a. Sharon holds Redacre in fee simple; Tim holds Brownacre in fee simple determinable.
b. Sharon holds Redacre in fee simple absolute; Tim holds Brownacre in fee simple defeasible, subject to a condition subsequent.
c. Tim may not transfer ownership of Brownacre without Grant's permission.
d. Grant has retained a right of reentry with regard to Brownacre.

48. A real estate transaction had a closing date of November 15. The seller, who was responsible for costs up to and including the date of settlement, paid the property taxes of $1,116 for the calendar year. On the closing statement, the buyer would be

a. debited $139.50.
b. debited $976.50.
c. credited $139.50.
d. credited $976.50.

49. An agreement that ends all future lessor-lessee obligations under a lease is known as a(n)

a. assumption.
b. surrender.
c. novation.
d. breach.

50. Aaron buys a house for $234,500. He makes a $25,000 cash down payment and takes out a $209,500 mortgage for 30 years. The lot value is $80,000. If Aaron wants to depreciate the property over a period of 27½ years, how much will the annual depreciation amount be, using the straight-line method?

a. $3,818.18
b. $4,709.09
c. $5,618.18
d. $8,527.27

51. A property manager leased a store for three years. The first year, the store's rent was $1,000 per month, and the rent was to increase 10 percent per year thereafter. The manager received a 7 percent commission for the first year, 5 percent for the second year, and 3 percent for the balance of the lease. The total commission earned by the property manager was

a. $840.
b. $1,613.
c. $1,936.
d. $2,785.

52. Against a recorded deed from the owner of record, the party with the weakest position is a

a. person with a prior unrecorded deed who is not in possession.
b. person in possession with a prior unrecorded deed.
c. tenant in possession with nine months remaining on the lease.
d. painter who is half-finished painting the house at the time of the sale and who has not yet been paid.

53. Jon, age 58, bought a home in 2008 for $346,000. Three years later, he sold the home for $374,800 and moved into an apartment. In computing Jon's income tax, what amount of this transaction is taxable?

a. $11,320
b. $16,980
c. $28,800
d. Nothing is taxable; Jon's capital gain is within the exemption guidelines.

54. Kevin moved into an abandoned home and installed new cabinets in the kitchen. When the owner discovered the occupancy, the owner had Kevin ejected. What is the status of the kitchen cabinets?

a. Kevin has no right to the cabinets.
b. The cabinets remain because they are trade fixtures.
c. Although the cabinets stay, Kevin is entitled to the value of the improvements.
d. Kevin can keep the cabinets if they can be removed without damaging the real estate.

55. Walter, Frank, and Joe are joint tenants. Joe sells his interest to Larry, and then Frank dies. As a result, which of the following statements is TRUE?

a. Frank's heirs are joint tenants with Larry and Walter.
b. Frank's heirs and Walter are joint tenants, but Larry is a tenant in common.
c. Walter is a tenant in common with Larry's and Frank's heirs.
d. Walter and Larry are tenants in common.

56. In a settlement statement, the selling price ALWAYS is

a. a debit to the buyer.
b. a debit to the seller.
c. a credit to the buyer.
d. greater than the loan amount.

57. The state wants to acquire a strip of farmland to build a highway. Does the state have the right to acquire privately owned land for public use?

a. Yes: the state's right is called condemnation.
b. Yes: the state's right is called eminent domain.
c. Yes: the state's right is called escheat.
d. No: Under the U.S. Constitution, private property may never be taken by state governments or the federal government.

58. Rhonda's estate was distributed according to her will as follows: 54 percent to her husband, 18 percent to her children, 16 percent to her grandchildren, and the remainder to her college. The college received $79,000. How much did Rhonda's children receive?

a. $105,333   c. $355,500
b. $118,500   d. $658,333

59. Which of the following is an example of external obsolescence?

a. Numerous pillars supporting the ceiling in a store
b. Leaks in the roof of a warehouse, making the premises unusable and therefore unrentable
c. Coal cellar in a house with central heating
d. Vacant, abandoned, and run-down buildings in an area

60. Which of the following phrases, when placed in a print advertisement, would comply with the requirements of the *Truth-in-Lending Act (Regulation Z)*?

a. "12 percent interest"
b. "12 percent rate"
c. "12 percent annual interest"
d. "12 percent annual percentage rate"

61. Which statement is *FALSE* regarding a capitalization rate?

a. The rate increases when the risk increases.
b. An increase in rate means a decrease in value.
c. The net income is divided by the rate to estimate value.
d. A decrease in rate results in a decrease in value.

62. The Equal Credit Opportunity Act makes it illegal for lenders to refuse credit to or otherwise discriminate against which of the following applicants?

a. Parent of twins who receives public assistance and who cannot afford the monthly mortgage payments
b. New homebuyer who does not have a favorable credit history
c. Single person who receives public assistance
d. Unemployed person with no job prospects and no identifiable source of income

63. When Polly died, a deed was found in her desk drawer. While the deed had never been recorded, it was signed, dated, and acknowledged. The deed gave Polly's house to a local charity. Polly's will, however, provided as follows: "I leave all of the real and personal property that I own to my beloved nephew, Robert." In this situation, the house *MOST LIKELY* will go to the

a. charity because acknowledgment creates a presumption of delivery.
b. charity because Polly's intent was clear from the deed.
c. nephew because Polly still owned the house when she died.
d. nephew because the deed had not been recorded.

64. If Margaret takes out a $90,000 loan at 7½ percent interest to be repaid at the end of 15 years with interest only paid annually, what is the total interest that Margaret will pay over the life of the loan?

a. $10,125
b. $80,000
c. $101,250
d. $180,000

65. After an offer is accepted, the seller finds that the broker was the undisclosed agent for the buyer as well as the agent for the seller. The seller may

a. withdraw without obligation to broker or buyer.
b. withdraw but would be subject to liquidated damages.
c. withdraw but only with the concurrence of the buyer.
d. refuse to sell but would be subject to a suit for specific performance.

66. To net the owner $90,000 after a 6 percent commission is paid, the selling price would have to be

a. $95,400.
b. $95,745.
c. $95,906.
d. $96,000.

67. Which of the following would *MOST LIKELY* be legal under the provisions of the *Civil Rights Act of 1968*?

a. A lender refuses to make loans in areas where more than 25 percent of the population is Hispanic.
b. A private country club development ties home ownership to club membership, but due to local demographics, all club members are white.
c. A church excludes African Americans from membership and rents its nonprofit housing to church members only.
d. A licensee directs prospective buyers away from areas where they are likely to feel uncomfortable because of their race.

68. It is discovered after a sale that the land parcel is 10 percent smaller than the owner represented it to be. The broker who passed this information on to the buyer is

    a. not liable as long as he only repeated the seller's data which he knew to be misrepresented.
    b. not liable if the misrepresentation was unintentional.
    c. not liable if the buyer actually inspected what she was getting.
    d. liable if he knew or should have known of the discrepancy.

69. On a residential lot 70 feet square, the side yard building setbacks are 10 feet, the front yard setback is 25 feet, and the rear yard setback is 20 feet. The maximum possible size for a single-story structure would be how many square feet?

    a. 1,000   c. 1,250
    b. 1,200   d. 4,900

70. All of the following are violations of the *Real Estate Settlement Procedures Act* (RESPA) EXCEPT

    a. providing a completed HUD-1 Uniform Settlement Statement to a borrower one day before the closing.
    b. accepting a kickback on a loan subject to RESPA requirements.
    c. requiring a particular title insurance company.
    d. accepting a fee or charging for services that were not performed.

71. The rescission provisions of the *Truth-in-Lending Act* apply to which of the following transactions?

    a. Home purchase loans
    b. Construction lending
    c. Business financing
    d. Consumer credit

72. A property has a net income of $30,000. An appraiser decides to use a 12 percent capitalization rate rather than a 10 percent rate on this property. The use of the higher rate results in

    a. a 2 percent increase in the appraised value.
    b. a $50,000 increase in the appraised value.
    c. a $50,000 decrease in the appraised value.
    d. no change in the appraised value.

73. The section of a purchase contract that provides for the buyer to forfeit any earnest money if the buyer fails to complete the purchase is known as the provision for

    a. liquidated damages.
    b. punitive damages.
    c. hypothecation.
    d. subordination.

74. In one commercial building, the tenant intends to start a health food shop using her life savings. In an identical adjacent building is a showroom leased to a major national retailing chain. Both tenants have long-term leases with identical rents. Which of the following statements is correct?

    a. If the values of the buildings were the same before the leases, the values will be the same after the leases.
    b. An appraiser would most likely use a higher capitalization rate for the store leased to the national retailing chain.
    c. The most accurate appraisal method an appraiser could use would be the sales comparison approach to value.
    d. The building with the health food shop will probably appraise for less than the other building.

75. A first-time homebuyer finds that he is unlikely to qualify for a mortgage under current interest rates. His parents agree to pay a lump sum in cash to the lender at closing to offset the high rate. What type of loan is this?

    a. Equity
    b. Participation
    c. Open-end
    d. Buydown

76. A $100,000 loan at 12 percent could be amortized with monthly payments of $1,200.22 on a 15-year basis or payments of $1,028.63 on a 30-year basis. The 30-year loan results in total payments of what percent of the 15-year loan's total payments?

    a. 146 percent   c. 171 percent
    b. 158 percent   d. 228 percent

77. According to a broker's CMA, a property is worth $125,000. The homeowner bought the property for $90,000 and added $50,000 in improvements, for a total of $140,000. The property sold for $122,500. Which of these amounts represents the property's market price?
    a. $90,000
    b. $122,500
    c. $125,000
    d. $140,000

78. What will be the amount of tax payable where the property's assessed value is $85,000 and the tax rate is 40 mills in a community in which an equalization factor of 110 percent is used?
    a. $2,337.50
    b. $3,090.91
    c. $3,700.40
    d. $3,740.00

79. In a settlement statement, how will a proration of prepaid water, gas, and electric charges be reflected?
    a. Debit to the seller, credit to the buyer
    b. Debit to the buyer, credit to the seller
    c. Debit to the buyer only
    d. Credit to the seller only

80. An apartment manager decides not to purchase flood insurance. Instead, the manager installs raised platforms in the basement storage areas and has the furnace placed on eight-inch legs. This form of risk management is known as
    a. avoiding the risk.
    b. controlling the risk.
    c. retaining the risk.
    d. transferring the risk.

81. A real estate broker was responsible for a chain of events that resulted in the sale of one of his client's properties. The broker is legally referred to as the
    a. initiating factor.
    b. procuring cause.
    c. responsible party.
    d. compensible cause.

82. A characteristic of a real estate salesperson who is an independent contractor is that he or she commonly receives
    a. more than 50 percent of her or his income in the form of a monthly salary or hourly wage.
    b. company-provided health insurance and other benefits.
    c. reimbursement for documented travel and business expenses.
    d. more than 90 percent of her or his income based on sales production.

83. In the cost approach to value, the appraiser makes use of
    a. the owner's original cost of the building.
    b. the estimated current replacement cost of the building.
    c. the sales prices of similar buildings in the area.
    d. the assessed value of the building.

84. Janet enters into an exclusive-agency buyer agency agreement with a real estate broker. Based on these facts, which of the following statements is TRUE?
    a. Janet is obligated to pay the broker's compensation regardless of who finds a suitable property.
    b. If Janet finds a suitable property without the broker's assistance, she is under no obligation to pay the broker.
    c. Janet may enter into other, similar agreements with other brokers.
    d. If Janet finds a suitable property without the broker's assistance, Janet will have to pay the broker's compensation.

85. An owner is usually concerned about how much money she can get when she sells her home. A competitive market analysis may help the seller determine a realistic listing price. Which of the following is *TRUE* of a CMA?

a. A competitive market analysis is the same as an appraisal.
b. A broker, not a salesperson, is permitted to prepare a competitive market analysis.
c. A competitive market analysis is prepared by a certified real estate appraiser.
d. A competitive market analysis contains a compilation of other similar properties that have sold.

86. An owner sells his fourplex. In regard to this situation, which of the following is *TRUE*?

a. The tenants may void their leases.
b. The lender may void the leases.
c. The current leases must be honored by the new landlord.
d. The current leases may be discharged by the previous landlord.

87. When appraising a single-family home, the appraiser would *NOT* consider which of the following in determining the value of a property?

a. Date sold
b. Racial demographics
c. Square feet of living area
d. Date of comparable sales

88. Which of the following is *NOT* an essential element of a contract?

a. Date
b. Consideration
c. Meeting of the minds
d. Signatures of the parties authorized to perform

89. One general rule of the Federal Do Not Call regulations is that

a. states must maintain separate do-no-call lists.
b. the national registry must be searched once a year.
c. real estate offices are exempt from the laws because they are not telemarketers.
d. it is illegal to make an unsolicited phone call to a number listed on the national registry.

90. Federal regulations on unsolicited e-mail

a. require commercial e-mails to include a physical address for the sender.
b. require prior permission of recipients in order to send e-mail to them.
c. require that e-mail lists be scrubbed every 31 days.
d. exempt phone calls to individuals with whom the office has a prior business relationship.

EXAM TWO PART TWO—ILLINOIS REAL ESTATE LAW AND PRACTICE

1. A transaction is closing on May 2 in a non-leap year. Which of the following is the correct proration of an annual charge of $560, using the statutory variation method?
   a. $188.78
   b. $189.68
   c. $190.78
   d. $191.98

2. Under Illinois law, what is the statutory ceiling on the prepayment penalty a lender may charge on loans secured by real estate that bear more than 8 percent annual interest?
   a. 1 percent
   b. 3 percent
   c. 8 percent
   d. There is none

3. All of the following are *TRUE* of leases in Illinois *EXCEPT* a(n)
   a. lease for 15 months would have to be in writing to be enforceable.
   b. lease for a term that begins one year after the date of signing would have to be in writing to be enforceable.
   c. lease for six months would have to be in writing to be enforceable.
   d. oral lease for 12 months could be enforceable.

4. What principle of landlord-tenant relations was established by the Illinois Supreme Court in 1972?
   a. Interest payments required on certain security deposits
   b. Landlord damages for a tenant's failure to vacate the premises
   c. Implied warranty of habitability in residential tenancies
   d. Landlord may forcibly remove a tenant without court action under the doctrine of "self-help"

5. In Illinois, if a landlord purposely fails to maintain an apartment building's furnace and plumbing, what option is available to a tenant whose apartment is without heat and water during the first three months of winter?
   a. Suit for constructive eviction
   b. Suit for actual eviction
   c. Suit for forcible detainer
   d. Suit for negligent default

6. Betty pays $1,250 per month for her apartment. If Betty refers three new tenants to the building's owner during the year, how much is she entitled to receive under the *Real Estate License Act of 2000* if the landlord's normal referral fee is $500 per new tenant?
   a. Nothing, unless Betty is a licensed real estate broker, salesperson, or rental-finding agent
   b. $1,000
   c. $1,250
   d. $1,500

7. All of the following properties are exempt from paying real estate taxes *EXCEPT*
   a. cities and counties.
   b. hospitals.
   c. educational institutions.
   d. condominiums.

8. Under the *Illinois Human Rights Act*, an "elderly person" is defined as any person who is over
   a. 40.   c. 62.
   b. 55.   d. 65.

9. The *Illinois Human Rights Act* specifically exempts all of the following *EXCEPT*
   a. gender-based discrimination in housing intended for single-gender occupancy.
   b. religious organizations giving preference in housing to members (unless membership is based on discriminatory factors).
   c. a three-unit apartment building, with the owner living in one of the units.
   d. a five-unit apartment building, in which one of the units is occupied by a resident manager.

10. Many of the residents of Randy's apartment building are elderly, and some are in poor health. To ensure that they are not disturbed, Randy politely declines to rent units to families or individuals who have young children. However, Randy provides such persons with a printed list of nearby apartment buildings that welcome children. Based on these facts, which of the following statements is *TRUE*?

    a. By providing a printed list of alternative comparable housing, Randy is in full compliance with the *Illinois Human Rights Act*.

    b. Because Randy's primary intent is to protect existing tenants' quality of life, and not to discriminate against prospective tenants who have young children, the *Illinois Human Rights Act* does not apply to this situation.

    c. Randy's policy violates the *Illinois Human Rights Act*.

    d. While Randy's policy, as stated, violates the *Illinois Human Rights Act*, he could add a "no children" provision to leases offered to new tenants and avoid violating the act.

11. What is the relationship between the Illinois agency statutes and the common law of agency?

    a. Illinois agency statutes supersede the common law of agency in Illinois.

    b. Illinois agency statutes and the common law of agency both govern agency relationships in Illinois.

    c. Agency statutes are simply an administrative codification of the common law of agency.

    d. The Illinois agency statutes govern broker's relationships with clients, while the common law of agency applies to salesperson relationships.

12. Which of the following is an example of a "ministerial act" under the Illinois agency law?

    a. Arguing the merits of an offer on behalf of a prospective buyer

    b. Helping prospective buyers determine an appropriate price range and geographic location for their home search

    c. Responding to general questions about the price and location of a specific property

    d. Assisting a buyer through the closing process

13. Gloria, a real estate broker, commonly names individual salespersons in her brokerage office as the exclusive agents of certain clients, leaving the other salespeople free to represent other parties in a transaction. Which of the following statements is *TRUE* regarding this practice?

    a. Because it is a common office practice, it is permitted as an exception to the general statutory prohibition against such arrangements.

    b. Designated agency arrangements such as this are specifically permitted by the Illinois agency law.

    c. This is an example of designated agency, which is an illegal relationship under the Illinois agency law.

    d. Gloria will be considered an undisclosed dual agent under these facts and will be in violation of Illinois law.

14. A broker decides to "sweeten" an MLS listing for a property by making a blanket offer of subagency. Is the broker's action acceptable?

    a. Yes, because Illinois law permits the creation of subagency relationships only through multiple listing services.

    b. Yes, because a subagency relationship may be created by either a blanket offer in an MLS or through a specific agreement between parties.

    c. No, because subagency is illegal under *Article 15 of the Real Estate License Act of 2000*.

    d. No, because subagency relationships may not be offered through an MLS in Illinois.

15. Salesperson Donna represents the seller in a transaction. When prospective buyers ask to look at the property, which of the following must Donna do?

    a. Tell them that they must first enter into a buyer representation agreement with another licensee.

    b. Clearly disclose in writing that Donna represents the seller's interests.

    c. Inform them that if a transaction results, a dual agency may be the best course of action.

    d. Show them the property without making any disclosures about Donna's relationship with the seller because the best time to close is at contract signing.

16. Several years ago, Unit 5B in the Grand Towers condominium was the site of a brutal and highly publicized murder. The unit was sold to an elderly woman who contracted the AIDS virus in a blood transfusion and died in the unit last year. As the agent for the woman's estate, what are your disclosure responsibilities to prospective purchasers of Unit 5B in this situation?
    a. You must disclose both the murder and the AIDS-related death.
    b. You are specifically required to disclose the AIDS death and may (at seller discretion) disclose the murder.
    c. You are specifically prohibited by federal law from disclosing AIDS.
    d. You must not disclose the murder, but you should disclose the AIDS-related death.

17. In Illinois, an unlicensed real estate assistant may perform which activity?
    a. Negotiate commission
    b. Prepare legal documents required for a closing
    c. Prepare and distribute flyers and promotional materials
    d. Explain simple contract documents to prospective buyers

18. Illegal discrimination might result in any of the following actions *EXCEPT*
    a. The need to do community service
    b. Loss of license
    c. Fines up to $25,000
    d. Loss of protection by errors and omissions insurance

19. Kate's unlicensed assistant, Tina, worked late nights and weekends to help ensure the successful closing of a difficult transaction. At Kate's direction, Tina's extra work included making several phone calls to the prospective buyers, encouraging them to accept the seller's counteroffer. Largely because of Tina's efforts, the sale went through with no problem. Kate wants to pay Tina a percentage of the commission, "because Tina has really earned it." Under Illinois law, what should Kate do?
    a. Illinois law permits Kate to compensate Tina in the form of a commission under the circumstances described here because Tina was clearly directed to do the work described.
    b. While Kate may not pay Tina a cash commission, Kate is permitted to make a gift of tangible personal property.
    c. Kate should pay no commission to Tina. Kate's direction and Tina's work violated Illinois law. Payment of commission would also violate the law.
    d. Kate may pay a commission to Tina only if Tina is an independent contractor.

20. If a buyer wants to have a clause included in the sales contract under which the seller offers assurances against the existence of werewolves, vampires, and trolls on the property, which of the following statements is *TRUE* in Illinois?
    a. The broker may include the clause because such standard supernatural disclosures are in general usage.
    b. Only the buyer or a licensed attorney may prepare the clause for inclusion in the sales contract.
    c. In Illinois, brokers are permitted to add additional clauses to blank form contracts, such as the clause described here, that do not directly involve the conveyance of title to real property.
    d. Under Illinois law, a frivolous clause, such as the one described here, is not permitted and any contract containing such a clause will be void.

21. Broker Rodney enters into a listing agreement with a seller. Under the terms of the agreement, when the property sells, the seller will receive a guaranteed $75,000. Any amount left over after the seller's $75,000 will constitute Rodney's compensation. Based on these facts, which of the following statements is *TRUE* in Illinois?

    a. This type of arrangement, called a *guaranteed sales agreement,* is illegal in Illinois, and Rodney will be disciplined for entering into it.

    b. This type of arrangement, called a *net listing,* is illegal in Illinois, and Rodney will be disciplined for entering into it.

    c. This is an example of a *guaranteed sales agreement,* which is permissible in Illinois if Rodney provides the seller with the necessary disclosures.

    d. This is an example of a *net listing,* which is discouraged (but not illegal) in Illinois.

22. In Illinois, which of the following in a listing agreement would result in the suspension or revocation of a licensee's license to practice real estate?

    a. A specified commission rate
    b. No specific termination date
    c. No broker protection clause
    d. A specific termination date

23. Which disclosure must be included in a listing contract under Illinois law?

    a. Anticipated seller closing costs
    b. Tax identification number
    c. Seller's net return
    d. Disposition of earnest money in the event of a purchaser default

24. Lou and Missy are a married couple living in Springfield, Illinois. Missy is the owner of their home. If Lou and Missy decide to sell their home and move to Wisconsin, who is required to sign the listing agreement?

    a. Both Lou and Missy must sign the listing.

    b. Because Missy is the sole owner of their home, she is the only party legally required to sign the listing.

    c. Because Lou and Missy are married, the signature of either spouse is legally sufficient.

    d. Lou is required to sign the listing only if Missy plans to use the capital gains exclusion.

25. From what source do Illinois local units of government receive their powers of eminent domain?

    a. A grant of authority signed by the governor
    b. Article 5 of the U.S. Constitution
    c. The Illinois Statehood Charter of 1818 and the Code of Administrative Procedure
    d. The Illinois Constitution and Code of Civil Procedure

26. Peg dies without leaving a will. If Peg owns real property in Illinois and has no heirs, what will happen to her real property?

    a. Peg's real property will be taken by the county in which it is located under the power of eminent domain.

    b. Ownership of Peg's real property will go to the state of Illinois through escheat.

    c. Peg's property will escheat to the county in which it is located.

    d. Peg's property will escheat to the county in which she last resided prior to her death.

27. Is there any limitation on an original grantor's right of reverter in Illinois?

    a. Yes: Both an original grantor's right of reverter and the enforceability of the underlying condition expire by law after 20 years.

    b. Yes: The original grantor's right of reverter continues for 40 years, although the underlying condition remains enforceable.

    c. Yes: Both the original grantor's right of reverter and the underlying condition automatically expire after 99 years.

    d. No: Under Illinois law there is no limitation on an original grantor's future interest.

28. Which of the following legal life estates could be available to a surviving husband in Illinois?

    a. Homestead
    b. Dower
    c. Curtesy
    d. A marital easement

29. How much of an estate of homestead is an individual entitled to in Illinois?

    a. $3,250   c. $15,000
    b. $5,000   d. $10,000

30. Elliot and Diane live in Moline, Illinois. They were married on July 10, 2006. On June 15, 2001, Elliot purchased Maroon Manor. On July 15, 2007, Diane inherited Riverview Terrace. On August 5, 2008, Elliot purchased Orion Farm. On August 10, Diane sold Riverview Terrace and bought Blackhawk Acres. Based on these facts, which of the following best describes the interests held by Elliot and Diane under Illinois law in the event the marriage is dissolved?

 a. Under the Illinois community property laws, Elliot and Diane are equal co-owners of all three properties.

 b. Maroon Manor and Blackhawk Acres are nonmarital property; Orion Farm is marital property.

 c. Maroon Manor is nonmarital property; Orion Farm is marital property; Blackhawk Acres is marital property by transmutation.

 d. All three properties are considered marital property.

31. Real property locations in Illinois are described by their geographic relation to all of the following EXCEPT the

 a. Second Principal Meridian.
 b. Third Principal Meridian.
 c. Fourth Principal Meridian.
 d. Fifth Principal Meridian.

32. How often is the assessed valuation of all real estate in Illinois adjusted by county authorities?

 a. Quarterly
 b. Annually
 c. Biennially
 d. Every three years

33. Nadia, an Illinois resident, was born on March 6, 1990. When will Nadia become of legal age?

 a. March 6, 2008
 b. March 7, 2008
 c. March 6, 2009
 d. March 7, 2011

34. If a minor enters into a contract in Illinois, what is the statutory period within which she or he may legally void the contract after reaching the age of majority?

 a. 6 months
 b. 1 year
 c. The contract may be voided only up to the date when the minor reaches the age of majority; after that date, the contract is binding.
 d. There is no statutory period.

35. Which of the following is essential to the validity of a deed in Illinois?

 a. A seal (or the word *seal*)
 b. Acknowledgment
 c. Granting clause
 d. Recording

36. In Illinois, the amount of consideration used to determine transfer taxes must be shown on a special form. What is the name of that form?

 a. The "Recording Form"
 b. The "Real Estate Declaration of Transfer"
 c. The "Blue Sheet"
 d. The "Tax Code Sheet"

37. How far back does a normal Illinois title search go?

 a. 15 years
 b. 40 years
 c. 75 years
 d. 125 years

38. All of the following are exempt from the provisions of the *Real Estate License Act of 2000,* EXCEPT a(n)

 a. property owner who sells or leases his or her own property.
 b. individual who receives compensation for procuring prospective renters of real estate.
 c. individual who is employed as a resident property manager.
 d. resident lessee who receives the equivalent of one month's rent as a "finder's fee" for referring a new tenant to the owner.

39. Which is a requirement for obtaining an Illinois broker's license?

 a. Having successfully completed 90 hours of approved real estate courses
 b. Being at least 18 years of age
 c. Being of good moral character
 d. Having been actively engaged as a licensed salesperson for at least three years

40. If Kayla successfully completed her Illinois real estate education requirement on November 1, 2007, what is the latest date on which she may take the state license exam?

 a. December 31, 2007
 b. November 1, 2009
 c. October 31, 2008
 d. October 31, 2010

41. What is the expiration date of every salesperson's license in Illinois?

    a. Their birthday, every other year
    b. April 30 of each odd-numbered year
    c. May 31 of each odd-numbered year
    d. Every other anniversary date of the individual salesperson's license

42. Broker Ken, an Illinois licensee, wants to open a branch office in a neighboring town. Ken applies for a branch office license and gives the branch a name that clearly identifies its relationship with his main office. Ken names Tony, a licensed Illinois real estate salesperson, as the branch office manager. Under these facts, will Ken receive approval for the branch office?

    a. Yes: Ken has fully complied with the requirements of the *Real Estate License Act of 2000*.
    b. No: Under the *Real Estate License Act of 2000*, brokers cannot have branch offices in more than one municipality.
    c. No: Branch office management requires a special license.
    d. No: the manager of a branch office must be a licensed real estate broker.

43. Max could tell that a prospective buyer would probably not make an offer if she knew the previous occupant of a property had died from complications due to AIDS and did not disclose that fact. Vince, an Illinois real estate broker, set up a "microbrokerage" real estate services outlet in a convenience store by placing a desk at the end of the snack food aisle. James waited outside an AMP testing facility and handed out brochures to prospective licensees on their way in to take the real estate exam, encouraging them to apply for a job at his office. Which, if any, of these individuals is subject to disciplinary action for violating the *Real Estate License Act of 2000*?

    a. Max only
    b. James only
    c. Max, Vince, and James
    d. Vince and James only

44. Which would be grounds for a disciplinary action?

    a. Being convicted of a felony in Illinois
    b. Advertising in a magazine that he or she is a member of the Chicago Association of REALTORS® when he or she is not
    c. Depositing escrow money into a personal account
    d. All of the above would be grounds for disciplinary action.

45. Salesperson Renee engaged in activities that constitute violations of the *Illinois Human Rights Act*, including blockbusting and discrimination on the basis of disability. Renee also cashed a $25,000 earnest money check from a prospective buyer and used the proceeds to buy a new car. Renee's employing broker was completely unaware of all of these activities. When Renee's violations are brought to the attention of the IDFPR, which of the following statements is *TRUE*?

    a. The employing broker will not have his or her license revoked as a result of Renee's violations.
    b. Renee's employing broker will be required to pay any fine imposed against Renee out of her or his own personal funds.
    c. Renee's violations are legally the responsibility of the employing broker, who will be subject to the same disciplinary action as Renee, regardless of whether she or he knew the violations had occurred.
    d. Renee's employing broker will be held liable for the *Human Rights Act* violations only.

46. A broker is convicted of a crime involving fraud in Wisconsin on November 9. On February 1 of the following year, the Wisconsin licensing agency notifies IDFPR of the conviction. Based on this information, which is *TRUE*?

    a. The broker should have called IDFPR first.
    b. IDFPR may refuse to renew the broker's license based on his Wisconsin conviction for a crime involving fraud.
    c. Because the conviction was not in Illinois, no discipline will occur.
    d. A conviction due to fraud does not constitute a violation of the Act.

47. Which of the following accurately describes the review process for a final administrative decision of the IDFPR?
   a. The accused may appeal a final administrative decision of the IDFPR directly to the Illinois Supreme Court.
   b. The accused may petition the circuit court of the county in which he or she resides. The circuit court's decision may be appealed directly to the Illinois Supreme Court.
   c. The accused may petition the circuit court of the county in which the property involved in the transaction that gave rise to the violation is located. The circuit court's decision may be appealed directly to the federal district court.
   d. The accused may request a rehearing by the IDFPR, but administrative decisions may not be appealed to any court.

48. If a limited liability company is convicted for the second time of engaging in real estate business activities without a license, what is the maximum penalty to which it may be subjected?
   a. A fine of no more than $2,000
   b. A fine of no less than $2,000 and no more than $5,000
   c. A fine of up to $10,000
   d. A fine of no less than $10,000 and no more than $25,000

49. Every Illinois salesperson who applies for renewal of his or her license must successfully complete a certain number of hours of continuing education courses in each two-year license renewal period. How many hours are required by Illinois law?
   a. Six
   b. Eight
   c. Nine
   d. Twelve

50. With regard to mortgage theory, Illinois is usually described as a(n)
   a. title-theory state.
   b. lien-theory state.
   c. intermediate-theory state.
   d. security-theory state.

51. Twenty years ago, Ron obtained a 30-year mortgage loan to purchase a home. The interest rate on the loan was 9.275 percent. Today, Ron is prepared to pay off the loan early. Based on these facts, which of the following statements is *TRUE* in Illinois?
   a. Ron's lender is entitled by statute to charge Ron a prepayment penalty equal to one year's interest on the current balance of the loan.
   b. Ron's lender is permitted by Illinois statute to charge Ron a prepayment penalty of no more than 8 percent of the current outstanding balance of the loan.
   c. Illinois does not take an official statutory position on the issue of prepayment penalties.
   d. Because Ron's interest rate is greater than 8 percent, the lender may not charge a prepayment penalty under Illinois law.

52. In Illinois, if a landlord wants to terminate a year-to-year tenancy, how much notice must the tenant receive?
   a. 7 days
   b. 30 days
   c. 60 days
   d. 4 months

53. In Illinois, which of the following is *TRUE* of an individual who wishes to engage only in the leasing of residential real property?
   a. He or she must obtain a salesperson's license and associate with a broker who specializes in residential leases.
   b. He or she may obtain a certified leasing-agent designation by passing a test.
   c. He or she may obtain a limited leasing-agent license by completing 15 hours of instruction and passing a written examination.
   d. He or she may engage in residential leasing activities without obtaining a license or other certification.

54. All of the following are exempt from the anti-discriminatory provisions of the *Illinois Human Rights Act* EXCEPT

    a. owner-occupied apartment buildings of ten units or any lesser number.

    b. private rooms in a private home occupied by the home's owner.

    c. rooms rented only to persons of one sex.

    d. private, single-family homes sold by their owners if the owner holds fewer than three properties, the home was last occupied by the owner, and it was sold without the assistance of a licensee and without the use of discriminatory advertising.

55. If an annual charge of $560 is prorated in October using the statutory variation method, which of the following will be the resulting daily charge?

    a. $1.51

    b. $1.53

    c. $1.54

    d. $1.56

56. Which of the following terms is NOT associated with water rights?

    a. Littoral

    b. Ingress

    c. Riparian

    d. Doctrine of prior appropriation

57. Zoning ordinances may regulate all of the following EXCEPT

    a. density.

    b. floor area ratios.

    c. downzoning.

    d. ownership in severality.

58. Which of the following is NOT true regarding option contracts?

    a. An option contract is classified as a unilateral contract.

    b. An option contract that has been exercised is classified as a bilateral contract.

    c. The option money may or may not be applied toward the purchase price.

    d. The seller is the optionee and the buyer is the optionor.

59. All of the following are assignable contracts EXCEPT a

    a. note.

    b. mortgage.

    c. lease.

    d. listing contract.

60. Which of the following would NOT terminate a listing contract?

    a. Death of the broker

    b. Destruction of the property

    c. Death of the sales associate

    d. Bankruptcy of the seller

EXAM THREE—ILLINOIS LICENSE LAW AND PRACTICE

1. Under the *Real Estate License Act of 2000*, what does "Advisory Council" refer to?

   a. The Real Estate Education Advisory Council
   b. The Advisory Council that enforces the Rules
   c. The framers of the license act itself
   d. A business management consulting body for local Associations of REALTORS®

2. Under the *Real Estate License Act of 2000*, what body does the Director oversee?

   a. Department of Real Estate Regulation
   b. The Real Estate Education Association
   c. Legislators Concerned for Real Estate
   d. The Division of Professional Regulation

3. Under the *Real Estate License Act of 2000*, which of the following need to be licensed?

   a. Personal assistants who only sit at public open houses
   b. Agents who do not collect rents on more than 25 units
   c. Those who work only with buyers (never take listings)
   d. All of the above

4. What is the primary purpose of the Real Estate Recovery Fund?

   a. It is a legal defense fund for REALTORS® who cannot pay their legal debts.
   b. It is to reimburse consumers who have been wronged by a licensee's actions.
   c. It is for IDFPR to use at will when a current year's budget is exceeded.
   d. It is used for recovery of unpaid commissions.

5. Which of the following statements regarding broker licensing is true?

   a. They now need to take 120 hours of classroom education.
   b. They no longer need to have a salesperson license for one year prior to taking the broker's exam.
   c. They may take prelicensing classes online if the courses are approved.
   d. All of the above are true.

6. What is the composition of the Real Estate Administration and Disciplinary Board?

   a. Nine members appointed by the Governor
   b. Eight members elected by local REALTOR® associations
   c. Eight members appointed by the Director
   d. Six members elected by the public

7. How long are the membership terms on "The Board"?

   a. Three-year staggered terms
   b. Two years each
   c. Four-year staggered terms
   d. Three years with a possible three-year renewal

8. The Real Estate Research and Education Fund each year receives what amount, and from what source?

   a. $100,000 from the state of Illinois
   b. $50,000 from voluntarily collected funds of licensees
   c. $125,000 from the Real Estate License Administration Fund
   d. $80,000 from licensees' fines placed in a Research and Education Fund escrow

9. Under the *Real Estate License Act of 2000*, who among the following could work in a limited way indefinitely without a specific license?

   a. Personal assistant hired by a broker-associate
   b. Leasing agent hired by a property management company
   c. Salesperson hired by a real estate sales office
   d. Broker working independently

10. The number of hours of continuing education that can be taken in one day

    a. is not regulated by the law.
    b. cannot be more than six hours.
    c. cannot be more than nine hours.
    d. can be up to twelve hours.

11. When does a salesperson's license expire?

    a. On the date it was first acquired, every two years

    b. On April 30 of each odd-numbered year

    c. On July 31 of each even-numbered year

    d. On January 1, every third year

12. Why is early discussion of agency so important under the *Real Estate License Act of 2000*?

    a. Working with a consumer may now be construed as an implied agency if nothing else has been stated.

    b. Working with a consumer may compel the consumer to pay a commission, whether or not a written agreement exists.

    c. If nothing is stated, subagency may be in effect.

    d. If nothing is stated, a minimum hourly fee may be demanded after the fact.

13. If you do not receive a license renewal form in the mail

    a. you must respond within three months of the date of the scheduled renewal.

    b. you must respond by the scheduled renewal date or you will only have two additional weeks grace period.

    c. you may renew your license up to six months later with a $25 fine.

    d. you must no longer practice real estate after the expiration date on your license.

14. Prelicense courses will have to be taken again if a license has been expired for more than

    a. six months.

    b. one year.

    c. eighteen months.

    d. two years.

15. Who would *NOT* need a signed written employment agreement in Illinois for working with a sponsoring broker?

    a. Leasing agent

    b. Salesperson

    c. Other brokers in the firm

    d. Co-op broker

16. Under the *Real Estate License Act of 2000*, a buyer to whom you are showing houses under a buyer-broker agreement is considered to be

    a. without a formal relationship.

    b. a customer.

    c. a client.

    d. a possible client.

17. Which statement could an Illinois buyer's agent appropriately make to his or her buyer client?

    a. "Here are the CMAs. I think they suggest the highest range you should pay is about $110,000–$120,000, but that's up to you."

    b. "The listing agent said the floors underneath the carpet are oak. Isn't that great?"

    c. "I know this neighborhood. Don't worry about radon."

    d. "There really isn't any way to get a list of released sex offenders' addresses in Illinois."

18. Employment agreements with a broker must cover at least

    a. supervision, duties, referral fees, and MLS requirements.

    b. referral fees, commission splits, and cooperation with other brokers.

    c. supervision, duties, compensation, and termination.

    d. salary and benefits agreed on.

19. Who needs to disclose material facts related to a transaction in Illinois?

    a. Listing agent

    b. Buyer's agent

    c. Sellers

    d. All of the above, if they have material information

20. What is always *TRUE* of licensed personal assistants under the *Real Estate License Act of 2000*?

    a. They must be licensed as brokers.

    b. They need an employment agreement with either the salesperson or the broker with whom they work day to day.

    c. They are usually paid directly by the person who selected them and with whom they work most closely.

    d. They need an employment agreement with the sponsoring broker and must be paid by the sponsoring broker.

21. What is *TRUE* about real estate advertising in Illinois under the *Real Estate License Act of 2000*?

   a. The company name must appear in a print ad for houses.
   b. Whenever the company name does appear, it must be in letters larger than the salesperson's name.
   c. Links on a salesperson's real estate Web site must routinely be approved by IDFPR.
   d. On an Internet site, the company name is usually not needed.

22. Which of the following would you *NOT* need to disclose in Illinois?

   a. To a buyer: the fact that the seller is your client
   b. To a seller's agent: the fact that your buyer client qualifies for the purchase price with only $5,000 to spare
   c. To a customer who is just starting to work with you: the fact that he or she is a customer, but that agency is possible and may very quickly be presumed in Illinois if nothing else is said
   d. To a buyer client: the fact that you hold a 1.1 percent interest in a property he or she wants to buy

23. What is *TRUE* about the typeface of ads under the *Real Estate License Act of 2000*?

   a. The name of the licensee should always be smaller than the name of the company.
   b. The name of the company should always be at least as large as the name of the licensee.
   c. The name of the company must appear first.
   d. There is no statement or rule regarding relative size of agent name and company name.

24. Who may pay compensation to a salesperson or broker associate in Illinois?

   a. Listing salesperson in the office
   b. Sponsoring broker
   c. Title company
   d. Mortgage company

25. Who may sue for commission in Illinois?

   a. The listing broker and listing salesperson
   b. The client
   c. The sponsoring broker
   d. Only the salesperson directly involved

26. Which of the following may *NOT* be offered to consumers in Illinois?

   a. Coupons to the local grocery store if they list
   b. Discounts on commission if they list
   c. A new television if they buy
   d. A finder's fee for referring client prospects

27. Which of the following may be offered to an Illinois licensee for referring business to a lawyer or loan officer?

   a. A weekend in Peoria
   b. A small stereo
   c. A cash amount under $200
   d. None of the above

28. What would *NOT* happen under the *Real Estate License Act of 2000* for offenses noted in the Act?

   a. License revoked
   b. $25,000 fine
   c. $5,000 fine
   d. Commissions seized

29. For which of the following could you be late in Illinois without affecting your license renewal?

   a. Student loans
   b. Illinois income tax
   c. Child support
   d. Mortgage

30. Dual agency conflict of interest is best avoided in Illinois by way of

   a. implied dual agency.
   b. designated agency.
   c. special agency.
   d. co-op agency.

31. Under the *Real Estate License Act of 2000*, when the license of any sponsoring broker is suspended or revoked, what is *TRUE* with regard to sales licensees' agreements with that sponsoring broker?

   a. They expire on the date of suspension.
   b. Each licensee has ten days in which to find another broker.
   c. A licensee can continue to work through the suspension.
   d. The licensee has 30 days in which to finish all deals.

32. A sponsored licensee can now sell "by owner"

a. if the broker agrees.
b. with the changes in the new license act.
c. only if he or she lives in the home.
d. only once per year.

33. An Illinois salesperson has been showing other agents' listings to a buyer but that buyer has not signed an agency agreement. Nothing else has been said. The buyer is

a. unrepresented.
b. a client.
c. a consumer.
d. a customer.

34. Real estate licensees are frequently referred to as *agents*. This is technically correct in Illinois because they are *ALWAYS* what?

a. General agents for the sponsoring broker
b. Universal agents for the seller
c. Special agents for the lender
d. General agents for consumers

35. Which of the following licensee statements would be appropriate in Illinois?

a. Licensee answering a call-in customer's question: "The standard commission is 6 percent."
b. Listing agent to buyer's agent: "List price is $200,000, but my seller will probably sell for about $195,000."
c. Buyers' agent to listing agent: "My buyers need to buy this weekend, so I think we can get this deal together."
d. Licensed salesperson to a licensed personal assistant: "Thanks for your help on this transaction, but I can't cut you a check."

36. How are the terms *statutory law* and *common law* intertwined historically in the law of agency in Illinois?

a. Illinois real estate law actively cites both common law and statutory law, but in a real estate conflict common law always supercedes.
b. Illinois real estate law is historically grounded in common law; the current statutory laws were influenced by it.
c. Common law dominates and supersedes statutory law in most real estate situations, but the statutes apply in all other cases.
d. Common law is federal; statutory law is state law.

37. An unlicensed individual who engages in activities for which a real estate license is required is subject to which of the following penalties?

a. A fine not to exceed $1,000
b. A fine not to exceed $5,000 and one year imprisonment
c. A civil penalty of $25,000 in addition to possible other penalties stipulated by law
d. A civil penalty not to exceed $25,000 and a mandatory prison term not to exceed five years

38. When a salesperson passes the license examination, the first proof of the eligibility to engage in real estate activities in Illinois is a

a. sponsor card.
b. pocket card.
c. license.
d. pass card.

39. Of the following types of insurance policies used in this state, which is *MOST LIKELY* to meet full replacement cost of a destroyed property (possibly exceeding the stated policy value)?

a. Actual cash value
b. Cash value with coinsurance
c. Basic "plus"
d. Guaranteed replacement cost

40. Under the *Real Estate License Act of 2000*, the exception to the rule that a licensee may accept compensation only from his or her sponsoring broker occurs

a. if the buyer chooses to pay his or her agent directly.
b. when assisting a FSBO and the FSBO wishes to compensate the agent.
c. when a transaction closes that was put together while the agent worked for a previous sponsoring broker.
d. when none of the above happens.

41. To qualify for a nonresident license, an out-of-state broker must do which of the following?

a. Be an active broker for at least five years immediately preceding application
b. Open a definite, permanent, and conspicuous place of business within Illinois
c. Take and pass the entire salesperson exam
d. Be licensed in a state that has enacted a reciprocal licensing agreement with Illinois

42. What should a buyer's agent check first if a buyer indicates he or she absolutely will *NOT* want to buy a home in a floodplain?

   a. The listings in the MLS computer
   b. The seller disclosure form for a given home
   c. Floodplain maps for the area(s) in which the buyer is interested
   d. House addresses available through FEMA

43. What will an Illinois agent's errors and omissions insurance certainly *NOT* cover?

   a. An agent who is being sued for failure to disclose urea-formaldehyde insulation
   b. An agent who is being sued because a client fell down the stairs at a showing
   c. An agent who obeyed seller instructions not to show a house to a certain ethnic group
   d. An agent who poorly handled a dual agency situation

44. The *Real Estate License Act of 2000* provides for fines up to

   a. $5,000.
   b. $10,000.
   c. $25,000.
   d. $50,000.

45. In Illinois, which of the following would be inappropriate?

   a. An attorney providing a cash referral directly to a salesperson for recommending the attorney in a transaction
   b. A buyer's agent for a client preparing multiple CMAs for the buyer
   c. A tenant receiving $1,000 in one year for referrals of tenants
   d. A licensed personal assistant showing a property

46. What is the guideline for when agency should be disclosed in Illinois?

   a. No later than 48 hours after meeting a customer
   b. No later than 72 hours after meeting a customer
   c. As early as possible
   d. During negotiations

47. How is the problem of dual agency often avoided today in Illinois?

   a. Companies must refer the buyer to another company.
   b. Companies do not disclose dual agency.
   c. One designated agent is assigned to each client.
   d. A transactional arbitrator is brought in.

48. What is the status of disclosed dual agency in Illinois in the first few years of the twenty-first century?

   a. Void
   b. Legal
   c. Illegal
   d. Voidable

49. Under the *Real Estate License Act of 2000*, what must be in writing?

   a. Grantee's signature on the deed
   b. All listings
   c. Exclusive-agency and exclusive-right-to-sell listings
   d. Agency between a buyer and a broker

50. Salesperson Jana Hall placed the following order with the telephone company: "List my name in the directory under the heading 'Real Estate,' as 'Jana Hall, Real Estate Salesperson, Residential Property My Specialty.'" Jana is also required to include

   a. her license number.
   b. the expiration date of her license.
   c. her street address.
   d. the name of her employing broker.

51. Who designates a salesperson or broker associate in Illinois to act as a "designated agent"?

   a. The state
   b. The seller or buyer
   c. The salesperson or broker associate himself, in signing a client agreement
   d. The sponsoring broker

52. Actions being brought against licensees under *Article 15* (Agency Relationships) of the *Real Estate License Act of 2000* must be taken

   a. within two years after the facts become known.
   b. within one year after the facts become known
   c. any time after the closing if negligence can be proven.
   d. within six months after closing.

53. Which one of the following situations would be allowed by Illinois law?

   a. An offer of subagency through the MLS
   b. Showing homes after one's license has expired, so long as one doesn't write the contract
   c. A listing agent refusing to present an offer to the sellers because it is a low offer
   d. A buyer's agent choosing not to mention to the listing agent that the buyers plan to tear down the house after purchase

54. In Illinois, licensees working through an MLS are NOT legally

   a. special agents to clients.
   b. general agents of their sponsoring broker.
   c. designated by their sponsoring broker as agents to clients.
   d. subagents.

55. Under the *Real Estate License Act of 2000*, which statement is *TRUE?*

   a. The person with whom a licensee works is always a customer if nothing else is said.
   b. The person with whom a licensee works is a client if nothing else is said.
   c. The person who works with buyers who do not want client status is called their *agent*.
   d. A client becomes a client only when the agency agreement is signed.

56. Who pays a licensed leasing agent?

   a. The owner of the properties being rented
   b. The tenant
   c. The sponsoring broker
   d. The previous tenant

57. How long may a leasing agent work without a license in Illinois, provided he or she is working to obtain a license and has a proper sponsor?

   a. 30 days
   b. 130 days
   c. 90 days
   d. 120 days

58. An Illinois licensee has listed a property whose owner had AIDS. The licensee should

   a. note that the owner has AIDS at the bottom of the disclosure sheet, per federal law.
   b. note that the owner has AIDS at the bottom of the disclosure sheet, per state law.
   c. do what seems right. There is no specific obligation to disclose, but if the agent feels it is best for all parties, he or she may do so.
   d. not mention this to anyone, unless the owner directs him or her to do so.

59. Which of the following is *TRUE* about leasing agents in Illinois?

   a. Leasing agents in Illinois may operate independently as long they are approved by IDFPR.
   b. While leasing agents are not licensed, a test indicating basic competence must be passed to work as a leasing agent.
   c. Leasing agents must have a sponsoring broker.
   d. Leasing agents may work without a license for 130 days if properly supervised.

60. A Champaign, Illinois, buyer's agent is showing properties to a young mother of three children whose safety is paramount to her. Which one of the following would NOT be appropriate?

   a. The agent tells the mother she can check addresses of convicted but released sex offenders on the Internet.
   b. The agent decides on his or her own to show only certain neighborhoods.
   c. The licensee checks properties surrounding an interesting subject property carefully for any signs of oil leaks, USTs, formaldehyde odors, gas odors, bogs, or fire/explosion hazards.
   d. The buyer's agent recommends radon testing, carbon monoxide detectors, and water testing.

61. Which of the following is outside the bounds of what an Illinois buyer's agent may do under law?

 a. Tell a seller (the seller's agent) that a buyer "qualifies" who really just barely qualifies for the seller's home.

 b. Check recent sales prices of homes in the area, mention the low ones to the listing agent, and use them as a basis to negotiate down.

 c. Indicate to Mr. and Mrs. Seller that a buyer has new work with a company in the area when he or she is just interviewing for a job.

 d. Threaten to report a listing agent to the local Association if a low offer isn't presented to the sellers.

62. Under the *Real Estate License Act of 2000*, which statement describes how a licensed personal assistant is paid?

 a. Whichever salesperson or broker he or she works for on a daily basis pays the assistant.

 b. Fees usually come straight from any closings in which the licensed assistant has participated.

 c. The cooperative broker fee covers the personal assistant.

 d. The sponsoring broker pays the licensed personal assistant.

63. In most transactions of residential real estate in Illinois, who pays for the local transfer tax stamps?

 a. The seller

 b. The seller or buyer, depending on rules of the municipality

 c. Buyer's attorney

 d. The buyer

64. In determining Illinois taxation, at what stage does one equalize property value?

 a. After determining assessed value

 b. Just after locating or determining fair market value

 c. After subtracting exemptions

 d. After the tax rate is applied to the property value

65. How much do local (city or town) tax stamps in Illinois cost?

 a. Vary by street

 b. $1.50 per $1,000

 c. $2.00 per $500

 d. Vary by town

66. Under the *Real Estate License Act of 2000*, who among the following would NOT need to work under a sponsoring broker in Illinois?

 a. A salesperson

 b. Another broker who is not a sponsoring broker (a *broker associate*)

 c. An appraiser

 d. A licensed personal assistant to a salesperson

67. In Illinois, if a salesperson leaves one firm to go to another, the salesperson's listings

 a. automatically go with the agent.

 b. stay with the broker unless the employment agreement stipulates otherwise.

 c. are canceled.

 d. are left to the discretion of the sellers.

68. If you lived in rural Illinois, who would it be best to contact for additional information regarding rural loans?

 a. IDFPR   c. FHA

 b. GNMA   d. USDA

69. Who would NOT receive a co-op fee in Illinois?

 a. The salesperson with the buyer (through the sponsoring broker)

 b. The listing broker

 c. The selling broker

 d. A buyer's agent (through the sponsoring broker)

70. If a salesperson is found guilty of violating the *Real Estate License Act of 2000*, his or her employing broker also may be disciplined by the IDFPR if the

 a. salesperson was a convicted criminal.

 b. broker had prior knowledge of the violation.

 c. broker failed to conduct the four-step pre-employment investigation of the salesperson's background and character required by the license law.

 d. broker failed to keep all local business licenses current.

71. A licensee must have written consent of the owners to advertise their house

    a. in the newspapers.
    b. by putting up a yard sign.
    c. on the Internet.
    d. in all of the above ways.

72. What projects does the transfer tax pay for in Illinois?

    a. Key state and county medical projects
    b. Illinois Department of Transportation (usually road projects)
    c. REALTORS® Defense Fund
    d. Affordable housing and land preservation

73. A will must include which heirs?

    a. Sisters and brothers
    b. Children
    c. Spouse
    d. Parents

74. What has replaced dower and curtesy in Illinois?

    a. Uniform Probate Code
    b. Spousal right of first choice
    c. Real estate by devise
    d. Life estate *pur autre vie*

75. Which type of ownership can be used only by a married couple in Illinois?

    a. Tenancy in common
    b. Joint tenancy
    c. Life estate
    d. Tenancy by the entirety

76. Which type of seller liens would a buyer MOST LIKELY agree to at an Illinois closing?

    a. Any liens existing at closing
    b. Mechanics' liens, because these often cannot be discovered prior to close
    c. Second mortgage liens, because these benefit the buyers
    d. An assumed mortgage

77. In Illinois, which type of contract might be considered held to be enforceable if entered into by someone under 18?

    a. Listing contract   c. Lease contract
    b. Sales contract   d. Land contract

78. Which type of will is enforceable in Illinois?

    a. Oral, so long as a person was there to hear it
    b. Holographic will
    c. Noncupative will
    d. Written will, signed and witnessed

79. In Illinois, which type of deed becomes null and void after one year if it is not recorded?

    a. General warranty deed
    b. Special warranty deed
    c. Bargain and sale deed
    d. Tax deed

80. An expired real estate license may be renewed in Illinois for how long?

    a. One year
    b. Two years
    c. Three years
    d. Five years

81. Which of the following is exempt from licensure?

    a. A hotel operator registered with the Illinois Department of Revenue
    b. A licensed auctioneer selling real estate at auction
    c. A time-share owner who refers no more than 20 prospective purchasers in any one year
    d. All of the above are exempt

82. Which of the following licenses expire on July 31, even years?

    a. Leasing agent license
    b. Broker license
    c. Salesperson license
    d. Appraiser license

83. Which of the following escrow records must be kept by a broker?

    a. Journal
    b. Ledger
    c. Monthly reconciliation statements
    d. All of the above must be kept

84. The principal to whom a real estate agent gives advice and counsel is a

    a. subagent.
    b. customer.
    c. client.
    d. fiduciary.

85. Which of the following is charged with the responsibility of administering the *Real Estate License Act 2000?*
   a. Secretary of State
   b. Bureau of Real Estate Professions
   c. Department of Professional Regulation
   d. Office of Banks and Trusts

86. The Real Estate Recovery Fund was
   a. established to provide a means of compensating people who have been harmed by a licensee's negligence.
   b. created to provide licensees with errors and omissions insurance.
   c. established to provide up to $100,000 for losses.
   d. created to recover escrow losses.

87. A broker who deposits earnest money in an escrow account must make sure that
   a. the account is state-insured.
   b. either buyer or seller has signed a written request form identifying who is to receive the interest.
   c. the money, when released, is at the direction of either principal.
   d. the account is FDIC insured.

88. A real estate developer who lives in Mississippi and is selling lots located in Mississippi from his company office in Illinois must be in compliance with which Act?
   a. *Illinois Interstate Commerce Act*
   b. *Illinois Development Act*
   c. *Illinois Land Plat Act*
   d. *Illinois Land Sales Registration Act*

89. The most important purpose of the *Real Estate License Act of 2000* is to
   a. protect the public.
   b. protect the real estate industry from fraudulent practices.
   c. regulate real estate businesses.
   d. regulate real estate practitioners.

90. Real estate licensees in Illinois must disclose all of the following EXCEPT
   a. material defects of which they have knowledge.
   b. any stigmas associated with the property.
   c. special compensation found outside the scope of their agency relationship.
   d. that they have an Illinois salesperson license.

91. Which appraisal licensing category allows an appraiser to appraise residential property of one unit to four units without regard to transaction value or complexity?
   a. Associate real estate appraiser
   b. Certified residential appraiser
   c. Certified general real estate appraiser
   d. None of the above

92. Appraisal licensing is required for which of the following?
   a. All federally related transactions
   b. For-sale-by-owner transactions
   c. Only commercial property transactions
   d. Commercial and industrial property transactions

93. Which of the following shows the receipt and disbursement of funds affecting a single particular transaction?
   a. Journal
   b. Ledger
   c. Reconciliation worksheet
   d. Master escrow account log

94. Which of the following shows the chronological sequence in which funds are received and disbursed for all transactions?
   a. Journal
   b. Ledger
   c. Reconciliation worksheet
   d. Master escrow account log

95. Which of the following identifies all escrow bank account numbers and bank name and address?
   a. Journal
   b. Ledger
   c. Reconciliation worksheet
   d. Master escrow account log

96. Escrow records must be maintained for at least
    a. three years.
    b. five years.
    c. seven years.
    d. ten years.

97. Illinois has reciprocity with which of the following states?
    a. Indiana
    b. Iowa
    c. Georgia
    d. All of the above

98. Which of the following is *TRUE* about the members of the Disciplinary Board?
    a. Members have no term limits.
    b. Members must be appointed by the IDFPR secretary.
    c. Six members must have real estate licenses.
    d. The governor appoints seven members.

99. Illinois recognizes which of the following estates?
    a. Homestead
    b. Curtesy
    c. Dower
    d. Community property

100. In Illinois, in order to be eligible for a homestead estate, an owner must
    a. file an eligibility form with the state agency.
    b. have an equity interest in the property.
    c. be married.
    d. reside in the property.

Web Link Directory

Chapter 1
American Society of Home Inspectors: www.ashi.org
Building Owners and Managers Association International: www.boma.org
Commercial Investment Real Estate Institute: www.ccim.com
Counselors of Real Estate: www.cre.org
Fannie Mae: www.fanniemae.com
Federal Reserve Board: www.federalreserve.gov
Freddie Mac: www.freddiemac.com
Ginnie Mae: www.ginniemae.gov
Institute of Real Estate Management: www.irem.org
National Association of Exclusive Buyer Agents: www.naeba.org
National Association of Independent Fee Appraisers: www.naifa.com
National Association of Real Estate Brokers: www.nareb.com
National Association of REALTORS®: www.realtor.org
Real Estate Buyer's Agent Council: www.rebac.net
Real Estate Education Association: www.reea.org
U.S. Department of Housing and Urban Development (HUD): www.hud.gov

Chapter 2
Manufactured Housing Institute: www.manufacturedhousing.org

Chapter 3
Comprehensive Loss Underwriting Exchange (CLUE): www.choicetrust.com
Department of Housing and Urban Development (HUD): www.hud.gov
Department of Housing and Urban Development's Office of Housing:
    www.hud.gov/offices/hsg/index.cfm
Federal Emergency Management Agency: www.fema.gov
U.S. Department of Veterans Affairs: www.va.gov

Chapter 4
Chicago Association of REALTORS® (CAR): www.chicagorealtor.com
Illinois Association of REALTORS® (IAR): www.illinoisrealtor.org

Chapter 5
Association of Real Estate License Law Officials: www.arello.org
Electronic Signatures in Global and National Commerce Act (E-Sign):
    www.ftc.gov/os/2001/06/esign7.htm
National Do Not Call Registry: www.donotcall.gov/default.aspx

Uniform Electronic Transaction Act (UETA): www.ncsl.org/programs/lis/CIP/ueta.htm

U.S. Department of Internal Revenue: www.irs.gov

U.S. Department of Justice, Antitrust Division: www.usdoj.gov/atr

Chapter 6

Illinois Department of Human Rights: www.state.il.us/dhr/

Chapter 7

Eminent Domain: www.realtor.org

Chapter 8

Illinois Condominium Property Act: www.condorisk.com/content/condoact/property_act.htm

Chapter 10

Illinois General Assembly: www.ilga.gov

IRS U.S. Dept of Treasury: www.irs.ustreas.gov

U.S. Department of Internal Revenue Service: www.irs.gov

Chapter 14

Applied Measurement Professionals Inc.: www.goamp.com

Illinois Department of Financial and Professional Regulation: www.idfpr.com/realestate

Illinois General Assembly: www.ilga.gov (click on Illinois Compiled Statutes, Chapter 225; ILCS 454)

Legal Information Institute: Mortgages: www.law.cornell.edu/topics/mortgages.html

Chapter 16

Fannie Mae: www.fanniemae.com

Farm Credit System: www.farmcredit.com

Farmer Mac: www.farmermac.com

Federal Reserve Board: www.federalreserve.gov

Freddie Mac: www.freddiemac.com

Ginnie Mae: www.ginniemae.gov

National Reverse Mortgage Lenders Association: www.reversemortgage.org

U.S. Department of Housing and Urban Development (HUD): www.hud.gov

U.S. Department of Veterans Affairs—Home Loans: www.homeloans.va.gov

U.S. Farm Service Agency: www.fsa.usda.gov

Chapter 17

ADA Homepage: www.usdoj.gov/crt/ada

HUD's Office of Healthy Homes and Lead Hazard Control: www.hud.gov/lea/leadhelp.html

Legal Information Institute: Landlord-Tenant Law: www.law.cornell.edu/topics/landlord_tenant.html

Chapter 18

American Management Association: www.amanet.org

Building Owners and Managers Association: www.boma.org

Building Owners and Managers Institute: www.bomi-edu.org
Equifax: www.equifax.com
Experian: www.experian.com
Illinois Division of Insurance: www.state.il.us/ins/
Institute of Real Estate Management: www.irem.org/home.cfm
National Association of Home Builders: www.nahb.com
National Association of Residential Property Managers: www.narpm.org
TransUnion: www.tuc.com
U.S. Department of Justice: www.usdoj.gov/crt/drs/drshome.htm

Chapter 19
American Society of Appraisers: www.appraisers.org
American Society of Farm Managers and Rural Appraisers: www.asfmra.org
Appraisal Foundation: www.appraisalfoundation.org
Appraisal Institute: www.appraisalinstitute.org
Illinois General Assembly: www.ilga.gov
International Right of Way Association: www.irwaonline.org
National Association of Fee Appraisers: www.naifa.com
National Association of Master Appraisers: www.masterappraisers.org

Chapter 20
Illinois Human Rights Act: www.state.il.us/dhr/
Illinois Land Sales Information: www.idfpr.com/DPR/RE/TSLS.asp
International Code Council: www.iccsafe.org
Interstate Land Sales Full Disclosure Act: www.hud.gov/offices/hsg/sfh/ils/
    ilshome.cfm
U.S. Department of Housing and Urban Development: Office of Housing:
    www.hud.gov/offices/hsg/index.cfm
U.S. Department of Housing and Urban Development: Housing Discrimination
    Complaints: www.hud.gov/complaints/landsales.cfm

Chapter 21
Americans with Disabilities Act (ADA) Home Page: www.usdoj.gov/crt/ada/
    adahom1.htm
Fair Housing Act: www.usdoj.gov/crt/housing/fairhousing/
    about_fairhousingact.htm
National Association of REALTORS®: Code of Ethics: www.realtor.org
National Fair Housing Advocate Online: www.fairhousing.com (click on Legal
    Research)
U.S. Department of Housing and Urban Development: Accessibility Guide-
    lines: www.hud.gov/library/bookshelf09/fhefhag.cfm
U.S. Department of Housing and Urban Development: Fair Housing:
    www.hud.gov/groups/fairhousing.cfm
U.S. Department of Housing and Urban Development: Fair Housing Laws and
    Executive Orders: www.hud.gov/offices/fheo/FHLaws
U.S. Department of Housing and Urban Development: Fair Housing Library:
    www.hud.gov/library/bookshelf09/index.cfm
U.S. Department of Housing and Urban Development: Housing Discrimination
    Complaints: www.hud.gov/complaints/housediscrim.dfm
U.S. Department of Housing and Urban Development: Public Service
    Announcement: www.hud.gov/offices/fheo/adcampaign.cfm

Chapter 22

Illinois Emergency Management Agency Radon Program:
    www.radon.illinois.gov
U.S. Environmental Protection Agency: www.epa.gov
U.S. Environmental Protection Agency: Asbestos: www.epa.gov/oppt/asbestos
U.S. Environmental Protection Agency: Carbon Monoxide: www.epa.gov/iaq/
    co.html
U.S. Environmental Protection Agency: CERCLA/Superfund: www.epa.gov/
    superfund/action/law/cercla.htm
U.S. Environmental Protection Agency: Compliance: www.epa.gov/
    compliance
U.S. Environmental Protection Agency: Formaldehyde: www.epa.gov/iaq/
    formalde.html
U.S. Environmental Protection Agency: Lead: www.epa.gov/lead
U.S. Environmental Protection Agency: Lead-Based Paint Disclosure Forms:
    www.epa.gov/lead/leadbase.htm
U.S. Environmental Protection Agency: Indoor Air Quality: Mold:
    www.epa.gov/iaq/molds
U.S. Environmental Protection Agency: Indoor Air Quality: Radon:
    www.epa.gov/iaq/radon
U.S. Environmental Protection Agency: Mold Remediation: www.epa.gov/
    mold/mold_remediation.html
U.S. Environmental Protection Agency's Office of Water: www.epa.gov/ow

Chapter 23

U.S. Department of Housing and Urban Development: RESPA: www.hud.gov/
    offices/hsg/sfh/res/respa_htm.cfm
U.S. Department of Housing and Urban Development: RESPA: Frequently
    Asked Questions: www.hud.gov/offices/hsg/sfh/res/respafaq.cfm

Glossary

abstract of title   The condensed history of a title to a particular parcel of real estate, consisting of a summary of the original grant and all subsequent conveyances and encumbrances affecting the property and a certification by the abstractor that the history is complete and accurate.

acceleration clause   The clause in a mortgage or deed of trust that can be enforced to make the entire debt due immediately if the borrower defaults on an installment payment or other covenant.

accession   Acquiring title to additions or improvements to real property as a result of the annexation of fixtures or the accretion of alluvial deposits along the banks of streams.

accretion   The increase or addition of land by the deposit of sand or soil washed up naturally from a river, lake, or sea.

accrued items   On a closing statement, items of expense that are incurred but not yet payable, such as interest on a mortgage loan or taxes on real property.

acknowledgment   A formal declaration made before a duly authorized officer, usually a notary public, by a person who has signed a document.

acre   A measure of land equal to 43,560 square feet, 4,840 square yards, 4,047 square meters, 160 square rods, or 0.4047 hectares.

actual eviction   The legal process that results in the tenant's being physically removed from the leased premises.

actual notice   Express information or fact; that which is known; direct knowledge.

adjustable-rate mortgage (ARM)   A loan characterized by a fluctuating interest rate, usually one tied to a bank or savings and loan association cost-of-funds index.

adjusted basis   *See* basis.

ad valorem tax   A tax levied according to value, generally used to refer to real estate tax. Also called the *general tax.*

adverse possession   The actual, open, notorious, hostile, and continuous possession of another's land under a claim of title. Possession for a statutory period may be a means of acquiring title.

affidavit of title   A written statement, made under oath by a seller or grantor of real property and acknowledged by a notary public, in which the grantor (1) identifies

himself or herself and indicates marital status, (2) certifies that since the examination of the title on the date of the contract no defects have occurred in the title and (3) certifies that he or she is in possession of the property (if applicable).

agency   The relationship between a principal and an agent wherein the agent is authorized to represent the principal in certain transactions.

agency coupled with an interest   An agency relationship in which the agent is given an estate or interest in the subject of the agency (the property).

agent   One who acts or has the power to act for another. A fiduciary relationship is created under the *law of agency* when a property owner, as the principal, executes a listing agreement or management contract authorizing a licensed real estate broker to be his or her agent.

air lot   A designated airspace over a piece of land. An air lot, like surface property, may be transferred.

air rights   The right to use the open space above a property, usually allowing the surface to be used for another purpose.

alienation   The act of transferring property to another. Alienation may be voluntary, such as by gift or sale, or involuntary, as through eminent domain or adverse possession.

alienation clause   The clause in a mortgage or deed of trust that states that the balance of the secured debt becomes immediately due and payable at the lender's option if the property is sold by the borrower. In effect this clause prevents the borrower from assigning the debt without the lender's approval.

allodial system   A system of land ownership in which land is held free and clear of any rent or service due to the government; commonly contrasted to the feudal system. Land is held under the allodial system in the United States.

American Land Title Association (ALTA) policy   A title insurance policy that protects the interest in a collateral property of a mortgage lender who originates a new real estate loan.

amortized loan   A loan in which the principal as well as the interest is payable in monthly or other periodic installments over the term of the loan.

annual percentage rate (APR) The relationship of the total finance charges associated with a loan. This must be disclosed to borrowers by lenders under the *Truth-in-Lending Act*.

anticipation The appraisal principle that holds that value can increase or decrease based on the expectation of some future benefit or detriment produced by the property.

antitrust laws Laws designed to preserve the free enterprise of the open marketplace by making illegal certain private conspiracies and combinations formed to minimize competition. Most violations of antitrust laws in the real estate business involve either *price-fixing* (brokers conspiring to set fixed compensation rates) or *allocation of customers or markets* (brokers agreeing to limit their areas of trade or dealing to certain areas or properties).

appraisal An estimate of the quantity, quality, or value of something. The process through which conclusions of property value are obtained; also refers to the report that sets forth the process of estimation and conclusion of value.

appreciation An increase in the worth or value of a property due to economic or related causes, which may prove to be either temporary or permanent; opposite of depreciation.

appurtenance A right, privilege, or improvement belonging to, and passing with, the land.

appurtenant easement An easement that is annexed to the ownership of one parcel and allows the owner the use of the neighbor's land.

asbestos A mineral once used in insulation and other materials that can cause respiratory diseases.

assemblage The combining of two or more adjoining lots into one larger tract to increase their total value.

assessment The imposition of a tax, charge, or levy, usually according to established rates.

assignment The transfer in writing of interest in a bond, mortgage, lease, or other instrument.

assumption of mortgage Acquiring title to property on which there is an existing mortgage and agreeing to be personally liable for the terms and conditions of the mortgage, including payments.

attachment The act of taking a person's property into legal custody by writ or other judicial order to hold it available for application to that person's debt to a creditor.

attorney's opinion of title An abstract of title that an attorney has examined and has certified to be, in his or her opinion, an accurate statement of the facts concerning the property ownership.

automated underwriting Computer systems that permit lenders to expedite the loan approval process and reduce lending costs.

automatic extension A clause in a listing agreement that states that the agreement will continue automatically for a certain period of time after its expiration date. In many states, use of this clause is discouraged or prohibited.

avulsion The sudden tearing away of land, as by earthquake, flood, volcanic action, or the sudden change in the course of a stream.

balance The appraisal principle that states that the greatest value in a property will occur when the type and size of the improvements are proportional to each other as well as to the land.

balloon payment A final payment of a mortgage loan that is considerably larger than the required periodic payments because the loan amount was not fully amortized.

bargain and sale deed A deed that carries with it no warranties against liens or other encumbrances but that does imply that the grantor has the right to convey title. The grantor may add warranties to the deed at his or her discretion.

base line The main imaginary line running east and west and crossing a principal meridian at a definite point, used by surveyors for reference in locating and describing land under the rectangular (government) survey system of legal description.

basis The financial interest that the Internal Revenue Service attributes to an owner of an investment property for the purpose of determining annual depreciation and gain or loss on the sale of the asset. If a property was acquired by purchase, the owner's basis is the cost of the property plus the value of any capital expenditures for improvements to the property, minus any depreciation allowable or actually taken. This new basis is called the adjusted basis.

bench mark A permanent reference mark or point established for use by surveyors in measuring differences in elevation.

beneficiary (1) The person for whom a trust operates or on whose behalf the income from a trust estate is drawn. (2) A lender in a deed of trust loan transaction.

bilateral contract *See* contract.

binder An agreement that may accompany an earnest money deposit for the purchase of real property as evidence of the purchaser's good faith and intent to complete the transaction.

blanket loan A mortgage covering more than one parcel of real estate, providing for each parcel's partial release from the mortgage lien on repayment of a definite portion of the debt.

blockbusting The illegal practice of inducing homeowners to sell their properties by making representations regarding the entry or prospective entry of persons of a particular race or national origin into the neighborhood.

blue-sky laws Common name for those state and federal laws that regulate the registration and sale of investment securities.

boot Money or property given to make up any difference in value or equity between two properties in an *exchange*.

branch office A secondary place of business apart from the principal or main office from which real estate business is conducted. A branch office usually must be run by a licensed real estate broker working on behalf of the sponsoring broker.

branch office license In Illinois, a separate license that must be obtained for each branch office a broker wishes to establish.

breach of contract Violation of any terms or conditions in a contract without legal excuse; for example, failure to make a payment when it is due.

broker One who acts as an intermediary on behalf of others for a fee or commission.

brokerage The bringing together of parties interested in making a real estate transaction.

brownfields Defunct, derelict, or abandoned commercial or industrial sites; many have toxic wastes.

Brownfields Legislation Provides federal funding to states and localities to clean up brownfields sites.

buffer zone A strip of land, usually used as a park or designated for a similar use, separating land dedicated to one use from land dedicated to another use (e.g., residential from commercial).

building code An ordinance that specifies minimum standards of construction for buildings to protect public safety and health.

building permit Written governmental permission for the construction, alteration, or demolition of an improvement, showing compliance with building codes and zoning ordinances.

bundle of legal rights The concept of land ownership that includes ownership of all legal rights to the land—for example, possession, control within the law, and enjoyment.

buydown A financing technique used to reduce the monthly payments for the first few years of a loan. Funds in the form of discount points are given to the lender by the builder or seller to buy down or lower the effective interest rate paid by the buyer, thus reducing the monthly payments for a set time.

buyer-agency agreement A principal-agent relationship in which the broker is the agent for the buyer, with fiduciary responsibilities to the buyer.

buyer's agent A real estate broker or salesperson who represents the prospective purchaser in a transaction. The buyer's agent owes the buyer/principal the statutory agency duties.

buyer's broker A residential real estate broker who represents prospective buyers exclusively. As the *buyer's agent*, the broker owes the buyer/principal the common-law or statutory agency duties.

CAN-SPAM Act Establishes requirements for commercial e-mail, spells out penalties for e-mail senders, and gives consumers the right to have e-mailers stop sending e-mails to them.

capital gain Profit earned from the sale of an asset.

capitalization A mathematical process for estimating the value of a property using a proper rate of return on the investment and the annual net operating income expected to be produced by the property. The formula is expressed as Net Income ÷ Rate = Value

capitalization rate The rate of return a property will produce on the owner's investment.

cash flow The net spendable income from an investment, determined by deducting all operating and fixed expenses from the gross income. When expenses exceed income, a *negative cash flow* results.

cash rent In an agricultural lease, the amount of money given as rent to the landowner at the outset of the lease, as opposed to sharecropping.

caveat emptor A Latin phrase meaning "Let the buyer beware."

certificate of reasonable value (CRV) A form indicating the appraised value of a property being financed with a VA loan.

certificate of sale The document generally given to the purchaser of delinquent property taxes at a tax foreclosure sale.

certificate of title A statement of opinion on the status of the title to a parcel of real property based on an examination of specified public records.

chain of title The succession of conveyances, from some accepted starting point, whereby the present holder of real property derives title.

change The appraisal principle that holds that no physical or economic condition remains constant.

chattel *See* personal property.

chlorofluorocarbons Nontoxic, nonflammable chemicals containing atoms of carbon, chlorine, and fluorine. Most often used in air conditioners, refrigerators, paints, solvents, and foam blowing applications.

Civil Rights Act of 1866 An act that prohibits racial discrimination in the sale and rental of housing.

closing statement   A detailed cash accounting of a real estate transaction showing all cash received, all charges and credits made, and all cash paid out in the transaction.

cloud on title   Any document, claim, unreleased lien, or encumbrance that may impair the title to real property or make the title doubtful; usually revealed by a title search and removed by either a quitclaim deed or suit to quiet title.

clustering   The grouping of homesites within a subdivision on smaller lots than normal, with the remaining land used as common areas.

code of ethics   A written system of standards for ethical conduct.

codicil   A supplement or an addition to a will, executed with the same formalities as a will, that normally does not revoke the entire will.

coinsurance clause   A clause in insurance policies covering real property that requires that the policyholder maintain fire insurance coverage generally equal to at least 80 percent of the property's actual replacement cost.

commingling   The illegal act by a real estate broker of placing client or customer funds with personal funds.

commission   Payment to a broker for services rendered, such as in the sale or purchase of real property; usually a percentage of the selling price of the property.

common elements   Parts of a property that are necessary or convenient to the existence, maintenance, and safety of a condominium or are normally in common use by all of the condominium residents. Each condominium owner has an undivided ownership interest in the common elements.

common law   The body of law based on custom, usage, and court decisions.

common law of agency   The traditional law governing the principal-agent relationship, superseded by statute in Illinois.

community property   A system of property ownership based on the theory that each spouse has an equal interest in the property acquired by the efforts of either spouse during marriage.

comparables   Properties used in an appraisal report that are substantially equivalent to the subject property.

comparative market analysis (CMA)   A comparison of the prices of recently sold homes that are similar to a listing seller's home in terms of location, style, and amenities.

competition   The appraisal principle that states that excess profits generate competition.

Comprehensive Environmental Response, Compensation, and Liability Act (CERCLA)   A federal law administered by the Environmental Protection Agency that establishes a process for identifying parties responsible for creating hazardous waste sites, forcing liable parties to clean up toxic sites, bringing legal action against responsible parties, and funding the abatement of toxic sites. *See* Superfund.

Comprehensive Loss Underwriting Exchange (CLUE)   A database of consumer claim history that allows insurance companies to access prior claim information in the underwriting and rating process.

comprehensive plan   *See* master plan.

computerized loan origination (CLO) system   An electronic network for handling loan applications through remote computer terminals linked to various lenders' computers.

condemnation   A judicial or administrative proceeding to exercise the power of eminent domain, through which a government agency takes private property for public use and compensates the owner.

conditional-use permit   Written governmental permission allowing a use inconsistent with zoning but necessary for the common good, such as locating an emergency medical facility in a predominantly residential area.

condominium   The absolute ownership of a unit in a multiunit building based on a legal description of the airspace the unit actually occupies, plus an undivided interest in the ownership of the common elements, which are owned jointly with the other condominium unit owners.

confession of judgment clause   Permits judgment to be entered against a debtor without the creditor's having to institute legal proceedings.

conformity   The appraisal principle that holds that the greater the similarity among properties in an area, the better they will hold their value.

consideration   (1) That received by the grantor in exchange for his or her deed. (2) Something of value that induces a person to enter into a contract.

construction loan   *See* interim financing.

constructive eviction   Actions of a landlord that so materially disturb or impair a tenant's enjoyment of the leased premises that the tenant is effectively forced to move out and terminate the lease without liability for any further rent.

constructive notice   Notice given to the world by recorded documents. All people are charged with knowledge of such documents and their contents, whether or not they have actually examined them. Possession of property is also considered constructive notice that the person in possession has an interest in the property.

contingency   A provision in a contract that requires a certain act to be done or a certain event to occur before the contract becomes binding.

contract A legally enforceable promise or set of promises that must be performed and for which, if a breach of the promise occurs, the law provides a remedy. A contract may be either *unilateral*, by which only one party is bound to act, or *bilateral*, by which all parties to the instrument are legally bound to act as prescribed.

contribution The appraisal principle that states that the value of any component of a property is what it gives to the value of the whole or what its absence detracts from that value.

conventional loan A loan that requires no government insurance or guarantee.

conversion The wrongful appropriation of property belonging to another; also, the process of changing a property's status from rental to condominium.

conveyance A term used to refer to any document that transfers title to real property. The term is also used in describing the act of transferring.

cooperating broker *See* listing broker.

cooperative A residential multiunit building whose title is held by a trust or corporation that is owned by and operated for the benefit of persons living within the building, who are the beneficial owners of the trust or stockholders of the corporation, each possessing a proprietary lease.

co-ownership Title ownership held by two or more persons.

corporation An entity or organization, created by operation of law, whose rights of doing business are essentially the same as those of an individual. The entity has continuous existence until it is dissolved according to legal procedures.

correction lines Provisions in the rectangular survey (government survey) system made to compensate for the curvature of the earth's surface. Every fourth township line (at 24-mile intervals) is used as a correction line on which the intervals between the north and south range lines are remeasured and corrected to a full six miles.

cost approach The process of estimating the value of a property by adding to the estimated land value the appraiser's estimate of the reproduction or replacement cost of the building, less depreciation.

cost recovery An Internal Revenue Service term for *depreciation*.

counteroffer A new offer made in response to an offer received. It has the effect of rejecting the original offer, which cannot be accepted thereafter unless revived by the offeror.

covenant A written agreement between two or more parties in which a party or parties pledge to perform or not to perform specified acts with regard to property; usually found in such real estate documents as deeds, mortgages, leases, and contracts for deed.

covenant of quiet enjoyment The covenant implied by law by which a landlord guarantees that a tenant may take possession of leased premises and that the landlord will not interfere in the tenant's possession or use of the property.

credit On a closing statement, an amount entered in a person's favor—either an amount the party has paid or an amount for which the party must be reimbursed.

curtesy A life estate, usually a fractional interest, given by some states to the surviving husband in real estate owned by his deceased wife. Most states have abolished curtesy.

datum A horizontal plane from which heights and depths are measured.

debit On a closing statement, an amount charged; that is, an amount that the debited party must pay.

decedent A person who has died.

dedication The voluntary transfer of private property by its owner to the public for some public use, such as for streets or schools.

deed A written instrument that, when executed and delivered, conveys title to or an interest in real estate.

deed in lieu of foreclosure A deed given by the mortgagor to the mortgagee when the mortgagor is in default under the terms of the mortgage. This is a way for the mortgagor to avoid foreclosure.

deed in trust An instrument that grants a trustee under a land trust full power to sell, mortgage, and subdivide a parcel of real estate. The beneficiary controls the trustee's use of these powers under the provisions of the trust agreement.

deed of trust *See* trust deed.

deed of trust lien *See* trust deed lien.

deed restrictions Clauses in a deed limiting the future uses of the property.

default The nonperformance of a duty, whether arising under a contract or otherwise; failure to meet an obligation when due.

defeasance clause A clause used in leases and mortgages that cancels a specified right upon the occurrence of a certain condition, such as cancellation of a mortgage on repayment of the mortgage loan.

defeasible fee estate An estate in which the holder has a fee simple title that may be divested on the occurrence or nonoccurrence of a specified event. There are two categories of defeasible fee estates: fee simple on condition precedent (fee simple determinable) and fee simple on condition subsequent.

deficiency judgment   A personal judgment levied against the borrower when a foreclosure sale does not produce sufficient funds to pay the mortgage debt in full.

demand   The amount of goods people are willing and able to buy at a given price; often coupled with *supply*.

density zoning   Zoning ordinances that restrict the maximum average number of houses per acre that may be built within a particular area, generally a subdivision.

depreciation   (1) In appraisal, a loss of value in property due to any cause, including *physical deterioration*, *functional obsolescence*, and *external obsolescence*. (2) In real estate investment, an expense deduction for tax purposes taken over the period of ownership of income property.

descent   Acquisition of an estate by inheritance in which an heir succeeds to the property by operation of law.

designated agent   A licensee authorized by a sponsoring broker to act as the agent for a specific principal in a particular transaction.

developer   One who attempts to put land to its most profitable use through the construction of improvements.

devise   A gift of real property by will. The donor is the devisor, and the recipient is the devisee.

devisee   A person who receives property by will.

discount point   A unit of measurement used for various loan charges; one point equals 1 percent of the amount of the loan.

dominant tenement   A property that includes in its ownership the appurtenant right to use an easement over another person's property for a specific purpose.

dower   The legal right or interest, recognized in some states, that a wife acquires in the property her husband held or acquired during their marriage. During the husband's lifetime the right is only a possibility of an interest; on his death it can become an interest in land.

dual agency   Representing both parties to a transaction. In Illinois, this is illegal unless both parties agree to it in writing.

due-on-sale clause   A provision in the mortgage that states that the entire balance of the note is immediately due and payable if the mortgagor transfers (sells) the property.

duress   Unlawful constraint or action exercised on a person whereby the person is forced to perform an act against his or her will. A contract entered into under duress is voidable.

earnest money   Money deposited by a buyer under the terms of a contract, to be forfeited if the buyer defaults but applied to the purchase price if the sale is closed.

easement   A right to use the land of another for a specific purpose, such as for a right-of-way or utilities; an incorporeal interest in land.

easement by condemnation   An easement created by the government or government agency that has exercised its right under eminent domain.

easement by necessity   An easement allowed by law as necessary for the full enjoyment of a parcel of real estate; for example, a right of ingress and egress over a grantor's land.

easement by prescription   An easement acquired by continuous, open, and hostile use of the property for the period of time prescribed by state law.

easement in gross   An easement that is not created for the benefit of any *land* owned by the owner of the easement but that attaches *personally to the easement owner*. For example, a right granted by Eleanor Franks to Joe Fish to use a portion of her property for the rest of his life would be an easement in gross.

economic life   The number of years during which an improvement will add value to the land.

electronic contracting   A process of integrating information in a real estate transaction between clients, lender, and title and closing agents electronically.

emblements   Growing crops, such as grapes and corn, that are produced annually through labor and industry; also called *fructus industriales*.

eminent domain   The right of a government or municipal quasi-public body to acquire property for public use through a court action called *condemnation*, in which the court decides that the use is a public use and determines the compensation to be paid to the owner.

employee   Someone who works as a direct employee of an employer and has employee status. The employer is obligated to withhold income taxes and Social Security taxes from the compensation of employees. *See also* independent contractor.

employment contract   A document evidencing formal employment between employer and employee or between principal and agent. In the real estate business this generally takes the form of a listing agreement or management agreement.

enabling acts   State legislation that confers zoning powers on municipal governments.

encapsulation   A method of controlling environmental contamination by sealing off a dangerous substance.

encroachment   A building or some portion of it—a wall or fence, for instance—that extends beyond the land of the owner and illegally intrudes on some land of an adjoining owner or a street or alley.

encumbrance Anything—such as a mortgage, tax, or judgment lien; an easement; a restriction on the use of the land; or an outstanding dower right—that may diminish the value or use and enjoyment of a property.

Equal Credit Opportunity Act (ECOA) The federal law that prohibits discrimination in the extension of credit because of race, color, religion, national origin, sex, age, or marital status.

equalization The raising or lowering of assessed values for tax purposes in a particular county or taxing district to make them equal to assessments in other counties or districts.

equalization factor A factor (number) by which the assessed value of a property is multiplied to arrive at a value for the property that is in line with statewide tax assessments. The *ad valorem tax* is based on this adjusted value.

equitable lien *See* statutory lien.

equitable right of redemption The right of a defaulted property owner to recover the property prior to its sale by paying the appropriate fees and charges.

equitable title The interest held by a vendee under a contract for deed or an installment contract; the equitable right to obtain absolute ownership to property when legal title is held in another's name.

equity The interest or value that an owner has in property over and above any indebtedness.

Equity in Eminent Domain Act Legislation that provides protections for private property owners when government seeks to acquire land for economic development projects.

erosion The gradual wearing away of land by water, wind, and general weather conditions; the diminishing of property by the elements.

escheat The reversion of property to the state or county, as provided by state law, in cases where a decedent dies intestate without heirs capable of inheriting, or when the property is abandoned.

escrow The closing of a transaction through a third party called an *escrow agent*, or *escrowee*, who receives certain funds and documents to be delivered on the performance of certain conditions outlined in the escrow instructions.

escrow account The trust account established by a broker under the provisions of the license law for the purpose of holding funds on behalf of the broker's principal or some other person until the consummation or termination of a transaction.

escrow instructions A document that sets forth the duties of the escrow agent, as well as the requirements and obligations of the parties, when a transaction is closed through an escrow.

estate (tenancy) at sufferance The tenancy of a lessee who lawfully comes into possession of a landlord's real estate but who continues to occupy the premises improperly after his or her lease rights have expired.

estate (tenancy) at will An estate that gives the lessee the right to possession until the estate is terminated by either party; the term of this estate is indefinite.

estate (tenancy) for years An interest for a certain, exact period of time in property leased for a specified consideration.

estate (tenancy) from period to period An interest in leased property that continues from period to period—week to week, month to month, or year to year.

estate in land The degree, quantity, nature, and extent of interest a person has in real property.

estate taxes Federal taxes on a decedent's real and personal property.

estoppel Method of creating an agency relationship in which someone states incorrectly that another person is his or her agent, and a third person relies on that representation.

estoppel certificate A document in which a borrower certifies the amount owed on a mortgage loan and the rate of interest.

ethics The systems of moral principles and rules that become standards for professional conduct.

eviction A legal process to oust a person from possession of real estate.

evidence of title Proof of ownership of property; commonly a certificate of title, an abstract of title with lawyer's opinion, title insurance, or a Torrens registration certificate.

exchange A transaction in which all or part of the consideration is the transfer of *like-kind* property (such as real estate for real estate).

exclusive-agency listing A listing contract under which the owner appoints a real estate broker as his or her exclusive agent for a designated period of time to sell the property on the owner's stated terms for a commission. The owner reserves the right to sell without paying anyone a commission if he or she sells to a prospect who has not been introduced or claimed by the broker.

exclusive-right-to-sell listing A listing contract under which the owner appoints a real estate broker as his or her exclusive agent for a designated period of time to sell the property on the owner's stated terms, and agrees to pay the broker a commission when the property is sold, whether by the broker, the owner, or another broker.

executed contract A contract in which all parties have fulfilled their promises and thus performed the contract.

execution The signing and delivery of an instrument. Also, a legal order directing an official to enforce a judgment against the property of a debtor.

executory contract A contract under which something remains to be done by one or more of the parties.

express agreement An oral or written contract in which the parties state the contract's terms and express their intentions in words.

express contract *See* express agreement.

external depreciation Reduction in a property's value caused by outside factors (those that are off the property).

facilitator *See* nonagent.

Fair Housing Act The federal law that prohibits discrimination in housing based on race, color, religion, sex, handicap, familial status, and national origin.

Fannie Mae A quasi-government agency established to purchase any kind of mortgage loans in the secondary mortgage market from the primary lenders. Formerly called Federal National Mortgage Association (FNMA).

Farm Credit System A federal agency of the Department of Agriculture that offers programs to help families purchase or operate family farms.

Farmer Mac A government-sponsored enterprise that operates similarly to Fannie Mae and Freddie Mac but for agricultural loans.

Farmer's Home Administration (FmHA) Agency of the federal government that provides credit assistance to farmers and other individuals who live in rural areas.

Federal Deposit Insurance Corporation (FDIC) An independent federal agency that insures the deposits in commercial banks.

Federal Home Loan Mortgage Corporation (FHLMC) A corporation established to purchase primarily conventional mortgage loans in the secondary mortgage market.

Federal National Mortgage Association (FNMA) *See* Fannie Mae.

Federal Open Market Committee (FOMC) A component of the Federal Reserve System; buys and sells U.S. government securities on the open market.

Federal Reserve System The country's central banking system, which controls the nation's monetary policy by regulating the supply of money and interest rates.

fee simple absolute The maximum possible estate or right of ownership of real property, continuing forever.

fee simple defeasible *See* defeasible fee estate.

feudal system A system of ownership usually associated with precolonial England, in which the king or other sovereign is the source of all rights. The right to possess real property was granted by the sovereign to an individual as a life estate only. On the death of the individual title passed back to the sovereign, not to the decedent's heirs.

FHA loan A loan insured by the Federal Housing Administration and made by an approved lender in accordance with the FHA's regulations.

fiduciary One in whom trust and confidence is placed; a reference to a broker employed under the terms of a listing contract or buyer agency agreement.

fiduciary relationship A relationship of trust and confidence, as between trustee and beneficiary, attorney and client, or principal and agent.

Financial Institutions Reform, Recovery, and Enforcement Act (FIRREA) This act restructured the savings and loan association regulatory system; enacted in response to the savings and loan crisis of the 1980s.

financing statement *See* Uniform Commercial Code.

fiscal policy The government's policy in regard to taxation and spending programs. The balance between these two areas determines the amount of money the government will withdraw from or feed into the economy, which can counter economic peaks and slumps.

fixture An item of personal property that has been converted to real property by being permanently affixed to the realty.

foreclosure A legal procedure whereby property used as security for a debt is sold to satisfy the debt in the event of default in payment of the mortgage note or default of other terms in the mortgage document. The foreclosure procedure brings the rights of all parties to a conclusion and passes the title in the mortgaged property to either the holder of the mortgage or a third party, who may purchase the realty at the foreclosure sale, free of all encumbrances affecting the property subsequent to the mortgage.

fractional section A parcel of land less than 160 acres, usually found at the edge of a rectangular survey.

fraud Deception intended to cause a person to give up property or a lawful right.

Freddie Mac *See* Federal Home Loan Mortgage Corporation (FHLMC).

freehold estate An estate in land in which ownership is for an indeterminate length of time, in contrast to a *leasehold estate*.

front footage The measurement of a parcel of land by the number of feet of street or road frontage.

functional obsolescence A loss of value to an improvement to real estate arising from functional problems, often caused by age or poor design.

future interest A person's present right to an interest in real property that will not result in possession or enjoyment until some time in the future, such as a reversion or right of reentry.

gap　A defect in the chain of title of a particular parcel of real estate; a missing document or conveyance that raises doubt as to the present ownership of the land.

general agent　One who is authorized by a principal to represent the principal in a specific range of matters.

general lien　The right of a creditor to have all of a debtor's property—both real and personal—sold to satisfy a debt.

general partnership　*See* partnership.

general warranty deed　A deed in which the grantor fully warrants good clear title to the premises. Used in most real estate deed transfers, a general warranty deed offers the greatest protection of any deed.

Ginnie Mae　*See* Government National Mortgage Association (GNMA).

government check　The 24-mile-square parcels composed of 16 townships in the rectangular (government) survey system of legal description.

government lot　Fractional sections in the rectangular (government) survey system that are less than one quarter-section in area.

Government National Mortgage Association (GNMA)　A government agency that plays an important role in the secondary mortgage market. It sells mortgage-backed securities that are backed by pools of FHA and VA loans.

government survey system　*See* rectangular (government) survey system.

graduated-payment mortgage (GPM)　A loan in which the monthly principal and interest payments increase by a certain percentage each year for a certain number of years and then level off for the remaining loan term.

grantee　A person who receives a conveyance of real property from a grantor.

granting clause　Words in a deed of conveyance that state the grantor's intention to convey the property at the present time. This clause is generally worded as "convey and warrant"; "grant"; "grant, bargain, and sell"; or the like.

grantor　The person transferring title to or an interest in real property to a grantee.

gross income multiplier　A figure used as a multiplier of the gross annual income of a property to produce an estimate of the property's value.

gross lease　A lease of property according to which a landlord pays all property charges regularly incurred through ownership, such as repairs, taxes, insurance, and operating expenses. Most residential leases are gross leases.

gross rent multiplier (GRM)　The figure used as a multiplier of the gross monthly income of a property to produce an estimate of the property's value.

ground lease　A lease of land only, on which the tenant usually owns a building or is required to build as specified in the lease. Such leases are usually long-term net leases; the tenant's rights and obligations continue until the lease expires or is terminated through default.

growing-equity mortgage (GEM)　A loan in which the monthly payments increase annually, with the increased amount being used to reduce directly the principal balance outstanding and thus shorten the overall term of the loan.

habendum clause　That part of a deed beginning with the words "to have and to hold," following the granting clause and defining the extent of ownership the grantor is conveying.

heir　One who might inherit or succeed to an interest in land under the state law of descent when the owner dies without leaving a valid will.

highest and best use　The possible use of a property that would produce the greatest net income and thereby develop the highest value.

holdover tenancy　A tenancy whereby a lessee retains possession of leased property after the lease has expired and the landlord, by continuing to accept rent, agrees to the tenant's continued occupancy as defined by state law.

holographic will　A will that is written, dated, and signed in the testator's handwriting.

home equity loan　A loan (sometimes called a *line of credit*) under which a property owner uses his or her residence as collateral and can then draw funds up to a prearranged amount against the property.

homeowner's insurance policy　A standardized package insurance policy that covers a residential real estate owner against financial loss from fire, theft, public liability, and other common risks.

homestead　Land that is owned and occupied as the family home. In many states a portion of the area or value of this land is protected or exempt from judgments for debts.

hypothecate　To pledge property as security for an obligation or loan without giving up possession of it.

implied agreement　A contract under which the agreement of the parties is demonstrated by their acts and conduct.

implied contract　*See* implied agreement.

implied warranty of habitability　A theory in landlord/tenant law in which the landlord renting residential property implies that the property is habitable and fit for its intended use.

improvement   (1) Any structure, usually privately owned, erected on a site to enhance the value of the property—for example, building a fence or a driveway. (2) A publicly owned structure added to or benefiting land, such as a curb, sidewalk, street, or sewer.

income approach   The process of estimating the value of an income-producing property through capitalization of the annual net income expected to be produced by the property during its remaining useful life.

incorporeal right   A nonpossessory right in real estate; for example, an easement or a right-of-way.

independent contractor   Someone who is retained to perform a certain act but who is subject to the control and direction of another only as to the end result and not as to the way in which the act is performed. Unlike an employee, an independent contractor pays for all expenses, Social Security, and income taxes, and receives no employee benefits. Most real estate salespeople are independent contractors.

index method   The appraisal method of estimating building costs by multiplying the original cost of the property by a percentage factor to adjust for current construction costs.

inflation   The gradual reduction of the purchasing power of the dollar, usually related directly to the increases in the money supply by the federal government.

inheritance taxes   State-imposed taxes on a decedent's real and personal property.

inoperative status   In Illinois, a license status that prohibits a licensee from engaging in real estate activities because he or she is unsponsored or his or her license has lapsed or been suspended or revoked.

installment contract   A contract for the sale of real estate whereby the purchase price is paid in periodic installments by the purchaser, who is in possession of the property even though title is retained by the seller until all payments are received in full. Also called a *contract for deed* or *articles of agreement for warranty deed*.

installment sale   A transaction in which the sales price is paid in two or more installments over two or more years. If the sale meets certain requirements, a taxpayer can postpone reporting such income until future years by paying tax each year only on the proceeds received that year.

interest   A charge made by a lender for the use of money.

interim financing   A short-term loan usually made during the construction phase of a building project.

Interstate Land Sales Full Disclosure Act   Federal law that regulates the sale of certain real estate in interstate commerce.

intestate   The condition of a property owner who dies without leaving a valid will. Title to the property will pass to the decedent's heirs as provided in the state law of descent.

intrinsic value   An appraisal term referring to the value created by a person's personal preferences for a particular type of property.

investment   Money directed toward the purchase, improvement, and development of an asset in expectation of income or profits.

involuntary alienation   *See* alienation.

involuntary lien   A lien placed on property without the consent of the property owner.

joint tenancy   Ownership of real estate between two or more parties who have been named in one conveyance as joint tenants. Upon the death of a joint tenant, the decedent's interest passes to the surviving joint tenant or tenants by the *right of survivorship*.

joint venture   The joining of two or more people to conduct a specific business enterprise. A joint venture is similar to a partnership in that it must be created by agreement between the parties to share in the losses and profits of the venture. It is unlike a partnership in that the venture is for one specific project only, rather than for a continuing business relationship.

judgment   The formal decision of a court on the respective rights and claims of the parties to an action or suit. After a judgment has been entered and recorded with the county recorder, it usually becomes a general lien on the property of the defendant.

judicial precedent   In law, the requirements established by prior court decisions.

Junk Fax Prevention Act   Prohibits faxing unsolicited fax advertisements or solicitations and does allow for an established business relationship exception.

junior lien   An obligation, such as a second mortgage, that is subordinate in right or lien priority to an existing lien on the same realty.

laches   An equitable doctrine used by courts to bar a legal claim or prevent the assertion of a right because of undue delay or failure to assert the claim or right.

land   The earth's surface, extending downward to the center of the earth and upward infinitely into space, including things permanently attached by nature, such as trees and water.

land contract   *See* installment contract.

latent defect   A hidden structural defect that could not be discovered by ordinary inspection and that threatens the property's soundness or the safety of its inhabitants. Some states impose on sellers and licensees a duty to inspect for and disclose latent defects.

law of agency *See* agency.

lease A written or oral contract between a landlord (the *lessor*) and a tenant (the *lessee*) that transfers the right to exclusive possession and use of the landlord's real property to the lessee for a specified period of time and for a stated consideration (rent). By state law leases for longer than a certain period of time (generally one year) must be in writing to be enforceable.

leasehold estate A tenant's right to occupy real estate during the term of a lease, generally considered to be a personal property interest.

lease option A lease under which the tenant has the right to purchase the property either during the lease term or at its end.

lease purchase The purchase of real property, the consummation of which is preceded by a lease, usually long-term. Typically done for tax or financing purposes.

leasing agent license In Illinois, a limited license for individuals who wish to engage only in activities related to leasing residential property.

legacy A disposition of money or personal property by will.

legal description A description of a specific parcel of real estate complete enough for an independent surveyor to locate and identify it.

legally competent parties People who are recognized by law as being able to contract with others; those of legal age and sound mind.

lessee *See* lease.

lessor *See* lease.

leverage The use of borrowed money to finance an investment.

levy To assess; to seize or collect. To levy a tax is to assess a property and set the rate of taxation. To levy an execution is to officially seize the property of a person to satisfy an obligation.

license (1) A privilege or right granted to a person by a state to operate as a real estate broker or salesperson. (2) The revocable permission for a temporary use of land—a personal right that cannot be sold.

lien A right given by law to certain creditors to have their debts paid out of the property of a defaulting debtor, usually by means of a court sale.

lien theory Some states interpret a mortgage as being purely a lien on real property. The mortgagee thus has no right of possession but must foreclose the lien and sell the property if the mortgagor defaults.

life cycle costing In property management, comparing one type of equipment with another based on both purchase cost and operating cost over its expected useful lifetime.

life estate An interest in real or personal property that is limited in duration to the lifetime of its owner or some other designated person or persons.

life tenant A person in possession of a life estate.

limited partnership *See* partnership.

liquidated damages An amount predetermined by the parties to a contract as the total compensation to an injured party should the other party breach the contract.

liquidity The ability to sell an asset and convert it into cash, at a price close to its true value, in a short period of time.

lis pendens A recorded legal document giving constructive notice that an action affecting a particular property has been filed in either a state or a federal court.

listing agreement A contract between an owner (as principal) and a real estate broker (as agent) by which the broker is employed as agent to find a buyer for the owner's real estate on the owner's terms, for which service the owner agrees to pay a commission.

listing broker The broker in a multiple listing situation from whose office a listing agreement is initiated, as opposed to the *cooperating broker*, from whose office negotiations leading up to a sale are initiated. The listing broker and the cooperating broker may be the same person.

littoral rights (1) A landowner's claim to use water in large navigable lakes and oceans adjacent to his or her property. (2) The ownership rights to land bordering these bodies of water up to the high-water mark.

loan origination fee A fee charged to the borrower by the lender for making a mortgage loan. The fee is usually computed as a percentage of the loan amount.

loan-to-value ratio The relationship between the amount of the mortgage loan and the value of the real estate being pledged as collateral.

location *See* situs.

lot-and-block (recorded plat) system A method of describing real property that identifies a parcel of land by reference to lot and block numbers within a subdivision, as specified on a recorded subdivision plat.

management agreement A contract between the owner of income property and a management firm or individual property manager that outlines the scope of the manager's authority.

manufactured housing Dwellings that are built off-site and trucked to a building lot where they are installed or assembled.

market A place where goods can be bought and sold and a price established.

marketable title   Good or clear title, reasonably free from the risk of litigation over possible defects.

market value   The most probable price property would bring in an arm's-length transaction under normal conditions on the open market.

master plan   A comprehensive plan to guide the long-term physical development of a particular area.

mechanic's lien   A statutory lien created in favor of contractors, laborers, and materialmen who have performed work or furnished materials in the erection or repair of a building.

Megan's Law   Federal legislation that promotes the establishment of state registration systems to maintain residential information on every person who kidnaps children, commits sexual crimes against children, or commits sexually violent crimes.

meridian   One of a set of imaginary lines running north and south and crossing a base line at a definite point, used in the rectangular (government) survey system of property description.

metes-and-bounds description   A legal description of a parcel of land that begins at a well-marked point and follows the boundaries, using directions and distances around the tract, back to the point of beginning.

mill   One-tenth of one cent. Some states use a mill rate to compute real estate taxes; for example, a rate of 52 mills would be $.052 tax for each dollar of assessed valuation of a property.

minimum services   A provision of the *Real Estate License Act of 2000* that requires licensees to perform a minimum level of service to clients.

ministerial acts   In Illinois, acts that a licensee may perform for a consumer that are informative and do not constitute active representation.

minor   Someone who has not reached the age of majority and therefore does not have legal capacity to transfer title to real property.

monetary policy   Governmental regulation of the amount of money in circulation through such institutions as the Federal Reserve Board.

month-to-month tenancy   A periodic tenancy under which the tenant rents for one month at a time. In the absence of a rental agreement (oral or written) a tenancy is generally considered to be month to month.

monument   A fixed natural or artificial object used to establish real estate boundaries for a metes-and-bounds description.

mortgage   A conditional transfer or pledge of real estate as security for the payment of a debt. Also, the document creating a mortgage lien.

mortgage banker   Mortgage loan companies that originate, service, and sell loans to investors.

mortgage broker   An agent of a lender who brings the lender and borrower together. The broker receives a fee for this service.

mortgagee   A lender in a mortgage loan transaction.

mortgage lien   A lien or charge on the property of a mortgagor that secures the underlying debt obligations.

mortgagor   A borrower in a mortgage loan transaction.

multiperil policies   Insurance policies that offer protection from a range of potential perils, such as those of a fire, hazard, public liability, and casualty.

multiple listing clause   A provision in an exclusive listing for the authority and obligation on the part of the listing broker to distribute the listing to other brokers in the multiple listing organization.

multiple listing service (MLS)   A marketing organization composed of member brokers who agree to share their listing agreements with one another in the hope of procuring ready, willing, and able buyers for their properties more quickly than they could on their own. Most multiple listing services accept exclusive-right-to-sell or exclusive-agency listings from their member brokers.

National Do Not Call Registry   A registry managed by the Federal Trade Commission that lists the phone numbers of consumers who have indicated their preference to limit the telemarketing calls they receive.

negotiable instrument   A written promise or order to pay a specific sum of money that may be transferred by endorsement or delivery. The transferee then has the original payee's right to payment.

net lease   A lease requiring that the tenant pay not only rent but also costs incurred in maintaining the property, including taxes, insurance, utilities, and repairs.

net listing   A listing based on the net price the seller will receive if the property is sold. Under a net listing the broker can offer the property for sale at the highest price obtainable to increase the commission. This type of listing is legal in Illinois.

net operating income (NOI)   The income projected for an income-producing property after deducting losses for vacancy, collection, and operating expenses.

nonagent   An intermediary between a buyer and seller, or landlord and tenant, who assists both parties in a transaction without representing either. Also known as a *facilitator*, *transaction broker*, *transaction coordinator*, and *contract broker*.

nonconforming use   A use of property that is permitted to continue after a zoning ordinance prohibiting it has been established for the area.

nonhomogeneity A lack of uniformity; dissimilarity. Because no two parcels of land are exactly alike, real estate is said to be *non-homogeneous*.

note *See* promissory note.

novation Substituting a new obligation for an old one or substituting new parties to an existing obligation.

nuncupative will An oral will declared by the testator in his or her final illness, made before witnesses and afterward reduced to writing.

obsolescence The loss of value due to factors that are outmoded or less useful. Obsolescence may be functional or economic.

occupancy permit A permit issued by the appropriate local governing body to establish that the property is suitable for habitation by meeting certain safety and health standards.

offer and acceptance Two essential components of a valid contract; a "meeting of the minds."

offeror/offeree The person who makes the offer is the *offeror*. The person to whom the offer is made is the *offeree*.

Office of Thrift Supervision (OTS) Monitors and regulates the savings and loan industry. OTS was created by FIRREA.

open-end loan A mortgage loan that is expandable by increments up to a maximum dollar amount, the full loan being secured by the same original mortgage.

open listing A listing contract under which the broker's commission is contingent on the broker's producing a ready, willing, and able buyer before the property is sold by the seller or another broker.

option An agreement to keep open for a set period an offer to sell or purchase property.

option listing Listing with a provision that gives the listing broker the right to purchase the listed property.

ostensible agency A form of implied agency relationship created by the actions of the parties involved rather than by written agreement or document.

package loan A real estate loan used to finance the purchase of both real property and personal property, such as in the purchase of a new home that includes carpeting, window coverings, and major appliances.

parol evidence rule A rule of evidence providing that a written agreement is the final expression of the agreement of the parties, not to be varied or contradicted by prior or contemporaneous oral or written negotiations.

participation mortgage A mortgage loan wherein the lender has a partial equity interest in the property or receives a portion of the income from the property.

partition The division of cotenants' interests in real property when the parties do not all voluntarily agree to terminate the co-ownership; takes place through court procedures.

partnership An association of two or more individuals who carry on a continuing business for profit as co-owners. Under the law a partnership is regarded as a group of individuals rather than as a single entity. A *general partnership* is a typical form of joint venture in which each general partner shares in the administration, profits, and losses of the operation. A *limited partnership* is a business arrangement whereby the operation is administered by one or more general partners and funded, by and large, by limited or silent partners, who are by law responsible for losses only to the extent of their investments.

party wall A wall that is located on or at a boundary line between two adjoining parcels of land and is used or is intended to be used by the owners of both properties.

patent A grant or franchise of land from the United States government.

payment cap The limit on the amount the monthly payment can be increased on an adjustable-rate mortgage when the interest rate is adjusted.

payoff statement *See* reduction certificate.

percentage lease A lease, commonly used for commercial property, whose rental is based on the tenant's gross sales at the premises; it usually stipulates a base monthly rental plus a percentage of any gross sales above a certain amount.

percolation test A test of the soil to determine if it will absorb and drain water adequately to use a septic system for sewage disposal.

periodic estate (tenancy) *See* estate (tenancy) from period to period.

personal property Items, called *chattels*, that do not fit into the definition of real property; movable objects.

physical deterioration A reduction in a property's value resulting from a decline in physical condition; can be caused by action of the elements or by ordinary wear and tear.

planned unit development (PUD) Planned combination of diverse land uses, such as housing, recreation, and shopping, in one contained development or subdivision.

plat map A map of a town, section, or subdivision indicating the location and boundaries of individual properties.

plottage The increase in value or utility resulting from the consolidation (*assemblage*) of two or more adjacent lots into one larger lot.

pocket card In Illinois, a card that must be carried by the licensee when engaging in real estate activities for which a license is required.

point of beginning (POB) In a metes-and-bounds legal description, the starting point of the survey, situated in one corner of the parcel; all metes-and-bounds descriptions must follow the boundaries of the parcel back to the point of beginning.

police power The government's right to impose laws, statutes, and ordinances, including zoning ordinances and building codes, to protect the public health, safety, and welfare.

polychlorinated biphenyls Used as an insulating material in dielectric oil and may be present in electrical equipment.

power of attorney A written instrument authorizing a person, the *attorney-in-fact*, to act as agent for another person to the extent indicated in the instrument.

prepaid items On a closing statement, items that have been paid in advance by the seller, such as insurance premiums and some real estate taxes, for which he or she must be reimbursed by the buyer.

prepayment penalty A charge imposed on a borrower who pays off the loan principal early. This penalty compensates the lender for interest and other charges that would otherwise be lost.

price-fixing *See* antitrust laws.

primary mortgage market The mortgage market in which loans are originated, consisting of lenders such as commercial banks, savings and loan associations, and mutual savings banks.

principal (1) A sum loaned or employed as a fund or an investment, as distinguished from its income or profits. (2) The original amount (as in a loan) of the total due and payable at a certain date. (3) A main party to a transaction—the person for whom the agent works.

principal meridian The main imaginary line running north and south and crossing a base line at a definite point, used by surveyors for reference in locating and describing land under the rectangular (government) survey system of legal description.

prior appropriation A concept of water ownership in which the landowner's right to use available water is based on a government-administered permit system.

priority The order of position or time. The priority of liens is generally determined by the chronological order in which the lien documents are recorded; tax liens, however, have priority even over previously recorded liens.

private mortgage insurance (PMI) Insurance provided by private carrier that protects a lender against a loss in the event of a foreclosure and deficiency.

probate A legal process by which a court determines who will inherit a decedent's property and what the estate's assets and liabilities are.

procuring cause The effort that brings about the desired result. Under an open listing the broker who is the procuring cause of the sale receives the commission.

progression An appraisal principle that states that, between dissimilar properties, the value of the lesser-quality property is favorably affected by the presence of the better-quality property.

promissory note A financing instrument that states the terms of the underlying obligation, is signed by its maker, and is negotiable (transferable to a third party).

property manager Someone who manages real estate for another person for compensation. Duties include collecting rents, maintaining the property, and keeping up all accounting.

property reports The mandatory federal and state documents compiled by subdividers and developers to provide potential purchasers with facts about a property prior to their purchase.

proprietary lease A lease given by the corporation that owns a cooperative apartment building to the shareholder for the shareholder's right as a tenant to an individual apartment.

prorations Expenses, either prepaid or paid in arrears, that are divided or distributed between buyer and seller at the closing.

protected class Any group of people designated as such by the Department of Housing and Urban Development (HUD) in consideration of federal and state civil rights legislation. Currently includes ethnic minorities, women, religious groups, the handicapped, and others.

puffing Exaggerated or superlative comments or opinions.

pur autre vie A life estate *pur autre vie* is a life estate that is measured by the life of a person other than the grantee.

purchase-money mortgage (PMM) A note secured by a mortgage or deed of trust given by a buyer, as borrower, to a seller, as lender, as part of the purchase price of the real estate.

quantity-survey method The appraisal method of estimating building costs by calculating the cost of all of the physical components in the improvements, adding the cost to assemble them and then including the indirect costs associated with such construction.

quiet title A court action to remove a cloud on the title.

quitclaim deed A conveyance by which the grantor transfers whatever interest he or she has in the real estate, without warranties or obligations.

radon A naturally occurring gas that is suspected of causing lung cancer.

range   A strip of land six miles wide, extending north and south and numbered east and west according to its distance from the principal meridian in the rectangular (government) survey system of legal description.

rate cap   The limit on the amount the interest rate can be increased at each adjustment period in an adjustable-rate loan. The cap also may set the maximum interest rate that can be charged during the life of the loan.

ratification   Method of creating an agency relationship in which the principal accepts the conduct of someone who acted without prior authorization as the principal's agent.

ready, willing, and able buyer   One who is prepared to buy property on the seller's terms and is ready to take positive steps to consummate the transaction.

real estate   Land; a portion of the earth's surface extending downward to the center of the earth and upward infinitely into space, including all things permanently attached to it, whether naturally or artificially.

real estate assistant   A licensed or unlicensed individual who assists a broker or salesperson in the real estate business.

real estate investment trust (REIT)   Trust ownership of real estate by a group of individuals who purchase certificates of ownership in the trust, which in turn invests the money in real property and distributes the profits back to the investors free of corporate income tax.

real estate license law   State law enacted to protect the public from fraud, dishonesty, and incompetence in the purchase and sale of real estate.

real estate mortgage investment conduit (REMIC)   A tax entity that issues multiple classes of investor interests (securities) backed by a pool of mortgages.

real estate recovery fund   A fund established to cover claims of aggrieved parties who have suffered monetary damage through the actions of a real estate licensee.

Real Estate Settlement Procedures Act (RESPA)   The federal law that requires certain disclosures to consumers about mortgage loan settlements. The law also prohibits the payment or receipt of kickbacks and certain kinds of referral fees.

real property   The interests, benefits, and rights inherent in real estate ownership.

REALTOR®   A registered trademark term reserved for the sole use of active members of the National Association of REALTORS®.

reconciliation   The final step in the appraisal process, in which the appraiser combines the estimates of value received from the sales comparison, cost, and income approaches to arrive at a final estimate of market value for the subject property.

reconveyance deed   A deed used by a trustee under a deed of trust to return title to the trustor.

recording   The act of entering or recording documents affecting or conveying interests in real estate in the recorder's office established in each county. Until it is recorded, a deed or mortgage ordinarily is not effective against subsequent purchasers or mortgagees.

rectangular (government) survey system   System established in 1785 by the federal government, providing for surveying and describing land by reference to principal meridians and base lines.

redemption   The right of a defaulted property owner to recover his or her property by curing the default.

redemption period   A period of time established by state law during which a property owner has the right to redeem his or her real estate from a foreclosure or tax sale by paying the sales price, interest, and costs. Many states do not have mortgage redemption laws.

redlining   The illegal practice of a lending institution denying loans or restricting their number for certain areas of a community.

reduction certificate (payoff statement)   The document signed by a lender indicating the amount required to pay a loan balance in full and satisfy the debt; used in the settlement process to protect both the seller's and the buyer's interests.

regression   An appraisal principle that states that, between dissimilar properties, the value of the better-quality property is affected adversely by the presence of the lesser-quality property.

Regulation Z   Implements the *Truth-in-Lending Act* requiring that credit institutions inform borrowers of the true cost of obtaining credit.

reinstatement   The activation of a suspended, revoked, or inoperative license.

release deed   A document, also known as a *deed of reconveyance*, that transfers all rights given a trustee under a deed of trust loan back to the grantor after the loan has been fully repaid.

remainder interest   The remnant of an estate that has been conveyed to take effect and be enjoyed after the termination of a prior estate, such as when an owner conveys a life estate to one party and the remainder to another.

rent   A fixed, periodic payment made by a tenant of a property to the owner for possession and use, usually by prior agreement of the parties.

rent schedule   A statement of proposed rental rates, determined by the owner or the property manager or both, based on a building's estimated expenses, market supply and demand, and the owner's long-range goals for the property.

replacement cost The construction cost at current prices of a property that is not necessarily an exact duplicate of the subject property but serves the same purpose or function as the original.

reproduction cost The construction cost at current prices of an exact duplicate of the subject property.

Resolution Trust Corporation The organization created by FIRREA to liquidate the assets of failed savings and loan associations.

restrictive covenants A clause in a deed that limits the way the real estate ownership may be used.

reverse-annuity mortgage (RAM) A loan under which the homeowner receives monthly payments based on his or her accumulated equity rather than a lump sum. The loan must be repaid at a prearranged date or on the death of the owner or the sale of the property.

reversionary interest The remnant of an estate that the grantor holds after granting a life estate to another person.

reversionary right The return of the rights of possession and quiet enjoyment to the lessor at the expiration of a lease.

right of survivorship *See* joint tenancy.

right-of-way The right given by one landowner to another to pass over the land, construct a roadway, or use as a pathway, without actually transferring ownership.

riparian rights An owner's rights in land that borders on or includes a stream, river, or lake. These rights include access to and use of the water.

risk management Evaluation and selection of appropriate property and other insurance.

rules and regulations Real estate licensing authority orders that govern licensees' activities; they usually have the same force and effect as statutory law.

sale and leaseback A transaction in which an owner sells his or her improved property and, as part of the same transaction, signs a long-term lease to remain in possession of the premises.

sales comparison approach The process of estimating the value of a property by examining and comparing actual sales of comparable properties.

salesperson A person who performs real estate activities while employed by or associated with a licensed real estate broker.

satisfaction of mortgage A document acknowledging the payment of a mortgage debt.

secondary mortgage market A market for the purchase and sale of existing mortgages, designed to provide greater liquidity for mortgages.

section A portion of a township under the rectangular (government) survey system. A township is divided into 36 sections, numbered 1 through 36. A section is a square with mile-long sides and an area of one square mile, or 640 acres.

security deposit A payment by a tenant, held by the landlord during the lease term and kept (wholly or partially) on default or destruction of the premises by the tenant.

seisin Possession of real property under claim of freehold estate (fee simple).

separate property Under community property law, property owned solely by either spouse before the marriage, acquired by gift or inheritance after the marriage, or purchased with separate funds after the marriage.

servient tenement Land on which an easement exists in favor of an adjacent property (called a *dominant estate*); also called a *servient estate*.

setback The amount of space local zoning regulations require between a lot line and a building line.

severalty Ownership of real property by one person only, also called *sole ownership*.

severance Changing an item of real estate to personal property by detaching it from the land; for example, cutting down a tree.

sharecropping In an agricultural lease, the agreement between the landowner and the tenant farmer to split the crop or the profit from its sale, actually sharing the crop.

single agency The representation of a single principal.

situs The personal preference of people for one area over another.

special agent One who is authorized by a principal to perform a single act or transaction; a real estate broker is usually a special agent authorized to find a ready, willing, and able buyer for a particular property.

special assessment A tax or levy customarily imposed against only those specific parcels of real estate that will benefit from a proposed public improvement like a street or sewer.

special service area (SSA) A taxing mechanism that can be used to fund a wide range of special or additional services and/or physical improvements in a defined geographic area within a municipality or jurisdiction.

special warranty deed A deed in which the grantor warrants, or guarantees, the title only against defects arising during the period of his or her tenure and ownership of the property and not against defects existing before that time.

specific lien A lien affecting or attaching only to a certain, specific parcel of land or piece of property.

specific performance   A legal action to compel a party to carry out the terms of a contract.

sponsor card   In Illinois, a card that certifies a new licensee's relationship with a broker and serves as a temporary permit to practice until a permanent pocket card is received.

square-foot method   The appraisal method of estimating building costs by multiplying the number of square feet in the improvements being appraised by the cost per square foot for recently constructed similar improvements.

statute of frauds   That part of a state law that requires that certain instruments, such as deeds, real estate sales contracts, and certain leases, be in writing to be legally enforceable.

statute of limitations   That law pertaining to the period of time within which certain actions must be brought to court.

statutory lien   A lien imposed on property by statute—a tax lien, for example—in contrast to an *equitable lien*, which arises out of common law.

statutory redemption   The right of a defaulted property owner to recover the property after its sale by paying the appropriate fees and charges.

steering   The illegal practice of channeling homeseekers to particular areas, either to maintain the homogeneity of an area or to change the character of an area, which limits their choices of where they can live.

stigmatized property   A property that has acquired an undesirable reputation due to an event that occurred on or near it, such as violent crime, gang-related activity, illness, or personal tragedy. Some states restrict the disclosure of information about stigmatized properties.

straight-line method   A method of calculating depreciation for tax purposes, computed by dividing the adjusted basis of a property by the estimated number of years of remaining useful life.

straight (term) loan   A loan in which only interest is paid during the term of the loan, with the entire principal amount due with the final interest payment.

subagent   One who is employed by a person already acting as an agent.

subdivider   One who buys undeveloped land, divides it into smaller, usable lots, and sells the lots to potential users.

subdivision   A tract of land divided by the owner, known as the *subdivider*, into blocks, building lots, and streets according to a recorded subdivision plat, which must comply with local ordinances and regulations.

subdivision and development ordinances   Municipal ordinances that establish requirements for subdivisions and development.

subdivision plat   *See* plat map.

sublease   *See* subletting.

subletting   The leasing of premises by a lessee to a third party for part of the lessee's remaining term. *See also* assignment.

subordination   Relegation to a lesser position, usually in respect to a right or security.

subordination agreement   A written agreement between holders of liens on a property that changes the priority of mortgage, judgment, and other liens under certain circumstances.

subrogation   The substitution of one creditor for another, with the substituted person succeeding to the legal rights and claims of the original claimant. Subrogation is used by title insurers to acquire from the injured party rights to sue to recover any claims the insurers have paid.

substitution   An appraisal principle that states that the maximum value of a property tends to be set by the cost of purchasing an equally desirable and valuable substitute property, assuming that no costly delay is encountered in making the substitution.

subsurface rights   Ownership rights in a parcel of real estate to the water, minerals, gas, oil, and so forth that lie beneath the surface of the property.

suit for possession   A court suit initiated by a landlord to evict a tenant from leased premises after the tenant has breached one of the terms of the lease or has held possession of the property after the lease's expiration.

suit to quiet title   A court action intended to establish or settle the title to a particular property, especially when there is a cloud on the title.

Superfund   Popular name of the hazardous-waste cleanup fund established by the Comprehensive Environmental Response, Compensation, and Liability Act (CERCLA).

Superfund Amendments and Reauthorization Act (SARA)   An amendatory statute that contains stronger cleanup standards for contaminated sites, increased funding for Superfund, and clarifications of lender liability and innocent landowner immunity. *See Comprehensive Environmental Response, Compensation, and Liability Act (CERCLA).*

supply   The amount of goods available in the market to be sold at a given price. The term is often coupled with *demand*.

supply and demand   The appraisal principle that follows the interrelationship of the supply of and demand for real estate. As appraising is based on economic concepts, this principle recognizes that real property is subject to the influences of the marketplace just as is any other commodity.

surety bond   An agreement by an insurance or bonding company to be responsible for certain possible defaults, debts, or obligations contracted for by an insured party. In the real estate business a surety bond is generally used to ensure that a particular project will be completed at a certain date or that a contract will be performed as stated.

surface rights   Ownership rights in a parcel of real estate that are limited to the surface of the property and do not include the air above it (*air rights*) or the minerals below the surface (*subsurface rights*).

survey   The process by which boundaries are measured and land areas are determined; the on-site measurement of lot lines, dimensions, and position of a house on a lot, including the determination of any existing encroachments or easements.

syndicate   A combination of people or firms formed to accomplish a business venture of mutual interest by pooling resources. In a *real estate investment syndicate* the parties own and/or develop property, with the main profit generally arising from the sale of the property.

tacking   Adding or combining successive periods of continuous occupation of real property by adverse possessors. This concept enables someone who has not been in possession for the entire statutory period to establish a claim of adverse possession.

taxation   The process by which a government or municipal quasi-public body raises monies to fund its operation.

tax credit   An amount by which tax owed is reduced directly.

tax deed   An instrument given to a purchaser after the expiration of the redemption rights. *See also* certificate of sale.

tax lien   A charge against property, created by operation of law. Tax liens and assessments take priority over all other liens.

tax sale   A court-ordered sale of real property to raise money to cover delinquent taxes.

tenancy by the entirety   The joint ownership, of property acquired by husband and wife during marriage. Upon the death of one spouse the survivor becomes the owner of the property.

tenancy in common   A form of co-ownership by which each owner holds an undivided interest in real property as if he or she were sole owner. Each individual owner has the right to partition. Unlike joint tenants, tenants in common have right of inheritance.

tenant   One who holds or possesses lands or tenements by any kind of right or title.

tenant improvements   Alterations to the interior of a building to meet the functional demands of the tenant.

testate   Having made and left a valid will.

testator   A person who has made a valid will.

tier (township strip)   A strip of land six miles wide, extending east and west and numbered north and south according to its distance from the base line in the rectangular (government) survey system of legal description.

time is of the essence   A phrase in a contract that requires the performance of a certain act within a stated period of time.

time-share   A form of ownership interest that may include an estate interest in property and that allows use of the property for a fixed or variable time period.

time-share estate   A fee simple interest in a time-share property.

time-share use   A right of occupancy in a time-share property, less than a fee simple interest.

title   (1) The right to or ownership of land. (2) The evidence of ownership of land.

title insurance   A policy insuring the owner or mortgagee against loss by reason of defects in the title to a parcel of real estate, other than encumbrances, defects, and matters specifically excluded by the policy.

title search   The examination of public records relating to real estate to determine the current state of the ownership.

title theory   Some states interpret a mortgage to mean that the lender is the owner of mortgaged land. On full payment of the mortgage debt the borrower becomes the landowner.

township   The principal unit of the rectangular (government) survey system. A township is a square with six-mile sides and an area of 36 square miles.

township strips   *See* tier.

trade fixture   An article installed by a tenant under the terms of a lease and removable by the tenant before the lease expires.

transfer tax   Tax stamps required to be affixed to a deed by state and/or local law.

trust   A fiduciary arrangement whereby property is conveyed to a person or institution, called a *trustee,* to be held and administered on behalf of another person, called a *beneficiary.* The one who conveys the trust is called the *trustor.*

trust deed   An instrument used to create a mortgage lien by which the borrower conveys title to a trustee, who holds it as security for the benefit of the note holder (the lender); also called a *deed of trust.*

trust deed lien   A lien on the property of a trustor that secures a deed of trust loan.

trustee   The holder of bare legal title in a deed of trust loan transaction.

trustee's deed   A deed executed by a trustee conveying land held in a trust.

trustor   A borrower in a deed of trust loan transaction.

undivided interest   *See* tenancy in common.

unenforceable contract   A contract that has all the elements of a valid contract, yet neither party can sue the other to force performance of it.

unilateral contract   A one-sided contract wherein one party makes a promise so as to induce a second party to do something. The second party is not legally bound to perform; however, if the second party does comply, the first party is obligated to keep the promise.

unit-in-place method   The appraisal method of estimating building costs by calculating the costs of all of the physical components in the structure, with the cost of each item including its proper installation, connection, etc.; also called the *segregated cost method*.

unit of ownership   The four unities that are traditionally needed to create a joint tenancy—unity of title, time, interest, and possession.

usury   Charging interest at a higher rate than the maximum rate established by state law.

valid contract   A contract that complies with all the essentials of a contract and is binding and enforceable on all parties to it.

VA loan   A mortgage loan on approved property made to a qualified veteran by an authorized lender and guaranteed by the Department of Veterans Affairs to limit the lender's possible loss.

value   The power of a good or service to command other goods in exchange for the present worth of future rights to its income or amenities.

variance   Permission obtained from zoning authorities to build a structure or conduct a use that is expressly prohibited by the current zoning laws; an exception from the zoning ordinances.

vendee   A buyer, usually under the terms of a land contract.

vendor   A seller, usually under the terms of a land contract.

voidable contract   A contract that seems to be valid on the surface but may be rejected or disaffirmed by one or both of the parties.

void contract   A contract that has no legal force or effect because it does not meet the essential elements of a contract.

voluntary alienation   *See* alienation.

voluntary lien   A lien placed on property with the knowledge and consent of the property owner.

waste   An improper use or an abuse of a property by a possessor who holds less than fee ownership, such as a tenant, life tenant, mortgagor, or vendee. Such waste ordinarily impairs the value of the land or the interest of the person holding the title or the reversionary rights.

will   A written document, properly witnessed, providing for the transfer of title to property owned by the deceased, called the *testator*.

workers' compensation acts   Laws that require an employer to obtain insurance coverage to protect his or her employees who are injured in the course of their employment.

wraparound loan   A method of refinancing in which the new mortgage is placed in a secondary, or subordinate, position; the new mortgage includes both the unpaid principal balance of the first mortgage and whatever additional sums are advanced by the lender.

zoning ordinance   An exercise of police power by a municipality to regulate and control the character and use of property.

Answer Key

Following are the correct answers to the review questions included in each chapter of the text. *In parentheses following the correct answers are references to the pages where the question topics are discussed or explained.* Suggested math calculations for some of the review questions can be found on pages 592 and 593. *If you have answered a question incorrectly, be sure to go back to the page or pages noted and restudy the material until you understand the correct answer.* The references for the Sample Examinations are to Chapter numbers.

CHAPTER 1
Introduction to the Real Estate Business

1. B (2)
2. B (6)
3. C (7)
4. C (7)
5. B (2, 3, 4)
6. D (4)
7. B (7)
8. A (3)

CHAPTER 2
Real Property and the Law

1. A (13)
2. B (15, 16)
3. C (18)
4. C (13)
5. D (16)
6. B (12)
7. A (15)
8. D (17)
9. B (14)
10. A (15)
11. B (13)
12. C (15)
13. D (12)
14. A (12)

CHAPTER 3
Concepts of Home Ownership

1. D (28)
2. B (26)
3. A (24)
4. B (24)
5. B (27)
6. D (27)
7. A (28, 29)
8. C (27)
9. C (28)
10. C (29)
11. C (27)
12. C (592)

CHAPTER 4
Real Estate Agency

1. C (37)
2. A (48)
3. A (37)
4. B (36)
5. C (48)
6. B (48)
7. D (46, 47)
8. C (47)
9. C (47)
10. C (51)
11. B (36)
12. A (37)
13. D (39)
14. B (49)
15. B (59)

CHAPTER 5
Real Estate Brokerage

1. B (63)
2. B (61)
3. B (64)
4. B (64)
5. D (68)
6. C (65)
7. D (61)
8. C (72)
9. A (592)
10. A (592)
11. C (72)
12. D (74)
13. C (74, 75)

CHAPTER 6
Brokerage Agreements

1. A (81)
2. C (81)
3. C (101)
4. A (81)
5. A (592)
6. D (82)
7. A (81)
8. D (85)
9. A (80)
10. D (592)
11. B (81)
12. B (64)
13. A (97)
14. B (97)
15. B (82)
16. A (592)
17. C (592)
18. C (82)

19. B (93)
20. C (97)
21. A (83)

CHAPTER 7
Interests in Real Estate

1. C (119)
2. A (111)
3. C (111, 112)
4. D (116)
5. A (112, 113)
6. D (115)
7. D (118, 119)
8. C (122)
9. A (108)
10. D (111, 112)
11. B (116)
12. A (114)
13. B (113)
14. B (120)
15. A (116)
16. D (120)
17. B (115)
18. A (115)
19. C (119)
20. C (110)
21. D (112, 113)
22. A (115)
23. B (112, 113)
24. B (113)

CHAPTER 8
Forms of Real Estate Ownership

1. D (131)
2. D (130)
3. A (130, 131)
4. B (139)
5. B (135)
6. D (133, 134)
7. B (129)
8. A (136)
9. C (142)
10. C (143)
11. C (138)
12. D (130)
13. D (133)
14. B (129)
15. B (129, 130)
16. C (141)
17. B (141)

18. B (130, 133)
19. D (139)
20. A (130)
21. D (143)
22. B (136)
23. A (132)
24. A (137)
25. B (130)
26. D (132)
27. A (140)

CHAPTER 9
Legal Descriptions

1. B (157)
2. D (152)
3. D (592)
4. B (150)
5. C (154)
6. C (154)
7. A (154)
8. A (154)
9. A (155)
10. D (592)
11. C (154)
12. D (592)
13. C (154)
14. D (156)
15. B (156)
16. B (592)
17. B (592)
18. B (592)
19. B (154)
20. C (154)
21. B (155)
22. A (152)
23. C (159)
24. C (152, 153)
25. B (160)
26. C (160)
27. C (160)

CHAPTER 10
Real Estate Taxes and Other Liens

1. D (169)
2. B (170)
3. B (177)
4. C (169)
5. B (171)
6. D (593)

7. C (171)
8. C (178, 179)
9. D (596)
10. C (169)
11. D (180)
12. C (177, 178)
13. B (169)
14. B (169)
15. D (178)
16. A (169)
17. B (171)
18. D (181)
19. B (173)
20. A (178, 179)
21. A (179, 180)
22. C (176)
23. A (175, 176)
24. A (593)
25. D (171)

CHAPTER 11
Real Estate Contracts

1. C (188)
2. B (192)
3. D (188)
4. B (189)
5. C (191)
6. D (193)
7. D (190)
8. A (209, 210)
9. A (210)
10. D (191)
11. D (211)
12. D (211)
13. D (212)
14. C (188)
15. B (189, 190)
16. A (191, 192)
17. B (189)
18. D (192)
19. B (211)
20. A (195)
21. C (209)
22. B (195)
23. B (195)
24. B (212)
25. D (191)
26. A (191)

CHAPTER 12
Transfer of Title

1. A (220)
2. A (220)
3. D (220)
4. A (221)
5. C (223, 234)
6. A (223)
7. D (223)
8. D (225)
9. B (224)
10. C (222)
11. B (219, 221)
12. B (221)
13. B (222)
14. C (227)
15. B (228)
16. D (227)
17. D (223)
18. A (223)
19. B (229)
20. D (229)
21. B (229)
22. C (229)
23. C (228)
24. B (229)
25. A (234)
26. B (225)
27. D (226, 227)
28. C (230)
29. C (230)
30. C (230)
31. B (593)
32. B (593)
33. D (593)
34. A (226, 227)

CHAPTER 13
Title Records

1. A (240)
2. A (241)
3. C (240)
4. A (240)
5. A (241)
6. D (243)
7. D (244)
8. D (242)
9. C (243)
10. A (243)
11. C (242)
12. C (246)
13. B (245)
14. D (245)
15. A (244)
16. B (241)
17. A (241)
18. A (241)
19. D (241)
20. D (240)
21. C (240)
22. B (240)
23. C (241)
24. B (244)

CHAPTER 14
Illinois Real Estate License Law

1. A (255, 256)
2. C (278)
3. C (259, 263)
4. B (263)
5. A (276, 277)
6. D (279)
7. C (278)
8. C (262)
9. A (260)
10. D (262)
11. C (263)
12. B (276)
13. B (255, 256)
14. D (273–276)
15. B (280)
16. A (275–276)
17. B (273–276)
18. D (271)
19. A (263)
20. D (256)
21. C (259)
22. D (264)
23. B (279)
24. A (259)

CHAPTER 15
Real Estate Financing: Principles

1. B (593)
2. A (287)
3. C (287)
4. A (288)
5. D (296)
6. B (290)
7. D (298)
8. D (292)
9. A (293, 295)
10. A (296)
11. B (593)
12. D (296)
13. B (297)
14. A (288)
15. B (291)
16. D (296)
17. B (297)
18. C (297)
19. A (298)
20. C (298)
21. C (294)
22. B (299)
23. C (294)
24. D (290)
25. D (297)
26. C (287)

CHAPTER 16
Real Estate Financing: Practice

1. D (319)
2. D (321)
3. C (308–309)
4. C (313)
5. B (306)
6. A (310)
7. B (305)
8. C (313)
9. B (319)
10. C (315)
11. B (323)
12. B (310)
13. B (308–309)
14. A (310)
15. B (309)
16. B (593)
17. B (312)
18. B (593)
19. B (593)
20. C (593)
21. D (593)
22. C (310)
23. A (26)
24. B (325)
25. D (111)

26. A (322)
27. B (315)
28. C (319)

CHAPTER 17
Leases

1. C (338)
2. C (337)
3. D (340)
4. C (334)
5. B (336)
6. D (332)
7. C (332)
8. B (332, 340)
9. B (340)
10. B (331)
11. B (337)
12. C (332)
13. C (593)
14. C (330)
15. A (330)
16. C (334)
17. C (332)
18. B (334)
19. A (339)
20. C (332)
21. C (342)

CHAPTER 18
Property Management

1. B (358)
2. A (351)
3. D (352)
4. C (358)
5. C (350)
6. B (357)
7. D (355)
8. B (355)
9. C (351)
10. A (351)
11. C (358)
12. C (358)
13. C (352)
14. B (357)
15. B (349)
16. A (352)
17. D (349)

CHAPTER 19
Real Estate Appraisal

1. C (374)
2. B (366)
3. B (368)
4. B (366)
5. D (368)
6. A (368)
7. D (372)
8. C (376)
9. A (593)
10. C (374)
11. C (374)
12. C (363)
13. B (374)
14. C (372)
15. D (593)
16. D (369)
17. B (593)
18. B (593)
19. B (372)
20. B (372)
21. D (368)
22. D (369)
23. D (374)
24. B (375)
25. A (372)
26. C (365)

CHAPTER 20
Land-Use Controls and Property Development

1. A (396)
2. A (393)
3. B (396)
4. C (391)
5. C (393)
6. A (391)
7. A (392)
8. D (391)
9. B (397)
10. A (397)
11. A (394)
12. C (394)
13. B (395)
14. B (395)
15. B (390)
16. D (394)
17. A (395)
18. A (395)

19. A (397)
20. A (391)
21. C (391)
22. B (390)

CHAPTER 21
Fair Housing and Ethical Practices

1. C (410)
2. A (414)
3. D (414)
4. B (411)
5. B (412)
6. A (412)
7. B (409)
8. B (413)
9. C (410)
10. B (405)
11. A (410)
12. B (405)
13. D (414)
14. C (407)
15. D (412)
16. D (408, 409)
17. A (415)
18. A (415)
19. C (409)

CHAPTER 22
Environmental Issues and the Real Estate Transaction

1. B (425)
2. C (426)
3. C (426)
4. A (425, 426)
5. A (435)
6. C (429)
7. B (438)
8. D (440)
9. C (433)
10. D (425)
11. C (426)
12. A (427)
13. B (426)
14. C (433)
15. D (434)
16. C (424)
17. B (424)
18. C (430)

CHAPTER **23**
Closing the Real Estate
Transaction

1. D (463)
2. B (449)
3. D (451)
4. A (449)
5. D (451, 452)
6. C (453)
7. C (450)
8. B (457)
9. B (457)
10. D (593)
11. C (457)
12. A (457)
13. C (593)
14. A (593)
15. C (457)
16. B (457)
17. D (453)
18. D (453)
19. B (455)
20. B (455)
21. C (455)
22. C (454)
23. B (593)
24. C (450)
25. A (460, 461)
26. D (460)

MATH CALCULATIONS FOR REVIEW QUESTIONS

CHAPTER **3**
12. $9,500 + $800 + $1,000 = $11,300

CHAPTER **5**
9. $8,200 ÷ .06 = $136,666.67
10. $2,520 × 2 = $5,040 ÷ $72,000 = .07 or 7%

CHAPTER **6**
5. $12,925 ÷ $235,000 = .055 or 5.5%
10. .065 × .40 = .026
    $9,750 ÷ .026 = $375,000
16. $153,500 × .06 × .40 = $3,684
17. $387,000 × .055 = $21,285. $387,000 − $21,285 = $365,715

CHAPTER **9**
3. 2 × 4 = 8
   640 ÷ 8 = 80
10. 43,560 × $2.15 = $93,654
12. 4 × 4 = 16
    640 ÷ 16 × $1,500 = $60,000
16. 4.5 × 43,560 = 196,020
    $78,400 ÷ 196,020 = .40
    150 × 100 = 15,000
    .40 × 15,000 = $6,000
17. 10 × 43,560 − 26,000 ÷ 5,000 = 81.92, rounded to 81
18. 400 × 640 ÷ 2 = 128,000 ÷ 43,560 = 2.94

CHAPTER **10**
6. $80,000 × .35 × .030 = $840
9. $47,250 × 1.25 × .025 = $1,477
24. $80,000 ÷ .333 × .95 ÷ 100 × 6 ÷ 2 = $760.00 (rounded)

C H A P T E R 12

31. $100,000 − $48,000 = $52,000 ÷ $500 = 104 × $.75 = $78

32. $80,000 − $50,000 = $30,000
     $30,000 ÷ $500 = 60 × $.75 = $45

33. $127,000 ÷ $500 = 254 × $.75 = $190.50

C H A P T E R 15

1. $120,000 × .03 = $3,600

11. $2,700 ÷ $90,000 = .03 or 3 points

C H A P T E R 16

17. $100,000 × .075 = $7,500 ÷ 12 = $625 interest
     $902.77 − $625.00 = $277.77
     $100,000 − $277.77 = $99,722.23

19. 9.41× 135 = $1,270.35

20. $85,000 × .115 = 9,775 ÷ 12 = $814.58
     $823.76 − $814.58 = $9.18

21. $114,500 × .80 = $91,600

22. $50,000 × .90 = $45,000
     $25,000 × .95 = $23,750
     $54,000 × .97 = $52,380.
     $45,000 + 23,750 + 52,380 = $121,130

C H A P T E R 17

13. $1,200 × 12 = $14,400
     $19,200 − 14,400 = 4,800 ÷ .04 = $120,000
     $120,000 + 150,000 = $270,000

C H A P T E R 19

9. $24,000 ÷ $300,000 = .08 or 8 percent

15. $112,000 − $53,700 ÷ $542,000 = 10.75 percent

17. $240,000 ÷ 65 × 5 = $18,462

18. $240,000 − $18,462 = $221,538

C H A P T E R 23

10. $1,800 ÷ 12 months = $150
     $150 × 6.5 = $975

13. $285,000 × .10 = $28,500
     $285,000 − $28,500 = $256,500
     $256,500 × .02 = $5,130 + $28,500 = $33,630

14. $300,000 × .30 = $90,000
     $90,000 − $22,000 = $68,000

23. $2,129 ÷ 365 = $5.83

Practice Exam One

The number in the parentheses refers to the Chapter of this book where information pertaining to the answer is located. Math calculations for the Sample Examinations begin on page 597.

(PART ONE)
1. B (10)
2. A (11)
3. A (11)
4. C (16)
5. C (16)*
6. B (6)
7. A (12)
8. A (21)
9. A (7)
10. D (8)
11. D (5)
12. A (15)
13. B (17)
14. A (19)
15. A (20)
16. C (5)*
17. D (4)
18. C (15)*
19. A (3)
20. B (7, 20)
21. D (6)*
22. B (9)*
23. B (15)
24. B (10)*
25. C (16)*
26. C (10)*
27. B (19)
28. C (9)*
29. C (15)*
30. B (6)*
31. A (11)
32. D (11)
33. B (11)
34. B (15)
35. B (11)
36. A (15)
37. D (19)*
38. B (6)
39. A (8)
40. A (13)
41. D (6)
42. B (17)
43. C (21)

44. B (15)*
45. D (10)
46. D (11)
47. C (20)
48. D (9)*
49. B (19)
50. B (10)
51. B (11)
52. B (8)
53. C (17)
54. D (11)
55. B (7)
56. C (15)*
57. A (7)
58. C (16)*
59. D (20)
60. B (11)
61. C (15)
62. A (21)
63. D (23)*
64. D (11)
65. B (12)
66. D (8)
67. B (23)*
68. D (21)
69. A (12)
70. A (19)
71. D (16)
72. D (8)
73. A (23)
74. D (23)
75. B (2)
76. C (7)
77. D*
78. B (6)
79. D (5)
80. D (17)
81. C (2)
82. A (20)
83. C (3)
84. B (5)
85. B (5)*
86. D (8)

87. C (21)
88. A (11)
89. C (6)
90. D (19

(PART TWO)
1. D (7)
2. A (11)
3. C (7)
4. B (7)*
5. B (8)
6. B (8)
7. B (9)
8. C (9)
9. D (8)
10. B (10)
11. B (10)
12. B (8)
13. B (6)
14. C (14)
15. D (6)
16. C (7)
17. A (6)
18. B (6)
19. A (11)
20. A (14)
21. D (14)
22. B (14)
23. A (12)
24. B (9)
25. B (14)
26. C (11)
27. D (15)
28. D (21)
29. B (12)
30. C (12)
31. C (12)
32. C (10)
33. B (17, 21)
34. B (12)*
35. D (13)
36. B (13)
37. C (14)

*   See Math Calculations beginning on page 601

38. C (14)
39. D (13, 14)
40. B (20)
41. B (15)
42. C (10)
43. D (10)*
44. B (11)
45. B (14, 21)
46. D (14)
47. B (14)
48. C (15)
49. D (14)
50. A (15)
51. C (14)
52. B (17)
53. C (14)
54. C (17)
55. B (20)
56. A (17)
57. C (4)
58. D (4)
59. B (2)
60. C (7)

Practice Exam Two
(P A R T O N E)
1. D (17)
2. D (2)
3. C (11)
4. B (15)
5. C (16)
6. D (4)
7. B (*)
8. D (21)
9. B (*)
10. B (15)*
11. B (11)
12. A (16)
13. D (6)
14. C (7)
15. D (4)
16. D (9)
17. B (12)
18. B (23)
19. C (6)*
20. A (19)
21. C (23)
22. B (17)
23. A (7)
24. B (23)
25. D (17)

26. D (16)*
27. C (16)*
28. B (4)
29. B (19)
30. D (23)
31. A (23)*
32. D*
33. A (11)
34. D (10, 13)
35. B*
36. A (6)
37. B (17)
38. D (6)
39. A (19)
40. C (19)*
41. D (12)
42. C (9)*
43. D (11)
44. D (18)*
45. C*
46. D (16)
47. A (7)
48. A (23)*
49. B (17)
50. C (19)*
51. C (18)*
52. A (13)
53. D (3)
54. A (2)
55. D (8)
56. A (23)
57. B (7)
58. B (12)*
59. D (19)
60. D (16)
61. D (19)
62. C (21)
63. C (12)
64. C (16)*
65. A (4)
66. B (6)*
67. B (21)
68. D (4)
69. C*
70. A (23)
71. D (16)
72. C (19)*
73. A (11)
74. D (19)
75. D (16)
76. C (16)*

77. B (19)
78. D (10)*
79. B (23)
80. B (18)
81. B (5)
82. D (5)
83. B (19)
84. B (6)
85. D (6, 19)
86. C (17)
87. B (19)
88. A (11)
89. D (21)
90. A (7)

(P A R T T W O)
1. B (23)*
2. D (15)
3. C (17)
4. C (17)
5. A (17)
6. B (17)
7. D (22)
8. A (21)
9. D (21)
10. C (21)
11. A (4)
12. C (4)
13. B (4)
14. D (4)
15. B (4)
16. C (4)
17. C (5)
18. A (14)
19. C (5)
20. B (11)
21. D (6)
22. B (6)
23. D (6)
24. A (6, 7)
25. D (20)
26. C (7, 12)
27. B (7)
28. A (7)
29. C (7)
30. C (8)
31. D (9)
32. B (10)
33. A (11)
34. D (11)
35. C (12)

36. B (12)
37. B (13)
38. B (14)
39. C (14)
40. D (14)
41. B (14)
42. D (14)
43. D (14)
44. D (14)
45. A (14)
46. B (14)
47. B (14)
48. D (14)
49. D (14)
50. C (15)
51. D (15)
52. C (17)
53. C (18)
54. A (21)
55. A (23)*
56. B (7)
57. D (20)
58. D (11)
59. D (6, 11)
60. C (6)

Practice Exam Three

1. A (14)
2. D (14)
3. D (14)
4. B (14)
5. D (14)
6. A (14)
7. C (14)
8. C (14)
9. A (14)
10. B (14)
11. B (14)
12. A (14)
13. D (14)
14. D (14)
15. D (14)
16. C (4, 14)

17. A (4)
18. C (14)
19. D (4, 14)
20. D (14)
21. A (14)
22. B (4)
23. D (14)
24. B (4)
25. C (14)
26. D (14)
27. D (14)
28. D (14)
29. D (14)
30. B (4)
31. A (14)
32. B (14)
33. B (4, 14)
34. A (4)
35. D (14)
36. B (4, 14)
37. C (14)
38. A (14)
39. D (3)
40. C (14)
41. D (14)
42. C (14)
43. C (21)
44. C (14)
45. A (5, 14)
46. C (4, 14)
47. C (14)
48. B (4, 14)
49. C (6, 14)
50. D (14)
51. D (4, 14)
52. A (4, 14)
53. D (4, 14)
54. D (4, 14)
55. B (4, 14)
56. C (14)
57. D (14)
58. D (4, 14)

59. C (14)
60. B (14)
61. C (14)
62. D (14)
63. B (12)
64. A (10)
65. D (12)
66. C (14)
67. B (6, 14)
68. D (16)
69. B (5)
70. B (14)
71. D (6, 14)
72. D (12)
73. C (12)
74. A (7)
75. D (8)
76. D (10)
77. C (11)
78. D (12)
79. D (10, 13)
80. B (14)
81. D (14)
82. A (14)
83. D (14)
84. C (4, 14)
85. B (14)
86. A (14)
87. D (14)
88. D (20)
89. A (14)
90. B (4)
91. B (19)
92. A (19)
93. B (14)
94. A (14)
95. D (14)
96. B (14)
97. D (14)
98. C (14)
99. A (7)
100. D (7)

MATH CALCULATIONS FOR SAMPLE EXAMINATIONS

Practice Exam One

(P A R T   O N E)

5. $412.50 × 12 = $4,950 ÷ $60,000 = .0825 = 8.25%

16. $2,593.50 × 2 = $5,187 ÷ .065 = $79,800

18. 10⅜ − 9¾ = ⅝
    5 points will increase yield by ⅝

21. $65,000 ÷ .94 = $69,149

22. 3 × 43,560 = 130,680 sq. ft.

24. $40,000 × .40 × 1.5 × .04 = $960

25. $60,000 × .90 = $54,000 × .01 = $540
    $60,000 × .10 = $6,000 + $540 = $6,540

26. $274,550 ÷ .85 = $323,000

28. 640 ÷ 4 = 160
    640 ÷ 4 = 160
    160 + 160 = 320 acres × $875 = $280,000 × .05 = $14,000

29. $38,500 × .04 = $1,540

30. $50,000 × .0775 = $3,875

37. $22,000 ÷ .08 = $275,000

44. $6,000 ÷ $150,000 = .04 or 4 points

48. 2 × 4 = 8.   640 ÷ 8 = 80
    4 × 4 = 16.   640 ÷ 16 = 40
    80 + 40 = 120 acres

56. $562.50 × 4 = $2,250
    $2,250 ÷ .075 = $30,000

58. $460 × 12 = $5,520 ÷ .08 = $69,000 loan
    $69,000 ÷ .80 = $86,250

63. $37,000 × .25 = $9,250 − $3,000 = $6,250

67. Count the actual number of days from March 16 through December 31: 291 days.
    $1,880.96 ÷ 365 = $5.153 × 291 = $1,500
    $84,500 − 67,600 = $16,900 down − $2,000 paid = $14,900
    $14,900 + 1,500 + 1,250 = $17,650

77. 90' + 175' + 90' + 175' = 540' × $1.25 = $662.50
    530' × 6.5' = 3,445 sq. ft. × $.825 = $2,842
    $662.50 + 2,842 = $3,505

85. $157,000 × .06 × .10 = $942

Practice Exam One

(P A R T   T W O)

4. $165,000 − $30,000 (their total homestead) = $135,000

29. $250,000 ÷ $500 = 500 × $.50 = $250

34. $185,000 ÷ $500 = 370 × $.25 = $92.50

43. $175,000 × .030 ÷ 2 = $2,625 on June 1st

Practice Exam Two

(P A R T   O N E)

7. 80' × $200 = $16,000 × .10 × .60 = $960

9. 9' × 12' × 8' = 864 cubic feet × $1.82 = $1,572 ÷ 2 = $786

10. $120,500 × .80 = $96,400

19. $195,000 × .075 × .65 = $9,506.25
26. $57,200 × .135 = $7,722 ÷ 12 = $643.50
     $666.75 − 643.50 = $23.25
     $57,200 − 23.25 = $57,176.75
27. $57,200 × .135 = $7,722 ÷ 12 = $643.50
31. $57,500 × .085 = $4,887.50 ÷ 360 = 13.576 × 14 = 190.07
     The bank will add interest on the day of closing.
32. $142,500 × 1.27 = $180,975
35. $193,600 ÷ $4.40 = 44,000 sq. ft. ÷ 200' = 220 feet
40. $142,000 − 18,000 = $124,000 value of building ÷ 31.5 years = $3,936.51
     $3,936.51 × 7 years = $27,556 depreciation
     $142,000 − 27,556 = $114,444
42. 2 × 4 × 4 = 32
     640 ÷ 32 = 20 acres that he owns.
     He wants to own 160 acres. 160 − 20 = 140 acres × $300 = $42,000
44. $795 × 3 = $2,385
     $2,385 + 1,200 + 900 = $4,485 × 12 = $53,820 × .085 = $4,574.70
45. 36' × 200' × 12' = 86,400 cubic feet ÷ 27 = 3,200 cubic yards × $1 × 12 = $38,400
48. 45 days to the end of the year.
     $1,116 ÷ 360 = $3.10 × 45 days = $139.50
50. $234,500 − 80,000 = $154,500 value of building ÷ 27.5 = $5,618.18
51. $1,000 × 12 × .07 = $840
     $1,100 × 12 × .05 = 660
     $1,210 × 12 × .03 = 435.60
     $840 + 660 + 435.60 = $1,936
58. 54% + 18% + 16% = 88%
     100% − 88% = 12% to the college
     $79,000 ÷ .12 = $658,333 × .18 = $118,500
64. $90,000 × .075 = $6,750 × 15 = $101,250
66. $90,000 ÷ .94 = $95,745
69. Subtract front setback 25' and rear setback 20' from 70': 70' − 45' = 25'
     Subtract side setback 10' and side setback 10' from 70': 70' − 20' = 50'
     50' × 25' = 1,250 sq. ft.
72. $30,000 ÷ .10 = $300,000
     $30,000 ÷ .12 = $250,000
     $300,000 − 250,000 = $50,000
76. $1,200.22 × 12 × 15 = $216,040
     $1,028.63 × 12 × 30 = $370,307
     $370,307 ÷ 216,040 = 1.71 or 171%
78. $85,000 × 1.10 × .040 = $3,740

Practice Exam Two
(P A R T   T W O)

1. January 1 to May 2 is 4 months and 2 days
    $560 ÷ 12 = $46.667 × 4 months = $186.667
    $46.667 ÷ 31 × 2 days = $3.011
    $186.667 + 3.011 = $189.68
55. $560 ÷ 12 ÷ 31 = $1.505 or $1.51

Index